UNIX®
Communications

UNIX®
Communications

Bart Anderson
Bryan Costales
Harry Henderson

The Waite Group

HOWARD W. SAMS & COMPANY
A Division of Macmillan, Inc.
4300 West 62nd Street
Indianapolis, Indiana 46268 USA

FIRST EDITION
THIRD PRINTING—1989

International Standard Book Number: 0-672-22511-5
Library of Congress Catalog Card Number: 87-81108

From The Waite Group, Inc.
Developmental Editor: Mitchell Waite
Managing Editor: James Stockford
Series Editor: Harry Henderson

From Howard W. Sams & Company
Acquisitions Editor: James S. Hill
Manuscript Editor: Diana C. Francoeur
Cover Artist: Kevin Caddell
Illustrator: Don Clemons
Indexer: Schroeder Editorial Services
Compositor: Shepard Poorman Communications Corp.

Printed in the United States of America

Contents

Part 2
UNIX News: USENET

Appendices

Preface

Two years ago, at the height of the MS-DOS® and IBM® PC revolution, mentioning "UNIX" and "communications" in the same breath would have elicited a rather large yawn from the vast majority of desktop computer users. Most people, including myself, would have guessed that *UNIX communications* referred to some incredibly complicated collection of devices, connecting expensive mainframe computers and running the esoteric, RAM-eating, user-unfriendly, and nongraphic UNIX operating system. Ugh. Only students, professors, and super scientists could use UNIX. Right?

Things seem to change fast in the computer field. Suddenly, UNIX, which has always had its devoted followers, is big time. Super low-cost 80286/80386 computers—running inexpensive versions of UNIX that are fully AT&T approved and accredited clones—are the rage. "UNIX offers more bang for the buck than MS-DOS" is heard. "Now everyone can use UNIX." Coincident with this UNIX explosion is the evolution of MS-DOS towards UNIX—though MS-DOS isn't there yet. UNIX is moving out in front and has the potential to become King of the operating systems. Will UNIX make it?

Hard to say, but one thing is definitely true: UNIX comes with communications facilities that you can use today, not years from now (as is the case with IBM's new OS/2 operating system). As you will see when you read this book, UNIX systems, from corporate mainframes to the AT clone on your desk, come with facilities for electronic mail (e-mail), worldwide news distribution, and programmable file transfer. It is UNIX's sophisticated and elegant set of communications tools and methodologies that this book is about.

I started playing with UNIX about three years ago. I probably would never have found out about it if not for Stewart Brand, who had the vision to set up the first public-access, regional-based UNIX conferencing system in the San Francisco Bay Area, called *The WELL*. The WELL is based on a 100-megabyte VAX 780 and a commercial user-friendly "shell" called *PicoSpan*. Pico, as the hackers call it, allows people who are not computer sophisticated to use The WELL as a bulletin board. It works great, is friendly, and keeps the complexity of UNIX away from the average user.

But the real magic for me came underneath the covers of PicoSpan. Typing `unix` at the Pico prompt put me in pure, wonderful UNIX (in Bourne or C Shell flavors). Now from the UNIX shell I could use e-mail to communicate with people in the regional area of San Francisco. I could use all of mail's fabulous features, like saving and loading files from the shell, running shell commands, sending group mail, and so on. I started using e-mail for communicating with my editors and authors and discovered that it allowed high-quality communications between people on wildly different schedules. For example, authors could upload and e-mail stuff to me late at night to save money on their phone bills. Mail replaced endless rounds of telephone tag and "while you were out" messages. But, and there is always the but, I had a lot of trouble learning to use the full features of the mail programs, mostly because the AT&T manuals were so unfriendly.

From the e-mail messages I received, I discovered that The WELL was a node in the wonderful UNIX USENET network. Here, I had access to thousands of professional people working every day in software, hardware, computer technology, and science—all connected together in a large "sharing" network that also had a bulletin board. This USENET network was INTERNATIONAL; it connected hundreds of UNIX computers all running the same "Netnews" software throughout the world. This was a much larger bulletin board than The WELL, and had a different type of user and a different caliber of information. It had tens of megabytes more information than I could ever sift through or find on The WELL. And the UNIX Netnews software had a great set of tools for reading and posting news items that was completely compatible with the UNIX shell, pipes, and scripts. The news software, like the shells, came in several flavors. As with UNIX mail, however, I had to struggle with the limited and rather cryptic documentation. It took me a long time to figure out everything it could do, and I'm still learning.

Finally, I grew more and more curious and bold about the technical side of UNIX communications. How does the Netnews software work? When I'm reading news and want to send a reply, how is the Netnews software integrated so that I end up in the editor of my choice? How can the e-mail program forward a message to a user located in Podunk, Iowa just by "looking" at the complex address I type in? How can I move files between the Macintosh™ on my desk and The WELL or other UNIX computers by using the *xmodem* or *kermit* programs? These and other questions led me to investigate the "UUCP" collection of programs, as well as other widely used file-transfer programs.

My business is developing thorough but friendly software guides, so I was interested in creating books that would share the excitement and power of UNIX communications with both new and advanced UNIX users. The bottom line was that I saw three potential books here—electronic mail, USENET, and UUCP—but no one subject was quite large enough to make a whole book. So I created *UNIX Communications*, which contains all three subjects in it (plus file transfer and conferencing). (Indeed, as you might have noticed, *UNIX Communications* is written by three authors.) I think you will find this to be a really helpful and useful book. I sure wish that I'd had it when I first discovered UNIX.

Mitchell Waite
The Waite Group

About the Authors

Bart Anderson left high-school teaching and newspaper reporting to work as a technical writer for The Waite Group, Racal-Vadic, Commodore-Amiga, and Hewlett-Packard. He is the coauthor of The Waite Group's *PC Lan Primer*.

Bryan Costales is senior systems programmer at EEG Systems Laboratory. He is the author of *C from A to Z* and of numerous articles on computer applications. He is a member of USENIX and ADPA, and is an award-winning art director of motion pictures. An avid volleyball player, he lives in northern California with his dog Zypher.

Harry Henderson is a free-lance technical writer and editor. He has edited, and contributed to, computer books for The Waite Group, Atari, Blackwell Scientific, Benjamin/Cummings, Wadsworth, and other publishers. He has a special interest in the UNIX operating system, and is the series editor for The Waite Group's *Tricks of the UNIX Masters*, *UNIX Bible*, and *UNIX Papers*.

Acknowledgments

I would like to thank Bart Anderson, a professional technical writer and the coauthor of Sams' *PC LAN Primer*, who wrote Part 1 on electronic mail. Bart's sensitive touch is particularly evident in the examples, which were carefully devised and tested on The WELL. Harry Henderson, coauthor of several Waite Group titles and series editor for The Waite Group/Sams' UNIX series (*UNIX Communications, UNIX Bible, UNIX Papers,* and *Tricks of the UNIX Masters*) authored Part 2 on USENET. Harry spent many late nights banging on the *readnews* and *rn* programs as he searched through dozens of newsgroups, looking for interesting information to put in his chapters. Bryan Costales, author of *C From A to Z* (Prentice-Hall/Simon & Schuster) and UNIX C programmer extraordinaire, humbly accepted and admirably accomplished the job of writing about the complex suite of UUCP programs. Bryan's attention to detail and his talent for lean, informative sentences are well-showcased in Part 3.

I extend my sincere appreciation to Harry Henderson, who edited a manuscript that was sometimes delivered electronically in incompatible word processing formats; who put up with constant e-mail queries while calmly asking for more clarity, more illustrations, and more information; and who accomplished all this while keeping up with Waite Group editing projects.

I would also like to thank The WELL computer conferencing system in Sausalito, California, and the entire community of UNIX users who created, and continue to maintain, e-mail, USENET, and the UUCP software. Indeed, these programs have allowed this book to be planned and executed almost completely electronically.

Finally, I give my sincere thanks to the people behind the scenes at Howard W. Sams who took our manuscript and turned it into a polished, marketable product that we are proud of: Jim Hill for understanding the potential of a communications book in the UNIX market and for taking the risk of acquiring the book, to Wendy Ford and Kathy Stuart Ewing for managing the book's production and for putting up with a potential logistical nightmare, to Diana Francoeur for her diligent editing and patience in dealing with three different authors, to Kevin Caddwell for his wonderful cover painting, to Glen Santner for turning my ideas into something Kevin could understand, and to all the other people at Howard W. Sams who one way or another were involved in making UNIX Communications a success.

Mitchell Waite
The Waite Group

First and foremost, I must thank George Jansen for helping me to revise and clarify my thinking, style, and language. Equal praise and thanks go to Mitchell Waite, of The Waite Group, for wanting to do this book in the first place, and to Bart Anderson for his germane editorial criticism.

I must also thank Alan Gevins and Nelson Morgan of EEG Systems Laboratory for their patience and support during the writing of this text.

Bryan Costales

Trademarks

Introduction

What does the phrase "UNIX Communications" mean to you? If you are a new UNIX user or someone who uses a UNIX system only casually, UNIX communications may simply mean keeping in touch with other users through electronic mail (e-mail), or perhaps chatting on-line using the *write* or *talk* program. If you are a more experienced user, UNIX communications for you probably includes access to *USENET*, the UNIX bulletin board system, which you can use to keep up with events and communicate with many other UNIX users by reading and posting "news" articles.

If you are a UNIX programmer, UNIX communications for you includes mastering the collection of programs, tools, protocols, and methods that make up the UUCP software. The UUCP facility provides the system support for mail, news, and other communications applications. Starting with the *uucp* program (*U*NIX to *U*NIX *C*o*P*y), the UUCP software and related programs allow transfer of text, binary, encoded, and encrypted files. There are also programs for the scheduling and management of file transfer jobs.

Finally, if you are a UNIX administrator (or "sysop"), UNIX communications also means the ability to install and maintain the Netnews software used to run the USENET bulletin board. It also means the regular cleaning up of mail and news directories, and the maintenance of links to other systems. In general, you as system administrator are responsible for meeting your users' needs for dependable communications and the regular flow of information. This requires a sound understanding of the UUCP software and the configuration options for the mail and news programs.

Of course, many of you belong in more than one of these categories—many system administrators, for example, write shell scripts and C programs to set up and maintain UNIX communications. Regardless of which categories currently describe your experience and interests, this book is designed to meet your present and future needs to master UNIX communications. Here is how *UNIX Communications* is organized.

UNIX Communications Fundamentals

Chapter 1 is a general introduction to UNIX communications. It shows the many ways you can communicate with UNIX, the different kinds of systems that can be used to run mail and other communications programs, and the ways in which the systems can be connected. This chapter also covers the basic concepts and conventions that will be used throughout the book. Even if you decide to skip a particular part of the book, you should read the discussion of concepts and conventions because it will help you to better understand the other chapters.

Chapter 2 presents a refresher course on the basic UNIX tools and ideas that you should know about in order to use UNIX mail and other communications programs. It quickly gets the beginner up to speed and provides a useful reference for the intermediate or casual user.

Part 1: Electronic Mail

Chapters 3 through 5 make up a complete tutorial on electronic mail for UNIX systems. Electronic mail under UNIX allows you to exchange letters and other text documents with other users, whether they are on the same UNIX computer or on one thousands of miles away.

The tutorial teaches you how to use the most advanced (as well as the most commonly used) UNIX e-mail program, called *mailx* (for System V) or *Mail* (for Berkeley UNIX). Chapter 3 presents the commands needed to perform all the basic e-mail functions, such as sending, reading, saving, and replying to mail. The following chapters (4 and 5) take you deeper into the more powerful capabilities of the mail program, showing you how to create folders, access shell commands, load files into mail documents, and much more. In addition, you are shown how to send remote mail to other UNIX systems, using the system of network addresses.

Part 2: USENET and Netnews

The second part of this book is an introduction and tutorial that will show you how to read and write news articles on USENET. USENET is a network of interconnected UNIX computers. These computers are found mostly in universities, scientific and engineering laboratories, and other technically oriented companies. USENET is not a commercial enterprise, such as Compuserve® or MCI Mail™, but rather is paid for by the companies and universities that make up the major "backbone" sites of the network.

USENET is easy to join. All it takes to connect to this network is to find another site willing to let you hook up! But to use USENET properly, you have to learn the "rules of the road" that the USENET community has devised for conserving resources and improving the quality of communication. This self-regulation has resulted in a unique, efficient, and useful bulletin and news program that is available anywhere in the world. The caliber of people using UNIX is high: in general, they are academic and professional users with a serious interest in UNIX and other technical topics. In addition, they are ready to share with you their opinions and ideas on philsophy, religion, politics, games, and hobbies.

This second part of *UNIX Communications* starts with a general introduction to USENET's history, structure, and operation (chapter 6). You will gain an overview of how USENET works and where you as a UNIX user fit in. Next, you'll find out through many examples just what kinds of information are available on USENET. The incredible variety ranges from conference notices and ads for rooms to rent, to philosophy and culinary arts, public-domain programs and source-code patches, reviews of the latest books and movies, and much more.

Chapters 7 through 10 cover the specific programs for reading and sending news in USENET, starting with the fairly simple news reading program *readnews*. Full discussions of the more powerful *rn* news reading program and the screen-oriented *vnews* program follow. Each of these chapters is stand-alone, so you can skip *readnews* and start with *rn* or *vnews* if you desire. Chapter 10 then shows you how to use *postnews*, the UNIX program for posting (sending) news on the USENET bulletin board. More than that, however, chapter 10 provides guidelines for effective communication, including how to respond to other users' articles and how to post your own articles courteously and responsibly.

Part 3: UUCP

If you are a programmer, system administrator, or someone who wants to know more about UNIX file transfer, you need to understand the UUCP software that underlies most mail, news, and other UNIX communications programs. Part 3 of *UNIX Communications* discusses all of the programs that make up the UUCP software.

Unlike the mail and news programs, which are interactive and command-driven, the UUCP software is used mainly in shell scripts and other programs to provide the needed communications facilities. Since the documentation for the UUCP programs in the standard UNIX manuals is often skimpy and lacks examples, many people have had trouble learning how to write file transfer programs. Chapters 11 through 17 discuss all of the important options for each of the UNIX communications tools in the UUCP package. These chapters give many clear, useful examples. They also provide some useful shell scripts to extend the power of the UUCP software and to serve as models for your own programming efforts. The discussion of UUCP is aimed at the intermediate to advanced UNIX user, with emphasis on learning to use the UUCP programs.

Finally, to help you see how the UUCP facilities fit together in a real-world communications process, chapter 18 follows an electronic mail message from its originating site to its remote destination, showing how the UUCP programs are called into play.

Appendices

The five appendices present a variety of important topics. Appendix A covers the simple */bin/mail* program, which you can use if the advanced mail program is not available on your system. Appendices B and C explain how to perform interactive, on-line UNIX communications with the *write* and *talk* programs and how to communicate between UNIX systems and micros with the popular *kermit* and *xmodem* error-checking, protocol-based transfer programs. Appendices D and E present resources for further study and exploration, including bibliographies.

What You Need to Get Started

In general, all you need to get started with this book is access to a UNIX computer. You may have an account on a UNIX computer at your company or at a local school or training center. You may own a UNIX computer and be running just a few terminals. You may even be running UNIX or a UNIX-like system on your personal computer. Any of these systems will allow you to learn how to use electronic mail.

However, in order to use *rn* and *readnews*, or to send e-mail to other UNIX sites, you will need to be connected to the USENET network. Fortunately, this isn't too difficult. If you are a user on a university UNIX system, it's very likely that you already have access to USENET. Some corporate sites also are connected to the net, particularly companies oriented toward research, technology, and software development. If you are taking any university courses, you might check to see if the school will give you an account on its UNIX system.

Another alternative that you may have is to get an account on a commerical, public-access UNIX system. At present, there are only a few public-access USENET machines, but we expect that, as UNIX continues to gain popularity, others will spring up. An example of such a system is The Whole Earth 'Lectronic Link in Sausalito, California (north of San Francisco). Known as "The WELL," this system is one of the first regional telecommunications services, appealing mainly to residents in the San Francisco Bay Area. It was set up by the revered Stewart Brand, publisher of the *Whole Earth Magazine* and the *Whole Earth Software Catalog*. The WELL provides a rich and easy-to-use shell called "PicoSpan."[1] The phone

1. The UNIX system is available to all users by typing `unix` at the PicoSpan prompt, and the full range of USENET programs is available, in addition to The WELL's own conferencing system.

number for The WELL is (415) 332-6106. (You will need a 300- or 1200-baud modem to sign up on The WELL.)

In addition to public-access conferencing systems, you may also find many companies that offer time-sharing on a UNIX system having access to USENET. This is particularly true near large technological centers, like Silicon Valley, Boston's Route 99, or Austin, Texas.

To practice using the UUCP software discussed in Part 3 of this book, you need a UNIX system that is connected to one or more other UNIX systems. Any system that offers USENET news also has access to other systems through the UUCP file transfer software, since the UUCP network is used to distribute news. But even if the system to which you have access doesn't offer USENET, it may be connected to other sites by modem, so you can still experiment with remote file transfers. UUCP software can also be used to transfer files over a serial cable or a LAN (local area network). Chapter 11 will show you how to find out what your system "looks like" on the UUCP network, and your system administrator may also be able to give you some guidance.

Our System

The authors for this book used various computer and software systems for accessing and using UNIX communications, including a Macintosh™ emulating a VT 100 terminal with a software program called MicroPhone, a COMPAQ® portable running *kermit*, an AT clone running Mirror and a Wyse terminal connected to a VAX® 780. Many example listings were obtained using our terminal programs with The WELL, the public-access UNIX system mentioned earlier. Key programming examples were tested on both System V and Berkeley UNIX.

As you can see, there are many ways to connect yourself to the world of UNIX communications. In our discussions we will always point out any significant differences among the major versions of UNIX, and any places where baud rate or specific terminal capabilities are important considerations.

A Bit of Advice

To communicate with others, you must talk to them, not hide in the closet. UNIX communications is the same way: to master it, you must reach out and communicate with other people. But because UNIX communications consists of words typed on keyboards and sent across phone lines, it has the potential to be an impersonal, cold medium, without the body language of face-to-face communications, or even the inflections of the human voice over the telephone. It is important, therefore, to be sensitive to the fact that at the other end of the terminal is a human being, and at the same time to be aware of, and to follow, some commonly accepted conventions that aid orderly communication. We have included dozens of examples with a variety of content so that you will be able to get a feeling for the generally accepted format of UNIX communications. Try to follow the advice we give on how to get your ideas across without offending people's feelings. Be an active, experimenting learner. Send messages, post new ideas, respond to questions, download and upload source code. You will find your appreciation for UNIX and its communications facilities will grow quickly.

UNIX Communications Fundamentals

1

Welcome to UNIX Communications

Welcome to the friendly world of UNIX® communications. This first chapter explains why UNIX and computer communication are a natural combination. It also describes the three areas of UNIX communications that are covered in this book (UNIX Mail, UNIX News, and UNIX File Transfer) and introduces basic concepts common to all of them. In addition, this chapter gives you examples that show how people are using UNIX to meet their communications needs. It also tells you where in the book you can find discussions of the various UNIX communications programs.

Why UNIX Communications?

If you work closely with people, you couldn't choose a better system to work with than UNIX. The UNIX operating system was designed for easy sharing of files and information. In addition, UNIX computers are easily linked to form communication networks serving hundreds, or even thousands, of users. The key to accessing this communication power lies in understanding the UNIX *communications* programs.

UNIX communications programs (such as electronic mail) are among the most often used UNIX programs, and are usually among the first programs a new user learns. Although UNIX is extensively documented, some of the most useful information on UNIX communications programs exists only in the minds of UNIX wizards and in highly technical manuals. This book aims to open up the world of UNIX communications to the general user.

UNIX and Computer Communications

UNIX is the leading multiuser computer operating system available today. It is suitable for machines ranging in size from the IBM® PC XT to Cray® II supercomputers. AT&T estimates that before 1985 about 200,000 UNIX licenses were issued. Now, the price for a two-user license has been reduced to $60, and a three-user license to $150. This has opened the door for the proliferation of UNIX on PCs.

Computer communications—the ability to transfer data from one user to another—has become the watchword of the computer industry for the 1980s, and should be even more important in the 1990s. We hear of local area networks (LANs), AppleTalk®, Ethernet™, and micro-to-mainframe links, but UNIX is an old pro at networking. UNIX-based computer networks have been around for twenty years! From the very beginning, communication between users was an essential part of the UNIX operating system. UNIX began as a joint effort of programmers at Bell Laboratories to create an operating system that would facilitate their work together. Since it was designed by programmers and not really marketed as a commercial product until fairly recently, UNIX has been able to remain an "open" system, with roadblocks to information exchange kept to a minimum.

Some Examples of Computer Communications

It's hard to visualize how computer communications work until you've actually done some communicating. Soon we will show you how to use the actual communications programs. In the meantime, the following examples should give you an idea of the possibilities that open up when users and computers are linked.

As we discuss the different scenarios, we'll introduce some common concepts of computer communications, like "dumb terminal" and "uploading a file." If you want more depth on any of these matters, consult one of the primers available on data communications and networks. We recommend the *PC Lan Primer* by The Waite Group (Indianapolis: Howard W. Sams, 1986).

User-to-User Communication on One Computer

The simplest example of computer communication is shown in figure 1-1. In this setup, two users on the same computer can send messages to each other via electronic mail, or they can exchange files and programs using basic UNIX commands. No special hardware or software is needed, and there are no compatibility problems.

Bookmark

HOWARD W. SAMS & COMPANY

DEAR VALUED CUSTOMER:

Howard W. Sams & Company is dedicated to bringing you timely and authoritative books for your personal and professional library. Our goal is to provide you with excellent technical books written by the most qualified authors. You can assist us in this endeavor by checking the box next to your particular areas of interest.

We appreciate your comments and will use the information to provide you with a more comprehensive selection of titles.

Thank you,

Vice President, Book Publishing
Howard W. Sams & Company

COMPUTER TITLES:

Hardware
- ☐ Apple 140 ☐ Macintosh I01
- ☐ Commodore I10
- ☐ IBM & Compatibles I14

Business Applications
- ☐ Word Processing J01
- ☐ Data Base J04
- ☐ Spreadsheets J02

Operating Systems
- ☐ MS-DOS K05 ☐ OS/2 K10
- ☐ CP/M K01 ☐ UNIX K03

Programming Languages
- ☐ C L03 ☐ Pascal L05
- ☐ Prolog L12 ☐ Assembly L01
- ☐ BASIC L02 ☐ HyperTalk L14

Troubleshooting & Repair
- ☐ Computers S05
- ☐ Peripherals S10

Other
- ☐ Communications/Networking M03
- ☐ AI/Expert Systems T18

ELECTRONICS TITLES:
- ☐ Amateur Radio T01
- ☐ Audio T03
- ☐ Basic Electronics T20
- ☐ Basic Electricity T21
- ☐ Electronics Design T12
- ☐ Electronics Projects T04
- ☐ Satellites T09
- ☐ Instrumentation T05
- ☐ Digital Electronics T11

Troubleshooting & Repair
- ☐ Audio S11 ☐ Television S04
- ☐ VCR S01 ☐ Compact Disc S02
- ☐ Automotive S06
- ☐ Microwave Oven S03

Other interests or comments: ____________________

____

____

Name ____________________

Title ____________________

Company ____________________

Address ____________________

City ____________________

State/Zip ____________________

Daytime Telephone No. ____________________

A Division of Macmillan, Inc.

4300 West 62nd Street Indianapolis, Indiana 46268 22511

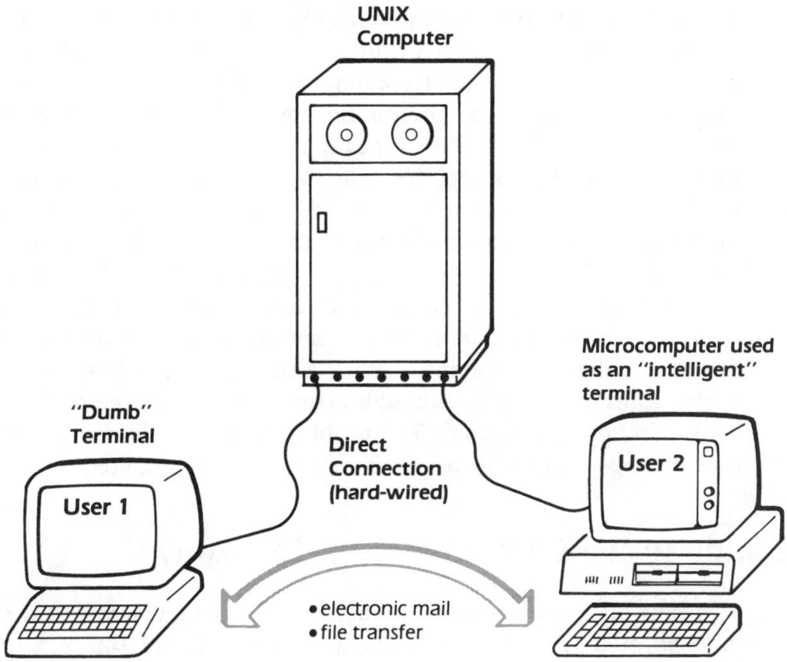

Figure 1-1. People on the same computer communicate with each other.

If this were a computer installation at a university (UNIX is used by approximately 90% of U.S. computer science departments), user #1 could send a message to another student in his computer language class:

```
Help! I have to write a paper on the FORTH programming language
by next week. Do you know of some good books on it?
```

User #2 would see the message when she checked her mail, and would send a message in return:

```
Relax. I've got an annotated FORTH bibliography on one of my
disks here. As soon as I find it, I'll upload it to the system
and mail it to you.
```

User #2 would then locate the file with the FORTH bibliography and include it in a mail message to user #1.

In figure 1-1, the UNIX setup on the left is a "dumb" terminal consisting of only a keyboard and a monitor. A *dumb* terminal has no intelligence (computer power) of its own; it allows you only to type information into the main computer and to display information presented by the computer.

The setup on the right is an "intelligent" terminal. An *intelligent* terminal (one with its own computing power) offers big advantages over a dumb terminal. If the main computer is heavily loaded with users, you can *download* your files (transfer them from the main computer to your personal computer) and continue to work on them using the computing power of your PC. With the PC, you can compose letters and documents locally with one of the word processors available for PCs (word processors that are usually faster and more powerful than the ones available on UNIX systems). Later, you can *upload* the text files (transfer them to the remote main computer).[2] Once the files are stored on the main computer, you can send them to other users with one of the UNIX mail programs.

In figure 1-1, both setups are directly connected with a wire or cable to the UNIX computer. This *hard-wired* connection, as it is also called, is simple and provides high-speed response. When a user presses a key, the computer seems to respond instantaneously, although actually the data is being sent at a rate of perhaps 9,600 bits per second. The problem with directly connected terminals is that they must be located in the same vicinity as the computer.

Talking to the Computer from Far Away

To access the computer from farther away than a few hundred feet, you must use a *modem* (modulator-demodulator), as shown in figure 1-2.

For this example, let's suppose that a travelling sales representative has set up a portable computer in a hotel room in Boston, and is using a modem to call the company's UNIX computer in Los Angeles. Over the telephone network, the sales representative can check his electronic mailbox to see if anyone has sent him messages. If so, he can fire off replies in a fraction of the time it would take with paper mail. It's a simple matter for him to upload a report to the main computer or to download a file with the latest competitive information onto his PC.

Central UNIX Computer Talks to Many Remote Users

The previous example showed only one remote user calling into a UNIX system. Figure 1-3 shows how many users in different locations can communicate with each other through a central UNIX computer. Users with modems call in over the public telephone network or through special *packet-switched* networks like Telenet™ (the packet-switched network can be cheaper over long distances).

On a *conferencing system*, such as The WELL (Whole Earth 'Lectronic Link) in Sausalito, California, users can send messages to one another with the UNIX mail programs, or they can participate in ongoing electronic conferences on such topics as "One-Person Businesses," "Spirituality," "Politics," and "UNIX." They

2. Think of the UNIX remote machine as being on a mountaintop. To send information, you must "up" load and to receive information you must "down" load it.

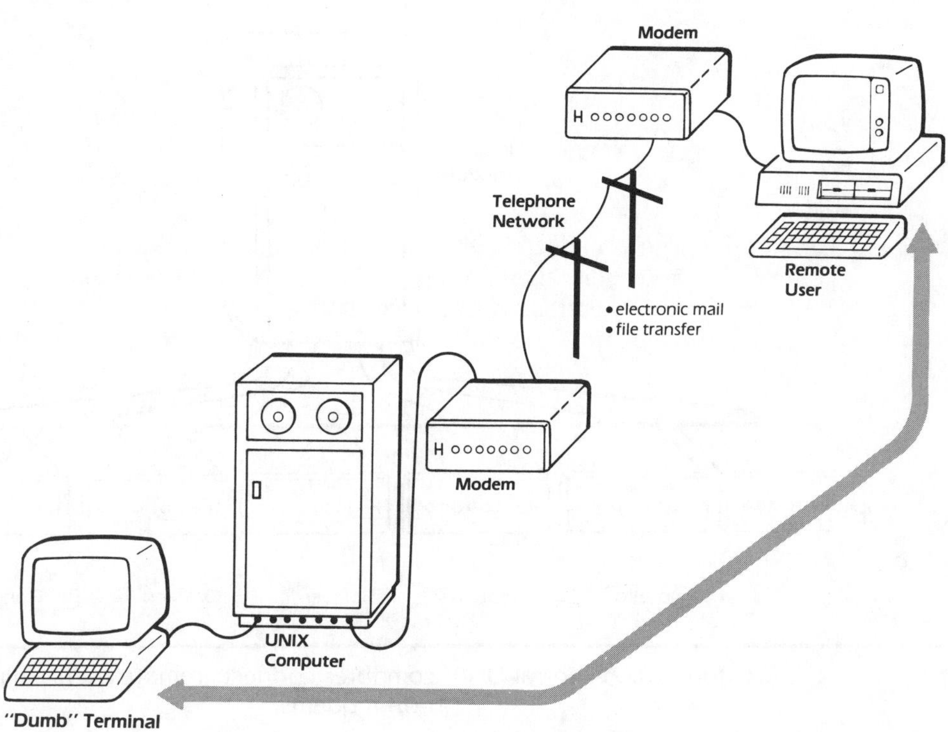

Figure 1-2. Modems allow the use of a computer from a distance.

can read news articles from around the world by using the Netnews software. This system serves as an intellectual forum for the discussion of new ideas and as a meeting place for people of similar interests.

The Limitations of Modem Speed

Users calling a UNIX computer often (but not always) have access to the same UNIX utility programs that are available to a directly connected user. The only limitation on the use of the programs is the speed of the modem. For example, a modem passing data at 300 bits per second (bps) takes 66 seconds to redraw a normal screen of text. Thus, a session with `vi` (the UNIX screen-oriented editor) can be excruciatingly slow as it updates the screen. Electronic mail also can be frustrating at 300 bps. In chapter 5, you'll learn some ways to tailor the mail program for slow 300-bps modems. A better solution is to purchase one of the 1200-bps modems, now very reasonably priced. For most users, 1200 bps is adequate. However, you can never have enough speed, and 2400-bps modems are gaining popularity. In 1986, modems with speeds of 9600 bps (and higher) have hit the marketplace.

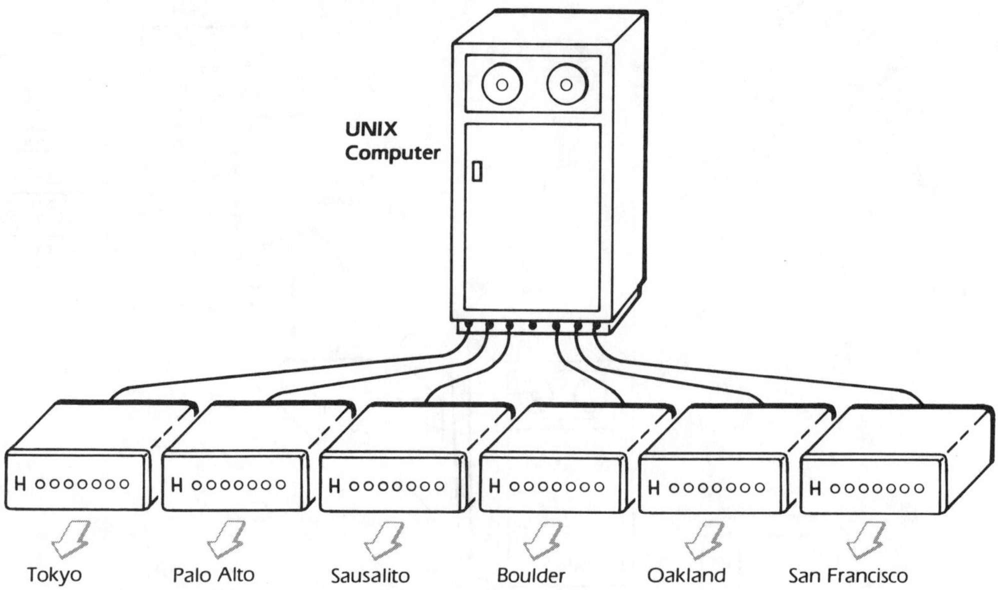

Figure 1-3. A central UNIX computer connects remote users calling in on modems.

New 9600-bps Modems

At prices in excess of $1500, the 9600-bps modems are too expensive for most individual users. For corporate use, however, where telephone communication between UNIX computers is necessary, they can be a godsend. Figure 1-4 shows a setup for transferring files between computers by using UUCP programs. (UUCP programs will be explained shortly.) When UNIX computers call one another, they often transfer megabytes of data and may tie up a phone line for hours. High-speed modems cut that time dramatically. For example, to send the text of the novel *Moby Dick* at 300 bps would take 23 hours. At 1200 bps, it would still take about 6 hours. With the new 9600-bps modems, it would take only 43 minutes!

Two UNIX Computers Talking Together

The two UNIX computers in figure 1-4 are shown connected by modems and the public telephone network. They could also be directly connected by cable, or they could be connected by *leased lines* (a private telephone connection). For highest speed, they could be connected by a local area network (LAN).

The programs that permit two UNIX machines to pass files to one another are

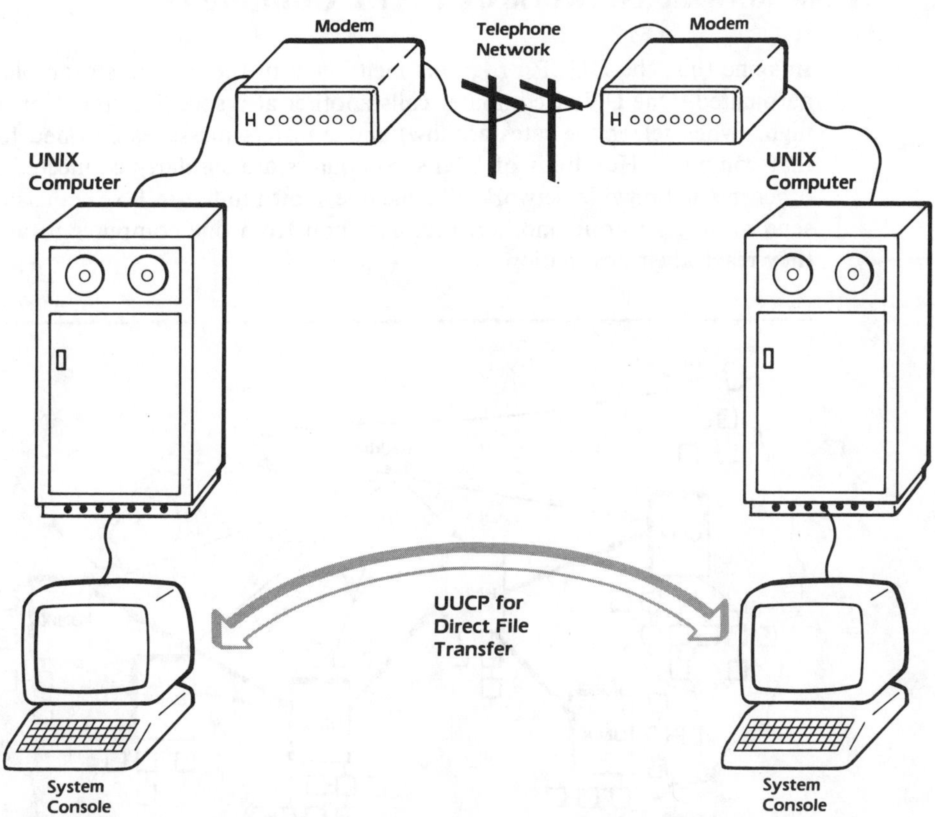

Figure 1-4. UUCP programs transfer files between UNIX computers.

known as the UUCP group of programs (UUCP stands for *U*NIX-to-*U*NIX *C*o*P*y).[3] Part 3 of this book is devoted to these programs. UUCP operations underlie the operation of many other UNIX communications programs. In fact, when you use a mail program to send a message to someone on another computer, the actual data transfer is handled by the UUCP programs. In most cases the Netnews software also uses UUCP.

The UUCP programs may be used directly. In figure 1-4, the systems administrators for two different UNIX systems could use the UUCP programs to transfer 5 megabytes of public-domain programs from one system to another.

3. A note on terminology. In this book we use the term *UUCP* (all caps) to refer to the UUCP group of file-transfer programs and to the network of links between the machines that run these programs. We use `uucp` (lowercase with a computer typeface) to refer to the specific utility of that name.

A Nationwide Network of UNIX Computers

Imagine this: the UUCP programs mentioned in the previous example have been automated. One UNIX computer calls another at a specified time (for instance, at night, when telephone rates are low) and transfers messages destined for users on that computer. Hundreds of UNIX computers are similarly connected to one another in a nationwide network, like the one shown in figure 1-5. Thousands of users send messages to one another; messages hop from one computer to another until they reach their destination.

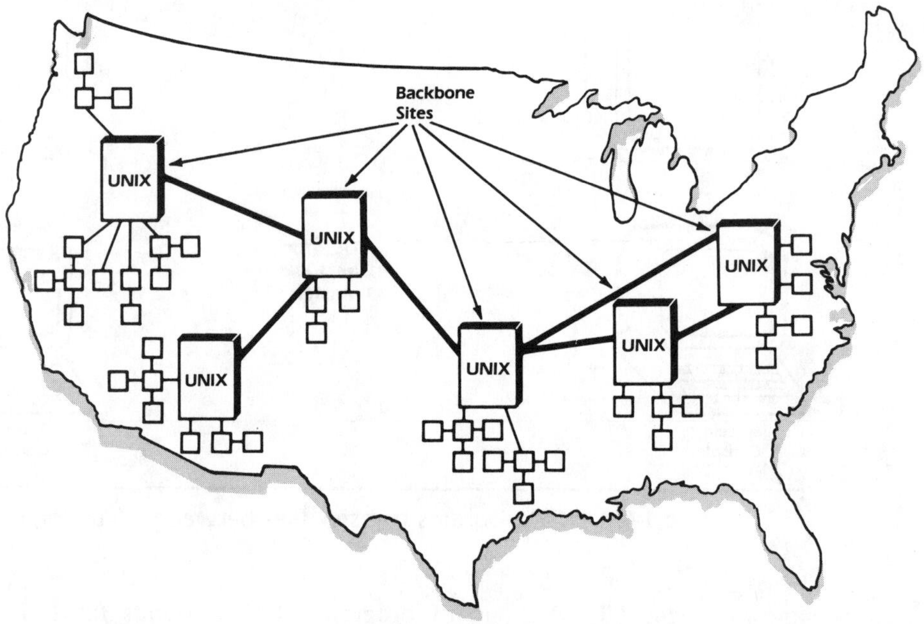

Figure 1-5. A network of UNIX computers links thousands of users.

Such a network does in fact exist—the UUCP network. Unbelievable as it may seem, this complex network functions on a cooperative basis, relying on volunteer administrators and on the goodwill of the institutions, companies, and research labs who own the computers.

The UUCP network does more than just move mail. A group of programs called Netnews runs continuously as USENET on the UUCP network. Hundreds of special "conferences" (called *newsgroups*) are organized on USENET, and users share ideas on this giant electronic bulletin board. (You will learn how to use USENET in Part 2 of this book.)

For example, when Commodore®'s Amiga® computer was introduced, a USENET conference was promptly formed to disseminate information, programs, and tips about the machine. From across the nation, hackers and would-be hackers contributed news, gossip, and advice. The creators of the Amiga in Los Gatos, California, read the articles and responded to them. As a result, bugs were speedily tracked down, and technical details (inevitably scarce when a new microcomputer is introduced) reached programmers and Amiga owners over USENET long before the details were available in published form.

Some UNIX Conventions

Before beginning our discussion of the communications programs, we will explain some of the conventions used in this book.

Commands

Special command keys are shown with an initial capital letter, like this: Escape, Delete. The carriage return is indicated as Return or Enter.

Commands using control characters are shown as Control-d, Control-n. In some UNIX programs, the prompts and help screens represent such commands as ^D, ^N. This is the same as Control-d and Control-n in our notation. In either case, you press the Control key and the letter simultaneously. You do not have to shift to capitalize the letter.

Typeface

For text representing programs, computer input and output, and the names of files, directories, programs, and variables, we will use a typeface that resembles what you see on the screen. It looks like this:

```
Welcome to UNIX Communications
Please enter your first command.
```

To indicate portions of the program that are input by the user, an italic version of this typeface is used in the programs:

```
lp myfile
```

Format Statements

Format statements show the proper *syntax*, or form, for using a particular command. For example:

```
cp filename directory_name
```

shows the format for using the copy command (`cp`) to copy a file into a different directory. The words `filename` and `directory_name` are placeholders for the names of the real file and directory. To use this command, you would have to enter the actual names of the file and the directory.

Variations between Systems

UNIX is remarkably standard for an operating system that has several different versions and runs on many different computers, from micros to mainframes. However, don't be surprised if some of the commands and options don't work exactly as described here—small differences in syntax and operation are inevitable. For example, on our system the electronic mail program is called by typing either `mail` or `Mail`.

You'll be able to solve small problems by experimenting and looking in a UNIX primer. You can also use the `man` command followed by a program name to read the on-line manual entry for that program. For more difficult problems ("How do I send a message to my cousin who's on a UNIX system at UCLA?"), you may have to turn to an experienced user or to the system adminstrator.

Bourne Shell and C Shell

There are several popular *shells,* or command processors, available for UNIX. The shells differ in how they handle certain commands and special characters. (We will discuss shells in chapter 2.) When we give program examples, we usually give them for the Bourne Shell (the `$` prompt). However, most of the examples will work as-is for the C Shell (`%` prompt), although you may have to "escape" certain characters, particularly in the chapters dealing with UUCP commands. For example, in the C Shell, when you are using an exclamation point to indicate a remote computer (`tortoise!`), you need to precede it with a backslash (\), like this:

```
% uucp alice.txt tortoise\!/uucp/alice.txt
```

Note that we always show the escape character (the backslash) when applicable. The escape character is ignored by the Bourne Shell if it is not needed.

Many of the examples in this book are taken from our home system, a 4.2BSD (Berkeley) system called The WELL (Whole Earth 'Lectronic Link), in Sausalito, California. However, we've been careful to make examples and explanations accurate for System V as well.

Where to Find More Information on UNIX

If you are just starting UNIX, you'll be able to pick up many of the basic UNIX commands from the overview in chapter 2. We also recommend that you read an introductory guide to UNIX, such as *UNIX Primer Plus*, by Waite, Martin, and Prata (Indianapolis: Howard W. Sams, 1983), if you have Berkeley UNIX; or, if you have System V, *UNIX System V Primer*, 2d ed., by the same authors (Indianapolis: Howard W. Sams, 1987). Keep a UNIX text at your terminal as you work through this book, and read about the UNIX commands as you encounter them. Soon you will have mastered the communications programs, and you will have a head start on UNIX as well. (More recommended UNIX books are described in Appendix E.)

Summary

Mastering the communications programs is essential to getting the most from a UNIX system. We have shown you several examples of computer communications on UNIX systems. In the next chapter, we'll cover the bare minimum of UNIX lore so that you can start sending and receiving electronic mail and explore the other UNIX communications facilities.

2

The UNIX Operating System

This chapter provides a quick introduction (or refresher) to the UNIX operating system, with a focus on those commands and concepts needed for UNIX communications. If you're completely at home with UNIX, you may want to skip this chapter and go on to chapter 3 ("Beginning Mail").

Why Learn about UNIX?

"Why should I learn about UNIX if all I want to do is send a message to someone down the hall?"

The quick answer is that you don't have to understand UNIX to send and receive mail. After you read the mail tutorial in chapter 3, you'll be sending messages in 10 minutes, and reading messages in 20. In fact, for many of your mail needs, you can probably get by with less than a dozen UNIX commands. Similarly, you can use USENET successfully without knowing any UNIX commands other than the names of the news programs themselves. (Using the UUCP programs successfully almost certainly requires some basic UNIX knowledge, however.)

Nonetheless, to get the most out of UNIX communications, you should become familiar with the basic UNIX system commands such as `cat`, `rm`, and `mkdir`. They can extend the power of the communications programs as well as make it easier for you to keep track of what you are sending or receiving. Let's see why.

UNIX Is Flexible

Even if you are not comfortable with computers in general or UNIX in particular, chances are that you will soon want to do more than send and read simple messages. Perhaps you'd like to use a more powerful word processor to write your mail than the default editor provided by the mail program. Or perhaps you'd like to print out all your messages from another user to put into a report.

Electronic mail is a good example of the flexibility that UNIX provides in contrast to most other operating systems. With electronic mail on most other operating systems, you're locked into one way of doing things. If the mail program asks you for the subject of a message that you want to send, you can be sure that it will always ask you for the subject of a message. The few people who understand a particular non-UNIX operating system may be able to change the way the mail program works, but this is often a laborious process.

UNIX, on the other hand, is an operating system whose middle name is "change." You don't want to be prompted for a message subject by the mail program? No problem! You change it with a one-line command. Perhaps you'd like to send your mail messages to a special printer. No problem on UNIX! You can set up your mail program so that the command `pipe` prints messages automatically. UNIX even provides the tools to encrypt your messages so that no one else can read them without a special keyword. Figure 2-1 contrasts the UNIX approach to that of most other operating systems.

Even though UNIX commands are easy to use and work well together, some learning *is* required. To do exactly what you want to do with UNIX, you might have to look up commands in the UNIX manuals or occasionally question the local UNIX guru. (Later on, you will see how USENET can help you with your UNIX questions and problems.)

How We Will Cover UNIX

This chapter provides a brief overview of UNIX, giving you the essentials you need to make use of the communications programs. Because the mail and the communications programs on UNIX are so intertwined with the operating system, we'll be explaining general UNIX concepts and commands thoughout the book. So, even if you are unfamiliar with UNIX, you will be able to follow along. If you are an experienced user, we'll refresh your memory about the commands so that you won't have to page through a reference book as often. However, it *is* useful to have a general guide to UNIX on hand, such as those we recommended in chapter 1 or those listed in Appendix E.

On-Line Help

UNIX offers on-line descriptions of its commands. At your system prompt, type `man`, a space, and then the name of the command you are interested in. For example, to see information on the `mailx` program, type:

man mailx

Several pages of information will be displayed on your terminal. If you type a space, the next page is shown. This information is actually from the on-line version

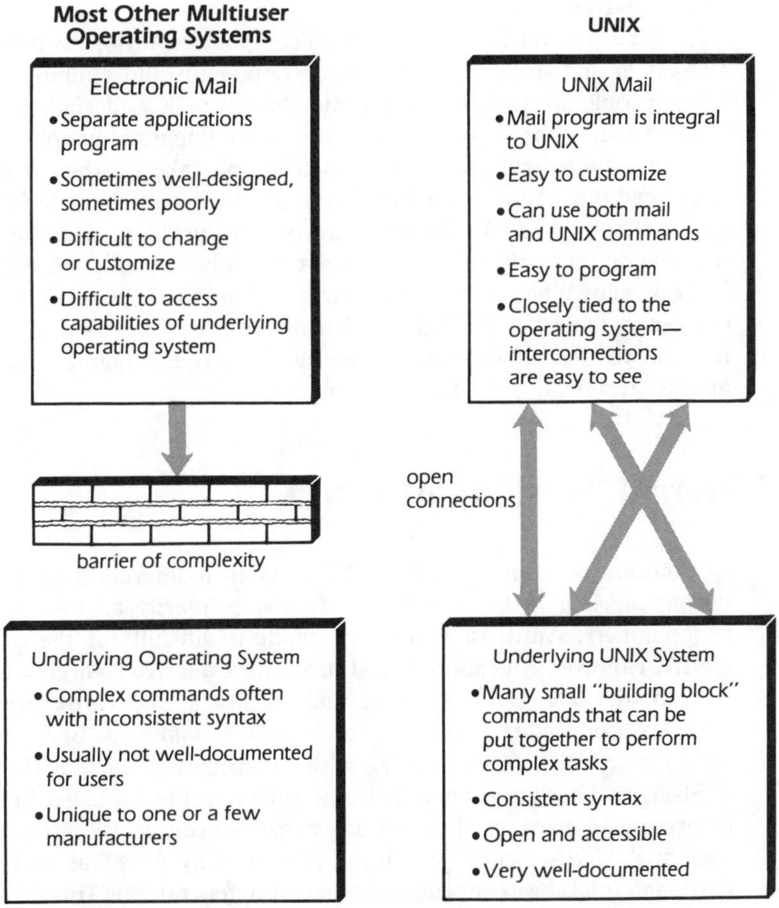

Most Other Multiuser Operating Systems
UNIX
Electronic Mail
• Separate applications program
• Sometimes well-designed, sometimes poorly
• Difficult to change or customize
• Difficult to access capabilities of underlying operating system
UNIX Mail
• Mail program is integral to UNIX
• Easy to customize
• Can use both mail and UNIX commands
• Easy to program
• Closely tied to the operating system—interconnections are easy to see
open connections
barrier of complexity
Underlying Operating System
• Complex commands often with inconsistent syntax
• Usually not well-documented for users
• Unique to one or a few manufacturers
Underlying UNIX System
• Many small "building block" commands that can be put together to perform complex tasks
• Consistent syntax
• Open and accessible
• Very well-documented

Figure 2-1. Electronic mail is flexible and versatile on UNIX.

of the standard UNIX manual for whatever version of UNIX your system is using. Unfortunately, for beginners this reference material can be more confusing than helpful. The on-line reference is really meant as a complete rundown for someone who already knows UNIX, or a reminder if you forget something. You may find it useful, for instance, in checking an option to a command.

Help from Human Beings

Perhaps the best sources of information are of the warm, mammalian variety. Go to other users, especially for questions that are specific to a particular system (for instance, how to print out a file on the little-used dot matrix line printer). Experienced users will often be able to clear up a problem with a few seconds of thought.

Once you know how to use electronic mail, you'll be able to use it to ask questions and receive answers.

A key person for the answers to complicated problems is the *system administrator*, the individual responsible for setting up and running the UNIX system. These people are usually enthusiastic about UNIX and glad to share their knowledge. However, they may get worn down from impatient neophyte users who ask the same questions again and again. Before you take up the system administrator's time, read the manual available at your site (for example, *The UNIX System User's Manual* from AT&T). Try to figure out the problem on your own. Sometimes, working on the problem until you solve it can be educational. But if frustration sets in, seek help. When you do ask your question, be as specific as possible. Not: "The computer doesn't work." But: "When I call up the `vi` editor, the cursor doesn't respond to the cursor control commands. I tried logging into my account with another terminal, but I had the same problem."

The Different Versions of UNIX

As you can see from figure 2-2, UNIX comes in different flavors. Born in Bell Labs during the late 1960s, UNIX was at first primarily an in-house tool for AT&T programmers. Antitrust regulations made it difficult for the company to market UNIX. However, educational institutions were allowed to license UNIX for minimal fees. In the late 1970s, students and faculty at the University of California at Berkeley produced their own version of UNIX, known as Berkeley UNIX or Berkeley Software Distribution (BSD), with enhancements such as the `vi` editor and the C Shell, an alternative command interpreter to the standard Bourne Shell. AT&T incorporated many of the Berkeley enhancements in its latest version of UNIX, System V. UNIX System V is being promoted by AT&T as an industry-wide standard, and it has been implemented on computers ranging from mainframes to minis to PCs. (Microsoft's XENIX® is available for IBM PC XTs and ATs, and is closely related to System V.)

You should learn which version of UNIX your system is running. The commands and syntax often differ slightly between versions. For example, to send a file to the line printer on System V, you would use the `lp` command; on other versions of UNIX, you would use `lpr`. Similarly, the powerful mail program described in the next few chapters is known as `mailx` on System V and as `Mail` on Berkeley UNIX, and it doesn't exist on earlier versions of UNIX.

Berkeley UNIX gives you a choice of the C Shell (`%` prompt) or the Bourne Shell (`$` prompt). Other versions of UNIX generally offer only the Bourne Shell.

UNIX Introduction or Refresher

The rest of this chapter introduces the key ideas of UNIX. There are about fifteen UNIX commands that you'll need to know to make it through the following `mailx`

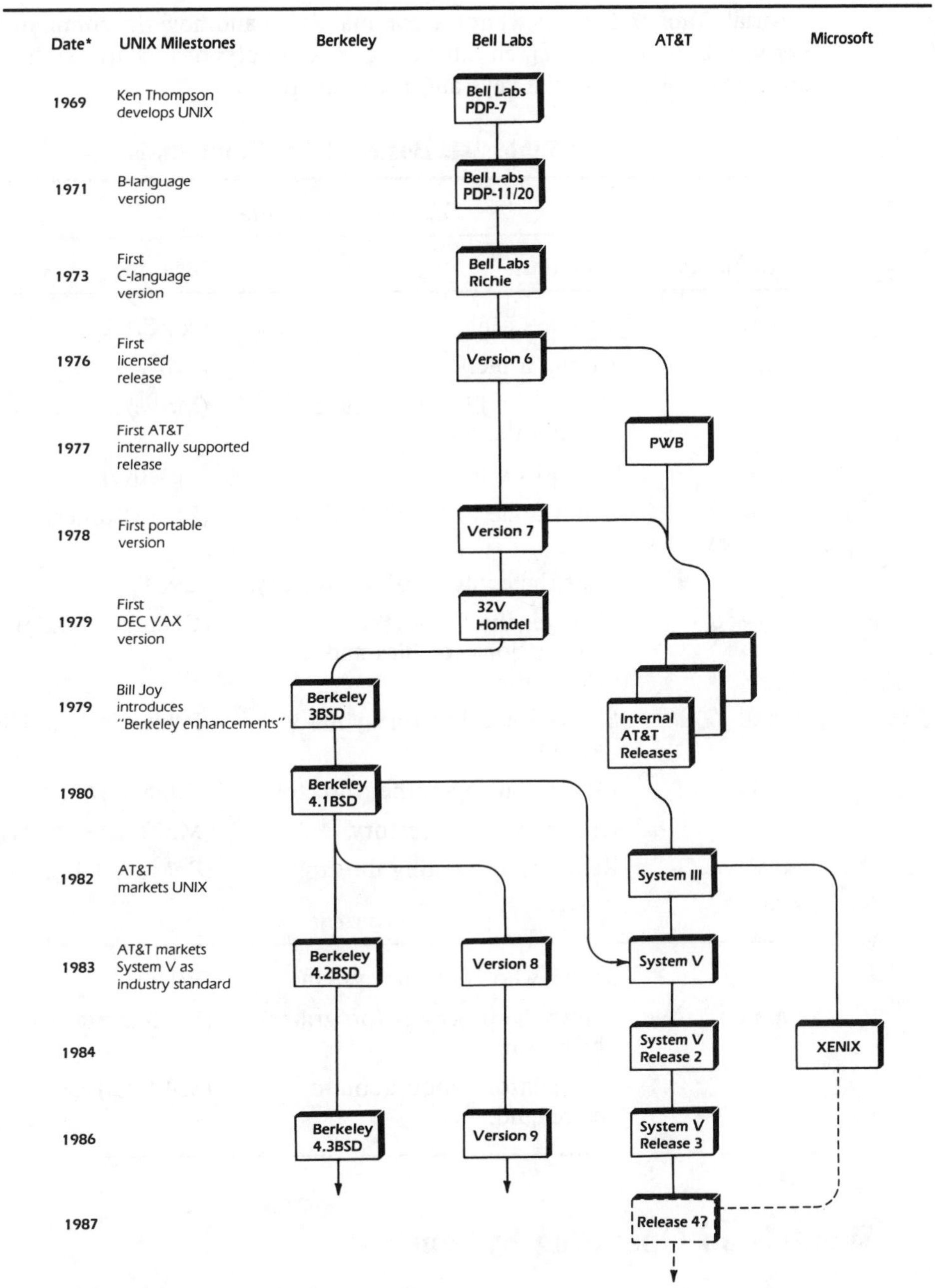

*All dates are approximate. Data from "4.2 BSD and 4.3 BSD as Examples of the UNIX System," Quarterman, Silbershatz, and Peterson, **ACM Computing Surveys** 17 (Dec 1985): 383.

Figure 2-2. The major lines of UNIX system development.

tutorial. Table 2-1 shows what the commands do and how the command names are derived. Later in the chapter, table 2-3 gives examples of how to use the commands, and table 2-4 lists special keys and their functions.

Table 2-1. Basic UNIX Commands

Command	Function	Meaning
	Files and Directories	
cat	Displays a file.	(conCATenate)
cp	Copies a file.	(CoPy)
mv	Renames a file or moves it within the file structure	(MoVe)
rm	Removes a file.	(ReMove)
lpr lp (Sys V)	Sends a file to the line printer.	(Line PRinter)
ls	Lists the contents of a directory.	(LiSt)
chmod	Changes the "mode" or permissions for files and directories.	(CHange MODe)
pwd	Shows what directory you are in.	(Print Working Directory)
cd	Moves you to another directory.	(Change Directory)
mkdir	Creates a new directory.	(MaKe DIRectory)
rmdir	Removes an existing directory.	(ReMove DIRectory)
	System	
who	Shows who is on the system.	(WHO)
ps	Shows the processes (programs) being run.	(Process Status)
man	Shows information about a command.	(MANual)

What Is an Operating System?

UNIX is an *operating system*—a large program that performs "housekeeping" chores for the computer and the computer user. It allows you to run programs; to examine, change, and delete files; and to perform many other essential tasks. An operating system offers users and programmers a convenient way to get at the computer's hardware and software resources. If a user wants to delete a file, for instance, all he or she has to do is issue a simple command to the operating system. The operating system takes care of all the technical details—changing entries in tables, freeing up disk space, etc. Thus, the user is insulated from the complexities of the hardware by the operating system.

Similarly, UNIX programs such as mail programs provide you with their own commands to do such things as display messages on the screen, save messages to a file, remove messages, and so on. The program does the work of telling the operating system what to do (by executing an appropriate UNIX command or making a "system call"). Thus, the program insulates you even more from direct dealings with the computer. But, when necessary, all the power of UNIX commands is still there to use directly. See figure 2-3.

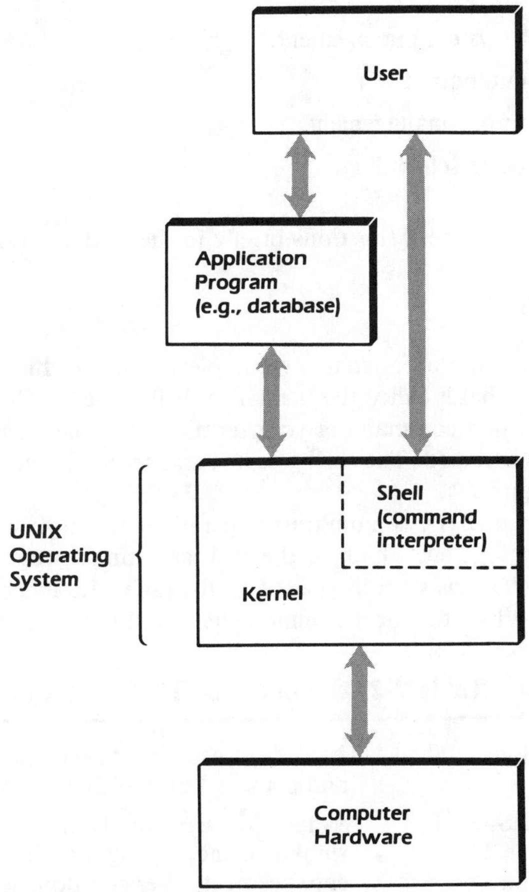

Figure 2-3. An operating system mediates between the user and the computer.

Having the operating system as a buffer between the user and the computer means that UNIX provides machine independence. For example, the ls command will always produce a list of files in a directory, regardless of which particular computer UNIX is running on. Similarly, a program written for UNIX will run on many different machines, with only minimal changes, provided the computer uses true UNIX and not a UNIX look-alike.

The Parts of UNIX

UNIX is made up of several modules, each with distinct tasks. At the center of the system is the *kernel*, the part of UNIX that deals directly with the hardware. The kernel contains primitive functions used by the housekeeping utilities:

- File system management.
- Input/output.
- Memory management.
- Process scheduling.

We'll discuss these functions briefly in the next several pages.

The Shell

To protect the user from the complexity and technicalities of the kernel, UNIX provides what is called the *shell*. The shell is the UNIX command interpreter. When you type in a command at your terminal, the shell accepts the command and sees that it is executed. The shell gets its name from the fact that it surrounds the kernel, as in figure 2-4.

Since UNIX is a multiuser operating system, it generates a new shell for each user that logs on. Think of the shell as a small program that each user interfaces with. UNIX has several types of shells, each with its characteristic prompt ($ or %). Table 2-2 lists the most common shells and prompts.

Table 2-2. Common UNIX Shells and Their Prompts

$	Bourne Shell	The default shell on AT&T systems; most widely used and standard on UNIX System V.
%	C Shell	Available on Berkeley UNIX Systems, with a syntax similar to the C programming language and with many enhancements over the Bourne Shell.
$	Korn Shell	A new shell with added features—"AT&T's answer to the C Shell."

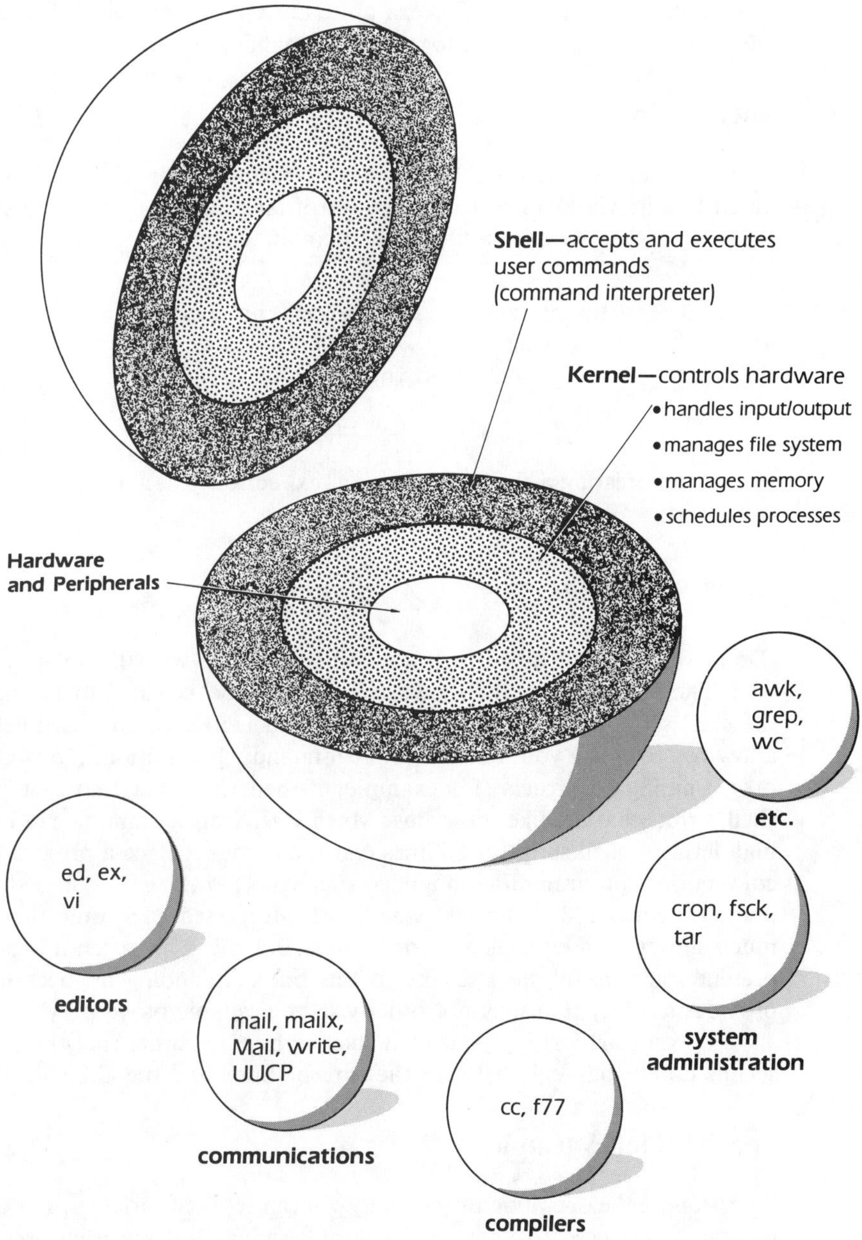

Figure 2-4. Structure of UNIX

In this book, we'll use examples from both the Bourne and the C Shells. Generally, commands that you enter in one shell will work in another. There are some exceptions, however. For example, the C Shell has an `alias` command that lets you rename and bundle together commands.

Shell Scripts

Shell scripts give UNIX much of its flexibility and power. Shell scripts are similar to batch files in MS-DOS or to a job control language in mainframe systems. At its simplest, a *shell script* is a file of shell commands:

```
echo  These users are currently on the system
who
echo Here is a "long" listing of your directory
ls -l
```

After creating a shell script with a text editor, you make it executable with the command:

```
chmod u+x script_name
```

(Don't worry about how this last command works; we will explain it later.)

The commands in the shell script can then be executed by typing the name of the shell script—just as if it were a standard UNIX command. Shell scripts thus allow you to create your own custom commands. In addition, the UNIX shells offer programming constructs (for example, if-then statements) so that you can write shell scripts that act like programs. Much UNIX programming can be done at this high level. A shell script of 20 lines can sometimes replace a program (written in a conventional programming language such as C) with many times that number of lines. Of course, shell scripts, which are interpreted each time they are run, are much slower than equivalent C programs. But this isn't often a problem. We will present some useful shell scripts in this book, including an occasional one that provides a utility that may not otherwise be available on your system.

If you start writing your own shell scripts, be aware that the syntax for shell scripts differs markedly between the Bourne Shell and the C Shell.

Special Shell Variables

To customize the operation of the shell, you can set shell variables. For example, some programs may need to know the type of terminal you are using; setting the `TERM` variable gives them that information. Similarly, setting `MAIL` tells UNIX where on the system the `mailx` program should look for incoming electronic mail. In chapter 5, you will learn about other variables that affect the operation of `mailx`, and you will learn how to set them.

Utility Programs

When you buy the UNIX operating system, you get much more than just the kernel and the shell. More than 200 utilities come with a typical version of UNIX, including programs such as:

`wc`	Word count utility
`ed` and `ex`	Line editors
`vi`	Screen editor
`nroff` and `troff`	Text formatters
`cc` and `f77`	Compilers

In addition, you can purchase applications programs such as database managers or word processors.

A Multiuser System

UNIX is both a "multiuser" and a "multitasking" operating system. As a *multiuser* system, UNIX allows up to several hundred users to access the same computer simultaneously, so that it appears to each user as if he or she has control of the machine. See figure 2-5.

As a multitasking system, UNIX allows each user to perform several tasks at once, as in figure 2-6. You can set the computer to formatting a text file, then issue a command to sort a large list, and even play a game while you're waiting for the computer to finish the other tasks.

Processes—"Programs in Execution"

The tasks initiated by a user are known as *processes*. A process is a program in execution. Processes are born, they live for a certain time, and they die. They even spawn "child" processes. On a UNIX machine, the same program code can run as several different processes. For example, when user #1 types `mailx` to start reading mail, the `mailx` program code begins running as a process for that user. When user #2 types `mailx`, UNIX begins running an identical version of `mailx` as a second process for user #2. Figure 2-6 shows a UNIX system running a `sh` (Bourne Shell) process for each of four users.

You might be wondering how you can really run several programs at once without confusing the computer (not to mention yourself). The answer is that you can run processes "in the background." Putting the command in the background allows you to use your terminal while the program is running. To tell UNIX to make a command a background task, add an ampersand character (&) at the end of a command line:

```
sort -o outfile infile &
```

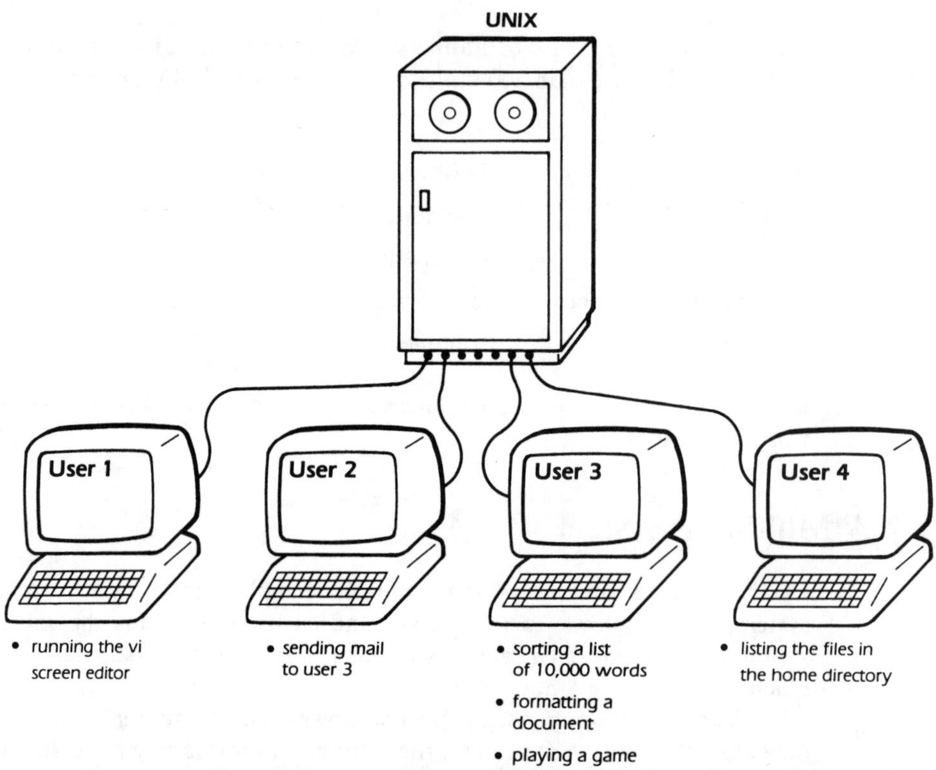

Figure 2-5. UNIX is a multiuser system.

The `-o` is an example of a UNIX command-line option (also called a *flag*). Many UNIX commands have options that are used to control how they work or what they work with. Here, the `-o` option is followed by a filename specifying where the output of the `sort` command is to be put.

The `sort` command sorts the file `infile` and puts the result in the file `outfile`, which can then be examined when the task is completed. Once you have typed the command, the computer does not wait for the sorting process to be completed. Instead, the shell prompt (`$` or `%`) is displayed. This means that you can enter another command right away, and the computer will start working on that command while the `sort` command continues working in the background. If that second command is also typed with an `&` to put it in the background, you can type a third command, and so on. Thus, you can have several commands running in the background. (But you can have only one command running at a time in the "foreground," since you can't enter another command while a command is running in foreground.)

To see the processes you are running, simply enter the `ps` (process status) command:

ps

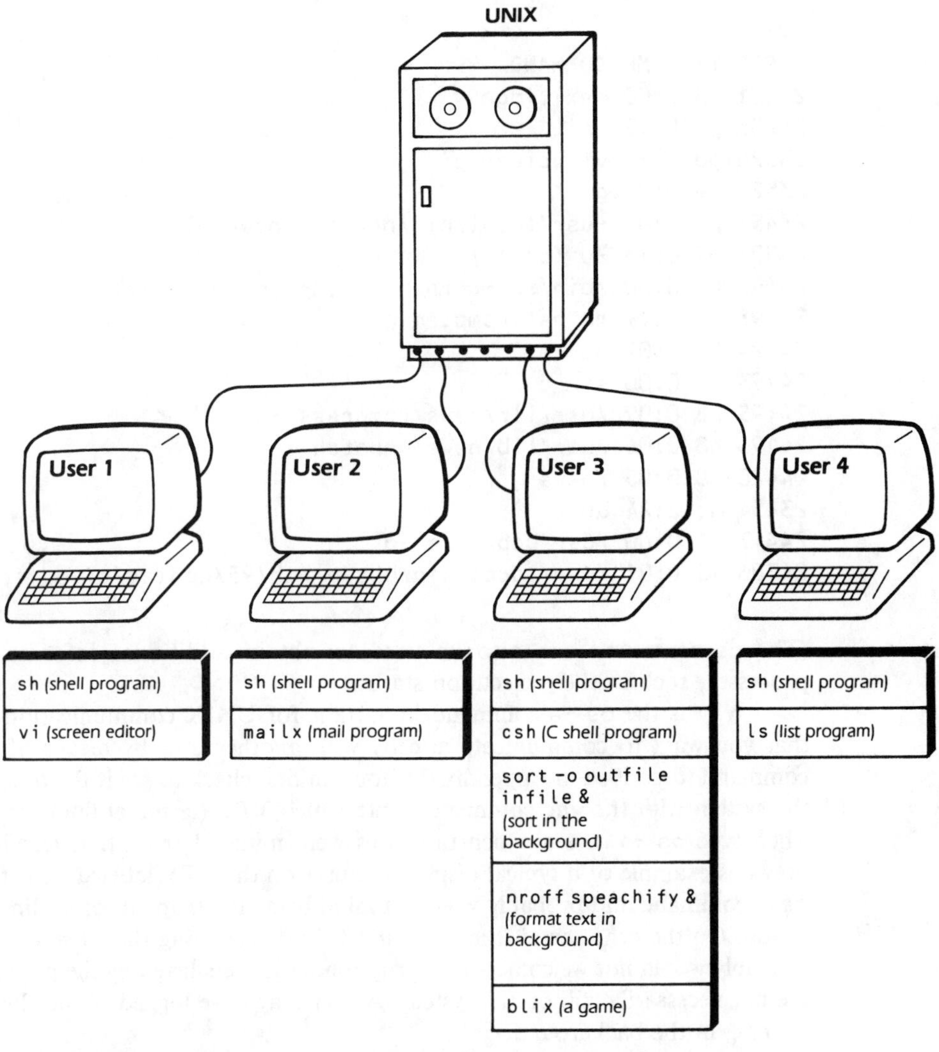

Figure 2-6. UNIX runs multiple processes (programs) for each user.

You might see a response like this:

```
  PID TT TIME COMMAND
24421 h4 0:01 ps
25131 h4 0:12 sort -o outfile infile &
```

If you want to see ALL the processes being run by all the users on the computer, enter the ps command with the -a flag:

ps -a

A typical display looks like this:

```
  PID TT TIME COMMAND
24401 i3 0:00 <exiting>
24255 pb 0:12 mail
23526 pd 0:28 vi wclean.c
23522 pe 0:22 g
23457 pf 0:09 -usr/local/bin/newcsh (newcsh)
23506 pf 0:16 -u (csh)
23697 h1 0:00 /bin/sh -c rn net.comp.amiga
23698 h1 0:29 rn net.comp.amiga
24424 h4 0:02 ps -a
24193 h8 0:00 sh -c
24195 h8 0:09 /usr/lib/news/compress -d
24196 h8 0:06 /usr/lib/news/unbatch
24420 h8 0:05 rnews
23454 hc 2:24 uw
24417 i1 0:00 /usr/ucb/more -d
24306 i3 0:01 /usr/local/bin/bbsed /uh/95/godlas/cf.buffer
```

(The `ps` command can also be used to obtain additional information about processes, such as their execution status.)

Why is the `ps -a` command important for UNIX communications? Suppose that you want to communicate directly with another user by means of the `write` command (described in Appendix B). You can first check to see if the other user is on the system with the `who` command. Note which TTY (terminal line) the user is on. Then type `ps -a` to see which processes were initiated from that terminal. In the previous example of a typical display, the user on the TTY labeled `pb` is running the `mail` command and probably wouldn't mind being interrupted for on-line communication. On the other hand, the user on TTY `pd` is running the `vi` screen editor and probably would not welcome an interruption. (All users listed by the `ps -a` command are not necessarily still on the system. A user may have logged off but left a process running in the background.)

UNIX Files

UNIX defines a *file* as a collection of data. The file may be a text file consisting of ASCII characters, or a program file consisting of binary data. Unlike files in many other operating systems, UNIX files have a very simple internal organization. There is no intrinsic block or record structure, nor are there nondata characters in the file (such as Control-z to mark the end of a file). Every regular UNIX file is simply a sequence of bytes, as illustrated in figure 2-7.

Names for UNIX files can be up to 14 characters long (longer in some ver-

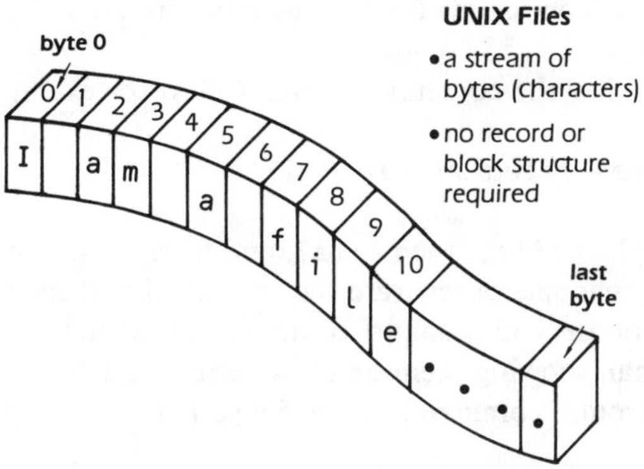

Figure 2-7. UNIX files are a sequence of bytes.

sions) and can include numbers and the underscore character (_). This makes it possible to give your files names that are readily understandable:

```
font_usage_man
simple_c_prog
JanSales1
JanSales2
```

It is important to realize that UNIX makes a distinction between upper- and lowercase in the names of files and commands. If you create a text file called `JanSales1`, you can't call it up as `jansales1`.

File Manipulation

In UNIX, the basic commands for manipulating files are straightforward, although the names of the commands are a bit cryptic. Sometimes, new users become impatient because these names are hard to remember. As they become familiar with the commands, however, they quickly see one of the benefits of the brevity—the commands are much faster to type!

Display a File (*cat*)

One of the most often used commands is the `cat` command—for viewing the contents of a file. Its seemingly nonintuitive name comes from the ability of the command to *conCATenate* (link together) several files. To display a file on your screen, use this format:

```
cat filename
```

You can stop and start the scrolling of the text with Control-s and Control-q. Alternative commands for viewing a file are pg on System V, and more on Berkeley UNIX.

To view the contents of several files, for example, type

```
cat file1 file2 file3
```

This displays file1, then file2, and then file3 on your screen. Note that UNIX requires that spaces separate the command and the filenames.

Suppose you want to combine several files and put them into one big file rather than showing them on the screen. The UNIX > redirection operator puts the output from a command into a file you specify. Thus, the command

```
cat file1 file2 file3 > bigfile
```

takes images of file1, file2, and file3, and writes them one after another into the file bigfile. The smaller files are thus concatenated into one large file. (The contents of the original files are not affected.)

Copy a File (*cp*)

The cat command can thus be used to copy files into other files. The more usual way to copy a file, however, is to use the cp command:

```
cp orig_file new_file
```

Here, UNIX automatically creates the file new_file and places in it a copy of orig_file.

Rename a File (*mv*)

The mv command is called *move* because, in addition to changing the name of a file, it can move a file from one directory to another. To rename a file, type mv followed by the original name and the new name:

```
mv old_name new_name
```

The difference between cp and mv is this: cp makes a copy of a file under the new name so that there are now two copies of the file in existence. The mv command, on the other hand, changes the name of the file. Only one copy of the file exists.

Delete a File (*rm*)

When you no longer need a file, it can be purged with the rm (remove) command:

```
rm obsolete_file
```

Be careful with the `rm` command—once you remove a file, there is usually no way to retrieve it.

Print a File (*lp* or *lpr*)

A file can be sent to your system's line printer with the `lp` command (on System V) or with `lpr` (on other versions of UNIX):

`lp filename` *(System V)*

or

`lpr filename` *(non-System V)*

This command causes the file to be *spooled*—copied onto a temporary file on a hard disk and then sent to the printer when the printer is free.

UNIX Directories

There may be thousands of files on a UNIX system. To make it easier for humans to work with them, UNIX organizes files into groups of related files, called *directories*. For example, when you log into a UNIX system, you are normally placed in your *home directory*, the collection of files you have copied or created for yourself.

List Files (*ls*)

To see the files in your directory, type

```
ls
```

You will see a display like the following:

```
News          dead.letter   mbox          read
after         dummy         mine          recordfolder
before        folders       opento        to_file
```

For more complete information on your files, use the `-l` option (long listing):

```
ls -l
```

You will see a display like the following:

```
drwxrwxr-x  2 bea           24 Jan 15  1986 News
-rw-r--r--  1 bea          638 Jan 30 01:02 after
-rw-r--r--  1 bea          587 Jan 30 01:01 before
```

```
-rw-------  1 bea      1438 Feb  5 02:15 dead.letter
-rw-r--r--  1 bea       546 Dec 18 23:36 dummy
drwxr-xr-x  2 bea       512 Feb  5 02:12 folders
-rw-------  1 bea     63399 Feb  5 02:17 mbox
-rw-r--r--  1 bea       385 Jan  1  1986 mine
drwxrwxrwx  2 bea       512 Jan 30 00:58 opento
drwxr-xr-x  2 bea        24 Nov  9 04:32 read
-rw-r--r--  1 bea     41207 Feb  9 04:43 recordfolder
-rw-r--r--  1 bea         1 Feb  5 02:13 to_file
```

The column on the left with the d's, r's, x's, and w's shows the *permissions* for a file—who can do what to it. (See the following discussion of the chmod command for more information.) The large numbers in the third column are the number of bytes in the file. The date and time on the right show when the file was last modified. On the far right are the names of the files. For more information on deciphering this long listing, consult a UNIX reference manual.

List Hidden Files (*ls -a*)

The ls command doesn't display files that begin with a period, since typically these "hidden" files are not accessed by the user. However, some of the UNIX communications programs do use hidden files. In later chapters, we'll look at two examples of such hidden files. In chapters 4 and 5, you'll learn how to change the .mailrc file in order to modify the operation of the mailx program; and in chapters 7, 8, and 9, we'll discuss the .newsrc file used by the news programs to keep track of news articles. To see if you have a .mailrc file, use the -a (all) option. You will see all the files in your directory, including those beginning with a period:

```
.              .rnlast        mbox
..             .rnsoft        mine
.login          News          folders
.mailrc         after         read
.newsrc         before        recordfolder
.plan           dead.letter   opento
.news.cf        dummy         to_file
.profile
```

Set Security (*chmod*)

UNIX is an *open* system, allowing ready access to files in the directories belonging to the system and to other users. Table 2-3 at the end of this chapter briefly explains how to restrict access to your files. For example, you enter:

chmod go-rwx mbox

to keep people from snooping in your `mbox` file (the file in which the `mailx` program puts messages you have read or saved).

The Current Directory

What does it mean to be *in* a directory (the *current* or *working* directory)? It means that you have ready access to the files in that directory and that your commands do not normally affect files in other directories. If you type

```
cat letter
```

you can see the contents of the file `letter` located in the current directory. If any files are named `letter` in other directories, they won't be displayed by this command.

To find the name of the current directory, type `pwd` (print working directory). You will see a pathname like

```
/user/jonas
```

The *pathname* tells where in the UNIX file system the directory is located. We'll explain pathnames in more detail shortly.

Wildcard Characters

The concept of the current directory is especially important in understanding the special wildcard characters * and ?. *Wildcard* characters let one filename stand for multiple files.

* **Matches any number of characters.**

`*`	=	all files
`f*`	=	all files beginning with `f`
`*.a`	=	all files ending with `.a`

? **Matches any single character.**

`????`	=	any 4-character filename
`f???`	=	any 4-character filename beginning with `f`
`??.a`	=	any 4-character filename ending with `.a`

If you enter a filename with a wildcard character, the shell applies the command to all files in the current directory that match the filename you give. For instance,

```
cat *
```

displays on the screen all the files in the current directory. Files in any other directory are not affected.

Wildcards and filename expansion are very useful UNIX capabilities. Unfortunately, the full set of wildcards and special symbols is not always available when communicating with other machines. We will point out those cases where wildcards CANNOT be used.

Make and Remove Directories (*mkdir* and *rmdir*)

In addition to containing files, UNIX directories can contain other directories. In turn, these directories can contain both files and yet other directories. This relationship of files and directories is illustrated in figure 2-8. The command for creating a directory is `mkdir` (make directory), and for removing a directory, it's `rmdir`.

The UNIX File Structure

The UNIX operating system is organized as a hierarchical file structure, that is, as an ordered relationship of files and directories. Figure 2-9 shows directories in a typical UNIX system. Note that the UNIX structure looks like a tree, turned upside down. At the top of this hierarchy is the root directory, symbolized by a forward slash (/).[1] Beneath the root directory are all the other directories and files in the UNIX system.

Pathnames show the way through the UNIX file structure. Follow our progress in figure 2-9 as we trace a path from the root to a user's directory. This directory has the pathname:

```
/user/simian/
```

By convention, the pathname begins with the root directory (the first slash). So, we start at the top of the UNIX file tree at the directory named:

```
/
```

From the root, we go to the directory named `/user`. On this system, `/user` is the directory that contains all the user directories. On other systems, this directory might be called `users` or `uh`; there's no standard name.

```
/user
```

From here we go to the home directory of the user named `simian`:

```
/user/simian
```

1. Note that the forward slash (/) is used for two purposes: to represent the root directory and to separate names and directories within a pathname.

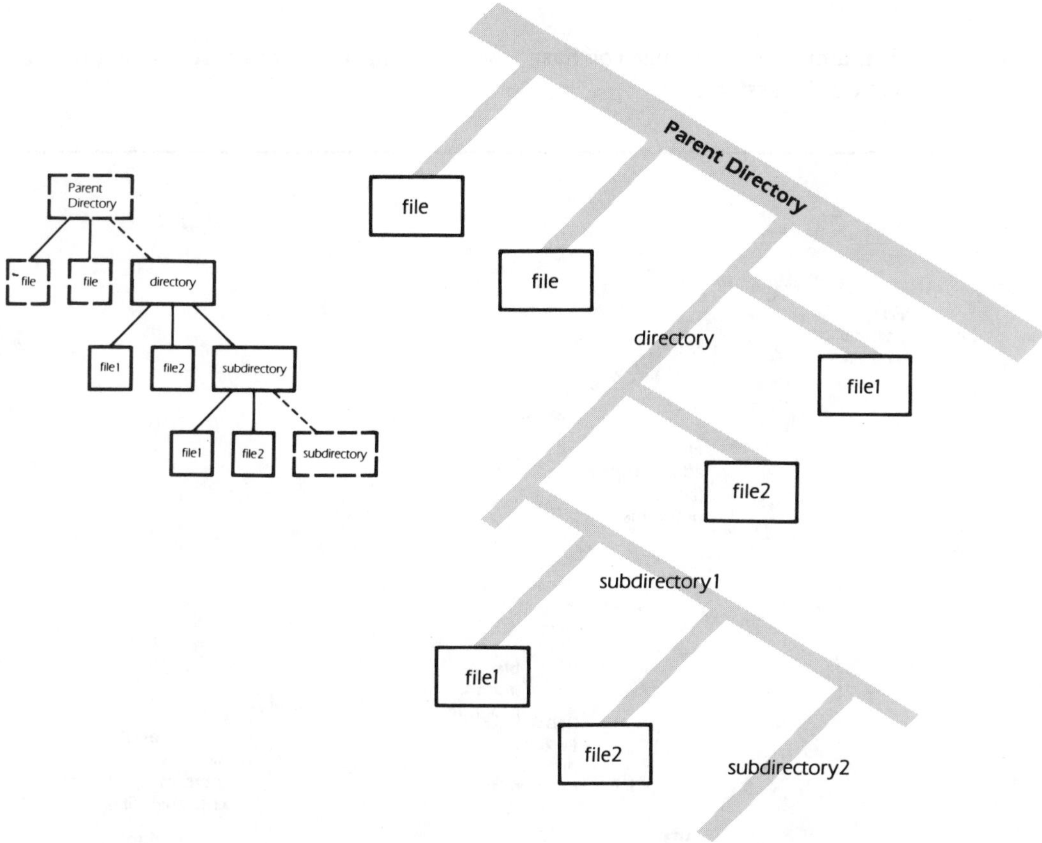

Figure 2-8. UNIX directories can contain both files and other directories.

If we wanted to, we could give a pathname for a file named `letter` in `simian`'s directory (see figure 2-10).

```
/user/simian/letter
```

Similarly, we could give a pathname for a file of the same name in the directory belonging to `tom`:

```
/user/tom/letter
```

Pathnames enable you to access files on the system, no matter which directory you are currently in. For example, if you are in `simian`'s directory, you can look at one of `tom`'s files with this command:

cat /usr/tom/letter

(This example assumes that `tom` hasn't protected his file `letter` from being read by others on the system.)

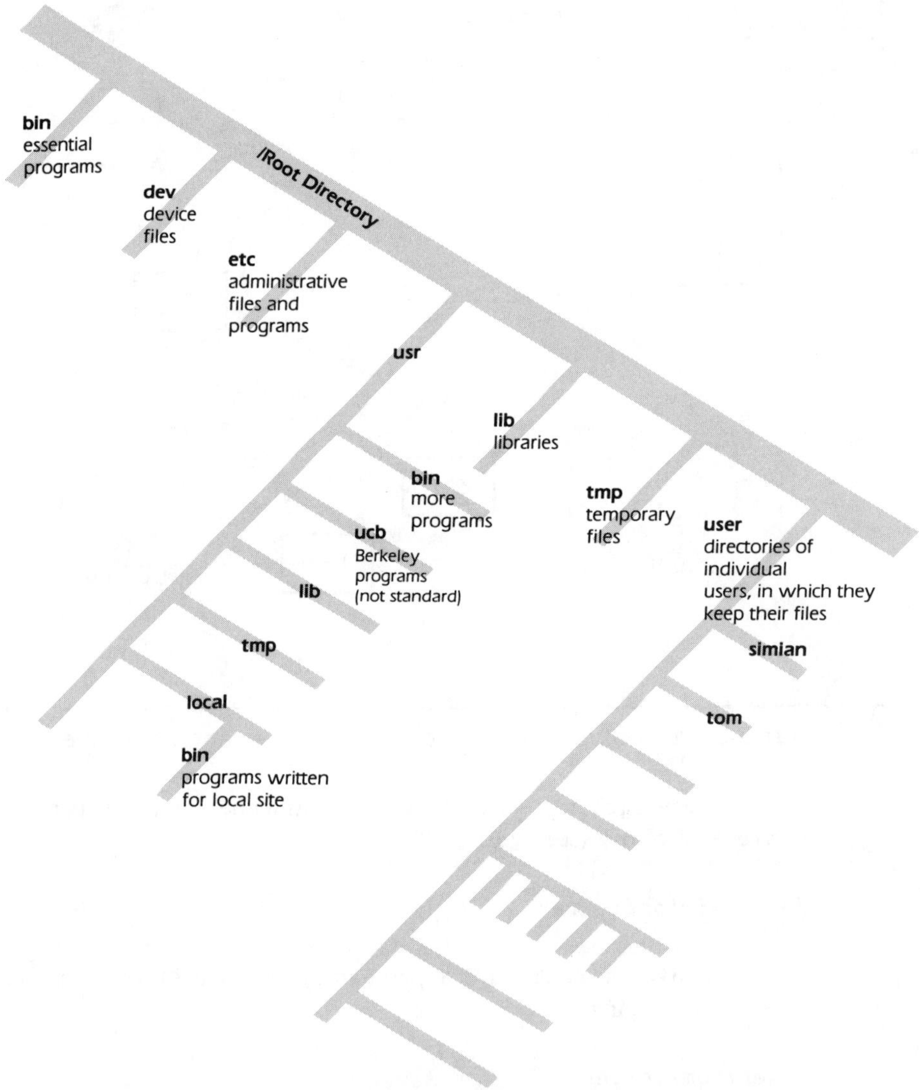

Figure 2-9. Typical UNIX directory structure.

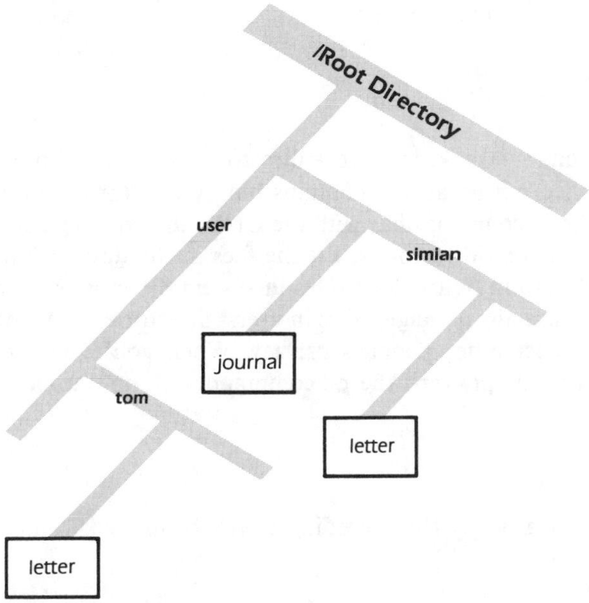

Pathnames

`/user/simian`	for the directory "simian"
`/user/simian/journal`	for the file "journal" in simian's directory
`/user/simian/letter`	for the file "letter" in simian's directory
`/user/tom/letter`	for the file "letter" in tom's directory

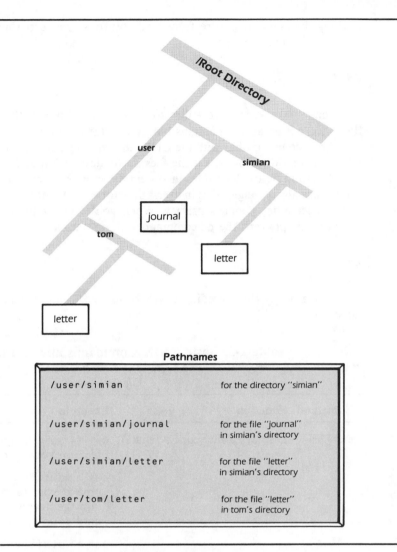

Figure 2-10. The pathname shows the position of a file in the directory structure.

Change the Current Directory (*cd*)

Using a lot of long pathnames to refer to files in other directories can quickly become awkward. If you are going to work with files in another directory, you can move to that directory with the `cd` command (change directory). For instance:

```
cd /user/tom
```

takes you to `tom`'s home directory. This directory now becomes your current or working directory. If you're feeling adventurous, you can tour other directories with a command such as:

cd /bin

This command takes you to a directory containing many of the UNIX commands. It's called *bin* because it contains binary files (program files).

To become familiar with the UNIX directory structure, it is a good exercise to cd to different directories, list the files in the directories, and so on. (Refer to the UNIX map in figure 2-9.) Files in system directories usually are protected, so you can't cause any damage. Files in users' directories may not be protected: be careful, and respect other people's privacy. When you're ready to return to your home directory, simply type the cd command with no pathname:

cd

For a list of the preceding UNIX commands, and examples of their use, see table 2-3.

Table 2-3. Basic UNIX Commands and Examples

Files

Command	Function	Example
cat	Displays a file (conCATenate).	cat file2 displays the contents of file2 on your terminal screen.
		cat > newfile1 takes what you type at your terminal and puts it into the new file named newfile, until you type Control-d.
		cat >> oldfile3 takes what you type at your terminal and adds it to the existing file named oldfile3, until you type Control-d.
cp	Copies a file (CoPy).	cp flim flam makes a copy of the file flim and calls it flam. (If flam is a directory, a copy of flim is put in that directory.)
mv	Renames a file (MoVe).	mv gappy happy changes the name of the file gappy to happy. (If happy is a directory, the gappy file is moved into it.)

Table 2-3. (cont.)

Command	Function	Example
	Files	
rm	Removes a file (ReMove).	rm Rodgers removes (deletes) the file Rodgers.
lpr lp (Sys V)	Sends a file to the line printer (Line PRinter).	lpr stuff sends the file stuff to the system line printer (for versions of UNIX other than System V). lp stuff sends the file stuff to the system line printer (for UNIX System V).
	Files and Directories	
ls	Lists the contents of a directory (LiSt).	ls lists the files and subdirectories in the current directory. ls -l gives a "long" listing of the current directory with complete information on each file. ls -a lists ALL the contents of the current directory, including files whose names begin with a period (such as .mailrc), which are not displayed by ls.
chmod	Changes the "mode" or permissions for files and directories (CHange MODe). *who*: u Login owner (user) g Group o Other users *op-codes*: + Add permissions - Remove permissions *permissions*: r Read w Write x Execute	chmod go-rwx mbox removes read, write, and execute permission on the file mbox for users in your group and all other users. This would prevent people from reading or changing the default file mbox in which messages that you've read are saved. (See chapter 3 for further explanation.) chmod ugo+rwx pubfiles opens the existing subdirectory pubfiles so that anyone can read, write, or execute the files in it.

Table 2-3. (cont.)

Command	Function	Example
	Directories	
pwd	Shows which directory you are in (Print Working Directory).	pwd displays your current directory.
cd	Moves you to another directory (Change Directory).	cd (with no directory name specified) returns you to your home directory.
		cd /user/reggie places you in the directory /user/reggie.
		cd .. places you in the directory "above" the current directory. If you were in /user /reggie, this command would put you in the /user directory.
mkdir	Creates a new directory (MaKe DIRectory).	mkdir Chap4 creates a new subdirectory called Chap4 in your current directory.
rmdir	Removes an existing directory (ReMove DIRectory).	rmdir budget87 deletes the directory budget87 (but only if the directory contains no files).
	System	
who	Shows who is on the system (WHO).	who displays the users currently logged onto the system.
ps	Shows the processes (programs) being run (Process Status).	ps displays the processes you are currently running.
		ps -a displays the processes being run by all users on the system.
man	Shows information about a command (MANual).	man mailx displays information about the mailx command and its options.
		man -k mail lists the UNIX commands that relate to the keyword mail.

Redirect Output (>)

The last concepts we'll cover concern the input and output for UNIX commands. UNIX allows you to *redirect* data between programs and files with the *redirection operators* shown in figure 2-11. This capability is very useful for communications tasks in which a file has to be processed through several stages.

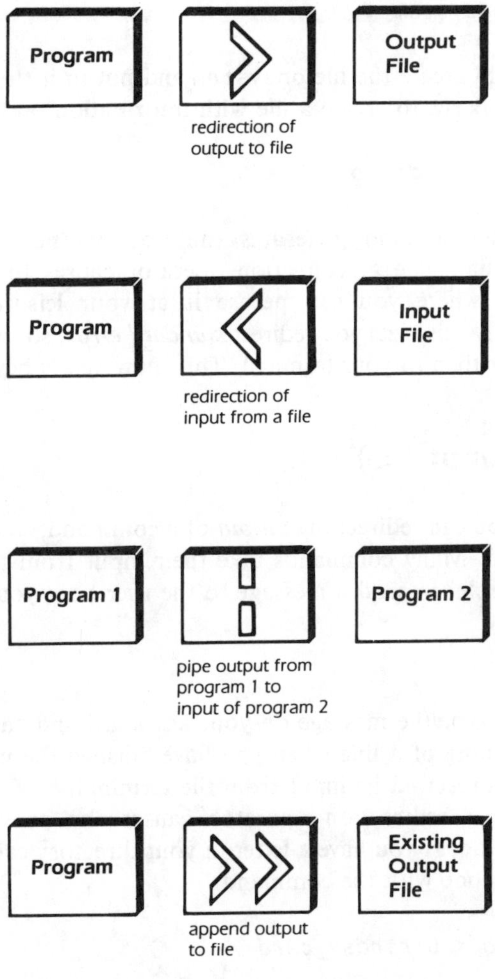

Figure 2-11. Redirection operators control input and output for programs.

Some commands don't need input, nor do they provide output. As we've just seen, `cd` simply returns you to your home directory. It neither expects nor produces data. It doesn't even display any information as it performs its task. Like most UNIX commands, it does its work silently without chatty messages to the user.

Other UNIX commands produce only an output; they require no input. For example, the who command generates a list of the users currently logged on your system. This list is sent to the standard output, normally considered to be your terminal. You can redirect the standard output to go someplace other than the terminal by using a redirection operator (> in this case). Let's say you want to save in a file the list produced by the who command. If you type

```
who > onsystem
```

UNIX will create the file onsystem and put in it the list of current users.

Similarly, to create a file with information on the pwd command, type:

```
man pwd > pwdinfo
```

The man command generates the text of the pwd entry in the UNIX on-line manual. The > redirection operator causes the text to be put into the file pwdinfo where you can peruse it at your leisure.

UNIX also lets you redirect *standard error*, so that error messages are sent to a file rather than to your terminal. This, however, is beyond the scope of this chapter.

Redirect Input (<)

Just as you can redirect the *output* of a command, so can you redirect the *input* of a command. Many commands take their input from the terminal (standard input). For example, to send a message to the user bob, you enter:

```
mail bob
```

You then type the message on your keyboard and enter Control-d (or a period) at the beginning of a line when you have finished the message. Thus, the mail command has received its input from the terminal.

The < redirection operator causes the program to get its input from a file instead. If you have a letter in your directory called birthday_card, you can send it to bob with the command:

```
mail bob < birthday_card
```

You've seen that the redirection operators > and < can be used to send a program's output to a file or to take input from a file. But what if you want a program to send its output, not to a file, but to another program? To see how this would work, let's build a simple utility to monitor the number of users on the computer. We can start with the who command, which displays on a separate line each currently logged-in user. If we could count the number of lines, we would have the number of users on the system. Fortunately, UNIX has a word count utility (`wc`) that will do just that. With the `-l` option, it produces a count of the lines in a file.

The problem now is to find a way to send the output of the `who` command to the `wc` program so that the lines produced by `who` can be counted. We could do it with a temporary file, by typing:

```
who > onsystem
wc -l < onsystem
```

But we can do it more directly with the UNIX *pipe* symbol (¦). This character tells UNIX to "pipe" the output from one program to the input of another program. Thus:

```
who ¦ wc -l
```

gives a count of the users on the system.

Combining UNIX Features

To keep a log of the number of users on the system, we can use the > operator to redirect the output of our monitor program to a file:

```
who ¦ wc -l > logfile
```

The count of users is placed in the file `logfile`. Unfortunately, every time the command is executed, it erases the previous contents of `logfile`—not much good for record-keeping. We need a way to add data to a file without destroying the old contents. For this purpose, UNIX provides the *append* operator, >>. The command

```
who ¦ wc -l >> logfile
```

adds the current number of users to the existing `logfile`. If we combine our new command with the `date` command (to display the time and date), we will have all we need for a shell script that records the time, date, and load on the computer:

```
date >> logfile
who ¦ wc -l >> logfile
```

All we have to do is use one of the UNIX editors to create this file, giving it the name we want for our script. If we make the shell script executable with `chmod u+x script_name`, we can run the shell script as if it were a standard UNIX command. We can even make the script execute at regular intervals with `crontab`—but that's beyond the scope of this introduction. You get the idea. Instead of

Instead of creating a new program from scratch with UNIX, we simply create a shell script from existing commands and redirection operators.

You may think that we've strayed from our subject of UNIX communications. Actually, you will soon see how UNIX commands can be used to enhance the communications programs. Indeed, most mail and news programs provide a command (called a *shell escape*) that allows you to "escape" to a shell so that you can execute UNIX commands, shell scripts, or other programs. In addition, shell scripts containing UUCP programs are often used to automate the transfer of files between machines.

Summary

This chapter has given you a bird's eye view of the UNIX operating system and its key features. We hope that it has helped you appreciate the beauty of UNIX:

- Easy programming by combining small building-block programs.
- A clean minimalist design with nothing extra, nothing unnecessary.
- A hands-on, open-access philosophy.

In addition to learning about the features of UNIX, you've learned (or reviewed) the UNIX commands that you will need in your daily use of UNIX communications. Tables 2-3 and 2-4 summarize the commands and special keys for you. Table 2-5 lists the mail commands that we'll cover.

Now—on to electronic mail!

Table 2-4. Special Keys and Their Functions

Key	Function
Control-c or Delete key	Interrupt character. Stops a command currently being executed (for instance, if you `cat` a file to display it on the screen but decide you don't want to see it all). Use Control-c to cancel the mail message you are currently composing.
Control-d	Removes you from the current environment. Use Control-d to exit the `mail` and `mailx` message editors. Note: at the `$` or `%` shell prompts, entering Control-d logs you off the system.
Control-h or Backspace key	Deletes the previous character. Used while entering commands and in the `mail` and `mailx` message editors.

Table 2-4. (cont.)

Key	Function
Control-s	Temporarily halts the current command being executed. Type Control-s to halt the scrolling of text on your terminal.
Control-q	Resumes the command that was halted by Control-s. Type Control-q to resume the scrolling of text.
Control-x or @ key	Deletes the current line of text being entered. Not implemented on all systems.

Table 2-5. Mail-Related Commands in UNIX

Command	Description	Where Covered
`mailx` (System V) `Mail` (BSD)	Extended mail programs for sending and reading electronic messages from other computer users.	Chapters 3–5
`uuname`	Shows which computers your system is connected to.	Chapter 4
`.mailrc`	Start-up file for mail. Modify this file to customize the `mailx` or `Mail` program.	Chapters 4, 5
`/bin/mail`	A rudimentary mail program for sending and reading messages with other users. Called "binmail" because it is located in the `/bin` directory.	Appendix A
`write`	Sends on-line message to another user.	Appendix B
`talk`	Instantaneously sends and receives messages.	Appendix B
`mesg`	Prevents other users from interrupting you with the `talk` or `write` command.	Appendix B
`chat`	New program for sending on-line messages among users.	Appendix B

Part

1

UNIX Mail

Part 1 focuses on the popular *UNIX mail* program, called `mailx` on UNIX System V and `Mail` on UNIX Berkeley (BSD) UNIX systems. (It may be called something else on your system.) To keep things simple, we will refer to it as the `mailx` program.

The three chapters in this part are a complete tutorial on UNIX mail, covering beginning to advanced concepts. You will learn all the concepts and commands necessary to exchange letters and other text documents with fellow UNIX users, whether they are on the same UNIX computer or on one thousands of miles away. Our discussion applies to both `mailx` and `Mail`, though we will point out differences between these programs where appropriate.

The coverage is divided into three levels:

- Beginning mail (Chapter 3)
- Intermediate mail (Chapter 4)
- Advanced mail (Chapter 5)

3

Beginning Mail

In this chapter, we'll whet your appetite for electronic mail (called *e-mail* for short) by showing you how it reduces the paperwork of an instructor at a community college. After a short discussion of the advantages of e-mail, we'll walk you through the basic operations of sending and reading messages on UNIX. You will learn to:

- Create and send a message to another user.
- See a listing of the messages that have been sent to you.
- Read your messages.
- Delete unwanted messages.
- Save messages to a file in your directory.

Finally, we'll peek behind the scenes to see how UNIX deals with files and directories when running e-mail. This background information will prepare you for the more advanced mail commands described in chapter 4.

Electronic Mail on UNIX

If you've never used electronic mail, you're in for some surprises. *Electronic mail* is a computerized mail delivery system. On UNIX, each user has an electronic mailbox called a *system mailbox*, as shown in figure 3-1. Messages from other users are delivered to your mailbox. These messages can be read and then saved or discarded.

You'll be surprised at how much easier it is to get work done when e-mail is available. Instead of making repeated phone calls to an elusive sales manager, you can ask your question in an electronic message. Instead of bothering with enve-

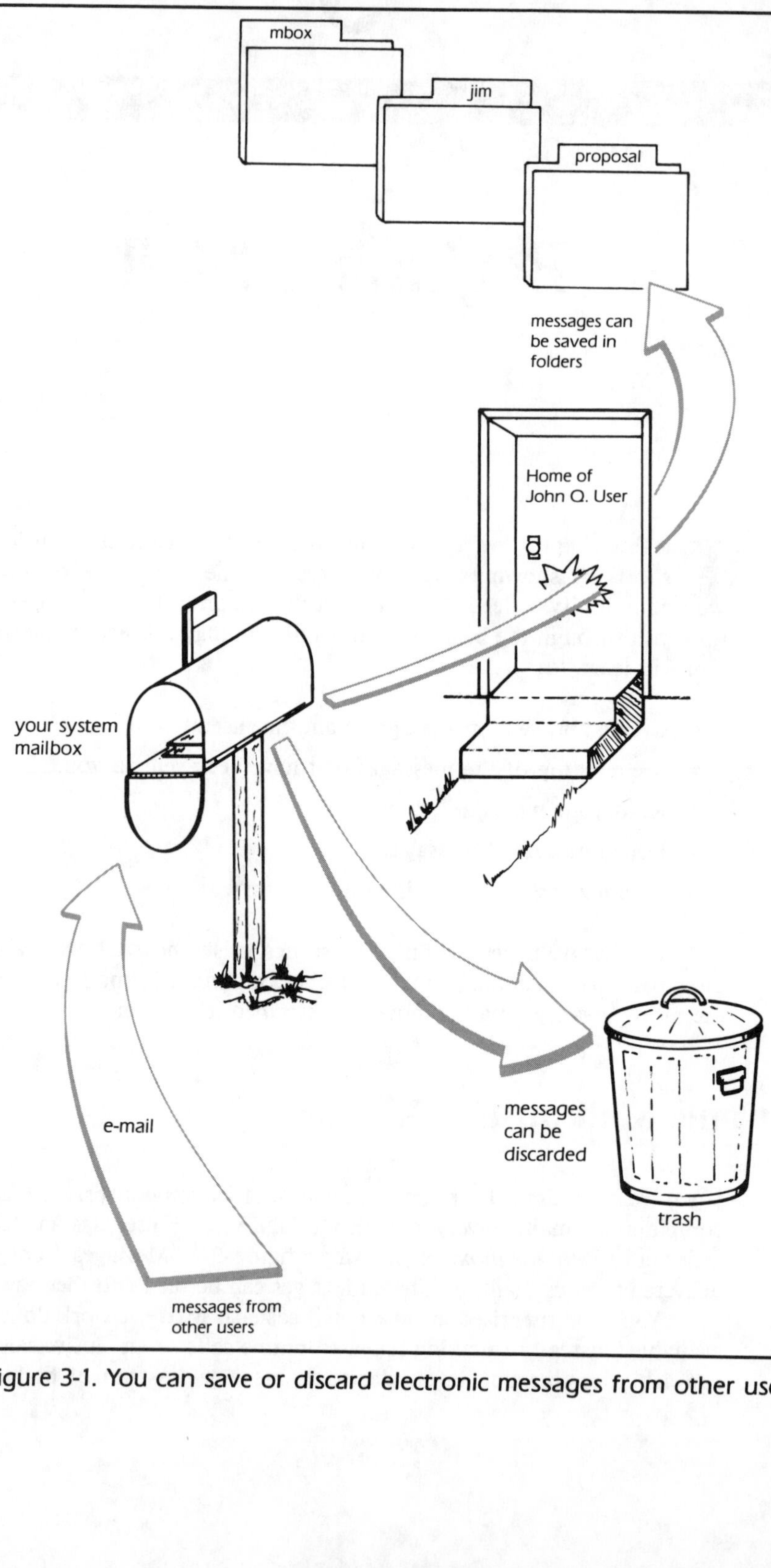

Figure 3-1. You can save or discard electronic messages from other users.

lopes, stamps, and address books, you can send your electronic mail with a few simple keystrokes. You don't have to wonder whether your first-class letter will take two days or a week to reach its destination.

But e-mail is more than just a replacement for conventional mail and telephone calls. It offers new forms of collaboration, such as conferencing. Electronic mail promises to become as widespread and indispensable as word processing. A few years from now, you'll ask, "How could we ever have gotten along without it?"[1]

A Mail Scenario

To see how electronic mail works in a real situation, let's follow an instructor at a community college as she handles her electronic correspondence from a UNIX terminal. (Although this example takes place in a college, the principles would be the same whether in a business, scientific, or academic setting.)

Sending Mail to a Group

Immediately after logging into the UNIX system, the instructor sends a short message to the 25 students in her Pascal class to let them know there's been a change in the class schedule. With one command the instructor sends out 25 identical copies of the note. (This beats standing in line for the photocopy machine!) The message is delivered almost instantaneously to the electronic mailboxes of each of the 25 students.

Reading and Replying to Mail

After telling the students about the schedule change, the instructor looks through her electronic mailbox by issuing a command to the UNIX system (`mailx` on System V, `Mail` on Berkeley UNIX).

The first message is from a student with a question about his term project.

---

1. Electronic mail has even begun to enter the history books. According to an article by David Hoffman and Bob Woodward in the *San Jose Mercury News* (Feb 13, 1987, p. 1), electronic messages were considered a source of evidence in the Tower Commission's investigation of the Iran-Contra scandal: "The panel, chaired by former Sen. John Tower, R-Texas, on Monday night received a huge new file of computer messages from the NSC [National Security Council] that were found in a special backup archive. . . . NSC officials were connected by a sophisticated computer system, through which they could send each other messages and memos. The system was designed to provide secure communications, and every message sent through it was preserved in an electronic archive."

He's having trouble with the topic he chose; may he switch to another? The instructor types a few lines, offering suggestions for a more realistic topic, and sends off her reply.

The second message is from the college bookstore: the 20 copies of the book on databases have been ordered, as she requested. The instructor dashes off a quick message reminding the bookstore that she had ordered 200 copies, not 20.

Saving and Printing Messages

The third and fourth messages are part of an ongoing discussion among three fellow teachers about the overuse of temporary instructors by community colleges. The instructor saves these messages in a file of e-mail, adding them to 30 other messages on the same subject. She sends this file to the laser printer so that she can review the responses later at her leisure.

Including a File in a Message

Her last message is from a programmer on a UNIX system 1500 miles away. The programmer has heard that she has compiled a list of inexpensive 1200-bps modems —could he get a copy? That's easily done. She sends him a short message and, with one more command, attaches the file that contains the list of modems. You can combine files and existing electronic messages in a message that you send to another user. (See figure 3-2.)

Advantages of E-Mail

Unlike telephone calls, electronic messages from other people won't interrupt you. You can read your e-mail when you choose. And if your system allows it, you can use a modem to read your e-mail from home or from any other remote location. You can see how e-mail allows you to handle correspondence quickly. When you read a message, you can reply to it immediately. All you need is your keyboard and terminal. If you want to edit the message, you can call up one of the UNIX editors. Sending a message requires only one simple command; there's no need to go to a post office or mail drop.

With the telephone, it's often difficult to get hold of the person you want. Much time is wasted playing "telephone tag": you call when he's out; when he returns your call, you're out. With electronic mail, if you have an idea, you can act on it immediately by creating a message and sending it. You don't need to consider whether the other person is available—you can act on a bright idea that comes at 2 a.m.!

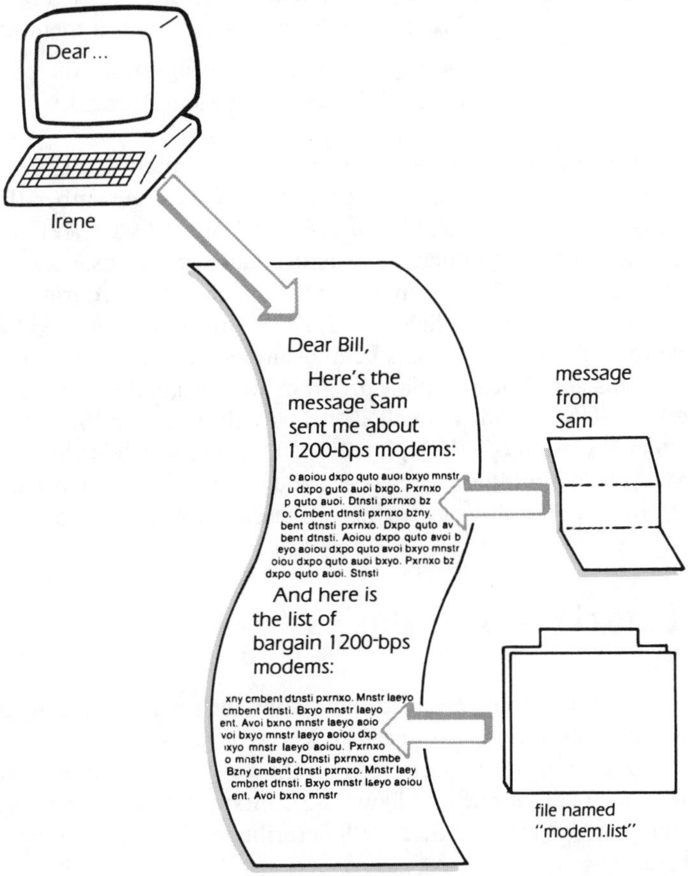

Figure 3-2. An electronic message can contain files or existing messages.

This immediacy makes electronic mail ideal for groups that need to inform their members of late-breaking events. The only hitch with electronic mail is that recipients must log into the UNIX system to know whether they have received any messages.

Other Versions of Mail

The `mailx` program described in this chapter isn't the only mail program available for UNIX. Other mail programs include:

`/bin/mail` The primitive UNIX mailer (`mail`) that lives in the `/bin` directory (see Appendix A).

`MH` A public-domain mail system from the Rand Corporation.

`AT&T Mail`	Part of the Unified Electronic Messaging Facility offered by AT&T; an elaborate system with a menu-driven interface.
`elm`	A screen-oriented mail program in the public domain, written by David Taylor of Hewlett-Packard.[2]

We've chosen the `mailx` program as our main focus because it's available on all Berkeley and System V versions of UNIX. (Remember that, unless otherwise specified, we will use `mailx` to refer to both AT&T's `mailx` and Berkeley `Mail`, since they are very similar in structure and commands.)

With about 200 commands and options, the program is both powerful and flexible—a tinkerer's delight. And, once you master the `mailx` program, you'll be able to understand the ideas behind any other mail program.

This sophisticated mail program was originally written by Kurt Schoens for Berkeley UNIX and was called `Mail` (with a capital `M`). When AT&T released its System V version of UNIX, it included `mailx`, which is almost identical to Berkeley `Mail`. The main difference between the two versions is that `mailx` has more custom options. (We'll point out further differences as they come up in the text.)

A Mail Tutorial—The Basics

Now let's talk about the basic commands for sending, reading, deleting, and saving messages—everything you need to know to get started.

Depending on how you call up the `mailx` program, it will be in either "write" mode or "read" mode (see figure 3-3). First we'll describe *write* mode (creating and sending messages), and then we'll describe *read* mode (reading, deleting, and saving messages).

Sending Messages

Sending mail is easy on UNIX. To send a message to a user named `leroy`, just enter:

`mailx leroy` *(System V)*

or

`Mail leroy` *(Berkeley)*

---

2. For a comparative survey of mailers and a discussion of the design features underlying them, see David Taylor's paper "All about UNIX Mailers" in *The UNIX Papers*, edited by The Waite Group (Indianapolis: Howard W. Sams, 1987).

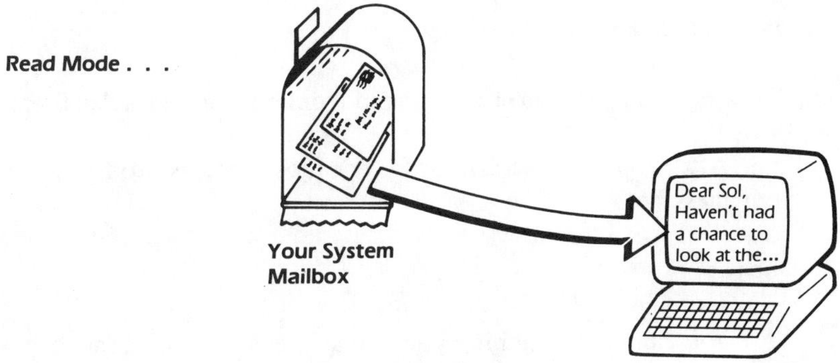

(A) **Read Mode:** To read your mail, type **mailx**, with no user name (for Berkeley users, type **Mail**).

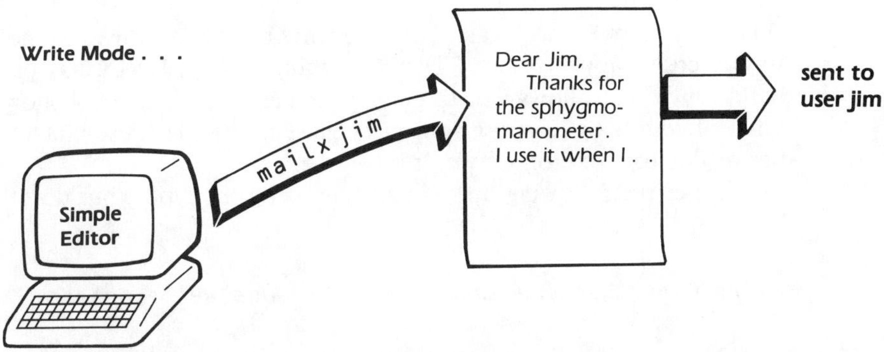

(B) **Write Mode:** To create a message and then send it, type **mailx user_name** (for Berkeley users, type **Mail user_name**).

Figure 3-3. The **mailx** program can be in **read** mode or **write** mode.

A good way to get acquainted with `mailx` is to send yourself some messages. In this way you'll be sure to have some messages in your system mailbox when we explain reading messages. Also, you won't have to worry about other people seeing your first efforts; feel free to experiment and try all the features of the program.

Log into your UNIX system and then enter the commands as they are shown in the following examples. (Although we don't show the prompt for the shell in use, you normally enter the same commands for both the Bourne and the C Shells.)

To e-mail yourself a letter, enter this command at the shell prompt (in this and the following examples, substitute your own login name for `william`):

mailx william *(System V)*

or

Mail william *(Berkeley)*

(We'll show only the mailx command from now on; Berkeley users please substitute Mail.)

After you press Return (or Enter), most systems prompt you for the subject of your message:

```
Subject:
```

You can enter anything you like at the subject prompt (or you can just press Return to leave it blank). This information tells the recipient of the message what the message is about, and it can help the recipient keep track of your message.

The Simple Message Editor

When you press Return again, you'll see that the cursor moves to the next line and stays there, waiting for you. There's nothing wrong. UNIX has placed you in a basic editor that allows you to enter your message. Chapter 4 shows how to use different editors to compose your message. For now, let's examine all the capabilities of this basic editor—it won't take long.

Enter the following line of text (including the typo), but don't press Return yet!

We're here, because we're here, because we're hhhere.

Now use your Backspace key to move the cursor left and erase the extra hh in hhhere. Try both Backspace and Control-h to see which works. (Some older "hard-copy" terminals use the pound sign (#) for erasing characters.) Now retype the line correctly.

The only other editing capability that some systems allow is to delete the entire line by pressing Control-x or the @ key. Experiment to see which (if any) works on your system.

As you can see, this message editor has severe limitations: after you press Return, the computer saves the line you've just typed; you can no longer change it with the message editor. If you notice a mistake on the first line while you are on the second line, you're stuck: there is no way to return to a previous line to correct it. You might add a line of explanation later in your message:

Oops! I meant "zoology" not "zoobirds" in line 1.

If the mistake is serious, you can cancel the entire message and start over, as we'll explain shortly. Or you can edit the message with a more powerful editor, as explained in chapter 4. The moral: use the default editor for "quick and dirty" messages. For messages that are longer or that need more polish, we'll show you how to bypass the default editor.

Send the Message

For now, let's just send this message. Press Return (to make sure that you're on a new line). Now type a single period and press Return again, like this:

```
mailx william
We're here, because we're here, because we're here.
.      ←type a period and press Return
EOT    ←UNIX responds
```

The single period is not inserted in the message; it merely tells the program that your message is complete. After you press Return, UNIX displays EOT (end of transmission). This means that UNIX accepted your message and sent it on its way.

Instead of a period, you can type Control-d:

```
mailx william
We're here, because we're here, because we're here.
^D     ←press Control and d keys simultaneously
EOT    ←UNIX responds
```

Be careful—once you send a message with Control-d or a single period, there's no way to recall it. It's like dropping a letter into a mailbox. (Think twice before you send that memo setting the boss straight!)

Cancel the Message

You can cancel a message while you're still writing it. You do this by issuing two *interrupt* characters. On our system, Control-c generates an interrupt character. Some systems accept the Delete key instead. Determine which key you should use on your system by cancelling a message to yourself. Type this message:

```
mailx william
Subject: testing cancel
Little we see in nature that is ours
```

Now, press Control-c (or the Delete key). You'll see a message like this:

```
(Interrupt--one more to kill letter)
```

To cancel the message, again press Control-c (or the Delete key). (There is also a way to cancel some messages even after they have been sent. This requires an understanding of how mail programs create UUCP jobs. See chapter 15.)

Send Mail to Several People

Lastly, let's see how to send the same mail simultaneously to more than one person. With nonelectronic mail, you'd have to make carbon copies or photocopies, or run off several copies of the letter on your printer. With electronic mail, you just add the login names of the additional recipients. For example,

```
mailx user1 user2 user3
```

sends the message you created to `user1`, `user2`, and `user3`. When we discuss *aliases* in chapter 4, you'll learn how to send mail to a group of people without having to name the people individually.

Experiment!

You now know the basics of sending mail. Play around with the program until you're comfortable with it. Some suggestions:

1. Create several messages and send them to yourself; you'll use these in the next section, which explains how to read mail. Which editing characters work on your terminal?
2. Find the login of a friend on your system and send messages to him or her.
3. Send a message simultaneously to yourself and your friend.

Sending Messages with *mailx*

1. To send mail, type `mailx user_name` (press Return) at the shell prompt (`$` or `%`), where `user_name` is the login name of the person to receive the message. For Berkeley UNIX, use `Mail user_name` instead.
2. After you issue the `mailx user_name` command, UNIX puts you into a simple editor so that you can create your message.
3. The editor responds to these commands (depending on your particular system):

`Return` or `Enter`	Start a new line
`Control-h`, `Backspace`, or `#`	Erase previous character
`Control-x` or `@`	Cancel current line
`Control-c` or `Delete`	Interrupt (to kill current message)

4. To end your message, press Return and type Control-d or a single period followed by another Return. UNIX automatically sends your message.

Understanding Message Headers

Each time you log into the UNIX system, the shell will tell you if you have any messages in your system mailbox:

```
You have mail.
```

UNIX makes it easy for you to see a summary of the messages that you have received. When you call up the `mailx` program, you will see a display of message *headers*. The purpose of headers is to quickly reveal some details about the received messages. For each message, the display tells you when the message arrived, who sent it, how long it is, the subject, etc. Imagine the messages as a large stack of envelopes sitting on your desk. You're going to be replying to some, saving others, throwing others away.

To read your message headers, type:

```
mailx
```

at the shell prompt. (Recall that in Berkeley UNIX, you will type `Mail`.) After you enter the command, you will see a display similar to figure 3-4.

```
Mail version 2.18 5/19/83.  Type ? for help.
"/usr/spool/mail/mike": 15 messages 9 new 14 unread
>U  1 rich      Sun Nov  2 10:50  128/6329 "Heather's project"
 U  2 lea       Mon Nov  3 03:44  44/1327 "Going to tradeshow?"
    3 lea       Mon Nov  3 06:54  13/335 "Vacation plans"
 U  4 rich      Mon Nov  3 13:33  16/583 "Bookstore offer"
 U  5 baabaa    Tue Nov  4 02:57  350/10870 "Rodin exhibit"
 *  6 heather   Tue Nov  4 09:41  14/464 "new class sked"
 N  7 rich      Tue Nov  4 09:45  15/356 "Re:  samples"
 N  8 rebus     Tue Nov  4 23:38  21/653 "UNIX Seminar"
 N  9 well!mck  Fri Nov  7 10:24  62/1844 "Format Codes Rev 0"
 N 10 chesley   Fri Nov  7 19:19  18/770 "No more games!"
&
```

Figure 3-4. Display of message headers.

If, instead of a display like this, you see an e-mail message scrolling across your screen, you are in the `/bin/mail` program. Ask your system administrator how to access the `mailx` program. (If your system doesn't have `mailx` or `Mail`, you can learn more about `/bin/mail` in Appendix A.)

This example shows only the first 10 messages of the 15 total messages that you've received. We know this from the second line of the display: `15 messages 9 new 14 unread`.

For each message you receive, `mailx` assigns a number. For example, the message `"Heather's project"` is message 1. You can use message numbers to identify the particular message(s) to be affected by a `mailx` command. Thus, the command `type 1` displays the contents of message 1.

Notice the > symbol to the left of the first message. This is a marker that keeps your place as you go through your messages. The message it points to is called the *current message*. When you issue a command with no message number, by default the command affects the current message. Thus, `type` (with no message number) displays the message pointed to by >.

Message Status

The letter before the message number (in column 1) indicates the status of the message. The letter `N` (New) marks messages that have been received since you last called up the `mailx` program. The letter `U` (Unread) identifies messages that weren't read in the previous mail session.

An asterisk (*) appears next to messages that have been saved to a file or folder while you have been using `mailx`. We'll explain how to save messages in a few pages.

A blank in column 1 means that the message has been read but not saved. (In this example, message 3 has been read but not saved.)

Login Name and Date

As you can see, there is a lot of information in the header display. Figure 3-5 shows the data fields for each message. We'll explain each field in turn.

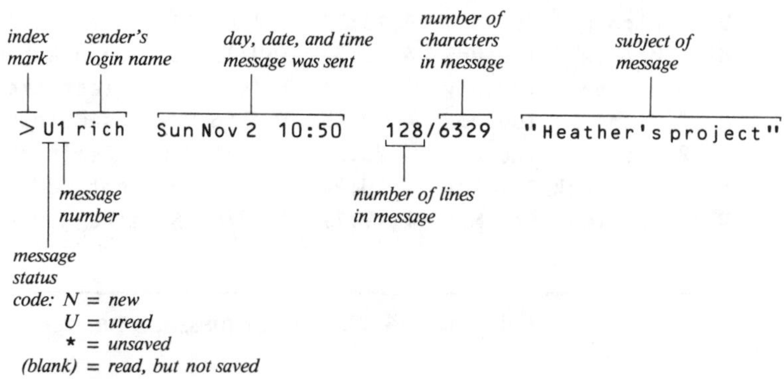

Figure 3-5. Meaning of a line in the **mailx** header display.

To the right of the message number is the login name of the person who sent the message. Some logins in figure 3-4 are `lea`, `rebus`, and `heather`. You can tell from the login entry whether a message was sent by a user on a different UNIX computer. For instance, `well!mck` in message 9 means that the message was sent by `mck`, a user on The WELL system. We'll explain how messages can be sent from one UNIX machine to another in chapter 4.

To the right of the sender is the day, date, and time that the message was sent.

The two numbers separated by a slash, such as **128/6329** in message 1, represent the number of lines and characters in the message. Thus, message 1 has 128 lines and 6329 characters (see figure 3-5).

The last entry in the header is the subject of the message, as entered by its sender.

Enter *mailx* Commands

Beneath the display of headers in figure 3-4, you will notice an ampersand (&) in the left margin. The ampersand is the prompt for the `Mail` program. (A question mark is the prompt for the `mailx` program.) When you see the & (or ?, depending on which program you have), you can begin entering commands for reading and handling your mail messages. There are more than 40 commands you can enter; in this section we'll cover the commands you need to get started. For a complete listing of the commands, see table 4-2 in the next chapter.

Commands can be entered with their full name, for example:

```
save
```

Some can be entered as an abbreviation—usually their first letter:

```
s
```

Experiment!

We recommend that you try the commands on your terminal as we explain them. Send yourself a group of messages and practice reading, deleting, and saving them. The `mailx` program is a powerful tool. Spend a little time now to get comfortable with it. When you want to leave the program, type

```
exit
```

or simply

```
x
```

Your messages won't be removed from the system mailbox, and you can practice with them again later.

To see a help screen on the most-used commands, enter `help` or a question mark (?). You can also consult tables 3-1 and 3-2 at the end of this chapter for a listing of the basic `mailx` commands.

Reading Messages

The easiest way to read the first message in `mailx` is simply to press Return. You'll see something like:

```
&    ←press Return
Message  1:
From rich Sun Nov  2 10:50:40 1986
Date: Sun, 2 Nov 87 10:50:10 pst
From: rich (Richard Keast)
To: mike
Subject: Heather's project
Did you know that Heather Chan (the paramedic) has received a lot
of good feedback about her project with the children's ward? You
might ask her what the clinic in Portland sent her.
&
```

Depending on how your system administrator has set up the `mailx` program, you may see additional lines of information preceding the text of the message. (In chapter 5, when we discuss the `.mailrc` file, you'll see how to suppress unneeded lines of information in the display of a message.) When reading a long message, you can use Control-s and Control-q to stop and start the scrolling of the text. Control-c interrupts the display of the message and returns you to the `mailx` prompt so that you can enter your next command. Control-c is useful if the message is long and you would rather not read it all now.

After the message has been displayed, you can cause the message headers to be redisplayed by typing:

headers

or simply

h

After the first message has been read, notice that in the header display the `U` notation that was formerly at message 1 has disappeared, indicating that the message has been read. This is illustrated in figure 3-6. Also, the index (>) points to message 1, indicating that commands will affect it by default.

To read the next message in the header display, press Return again. You can continue reading all your messages in this fashion—simply by pressing Return for the next message.

If you want to read a particular message, just type its message number. For example, to display message 5, type:

5

```
>    1 rich      Sun Nov  2 10:50  128/6329 "Heather's project"
 U   2 lea       Mon Nov  3 03:44  44/1327 "Going to tradeshow?"
     3 lea       Mon Nov  3 06:54  13/335 "Vacation plans"
 U   4 rich      Mon Nov  3 13:33  16/583 "Bookstore offer"
 U   5 baabaa    Tue Nov  4 02:57  350/10870 "Rodin exhibit"
 *   6 heather   Tue Nov  4 09:41  14/464 "new class sked"
 N   7 rich      Tue Nov  4 09:45  15/356 "Re:  samples"
 N   8 rebus     Tue Nov  4 23:38  21/653 "UNIX Seminar"
 N   9 well!mck  Fri Nov  7 10:24  62/1844 "Format Codes Rev 0"
 N  10 chesley   Fri Nov  7 19:19  18/770 "No more games!"
&
```

Figure 3-6. Header display after reading a message.

Several other commands can be used to display a message on the screen: `type`, `t`, `print`, `p`. Any of these commands will enable you to read message 5:

```
type 5
t 5
print 5
p 5
```

If You Have More Than Ten Messages

Normally, `mailx` displays only 10 message headers at once. In this example, however, we have 15 messages. We know that we have 15 messages because the `mailx` program said so when we first called it up:

```
"/usr/spool/mail/mike": 15 messages 9 new 14 unread
```

To see the remaining 5 message headers, type:

```
z+
```

or simply

```
z
```

In this example, the display would look like this:

```
>N 11 mitch       Sat Nov  8 10:16  15/472 "Re:  TWG CODES REV 0"
 N 12 bea         Sat Nov  8 14:18  11/296 "Re:  test reply on saturday"
 N 13 bea         Sat Nov  8 14:26  18/392 "to carolyn richmond's defunct"
 N 14 MAILER-DAEMON Sat Nov 8 14:26 30/746 "Returned mail: User unknown"
 N 15 jim         Sat Nov  8 22:41  14/378 "Re:  TWG CODES REV 0"
```

To see the previous display of message headers, enter:

```
z-
```

Daemons

You may be wondering about the line in the previous display:

```
N 14 MAILER-DAEMON Sat Nov 8 14:26 30/746 "Returned mail: User
unknown"
```

What's a "daemon"? Have we somehow stumbled into a Dungeons and Dragons game? Actually, a *daemon* is a process (a program in execution) that performs a task for the operating system on a regular basis. For example, a printer daemon is a process that regularly checks to see if there are files in the printer queue; if so, it sends them to the printer. A mailer daemon is responsible for delivering mail on the system. (It's your friendly mail carrier.) In this example, the daemon is reporting that the user to whom you tried to send the message doesn't exist, at least not under the name specified.

Replying to Messages

As you read your messages, you can use the `Reply` command to send an immediate response to a message. Type `Reply` or `R` and you will be placed in the message editor for composing a message. Write your message just as described earlier, using Control-d or a single period to exit the editor and send the message. The program automatically sends the message only to the person who originated the message.

For example, suppose you receive a message like this:

```
Message  21:
From dill Sun Nov  16 20:50:40 1987
Date: Sun, 16 Nov 87 20:50:10 pst
From: dill (Dillon Thomas)
To: mike
Subject:  June Vacation
So what's it going to be--yes or no?
```

At the `mailx` prompt, type `Reply 21` (`R 21`), or just `R` if 21 is the current message. The program automatically fills in the subject from the message to which you are replying:

```
Subject: Re: June Vacation
```

Now type the text of your response as described earlier under "Sending Mail." Send the message by typing a single period or Control-d in column 1.

Note that UNIX also offers the `reply` or `r` command (lowercase `r`). There is a distinct difference between the `reply` and `Reply` commands when the original message was sent to other people in addition to you. The message that you send with `reply` is sent not only to the person who wrote the message, but to everyone else who received it. (See figure 3-7A.) This includes anyone on the `To:` and `Cc:` (carbon copy) lists included with the message. You may not want everyone to read your reply—perhaps it's a response to a job opening. In the case of figure 3-7B, you send your reply to just the originator of the message by using the `Reply` command (with a capital `R`).

Saving Messages to the *mbox* File

Once you are receiving messages regularly, you have to decide what to do with them. Many of them you'll want to save for future use. The `mailx` program provides a file called a *system mailbox* to hold your received messages. However, if you leave all your messages in your system mailbox, it will soon grow big and unwieldy.

The `mailx` program solves this problem by providing another file called `mbox` in your home directory. If you read a message and then leave the program with the `quit` command, your message is automatically saved in this catch-all `mbox` file. These messages are then removed from the system mailbox. (Note that if you leave the program with `exit` instead of `quit`, your system mailbox remains as is—no messages are removed.)

You can also save a message in `mbox`, regardless of whether you have read it, by using the `save` command. For example, to save the current message to `mbox`, enter:

```
save
```

Messages That "Disappear"

The automatic transfer of messages to the `mbox` file may seem confusing at first. One day you read your messages; a day later when you call up the `mailx` program, all your messages seem to be gone! They're really safe and sound in your `mbox` file.

It's easy to check this out for yourself. Read or save several messages in the header display. Leave the program with `quit`. Now call up the `mailx` program again, but this time tell it to read the `mbox` file instead of the system mailbox. You do this with the `-f` flag:

```
mailx -f mbox
```

The `-f` flag tells the program to read messages in the specified file. With the `-f` flag, you can access messages in any file—in your directory or in the directory of another user. (If you don't specify a file, the program automatically reads the `mbox` file; so `mailx -f` is all you really need to read `mbox`.)

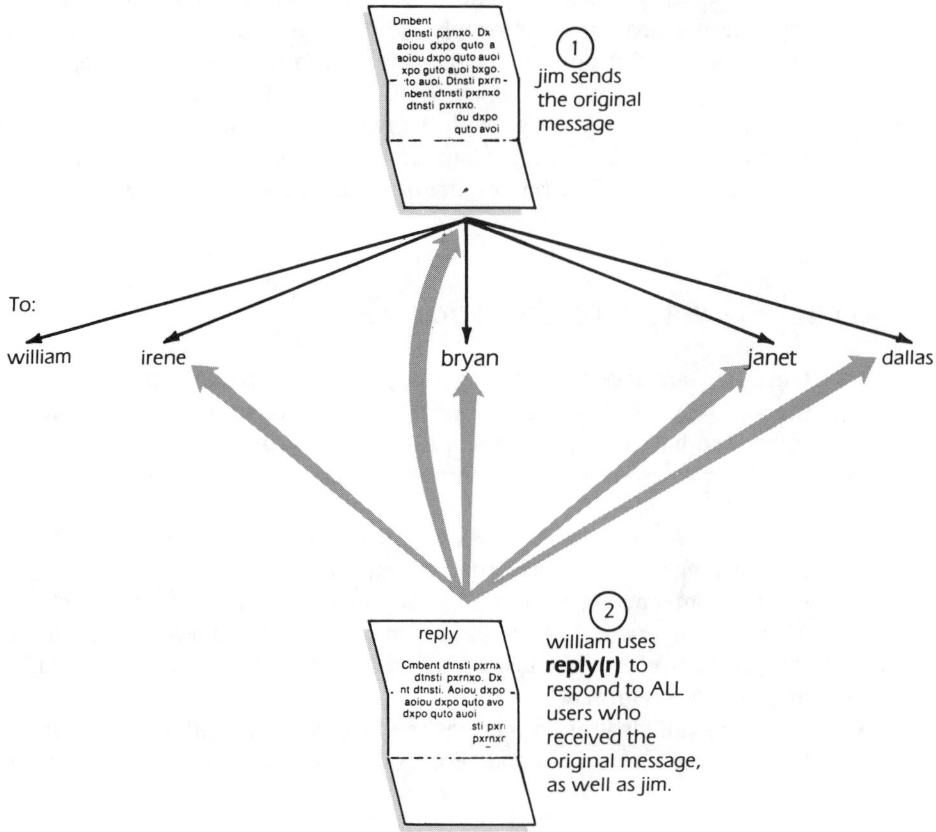

(A) To reply to everyone who received the original message, use **reply** (lowercase **r**).

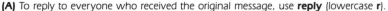

Figure 3-7. Using **reply** and **Reply**.

Saving Messages to Files

Saving to `mbox` only postpones the problem of what to do with your messages, however. If you receive a lot of e-mail, `mbox` will soon grow large and unwieldy. Messages on all subjects and from different users are saved together in `mbox` with no order or organization.

A better way to store your messages is in files. See figure 3-8. To organize your correspondence, you can name files after the person who sent the message or after the subject of the message. (Experiment to see which form of organization works best for you.) You can even save a message to two (or more) different files.

To save a message to a file, just enter the `save` command followed by a

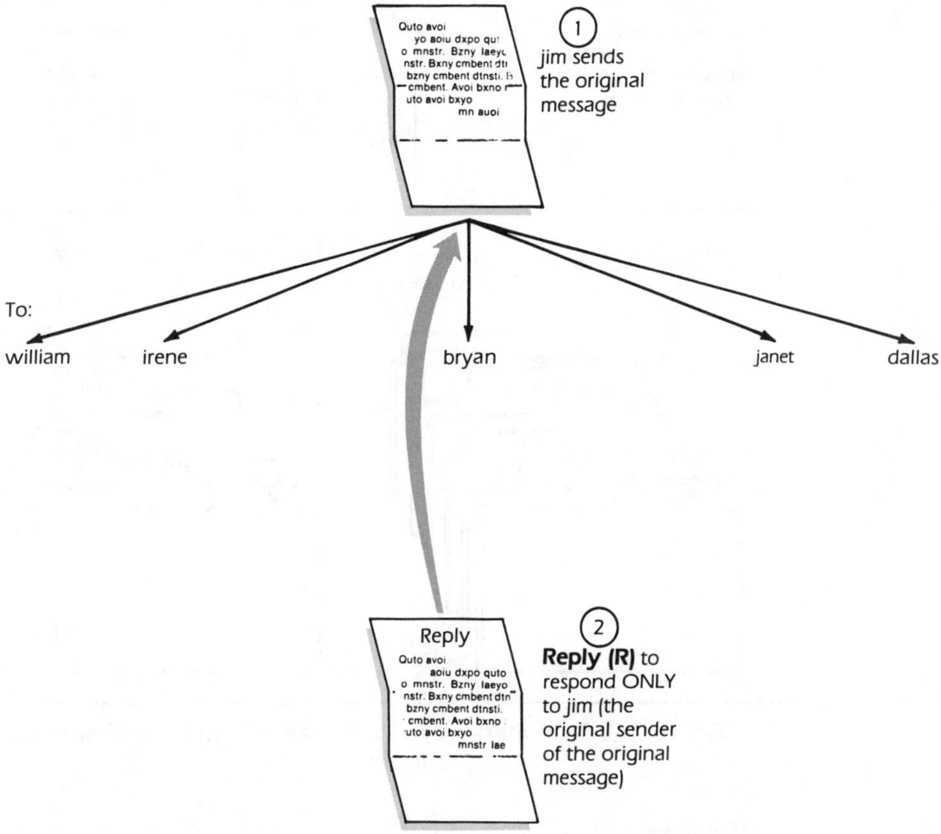

(B) To reply only to the sender of a message, use **Reply** (capital **R**).

Figure 3-7. (cont.)

filename. If the file exists, the message will be added to the file. If the file doesn't exist, a new file will be created automatically. For instance, to save message 5 to the file named `rodin`, enter:

`save 5 rodin`

You will see a display like:

```
"rodin" [New File] 350/10870
```

As the message says, the new file contains 350 lines and 10,870 characters. (Remember that you can enter most commands with an abbreviation—`s` instead of `save`.) If the file you name already exists, your message will be *appended* (added to) the contents of the existing file.

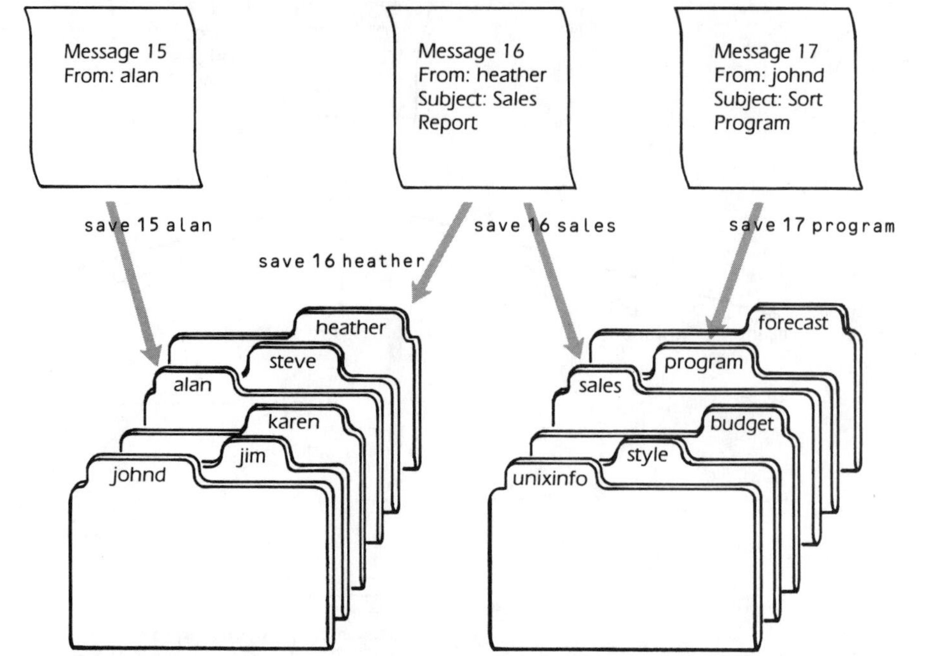

Figure 3-8. Save messages in files named after the sender or the subject (or both).

If you enter:

```
s newproposal
```

you save the current message (the one pointed to by the >) into the file named `newproposal`.

After saving a message, if you then display the message headers (with the command `headers` or `z`), you will see an asterisk (*) next to the message number of any saved messages. If you `quit` the program, the saved files will no longer appear in the message header display in future sessions (that is, they are deleted from the system mailbox). In the next chapter, we'll describe *folders*, a more sophisticated method for organizing your mail messages.

Keeping Your Messages Private

You have seen how `mailx -f` allows you to read messages in any file. Conversely, this means that YOUR messages can be read by other people. To ensure that your messages are private, you will have to change the permissions (access rights) for the files in your home directory. To protect your mbox file, for example, enter the chmod (change mode) command:

```
chmod go-rwx mbox
```

This removes the read (r), write (w), and execute (x) privileges for people in your group (g) and for any other users on the system (o).

Command Power with Message Lists

By specifying a message number, you can execute a mailx command on any message in the header display. With "message lists," you can execute a command on many different messages at once. A *message list* specifies a group (or list) of messages. It is typed on the same line as the command. There are several forms of message lists. For example, to save messages 2, 4, and 6 to the file memos, just separate the message numbers with spaces:

```
save 2 4 6 memos
```

To save a range of messages, type:

```
save 1-5 memos
```

(This saves messages 1 through 5.)

To save ALL messages, use the asterisk character:

```
save * memos
```

You can also select messages by the information they contain in their headers. The ability to select all messages sent by another user is a big timesaver. For example, to save all the messages sent by uriah, simply type:

```
save uriah uriah_file
```

All the messages from uriah are saved in the file uriah_file.

To select messages that contain a particular word in the subject field (Subject:), use the slash character (/). For example, if you have an ongoing discussion about calculus, you could save these messages into a file named calc_ideas by using the command:

```
save /calculus calc_ideas
```

All messages with the string "calculus" occurring in the subject field are saved. Messages with "Calculus" or "CALCULUS" would be saved also because upper-

or lowercase is ignored. Table 3-1 shows some sample message lists and the messages they specify.

Table 3-1. Message Lists for *mailx* Commands

Sample Message List	Messages Specified
`No message list`	Current message.
`12`	Message 12.
`12-20`	Messages 12 through 20.
`*`	All messages.
`john`	All messages sent by `john`.
`/reorg`	All messages that have `reorg` in the subject line.

Printing Hard Copies of Messages

Instead of reading your messages on the terminal screen, you can send them to the printer. Depending on your system, you may be able to enter a command like:

```
save 5 ¦ lp
```

This is an example of the UNIX pipe facility described in chapter 2. A pipe is indicated by the symbol ¦. The output of the `save 5` command is sent (or piped) to the `lp` command, the System V command for printing text on the line printer. For other versions of UNIX, substitute `lpr` for `lp`. The syntax for printing text may be slightly different at your site. (Of course, if you are a remote user who is accessing the UNIX system from a personal computer, you probably don't want to print messages on the line printer at the UNIX site. Most communications programs that run on PCs have a way to save text from the screen to a disk file. Check the documentation for your communications program.)

Deleting Messages

Sooner or later you will want to clean out your old, useless messages. Otherwise, you may get a gentle hint from your system administrator to do something about the 240K of disk space being taken up by your `mbox` file. The command to delete messages is:

```
delete message_list
```

You can specify a message list for `delete` just as you can for `save`. For example, to remove messages 11 through 19, enter:

```
delete 11-19
```

To remove all messages from user sam, enter:

```
delete sam
```

Remember, if you don't specify message numbers, the command affects only the current message. Typing delete or d removes only the current message.

Undelete Messages

Be careful when you delete messages. If you quit the mailx program, the deleted messages are permanently gone and cannot be retrieved. However, if you discover your mistake *before* leaving the program, all is not lost. In that case you can restore the deleted messages with the undelete command:

```
undelete message_list
```

The usual conventions about message lists apply for undelete. For instance, to bring back all messages that were deleted in the current mail session, type:

```
undelete *
```

Leaving *mailx*

When you're finished with your e-mail, you can leave the mailx program in two different ways. If you type:

```
quit
```

or

```
q
```

you will see a message like the following and will be returned to the standard shell prompt:

```
Saved 4 messages in mbox
Held 5 messages in /usr/spool/mail/bea
```

In this example, four messages were put into the mbox file (because you read or saved them to mbox). These messages won't appear in the header display the next time you use the mailx program. Five other messages remain in the system mailbox. Any messages you didn't read will reappear in the header display (marked with a U for "Unread") when you call up the program again.

If you DON'T want any messages removed from your system mailbox when you leave `mailx`, enter:

exit

or

x

All your messages will be retained and will appear in the message header display when you next call up the program. We'd suggest using the `exit` command until you are completely familiar with the program—it's easier to keep track of your messages.

Table 3-2. Basic Commands for *mailx*

Command	Function	Example
	Display Messages	
next msg_list* (n, +, Return)	Displays the first message in the message list msg_list. If no message list, displays the next message.	Pressing Return displays the next message.
print msg_list (p) type msg_list (t)	Displays the messages specified by the message list. If no message list, displays the current message.	p 5 displays message 5. t jim displays messages from user jim.
	Display Message Headers	
headers msg_list (h)	Displays the group of message headers containing the specified message. If no message list, displays the current group of headers.	h displays the current group of headers. h 12 displays the headers containing message 12.
z, z+	Displays the next group of message headers.	z displays the next group of headers.
z-	Displays the previous group of message headers.	z- displays the previous group of headers.
from msg_list (f)	Displays the headers of messages from senders specified by the message list.	f elise displays the headers of messages sent by elise.
Reply msg_list (R)	Both Reply and reply allow you to reply to the message specified. You are put into the default message editor.	R 15 lets you send a response to the sender of message 15.

Table 3-2. (cont.)

Display Message Headers		
Command	**Function**	**Example**
	With Reply (capital R), your reply is sent only to the person who sent you the original message.	
reply msg_list (r)	With reply (lowercase r), your reply is sent to the originator and to everyone who received the original message.	r 5 lets you send a response to the sender and recipients of message 5.
save msg_list filename (s)	Saves the specified messages to the file named. If no file is named, messages are saved by default in the file mbox.	s saves the current message in mbox. s 3 sys_admin saves message 3 in the file sys_admin.
delete msg_list (d)	Deletes the specified messages. Deletes the current message if no message list.	d 1-12 deletes messages 1 through 12.
undelete msg_list (u)	Restores the specified messages that have been deleted in the current mail session.	u * undeletes all messages deleted during the current mail session.
quit (q)	Quits the mailx program and returns you to the shell prompt ($ or %). Messages that were deleted, saved, or read in the current session are removed from your system mailbox.	q ends the mailx session, making changes to your system mailbox.
exit, xit (ex, x)	Exits the mailx program and returns you to the shell prompt ($ or %). Messages that were deleted, saved, or read in the current session are NOT removed from your system mailbox.	x ends a mailx session without making changes to your system mailbox.

*msg_list is a message list. It designates the messages to be affected by your command, as in table 3-1. It can refer to an individual message (7) or to a range of messages (1-5). The symbols in parentheses are abbreviations that you can enter instead of the full command.

Shortcuts

As you become more adept at handling your e-mail, you'll discover many shortcuts and alternative methods in the multitude of `mailx` commands. For example, `dt` or `dp` is a one-step command to delete the current message and display the next. Another helpful command is `shell`, which lets you escape to a shell and enter shell commands (like `ls`) until you type Control-d. For a complete listing of all the commands, consult your UNIX manual or table 4-2 in the next chapter.

A Look behind the Scenes

Before we move on to more advanced `mailx` operations, let's stop to see what the program is doing behind the scenes. Understanding the underlying mechanism of `mailx` will help you make sense of the approximately 200 commands and options.

The System Mailbox

As you learned earlier, each user is assigned a system mailbox. This mailbox is a file in which incoming messages are stored. On System V, the mailbox of user `eric` typically has the pathname `usr/mail/eric`. On a Berkeley system, it's usually `usr/spool/mail/eric`. You can display the contents of your system mailbox by entering the `cat` command:

cat /usr/mail/eric *(System V)*

or

cat /usr/spool/mail/eric *(Berkeley)*

Figure 3-9 shows the system mailbox and the other files that `mailx` deals with. The "folders" in the lower right of the figure are a special kind of file that we'll cover in chapter 4.

When you call up the `mailx` program, you will see a listing of the messages currently stored in your system mailbox file. The program copies the contents of your mailbox to a temporary file for the duration of your mail session. (This is what makes it possible to "undelete" messages, for example.) As you go through your e-mail, the messages in your temporary file are marked for deletion if you enter the `delete` command or if you save the message in another file. Since messages you read are automatically saved in mbox, these are marked for deletion in the temporary file.

Because you are working on a temporary file, the changes you specify for the system mailbox are not final until you leave the program. If you `quit` the program,

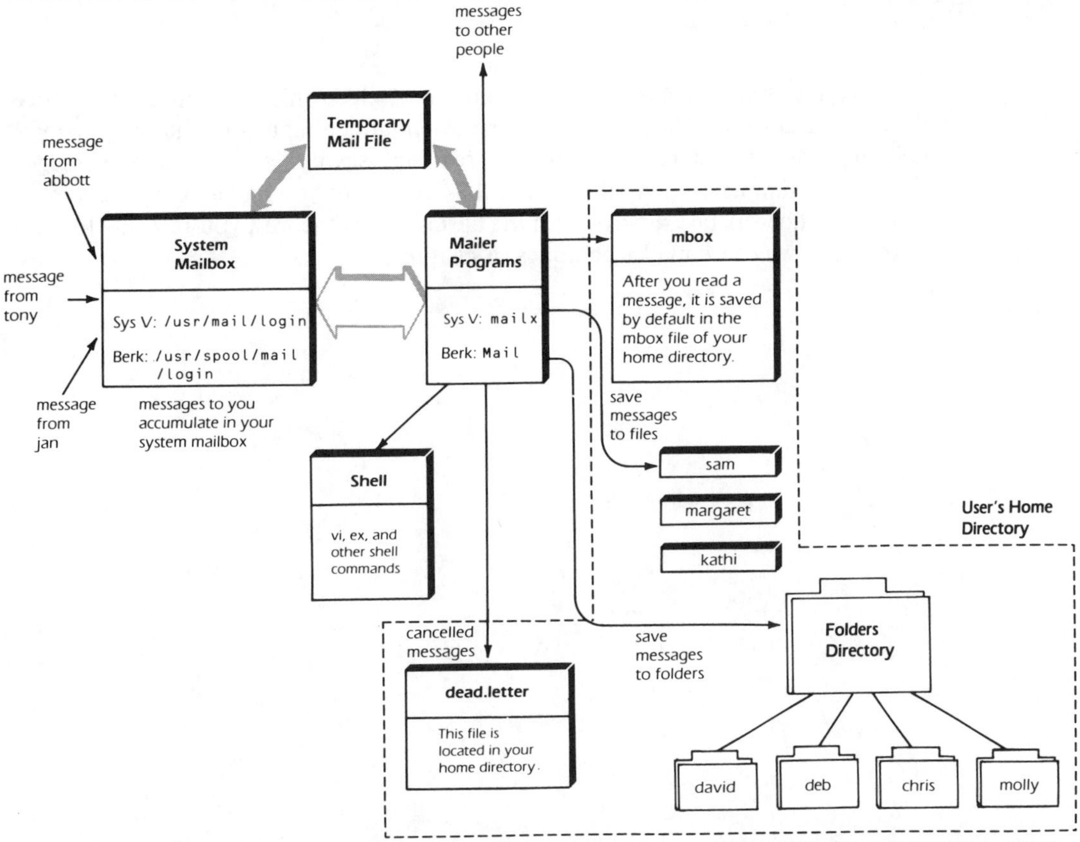

Figure 3-9. The underlying structure of **mailx**.

the temporary mail file replaces the former system mailbox, and the changes are made permanent. If you `exit` the program, the temporary mail file is abandoned and the existing system mailbox stays as it was.

The *dead.letter* File

Figure 3-9 also shows what happens to messages you cancel. If you cancel the message you're sending, the message is stored in the `dead.letter` file in your home directory. Only the most recently cancelled message is kept in `dead.letter`. If you decide to send the message later on, you can insert `dead.letter` into your message. (Chapter 4 will show you how to insert files into messages.) As you can see, the `mailx` program is not as complex or mysterious as it first appears. It simply offers a convenient user interface for manipulating files (and parts of files).

Summary

This chapter showed some of the advantages of electronic mail: its speed, convenience, and flexibility. You've learned the essential commands for handling e-mail, including the procedures for sending, reading, saving, and deleting messages. (These were summarized in tables 3-1 and 3-2.) Finally, you had a quick overview of how `mailx` does its tasks. Now, with the basics out of the way, you're ready to move on to the advanced e-mail techniques in chapter 4.

4

Intermediate Mail

In the last chapter you learned the essentials of using the `mailx` program. Now you'll learn how to make your `mailx` program faster and more flexible. This chapter shows you how to:

- Use "tilde" commands to gain more control over the messages you create.
- Create messages with `vi` and other editors.
- Insert existing files and messages into the message you're writing.
- Prepare messages off-line on your PC.
- Send messages to users on UNIX computers other than yours.
- Customize the operation of the `mailx` program by adding commands to your `.mailrc` file.
- Send messages to a group by using an "alias."
- Organize the messages you receive into convenient folders.

Tilde Commands—Power from Inside the Message Editor

While reading your e-mail messages, you handle the messages by entering the appropriate commands at the `mailx` prompt. When writing messages, you issue "tilde" commands, so named because they begin with a *tilde* (~). Tilde commands allow you to create text with your choice of editors, to insert text into messages, to change entries in your message heading, and much more. Tilde commands are also known as *tilde escapes* because you use them to "escape" from the editor to enter a command. (Tables showing all the `mailx` and tilde commands appear at the end of this chapter.)

For customizing the operation of `mailx`, there's yet another set of "commands," which will be described in chapter 5. (Actually, they are called *mailx variables*.) Table 4-1 summarizes the three types of commands and variables available in `mailx`.

Table 4-1. Types of Commands and Variables Available in *mailx*

Type	When Used	Examples
mailx Commands (Chapter 3)	Entered while reading messages.	`type` displays the contents of a message. `save` saves a message to a file.
Tilde Commands (Chapter 4)	Issued while writing messages.	`~v` invokes full-screen editor. `~r` inserts a file into a message.
mailx Variables (Chapter 5)	Set to customize `mailx` (e.g., in the `.mailrc` file).	`dot` allows a period to terminate input for a message. `VISUAL` determines the editor to be invoked by `~v`.

Using a More Powerful Editor and Displaying Text

When you first used the `mailx` program, you were probably disappointed by the limitations of the default message editor. It has almost no real editing capabilities. Thus, if you make a mistake on the first line of your message, you can't correct it. With the tilde commands, however, it's easy to access the power of a full-fledged text editor.

Tilde Commands to Invoke an Editor or Print Text

`~e`	Call up an editor (`ed` or `ex` by default).
`~p`	Print (display on the screen) the message you have created.
`~v`	Call up a full-screen editor (`vi` by default).

Invoking the *vi* Full-Screen Editor (~ *v*)

Suppose you have started a message like this:

```
Sounds llllike you're really weighed down with all those
```

```
projects.  Before you burn yourself out, talk to me.  Maybe we
can rearrange the schedule or postpone some of the less-
critical assignments.
```

Looking over this message before you send it, you see the misspelling `llllike` in the first line. With the default message editor, there's not much you can do about it: either apologize for it on the next line or cancel the message (by pressing Control-c twice) and start over again.

Here's where the tilde commands come to the rescue. While you're still in the message editor, type `~v` at the left margin of a line, like this:

```
Sounds llllike you're really weighed down with all those
projects.  Before you burn yourself out, talk to me.  Maybe we
can rearrange the schedule or postpone some of the less-
critical assignments.
~v
```

You'll find yourself in UNIX's full-screen `vi` editor, editing the text that you have written so far. You can move the cursor to the misspelled word, fix it, and return to the mail program. Even though `vi` is more primitive than word processors available on PCs, it is still light-years ahead of the default message editor: `vi` has complete editing facilities. As one `vi` enthusiast said, "You can do anything with `vi`." If you are not familiar with `vi`, either of the UNIX guides we suggested in chapter 1 can help you. Also, the *UNIX Bible* mentioned in Appendix E has particularly good sections on both the `ex` and the `vi` editors. (Because `vi` has so many commands and options, the explanation of `vi` in the UNIX manual can be confusing for beginners.)

Exiting *vi* to the Message Editor

When you finish editing your message, exit the `vi` program as you normally would (for instance with the Escape `ZZ` or Escape `:wq` sequences). You will return to the default e-mail message editor. You can add more text within the normal message editor, issue other tilde commands (such as to reenter `vi`), or end the message in the usual way—by typing either Control-d or a period in column 1.

Users of `mailx` are sometimes puzzled when they exit the `vi` editor and just see a blinking cursor—has the program bombed? No, you're still in the taciturn `mailx` message editor. Remember that after you leave the `vi` editor, your message is unfinished as far as `mailx` is concerned.

If ~*v* Doesn't Invoke *vi*

Most systems have been set up so that `~v` invokes `vi`. If your system hasn't been set up like this, the next chapter shows you how to do it by setting the `VISUAL` variable. If you prefer that a different editor be invoked by `~v`, you can set the `VISUAL` variable to that editor. (Chapter 5 shows how to set `mailx` variables.)

Invoking the *ex* Line Editor (~*e*)

Just as you can invoke the `vi` screen editor, so can you invoke the `ed` or `ex` line editors. To use `ed` or `ex`, enter the following command at the left-hand margin:

```
~e
```

Most people prefer `vi` for composing and editing messages—for most users, a line editor is a waste of time. However, if you are communicating with a slow modem or over a poor phone line, you may want to use a line editor to avoid the delays caused by `vi`'s redrawing of the screen. The line editor is also needed if your PC cannot emulate one of the terminals recognized by your UNIX system.

As with `~v`, you can change the editor that `~e` calls up. Normally it is set for `ed` or `ex`, but you can change this by setting the `EDITOR` variable. Again, read how to do this in chapter 5.

Seeing What You've Written So Far (~*p*)

To review the message you've written so far, enter

```
~p
```

in the left margin. The program will display your entire message on the screen. The `~p` command is handy if part of your message has scrolled off the screen, if it has become garbled because of telephone line noise, or if you've edited your message and you want to see how it looks.

Adding to Your Message

Once you become heavily involved in electronic mail, you'll find the next set of commands indispensable. These commands allow you to copy files and other text into the message you're creating.

Tilde Commands to Insert Files/Messages into Your Message

`~!< command`	Insert the output of the specified UNIX command (System V only).
`~d`	Insert the file `dead.letter`.
`~f message_list`	Insert a message(s).
`~m message_list`	Insert a message(s), right-shifted by a tab.
`~r filename`	Insert a file.

Inserting a File (~*r*)

Suppose you want user `jones` to look over a budget proposal you're preparing for your department. If the proposal were printed on paper, you'd have to photocopy it and arrange for it to be delivered. With `mailx`, you need only enter:

```
~r budget.drft
```

where `budget.drft` is the filename of the budget proposal. The `mailx` program automatically inserts the file in your message and displays the number of lines and words in the file:

```
"budget.drft" 108/4380
```

The capability for inserting files in messages makes `mailx` suitable for much more than just short messages. For example, writers can send their editors a copy of a manuscript. Programmers can send source code to one another. A teacher who finds that students are puzzled by a topic can quickly type some notes and a reading list and send them to the students in time for the next class meeting. Handouts or form letters can be created and then inserted as needed with `~r`.

Inserting a Message into the Message You're Writing (~*f*)

It is often convenient to include messages from other people in the message you're writing. For example, to insert message 1 into the current message, enter:

```
~f 1
```

In your message, you would type:

```
Last week you said you wanted more information on the GIMCRACK
database.  Sam Johnson sent me a message that explained it
pretty well.  Here's what he said:
~f 1
```

Like `mailx` commands, tilde commands allow you to specify a message list rather than just one message. The following box shows how to specify a message list when forwarding a message.

Forwarding Messages by Specifying Message Lists

`~f 1-4`	Insert messages 1 through 4.
`~f *`	Insert all messages.
`~f hoffman`	Insert all messages from user `hoffman`.

Inserting an Indented Message (~*m*)

The `~m` command is almost identical to `~f`. It, too, inserts another message into the message you're composing. The difference is that, when the recipient gets the message, the quoted message will be shifted to the right by one tab stop, setting it apart from the main message.

Inserting the *dead.letter* File (~*d*)

When you use Control-c to cancel a message that you are composing, the partial message is saved in the `dead.letter` file located in your home directory. Whatever previously existed in `dead.letter` is overwritten.

To insert the last cancelled message into the message you're currently composing, enter the `~d` command:

```
~d
```

You can see that this is just a shorthand form for

```
~r dead.letter
```

Inserting Output from a UNIX Command (~!<)

In addition to files and messages, the output from UNIX system commands can be inserted into your message (System V only). The format is:

```
~!< command
```

Let's say that you want to send a friend a listing of all the files in your directory. There are several ways you can do this. For instance, from the shell you can redirect the output of `ls` to a file. Then when creating your message, you can insert this file in your message. System V provides a more direct way of doing it, however. While writing your message, you enter:

```
~!< ls
```

The output from the shell command `ls` will be automatically inserted into your message. This tilde command uses the exclamation mark (`!`) for escaping to the shell to execute the UNIX command, and uses a redirection character (`<`) to take input from the command that follows.

Changing Information in the Message Header

Information about a message is contained in the heading that precedes the text. For example:

```
To: amadeus
Subject: Compositions
```

or

```
To: peter
Subject: Re: a cottage for sale
Cc: beatrix
```

While you are writing a message, you can change or add to the information currently in the `To:`, `Subject:`, `Cc:`, and `Bcc:` fields.

Tilde Commands to Change the Header of Your Message

`~c user_names`	Add names to the `Cc:` list.
`~b user_names`	Add names to the `Bcc:` list (System V only).
`~h`	Change information in the header (`To:`, `Subject:`, `Cc:`, and `Bcc:`).
`~s string`	Specify a new subject in the header.
`~t user_names`	Add names to the `To:` list.

Specifying a Subject for the Message (~*s*)

Before you begin writing a message, `mailx` will usually prompt you for a subject. If you are replying to a message, the program will automatically create a subject for you, using the subject of the original message:

```
Subject: Re: cottage for sale
```

The recipients of your messages will see the subject labels when they look at the display of message headers. You can easily change the subject in midstream with the `~s` command. This command replaces the existing subject entry with the string of text that you specify. For instance, to assign puns as the subject of your message, type:

```
~s puns
```

Adding More Names to the *To:* List (~*t*)

Anyone on the `To:` list of your message header will receive a copy of your message. Normally you specify a recipient when you enter the message editor (for example, `mailx jimbo`). With the `~t` command, you can easily name more people to receive the message. In the middle of writing a memo, for example, you realize that other people would be interested in reading this memo. You can add them to the `To:` list by typing:

```
~t joan mavis
```

Adding Names to the *Cc:* and *Bcc:* Lists (~*c*, ~*b*)

A copy of your message is received by anyone on the `Cc:` (carbon copy) list, just as a memo in an office is also delivered to the people listed after `Cc:`. Let's say that you're writing to `jones`, and you realize that you want to send carbon copies of your message to `mac` and `jeri`. You can send the copies with the `~c` command, like this:

```
~c mac jeri
```

System V offers a similar command (`~b`) for adding names to the `Bcc:` (blind carbon copy) list. A *blind carbon copy* is a copy that does not show in its header the names of the other recipients of the message. (A normal carbon copy has all the header information in the original, including the names of all recipients.)

Changing Header Fields (~*h*)

You can easily make changes to ALL the relevant header fields by entering this tilde command:

```
~h
```

The `mailx` program will prompt you for changes to the `Subject:`, `To:`, and `Cc:` fields in turn. To change an entry, use the Backspace key to delete unwanted characters; then type in the revised version and press Return. If you don't want to change the field, just press Return.

Miscellaneous Tilde Commands

We'll conclude our discussion of tilde commands with some that don't fit neatly into any category. Before we discuss these miscellaneous commands, however, you should know that there are still more tilde commands available. System V has some others, which you can read about in table 4-3 or in your UNIX manual. Of particular interest are the `~A`, `~a`, and `~i` commands, which insert strings of text that you have predefined.

Other Tilde Commands

`~w filename`	Write (save) the message to the file `filename`.
`~?`	Display the list of tilde commands.
`~! command`	Execute a shell command.
`~: command`	Execute a `mailx` command.
`~¦ command`	Pipe the message through a command.
`~~`	Print a tilde in text.

Writing a Message to a File (~ *w*)

As you're composing your message, you may decide to keep a copy of what you've written. Enter the `~w` command to write the existing message to a file:

```
~w my.file
```

An alternative method of saving your message is to add yourself to the `To:` or `Cc:` list with the `~t` or `~c` commands described previously. You then receive a copy of the message when it is sent, just as the other recipients do.

Displaying the List of Tilde Commands (~ ?)

To refresh your memory about the tilde commands, enter:

```
~?
```

You will see a list of the tilde commands and a brief description of each.

Performing a Shell Command (~ !)

Have you ever wanted to see a listing of your files while you are writing a message? The `~!` command lets you temporarily escape to the UNIX shell to execute commands at the `$` or `%` prompts. For example:

```
~!ls -l
```

gives a "long" listing of all the files in your directory. After the command is executed, you are returned to the message editor to continue writing your message. There are many other UNIX system commands that are useful while you are sending mail. For example, suppose you are writing a letter and you want to send someone else a copy. But what's her login name? You're not sure? If you have a BSD system, you can use the `finger` command like this:

```
~! finger joanne
```

to find out her login name, plus other information about her. If you have System V, you can use `grep` to get a similar result:

```
~! grep joanne /etc/passwd
```

Performing a *mailx* Command (~:)

Suppose you want to execute a `mailx` command such as `headers` or `type` from inside the message editor. The `~!` gives you access only to the UNIX shell commands. For `mailx` commands, use `~:` instead. For example, say you're writing a message to `tim` and want to quote the message he sent you. Unfortunately, you can't remember what the message number was. Tilde commands to the rescue. First, you display headers for all the messages `tim` sent you with the command:

```
~:from tim
```

Message 5 on the header display looks like the message you want. Then, you verify its contents by entering:

```
~:type 5
```

Finally, you insert the message with:

```
~r 5
```

Piping Your Message through a Command (~ |)

In chapter 2, we explained that the pipe character (¦) is used to send the output from one program to the input of another program, as if they were connected by a pipe. For example,

```
who ¦ wc -l
```

takes the output of the `who` command (a listing of the users on the system) and sends it to the `wc -l` command (which counts the number of lines). The `wc -l` command then outputs the result to the screen.

With `~¦`, you can pipe the message you are currently writing through a specified command. The output of that command then replaces the message. The pipe command is often used with the `fmt` program available on many systems for formatting messages. The program is invoked like this:

```
~¦ fmt
```

Your message will be replaced by a nicely formatted version.

Since the output of the command in the ~¦ replaces the existing message, you WOULD NOT enter a command like:

```
~¦ wc
```

The output of the `wc` (word count) program is a count of the characters, words, and lines in a file. The preceding command deletes the text of your message and replaces it with the three numbers that are the output of `wc`—not a result that you would normally want.

Printing a Tilde in Your Text (~ ~)

By default, the message editor interprets a tilde in column 1 as part of a tilde command. If you want to print a tilde character in your text and not have it interpreted as a tilde command, enter two consecutive tildes:

```
~~
```

Sending Messages Written on Your PC

If you're using a PC (as opposed to a terminal) to communicate with a UNIX system, you may want to create messages on your PC rather than on the remote UNIX system. Why would you want to do this?

For one, there is a greater selection of word processors available for microcomputers. You can choose the word processor you like and are familiar with, rather than be stuck with the editor that happens to be on your UNIX system. If you're accustomed to a particular word processor, you may not want to invest the time to learn another one.

A second consideration is telephone and computer charges. To access a commercial UNIX system, you might pay between $4 and $10 per hour, depending on the time of day. Rather than handle your e-mail on-line, it's more cost effective to download e-mail to your PC (by using the **SAVE** feature on your communications software). You print out your e-mail messages on your local printer and then compose your responses with your favorite word processor.

Creating a Pure ASCII File

Whichever word processor you use to write messages, select the option that creates a pure ASCII file (one without any special formatting characters). For example, in WordStar® choose the "nondocument" mode. If you send a file with nontext characters, the recipients of your message may have problems reading it.

Sending the File to UNIX

When you are finished writing your messages on the PC, log into the UNIX system. At the UNIX prompt, enter:

```
cat > my.file
```

This tells UNIX to take the input from the standard input (i.e., whatever you enter at your keyboard) and put it into a file named `my.file`.

To upload a file to a UNIX sytem, you don't have to type text on your keyboard. Just use the **SEND-ASCII** feature provided with your communications software. (When we talk about functions such as **SAVE** or **SEND-ASCII** we are using generic names. Your particular software will probably have a different name for the function.) Most good communications programs have a command that will send a file as a stream of ASCII characters over the telephone line to another computer. The UNIX system doesn't care whether you type the ASCII characters on your keyboard or send them with the **SEND-ASCII** feature. In either case, it will put the characters into the file that you have specified with the `cat > filename` command. After your file is transferred, enter Control-d. You now have a UNIX file containing the message you composed on your PC.

Sending the File as a Message

There are two ways to send this file as a message. The simplest way is to use redirection. For a single recipient, type:

```
mailx pkdick < my.file
```

For a group, type:

```
mailx jim lonnie lynn < my.file
```

The less-than character (`<`) directs the `mailx` program to take its input from the file named `my.file`. The file will then be sent as mail to the users you specify.

A second way to send a file as a message involves the `~r` command we discussed a few pages earlier. At the UNIX shell prompt, enter the command to send a message. For example,

```
mailx jim
```

Then, in the message editor, insert the file with the tilde command:

```
~r my.file
```

While you're in the message editor, you can add any additional text you desire. Send the message by typing Control-d or a single period in column 1.

Writing a Message on Your PC and Sending It as E-Mail

1. Create the message on your PC by using your favorite word processing program. Set the program to produce a pure ASCII file. Save the message to a file.
2. Log into the UNIX system in your usual way.
3. At the UNIX prompt, enter:

   ```
   cat > filename
   ```

4. Upload the file to UNIX with the `SEND-ASCII` command in your communications software.
5. After the file is transferred, type Control-d.
6. Enter the command:

   ```
   mailx user_name < filename
   ```

   OR

   From within the `mailx` message editor, enter the tilde command:

   ```
   ~r filename
   ```

   and add any additional text you wish.
7. End your message in the usual way (by typing either Control-d or a single period in column 1).

Sending Messages to People on Other Computers

So far our discussion of e-mail has centered on users on the same computer. But there are hundreds of thousands of users on other UNIX machines, and UNIX provides a way for you to reach them. Literally thousands of UNIX computers are connected in an informal, voluntary network called the *UUCP network*, after the `uucp` file-transfer program (which is covered in detail in Part 3 of this book). No one knows exactly how many UNIX sites are involved in the UUCP network—probably more than 5000.

If your computer has a connection to the UUCP network, you can send messages to anyone on this network virtually for free. The bad news is that it may take some research to find the right *address* (the route your message takes through the network).

An address looks like this:

```
hplabs!nike!sunybcs!tenny
```

In this example, the message is routed first to the UNIX computer named `hplabs`, then to the one named `nike`, and finally to the one named `sunybcs`. At `sunybcs`, the message is delivered to the user named `tenny`. Note that the last name given is the actual user; all the preceding names (separated by exclamation points, called *bangs* in UNIX jargon) are the UNIX computers through which the message is routed.

Still, the bad news isn't that bad—many people are happy with the UUCP network. Says one network user:

> I have talked with over 50 people with addresses a mile long, spread out all over the United States and Canada now, and the network seems pretty darn reliable. Only a few times did the delays become excessive (one to two weeks worst case). Average was one to two days for turnaround.

Many able minds are at work trying to simplify the addressing scheme for UNIX computers. In the meantime, the resources of the anarchistic, marvelous UUCP network are at your disposal—if you can figure out user addresses. Let's see how to do it.

When Two UNIX Computers Are Connected to Each Other

Your brother is on one UNIX system, and you are on another. Can you send mail to each other?

By phone, call him while he is at his terminal. Ask him for the "nodename" of his UNIX system. (The *nodename* is the name by which the system is known on the network.) If he doesn't know the nodename, it's easy enough for him to find it. At the UNIX shell prompt, have him enter:

uname -n *(System V)*

or

uuname -l *(Berkeley)*

The computer replies:

```
hoptoad
```

(or whatever the correct name is). To find your own nodename, type the same command. You'll see something like:

```
well
```

In this example, his UNIX computer is called `hoptoad`; yours is called `well` (Whole Earth 'Lectronic Link).

The next step is to see if the two computers are connected, either with a hard-wire (cable) connection or by a telephone/modem connection. At your terminal, type in:

uuname

You will see a list of all the computers to which your system is connected. For `well`, it is:

```
acad
aci
amiga
apple
arete2
cicomsys
cogsci
commem
copper
cosys
cpro
dual
eakins
esivax
fico2
forum1
iquery
hoptoad
hplabs
island
itivax
kdavis
lll-crg
lll-lcc
msudoc
m-net
micropro
notavax
picuxa
```

```
polliwog
portal
proper
ptsfa
r2d2
rencon
russs
simbrg
triton1
usenix
unicom
vanguard
vecpyr
xanadu
```

Since hoptoad is on the list, your computer and his are directly connected, and you can easily send a message to your brother. To send him a message, enter:

```
mailx hoptoad!chris
```

> When you're sending mail to remote systems, keep in mind that the message may not be sent immediately. When one UNIX system is connected to another by telephone lines and modems, the systems may call each other at regular intervals. Only then are messages transferred to the other system.

If Your Computer Isn't Connected to the Other System

You can see that remote mail is relatively straightforward when the other system communicates directly with your system. What if the system to which you want to send messages ISN'T on the uuname list? It is still possible to send e-mail—it just takes a little work to figure out the address.

The basic idea is that the UNIX UUCP network is organized around several major "backbone" UNIX computers. Thus, you may be able to have your message forwarded from site to site, until it reaches its destination as in figure 4-1. The key is to figure out how you can reach one of the major backbones.

If the computer systems were named as shown in figure 4-1, you could send a message to clara on the system named othersite with this command:

```
mailx backbone1!backbone2!backbone3!offshoot1!othersite!clara
```

Your message would be sent from one computer to another until it reached the system othersite.

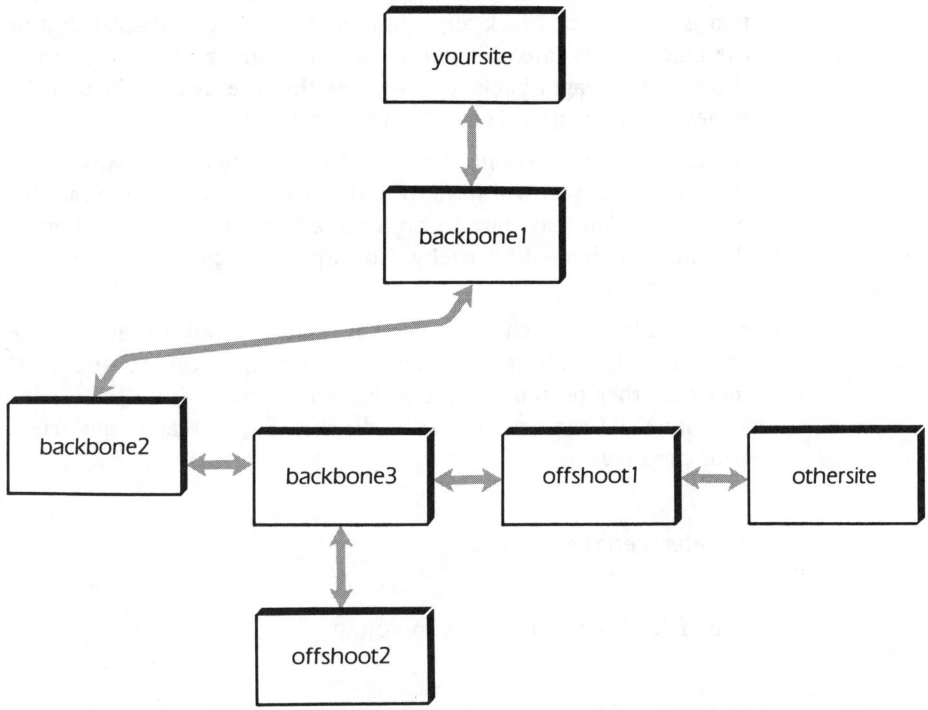

Figure 4-1. Part of a UNIX network.

Finding a Remote Address

If you are lucky, your system has a program called `uuhosts` to help you find the address of a remote UNIX computer. To find a path to the `hplabs` system, you would type:

```
uuhosts hplabs
```

You will see a display of paths to the remote computer, as well as other address information.

If your system does not have `uuhosts`, then follow these steps to find a path to a remote computer:

1. Establish which backbones you both can reach. That is the key. Both you and the other party need to have a map of the backbones. A recent map of the backbone sites (downloaded from USENET) is shown in figure 4-2. The names may change over time, so check with your system administrator.

2. With the uuname command, get a list of the computers to which your system is connected. Mark any computers on the uuname list that are also on the map. For example, if you look at the uuname listing for the well shown a few pages back, you will see that the well talks to four backbones: hplabs, glacier, lll-lcc, and lll-crg.

   If there are no backbone sites on your uuname listing, your job will be a bit more difficult: you will have to find out which of the uuname sites talks to a backbone. You may have to do a uuname on a remote machine to find out that information—a bit tricky. Consult the discussion of the uux command in chapter 14.

3. Now you know which machines you both can talk to, and you're ready to determine the addresses. Assuming that you are on the well, let's suppose that the other person can get to hplabs. Great—from the uuname list you see that YOU can get to hplabs directly. So, to reach your friend, address your messages as:

   hplabs!remote!friend

   Your friend sends messages to you at:

   hplabs!well!you

   But suppose your friend can talk only to ihnp4. From the map you see that you can access ihnp4 with hplabs!qantel!ihnp4 or with lll-lcc!qantel!ihnp4. Which address do you use? Hard to say. It depends on which is the more reliable. Try both. Your friend replies and tells you when the letter arrived. From the difference in time you can tell which address is faster.

4. You may experience problems sending mail via a particular backbone site. In this example, let's say that the hplabs connection with the well is unreliable or infrequent. In that case you can try sending to a larger nonbackbone site to which you are directly connected. This site may provide a better path to a common backbone site. For example, the well is connected to ptsfa, a large UNIX computer with connections to many other systems. So you can try:

   ptsfa!ihnp4!remote!friend

   The ptsfa machine might have a better connection with ihnp4 than hplabs does, and this new address would speed up mail.

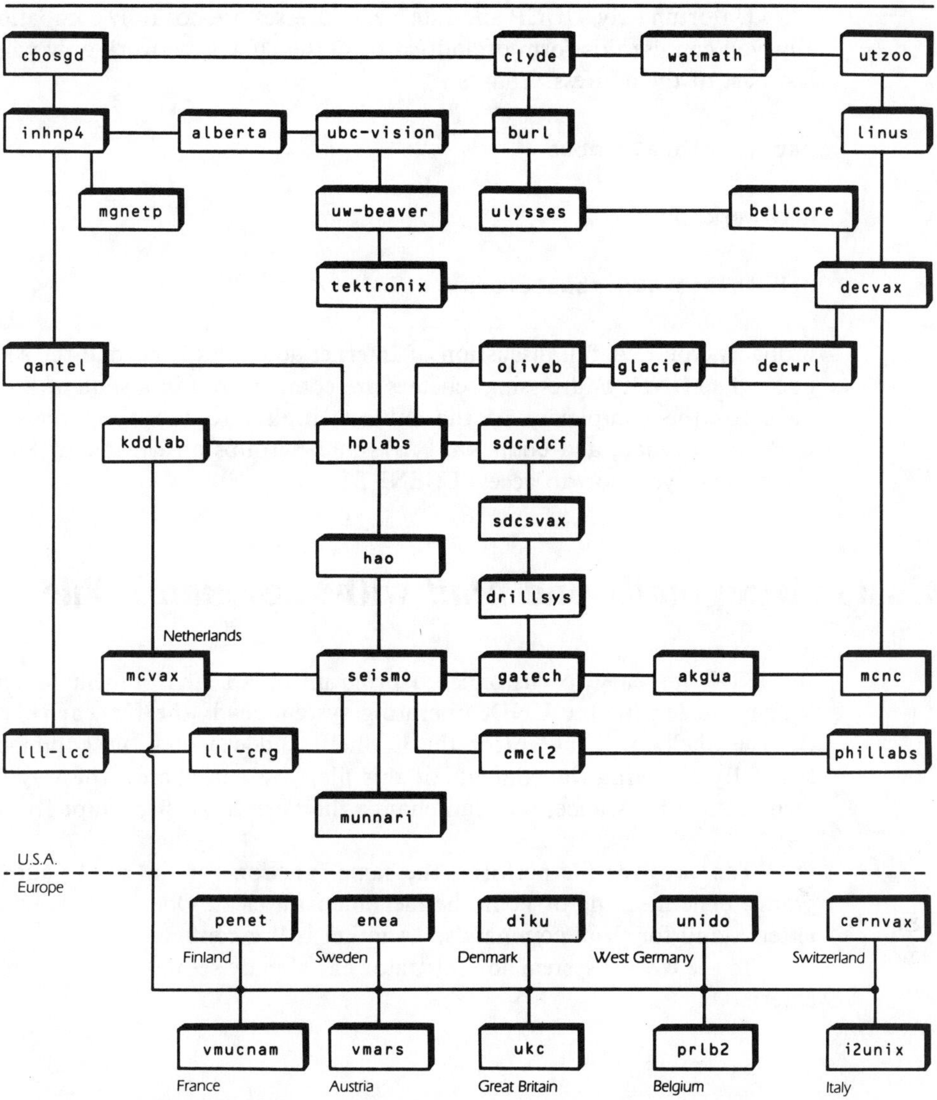

Figure 4-2. Map of the backbone sites in the UNIX network.

Internet Addresses

Another way to address messages is with an Internet address. These are commonly used on ARPANET (The Defense Department's *A*dvanced *R*esearch *P*rojects *A*gency *NET*work, which includes many academic institutions). An Internet address looks like this:

```
clara@nimbus
```

Unfortunately, UUCP and Internet addresses are not fully compatible. Generally, you can use this form of address from the UUCP network only when it is the last part of the address. That is:

```
nebula!clara@nimbus
```

may work, but

```
nebula!site4@nimbus!clara
```

probably won't. A full discussion of Internet addresses is beyond the scope of this book. The UNIX addresssing schemes are complex and in a state of flux. To get a taste for the complexity of the subject, look into the `comp.mail.headers`, `comp.mail.uucp`, and `comp.mail.misc` newsgroups on USENET. (Part 2 of this book shows you how to access USENET.)

Customizing *mailx* and *Mail* with the *.mailrc* File

In UNIX, it's easy to customize a program or an environment to your needs. When you log in, the UNIX operating system reads the file `.profile` (for the Bourne Shell) or `.login` (for the C Shell) and executes the commands found there. By changing the contents of this file, you can change the way the system responds. For instance, you can change the normal shell prompt from `$` or `%` to `Yes?`.

The `.mailrc` file performs the same function for the `mailx` and `Mail` programs. (The meaning of `rc` in the filename isn't clear. One explanation is that the letters stand for "run commands." Another is "re-configure.")

To see if your system administrator has already set up a `.mailrc` file for you, enter:

```
ls -a
```

Remember that files beginning with a period aren't displayed by the normal `ls` command.

Check the contents of the file with the command:

```
cat .mailrc
```

On your screen you may see several commands displayed, such as `set dot`. The `mailx` and `Mail` programs can be customized with commands like these. (Chapter 5 explains all of the possible settings.) Let's see how you can change the `.mailrc` file.

Modifying the *.mailrc* File

Since `.mailrc` is a text file like any other, you can edit it with an editor such as `vi`. If `.mailrc` doesn't exist, you can create it. A quick way to create or add to the `.mailrc` file is with the command:

```
cat >> .mailrc
```

The >> characters tell UNIX to append the text you type to the `.mailrc` file. (This is much safer than `cat > .mailrc`, which deletes the previous contents of the `.mailrc` file.)

After you enter the `cat` command, the cursor drops down a line and waits for you to enter your text—just as the `mailx` message editor does. Like the `mailx` message editor, this method provides the same minimal editing capabilities. When you're finished entering your text, type Control-d. Your `.mailrc` file should now be changed. To make sure the new `.mailrc` file is what you want, type:

```
cat .mailrc
```

The contents of the new `.mailrc` file will be displayed. The next time that you call up the `mailx` program, it will respond to the commands you have entered in the `.mailrc` file.

Using Aliases to Send Messages to a Group

When you regularly send messages to a particular group of UNIX users, you can save yourself a lot of typing by setting up an "alias" for the members of the group. In `mailx`, an *alias* is a name that stands for several users. When you send a message to that alias, the message goes to each of the users. For example, if the members of your department are `ray`, `libby`, `curt`, and `bob`, you can create an alias by entering this `alias` command at the `mailx` prompt:

```
alias docdept ray libby curt bob
```

You can now send a message to everyone in the department by typing:

```
mailx docdept
```

By entering the `alias` command in the `.mailrc` file, you don't have to reenter the command every time you call up the `mailx` program. Your aliases will be automatically available for use.

Using *alias* to Avoid Lengthy User Names

The `alias` command can save you from typing lengthy user names. For example, you might want a short alternative for a name:

```
alias bz brzhenski
```

Now you can send a letter with:

```
mailx bz
```

You might also want a shorter way to specify long addresses. For instance:

```
alias clara guru!wombat!alice!nimbus!clara
```

The new address is now `clara`.

Using Folders to Organize Your Mail

If you receive lots of mail, you'll love folders. *Folders* provide a convenient way to organize all the messages you want to save. Folders let you save all your messages to files in one convenient subdirectory. Let's see why you would want to do this. The most rudimentary way to save your mail is to use `mbox`. If you enter a command like `save` (without specifying a filename), the current message is automatically saved to `mbox`. In addition, when you read a message, it is saved by default in `mbox` when you leave the program with the `quit` command.

The problem is that `mbox` soon becomes large and unwieldy. It becomes difficult to find the messages you want when there are 50 messages in `mbox` from a dozen different users!

A better way to save messages is to use individual files. Specify the filename after the `save` command. For example, enter a command like `save 5 sam` to copy message 5 into the file named `sam`. The disadvantage of saving messages to files is that if you receive a lot of mail from many users, your home directory will soon become crowded with dozens of message files. It will be hard to keep track of them all.

To remedy the overcrowding, you can create a subdirectory especially for mail files. In figure 4-3 `mymail` has been set up as a subdirectory in the home directory of the user `eric`.

This new subdirectory makes it much easier to keep track of your mail files, and your home directory is less crowded. The only problem is that to save a file, you must write out the pathname for the new mail files. For example, to save message 4 you enter:

```
save 4 mymail/jim
```

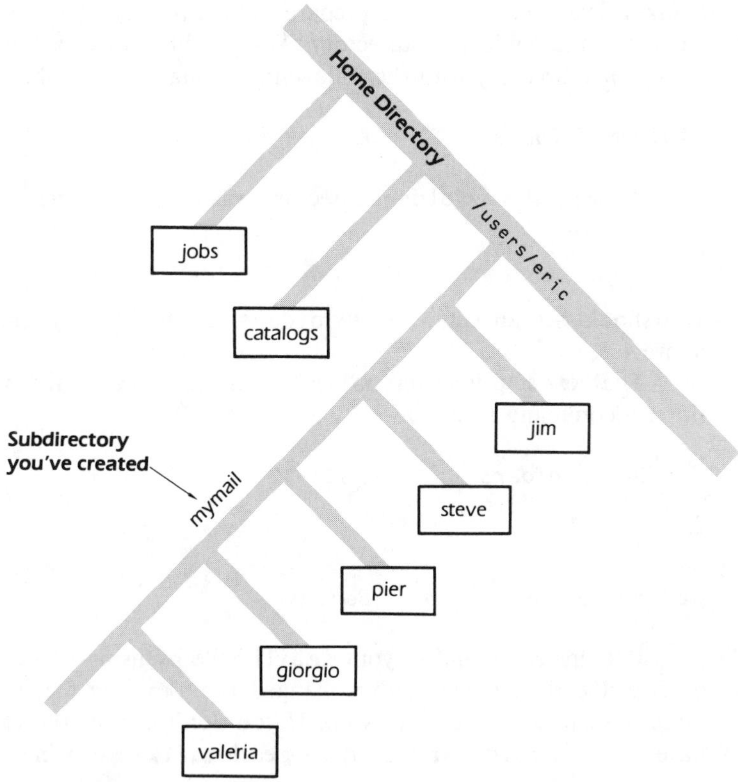

Figure 4-3. Saving messages in a special subdirectory.

Saving Messages in Folders

Folders operate in much the same way as the subdirectory described above. You again set up a special subdirectory for mail messages. But, to save a message to a folder, you just type a plus sign (+) instead of writing the subdirectory name. The program saves the messages to a file in the subdirectory you've created for your folders.

For example, to save message 4 to the `jim` folder, simply enter:

```
save 4 +jim
```

> A *folder* is simply a file in a specially designated subdirectory.

Preparing the Folders

It takes several commands to prepare folders for use. The first step is to choose a name for the folders subdirectory. You might choose a name like `myfolders`. Create this directory with the following command at the shell prompt:

```
mkdir myfolders
```

To see if the `myfolders` directory was created, enter:

```
ls
```

You should see an entry for `myfolders`. Your directory structure will resemble figure 4-4.

The next step is to tell `mailx` to store messages in the `myfolders` directory. Enter a command like:

```
folder=myfolders          (System V)
```

or

```
set folder=myfolders      (Berkeley)
```

Put this command in your `.mailrc` file by using `vi` or `cat >> .mailrc`, as described earlier. Once you've changed the `.mailrc` file, the program sets the `folder` variable when it starts up. If you don't change the `.mailrc` file, you will have to set the `folder` variable during each `mailx` session in which you use folders.

Using Folders

To save a message to a folder, use a command like this:

```
save +giorgio
```

This saves the current message to the folder named `giorgio` (the complete pathname of the folder might be something like `/users/eric/myfolders/giorgio`).

To save message 5 to the folder named `steve`, enter:

```
save 5 +steve
```

To save all the messages from user `jim` to the folder named `jim`, enter:

```
save jim +jim
```

Remember that you can save messages by subject area, as well as by the name of the sender:

```
save 7 +book_ideas
```

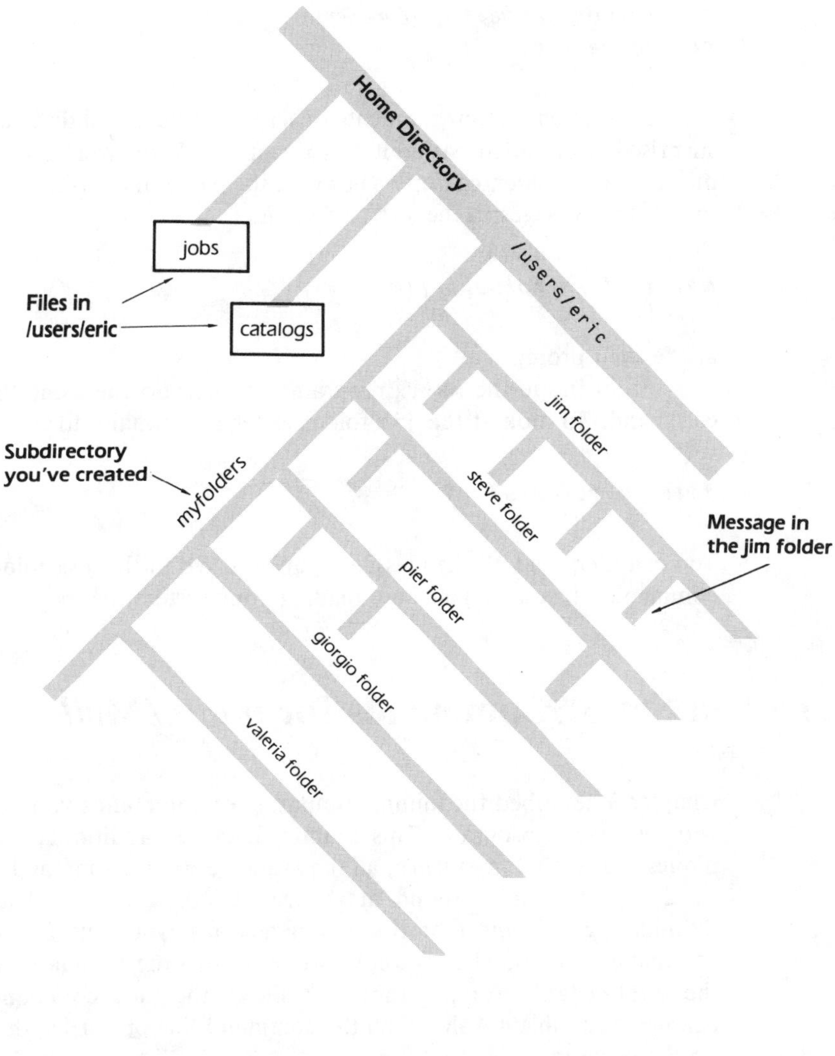

Figure 4-4. The **myfolders** subdirectory holds folder files.

As you become more familiar with `mailx`, you'll develop your own ways to organize your correspondence. For example, you might change the name of your folder subdirectory every month:

```
folder=janmail          (System V)
folder=febmail
```

or

```
set folder=janmail     (Berkeley)
set folder=febmail
```

It takes only a few moments to set up a folders subdirectory, and you will be surprised how much easier it is to keep track of your e-mail. To look at the messages in a folder, call up `mailx` with the `-f` command-line option. For example, to see the messages in the `jim` folder, enter:

```
mailx -f /myfolders/jim
```

at the shell prompt.

From inside the `mailx` program, you can do the same thing with the `file` command. To look at the `jim` folder, enter a command like:

```
file /myfolders/jim
```

You can then read all the messages you've saved in the `jim` folder and issue `mailx` commands, just as if you were reading your system mailbox.

The Full Set of Commands for *mailx/Mail*

Chapter 3 described the minimum number of commands you needed to get started with the `mailx` program. This chapter described additional commands and techniques. For your convenience, all the available `mailx` commands have been summarized in three tables found at the end of this chapter. The tables may look intimidating, but most of the commands are synonyms or minor variations of commands that you already know. Table 4-2 lists the commands you can enter from the `mailx/Mail` prompt. Table 4-3 shows the tilde commands covered in this chapter, and table 4-4 shows all the command-line options with which you can call up the program.

Summary

In this chapter you have learned almost all the commonly used features of `mailx` and `Mail`. Tilde commands give you access to the program while you are composing messages. Among the many tilde commands, `~v` invokes the `vi` editor and `~r` inserts a file into the message you're writing.

UNIX offers you a way (albeit cumbersome) to send messages to users on other UNIX computers. One way is to trace a route between you and the other user and specify it with an address like hplabs!nike!sunybcs!tenny!.

By adding commands to the .mailrc file in your home directory, you can configure the mailx program to your liking. For example, by adding an alias statement, you can specify an entire group of recipients with a one-word alias.

A second candidate for inclusion in the .mailrc file is a folder statement that enables you to easily save messages to files in the folders subdirectory.

In addition to alias and folder, there are many more commands that can be added to .mailrc to modify the operation of the mailx program. Chapter 5 will show you the multitude of ways you can customize mailx.

Table 4-2. The *mailx/Mail* Commands

Command	Abbreviation	Meaning
!command		Execute the shell command specified by command.
#		Comment (e.g., in .mailrc files).*
=		Displays number of current message.*
?		Displays list of mailx/Mail commands.
-		Displays previous message (e.g., -3 means back up 3 messages from current message and print message).
alias	a	Defines a single name for a set of user names.
alternates	alt	Tells mailx/Mail alternate names for a user name. With no argument, lists your alternate names (see chapter 5).
chdir	cd	Changes current directory. If no argument, changes to your home directory.
copy	co	Copies message to a file (or folder). Does not earmark for deletion when you quit (q) the mail program.
Copy		Copies message to a file which is named after the sender of the message.*
delete	d	Deletes messages (see undelete).
discard		Suppresses display of the specified header fields when displaying messages. (Same as ignore.) Print and Type override this command.*
dp or dt		Deletes current message and displays next message.

*The asterisk indicates commands exclusive to System V.

Table 4-2. (cont.)

Command	Abbreviation	Meaning
echo		Displays the specified string (e.g., in .mailrc file).
edit	e	Invokes editor for a given message or messages.
else		Conditionally executes mailx commands. Used with if.
endif		Marks the end of an if statement. See if.
exit	ex, x, xit	Leaves mailx/Mail program, retaining all messages in mailbox EXACTLY as at beginning of mail session.
file	fi	Begins reading a new file of messages. Special symbols: % current mailbox %name mailbox of another user # the last file read & your mbox +folder a folder (Berkeley only)
folder	fo	Same as file.
folders		Lists your folders.
followup		Replies to a message. Your reply is saved in a file named after the original sender of the message.*
Followup		Replies to the first message in a message list. Your reply is sent to the sender of each message in the message list and is saved in a file named after the sender of the first message.*
from	f	Displays header lines of messages in the message list specified.
group		Same as alias.
headers	h	Displays group of header lines containing the specified message.
help		Prints a brief summary of mailx commands.
hold	ho	Retains the specified messages in the mailbox; they won't be moved to mbox. Same as preserve.
if send		Conditionally executes Mail commands in the

*The asterisk indicates commands exclusive to System V.

Table 4-2. (cont.)

Command	Abbreviation	Meaning
¦receive		.mailrc file, depending on whether you are reading (if receive) or sending (if send) mail. Used with endif (Berkeley only).
if s¦r		Conditional execution of mailx commands in the .mailrc file, depending on whether you are reading (if r) or sending (if s) mail. Used with endif and else.* The mailx commands after if s will execute up to an else or endif, if the program is in send mode. The commands after if r are executed only in receive mode.
ignore		Suppresses display of the specified header fields when displaying messages. (Same as discard.) Print and Type override this command.
list		Lists mailx/Mail commands.
mail	m	Sends mail to specified names.
mbox		Saves the specified messages in mbox when you quit.
next	n, +, Return	Displays the next message or the message specified.
pipe	¦	Pipes the message through the specified command. With no arguments specified, pipes the current message through the command designated by the cmd variable. With the page variable set, each message has a form feed inserted after it.*
preserve		Keeps the specified messages in your mailbox when you quit. Same as hold.
print	p	Displays specified messages.
Print	P	Displays specified messages, including all header fields.
quit	q	Leaves mailx, updating system mailbox and mbox as appropriate.
reply respond	r	Composes a reply to a message, sending it to the author of the original message and to all the people, except you, who received the message.
Reply Respond	R	Composes a reply to a message, sending it ONLY to the author of the original message.

*The asterisk indicates commands exclusive to System V.

Table 4-2. (cont.)

Command	Abbreviation	Meaning
save	s	Appends messages to a file. If no file is specified, saves to mbox.
Save		Saves the specified messages in a file named after the sender of the first message.*
set	se	Sets binary or valued options (see chapter 5).
shell	sh	Creates a shell in which you can enter UNIX commands. When you leave the shell, you are returned to mailx/Mail.
size		Displays the size (in characters) for the specified messages.*
source	so	Executes the mailx/Mail commands in the specified file.
top	to	Prints the first so many (5 by default) lines of each message in the message list.
touch		Moves messages in the message list to mbox when you quit, unless the messages are specifically saved to a file.*
type	t	Displays specified messages. (Same as print.)
Type	T	Displays specified messages, including all header fields. (Same as Print.)
unalias		Removes one or more aliases from the list of aliases (Berkeley).
undelete	u	Recovers messages in the message list that have been deleted in the current mail session.
unset		Undoes the operation of a set command (see chapter 5).
version		Displays the version and release date of the program.*
visual	v	Invokes visual editor on a list of messages.
write	w	Appends messages to a file; doesn't include headers. Otherwise, similar to save.
xit	x	Synonym for exit.
z+	z	Scrolls to next screenfull of headers.
z-		Scrolls to previous screenfull of headers.

*The asterisk indicates commands exclusive to System V.

Table 4-3. Tilde Commands

Escape	Arguments	Description
~!	command	Executes shell command.
~.		Ends the message.*
~:	mail_cmd	Executes a mailx command while composing a message.
~_	mail_cmd	Same as ~:.
~?		Displays a list of tilde commands.
~¦	command	Pipes message through command. Output of the command replaces message.
~~		Inserts a tilde in message.
~<	filename	Reads in the specified file. Same as ~r.*
~<!	command	Executes a system command and inserts the output in the message.*
~a		Inserts the string defined by the mailx variable sign into the message (see chapter 5).*
~A		Inserts the string defined by the mailx variable Sign into the message (see chapter 5).*
~b	name...	Adds names to the Bcc: field.*
~c	name...	Adds names to the Cc: field.
~d		Inserts dead.letter into message.
~e		Calls up text editor (ed or ex).
~f	messages	Inserts specified messages into the message.
~h		Allows interactive changes to the header fields.
~i	variable	Inserts the text defined by the variable into the message.*
~m	messages	Inserts specified messages, right-shifting them by one tab stop.
~p		Displays message text as it currently stands.
~q		Cancels the letter. Same as Control-c.
~r	filename	Inserts the specified file into the message.
~s	string	Sets Subject: field to string.
~t	name...	Adds names to To: field.
~v		Calls up screen editor.
~w	filename	Writes message to file, not including headers.
~x		Exits same as ~q, except that message is not saved in dead.letter

* The asterisk indicates tilde commands exclusive to System V.

Table 4-4. Command-Line Options

Flag	Description
-e	Tests for presence of mail.*
-f file	Reads messages from the specified file instead of from the system mailbox. If no file is specified, reads mbox.
-F	Saves the message created to a file named after the first recipient.*
-H	Prints a header summary only.*
-i	Ignores tty interrupt signals.
-n	Prevents reading of Mail.rc or Mailx.rc (see chapter 5).
-N	Prevents the initial display of headers.
-s string	Sets the Subject: header to the string specified.
-u name	Reads messages in the mailbox of the user specified.

* The asterisk indicates command-line options exclusive to System V.

5

Advanced Mail

By now you should be feeling comfortable with the `mailx` program. You should have a grasp of the basic commands as well as the more sophisticated features, and you should be using `mailx` regularly. As you send and receive messages, you may find yourself wishing that you could change this or that detail of the program. In fact, you can change many of the functions and features of `mailx`. This chapter will show you how to:

- Change individual options (`mailx` variables) by entering `set` and `unset` commands at the `mailx` prompt.
- Configure your `mailx` program automatically by setting variables in the `.mailrc` file.
- Customize almost every aspect of the program by changing options.

We'll describe in detail the more than 40 options available to you. Technically, these options are called *mailx variables*. They are settings that `mailx` uses to control its operation and are similar to the environmental variables (like `TERM`) that are set for the shell.

Setting *mailx* Variables

To modify the operation of `mailx`, you change `mailx` variables with the `set` and `unset` commands. For example, in the last chapter, you saw that folders are activated with a command like:

```
set folder=myfolders
```

After mailx executes this statement, the value of the folder variable is set to myfolders, the name for the new folders directory. Because the folder variable can be assigned a value, it is known as a *valued variable*. Other valued variables are set to a numerical value. For instance, to set the number of headers shown in the header display, enter a command like:

```
set screen=15
```

The screen variable now has a value of 15; when you read your mail, 15 headers will be displayed on the screen, instead of the usual default value of 10.

Other mailx variables can be set only to ON or OFF; these are known as *binary variables*. An example of a binary variable is:

```
set dot
```

This statement allows you to terminate input by typing a period in the first column of a message. To disable this feature, you unset it with a command like:

```
unset dot
```

The unset command is used to disable options that are set by default or that have been set in a system-wide configuration file, which we'll describe later.

Determining Which Variables Are Set

You can easily find out which variables are currently set for your mailx program. At the mailx prompt, enter:

```
set
```

You might see a display like:

```
append
ask
escape  :
folder  myfolders
keep
record  mymesgs
```

Let's take a closer look at the meaning of the variables in this display. We'll briefly explain each setting in order to give you a taste of what mailx options do. If some of the options don't make sense to you now, don't worry. Each option will be fully explained later in the chapter.

In this example, the append variable means that messages are appended to the mbox file. The ask variable is unique to Berkeley UNIX; it causes the program to prompt you for a subject when you create a message. (Prompting for the subject is automatic in System V.) The valued variable escape means that instead of typing a tilde (~) to issue tilde commands in the editor, you enter a colon (:). Another valued variable folder is assigned the name of the folders directory, in this case myfolders. The keep variable means that your system mailbox is not deleted when it is empty but is retained with the access permissions you have assigned it. The last variable, record, will be a joy to anyone who likes to keep records; it puts a copy of all your outgoing messages in a file, here named mymesgs.

Automatically Configuring *mailx* with the *.mailrc* File

It would be no fun if you had to set every option at the mailx prompt before you started your mail session. Fortunately, you don't have to. As you learned in chapter 4, mailx executes the commands it finds in the .mailrc file every time you call up the program. By adding the appropriate set and unset statements to your .mailrc file, you can have mailx automatically set your options at the start of each session.

To change the .mailrc file, you can use an editor like vi or the command:

```
cat >> .mailrc
```

With the cat command, you type in the commands that you want to add to your .mailrc file, and you end your input with Control-d.

To produce the settings in our example, enter the following commands in your .mailrc file:

```
set append
set ask
set escape=:
set folder=myfolders
set keep
set record=mymesgs
```

Here's another, more complicated, .mailrc file that combines both variables and commands:

```
set ask quiet askcc escape=@
set SHELL=/bin/csh
set VISUAL=/usr/ucb/vi
set toplines=2
set folder=/uh/31/bea/.mbox
set crt=22
alias kenneman km
alias party izzy hoptoad!johnboy jjb dinah well!mozart
```

You'll learn the meanings of these variables later in the chapter. For now, we'll just point out a few items of interest.

Note the first line:

```
set ask quiet askcc escape=@
```

This is a short way to set several options at once. This line replaces:

```
set ask
set quiet
set askcc
set escape=@
```

The last two lines of the `.mailrc` example show that aliases can be defined in a `.mailrc` file:

```
alias kenneman km
alias party izzy hoptoad!johnboy jjb dinah well!mozart
```

Notice that `alias` is not a variable but a command in its own right; no `set` or `unset` command is needed. Two other commands often found in a `.mailrc` file are `ignore` and `alternates`. We'll talk about these later in this chapter.

The System-Wide Configuration File

There's still one more way that `mailx` variables can be set. If you enter the `set` command, you may see settings for variables that you didn't set. Who set them? The answer is that there's another file, called a *system-wide configuration file*, that is similar to `.mailrc`. The difference between the two files is that your `.mailrc` file sets variables for your personal program, whereas the system-wide configuration file sets variables for ALL users. If you don't like any of these system-wide settings, you are not stuck with them, however. We'll explain how to override system-wide settings in a moment.

When you call up the `mailx` program, it first executes the commands that it finds in a system-wide configuration file. Only afterwards does it execute the commands in your personal configuration file (`.mailrc`). This is illustrated in figure 5-1.

The system-wide configuration file has different names, depending on the system. On a Berkeley system, it may appear as `/usr/lib/Mail.rc`. On other systems, it may be `/usr/lib/mailx/mailx.rc`. Here is an example of the `Mail.rc` file for a Berkeley system:

```
set append
set dot
set save
```

```
set ask
set escape=:
ignore Received Message-Id Via Status
```

The statements are similar to the ones in the sample `.mailrc` files we discussed earlier. The only line that may puzzle you is the last one. This `ignore` command (it's a command, not a variable) prevents the display of four seldom-used lines of information at the beginning of each message.

It's important to know about the system configuration file because it may set options that you wish to disable. This sample file, for example, sets the `dot` option. If you want to disable it, enter this command in your `.mailrc` file:

```
unset dot
```

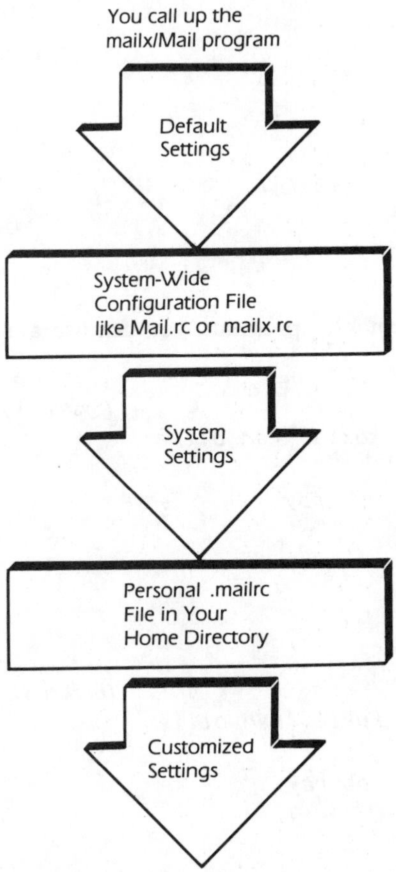

Figure 5-1. The **mailx** program first reads the system-wide configuration file and then reads **.mailrc**.

Because your `.mailrc` file is read after the system file, your `unset` command is read last and the `dot` feature is disabled.

Programming a *.mailrc* File

You can make `.mailrc` respond differently, depending on whether you're sending or receiving mail. (Remember that to enter *receive* mode, you type `mailx` or `Mail`; to enter *send* mode, you type a command like `mailx anna` or `Mail anna`.)

To enable the `dot` option only while you're reading mail, you could enter these statements in your `.mailrc` file:

```
if r            (System V)
set dot
endif
```

or

```
if receive      (Berkley)
set dot
endif
```

For a more complex program, you can use `else`:

```
if s                              (System V)
alias dept kukla fran ollie
else
alias dept bob ray
endif
```

or

```
if send                           (Berkeley)
alias dept kukla fran ollie
else
alias dept bob ray
endif
```

These statements give the alias `dept` a variable meaning. When you call up the `mailx` program in send mode, messages sent to `dept` are delivered to `kukla`, `fran`, and `ollie`. In receive mode, they are delivered to `bob` and `ray`.

How We Will Cover the Options

Now that you know how to set options and change your `.mailrc` file, you're ready for the options themselves. You can read through the option descriptions now or refer back to them as needed. To make the discussion easier to follow (and easier to reference), we cover the options by subject matter. Here is the order we'll follow:

- Sending mail.
- Tilde commands.
- Messages and displays while reading mail.
- Commands for reading mail.
- Folders.
- Files and the `mailx` program.
- Names and addresses.

Table 5-1 lists the options that we cover and gives a brief description of what each does. If the sheer number of options seems intimidating, remember that `mailx` behaves sensibly right out of the box. If you're happy with the way it works, there is no need to change anything. If you do want to change the behavior of `mailx` to suit your needs or way of working, we suggest setting just one or two variables (or giving one or two commands) at a time and observing the effects. Changing many things at once makes it hard to see what is going on. It is also a good idea to keep a copy of your old `.mailrc` file, calling it perhaps `.oldmailrc`. Retaining the old file allows you to return to your old environment and start over if necessary.

Table 5-1. The *mailx* Options

	Sending Mail
`ask` (b, Berk)	Prompts for a subject. (Default: disabled)
`asksub` (b, V)	Prompts for a subject. (Default: enabled)
`dot` (b)	Exits editor with a period. (Default: disabled)
`ignore` (b)	Ignores interrupt characters. (Default: disabled)
`ignoreeof` (b)	Prevents Control-d from ending message. (Default: disabled)
`nosave` (b, Berk)	Stops the saving of cancelled messages. (Default: disabled)

b = binary option (set or not set); v = valued option (e.g., filename or number);
Berk = Berkeley UNIX only; V = System V only.

Table 5-1. (cont.)

	Sending Mail
`askcc` (b)	Prompts for carbon copies. (Default: disabled)
`record` (v)	Keeps a record of messages you send. (Default: disabled)
`save` (b, V)	Enables the saving of cancelled messages. (Default: enabled)
`showto` (b, V)	Shows the recipient of messages. (Default: disabled)
`sendmail` (v)	Specifies a program for delivering mail. (System V default: `mail`)
	Tilde Commands
`EDITOR` (v)	Defines the `~e` editor. (System V default: `ed`)
`escape` (v)	Defines the escape character. (Default: tilde `~`)
`sign` (v, V)	Defines the string inserted by `~a`. (Default: none)
`Sign` (v, V)	Defines the string inserted by `~A`. (Default: none)
`VISUAL` (v)	Defines the `~v` screen editor. (System V default: `vi`)
	Messages and Displays While Reading Mail
`crt` (v)	Specifies the number of lines per message display. (Default: none)
`header` (b, V)	Enables header display. (Default: enabled)
`ignore`	Suppresses display of header fields. (A command; no default)
`noheader` (b, Berk)	Suppresses header display. (Default: disabled)
`PAGER` (v, V)	Specifies the pager program for long messages. (System V default: `pg`)
`prompt` (v, V)	Changes `mailx` prompt. (System V default is ?)

b = binary option (set or not set); v = valued option (e.g., filename or number); Berk = Berkeley UNIX only; V = System V only.

Table 5-1. (cont.)

	Messages and Displays While Reading Mail
`quiet` (b)	Suppresses opening messages. (Default: disabled)
`screen` (v)	Specifies the number of headers displayed.
	Commands for Reading Mail
`autoprint` (b)	Makes `delete` act like `dp`. (Default: disabled)
`cmd` (v, V)	Sets a default command for the `pipe` command. (Default: none)
`hold` (b)	Prevents messages you read from "disappearing." (Default: disabled)
`keepsave` (b)	Prevents messages you save from "disappearing." (Default: disabled)
`page` (b, V)	Inserts a form feed after each message. (Default: disabled)
`SHELL` (v)	Specifies the shell to escape to. (System V default: `sh`)
`toplines` (v)	Specifies the number of lines `top` displays. (Default: 5)
	Folders
`folder` (v)	Defines the folders directory. (Default: none)
`LISTER` (v, V)	Defines the command to list your folders. (Default: `ls`)
`outfolder` (b, V)	Places files of outgoing messages into the folders directory. (Default: disabled)
	Files and the* mailx *Program
`append` (b)	Appends messages to `mbox`. (Default: disabled)
`DEAD` (v, V)	Defines a new dead letter file. (Default: `$HOME/dead.letter`)
`keep` (b)	Preserves your system mailbox file. (Default: disabled)

b = binary option (set or not set); v = valued option (e.g., filename or number);
Berk = Berkeley UNIX only; V = System V only.

Table 5-1. (cont.)

	Files and the* mailx *Program
`MBOX` (v, V)	Defines a new default file for saving messages. (Default: `$HOME/mbox`)
	Names and Addresses
`allnet` (v, V)	Allows for accounts on different systems. (Default: disabled)
`alternates`	Tells `mailx` that you have accounts on different systems. (A command; no default)
`conv` (v, V)	Converts UUCP addresses to another format. (Default: disabled)
`metoo` (b)	Lets you receive a copy of messages you send. (Default: disabled)
`onehop` (b, V)	Prevents rewriting of remote addresses. (Default: disabled)

b = binary option (set or not set); v = valued option (e.g., filename or number); Berk = Berkeley UNIX only; V = System V only.

Options for Sending Mail

It's much simpler to send messages than to read them with `mailx`. Yet even in this seemingly straightforward process, you can set options to change the way you create and send messages.

Prompting for a Subject: *ask* (Berk)

When you begin to write a message, the `Mail` program can prompt you for a `Subject:`. Enable this feature with the line:

```
set ask
```

To disable the feature, enter:

```
unset ask
```

By default, `ask` in Berkeley `Mail` is disabled.

Prompting for a Subject: *asksub* (V)

The asksub option in System V is similar to the ask option in Berkeley Mail. However, in System V mailx, asksub is enabled by default, and you are automatically prompted for a subject. If you don't want to be prompted for a subject, disable asksub with an unset command.

Exiting the Editor with a Period: *dot*

When you are finished writing a message, you exit the system's simple editor with a Control-d. By setting the dot option, you can exit the editor by typing a period (.) in the first column. The following line allows you to exit the editor with a period:

```
set dot
```

By default, dot is disabled.

Preventing Control-d from Ending a Message: *ignoreeof*

If you prefer that Control-d in column 1 NOT terminate a message, then you must set ignoreeof, like this:

```
set ignoreeof
```

The eof in ignoreeof stands for End-of-File (Control-d). The default is for ignoreeof to be disabled. In other words, Control-d is normally used to end a message.

Ignoring Interrupt Characters: *ignore*

As you're typing your message, you can enter the interrupt character twice to cancel your message. (The interrupt character may be Control-c or the Delete key, depending on your system and terminal settings.) If you are communicating by modem and have a noisy telephone connection, spurious interrupt characters may cause your message to be cancelled.

To prevent mailx from responding to interrupt characters, enter this line:

```
set ignore
```

By default, ignore is disabled.

Disabling the Saving of Cancelled Messages: *nosave* (Berk)

If a message you write is cancelled with an interrupt character (Control-c or Delete key) or if it cannot be delivered, the message is placed by default in the file `dead.letter` in your home directory. To disable this feature in Berkeley `Mail`, enter:

```
set nosave
```

Enabling the Saving of Cancelled Messages: *save* (V)

The `save` option in System V `mailx` is the reverse of the Berkeley `nosave` option. By default, `save` is enabled; cancelled and undelivered messages are saved in `dead.letter`. Unset `save` to disable the feature in System V.

Prompting for Carbon Copies: *askcc*

After you've finished entering your message, the `mailx` program can prompt you for the names of people to put on the carbon copy `Cc:` list. The login names you type after the `Cc:` prompt will receive your message, just as the names on the `To:` list will.

To have the program automatically ask you for a `Cc:` list, enter this line:

```
set askcc
```

By default, `askcc` is disabled.

Keeping a Record of Messages You Send: *record*

If you want to keep a record of all the messages you send, enter a line like:

```
set record=mymesg
```

where `mymesg` is the name of the file in which your outgoing messages should be stored. Later you can read this file by entering `file mymesg` at the `mailx` prompt (where `mymesg` is the name of the file you have assigned to `record`). By default, `record` is disabled.

The System V `mailx` program offers other ways to save copies of your messages. The commands `Copy`, `followup`, `Followup`, and `Save` (see table 4-2) save copies of messages in files named after your correspondent. This is frequently more useful than having just one file that contains all of your messages.

If you want to place the `record` or other record-keeping files in your folders directory, see the `outfolder` option described under "Options for Folders" later in this chapter.

Showing the Recipient of Messages: *showto* (V)

There is one problem with the previous scheme described for keeping copies of outgoing messages. All the messages placed in the file are FROM YOU. But when you use `mailx` to read the record-keeping file, the header display shows whom the message is FROM. All the messages will be labelled as being from you—not very informative.

Correct this by setting the `showto` option (System V only):

```
set showto
```

The header display for your record-keeping file will then display TO WHOM the messages were sent. By default, `showto` is disabled.

Specifying a Program for Delivering Mail: *sendmail*

The actual delivery of messages is not handled by `mailx` but by another program. In the case of System V `mailx`, the delivery program is `mail` (otherwise known as `/bin/mail`). You can choose a different mail delivery program by setting the valued variable `sendmail`. Most users should stick with the default mail delivery program, however.

Tilde Commands

To issue a command from within the simple editor, you type a tilde (~) in the first column, followed by one of the tilde commands described in chapter 4. The tilde is known as the mail "escape" character because it allows you to leave the e-mail editor to perform other functions.

Defining the Escape Character: *escape*

Suppose that it's awkward or impossible to type a tilde on your terminal. The `escape` option allows you to substitute another character as the escape character. For example, to change the escape character from a tilde to a colon (:), use this line in your `.mailrc` file:

```
set escape=:
```

Thereafter, enter a colon within the editor when you want to use the tilde commands. For example, `:v` would place you in the screen editor, and the command `:r bigdoc` would insert the file `bigdoc` in your message. The `mailx` program will now no longer respond to tildes.

Defining the ~*e* Editor: *EDITOR*

In chapter 4, you learned that you could invoke a system editor (like `ed` or `ex`) with the `~e` tilde command. In System V, the default editor is `ed` (although the system administrator can change this by using a system-wide configuration setting). You can name the editor that will be called up with `~e` by setting the `mailx` variable `EDITOR` to the pathname of the editor you want. For example, this line:

```
set EDITOR=/usr/local/bin/new_editor
```

sets the `~e` editor to `new_editor` in the `usr/local/bin` directory. Ask a knowledgeable user or the system administrator for the pathname of the editor you want.

Defining the ~*v* Screen Editor: *VISUAL*

The `mailx` variable `VISUAL` names the editor that will be called up with the `~v` tilde command, just as `EDITOR` does for `~e`. In System V, the default is `vi`. Like `EDITOR`, `VISUAL` can be set to the pathname of whichever editor you want. For example:

```
set VISUAL=/usr/local/bin/new_screen_ed
```

means that `~v` will invoke the `new_screen_ed` in the `usr/local/bin` directory. (The name "visual" indicates that this option is intended to name a screen-oriented editor such as `vi`, rather than a line editor such as `ex`. But you can set `VISUAL` to any editor you wish.)

Defining the String Inserted by ~*a*: *sign* (V)

System V allows you to insert an *autograph* string in a message with the `~a` command. (In other communications and news programs, this string is sometimes called a *signature*.) Define the string to be inserted with a command like:

```
set sign="Your obedient servant, Uriah"
```

The `sign` variable has no default value.

Defining the String Inserted by ~*A*: *Sign* (V)

You can insert an alternate autograph string with the `~A` command. Define the alternate string with a command such as:

```
set String="Remember--work makes life sweet!"
```

The `Sign` variable has no default value.

Options for Messages and Displays While Reading Mail

Once you have called up `mailx` to read your mail, the program displays several items of information. Some people find these displays a nuisance, so `mailx` provides options to suppress them. You can also change the way headers and messages are displayed on the screen.

Suppressing the Opening Message: *quiet*

When you enter `mailx` to read messages sent to you, the program displays an opening message and version number. A typical opening looks like:

```
Mail version 2.18 5/19/83. Type ? for help
```

You can instruct the `mailx` program NOT to display this information with the line:

```
set quiet
```

By default, `quiet` is disabled.

Suppressing the Header Display: *noheader* (Berk)

Following the opening line of `mailx` information, the program displays the headers of your first 10 or so messages. To disable this display in Berkeley `Mail`, enter:

```
set noheader
```

You might want to disable the header display if you are communicating with your UNIX system using a slow modem. The default setting is for headers to be displayed (`noheaders` is disabled).

Enabling the Header Display: *header* (V)

The System V `header` option is the reverse of Berkeley's `noheader`. The `header` option is set by default in System V, enabling the display of headers. Unset `header` to disable the header display.

Specifying the Number of Headers Displayed: *screen*

With the `screen` option, you can change the number of headers in the header display. To see headings for 15 messages at once, enter:

```
set screen=15
```

Suppressing the Display of Header Fields: *ignore*

When you enter a command to display a message, you see more than just the message text. At the top of each message you see a number of header fields, such as:

```
From bea Tue Nov 25 08:31:59 1987
Received: by well.UUCP (4.12/4.7)
id AA02116; Tue 25 Nov 87 08:31:15 pst
Date: Tue, 25 Nov 87 08:31:15 pst
From: bea (Bart Anderson)
Message-Id:  <8611251631.AA07322@well.UUCP>
To: miranda
Subject: Re:  glad tidings
Cc: novio
Status: O
```

Some of these header fields may be of no interest to you and serve only as distractions. You can prevent the display of individual fields with a command like:

```
ignore Received
```

You can name more than one header field in the same `ignore` command. To avoid the display of all the less-interesting fields, enter this line in your `.mailrc` file:

```
ignore Received Message-Id Via Status
```

Only the display of header fields is suppressed; the `ignore` command does not actually delete them from the message file. The `Print` and `Type` (initial caps) commands override the `ignore` command and display messages with all header fields. Note that `ignore` is a *command*; it is not a variable and does not require the `set` command. Don't confuse this with the `mailx` variable also named `ignore`, which causes `mailx` to ignore interrupt characters.

Changing the *mailx* Prompt: *prompt* (V)

By default, the mailx prompt for System V is a question mark (?), and for Berkeley systems the Mail prompt is an ampersand (&). You can change the mailx prompt to the text string you want with the prompt option (System V only). To change the prompt to "mailx," enter this line:

```
set prompt="mailx: "
```

From that point on, your program will display:

```
mailx:
```

and await your input. This might be useful if you regularly use more than one mail program.

Specifying the Number of Lines per Message Display: *crt*

If you are viewing a long message, you can stop and start the scrolling of the display with Control-s and Control-q. However, you may prefer to view messages through a *pager program*. The pager program displays a screenfull of text and then pauses until you press a key before it displays the next screenfull. If you want a pager program, set crt equal to the minimum number of lines to be displayed before the pager program is invoked. For 22 lines of text to be displayed as a screenfull, enter:

```
set crt=22
```

If you are communicating with a slow modem, you may want to set a smaller number for crt. In System V mailx, the pager program is pg; in Berkeley Mail, it's more. By default, crt is not set and a pager program is not invoked.

Specifying an Alternative Pager Program: *PAGER* (V)

When you are displaying long messages (longer than the number of lines in the crt setting just described), the program can invoke a paging program. On System V mailx, you can select a different paging program than the default pg by setting the PAGER variable. You can also choose different options for pg. For example, the following line causes pg to be called up with the -c flag so that it homes the cursor and clears the screen before displaying the next screenfull.

```
set PAGER="pg -c"
```

Command Options for Reading Mail

The mailx program offers a bewildering variety of commands for reading and handling the messages that you receive. As if this variety weren't enough, you can set options to customize many of the commands to your liking.

Specifying the Number of Lines That *top* Displays: *toplines*

The top command (issued at the mailx prompt) allows you to see the first few lines of the specified message. You can change the number of lines that top displays by setting the toplines option. For example, if you want 10 lines displayed instead of the default of 5, enter this line:

```
set toplines=10
```

Afterwards, the top command displays the first 10 lines of a message.

Making *delete* Act like *dp*: *autoprint*

The autoprint option comes in handy when you're reading through a large number of messages. Often you will want to discard the message that you're currently viewing and go on to the next message. To do this, you must first delete the current message and then ask for the next message to be displayed. You can reduce this procedure to one step with the dt or dp command.

If you continually use dt or dp, you may want to automate the process. With the autoprint option set, if you delete a message, the next message is automatically displayed. Enable this feature with the line:

```
set autoprint
```

By default, autoprint is disabled.

Preventing Messages You Read from Disappearing: *hold*

When you quit the mailx program, the messages you have read in that session are automatically added to the mbox file in your home directory and deleted from your system mailbox. The next time you call up mailx, you won't see those messages in the header display. This can be disconcerting to new e-mail users—their messages keep disappearing! (And the mbox file keeps growing.) To keep messages from disappearing, enter:

```
set hold
```

Afterwards, the messages you read ARE NOT deleted from the system mailbox, and they are not automatically saved in `mbox`. Instead, messages remain in the system mailbox unless you explicitly save or delete them. By default, `hold` is disabled.

Preventing Messages You Save from Disappearing: *keepsave*

The `keepsave` option is very similar to `hold`. Instead of protecting the messages that you have *read*, `keepsave` protects the messages you have *saved*.

With normal `mailx` operation, if you save messages with the `save` command, the messages will be deleted from the system mailbox when you leave the program with the `quit` command. However, if you enter:

```
set keepsave
```

the operation of `mailx` is altered so that messages you save are NOT automatically deleted from the system mailbox. Both `hold` and `keepsave` might be good options to set for new users. By default, `keepsave` is disabled.

Specifying the Shell to Which You Escape: *SHELL*

When you are inside the `mailx` program, you can escape to the shell with the `SHELL` command. Afterwards, you can enter UNIX commands like `who` and `ls`; entering Control-d returns you to the `mail/Mailx` program. (You can also execute shell commands by prefacing them with an exclamation point (!) at the `mailx` prompt, for example, `!ls`).

On some systems (e.g., Berkeley systems), you have a choice between shells. The Berkeley system offers both the C Shell (`%` prompt, invoked with the `csh` command) or the Bourne Shell (`$` prompt, invoked with the `sh` command).

You can change the shell to which you escape with a line like this:

```
set SHELL=/bin/sh
```

Note that the System V default for `SHELL` is `sh`.

Setting a Default Command for the Pipe Command: *cmd* (V)

When you are in the `mailx` program, you can process mail messages through another program with either the `pipe` or the `¦` command. For example, you might enter:

```
pipe 3 nroff
```

or

```
| 3 nroff
```

These commands would pipe the text of message 3 through the `nroff` program, causing it to be formatted.

If you regularly pipe messages through a certain command, you can make that command the default for the `pipe` command. Just set `cmd` equal to the desired command. For instance:

```
set cmd=nroff
```

Now, to format a message with `nroff`, all you need enter is:

```
pipe 3
```

Message 3 is sent to `nroff`, the default pipe command that you specified.

If you want to send messages to the printer with the pipe command, enter a line like this:

```
cmd=lp
```

(Other printing commands may be available on your system. Use the appropriate command on your system for sending a file to the printer.) Now you can send messages to the printer with a mail command like:

```
pipe 1-5
```

Messages 1 through 5 are sent to your system printer. There is no default setting for `cmd`.

Inserting a Form Feed after Each Message: *page* (V)

If you use the `pipe` command to send messages to your system printer, you might want to enter the line:

```
set page
```

This option causes a form feed to be inserted between messages that are sent with the pipe command. Each message will then start printing on a new page. By default, the `page` option is disabled.

Options for Folders

Chapter 4 showed you how to simplify the saving of messages by creating a folders directory. Figure 4-4 in the previous chapter shows a folders directory containing several files named after correspondents.

To save a message to the folder `giorgio` located in the directory named `myfolders`, enter a command like:

```
save 4 +giorgio
```

As you can see, a + is used to prefix the name of the folder in which the message will be saved, and `mailx` takes care of finding the correct pathname (`/users/eric/myfolders/giorgio` for example).

Defining the Folders Directory: *folder*

In order to use folders, you must first create the folders directory with the `mkdir` command (e.g., `mkdir myfolders`). You must next tell the `mailx` program about the folders directory with the `folder` option. You set `folder` to the name of the directory you choose to hold your folders. For instance:

```
set folder=myfolders
```

By default, the `folder` feature is disabled.

Changing the Command to List Your Folders: *LISTER* (V)

You can see a list of all your folders with the `folders` command. By default, the System V `mailx` program uses the `ls` command to display the files. By specifying a value for the `LISTER` variable, you can change the command that lists folders (System V only). For example, to get a detailed listing of the folders, you can enter:

```
set LISTER="ls -l"
```

Placing Files of Outgoing Messages into the Folders Directory: *outfolder* (V)

If you save messages in folders, you'll probably want to set the `outfolder` option (System V only) by entering:

```
set outfolder
```

Afterwards, any files created to save outgoing messages are placed in the directory set by the `folder` variable. These files may be created with the `Copy`, `followup`, `Followup` and `Save` commands, as well as automatically by the `record` variable. By default, `outfolder` is disabled.

Options for Files and the *mailx* Program

As you saw in figure 3-9, the `mailx` program interacts with other files while it performs its tasks. Several options allow you to change the names of the files, as well as the way `mailx` deals with them.

Preserving Your System Mailbox: *keep*

The system mailbox temporarily stores the messages that other users have sent you. For a user with the login name of `eric`, this mailbox is the file `/usr/mail/eric` on System V. On a Berkeley system it is `/usr/spool/mail/eric`.

If your system mailbox is emptied (i.e., all messages are deleted), the system mailbox file is normally removed. When messages are again sent to you, the file is re-created. However, you may have changed the permissions on your original mailbox to prevent other users from reading your mail. In this case, when the file is re-created, it may not have the permissions you desire. The `keep` option prevents this from happening by not allowing the system to remove the system mailbox file. With the `keep` option, if the mailbox is empty, the file is merely truncated to zero length—but not removed. Invoke the `keep` option with the line:

```
set keep
```

By default, `keep` is disabled.

Defining a New Dead Letter File: *DEAD* (V)

When you cancel a message by entering two interrupt characters, the message as it stands at that time is saved by default in the file `dead.letter` located in your home directory. You can cause the program to save cancelled messages in a different file by setting the `DEAD` variable (System V only). For example, to specify `newdead` as the dead letter file, you would enter:

```
set DEAD=$HOME/newdead
```

The environmental variable `$HOME` stands for your home directory; thus, `$HOME /newdead` puts the file `newdead` in your home directory.

Specifying a New Default File for Saving Messages: *MBOX* (V)

When you `quit` the `mailx` program, messages that you have read are saved by default in the file `mbox` located in your home directory. For example, if you read all your messages with the `print *` command and then `quit`, all the messages will be placed in the `mbox` file.

Just as you can change the dead letter file with `DEAD`, so can you change the name of the default `mbox` file with the `MBOX` variable (System V only). For example,

```
set MBOX=$HOME/newmbox
```

means that, by default, messages will be saved in the file `newmbox` in your home directory.

Appending Messages to *mbox*: *append*

Normally when a message is saved in `mbox`, it is *prepended*. This means that the most recently saved message will appear first in the header display when you examine `mbox`. Prepending and appending are shown in figure 5-2.

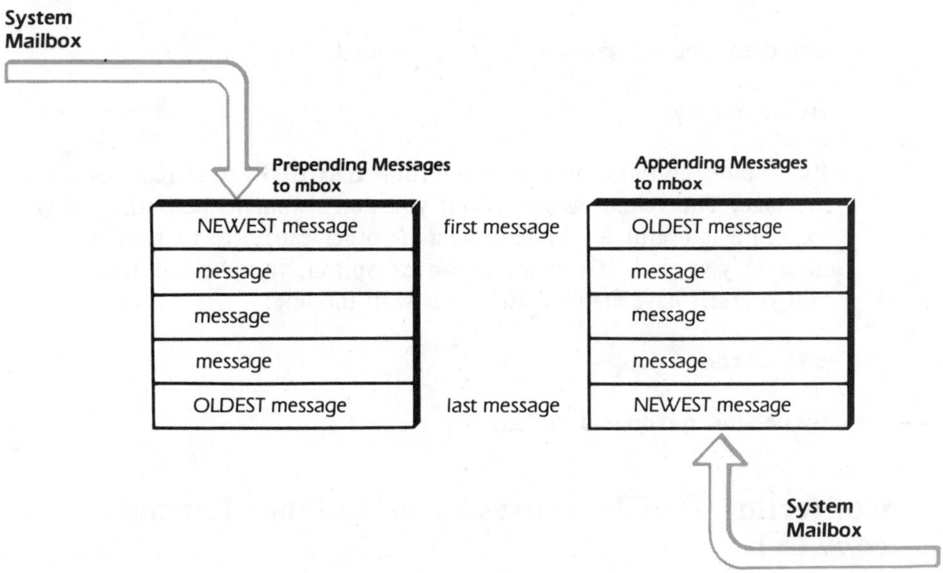

Figure 5-2. Messages can be prepended or appended to the **mbox** file.

To *append* messages to `mbox` rather than prepend them, set the `append` option, as follows:

```
set append
```

By default, `append` is disabled.

Options for Names and Addresses

The last group of options affects how `mailx` deals with user names and addresses. Addresses, as you remember from chapter 4, specify a pathway from machine to machine so that messages can be sent to users on other UNIX computers.

Receiving a Copy of Messages That You Send: *metoo*

When you are sending mail to a group, your name will commonly appear in the group alias, since you are often part of the group. The `mailx` program assumes that you do not want to receive a copy of a message that you yourself have created, so your name will be removed from the list of recipients before the message is sent.

For instance, if you have the login name of `ian` and you are formulating a budget with a group of coworkers, you can set up this alias:

```
alias budget ian sally silvana richard sam
```

You then send messages with this command:

```
mailx budget
```

By default, everyone in the alias group EXCEPT YOU receives a copy of your message. The system assumes that you don't want to be bothered. However, you may find it useful for management or other purposes to have a record of every message you send. If you set the `metoo` option, you also will receive messages that you yourself have created. Enable it with the line:

```
set metoo
```

By default, `metoo` is disabled.

Converting UUCP Addresses to Another Format: *conv* (V)

In System V, the `conv` variable can be set to a specific address format. Afterwards, UUCP addresses are converted to the format specified. (Remember that UUCP addresses look like this: hplabs!well!paula.) By default, conv is disabled. If you are regularly sending mail to another network (such as ARPANET), you may want to use conv.

Allowing for Accounts on Different Computers: *allnet* (V)

If you communicate with people who have accounts on several systems, you may want to set the allnet option (System V only). To explain allnet, let's say that you exchange messages with someone named sylvia who has accounts on three different machines: hpitg, ubass, and pclabs. Thus, messages from sylvia may be sent from one of three different addresses:

```
hpitg!sylvia
ubass!sylvia
pclabs!sylvia
```

If allnet is set with the line:

```
set allnet
```

the mailx program treats all three of those network names as identical. In message lists, the program would look only at the login name sylvia, rather than at the system names. By default, allnet is disabled.

Telling *mailx* about Your Accounts on Different Systems: *alternates*

The allnet option just described tells the mailx program that a mail recipient may appear on different machines. To tell the program that YOU may appear on different machines, use the alternates command. Afterwards, the mailx program removes your alternate names from the list of recipients when you are replying to a message. This prevents you from sending duplicate messages to yourself at each of your other addresses.

Note that alternates is a command, not an option; no set command is needed. Also, the use of alternates does not override record if the latter is turned on.

If your login name were eric and you had accounts on several machines, you could enter the following line to tell your computer the different names by which you might be known:

```
alternates vadic!eric calplan!eric csy!eric
```

Afterwards, if mailx sees a list of recipients that includes vadic!eric and csy!eric, it would not send your message to your accounts on those machines.

To see a list of current alternate names, you can enter alternates with no arguments.

Preventing Rewriting of Remote Addresses: *onehop* (V)

Normally, when you reply to a message that was sent to several people, the addresses of the other recipients are rewritten so that they are relative to the sender's machine. If you enter:

```
set onehop
```

the addresses are no longer rewritten. For networks in which each machine can send messages directly to other machines, setting onehop means that mail is delivered more quickly, since it doesn't get routed through intermediate machines. By default, onehop is disabled.

Summary

This chapter showed you the huge array of variables that you can set for mailx. You learned how to customize mailx by changing options (mailx variables). At the mailx prompt, individual options can be enabled with the set command or disabled with unset. To automatically configure your program whenever you run it, you can enter set and unset commands in the .mailrc file in your home directory. A similar file (called mailx.rc or Mail.rc) can configure the mailx program for every user on the system.

We described more than 40 options with which you can change almost every aspect of the mail program. Table 5-1 listed all the options and gave a brief description of what each does.

This concludes our discussion of the mailx program and of electronic mail. (Remember that there is also a tutorial on /bin/mail in Appendix A.) We hope that we have made using electronic mail easy, productive, and more fun!

Let's now move on to another aspect of UNIX communications, the USENET news network.

Part

2

UNIX News: USENET

Part 2 presents *USENET*, the UNIX communications network that is one of the best electronic networks available. This network is international, connecting UNIX users all over the United States, Canada, Europe—indeed, the world.

The next five chapters show you how to use the USENET Netnews software to read, reply to, and post news articles on hundreds of subjects.

The coverage is divided into five areas:

- Introduction to USENET (chapter 6)
- `readnews`, a simple news reading program (chapter 7)
- `rn`, a more-powerful news reading program (chapter 8)
- `vnews`, a screen-oriented news reading program (chapter 9)
- `postnews`, a news writing program for sending (posting) news (chapter 10)

6

Introduction to USENET

Part 1 of this book showed how individuals can use the UNIX mail programs for private communications. In addition to private communications, however, most of us regularly receive public communications: newspapers, magazines, professional journals, newsletters, and so on. USENET can be thought of as a cross between a magazine and a high-quality CB radio. Like a magazine, it has many articles related to specific topics. However, there is usually no magazine editor, so the writing is informal and has much of the give-and-take heard in the casual conversation of CB radio users.

What Is USENET?

USENET is a network available to UNIX users for sending messages (or "news articles") that can be read and responded to by other users. Participating in USENET is like subscribing to a collection of electronic magazines. These "magazines," called *newsgroups*, are devoted to particular topics, ranging from questions about UNIX, programming languages, and computer systems to discussions of politics, philosophy, science, and recreational activities. Any participating user can write and submit articles on any topic and, in turn, read articles submitted from UNIX sites all over the world. The collection of programs that makes this exchange possible is called *Netnews*.

Here are some of the items you can find on USENET:

- Program source code for utilities and games.
- News and reviews of the latest software and hardware.
- Employment, consulting, and other business contacts.
- Answers to your questions about bugs and compatibility.

- Discussions on artificial intelligence (AI) research, space, and technology.
- Announcements and classified ads.
- Discussions on politics, philosophy, and religion.
- "Play by mail" games and game hints.

This list is only a sampling of the possibilities. There are over 400 newsgroups available on USENET today, and more are being created every month. (We will look at how newsgroups are organized later.)

Overview of USENET

In this and the following four chapters, we'll show you how USENET works and how to get the most out of it. In this chapter we'll give you an overview of USENET, including:

- How USENET began and how it is organized.
- How to participate in USENET.
- How news is sent to and from your site.
- How news is processed by your site.
- Interface programs for reading and posting news.
- A `readnews` example session with a look behind the scenes.

This material will prepare you to use the four programs explained in chapters 7 through 10. These are the programs that enable you to read and write news articles on USENET. Three of them, `readnews`, `rn`, and `vnews`, are used for reading and replying to news articles. The fourth, `postnews`, is used to send, or *post*, original news articles. After finishing Part 2, you will be able to compare these programs and choose the ones that best suit your needs.

USENET History and Organization

USENET can best be described as a kind of grass roots network based on controlled anarchy. In contrast to the formal computer networks operated by the Defense Department and other government agencies and large companies, many of which have been in existence for years, USENET grew from the ground up without a formal structure.

The fertile ground from which this network sprung was the widespread acceptance of UNIX in universities, engineering and scientific companies, and research agencies. Students and researchers in all fields had a need to share technical information and observations about their work. They needed a means of communication that was less formal and faster than traditional media such as journals and conferences. They wanted a way that enabled them to speak freely without worrying about heavy-handed controls and regulations. And the basis for such a medium was already in place: the widespread connection of UNIX sites through UUCP and other networks.

With the `uucp` program (see Part 3), files could be sent between users on different machines. The files could be informally shared, but there was no method for regular distribution of a file to a whole group of users, and no easy way for users to browse or find material they were interested in. A set of programs that would provide automatic distribution of articles and easy access to them was needed.

The Netnews software that made USENET possible was developed by Tom Truscott and James Ellis at Duke University in 1979. USENET started out with just two sites: Duke University and the neighboring University of North Carolina. The first news programs were simply shell scripts that moved files back and forth between the two sites. The programs were then rewritten in C and released to the public in 1980 by Tom Truscott and Steve Daniel. This set of programs was known as "Netnews Release A."

Besides taking care of the distribution and management of files containing news, a news system must provide ways that users can access, read, and send (post) news articles. The first version of the front-end software that allowed users to read and post news articles was intended to distribute news for the USENIX Association, a professional organization for UNIX users—thus, the network was given the name *USENET*.

After these first Netnews programs were described at the 1980 USENIX conference, word began to spread and interest in USENET began to grow. People at other UNIX sites wanted to use the software. At the University of California, Berkeley, Mark Horton and Matt Glickman started to run USENET, and in 1982 they revised the Netnews programs to create the "B" version. This version of the software added new features, including a better organization of topical newsgroups and the ability to accommodate the growing number of sites. Since then, Version B has gone through many releases that have added new features to make it easier for users to manage the news. (At the time of writing, release 2.11 of Version B is being installed.) Users at Bell Labs, the other bastion of UNIX development, also became interested and provided helpful facilities. USENET now has over 5000 participating sites with over 150,000 users. The net has become international, with users in Australia, Asia, and Europe, as well as North America.

USENET has experienced explosive growth in the last few years. Now that inexpensive UNIX systems (such as AT clones and various kinds of work stations) are available, it is likely that USENET will grow even more rapidly in years to come.

Participating in USENET

Since USENET capability isn't built into any version of UNIX, how does a site obtain access to USENET? And how does a user start using it?

USENET for Administrators

Most traditional computer networks are administered. This means that whether the network is commercial (such as CompuServe® or The Source℠) or is run by an individual as a benefit for the community (such as most bulletin boards), it is controlled by one person or group who establishes policy and rules for usage and who maintains the message base, the equipment, and so on.

USENET is different. There is no membership application, no dues, and, indeed, almost no organization. If you have a UNIX system and a modem, you can join simply by asking an existing USENET user (via e-mail) to send you the Netnews software (which is free) and then asking that user, or another, to exchange news articles with you. Good sources for the Netnews software include nearby universities or other sites that may already be connected to your UNIX system. (See Part 3 of this book for information on determining to which sites your system is connected. Also see Appendix D for information on USENET.) The Netnews software gives you access to the news being forwarded from all the other sites on the net and gives you the ability to write news that will be distributed throughout the network. (It is considered courteous for a new USENET user, once established, to offer to help potential new users in the area, thus continuing the sharing.)

After you have received the software necessary to participate in USENET, you must set up the required directories and files, and configure the software for your needs. You can then invite users of your machine to read and post messages. (The actual details of configuring and managing the Netnews software are rather complex and beyond the scope of this book. See Appendix D for some sources that can help you get started, however.)

USENET for Users

Fortunately, as a user on a UNIX system that has access to USENET, you do not need to know the details of how the Netnews software works. If you want to read news articles and respond to them with your own articles, all you have to do is run one of the news reading programs: `readnews`, `rn`, or `vnews`). If you want to write an original article (one that is not a response to another article), you run `postnews`. These programs are similar in complexity to the various UNIX editors (`ex`, `vi`, `emacs`, etc.). That is, in one session you can learn enough to get around, and then you can later explore the advanced features and options. Our tutorials on these programs in the following chapters are designed to get you started quickly, as well as to provide you with reference materials for mastering the more advanced features of the programs.

How the Netnews Software Is Constructed

USENET can be thought of as a series of layers that start with the physical connections between machines and that culminate in the interface programs that you, the user, can use to read and post news.

Layers of Connections

As figure 6-1 shows, USENET starts at the bottommost layer with the physical connection of machines, which may be via modems and phone lines, or cables, connectors, and a LAN (local area network). The next layer consists of the low-level networks that manage the transfer of files between machines. These could be a sophisticated LAN, a network such as Ethernet or ARPANET, or simply the capability of machines to use the UUCP software to dial each other and establish a connection. Indeed, UUCP is the most widespread of such facilities, since it is available on nearly every UNIX system. (Part 3 discusses the UUCP software in detail.) News articles are normally sent and received as UUCP batch jobs.

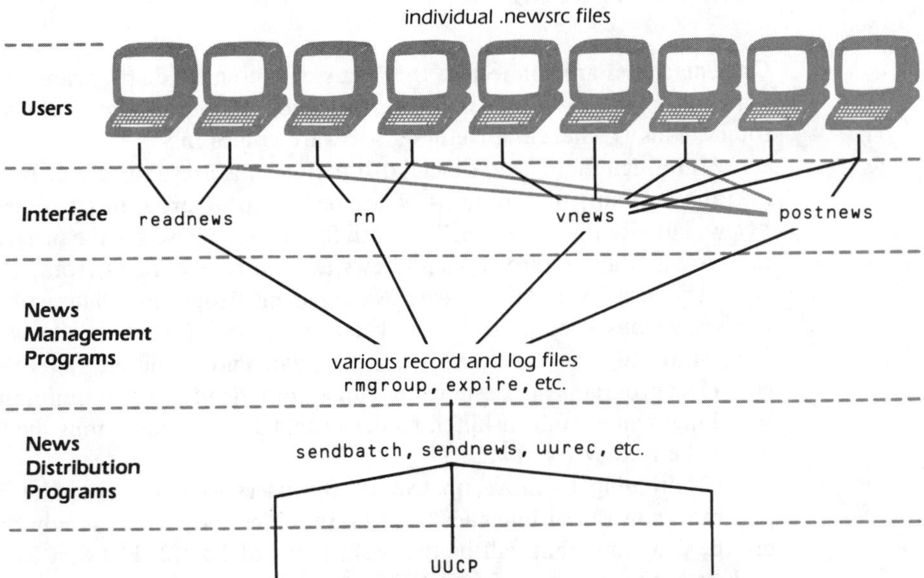

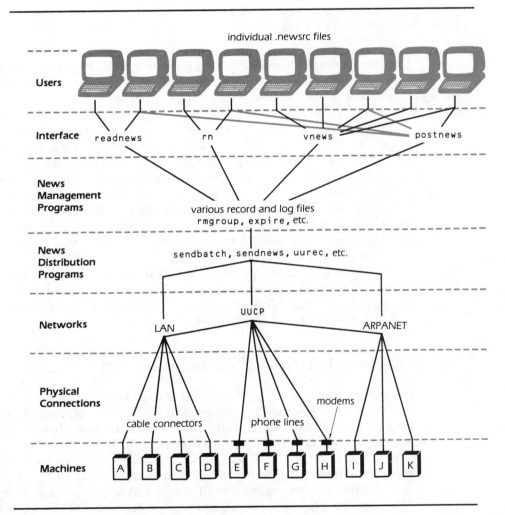

Figure 6-1. Layers of connections in USENET.

USENET can use almost any existing connection between two machines. For example, in a complicated situation, UUCP software might run on top of a local area network, with the Netnews software in turn using UUCP. In figure 6-1, all machines run the Netnews software, and all machines can reach each other via UUCP, sometimes going through another net. Machines A, B, C, and D happen also to be part of a LAN; machines E, F, G, and H are simply using UUCP; and machines I, J, and K are members of ARPANET (the Defense Department's *Ad*vanced *R*esearch *P*rojects *A*gency *NET*work, which has many nonmilitary as well as military/defense users). As a USENET user, you normally don't have to worry about how machines are connected. Our point in bringing up the matter is to show the versatility of USENET.

How Netnews Works

Once machines are connected, the next step is to provide programs that can disseminate and manage the *newsbase*, or collection of thousands of articles on scores of topics. This is where the Netnews software comes in.

Although there is no official distinction, it is useful to divide Netnews software into three groups of programs. The first group of programs is represented by the "News Distribution Progams" layer in figure 6-1. These are the programs that allow the system administrator to send news to, and receive news from, other machines.

The next layer is the "News Management Programs." These programs involve necessary housekeeping tasks for keeping up with the flow of news into the site. They allow the system administrator to update and prune the system's news directories. (The programs are designed to run automatically with a minimum of attention. But things can get out of kilter, so the system administrator must be knowledgeable about the Netnews software.)

Continuing to move up toward the users in figure 6-1, the final group of programs consists of interfaces that users can employ to read and post news. These are the programs that will be the main focus of Part 2. But first let's take a closer look at how the layers of USENET work together.

Distribution of Articles throughout the Net

In chapter 4 you saw a UUCP map that showed connections among a group of UNIX machines. The same connections that allow for the sending and forwarding of electronic mail allow for the distribution of USENET news. Indeed, the Netnews software sometimes uses midlevel mail programs to send news articles, and these programs in turn use UUCP, as you will see in Part 3 of this book. A Netnews distribution network can be thought of as an overlay on the UUCP map.

In figure 6-1, we implied that all sites in USENET are connected by UUCP. This is theoretically true in that, in most cases, a path could be constructed between any two machines. In practice, however, it would be very expensive and slow if each site had to send its news articles to every other site, usually through several intermediates. In fact, as with the uucp file transfer program, each site normally communicates directly only with selected nearby sites.

In Part 1, you saw that sites can serve as backbone sites for UUCP file transfers, such as remote mail. Just as some sites serve as a kind of regional clearinghouse or as a gateway between networks for remote mail and other uucp file transfers, many of the same sites have committed themselves to supporting USENET by serving as backbone sites for USENET. In Netnews terms, a *backbone site* is a system that:

- Collects news posted from many nearby sites.
- Receives news from at least two other backbone sites.
- Forwards the news from its region to at least two other backbone sites.
- Feeds all the news it has received to local sites.

Figure 6-2 shows how news is collected and forwarded by a backbone site. Let's say you are a user on a small installation (or even a micro) at site A. Site A is a *leaf node*, meaning that it communicates with only one other site—the site that feeds it news. That is, there is one site above it in the tree, and none below it.

You post a message using the postnews program or by using the reply option in one of the news interface programs (all of these programs will be discussed in coming chapters). The message could be an announcement like this:

```
From: Marcella.Zaragoza@ISL1.RI.CMU.EDU
Subject: Seminar - Understanding How Devices Work (CMU)
Date: 30 Jan 87 15:45:09 GMT

                        AI SEMINAR

TOPIC:      Understanding How Devices Work: Functional
                Representation of Devices and
                Compilation of Diagnostic Knowledge

SPEAKER:    B. Chandrasekaran
                Department of Computer & Information Science
                The Ohio State University
                Columbus, OH 43210

PLACE:      Wean Hall 4605

DATE:       Wednesday, February 4, 1987

TIME:       10:00 a.m.

                        ABSTRACT
```

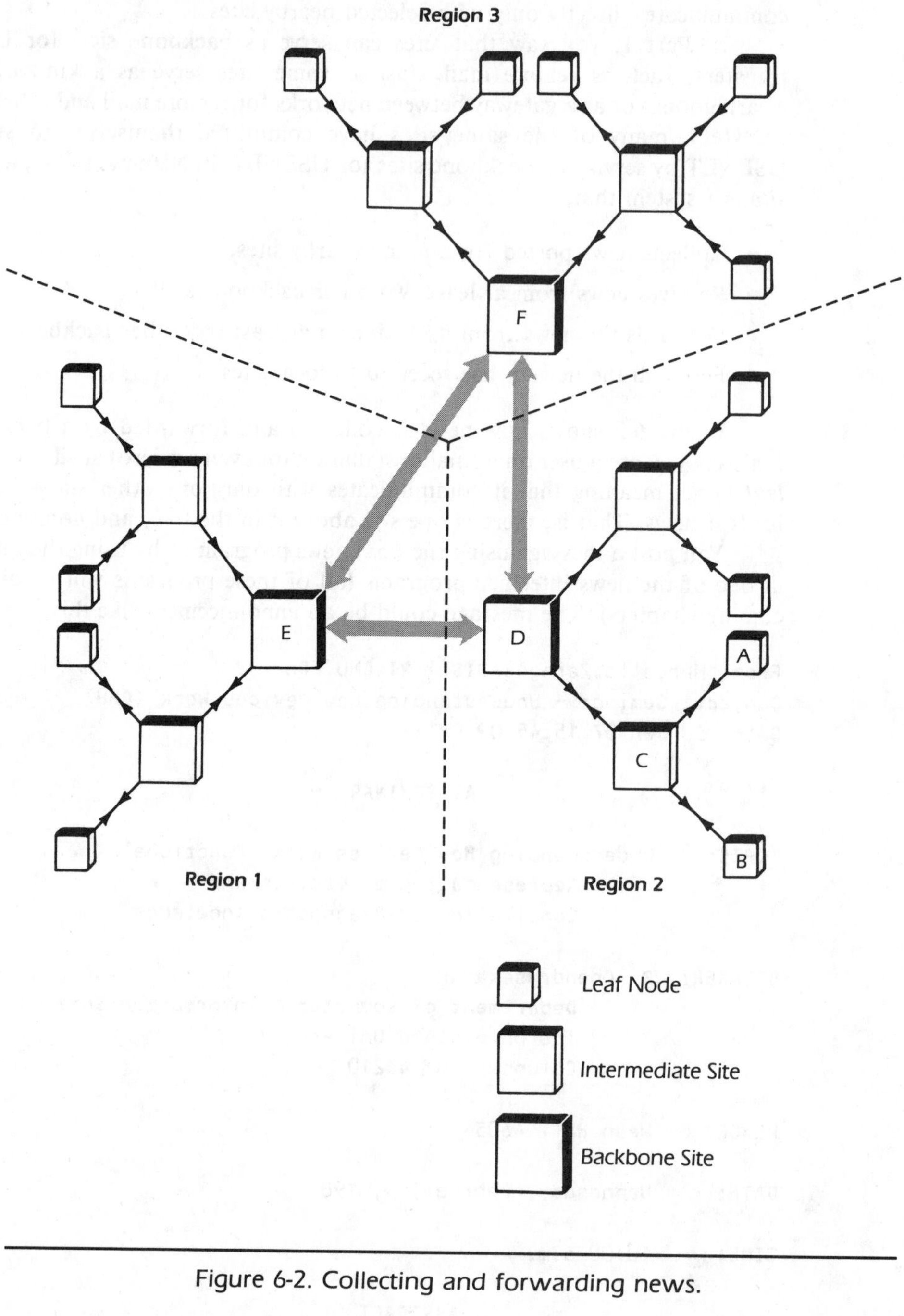

Figure 6-2. Collecting and forwarding news.

(We have omitted part of this and of other example articles to save space.)

Like a mail message, the article has header fields showing its origin, date, and so on. A news article is in fact very similar to the mail messages discussed in Part 1 of this book. This is intentional: the news article format is designed to be compatible with mail. This compatibility means that Netnews can take advantage of the flexibility of the mail system. We will look at these header fields in more detail when we look at reading and writing news.

Back to our example. Your message goes to another machine near you—your news feed at an intermediate site called C. (Note that leaf sites A and B are both *fed* from C. This means that they get copies of all available news articles from site C and that they send any news they originate to that site.) From site C, your news article goes to site D, which is the regional backbone site. Your news, plus any news from sites A and C and from the other sites in your region, is forwarded by backbone site D to the backbone for the adjacent region (site E). In reality, a given region can have many more layers of connections, but the principle is the same.

A *region*, by the way, is not a particular geographic area but rather a group of sites that find it economical to serve each other's needs. Since telephone costs increase roughly with distance, there is some correlation with geography, of course.

Each backbone site in turn collects news postings from its region as well as news forwarded by two or more adjacent backbones, and sends all this news on to two or more other backbones. By this system of relayed messages, each backbone eventually receives messages originated from all over the net.

Each backbone distributes the news it has received from other backbones to secondary sites in its region. Eventually, your article is distributed all over the net, and your system has received news from everywhere, but most sites have not had to pay for more than (usually) a local call. This method of news distribution is often called the "flooding algorithm" because of the way that the news spreads like water flooding into a system of rivers, tributaries, and streams. Figure 6-3 shows how an article can be propagated through the entire net in this way. (We should note that not all news is distributed worldwide. Some newsgroups are intentionally designed for local news, and any message can have its distribution restricted to a local area. More on this later.)

Backbone Sites and USENET Administration

The cost of USENET for local sites is modest, but the same cannot be said of the backbone sites. They often run up a considerable monthly phone bill in forwarding news to the next backbone, and someone has to spend quite a few hours a week administering the news. In general, backbones distribute a wide variety of newsgroups, many of them of only peripheral interest to the institution sponsoring the site. Many of the sites are academic institutions that see USENET as a valuable resource for the dissemination of knowledge and as an aid to researchers. Many corporate sites see USENET as a public service as well as a tool for their employees' professional development.

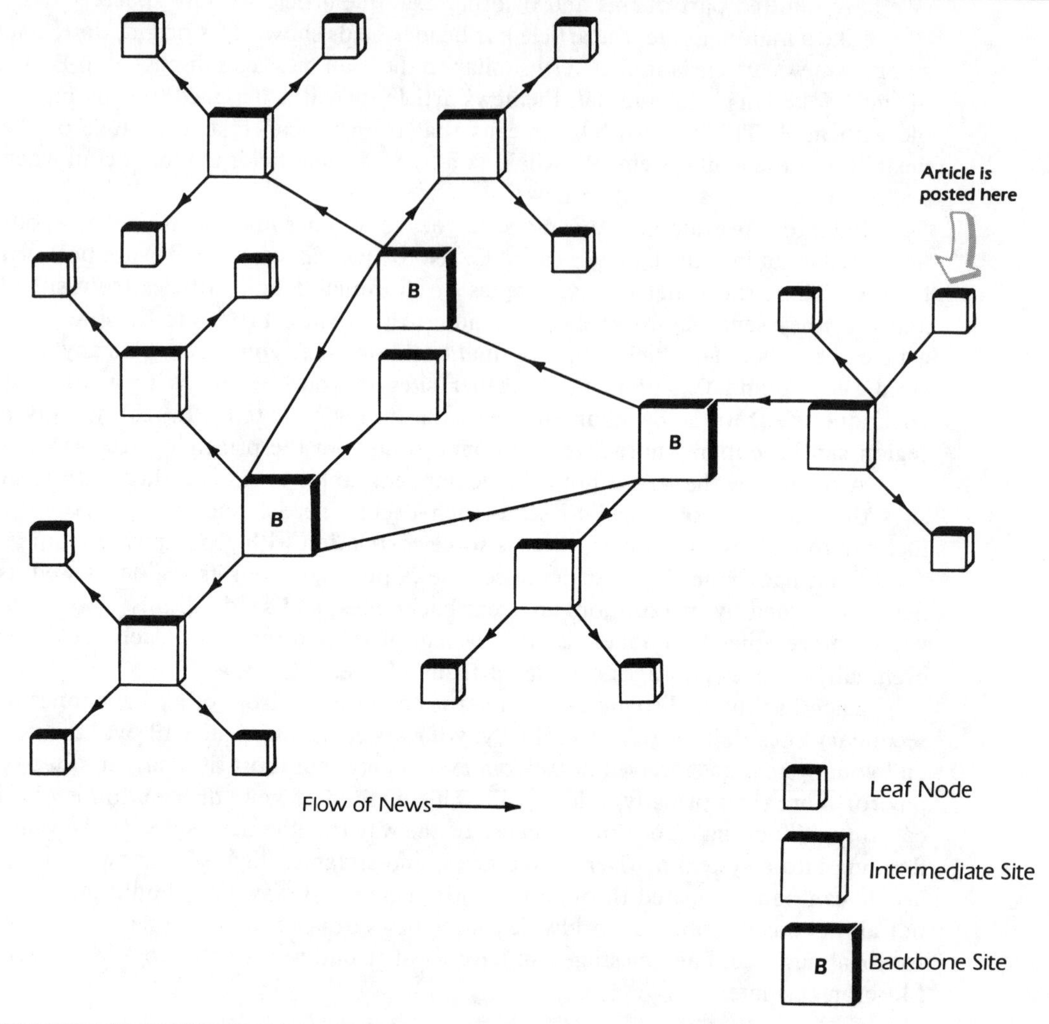

Figure 6-3. Propagating news.

However, newsgroups (topics) that seem to be of very limited interest, or that have been taken over by *flaming,* or heated personal arguments, may be dropped by the backbones. (This means that not all news articles are available at a given site. Some may not be distributed by the backbone. Others may be rejected by the local site itself for reasons of cost, space, or computing resources. But most sites have a good selection of the most important and interesting newsgroups.)

The closest that USENET comes to a government is in the policies enforced by the backbone sites. Of course, any site is free to create or distribute any newsgroup. Any backbone is also free to forward it or reject it. In a very real sense, USENET is a marketplace of ideas. And, in general, it is a marketplace that allows a great deal of freedom while expecting a reasonable degree of responsibility and courtesy. We will have more to say about the latter in chapter 10.

Administering the News at the Local Site

Now that you have seen how a message can travel from your site to every site on USENET, and how messages from everywhere else can travel to your site, let's look at the user end. How is all this news made accessible to you and other users?

To review, you get news because your backbone site is receiving news packets from all over the net. The backbone gives your site (or a local site connected to yours) a *news feed*, or stream of news. Thus, you have potential access to any article originated anywhere on the net.

The Arrival of News at the Local Site

When news articles arrive in your system, they usually go into a "spool" directory similar to that used by UUCP (see Part 3 of this book). A *spool* is a temporary storage place for data. This directory usually has a name like `usr/spool/news`. After being processed by the Netnews software (see the next section), articles are usually stored in a directory called `/usr/lib/news`. (You may want to do some exploring on your system to see where it stores news. Pathnames will vary from system to system.) The news directory will probably look something like this if you list it with `ls`:

```
ls /usr/news
batch     etc      mi       news     src
ca        lib      misc     rec      talk
comp      local    mod      sci      temp
control   maps     na       social
```

If you look at the actual `/news` directory on your system, you will find a different set of files than those we've shown here. We're showing only some of the most important. We'll discuss what some of these directories are used for in the next few sections. For now, we'll note that many of them (`ba`, `ca`, `comp`, `misc`, `mod`, `na`, `news`, `rec`, `sci`, `soc`, `src`, and `talk`) are distribution areas or topic areas containing newsgroups as subdirectories. For example, `ba` is the subdirectory for newsgroups related to the San Francisco Bay Area, whereas `comp` is the subdirectory for newsgroups related to different sorts of computer systems. (We will be looking at the structure of newsgroup names in more detail soon.) Some directories, such as `etc`, `lib`, and `src`, contain the Netnews software itself or files used by the software. The `batch` directory contains shell scripts that run background Netnews processes.

The Processing of Incoming News

The Netnews software at the local site has to do regular housekeeping to keep the news up to date. The software also has to keep track of which newsgroups a given user wants to be shown, and which articles he or she has already seen. We will look at three general areas handled by the Netnews software at the local site:

1. Receiving, filtering, and storing news.
2. Updating the newsbase.
3. Enabling users to read, reply to, and generate news.

We will not go into all the details of news processing here, rather we'll try to get a broad picture of what is going on. There are two key files that are important for news processing at a site: the *system file* and the *active file.*

The Site's System File

The system file, /news/lib/sys, contains the site's *subscription list*, that is, a set of patterns that determine which newsgroups the site will accept. If an incoming newsgroup does not meet the specifications in the system file, it and its articles are not accepted by the site.

In addition, the system file contains the subscription lists for sites that your site is exchanging news with. The advantage of a subscription list is that it saves time and money at both ends if you don't send stuff someone doesn't want. Here is an example of a sys file:

```
cat /news/lib/sys
#       Whole Earth 'Lectronic Link, Sausalito, California, Sep 14, 1985
#       Running Version 2.10.3 USENET Software
#
#       If you change something in this file, please notify
#       usenet and change the modify date at the top.
#
well:local,net,world,comp,news,sci,rec,misc,soc,talk,mod,na,usa,ca,ba,well,
hackintosh,mi,to.well::
#
####    WELL's primary netnews feed
#
# Pacific Bell, San Francisco, California
#
ptsfa:net,world,comp,news,sci,rec,misc,soc,talk,mod,na,ba,ca,usa,to.ptsfa:
F:/well/news/batch/ptsfa
#
####    WELL's leaf nodes
#
```

```
# MicroPro International, San Rafael, California
#
#
#micropro:net,mod,na,usa,ca,ba,to.well:FL3:/well/news/batch/micropro
#micropro:net,fa,mod,na,ba,ca,usa,to.micropro\
#   !net.flame,!net.religion,!net.politics,!net.philosophy,\
#   net.religion.jewish\
#   :F:/well/news/batch/micropro
#
```

Note that the file starts with information about the site, which happens to be The WELL (Whole Earth 'Lectronic Link, a conferencing system). Then comes the site's subscription list.

The main newsfeed site (source for exchanging news) for The WELL happens to be Pacific Bell in San Francisco (`ptsfa`). The subscription list for Pacific Bell is then given (it includes nearly everything).

The next site, Micropro, is the first of many leaf nodes of The WELL (only this one is shown here). As we explained earlier, leaf nodes are the sites that are fed from a backbone (or an intermediate site, such as The WELL in this case). You can see that the subscription list for Micropro is rather complex. It starts out by accepting broad categories of newsgroups (`na`, `net`, etc.) but then excludes specific newsgroups that aren't wanted. Exclusion is indicated by prefixing the newsgroup name with an exclamation point.

The Site's Active File

The `/news/lib/active` file serves two main purposes. First, it is an up-to-date list of all the valid newsgroups (regardless of whether the site subscribes to them). Second, numbers after the name of each newsgroup record the earliest and latest articles received. The Netnews software uses this information to remove expired articles and to check for duplicates. A part of an `active` file might look like this:

```
cat /news/lib/active
comp.sys.amiga 00293 00006 y
comp.sys.apollo 00000 00000 y
comp.sys.apple 00117 00002 y
comp.sys.atari.8bit 00034 00008 y
comp.sys.atari.st 00176 00005 y
comp.sys.cbm 00049 00002 y
comp.sys.hp 00019 00002 y
comp.sys.ibm.pc 00287 00004 y
comp.sys.ibm.pc.digest 00000 00000 y
comp.sys.m6809 00022 00002 y
```

The first field in each line is the name of the newsgroup. (The newsgroup naming scheme is described later.) The second field is the highest article number that has been received for this newsgroup. The third field is the lowest article number that has not yet expired. The last field is a `y`, `n`, or `m` (moderated groups). It indicates whether a user at this site is allowed to post news to the group. (Some newsgroups can be read but not posted to. These are called *read-only* groups, and are often newsgroups "ported" over from another network, such as ARPANET.

Figure 6-4 shows the functions of the `sys` (system) and `active` files. Newsgroups excluded by the `sys` file are not accepted. Thus, newsgroup 3 is rejected out of hand. In accepted newsgroups, articles already received by the system are rejected: for example, article A of newsgroup 2. When the articles are processed against the `sys` file, article *numbers* are assigned. This means that article numbering is different on each system.

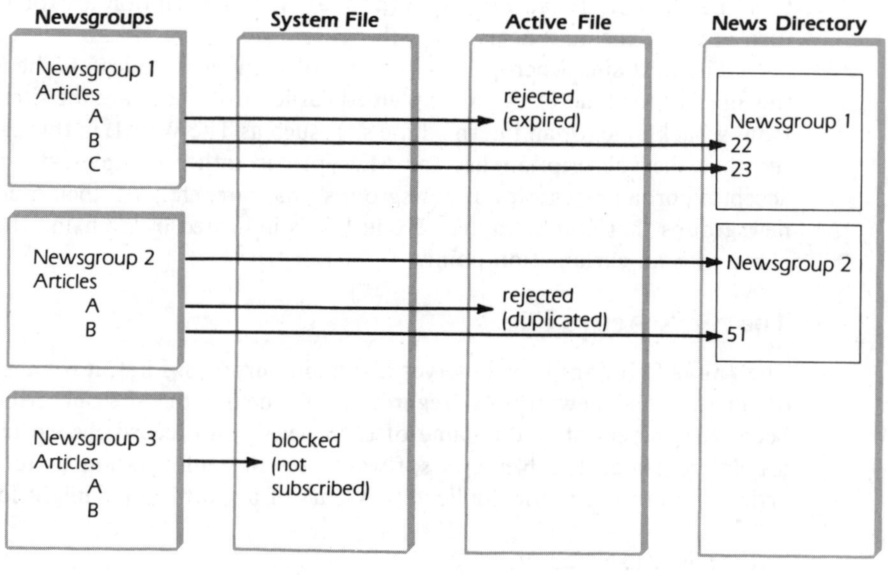

The **sys** file controls which newsgroups are accepted. The **active** file checks the validity of newsgroups and checks for expired and duplicate articles.

Figure 6-4. Filtering the incoming news.

In addition to news articles, there are incoming *control articles.* These are not articles that can be read by humans but rather ones that tell the Netnews software at the site to do such things as add a newly established newsgroup to the active list or remove a defunct one. The use of control articles is an elegant mechanism: it uses the regular news stream to keep the site up to date and ensures that under normal conditions the `active` file at the site is always current.

Figure 6-5 shows these two processes. Incoming control articles are causing one newsgroup to be added and one removed. Meanwhile, the local Netnews software is checking the `active` file and removing expired articles.

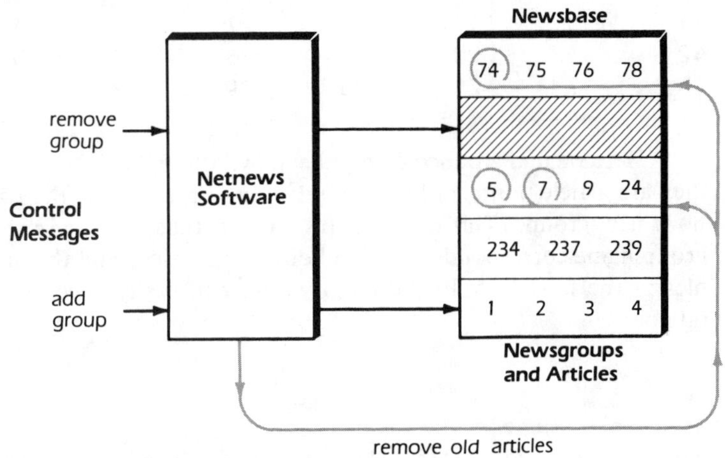

Figure 6-5. Updating the newsbase.

More about Newsgroups

We have been concentrating on the mechanics of news and the way it is processed. Let's now look at how the news is organized into newsgroups, both in terms of directories and files and in terms of the names of the groups themselves.

Storage of Newsgroups in the UNIX File System

Once the news has been filtered, it is stored in the `news` directory. As mentioned before, the news is placed into newsgroups by distribution area (`ca` for California, for example) or by broad topic (`rec` for recreations, arts, or hobbies, for example). Now let's look at how the newsgroups are named and organized.

From the `news` directory, let's go to the particular subdirectory that is also called `news`. This subdirectory represents a class of newsgroups that is concerned with discussion of how Netnews itself works, announcements for users and system administrators, and so on. Let's `cd` to that directory and then do a listing with `ls`:

```
cd news
ls
misc            stargate          sysadmin
```

Now let's look at the subdirectory `misc`:

```
cd misc
ls
10    14    18    22    26    3     33    5     9
11    15    19    23    27    30    34    6
12    16    20    24    28    31    35    7
13    17    21    25    29    32    4     8
```

Here we find a bunch of numbers. What are they? You have probably guessed: they are article numbers for currently stored articles for the `misc` subgroup of the `news` newsgroup. (This newsgroup's name is thus `news.misc`. Note how the newsgroup name corresponds to the subdirectories used, and the articles themselves are files in the lowest-level subdirectory.) We can easily check out one of the article numbers:

```
cat 12
Xref: well news.misc:12 junk:91
Path: well!ptsfa!lll-lcc!lll-crg!rutgers!mit-eddie!husc6!necntc!frog!guest
From: guest@frog.UUCP (RX/FTP user)
Newsgroups: news.misc,news.groups
Subject: Information requested on success
Message-ID: <1123@frog.UUCP>
Date: 12 Nov 86 03:13:16 GMT
Reply-To: jon@frog.UUCP (jon)
Distribution: net
Organization: Superfrog Heaven [ CRDS, Framingham MA ]
Lines: 9

I am attempting to contribute constructive verbosity to the net.
However, in this learning curve, I am having trouble finding much on-line
help to sort out questions I have.
It would be very helpful if there were some help files in a central
location for all to study at their leisure.
```

Names and Organization of Newsgroups

We have seen that the directories and subdirectories into which articles are organized correspond to newsgroups. The purpose of newsgroups is to organize news by distribution areas or topics to make the news manageable, for both administrators and users. A given site may receive several thousand articles a week. Hardly anyone would have the time or interest to read them all. News also takes up space on disk, so systems that are pressed for space are likely to accept only a portion of the more than 400 available newsgroups. We have seen that the `sys` file can be used to restrict the newsgroups accepted by a given site.

Naming Newsgroups

Newsgroup names start with a prefix that indicates either topic area or geographical and institutional interest. The topic areas are as follows:

`comp.`	Computers
`sci.`	Science and technology
`rec.`	Recreation/arts/leisure
`news.`	USENET itself
`soc.`	Society, social issues
`talk.`	High-volume discussions
`misc.`	Miscellaneous

Each of these topic areas has one or more subtopics. For example, under `comp.` we have several broad subtopics, such as `sys.` (computer systems), `lang.` (computer languages), and `unix.` (guess what?). These are then often broken down still further into specific topics, such as `comp.sys.apollo` (Apollo workstations), `comp.sys.ibm-pc`, and `comp.unix.questions`.

The geographical areas (local groups) that you see will depend on your location. Here are some examples:

`na.`	North America
`ca.`	State (California)
`ba.`	Local (San Francisco Bay Area)

Thus, `ba.announce` would be a newsgroup for general announcements of interest to San Francisco Bay Area residents.

Here are some examples of organizational subdivisions:

`att.`	AT&T
`well.`	Site-specific (The WELL conferencing system)

Each site usually has its own site-specific group for local news.

Only one of the high-level prefixes (topical, geographical, organizational) is used for a given group. It is followed by one or more additional elements indicating topics and subtopics. Figure 6-6 shows how some newsgroup names are constructed.

The `talk.` prefix is something of an anomaly: it was created to identify groups likely to have high volume (both in terms of number of articles and heat of debate). It enables sites that don't want such groups to easily identify and exclude them, and it enables users to avoid reading them if they are received.

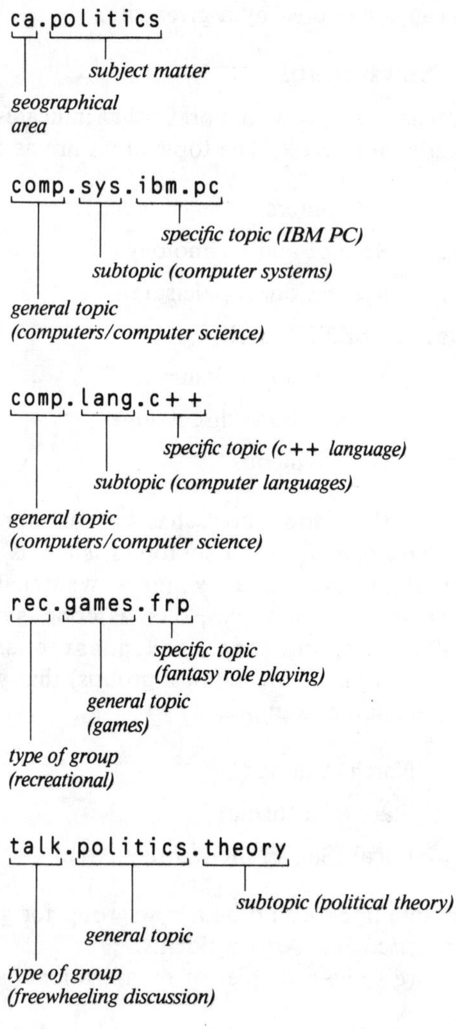

Figure 6-6. Examples of newsgroup names.

A Newsgroup Sampler

If you are not sure what a newsgroup covers, you can list the file `/usr/lib/news/newsgroups`, which contains a list of all currently active newsgroups and has a brief description of each. If you want to find out which newsgroups deal with UNIX, you can use `grep` like this:

grep unix /usr/lib/news/newsgroups

(Your news directory path may be different.)

Here is a listing of the newsgroups that were active at the time of writing.

Newsgroup	*Description*
comp.ai	Artificial intelligence discussions.
comp.ai.digest	Digest on artificial intelligence.
comp.arch	Computer architecture.
comp.binaries.amiga	Binary—postings for the Commodore Amiga only.
comp.binaries.atari.st	Binary—postings for the Atari ST only. (Moderated)
comp.binaries.mac	Binary—postings for the Apple Macintosh only.
comp.bugs.2bsd	Reports of UNIX version 2BSD related bugs.
comp.bugs.4bsd.ucb-fixes	Bug reports/fixes for BSD UNIX. (Moderated)
comp.bugs.4bsd	Reports of UNIX version 4BSD related bugs.
comp.bugs.misc	General bug reports and fixes (includes V7 and UUCP).
comp.bugs.sys5	Reports of USG (System III, V, etc.) bugs.
comp.cog-eng	Cognitive engineering.
comp.compilers	Discussion about compiler construction, theory, etc.
comp.databases	Database and data management issues and theory.
comp.dcom.lans	Local area network hardware and software.
comp.dcom.telecom	Telecommunications.
comp.dcom.modems	Data communications hardware and software.
comp.doc	Archived public-domain documentation.
comp.doc.techreports	Announcements and lists of technical reports.

comp.edu	Computer science education.
comp.emacs	EMACS editors of different flavors.
comp.graphics	Computer graphics, art, animation, image processing.
comp.lang.ada	Discussion about Ada.
comp.lang.apl	Discussion about APL.
comp.lang.c	Discussion about C.
comp.lang.c++	The object-oriented C++ language.
comp.lang.forth	Discussion about Forth.
comp.lang.fortran	Discussion about FORTRAN.
comp.lang.lisp	Discussion about LISP.
comp.lang.misc	Different computer languages not specifically listed.
comp.lang.modula2	Discussion about Modula-2.
comp.lang.pascal	Discussion about Pascal.
comp.lang.prolog	Discussion about PROLOG.
comp.lang.smalltalk	Discussion about Smalltalk 80.
comp.laser-printers	Laser printers.
comp.lsi	Large-scale integrated circuits.
comp.mail.headers	Gatewayed from the ARPA header-people list.
comp.mail.maps	Various maps, including UUCP maps.
comp.mail.misc	General discussions about computer mail.
comp.mail.uucp	Mail in the UUCP network environment.
comp.misc	General topics about computers not covered elsewhere.
comp.newprod	Announcements of new products of interest to readers.
comp.org.decus	DEC Users' Society newsgroup.
comp.org.usenix	USENIX Association events and announcements.
comp.os.cpm	Discussion about the CP/M operating system.
comp.os.eunice	The SRI Eunice system.
comp.os.fidonet	FidoNew digest, official newsletter of FidoNet Assoc.

`comp.os.minix`	Discussion of Tanenbaum's MINIX system.
`comp.os.misc`	General OS-oriented discussion not carried elsewhere.
`comp.os.os9`	The OS9 operating system.
`comp.os.research`	Operating system theory and issues.
`comp.periphs`	Peripheral devices.
`comp.protocols`	Computer communication protocols.
`comp.protocols.appletalk`	The Appletalk protocol.
`comp.protocols.kermit`	The Kermit protocol and Kermit programs.
`comp.protocols.tcp-ip`	The TCP-IP protocol.
`comp.risks`	Risks to the public from computers and users.
`comp.soc`	Discussions of computers and society.
`comp.sources`	For the posting of software packages and documentation.
`comp.sources.amiga`	Source code—postings for the Amiga only. (Moderated)
`comp.sources.atari.st`	Source code—postings for the Atari ST only. (Moderated)
`comp.sources.bugs`	For bug fixes and features discussion pertaining to items in `comp.sources`.
`comp.sources.d`	For any discussion of source postings.
`comp.sources.games`	Postings of recreational software.
`comp.sources.mac`	Software for the Apple Macintosh.
`comp.sources.misc`	Source code that fits in no other category.
`comp.sources.unix`	Source code for UNIX systems.
`comp.sources.wanted`	Requests for software and fixes.
`comp.std.c`	C language standards.
`comp.std.internat`	Discussion about international standards.
`comp.std.misc`	Standards that don't fit in other groups.
`comp.std.mumps`	Discussion for the X11.1 committee on MUMPS.
`comp.std.unix`	Discussion for the P1003 committee on UNIX.

comp.sys.amiga	Discussion about the Amiga micro.
comp.sys.apollo	Discussion about Apollo computers.
comp.sys.apple	Discussion about Apple micros.
comp.sys.atari.8bit	Discussion about 8-bit Atari micros.
comp.sys.atari.st	Discussion about 16-bit Atari micros.
comp.sys.att	Discussion about AT&T microcomputers.
comp.sys.cbm	Discussion about Commodore micros.
comp.sys.dec	Discussion about DEC computer systems.
comp.sys.hp	Discussion about Hewlett-Packard equipment.
comp.sys.ibm.pc	Discussion about IBM personal computers.
comp.sys.ibm.pc.digest	Digest on IBM personal computers.
comp.sys.intel	Discussion about Intel systems and parts.
comp.sys.m6809	Discussion about 6809's.
comp.sys.m68k	Discussion about 68k's.
comp.sys.mac	Discussion about the Apple Macintosh and Lisa.
comp.sys.mac.digest	Macintosh digest.
comp.sys.masscomp	Discussion of the Masscomp line of computers.
comp.sys.misc	Micro computers of all kinds.
comp.sys.nsc.32k	National Semiconductor 32000 series chips.
comp.sys.pyramid	Pyramid 90X computers.
comp.sys.ridge	Ridge 32 computers and ROS.
comp.sys.sequent	Sequent systems, especially Balance 8000.
comp.sys.sun	Sun Work Station computers.
comp.sys.tandy	Discussion about TRS-80's.
comp.sys.ti	Discussion about Texas Instruments.
comp.sys.vax	DEC's VAX line of computers.
comp.sys.workstations	Workstations (general).
comp.terminals	All sorts of terminals.
comp.text	Text processing.
comp.unix	General UNIX discussions. (Moderated)

`comp.unix.questions`	UNIX neophytes group.
`comp.unix.wizards`	Discussions, bug reports, and fixes on and for UNIX.
`comp.unix.xenix`	Discussion about the XENIX OS.
`comp.windows.misc`	Discussion of windowing software.
`comp.windows.news`	News and reports on windowing software.
`comp.windows.x`	Discussion about the X Window System.
`misc.consumers`	Consumer interests, product reviews, etc.
`misc.consumers.house`	Discussion about owning and maintaining a house.
`misc.forsale`	Short, tasteful postings about items for sale.
`misc.handicap`	Items of interest for/about the handicapped. (Moderated)
`misc.headlines`	Current interest: drug testing, terrorism, etc.
`misc.invest`	Investments and the handling of money.
`misc.jobs`	Job announcements, requests, etc.
`misc.kids`	Children, their behavior and activities.
`misc.legal`	Legalities and the ethics of law.
`misc.misc`	Various discussions not fitting in any other group.
`misc.psi`	Discussion of paranormal abilities and experiences.
`misc.taxes`	Tax laws and advice.
`misc.test`	For testing of network software. Very boring.
`misc.wanted`	Requests for things that are needed (NOT software).
`news.admin`	Comments directed to news administrators.
`news.announce.conferences`	Calls for papers and conference announcements.
`news.announce.important`	General announcements of interest to all.

news.announce.newusers	Explanatory postings for new users.
news.config	Postings of system downtimes and interruptions.
news.groups	Discussions and lists of newsgroups.
news.lists	News-related statistics and lists. (Moderated)
news.misc	Discussions of USENET itself.
news.newsites	Postings of new site announcements.
news.software.b	Discussion about B news software.
news.software.notes	Notesfile software from the University of Illinois.
news.stargate	Discussion about satellite transmission of news.
news.sysadmin	Comments directed to system administrators.
rec.arts.books	Books of all genres, shapes, and sizes.
rec.arts.comics	The funnies, old and new.
rec.arts.drwho	Discussion about Dr. Who.
rec.arts.movies	Discussions of movies and moviemaking.
rec.arts.movies.reviews	Reviews of movies. (Moderated)
rec.arts.poems	For the posting of poems.
rec.arts.sf-lovers	Science fiction lovers' newsgroup.
rec.arts.startrek	Star Trek, the TV show and the movies.
rec.arts.tv	The boob tube, its history, and past and current shows.
rec.arts.tv.soaps	Postings about soap operas.
rec.arts.wobegon	"A Prairie Home Companion" radio show discussion.
rec.audio	High fidelity audio.
rec.autos	Automobiles, automotive products and laws.
rec.autos.tech	Technical aspects of automobiles et. al.
rec.aviation	Aviation rules, means, and methods.
rec.bicycles	Bicycles, related products and laws.
rec.birds	Hobbyists interested in bird watching.

`rec.boats`	Hobbyists interested in boating.
`rec.food.cooking`	Food, cooking, cookbooks, and recipes.
`rec.food.drink`	Wines and spirits.
`rec.food.recipes`	Recipes from the USENET Cookbook (troff and text).
`rec.food.veg`	Vegetarians.
`rec.games.board`	Discussion and hints on board games.
`rec.games.bridge`	Hobbyists interested in bridge.
`rec.games.chess`	Chess and computer chess.
`rec.games.empire`	Discussion and hints about Empire.
`rec.games.frp`	Discussion about fantasy role-playing games.
`rec.games.go`	Discussion about Go.
`rec.games.hack`	Discussion, hints, etc., about the Hack game.
`rec.games.misc`	Games and computer games.
`rec.games.pbm`	Discussion about play-by-mail games.
`rec.games.rogue`	Discussion and hints about Rogue.
`rec.games.trivia`	Discussion about trivia.
`rec.games.video`	Discussion about video games.
`rec.gardens`	Gardening, methods and results.
`rec.guns`	Firearms.
`rec.ham-radio`	Amateur Radio practices, contests, events, rules, etc.
`rec.ham-radio.packet`	Discussion about packet radio setups.
`rec.humor`	Jokes and the like. May be somewhat offensive.
`rec.humor.d`	Discussions on the content of `rec.humor` articles.
`rec.mag`	Magazine summaries, tables of contents, etc.
`rec.mag.otherrealms`	*Otherrealms* science fiction/fantasy magazine.
`rec.misc`	General topics about recreational/participant sports.

rec.motorcycles	Motorcycles and related products and laws.
rec.music.classical	Discussion about classical music.
rec.music.folk	Folks discussing folk music of various sorts.
rec.music.gaffa	Progressive music discussions (e.g., Kate Bush).
rec.music.gdead	A group for (Grateful) Dead-heads.
rec.music.makers	For performers and their discussions.
rec.music.misc	Music lovers' group.
rec.music.synth	Synthesizers and computer music.
rec.nude	Hobbyists interested in naturist/nudist activities.
rec.pets	Pets, pet care, and household animals in general.
rec.photo	Hobbyists interested in photography.
rec.puzzles	Puzzles, problems, and quizzes.
rec.railroad	Real and model train fans' newsgroup.
rec.scuba	Hobbyists interested in SCUBA diving.
rec.skiing	Hobbyists interested in skiing.
rec.skydiving	Hobbyists interested in skydiving.
rec.sport.baseball	Discussion about baseball.
rec.sport.basketball	Discussion about basketball.
rec.sport.football	Discussion about football.
rec.sport.hockey	Discussion about hockey.
rec.sport.misc	Spectator sports.
rec.travel	Travelling all over the world.
rec.video	Video and video components.
rec.woodworking	Hobbyists interested in woodworking.
sci.astro	Astronomy discussions and information.
sci.bio	Biology and related sciences.
sci.crypt	Different methods of data encryption /decryption.
sci.electronics	Circuits, theory, electrons, and discussions.

`sci.lang`	Natural languages, communication, etc.
`sci.math`	Mathematical discussions and pursuits.
`sci.math.stat`	Statistics discussion.
`sci.math.symbolic`	Symbolic algebra discussion.
`sci.med`	Medicine and its related products and regulations.
`sci.misc`	Short-lived discussions on subjects in the sciences.
`sci.philosophy.tech`	Technical philosophy, math, logic, etc.
`sci.physics`	Physical laws, properties, etc.
`sci.research`	Research methods, funding, ethics, and whatever.
`sci.space`	Space, space programs, space-related research, etc.
`sci.space.shuttle`	The space shuttle and the STS program.
`soc.college`	College, college activities, campus life, etc.
`soc.culture.african`	Discussions about Africa and things African.
`soc.culture.celtic`	Group about Celtics (not basketball!).
`soc.culture.greek`	Group about Greeks.
`soc.culture.indian`	Group for discussion about India and things Indian.
`soc.culture.jewish`	Group for discussion about Jewish culture and religion.
`soc.culture.misc`	Group for discussion about other cultures.
`soc.human-nets`	Computer-aided communications digest.
`soc.misc`	Socially oriented topics not in other groups.
`soc.motss`	Issues pertaining to homosexuality.
`soc.net-people`	Announcements, requests, etc., about people on the net.
`soc.religion.christian`	Discussions on Christianity and related topics.
`soc.roots`	Genealogical matters.

`soc.singles`	Newsgroup for single people, their activities, etc.
`soc.women`	Women's rights, discrimination, etc.
`talk.abortion`	All sorts of discussions and arguments on abortion.
`talk.bizarre`	The unusual, bizarre, curious, and often stupid.
`talk.origins`	Evolution versus creationism (sometimes hot!).
`talk.philosophy.misc`	Philosophical musings on all topics.
`talk.politics.arms-d`	Disarmament issues.
`talk.politics.misc`	Political discussions and ravings of all kinds.
`talk.politics.theory`	Theory of politics and political systems.
`talk.religion.misc`	Religious, ethical, and moral implications.
`talk.religion.newage`	Esoteric and minority religions and philosophies.
`talk.rumors`	For the posting of rumors.

Note that some groups are moderated or have moderated versions. Netnews version 2.11 handles this automatically.

News and the User

All of this obtaining, filtering, and storing of news is well and good, but the news must start with someone reading something at a terminal and typing something in reply. The purpose of processing news is ultimately communication between human beings. The final aspect of Netnews that we will discuss in this chapter concerns the facilities that enable users to read, reply to, and write news.

News is read, and articles are written or replied to, with the use of Netnews *interface programs*. These consist of:

- `readnews` Basic news reading and replies.
- `rn` Advanced news reading and replies.
- `vnews` Screen-oriented news reading and replies.
- `postnews` Posting of new articles.

These interfaces rely on lower-level programs such as `sendnews` to actually post the articles to the net. (We do not cover the lower-level programs in this book because they do not involve users directly.) The last section of this chapter will further explain these interfaces (what they have in common and their differences), and then each program will be covered thoroughly in a later chapter.

The interfaces are used with three other kinds of programs: pagers, editors, and mailers. *Pagers* are programs like `more` (on BSD) or `pg` (on System V) that control how successive portions of a message appear on the screen. The regular UNIX *editors* are of course used to write mail replies and articles. *Mailers* are used to mail direct replies to article authors. As you will see later, each of the news interfaces allows you to specify pager, editor, and mailer if you don't like the defaults provided. Figure 6-7 shows how the interface end of Netnews works.

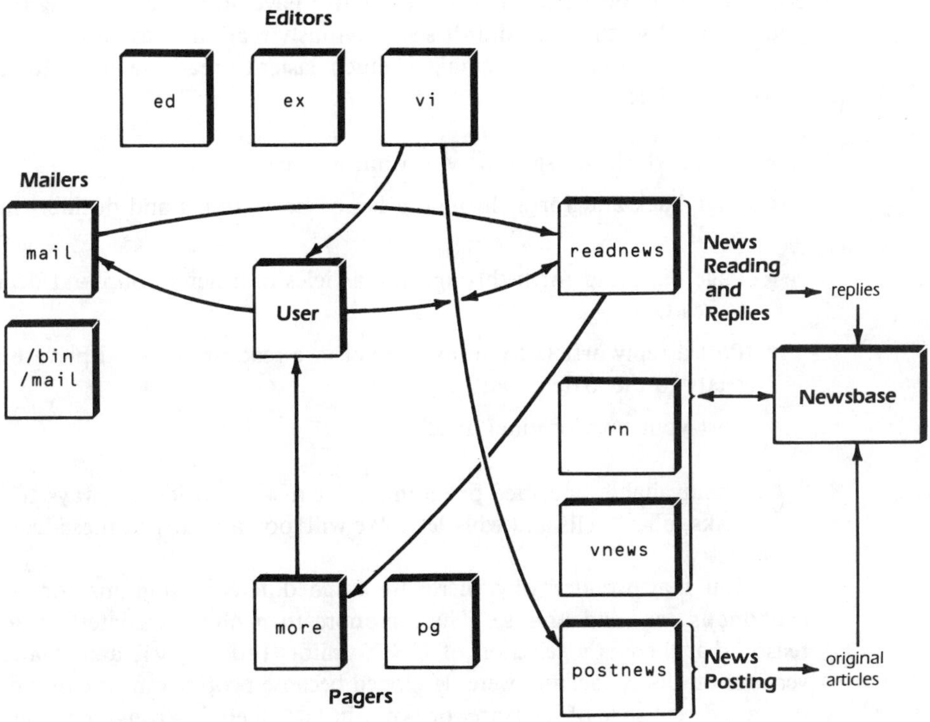

Figure 6-7. Netnews user interface.

In figure 6-7, a user is using `readnews` to read and reply to articles. With the `more` command, the user can view each part of the article. If the user decides to respond to the article by mail, `vi` can be used to edit the reply, and `mail` to send the reply directly to the article's author. Alternatively, the user can post a separate response article, again using `vi`, or write a completely original article using `postnews` and `vi`. Let's take a closer look at the Netnews user interface.

User Interfaces

Now that you have an overview of how news is sent, received, and processed by your site, it is time to look at the programs that are most important to you as a USENET user: the Netnews user interfaces.

We have seen that news articles are simply UNIX text files stored neatly in directories corresponding to their newsgroups. If you wanted to, you could read any news that arrived at your site simply by finding and displaying these files. However, chances are that you would have to wade through many articles you were not interested in. You would have no way to either post a reply or (easily) send e-mail to an article's author. You would also have no way of keeping track of what you had read so that you didn't see previously read articles again.

The Netnews interfaces make it much easier to read the news. In general, they make it possible for you to:

- Select which newsgroups you want to see.
- Page back and forth through a list of newsgroups and decide which to read.
- Page back and forth through the articles in a newsgroup and decide which to read.
- Post a reply article to an article you are reading, or send private mail directly to the article's author.
- Post your own original articles.

The available interface programs offer a wide variety of ways to accomplish these tasks, plus "bells and whistles." We will look at many of these features in later chapters.

You may wonder why there are three different programs for reading news (`readnews`, `rn`, and `vnews`). There is more than one news interface for the same reason that there is a selection of UNIX editors (`ed`, `ex`, `vi`, and `emacs`). Different versions of UNIX facilities were developed because people wanted either new capabilities, a different style of interface, or both. In fact, there is a rough parallel between the three news interfaces and the various editors. Just as `ed` is the oldest, simplest, most basic UNIX editor, `readnews` is the original news interface for USENET. Because of this, `readnews` has guaranteed availability on any system that supports USENET, whereas the other two, though widespread, do not have this general availability. (The `vnews` interface is like the `vi` editor in that it is screen-oriented; `rn` is a bit like the `emacs` editor in its power and complexity.) Just as all editors have to have certain capabilities, such as the ability to add, insert, delete, and change lines of text, all news interfaces have to be able to select, read, and page through news articles. Learning how to use readnews will give you the concepts you need to use a more sophisticated interface later on. Therefore, we suggest that you start with readnews.

After you master readnews, where should you go from there? You could, of course, learn both rn and vnews, and we urge you to at least look over both of those chapters so that you can see what additional capabilities these interfaces offer. Your choice of where to go next depends roughly on whether you want advanced functionality (rn) or ease of use (vnews). Certainly, if you're happy where you are, stay with readnews.

To post news, you don't have to worry about making choices. In most cases there is only postnews. Note that replying to an *existing* article is normally done within readnews, rn, or vnews, but originating (posting) a *new* article is done with postnews.

A Quick Tour of *readnews*

Chapter 7 will cover readnews in detail. So, for now, let's take just a quick look at how a news reading program is used. We'll start by invoking the readnews program.

```
readnews -n comp.unix.all
```

The default for news reading programs presents all available newsgroups (unless you have previously "unsubscribed" to some). Here, we use a command-line option that specifies a particular set of newsgroups—those that begin with the element comp.unix. (Each news reading program has a set of command-line flags that you can use to specify such items as the groups or set of groups that you want presented to you, the amount of information you want to see in article headers, and many other options.)

The readnews program presents us with the name of the first newsgroup, followed by the header of the first article in the group that we have not previously read:

```
-----------------------------
Newsgroup comp.unix.questions
-----------------------------

Article 1205 of 1408, Feb 20 09:30.
Subject: Re: USENIX / UNIFORUM info wanted
Path: ..!dartvax!andyb (Andy Behrens @ Burlington Coat Factory,
Lebanon, NH)
(9 lines) More? [ynq] y
```

The *.newsrc* File

But how does the news reading program know what we've read or haven't read? The answer is the `.newsrc` file. A `.newsrc` is created by the Netnews software for each user and is normally kept in the user's home directory. Among other things, the `.newsrc` file keeps a list of the individual newsgroups to which you have subscribed (as well as those you have rejected) and the numbers of the articles that you have read in each group. This list is updated each time you run an interface program (unless you specifically say not to). The default is for the news reading program to show you subscribed newsgroups in the order in which they appear in your `.newsrc`. Within a newsgroup, the program compares the article numbers following the group name with the numbers of the available articles, and shows you only those that you haven't yet read. Here's an excerpt from a `.newsrc` file:

```
ca.wanted: 1-147,283
comp.ai: 1-577,1044,1059
comp.sys.amiga:
comp.sys.binaries.amiga: 1-1
comp.sources.amiga: 1-12
news.announce: 1-12
news.announce.newusers: 1-86
comp.society: 1-72
comp.compilers: 1-92
```

Note that ranges of consecutive articles are indicated by hyphens, while isolated articles and ranges are separated by commas.

Obtaining a *.newsrc*

When you read news for the first time, you won't have a `.newsrc`. Normally, the interface will create one for you, using your site's default *subscription list*. An example of such a list is:

```
all,all.announce,!junk,!control,!test
```

This list indicates that the site will accept (and start new users with) newsgroups that begin with any prefix, and any newsgroup that ends in `.announce`, but the site will reject any newsgroup beginning with `junk`, `control`, or `test`.

Now let's continue reading our article. After the article header is displayed, the following prompt is given:

```
(9 lines) More? [ynq] y
```

This prompt asks if we want to see more of the article. We type `y` for yes:

```
UniForum is an annual event sponsored by /usr/group.  It comprises
a trade show, conferences, workshops, and tutorials.

The best source of information is
        /usr/group
        4655 Old Ironsides Dr., #200
        Santa Clara, CA 95054
        (408) 986-8840

Article 1206 of 1408, Feb 20 12:12.
Subject: LINK_TIMEOUT environment variable
Path: ..!ethz!heiser (Gernot Heiser @ CS Department, ETH Zuerich,
Switzerland)
(13 lines) More? [ynq] N
```

After the complete article has been displayed, the header for the next article is printed. Let's say we decide that this article is too technical, and we don't want to read any more articles in `comp.unix.questions`. We type `N`, which means "go to the next newsgroup":

```
-------------------------
Newsgroup comp.unix.wizards
-------------------------

Article 192 of 1379, Nov 23 21:39.
Subject: Re: stopped jobs don't always disappear (after logout)
Path: ..!hpisoa1!davel (Dave Lennert)
(30 lines) More? [ynq]
```

And so we find ourselves in `comp.unix.wizards`. Probably NOT an improvement if we want light reading!

This brief tour has shown that:

- You can specify which newsgroup(s) you want to start with.
- You are shown new articles in each newsgroup you visit.
- You can jump to another newsgroup.

As you'll see in later chapters, there's much more to learn about reading news, but we hope that this quick tour has shown you that reading news is not really difficult or mysterious.

General Concepts of News Interfaces

As we prepare to move on to the detailed tutorials of chapters 7 through 10, let's mention a few more things about news reading programs in general. These concepts will help you understand what is going on.

Setting Options

In the preceding example, you saw that a command-line flag can modify the behavior of the news reading program. We asked to see just the UNIX `comp` newsgroups by specifying `-n comp.unix.all`. The sets of command-line options used by `readnews` and `vnews` are very similar, whereas those used by `rn` are quite different.

Many options can also be set by using *environmental variables*. These are values maintained by the shell and used to specify aspects of your environment. You were introduced to some of these in Part 1 of this book. Just as `mailx` provides variables to which you can give values (i.e., turn "on" or "off") that affect the behavior of the mail program, the news programs also provide sets of such variables. They can be placed in your `.login` file (for C Shell users) or in your `.profile` file (for Bourne Shell users). Some of the news programs also allow you to put the variable settings in special files that can be read by the program, just as `mailx` lets you set variables in your `.mailrc` file. To refresh your memory, the general way to set environmental variables at the shell level is, for the C Shell:

```
setenv EDITOR "/usr/ucb/vi"
```

and for the Bourne Shell:

```
EDITOR=/usr/ucb/vi
export EDITOR
```

Both examples tell the Netnews programs that you want `vi` when you are given an editor for writing mail responses or news articles.

Editing Your *.newsrc* File

As you have already seen, you can control which newsgroups will be presented to you when you read news. A good way to customize your news environment is to edit your `.newsrc` file directly. First, you should let `readnews` or another interface generate a complete `.newsrc` file for you. (The news reading programs do this automatically if they don't find `.newsrc` in your home directory.) The new `.newsrc` will include all newsgroups subscribed to by your site (that is, all newsgroups in the `active` file, except those excluded by your site's subscription list in the `sys` file).

Then you can edit the `.newsrc` with any editor. To "unsubscribe" to a newsgroup, place an exclamation point immediately after the newsgroup name (replacing the colon between the name and the article numbers if any). The news software will skip over this newsgroup in the future and will not show you any news from it.

```
comp.compilers: 1-125
comp.sys.apollo! 23-54,77
comp.sys.ibm.pc.digest
comp.laser-printers: 1-24,28,30
```

Here, we have unsubscribed to `comp.sys.apollo`.

You can also use an editor to move newsgroups around in `.newsrc` so that you will see the more important ones first. These techniques can help you select a useful subset of the vast volume of news available on most systems.

Summary

In this chapter you have seen how USENET came about and how it is organized and maintained. You also were introduced to the Netnews user interface (user news programs). You saw how news is distributed, processed, and administered; how to access USENET; and how newsgroups are named.

In chapter 7 you will begin to get practical experience by experimenting with the `readnews` interface.

7

Reading News with *readnews*

The readnews program is the oldest USENET news reading interface and is the one that you will find on any system that participates in USENET. Although rn presents information more efficiently and has many more options, and vnews has the advantage of a screen-oriented interface, readnews has a respectable balance of power and simplicity.

Starting *readnews*

The simplest way to run readnews is to type readnews at the UNIX prompt. If the system can't find readnews, you might try asking the system administrator if the site belongs to USENET and, if so, what the pathname to readnews is (it's usually in /usr/bin). (If the site does not belong to USENET, you might be able to convince the system administrator to join.)

Don't be surprised if, after starting readnews, nothing happens for as long as several minutes. The readnews program has found that you don't have a .newsrc file, and it is happily constructing one for you. (Recall from chapter 6 that the initial .newsrc is set up by consulting the active file and screening newsgroups through the site subscription list.)

Eventually, you will see a display similar to this:

```
--------------------
Newsgroup news.misc
--------------------

Article 3 of 69, Nov  7 12:14.
Subject: net.news is being renamed news.misc
Path: ..!cbosgd!mark (Mark Horton @ AT&T Bell Laboratories, Columbus, Oh)
```

```
Newsgroups: net.news,news.misc
(12 lines) More? [ynq]
```

The newsgroup you see will of course depend on which available groups at your site happen to have news. After the newsgroup name, the header for the first article found is shown. In our example, the display shows the newsgroup name, the article number (3), and the total number of current articles in the newsgroup (69). The `Subject:` line gives a brief statement by the author of what the article is about. (This can help you decide whether to read the article or skip over it.) The `Path:` line gives the path from the site of the article's author to your site. (This path will be used by your mailer if you choose to mail a reply to the author. The commands for mailing a reply will be described later.) A list of all newsgroups to which the article has been posted follows on the `Newsgroups:` line.

The prompt line tells you how many lines are in the article and asks you if you want to see `More?`. At the `More?` prompt, a number of responses are possible. Before we look at them, however, let's explain how we will present the news programs.

In this chapter, as well as in chapters 8 through 10, we will cover groups of related commands. For each group we will discuss the specific commands in the group, explaining what they do and giving appropriate examples. A screened box will contain a summary of each group of commands. The summary will make it possible for you to quickly review material or look up specific commands. We recommend that you sit down at a terminal and try out the commands as you read about them, using the news on your own system.

Reading Articles in a Newsgroup

When an article header is displayed, there are many commands that you can use to tell `readnews` what you want to do with the article. In the `More?` prompt, `readnews` suggests the most important or likely commands in brackets: `[ynq]`. Pressing Return is the same as typing the first command suggested. Thus, to continue reading this article, you can type `y` or simply press Return:

```
(12 lines) More? [ynq] y
This newsgroup is being renamed from net.news to news.misc.
This renaming will gradually take place over the next few weeks.
More and more messages posted to this newsgroup will be aliased
into the new newsgroup as they pass through the net, and people
will begin to post to the new group.  After a few weeks, the
old name will be removed.

This note is to inform you of the renaming so you can begin to
read the new group as well as the old group.

          Mark Horton
          Director, the UUCP Project
```

After you come to the end of an article, the next article's header is displayed. You can skip articles by typing n (for "no more of this article" or "next") each time you are asked More?

```
Article 4 of 69, Nov  7 20:36.
Subject: The 50% rule is in--now what?
Path: ..!brahms!weemba (Matthew P Wiener @ University of California,
Berkeley)
(16 lines) More? [ynq] n

Article 5 of 69, Nov  9 03:40.
Subject: Re: The 50% rule is in--now what?
Summary: Rn needs friendlier rejection.  Experimentation next.
Path: ..!mecc!sewilco (Scot E. Wilcoxon @ MN Ed. Comp. Corp., St.
Paul, MN)
(24 lines) More? [ynq] n
```

One of the first things to learn about any program is how to exit it gracefully. There are two ways to end a session with readnews. The normal command is q (quit), which updates your .newsrc (records the articles you have read, etc.) and returns you to the UNIX prompt. The x (exit) command exits readnews without updating your .newsrc. This feature might be useful if you want to read everything over again or if you think you have made a mistake that affects your .newsrc.

Basic Commands for Reading Articles in *readnews*

y	Yes, read this article.
n	No, go to the next article in the newsgroup.
q	Quit readnews and update .newsrc.
x	Quit readnews but don't update .newsrc.

We now know how to march through the newsgroup one article at a time. But suppose we change our mind and want to return to an article we've already skipped over? After typing n at the More? prompt for article 5 in the previous example, we find ourselves looking at the header for article 6. We can back up by typing p, for "show me the previously displayed article":

```
Article 6 of 69, Nov  9 14:12.
Subject: Re: The 50% rule is in--now what?
Path: ..!chinet!rissa (Garret and Trish @ chi-net, Public Access
UN*X, Chicago IL)
(51 lines) More? [ynq] p
```

```
Article 5 of 69, Nov  9 03:40.
Subject: Re: The 50% rule is in--now what?
Summary: Rn needs friendlier rejection.  Experimentation next.
Path: ..!mecc!sewilco (Scot E. Wilcoxon @ MN Ed. Comp. Corp.,
St. Paul, MN)
(24 lines) More? [ynq] -
```

We're now back at article 5. You can "toggle" between the current and the previous articles by typing a hyphen (-), as shown in the preceding example. Since we were looking at article 6 before we arrived at article 5, the result is that we go back to the previously shown article, article 6 in this case:

```
Article 6 of 69, Nov  9 14:12.
Subject: Re: The 50% rule is in--now what?
Path: ..!chinet!rissa (Garret and Trish @ chi-net, Public Access
UN*X, Chicago IL)
(51 lines) More? [ynq] -
```

And another - would return us to article 5, since that article is now the one previously shown:

```
Article 5 of 69, Nov  9 03:40.
Subject: Re: The 50% rule is in--now what?
Summary: Rn needs friendlier rejection. Experimentation next.
Path: ..!mecc!sewilco (Scot E. Wilcoxon @ MN Ed. Comp. Corp., St.
Paul, MN)
(24 lines) More? [ynq] b
```

But here we typed `b` at the last prompt. The `b` command always means "back one article," regardless of which article was last shown. So it will move us to article 4:

```
Article 4 of 69, Nov  7 20:36.
Subject: The 50% rule is in--now what?
Path: ..!brahms!weemba (Matthew P Wiener @ University of California,
Berkeley)
(16 lines) More? [ynq]
```

If you remember the number of an article you've seen before (or if you've obtained the number from a list of article titles with `readnews -l` —see "Options for Controlling Form of Output" in this chapter), you can jump directly to the article by typing the article number.

Commands for Moving Back and Forth in a Newsgroup with *readnews*

`p`	Reprint previous article, but don't change position.
`-`	Go back to last article displayed (toggle).
`b`	Go back to previous article (not a toggle).
`number`	Move to article having same number as `number`.

Saving, Marking, and Killing Articles

While you are looking at articles in a newsgroup, you can tell `readnews` that you want to save the current article in a file in your home directory:

```
Article 4 of 69, Nov  7 20:36.
Subject: The 50% rule is in--now what?
Path: ..!brahms!weemba (Matthew P Wiener @ University of California,
Berkeley)
(16 lines) More? [ynq] s
./Articles: Appended
```

Since we didn't give a filename, `readnews` appended the article to a file called `Articles` in our home directory. (It will create this file if necessary.) If we had given a filename or path, it would have used that instead. For the benefit of people who are used to the UNIX editors, the `w` (write) command will also work.

Suppose you're not sure what to do with the article, but you would like to see it again. You can mark the article as "unread" by typing `e` at the `More?` prompt. By default, `readnews` marks articles that have been shown to you as having been read, and, at the end of the session, it updates your `.newsrc` file accordingly. This means that you will not see the article in future sessions. (What the `e` command actually does is to erase the record of the article as having been read; thus, you will see it again in the next session.)

```
(16 lines) More? [ynq] e
Holding article 4
```

The message says that the article is being "held." When we next enter the newsgroup (later this session or in another session), we will be shown the article again, as though we hadn't read it at all. Remember, however, that the `e` command is not good for long-term storage of articles. As mentioned in the last chapter, news articles are normally removed from the system after they are two weeks old. Use `s` if you want to save an article for permanent reference.

The + command also marks an article as unread. The difference between e and + is that + skips over the *next* article and marks it as unread (it is like a combination of n and e), whereas e marks the *current* article as unread.

The opposite of marking an article unread is marking it "read." Any article that you read is of course marked as "read" unless you unmark it with a command such as e. The n command also marks the current article as read when it skips to the next article. To catch up with a newsgroup without actually reading all the articles, you can use the K (kill) command. The K command marks ALL the remaining articles in a newsgroup as "read" and then skips you to the next newsgroup. Figure 7-1 shows graphically where articles end up after being disposed of by various commands.

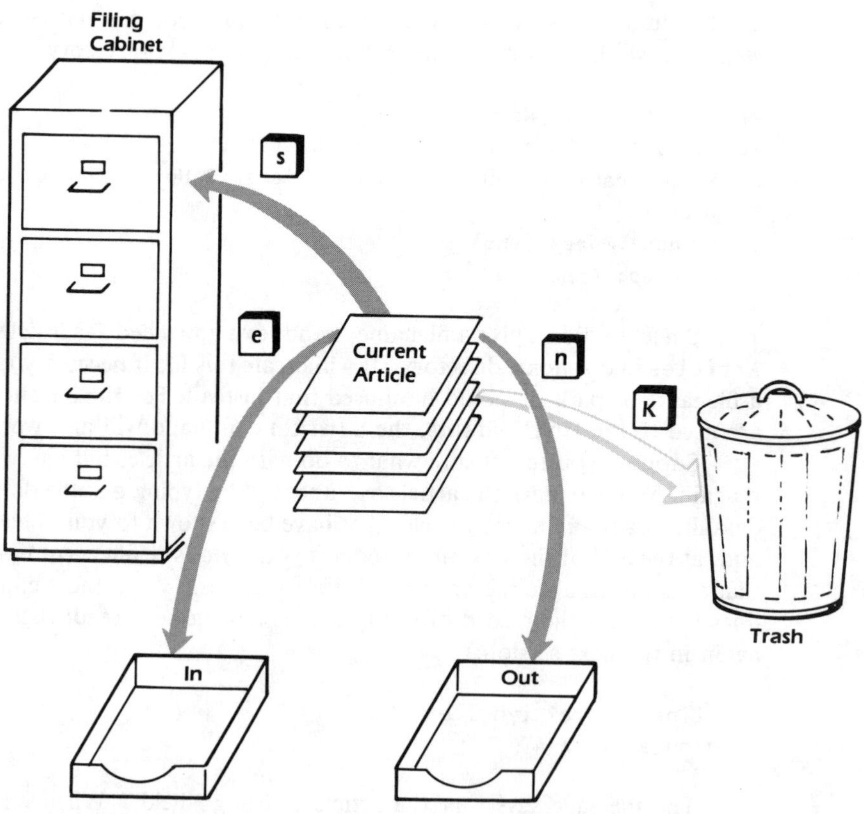

Figure 7-1. Disposition of articles in **readnews**.

```
Article 15 of 125, Nov 12 12:08.
Subject: Re: The Woz and the Apple IIGS, //x
```

```
Path: ..!PSUVM.BITNET!B5U (B5U @ The ARPA Internet)
(30 lines) More? [ynq] K

-----------------------------
Newsgroup comp.sys.atari.8bit
-----------------------------
Article 9 of 37, Nov 10 08:07.
Subject: Thank you
Keywords: Train Dispatcher
Path: ..!topaz!appelbau (Marc L. Appelbaum @ Rutgers Univ., New Brunswick,
N.J.)
(10 lines) More? [ynq]
```

The K command performs its murder silently: the evidence of the deed is that you now see the name of the next newsgroup and the header of the first article in that newsgroup.

Special Kinds of Reading: Digests and Encrypted Articles

There are two special kinds of articles that you need to tell readnews about in order to read them properly.

One kind of article is a digest. A *digest* is a collection of articles (perhaps the archives of an earlier discussion). Separate articles have been packed together into one article to save space and processing. If you use the normal y command to start reading the article, the special digest header section will be printed, but then the articles within the digest will run together:

```
Article 314 of 318, Feb 24 17:54.
Subject: Arms-Discussion Digest V7 #105
Path: ..!XX.LCS.MIT.EDU!ARMS-D-Request (Moderator @ The ARPA Internet)
(288 lines) More? [ynq] y
Arms-Discussion Digest                    Tuesday, February 24, 1987 8:54PM
Volume 7, Issue 105

Today's Topics:

                          administrivia
                     SLBMs in the Great Lakes
               Re: Soviet Analysis of Popular Music
                          Occupation of US
                          Submarine Basing
          Economics of SDI (and other military expenditures)
                            SLBM Basing
```

```
------------------------------------------------------------------------
Date: Sat, 21 Feb 1987  21:50 EST
From: LIN@XX.LCS.MIT.EDU
Subject: administrivia

==>> The name below has been removed since my mailer doesn't recognize the
host MASON

--More--
```

Digest articles are usually easier to read if they are broken down into separate articles. Type d at the More? prompt for a digest article if you want to read the digest as individual articles. The reading procedure is then the same as for regular articles. The same title information as in the preceding example is shown, but then you see:

```
Date: 25 Feb 87 07:43:00 PST
From: "ESTELL ROBERT G" <estell@nwc-143b.ARPA>
Subject: barrage attacks on subs
Reply-To: "ESTELL ROBERT G" <estell@nwc-143b.ARPA>
Digest article 1 of 5 (27 lines) More? [ynq] n

Date: Wed, 25 Feb 87 09:42:05 PST
From: pom%under.s1.gov@mordor.s1.gov
Subject:      Occupation of US
Digest article 2 of 5 (60 lines) More? [ynq]
```

Notice that a regular article header is printed for Digest article 1 of 5. You can now use the regular article movement commands (such as n) to move through the articles in the digest. You can also save the individual articles to a file, reply to them (discussed later), and so on.

Another command, D (note that case does make a difference here, as with so many UNIX commands), *decrypts* (decodes) an article. An *encrypted* article is one whose text has been coded by a *Caesar cypher.* This normally means that each original, typed letter is replaced by one 13 letters farther down the alphabet, wrapping around the letter "a" if necessary. For example:

```
Why did the chicken cross the road?
```

will appear as:

```
Jul qvq gur puvpxra pebff gur ebnq?
```

if you use the ordinary article reading commands. The D command decrypts the article and shows you the original text.

The purpose of encryption is to conceal puzzle answers, movie or book endings, game hints, and off-color or otherwise offensive jokes (found in `rec.humor`) from people who don't wish to see them.

Here's a summary of the article saving and special-purpose reading commands:

Article Saving and Special Reading Commands in *readnews*

s	Append article to `Articles` file, or to named file if given.
e	Mark article as unread; present it next time.
+	Skip next article; mark it as unread.
K	Mark remaining articles as read; go to next newsgroup.
d	Break up a digest article into separate articles.
D	Decrypt an enciphered article.

Replying to Articles

Sooner or later, you're going to have strong feelings one way or the other about something you read. There are two basic ways to respond to articles: posting a follow-up article and sending mail to the article's author.

In most cases, mailing a response to the author is preferred. Some of these cases include responding to an advertisement or asking a question that you don't think would be of general interest to thousands of other users. In chapter 10 we will look at the *netiquette*, or customs and recommended practices, for posting articles in connection with `postnews`. There, we will look in more detail at the criteria for replying by mail versus posting follow-up articles. In this and the next two chapters, we will present only the mechanics of posting follow-up articles and replying by mail in each news reading program. We do recommend that you read chapter 10 before posting follow-up articles, however.

Posting a Follow-up Article

Let's say that you have been reading an article claiming that C is a really easy-to-use programming language. You can post a follow-up article to the currently displayed article by typing the `f` command at the `More?` prompt:

```
----------------
Newsgroup comp.lang.c
----------------

Article 291 of 313, Nov 15 12:29.
```

```
Subject: C is easy to learn
Path: ..!amdahl!hdl (Hilda Doolittle)
(8 lines) More? [ynq] f
```

You will be asked to summarize your article. This pause gives you another opportunity to think about what you want to say.

```
Please enter a short summary of your contribution to the discussion
Just one or two lines ...    (end with a blank line)
>C is NOT easy to learn
>    ←press Return
```

After pressing Return at the start of a line, you are asked whether you want to include a copy of the article to which you are replying in your follow-up article. If you type y, readnews will include the text of the original article, prefixing each line with a greater-than symbol (>). If the article to which you are replying was itself a reply to an earlier article, the lines in the existing article that are already preceded by > will have a second one attached, and so on, like this:

```
>> I think the Dodgers are the greatest baseball team ever
> Clearly, you don't understand baseball statistics. Why...
  The whole question of what is the "best" team is dubious...
```

In the example, the first line is from the original article, the second line from a follow-up to that article, and the third line part of the follow-up to the follow-up article.

Quoting the original article by having readnews include the article in the follow-up makes it easier for people reading the follow-up to know what you are talking about. You should, however, edit out all but the necessary quoted lines to save space. Remember that saving space also means saving time for thousands of readers.

```
Do you want to include a copy of the article? y
OK, but please edit it to suppress unnecessary verbiage, signatures, etc.
```

In response to the problem of unnecessary quoting, a strongly held custom known as the *50% rule* has been adopted. This means that no more than half of your article should consist of quoted material from other articles. The assumption behind this rule is that, if you have quoted at length adding only a brief comment, it would be better to send your comment by electronic mail to the article's author. This avoids cluttering up the net with articles that mainly repeat earlier articles. And regardless of the length of your own comments, you should quote only enough of the original article to identify what you're responding to. Like many such customs on USENET, the 50% rule is controversial, but not bad as a guide. Some, but not all, Netnews software automatically enforces this rule.

After you decide whether you want to quote the original article, you are placed in the editor to draft your response. Our editor happens to be `vi`; your system may have a different default, or you may have chosen a different editor (see "Using Environmental Variables" further on).

The editor starts with the header of the original article in the edit buffer, together with any quoted material. This is reflected by the 16 lines that are already in the buffer in our example case below. (We will defer discussion of editing headers to chapter 10.) You then type your response, using the editor as usual, and exit the editor with `wq`:

```
No lines in the buffer
"/tmp/post016472" 16 lines, 485 characters
C is not easy to learn for normal people. It is not easy to
make sense of function names like "printf" and "scanf." I
won't even mention the problems with pre- and postincrementing.
:wq
"/tmp/post016472" 19 lines, 665 characters
```

Next, you are asked what you want to do with your article. You can choose from the following commands:

- `s` Send (post) the article.
- `e` Edit (revise) the article.
- `l` List (display) the text of the article.
- `w` Write (save) the article to a file.
- `q` Quit without posting the new article.

```
What now? [send, edit, list, quit, write] s
Posting article...
Article posted successfully.
(8 lines) More? [ynq]
```

You are informed that the posting was successful (this may take a minute or two, especially on a slow system). You are then returned to the `More?` prompt for the current article.

The `fd` command is similar to `f`, except that it does not put the headers of the article in the editor buffer. This feature can be useful if you want to change the header substantially (see chapter 10).

Responding by Mail

As we mentioned earlier, you will often respond by sending mail directly to the article's author rather than by posting a follow-up article. The Netnews interfaces make this very easy to do. They provide you with the author's e-mail address (the path) and a subject, and let you use either the editor or the mailer to compose your message. Let's see how this works.

At the More? prompt for the article to which you want to respond by mail, type r. (Think of r as "respond by mail," and f as "follow-up.")

```
Article 313 of 313, Mon 15:46.
Subject: 1982 Honda for Sale
Summary: Nice car, well cared for
Path: ptsfa!jd (John Davidson)
(5 lines) More? [ynq] r
```

Again, you are placed in your editor. This time we will edit the Subject: to make it reflect the fact that we are replying to the ad, and we will edit the Summary: to reflect the fact that we are interested in the car under certain conditions. When we exit the editor, the reply is automatically sent (so check your work first!).

```
No lines in the buffer
No lines in the buffer
"/tmp/fol016461" 3 lines, 46 characters
To: ptsfa!jd
Subject: Re: Your Car Ad
Summary: I'll pay $2000 if car is in good shape
I'll offer you $2000 cash for the car if we can arrange to have a
mechanic satisfactory to both of us check it over. If you're
interested, call my office at...
:wq
"/tmp/fol016461" 7 lines, 201 characters
Sending reply.
```

Notice that the path: in the original article becomes the To: field in our letter. (Many systems use the From: line instead of the Path line for the address in replies.) This means that the mail program has been automatically provided with the information needed for the letter to be delivered. (Occasionally, this will not work properly, for example, when the path is in a non-UUCP format.)

The rd command is similar to r, but it puts you directly in the mailer rather than in the editor buffer. You simply write your letter and exit the mailer as usual:

```
To: ptsfa!jd
Subject: Re: Your Car Ad
Summary: I'll pay $2000 if car is in good shape
I'll offer you $2000 cash for the car if we can arrange to have a
mechanic satisfactory to both of us check it over. If you're
interested, call my office at...
^D
EOT
```

This can be a little quicker if you are writing a short response. If you change your mind and decide you want to edit, you can get the editor from your mailer (see Part 1 of this book).

Cancelling an Article or Reply

You can cancel an article you have posted (with `postnews`), and you can also cancel a reply. To do so, you must move to the point at which you see the article's `More?` prompt. Do this by using the article movement commands discussed earlier. Typing `c` will cancel the article. Only the author of the article or the "superuser" (usually the system administrator) can cancel an article. Since the cancellation has to be sent over the net as a control message, it will take a while for the cancellation to take effect everywhere. (If you are a real UUCP whiz, you can stop the article from even leaving your site by using the methods for killing UUCP jobs given in chapter 15.)

Here's a summary of the response commands:

Commands for Responding to an Article in *readnews*

`f`	Write a follow-up article in your editor and post it.
`fd`	Write a follow-up article; do not include header.
`r`	Reply by mail to article author, using editor.
`rd`	Reply by mail to article author, using mailer directly.
`c`	Cancel an article you have posted.

Using Informational Commands

The *informational commands* are a group of commands that will provide you with additional information or that will change the way information about articles is displayed. One of the most important of these is the ? command. By typing ? anytime you are at the `More?` prompt, you can get a brief command summary. For your convenience, this command summary appears at the end of the chapter so that you can use it as a reference.

You can also see a more complete header for the current article by typing `h` (header):

```
Article 4 of 125, Nov  5 20:01.
Subject: SOS-ProDOS compatibility
Path: ..!ISUMVS.BITNET!F1.EGS ("E. G. Schnoebelen" @ The ARPA Internet)
(24 lines) More? [ynq] h
```

```
--------
Article 4 of 125: <8611102040.AA04271@ucbvax.Berkeley.EDU>
Subject: SOS-ProDOS compatibility
From: F1.EGS@ISUMVS.BITNET ("E. G. Schnoebelen")
Path: ptsfa!lll-lcc!lll-crg!rutgers!sri-spam!sri-unix!hplabs!decwrl!ucbvax
!ISUMVS.BITNET!F1.EGS
Organization: The ARPA Internet
Newsgroups: comp.sys.apple
Date: 6 Nov 86 04:01:32 GMT
Sender: daemon@ucbvax.BERKELEY.EDU
--------
(24 lines) More? [ynq] H
--------

Article 4 of 125: <8611102040.AA04271@ucbvax.Berkeley.EDU>
Relay-Version: version B 2.10.3 4.3bsd-beta 6/6/85; site well.UUCP
Path: well!ptsfa!lll-lcc!lll-crg!rutgers!sri-spam!sri-
unix!hplabs!decwrl!ucbvax
!ISUMVS.BITNET!F1.EGS
From: F1.EGS@ISUMVS.BITNET ("E. G. Schnoebelen")
Newsgroups: comp.sys.apple
Subject: SOS-ProDOS compatibility
Message-ID: <8611102040.AA04271@ucbvax.Berkeley.EDU>
Date: 6 Nov 86 04:01:32 GMT
Date-Received:
Sender: daemon@ucbvax.BERKELEY.EDU
Organization: The ARPA Internet
Lines: 24
--------

(24 lines) More? [ynq]
```

Note the three different header lengths shown in the preceding example. The default (which we have been using in most of our examples) shows only article identification, subject, and path. If you type h while looking at an article, a longer header with more information about the sender and how the article got to you will be displayed. Typing H produces a header that goes all out for verbosity, including identifying the software that was used to relay or forward the news. (The contents of the header will vary with the version of Netnews software being used.) You probably won't need this one unless you are tracing net pathways or debugging the Netnews software.

Occasionally, you may be reading articles and forget which newsgroup you are in. You could display an article and check the header, but there's a faster way. Type # (think of it as "number"):

```
Article 15 of 125, Nov 12 12:08.
Subject: Re: The Woz and the Apple IIGS, //x
Path: ..!PSUVM.BITNET!B5U (B5U @ The ARPA Internet)
(30 lines) More? [ynq] #
Article 15 of 125: newsgroup comp.sys.apple
(30 lines) More? [ynq]
```

Typing # gives you the article number, number of articles in the newsgroup, and the newsgroup name. This is most useful when you have been reading a long article with several pages of text and the header has long since scrolled off the screen. Here is a summary of the informational commands:

Informational Commands in *readnews*

?	Help: show command summary.
h	Show lengthy header for current article.
H	Show very lengthy header for current article.
#	Show current article number, number of articles, and newsgroup name.

Moving between Newsgroups

So far we have been looking at articles within a single newsgroup. There are also commands that let you move between newsgroups. When you reach the end of the last article in a newsgroup, you will automatically be moved to the next newsgroup (usually the next subscribed group in your `.newsrc`).

Here we are back in the newsgroup `news.misc`. We can type **N** to move to the next newsgroup:

```
Article 5 of 69, Nov  9 03:40.
Subject: Re: The 50% rule is in--now what?
Summary: Rn needs friendlier rejection.  Experimentation next.
Path: ..!mecc!sewilco (Scot E. Wilcoxon @ MN Ed. Comp. Corp., St. Paul, MN)
(24 lines) More? [ynq] N

-----------------------
Newsgroup news.stargate
-----------------------

Article 1 of 1, Nov  7 12:15.
Subject: net.news.stargate is being renamed news.stargate
```

```
Path: ..!cbosgd!mark (Mark Horton @ AT&T Bell Laboratories, Columbus, Oh)
Newsgroups: net.news.stargate,news.stargate
(12 lines) More? [ynq] P
```

As you can see, **N** moves you to the next newsgroup and shows you the first article in that newsgroup. You can also give the name of a newsgroup with the **N** command. In that case, you will jump to that newsgroup if it is a valid group and has news. Remember that the commands for moving between *newsgroups* are *capital* letters, and those for moving between *articles* within a newsgroup are *lowercase* letters. Thus, n gives you the next article in the current newsgroup, whereas **N** moves you to the next newsgroup. Figure 7-2 graphically shows the results of some movement commands.

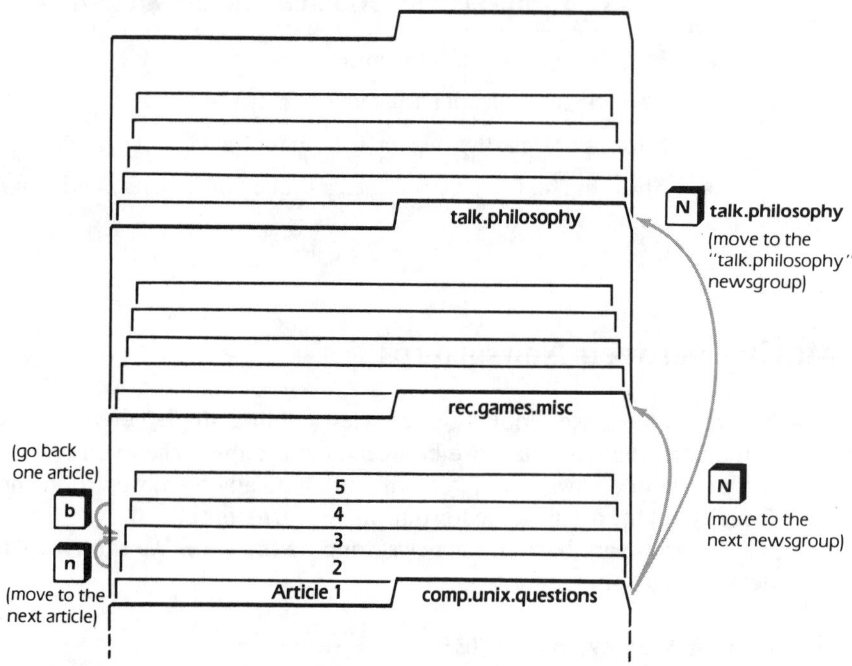

Figure 7-2. Results of some movement commands in **readnews**.

At the last More? prompt in the preceding example, we typed P. This moves us to the previously shown newsgroup:

```
------------------
Newsgroup news.misc
------------------

Article 4 of 69, Nov  7 20:36.
```

```
Subject: The 50% rule is in--now what?
Path: ..!brahms!weemba (Matthew P Wiener @ University of California,
Berkeley)
(16 lines) More? [ynq] U
Unsubscribing to newsgroup: news.misc
```

The U command *unsubscribes* the current newsgroup. This means that the newsgroup is marked in your .newsrc as not wanted. You can always resubscribe by going into .newsrc with an editor and removing the ! from the end of the group name.

Commands for Moving between Newsgroups in *readnews*

- N Move to next newsgroup (or named newsgroup if given).
- P Move to previous newsgroup.
- U Unsubscribe to current newsgroup.

Using a Shell from *readnews*

As you saw in Part 1 on mail programs, it is sometimes useful to be able to run regular UNIX commands from within a UNIX communications program. For example, you might want to use grep to find a name in your address list while writing a news article. You don't want to have to exit news and start over again. In common with many other UNIX programs, readnews offers a *shell escape* facility. If you type an exclamation point (!) at the More? prompt, you are given a standard UNIX shell. The rest of the commands you type on that line will be treated as input to that shell. (You can also set which shell you will be given: see the later discussion on environmental variables further on in this chapter.)

Besides the shell escape facility, readnews provides a useful environmental variable, $A. This variable refers to the article (file) you are currently looking at. It allows you to use UNIX commands to manipulate whichever article you are reading. For example:

```
Article 15 of 125, Nov 12 12:08.
Subject: Re: The Woz and the Apple IIGS, //x
Path: ..!PSUVM.BITNET!B5U (B5U @ The ARPA Internet)
(30 lines) More? [ynq] ! head $A >> index
```

Here, we typed ! and then used the head UNIX command to print the first ten lines of the current article (represented by $A) and append them to a file called index. This file might be used to keep track of information on articles we have recently read. If, later in the session, we've forgotten which newsgroup and number an interesting article had, we could `grep` into this file and get the information.

```
! cat $A ¦ lp
```

This example sends the current article to the line printer via a pipe.

Using a Shell from *readnews*

!	Start a shell; rest of line is input to shell.
`$A`	Environmental variable representing article.

Using Option Flags in *readnews*

In addition to giving commands *during* a session, you can also control the behavior of `readnews` at startup. In fact, option flags can be given either on the command line when you start `readnews` or on an options line in your `.newsrc`. To set up options in your `.newsrc`, simply start the *first* line of your `.newsrc` with a line that begins:

```
options
```

For example, the line

```
options -n comp.unix.all
```

uses the `-n` (newsgroups) option to tell `readnews` to start by displaying newsgroups that begin with `comp.unix`. (See the option descriptions that follow for more details.) If your options take up more than one line, start the second line with a space or tab character to let `readnews` know that the line is a continuation.

Now let's look at the options available with `readnews`. To experiment with them, try invoking `readnews` with various combinations of options. When you find options that are useful, you can make them into defaults by putting them in the options line in your `.newsrc`, as described previously.

Options for Newsgroup and Article Selection

Here are some options that you can use to control which newsgroups and/or articles will be presented by `readnews`.

Options for News Selection in *readnews*

`-n` (newsgroups)	Select specified newsgroups.
`-t` (titles)	Select all articles whose titles contain one of the strings specified.
`-a` (date)	Select all articles that were posted after the specified date.
`-x`	Select all articles, regardless of whether they've been read before (that is, ignore the `.newsrc` file).

Here are some examples using these options. Note that options can be combined.

```
readnews -n comp.sys.all,rec.games.hack
```

This tells `readnews` to begin with all newsgroups relating to computer systems and all articles in the newsgroup devoted to the `hack` game. Note that "`all`" functions like the UNIX wildcard character `*`, matching anything that follows it.

```
readnews -n comp.unix -t vi
```

This tells `readnews` to find articles in the UNIX discussion group whose titles mention `vi`. (Note: if you use symbols special to the shell, they must be quoted.)

```
readnews -n all -a last thursday
```

This means that from all newsgroups you will see only those articles posted after (`-a`) last Thursday (`readnews` is smart enough to know about days of the week, as well as last week).

```
readnews -x -n comp.lang.lisp
```

This says that you want to read all articles on the Lisp language, regardless of whether you've seen them before.

Options for Controlling Form of Output

Here are some examples of controlling the output format. Let's look at the titles of all articles in newsgroups starting with `news`. Using the `-l` flag means that we don't want the articles marked as "read" (after all, we won't have seen their actual text yet):

```
readnews -l -n news > titles @
news.sysadmin/1      net.news.sa is being renamed news.sysadmin
news.sysadmin/2      News feed needed
news.sysadmin/3      Sites to be removed unless updates are received
news.sysadmin/4      Re: Sites to be removed unless updates are received
news.sysadmin/5      Re: Sites to be removed unless updates are received
news.sysadmin/6      Sites to be removed unless updates are received
news.sysadmin/7      Generic Problem with Ultrix/BSD dump/restore
news.sysadmin/8      Re: Sites to be removed unless updates are received
news.sysadmin/9      Re: Generic Problem with Ultrix/BSD dump/restore
news.sysadmin/10     Re: Sites to be removed unless updates are received
```

The `-l` option is handy for browsing through the article titles at your leisure. You can then go back into `readnews` and read the articles you want by jumping to the appropriate article numbers. A way to do this would be:

```
readnews -l -n news -p > titles &
```

Options for Output Control in *readnews*

- `-l` Output only article titles, do not update `.newsrc`.
- `-e` Output the titles, and update `.newsrc`.
- `-r` Output articles in reverse order (by article number).
- `-f` Show original articles only, not follow-ups.
- `-h` Use shorter article headers.
- `-s` Output site and user subscription list (such as from `.sys` file and user's options line in `.newsrc`).
- `-p` Send all articles to standard output without asking questions. This option is usually used for sending articles to the printer or to a file.
- `-u` Update `.newsrc` every 5 minutes.

Here, the command works as it did before, except that the `-p` command sends the titles found directly to standard output, without the normal interactive session. The output is redirected to the file titles for later viewing, and the ampersand (&) at the end of the line puts the whole command in the background so that you can continue while readnews is working.

Of the other options given, -r is useful when you want to see the latest news first, perhaps on a fast-breaking news topic where old news is not good news. The -h option's shorter headers save reading time, particularly on overloaded systems or on slow 300-baud phone lines. If you have a particularly bad line and are prone to being dropped, you can use the -u option to have your .newsrc updated frequently while you work. The -s option is useful for showing you which newsgroups you are NOT receiving. (It is useful to compare this information with the active file in the /news directory.) And the -f option can speed up reading if you don't want to read the dozens of often uninformative follow-up articles that accumulate around certain topics. For example, you might want just the announcements relating to some political topics, not the endless pros and cons that accompany them.

Options for Alternate Interfaces

All of the preceding discussion in this chapter has been based on the default readnews interface. There are two optional interfaces you can select with option flags, however. These interfaces are two variants of a mail-type interface. For example:

```
readnews -M -n news
"/tmp/M1011769": 17 messages 17 new
& headers
>N  1 cbosgd!mark Fri Nov  7 11:59  20/725 "net.news.sa is being renamed"
 N  2 rlw       Wed Nov 12 11:14  31/995 "News feed needed"
 N  3 cbosgd!tgt Fri Nov 14 07:40  98/3093 "Sites to be removed unless up"
 N  4 cit-vax!mangler Sat Nov 15 02:18  26/1053 "Re: Sites to be removed
unles"
 N  5 amdahl!gam Sat Nov 15 13:43  39/1360 "Re: Sites to be removed unles"
 N  6 cbosgd!tgt Sat Nov 15 19:38  98/3097 "Sites to be removed unless up"
 N  7 cbmvax!grr Sun Nov 16 10:59  29/1454 "Generic Problem with Ultrix/B"
 N  8 sbcs!root Sun Nov 16 11:59  45/2021 "Re: Sites to be removed unles"
 N  9 prls!ems Tue Nov 18 00:50  40/1802 "Re: Generic Problem with Ultr"
 N 10 decwrl!reid Tue Nov 18 11:59  26/1219 "Re: Sites to be removed unles"
```

If you have ever used mail, you'll recognize this format. The & prompt is the one used by mail (specifically, mailx or Mail). Note that we used the headers command, which works the same way as in mail, to show headers for the first ten messages. To see the text of a message, we use another mail-type command, p, with a message number:

```
& p1
Message  1:
From ptsfa!lll-lcc!lll-crg!rutgers!clyde!cbatt!cbosgd!mark Fri Nov  7
11:59:20 1986
Full-Name: Mark Horton
Newsgroups: net.news.sa,news.sysadmin
Subject: net.news.sa is being renamed news.sysadmin
Article-ID: news.sysadmin/1

This newsgroup is being renamed from net.news.sa to news.sysadmin
&
```

(This message is actually longer; we've shown only the first line to save space.) Other `mail`-like commands are also available, such as `d` to delete messages and `s` to save a message in a file.

When would you use this interface? You can use it to allow someone to read news messages who hasn't yet learned to use `readnews`. Since it has a very compact header format, this interface is probably best for reading a single newsgroup with relatively few messages, when you don't need the full flexibility of the standard `readnews` interface. The messages are simply provided in a stack, and there is no way to automatically skip to the next or preceding newsgroup.

In addition to `-M`, the `-c` option can also be used to provide a `mail`-type interface. This command uses the format of the old `/bin/mail` mailer:

```
readnews -c -n net.games


------------------
Newsgroup net.games
------------------


Article 1467 of 1534, Nov 10 16:27.
Subject: Sorcerer hint requested
Path: ..!deneb!ccs026 (The Doctor @ University of California, Davis)

    I am fairly sure I have everything necessary to win Sorcerer
except the scroll to make me immune to possession.  My guess is
that it lies across the mine field.  Any hints on how to get
across?
                            Thanks in advance,
                            Mike Keihl
                            {ucbvax,lll-crg,dual}!ucdavis!deneb!ccs026
                            makeihl@ucdavis.BITNET

(n)ext re(p)rint (w)rite (q)uit (r)eply (c)ancel -[n] +[n] (f)ollowup
(N)ext (U)nsubscribe (v)ersion
```

This interface is interesting in that it provides both the header and the article at once. It also provides a small but functional set of commands. A disadvantage of this interface is that you will probably see more of many articles than you wanted to. This interface is best for newsgroups in which you usually want to read all of each article. (You can learn about `/bin/mail` commands in Appendix A.)

Options for Interfaces in *readnews*

`-M`	Interface like `mailx`.
`-c`	Interface like `/bin/mail`.

Using Environmental Variables

As you saw at the end of chapter 6, the Netnews interfaces also provide environmental variables as a means to control operations. Here are the ones used by `readnews`:

Environmental Control Variables for *readnews*

`EDITOR`	The editor to be used for writing follow-up articles.
`MAILER`	The mailer to be used for sending replies.
`PAGER`	The program to be used for paging article text.
`SHELL`	The shell to be run by the `!` command.
`NEWSBOX`	The file or directory to save articles in.
`NAME`	Your full name to be used in the header of articles posted by you.
`ORGANIZATION`	The name of your organization/site to be used in the header of articles posted by you.
`NEWSOPTS`	Options for `readnews`.

The first five variables, `EDITOR`, `MAILER`, `PAGER`, `SHELL`, and `NEWSBOX` are set by giving the pathname of the program or file to be used. The defaults are usually `/usr/ucb/vi`, `/bin/mail`, and `/usr/ucb/more`, for `EDITOR`, `MAILER`, and `PAGER`, respectively, at least on BSD systems. The default shell is usually `/bin/sh`. The default for `$NEWSBOX` is your home directory. At the end of chapter 6, you learned how to set environmental variables. For example:

```
setenv MAILER /bin/mail
```

in the C Shell, or

```
MAILER= "/bin/mail"
export MAILER
```

in the Bourne Shell. We will show just the C Shell version for the rest of our examples. Note that pathnames usually must be quoted in the Bourne Shell, unlike the C Shell.

The next two environmental variables are essentially strings that provide information to be used in articles you post. The default for **NAME** is the comments field of your ID in the /etc/passwd file. The default for **ORGANIZATION** is the site name information known to readnews. It can be useful for you to set these variables to new values if the defaults don't really apply to you (for example, if you are a guest user on someone else's system):

```
setenv NAME "Emperor Norton I"
setenv ORGANIZATION "The Emerald City of Oz"
```

Note that strings should be quoted.

Finally, the **NEWSOPTS** variable can hold a string of command-line options for readnews. These options should be written just as they would appear on the command line or on the options line in .newsrc. (Thus, there are actually three ways to set most readnews options: the command line, the options line in the .newsrc, and the **NEWSOPTS** environmental variable.) For example:

```
setenv NEWSOPTS "-h -n comp.sys.all"
```

Summary

You now know everything that is important to know about readnews. (We've left out a few obscure items.) You have learned the basic navigation of the newsbase. You know how to start up readnews and how to read and reply to news. You have learned how to run UNIX commands from readnews, and you've been introduced to the command-line options and environmental variables in readnews.

We suggest that you practice using readnews. This would also be a good time to reread the discussion of Netnews interfaces at the end of the last chapter and to decide which interface you would like to try next. (If you want to start posting original articles, see chapter 10 on using postnews.)

The next chapter presents rn, which adds many capabilities not found in readnews. We'll close this chapter with the readnews "help" listing as displayed by the ? command.

The **readnews** *Help Listing*

Command	Meaning
y	Yes. (Or just press return.) Prints this article and goes on.
n	No. Goes on to next article without printing current one.
d	Digest. Breaks a digest article up into separate articles.
q	Quit. Update .newsrc if -l or -x not used.
U	Unsubscribe. You won't be shown this newsgroup anymore.
c	Cancel an article you posted.
r	Reply. Reply to article's author via mail.
f [title]	Submit a follow-up article.
N [newsgroup]	Go to next newsgroup or named newsgroup.
s [file]	Save. Article is appended to file (default is "Articles").
s ¦program	Run program with article as standard input.
e	Erase. Forget that an article was read.
h	Print verbose header. Use H for extremely verbose header.
!	Shell escape.
<number>	Go to message #<number> in this newsgroup.
-	Go back to last article.
b	Back up one article in the current group.
K	Mark the rest of the articles in current group as read.
x	Exit. Don't update .newsrc.
v	Version. Print current news version number.

c, f, r, e, h, and s can be followed by -'s to refer to the previous article

8

Reading News with *rn*

As you saw in chapter 7, `readnews` is a relatively simple program. In addition to allowing you to move through the newsgroups and to read articles, it provides the basic functions for saving articles, marking them as read or unread, unsubscribing to newsgroups, and so on. It also allows you some control over your environment through options that can be set in various ways.

Still, the `readnews` program is limited to the basics, and many of the original users of `readnews` began to wish for more features. Let's look at some desirable features for a news reading program.

One of the most important features is the capability to follow a thread of articles on the same subject. The ordering of articles by number based on when they were received may be an easy way for computers to keep track of articles, but it isn't really the way people want to read about something. We want to read an original article, its responses and offshoots—the developing discussion of a topic in context. We want the sense of participation in a conversation.

Another desirable feature is the capability to use patterns and "regular expressions" to select a set of newsgroups or to find a set of articles within the same newsgroup. *Regular expressions* (patterns that are matched against strings according to a set of rules) are a pervasive UNIX feature familiar to many users. By using them, you can often save yourself a lot of typing.

On the matter of saving keystrokes, many commercial applications (particularly in the MS-DOS world) now have a *macro* facility. Macros allow you to define one or two keystrokes as the equivalent of a command or a series of commands. Since there is so much news to read and process on USENET, having a macro facility could be a timesaver.

Still another useful feature is the capability to apply a command (such as marking an article as read) to a range of articles or to a set of articles based on patterns. It is also useful to be able to automatically filter out unwanted articles. This can save time and reduce tedium.

The Powerful *rn* Program

In response to the desire for such features, the `rn` news reading program was developed. It has all the features we've mentioned and many more. In addition, it is designed to show relevant information quickly and give you the ability to act on it globally (that is, affect large numbers of articles with one command). Because of the way `rn` presents information, its author, Larry Wall, claims that: "Whether or not it's faster, it *seems* faster."

This power does not come without a trade-off, however. If you want to compare `readnews` to a simple but effective hunting knife, you must compare `rn` to the granddaddy of all Swiss Army knives. There are a huge number of `rn` commands: the `rn` manual entry is about five times the length of that for `readnews`. But don't let this overwhelm you. As with a Swiss Army knife, you can do useful work with the main blade and then learn how to use the accessories. The `rn` program is now widely available in the USENET world, and most people who have mastered it are glad they did.

This chapter will help you master `rn`. We will use the same approach as before, presenting small groups of related commands, illustrating them, and providing a summary for reference.

The `rn` program groups its commands in three levels: the newsgroup selection level, the article selection level, and the pager level, as shown in figure 8-1. We will follow this organization, but we won't overwhelm you by presenting all of the `rn` commands at each level before proceeding to the next. Rather, we'll cover the most commonly used commands for each level first, and then we'll go back and discuss such things as applying commands by pattern, kill files, and macros.

Starting *rn*

Start the `rn` program by typing the letters `rn` at the UNIX prompt. (There are command-line options and switches that can also be specified at this time. These are discussed later.) If you do not have a `.newsrc` file, `rn` will create one for you from the `active` file in the system news directory and the system subscription list. (This file-creation process is a bit faster than it is in `readnews`, averaging about a minute.) While the file is being set up, `rn` will give you some helpful information, since it assumes you are a first-time user because you don't have a `.newsrc`. The following will give you an example of `rn`'s friendly, helpful personality:

```
rn
Trying to set up a .newsrc file--running newsetup...

Creating .newsrc in /uh/21/hrh to be used by news programs.
Done.
```

```
If you have never used the news system before, you may find the articles
in news.announce.newuser to be helpful.  There is also a manual entry for
rn.
To get rid of newsgroups you aren't interested in, use the 'u' command.
Type h for help at any time while running rn.
(Revising soft pointers--be patient.)
Unread news in ca.general                77 articles
Unread news in ca.news                    1 article
Unread news in ca.news.group              1 article
Unread news in ca.politics                2 articles
Unread news in ca.unix                    3 articles
etc.

********  77 unread articles in ca.general--read now? [ynq]
```

If you already have a `.newsrc`, `rn` first backs it up under the name `.oldnewsrc` and then works with the copy, for safety's sake. Both you and `rn` will cause changes to take place in the `.newsrc` during your news session. The backup ensures that you can start over from the condition at the end of the last session if something goes wrong with the system or if you decide that you want to reverse a decision.

The `rn` program checks the `.newsrc` file for consistency with the files in the system news directory. Not only does it check more items than `readnews` does, it also (unlike the latter program) keeps you informed about what is happening. This process can take quite a while and quite a few keystrokes, but have patience—in subsequent sessions you'll be asked about newsgroups only occasionally. Here are some of the problems and situations that `rn` deals with:

- Newsgroups in your `.newsrc` file that no longer exist (that is, are not found in the `active` file). This can happen if a newsgroup is dropped by the net or is renamed. These are called *bogus newsgroups*.
- Newsgroups recently added to USENET that do not appear in your `.newsrc`. For each such group, you are asked if you want to subscribe.
- Inconsistencies between your `.newsrc` and the system news files. Various problems can cause the "soft pointers" (which `rn` uses to keep track of what you have read) to no longer correspond to the system news files. A *spool file* (the place where news is initially stored in the system) could be missing. Whatever the problem, `rn` will advise you and adjust your `.newsrc`.

It is not necessary for most users to worry about these problems. Here are some examples of questions you might be asked by `rn`:

```
rn
Unread news in ca.general                  77 articles
Warning!  Somebody reset ca.news.group--assuming nothing read.
(Revising soft pointers--be patient.)
Unread news in ca.news.group                9 articles
Warning!  Bogus newsgroup: ca.news.lists
Unread news in ca.wanted                  124 articles
Unread news in mod.ai                     465 articles
etc.
Checking out your .newsrc--hang on a second...
Newsgroup ca.unix not in .newsrc -- add?  [yn] y
Put newsgroup where?^
Moving bogus newsgroups to the end of your .newsrc.
Delete bogus newsgroups? [ny] y

********  77 unread articles in ca.general--read now? [ynq]
```

In this listing, rn started to find unread news. Then it discovered that the pointers that indicate the first and last articles read for ca.news.group were out of sync with the system news files. This can happen because of incompatibilities in news software, the mistake of a system administrator, or a mistake you make in editing your .newsrc outside of rn. When this happens, rn simply resets the pointers, marking the whole newsgroup "unread."

Next, rn found that the newsgroup ca.news.lists was not in the active file. This can happen when a newsgroup has been removed from USENET but is still in your .newsrc or if the active file has not been maintained properly. Thus, rn notified us that this is a bogus newsgroup.

Then rn found out that ca.unix was a valid newsgroup in the active file but was not in our .newsrc. (This may be because USENET just added it.) We were asked whether we wanted to add it to our .newsrc, and we typed y for yes. We were then asked where to put it, and we responded with ^, which stands for "at the beginning of the .newsrc." Adding the newsgroup to the .newsrc means that we are automatically subscribed to it, and we will see any articles posted to this group. We decided we would like to watch this group for a while to see if it was worth reading, so we put it at the front of our .newsrc, where we would always see it first. (We will discuss other places you can put or move newsgroups later.)

Finally, rn moved the bogus newsgroup (ca.news.lists) that it had found to the end of the .newsrc. If we have reason to believe that the newsgroup will be properly installed shortly, we can leave it there and move it after it becomes valid (rn will continue to report the group as bogus unless it is reinstated by the net). If we think the newsgroup is going to remain bogus (perhaps it follows an older naming scheme and has been renamed), we can do as we've done here and tell rn to get rid of it for good by saying "yes" (y) to the question about deleting bogus newsgroups.

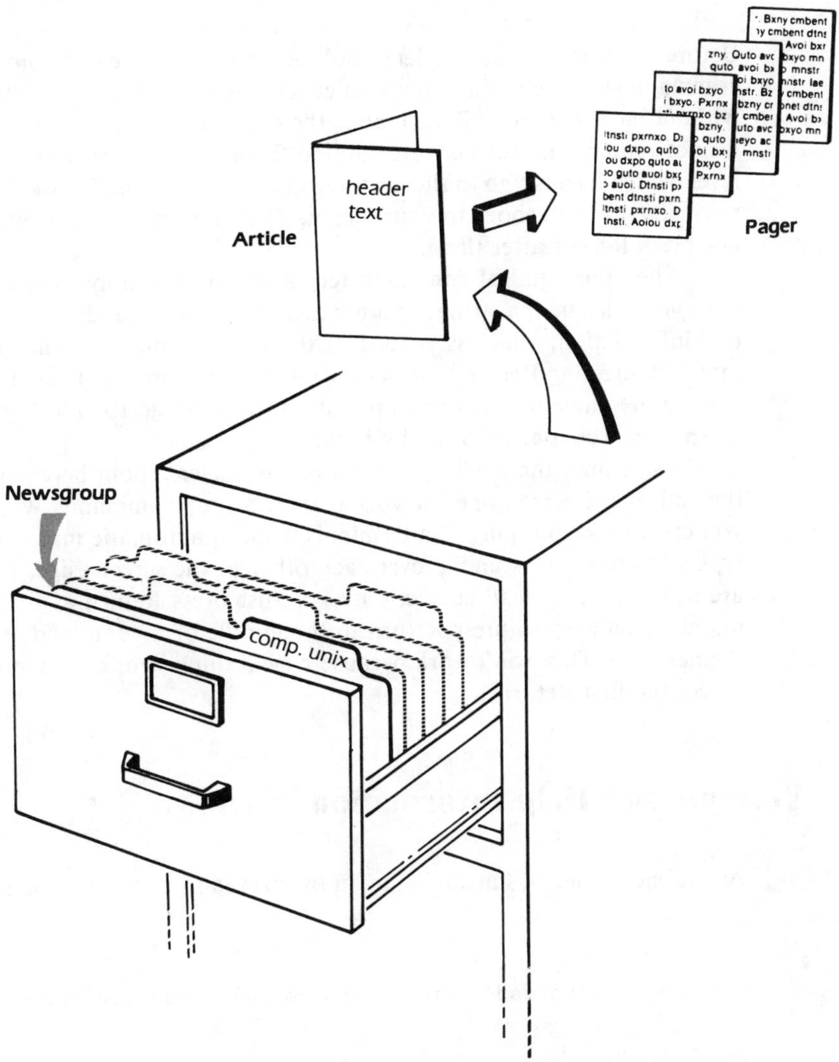

Figure 8-1. Three levels of **rn**.

If your `.newsrc` is badly out of date (perhaps you have not been reading news for some time, or you have been using `readnews` or another news reading program), it may take a few minutes for `rn` to do the revision and ask the necessary questions. In later sessions there should be only the occasional message or offer of a new newsgroup. (The `rn` documentation warns that using other news programs such as `readnews` may scramble the order of newsgroups in your `.newsrc`. Such effects will vary with the version of the Netnews software that you are using.)

Entering *rn* Commands

Before we start to use `rn`, let's look at how we will enter commands. Many `rn` commands require typing only a single character (occasionally with a control key), without having to press Return after the command. These commands are ones that do not require any further information from the user, such as `n` at the newsgroup level, which means "go to the next newsgroup with unread news." These commands normally are not echoed to your screen. They are acted on immediately; you should not press Return after them.

The other kind of command requires that you supply some additional information: a filename, a string, or a number. These commands wait for you to provide this information, which is echoed to the screen. You must end this kind of command by pressing Return. An example is the `g` command at the newsgroup level. It expects the name of a newsgroup that you want to go to. Thus, you might type: `g comp.sys.ibm.pc`, followed by Return.

Sometimes there will appear to be insufficient room between the prompt and the end of the screen line for you to enter a long command. With most terminals you can just keep typing. On terminals without automatic margins, characters you type will appear to stumble over each other at the screen edge, but the characters are actually being read correctly by `rn`. Just press Return at the end of the command. (Don't try to press Return in the middle of a command and continue it on the next line. This won't work because `rn` will think your command is finished when it sees the first Return.)

Prompts and Help Information in *rn*

At the end of the `rn` startup listing in the preceding example, you saw the following prompt:

```
******** 106 unread articles in comp.ai--read now? [ynq]
```

Notice that `rn` suggests the most common commands applicable in a given situation. In this case, these commands are "Yes, I want to read this newsgroup," "Show me the next newsgroup," and "I want to quit." Pressing the space bar is equivalent to typing the first suggested command: thus, pressing the space bar here is the same as typing `y`.

There are actually many more commands available in most situations than are shown in the prompt. Each of the three levels of `rn` commands (newsgroup, article, and pager) has its own listing of "help" information. Typing `h` at the prompt gets you the help for the corresponding level. If you can capture and print these help listings, they may prove helpful at the terminal. We will also print them for you at the end of this chapter.

The Newsgroup Selection Level

Once `rn` is satisfied with your `.newsrc` (actually, the copy, but we'll refer to it as `.newsrc` from now on), `rn` enters the newsgroup selection level. It will start at the beginning of your `.newsrc`, looking for unread news, unless you specified a newsgroup on the command line when you invoked `rn`. Here, we specified `comp.ai` on the command line, having decided to start by looking for news about computers and to begin with the first `comp.` group:

```
rn comp.ai
Unread news in comp.ai                    106 articles
Unread news in comp.arch                  145 articles
Unread news in comp.bugs.2bsd               2 articles
Unread news in comp.bugs.4bsd              99 articles
Unread news in comp.bugs.misc               7 articles
etc.

******** 106 unread articles in comp.ai--read now? [ynq] n
```

This command restricts `rn` to looking at just the `comp.ai` newsgroup. But, as you will see, you can easily move on to other groups without having to start over. (Note that, in `rn`, newsgroups are specified with just the group name, not the `-n name` used by `readnews`. In fact, if you use the latter, some versions of `rn` will remind you that "this is not readnews.")

The `rn` program begins by listing some newsgroups that have unread news in them. It then asks you whether you want to read the first newsgroup, `comp.ai`. Note that it does not assume that you wish to read the first article in the first group. It gives you the opportunity to start reading, but it remains at the newsgroup level until you tell it to enter the article level. This means that you can flip through your `.newsrc` easily without seeing a lot of unwanted article headers. This behavior is particularly useful on slow (1200-baud or less) connections.

Moving through the Newsgroups

Now let's continue at the newsgroup level and see what we can do. The basic commands for moving through the newsgroups are very similar to the ones for `readnews`, so if you have read the last chapter you will already be familiar with them. In the listing that follows (and in many others in this chapter), we have shown, for illustrative purposes, the key that was typed for each command. Remember that most `rn` commands will not be echoed on your screen.

Also, we have sorted our `.newsrc` alphabetically so that you can see the order of the groups in the `.newsrc`. This helps to illustrate the operation of the commands. Instead of sorting your `.newsrc` alphabetically for actual use, you'll probably arrange it by topics or areas of importance. We will show you how to rearrange your .newsrc from within rn later.

Here are some examples of how you can move through the newsgroups and check for the ones that have unread news. Note that the prompt for identifying newsgroup level is read now? [ynq].

First, you can move to the next newsgroup having unread news by typing n, or to the previous newsgroup by typing p:

```
******** 145 unread articles in comp.arch--read now? [ynq] n
********   2 unread articles in comp.bugs.2bsd--read now? [ynq] p
```

Here, we started in the newsgroup comp.arch. Rather than reading it now, we typed n at the read now? prompt. (You can think of the n command as either "next group" or "no, I don't want to read this newsgroup now." In any case, it takes you to the next newsgroup, comp.bugs.2bsd in our example.

Next, we typed the p command, which returned us to the previous newsgroup, comp.arch. The - command toggles between the current and the previously displayed newsgroup:

```
******** 145 unread articles in comp.arch--read now? [ynq] -
********   2 unread articles in comp.bugs.2bsd--read now? [ynq] 1
```

Here, we moved back to comp.bugs.2bsd, the previously displayed newsgroup. We then typed 1 to go to the very first newsgroup in our .newsrc, which happens to be ba.news.group. (Only the number 1 works. You cannot type an arbitrary number to move to the newsgroup having the corresponding position in your .newsrc.)

```
********   0 unread articles in ba.news.group--read now? [ynq] ^
******** 106 unread articles in comp.ai--read now? [ynq] $
******** End of newsgroups--what next? [npq]
```

As you can see, you can also use ^ (the caret symbol) to mean the first newsgroup in your .newsrc, and $ to mean the last one. (The meaning of first and last for these symbols is a pervasive UNIX convention, being part of the system of regular expressions. For example, the UNIX editors and programs such as grep use ^ to mean "beginning of a line or string" and $ to mean "end of a line or string.")

It is important to distinguish between commands that go to the first group with unread news, and those that go to the first group regardless of whether it contains unread news. The n, p, and ^ commands search for groups with unread news. N and P (note the uppercase) work like n and p, except that they look for the next and previous groups, respectively, regardless of whether they contain unread news. Likewise, typing 1 gets you the first newsgroup, regardless of whether it has unread news.

The uppercase N and P might be useful if you want to reread a newsgroup or perhaps "unsubscribe" to it, or if you just want to refresh your memory about which groups exist.

Note that, when we typed **$**, we were positioned at the end of the last newsgroup, thus the prompt: `End of newsgroups--what next?` This position is useful for some commands that we will discuss later.

Moving through Newsgroups in *rn*

`n`	Go to the next newsgroup with unread news.
`N`	Go to the next newsgroup, regardless of status.
`p`	Go to the previous newsgroup with unread news.
`P`	Go to the previous newsgroup, regardless of status.
`-`	Go to the previously displayed newsgroup (toggle).
`1`	Go to the first newsgroup.
`^`	Go to the first newsgroup with unread news.
`$`	Go to the end of the newsgroup list.

Reading Articles: A Quick Preview

As we noted earlier, our presentation follows the levels used by `rn` itself: starting at the newsgroup level, then the article level, then the pager level. But we know that if you're trying out these commands at your terminal, you probably want to start reading articles right away. To start reading articles immediately, follow the procedure in the box "How to Read an Article in *rn*."

How to Read an Article in *rn*

1. At the `read now?` prompt, type `y` or press the space bar to indicate that you want to start reading articles in the current newsgroup. The header of the first article will be shown.
2. When the prompt `--MORE--` appears, type a space to continue reading screenfulls of the text of the article, or type `q` or `n` to jump ahead to the end of the article.
3. At the end of the article, you will see the prompt `--what next?--`. Type an `n` or press the space bar to begin the display of the next article. Type a `q` to go to the end of the newsgroup, where you can use the newsgroup commands we have been discussing to go to another newsgroup. (More article selection level commands will be discussed later.)

Selecting Newsgroups by Name or Pattern

The point at which rn surpasses readnews lies in its capability to search for newsgroups by pattern as well as by name. First, we can use the g (go) command to move to the named newsgroup:

```
********   0 unread articles in comp.ai--read now? [ynq] g comp.sys.amiga
```

(If the group cannot be found, you are not moved from your current location.) Note that the space after the g is optional; we could have typed: gcomp.sys.amiga.

We can also search by pattern. Suppose, after reading the Amiga news, that we want to find out what the Atari people have to say. But we don't remember the name of the Atari group. We can use a pattern like this to search for any group with Atari in its name:

```
******** 1307 unread articles in comp.sys.amiga--read now? [ynq] /atari
Searching...
********  76 unread articles in comp.sys.atari.8bit--read now? [ynq] ?amiga
Searching...
```

We've found a group called comp.sys.atari.8bit. The / command looks for the first newsgroup matching the pattern specified. When we typed /atari, we were placed in comp.sys.atari.8bit. (The group for the 16-bit Atari ST is next after this one in our .newsrc, so we can type an n to get there.) You can see from this example that the pattern is matched if it occurs anywhere in the newsgroup name.

The ? command does the same sort of search, but it scans backward (toward the beginning of your .newsrc). Thus, if we type ?amiga, we end up back in comp.sys.amiga. (The use of / for a forward search and ? for a backward search is a common UNIX convention found in the editors and other programs.) When rn is searching backward or forward and finds one end of the file (the beginning or the end), it wraps around to the other end and continues to the point where it started the search. If it doesn't find the pattern you were searching for, it tells you.

Let's say we now try to find groups with unix in their names:

```
******** 1307 unread articles in comp.sys.amiga--read now? [ynq] /unix
Searching...
******** 249 unread articles in comp.unix.questions--read now? [ynq] /unix$
Searching...
[0 unread in comp.unix--skipping]
```

Our first search finds comp.unix.questions. Next, we searched for unix$. Like grep, the $ anchors its search on the end of the line. It matches only groups whose names *end* with unix. The newsgroup comp.unix was found, but it happened to have no unread articles. Thus, it was skipped. The search went on and found mod.std.unix:

```
********  22 unread articles in mod.std.unix--read now? [ynq] /^comp.
Searching...
********   3 unread articles in comp.os.misc--read now? [ynq]
```

Our final search is for `^comp.`. This search is anchored on the *front* of the string, so we end up with the first `comp.` group in our `.newsrc`. Remember the special meanings of ^ and $; you will see that `rn` uses them in other contexts as well. Figure 8-2 illustrates anchoring a search.

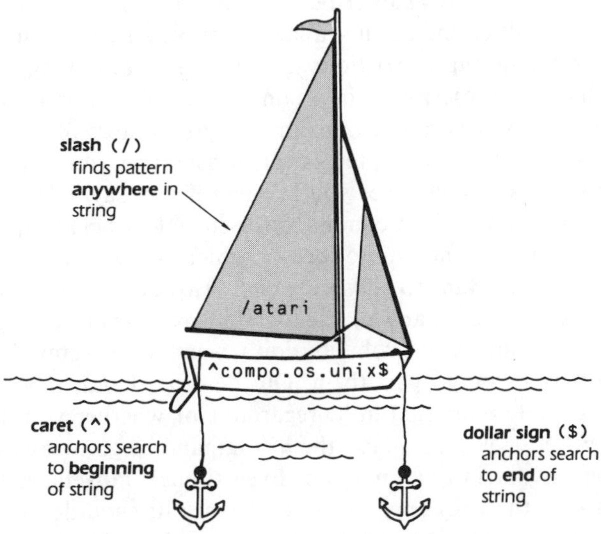

Figure 8-2. Anchoring a search.

Selecting Newsgroups by Name or Pattern in *rn*

`gnewsgroup`	Go to the named newsgroup.
`/pattern`	Search forward for newsgroup matching the pattern.
`?pattern`	Search backward for newsgroup matching the pattern.

Note: Following UNIX convention, `^pattern` means "match the beginning of the newsgroup name"; `pattern$` means "match the end of the newsgroup name."

Newsgroup Management Commands

While you are working your way through your .newsrc, you can also perform some tasks that will help you manage your news flow. You can unsubscribe or subscribe to newsgroups, add newsgroups not found in your .newsrc, and mark newsgroups as read or unread.

The u command unsubscribes the current newsgroup. For example:

```
******** 145 unread articles in comp.arch--read now? [ynq] u
Unsubscribed to newsgroup comp.arch
```

There is no "subscribe" command as such in rn. When you start using rn, you are subscribed to all available groups. Any "options line" in your .newsrc, or other newsgroup restrictions used by readnews, is ignored by rn. This is because rn handles subscription in a number of different contexts. As noted earlier, if, on startup, rn finds newsgroups in the system news file that are not in your .newsrc (presumably newly created ones), it asks you whether you want to add them and automatically subscribes you to them if you say y (yes).

If you use the g command (discussed earlier) to go directly to a newsgroup to which you have not subscribed or which is not in your .newsrc, you will be asked whether you want to subscribe to it. However, regular newsgroup movement commands (such as n and p) silently skip over unsubscribed groups. This behavior is sensible, since you probably don't want to be reminded of unsubscribed groups every time you go past them. On the other hand, if you ask for a group, you are presumably interested in it, regardless of whether you have subscribed to it.

Let's say that we use the g command to go to ca.news, but rn finds that this group is not in our .newsrc. Even though movement through the newsgroups is based on the .newsrc, rn also looks over its shoulder at the active newsgroups file for our site, so it knows that ca.news exists. We are asked if we want to add it to our .newsrc:

```
********   2 unread articles in comp.bugs.2bsd--read now? [ynq] g ca.news
Newsgroup ca.news not in .newsrc--add? [yn] y
```

(If the newsgroup had been in our .newsrc but was unsubscribed, we would have been asked whether we wanted to subscribe to it.) Since we typed y in response to rn's question about adding ca.news, we are then asked where in our .newsrc to put the newsgroup. If you're not sure how to tell rn where to put the group, you can type h for help:

```
Put newsgroup where? [$^.L] h

Type ^ to put the newsgroup first (position 0).
Type $ to put the newsgroup last (position 249).
Type . to put it before the current newsgroup (position 17).
Type -newsgroup name to put it before that newsgroup.
```

```
Type +newsgroup name to put it after that newsgroup.
Type a number between 0 and 249 to put it at that position.
Type L for a listing of newsgroups and their positions.

Put newsgroup where? [$^.L] +ba.news
```

You will see that ^ (the caret symbol) and $ have meanings similar to the ones they have for newsgroup movement commands. Typing ^ puts the newsgroup at the beginning of `.newsrc`, called position 0 rather than 1 in the fine old programmer's tradition. The $ is position 249 because there are that many newsgroups in our `.newsrc`. You can also type a number to put the newsgroup in that position, or you can type `+name` or `-name` to put it after or before the specified newsgroup. So, to put `ca.news` after `ba.news`, we replied: `+ba.news`, thus grouping our two regional newsgroups together. Figure 8-3 shows the possible places to put a newsgroup. These locations also apply to moving already existing newsgroups, a topic that is discussed a little later.

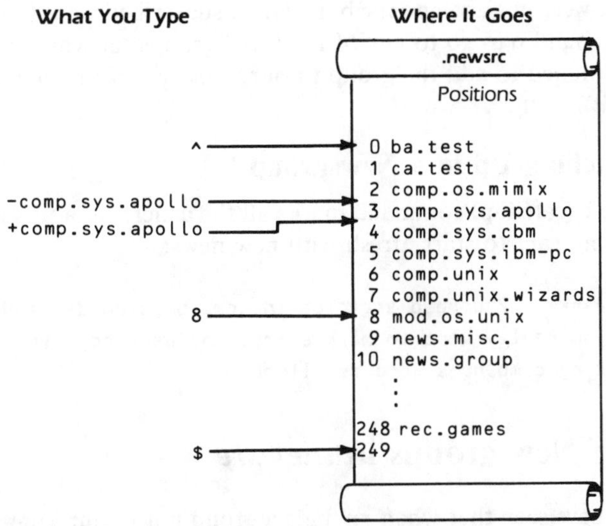

Figure 8-3. Placing or moving a newsgroup.

Suppose that, after several months of news reading, you're not sure which decisions you have made over many sessions about subscribing and unsubscribing to newsgroups. You could, of course, use the `cat` or `more` UNIX commands to examine the contents of your `.newsrc` directly, or possibly you could use `grep` to do pattern searching. (Recall that newsgroups to which you have unsubscribed are preceded by an exclamation point.)

But you can let `rn` do most of this work for you. The `l` command, followed by a string, lists unsubscribed newsgroups containing that string. For example, suppose you want to check on the "talk" groups:

```
********  99 unread articles in comp.bugs.4bsd--read now? [ynq] ltalk
Completely unsubscribed newsgroups:
talk.abortion
talk.rumors
[Type Return to continue]

Unsubscribed but mentioned in .newsrc:
mod.protocols.appletalk
talk.bizarre
talk.philosophy.misc
talk.politics.misc
talk.politics.theory
talk.religion
talk.religion.misc
```

The `rn` program first looked for groups that were not even in our `.newsrc` but whose names matched the string `talk`. It found two: `talk.abortion` and `talk.rumors`. After we pressed Return as requested, a number of "talk" groups that were in our `.newsrc` but were unsubscribed were found. We could now use the command `g` to go to any of the listed groups, at which point we would be asked if we wanted to add the group to our `.newsrc` (if missing) or subscribe to the group (if it's in the `.newsrc`).

Catching Up in a Newsgroup

The `c` (catchup) command marks all the articles in a newsgroup as read. It is useful if you want to start afresh with new news:

```
********   2 unread articles in comp.bugs.2bsd--read now? [ynq] c
Do you really want to mark everything as read? [yn] y
Marking comp.bugs.2bsd as all read.
```

Moving Newsgroups in *.newsrc*

We have seen that when `rn` finds a group not in our `.newsrc`, it asks us if we want to add it, and then where to put it. In addition, we can move a group that is already in our `.newsrc` to a different location by using the `m` command:

```
********   2 unread articles in comp.bugs.4bsd--read now? [ynq]
m comp.sys.amiga
Put newsgroup where? [$^.L] 220
```

In response to the newsgroup level prompt, we typed `m comp.bugs.4bsd`. We were asked where to put the newsgroup, and we decided to bury it in position 220 in our `.newsrc`. Perhaps we were tired of reading bug reports! The same placement options are available here that were listed in our earlier discussion of adding groups with the `g` command. These options included: ^, $, a number, or a position relative to another newsgroup (`+name` and `-name`).

In addition, the `a` command (discussed in the next section) allows you to search for newsgroups by pattern and to add any new ones you find.

Checking Your *.newsrc* Status

You can get an overview of the status of all newsgroups in your `.newsrc` by using the `L` command. Its output will look like this:

```
#  Status   Newsgroup
0 (UNSUB)   ba.food! 1-119
1 (UNSUB)   ba.general! 1-714
2 (UNSUB)   ba.news! 1-1151
3    362    comp.sys.apple: 1-102
4      1    ca.news: 1-18
5 (UNSUB)   ba.news.config! 1-108
etc.
```

The newsgroups are listed in the order in which they appear in the `.newsrc`. The status can be one of the following:

`READ`	No unread articles in this newsgroup.
`number`	The number of unread articles in this newsgroup.
`UNSUB`	Unsubscribed newsgroup.
`BOGUS`	"Bogus" newsgroup (not in `active` file).
`JUNK`	A line in `.newsrc` not corresponding to a newsgroup, such as an options line for `readnews`.

Running the `L` command can give you an indication of how thoroughly you are reading your news, as well as ideas for possible rearrangement of your `.newsrc`.

Commands for *.newsrc* Management in *rn*

`u`	Unsubscribe to the current newsgroup.
`c`	"Catch up" in current newsgroup (mark all articles as read).
`lstring`	List newsgroups not subscribed to whose names contain `string`.
`mname`	Move the named newsgroup to another location in `.newsrc`.
`L`	Show status of newsgroups from `.newsrc`.

Selecting a Subset of Newsgroups

Even with the commands we have now seen, the `.newsrc` can become an unwieldy beast, since it can contain several hundred newsgroups. On any given day this represents thousands of articles. The `rn` program gives us a way to cope with this news glut by specifying a subset of newsgroups to work with. The `o` command selects for display those newsgroups matching a specified pattern. (The rules for specifying patterns are the same as for the `/` command discussed earlier under searching for newsgroups.) For example, if you want to concentrate on news about computer systems, you can enter the following:

```
******** 9 unread articles in comp.bugs.4bsd--read now? [ynq] o comp.sys

******** 360 unread articles in comp.sys.apple--read now? [ynq] n
********  76 unread articles in comp.sys.atari.8bit--read now? [ynq] n
******** 410 unread articles in comp.sys.atari.st--read now? [ynq] n
********  20 unread articles in comp.sys.att--read now? [ynq] n
********  58 unread articles in comp.sys.cbm--read now? [ynq] n
********  26 unread articles in comp.sys.hp--read now? [ynq] n

Restriction comp.sys still in effect.

******** End of newsgroups--what next? [npq]
```

Here we specified that we wanted to see the subset of newsgroups containing `comp.sys`. We used the `n` command to flip through some of these groups, only a portion of which are listed above. When we got to the last matching group, we were reminded that the restriction to `comp.sys` is still in effect. This means that the various commands such as `n` and `p` or other search commands will treat this subset as though it were the whole `.newsrc`. We now have a much more manageable list of newsgroups, perhaps 25 instead of 250. To remove this restriction and again use the whole `.newsrc`, we type `o` without any pattern.

We can also set a subset and add any new newsgroups (i.e., groups not in our `.newsrc`) that match the pattern used to define the subset. We do this with the `a` command. For example, `a comp.lang` selects the various newsgroups involving computer language. Once you have responded to any questions about adding groups, `a` behaves just like `o`. Also, an `a` command removes any old restriction set by an `o` command, and vice versa.

Selecting a Subset of Newsgroups in *rn*

`opattern`	Select and display only newsgroups matching pattern.
`apattern`	Add new newsgroups matching pattern; then select as above.

The Article Level

Although there are some other commands that work at the newsgroup level, we've now covered the most important functions. Let's move on to the selection of articles within a newsgroup. Here, too, you'll find that `rn` has plenty of options, including more pattern-searching commands.

Starting to Read an Article

Earlier, we presented a "quick start" procedure for those of you who wanted to read articles right away. We have now come to the detailed discussion of the article selection level.

As you have seen repeatedly, `rn` at the newsgroup level always shows you the current newsgroup and asks you if you want to read it:

```
******** 888 unread articles in comp.sys.ibm.pc--read now? [ynq] y
Article 200 (887 more) in comp.sys.ibm.pc:
From: cjdb@sphinx.UChicago.UUCP (Charles Blair)
Subject: Re: Keyboard repeat speed-up program for AT
Message-ID: <824@sphinx.UChicago.UUCP>
Date: 19 Nov 86 15:11:27 GMT
References: <282@rocky2.UUCP>
Reply-To: cjdb@sphinx.UUCP (Charles Blair)
Distribution: net
Organization: University of Chicago Library Computer Systems
Lines: 31

--MORE--(28%)
```

By typing `y` (or just a space) at this prompt, you are shown the first unread article in the newsgroup: in this case, `comp.sys.ibm.pc`. The full header is shown (this can be modified by various options discussed later). You can also see the `--MORE--` prompt at the bottom of the screen. It says that 28% of the file (article) has been shown (this 28% is the header in this case, with the balance being the article text).

Pagers are programs that present screenfulls of text at a time. The pager used by `rn` is very similar to the `more` program used in BSD UNIX. Because your terminal may not be equipped to handle all the pager functions, the behavior of `rn` at the pager level may differ slightly from what we describe here. However, we will not cover all the pager functions here, only those that are most useful for reading news articles.

You can continue to read the article by pressing the space bar at each `MORE` prompt. You can use `b` to back up a page if you missed something. We'll cover the other paging commands later.

We'll continue with the article level in a moment. First, though, let's show a useful alternative way of moving from the newsgroup level to the article level. Typing the = command at the current newsgroup lists all the unread articles and their subject lines, one page at a time:

```
******** 888 unread articles in comp.sys.ibm.pc--read now? [ynq] =
200 Re: Keyboard repeat speed-up program for AT
258 Re: MS Windows - Anyone out there?
259 ARC5.12
542 Lots of questions
654 Re: Microsoft Fortran graphics
655 Re: Some Questions
656 Re: Mainframes vs micros
657 New MORE.COM program (works like "less")
658 PcWrite V2.4 (or something)
659 Re: Mainframes vs micros
660 Re: printing > 10 files
661 Re: C compilers?
662 Re: A dream about breaking copy protection!
663 Re: Who makes array processors for AT (or XT, PC)??
664 Looking for a free regexp package
665 PC6300 bell
666 Re: A dream about breaking copy protection!
667 Re: Lots of questions
668 Re: dbase III frustration ended!
669 How do I BSAVE?
670 Re: PC/AT Configuration Questions
671 Re: MS-DOS Versions
672 Re: MS-DOS Versions
[Type space to continue]
```

To get to the next page, press the space bar to continue or type another key to stop the display. This display gives you a kind of table of contents to the newsgroup. By reading the listing, you can decide which articles to jump to or which subject threads to follow. (The commands for these procedures will be discussed shortly.) The = command provides a good overview of what is being talked about in a newsgroup. After the subject display is finished, you are positioned at the first unread article in the newsgroup, just as though you had typed y at the newsgroup prompt.

Starting to Read a Newsgroup (at Newsgroup Level) in *rn*

y or space	Start reading current newsgroup.
=	List subjects; then start reading.
.command	Execute an article-level command; then start. (See next section for commands.)

Moving through Articles in a Newsgroup

Once we've entered the article level, we can move back and forth through the articles in the newsgroup. The commands used for basic movement will be very familiar to you: they are the same as the basic commands for moving among newsgroups in the `.newsrc`, except that here the commands apply to articles, not newsgroups. Let's say we have responded `y` at the newsgroup selection level and have been shown the header of the first article, which includes the number of articles remaining in the newsgroup and the newsgroup name:

```
Article 659 (428 more) in comp.sys.ibm.pc:
From: sam@lanl.ARPA (Sam A Matthews)
Subject: Re: Mainframes vs micros
Message-ID: <10781@lanl.ARPA>
Date: 23 Dec 86 00:06:56 GMT
References: <653@imsvax.UUCP> <1397@cit-vax.Caltech.Edu>
Reply-To: sam@a.UUCP (Sam A Matthews)
Organization: Los Alamos National Laboratory
Lines: 29

--MORE--(22%)n
```

We typed `n` at the `--MORE--` prompt, having decided to skip over the article itself. We are shown the next article:

```
From: boykin@custom.UUCP
Subject: Re: printing > 10 files
Message-ID: <109@custom.UUCP>
Date: 20 Dec 86 16:10:24 GMT
References: <88@bcsaic.UUCP>
Organization: Custom Software Systems; Natick, MA
Lines: 22
```

After the article header, and as long as there is still more text to be read in an article, you will see the `more` prompt. Typing a space gets you another page of text. Typing `q` jumps you to the end of the article and leaves the article marked as unread. Typing `n` also jumps you to the end of the article but marks the article as read. At the end of an article, you will see a prompt like this:

```
End of article 540 (of 832)--what next? [npq]
```

At the end of an article you can type:

`n` Go to the next unread article.

`N` Go to the next article, even if already read.

p Go to the previous unread article.

P Go to the previous article, even if already read.

The catch here is that p (go to previous unread article) will not work as you might expect if you have been using n to skip over articles after seeing their headers. The n command marks articles as read as you skip over them. Therefore, p, which goes back looking for *unread* articles, will not show you any articles you skipped over with n. But remember that you can use P and N to show you articles whether or not they have been marked as read.

There are three other useful commands for moving through articles. The - command is a toggle that shows the previously displayed article. The ^ command goes to the first unread article in the newsgroup. (You can also specify an article by its number within the newsgroup: thus, we could type 659 at the MORE prompt and again see that article. Reading status does not affect this command.)

Finally, the $ goes to the end of the newsgroup (just past the last article). The What next? prompt reminds us that we are no longer "in" an article, as we were each time that we saw the MORE prompt. The article selection commands that we have just seen, and quite a few more, can be used at this prompt also.

Basic Article Selection Commands in *rn*

n or space	Get next unread article.
N	Get next article, even if read.
p	Get previous unread article.
P	Get next article, even if read.
-	Get previously displayed article (toggle).
^	Get first unread article in newsgroup.
number	Get article with specified number.
$	Go to end of newsgroup.

```
Article 659 (428 more) in comp.sys.ibm.pc:
From: sam@lanl.ARPA (Sam A Matthews)
Subject: Re: Mainframes vs micros
Message-ID: <10781@lanl.ARPA>
Date: 23 Dec 86 00:06:56 GMT
References: <653@imsvax.UUCP> <1397@cit-vax.Caltech.Edu>
Reply-To: sam@a.UUCP (Sam A Matthews)
Organization: Los Alamos National Laboratory
Lines: 29
```

```
--MORE--(25%)$
End of newsgroup comp.sys.ibm.pc.  (428 articles still unread)

What next? [npq]
```

Searching for Articles by Pattern

Just as `rn` lets us use patterns to find newsgroups, it also lets us use them to find articles within a newsgroup. We can match patterns against the subject, the whole header, or the whole article. For example, we can look for articles that refer to the C Shell (Csh) in their `Subject:` header lines by using the string `Csh` preceded by a slash `/`:

```
End of article 474 (of 743)--what next? [npq] /Csh
Searching...
...500...550...600...650...700

Not found.
```

No luck on that search. What about an article on System V (often abbreviated SV)?

```
End of article 474 (of 743)--what next? [npq] /SV
Searching...
...500
Article 508 (254 more) in comp.unix.questions:
From: monkey@unixprt.UUCP (Monkey Face@unixprt)
Newsgroups: comp.unix.wizards,comp.unix.questions,comp.bugs.sys5
Subject: Remote File Sharing (RFS) - SVR3
Keywords: RFS, SVR3
Message-ID: <261@unixprt.UUCP>
Date: 1 Jan 87 01:21:28 GMT
Organization: uni-xperts - Unix System and Networking Consultants
Lines: 12
```

After searching for a few seconds and reporting that it had moved past article 500, `rn` found an article with `SV` in the subject (it happens to be part of the string `SVR3`).

But this pattern-matching search command is even more versatile. The basic search command is a slash `/`, followed by a pattern, followed optionally by modifiers that specify the part of the article to be checked. In the preceding listing, we first did a search for `Csh` (that is, the C Shell) anywhere in the subject line of the article (which is the default field to check). By the way, you don't have to worry about case sensitivity: the default is to match regardless of case, so `Csh` will match `csh`. The `rn` program displays a running report of its progress in checking the articles.

When a matching article is found, the first page (header) is displayed with the `MORE` prompt, exactly as though you had used one of the basic article selection commands.

Let's look at a few more examples of searching. We can search for AT&T in *any* header field:

```
--MORE--(46%) /AT&T/h
Searching...
Article 538 (254 more) in comp.unix.questions:
From: ekrell@ulysses.homer.nj.att.com (Eduardo Krell)
Newsgroups: comp.unix.wizards,comp.unix.questions
Subject: Re: Remote File Sharing (RFS) - SVR3
Keywords: RFS, SVR3
Message-ID: <1583@ulysses.homer.nj.att.com>
Date: 5 Jan 87 14:15:25 GMT
References: <261@unixprt.UUCP> <371@oblio.UUCP> <10938@sun.uucp>
Reply-To: ekrell@ulysses.UUCP (Eduardo Krell)
Organization: AT&T Bell Laboratories, Murray Hill
Lines: 28
```

Searching for Articles by Pattern in *rn*

A search command consists of `/` (forward search) or `?` (backward search), plus a pattern, plus optional modifiers. More than one modifier can follow the `/` or `?`, for example: `/awk/ar`.

`/pattern`	Scan forward for article with `pattern` in subject line.
`/pattern/h`	Scan forward for article with `pattern` anywhere in header.
`/pattern/a`	Scan forward for article with `pattern` anywhere in the article.
`/pattern/r`	Scan already read articles also.
`/pattern/c`	Make search case-sensitive (ordinarily lower- and upper-case match).
`?pattern`	Scan backward for article with `pattern` in subject line. This can also be combined with the modifiers given above: for example, `?pattern?a`.
`/`	Repeat previous forward search.
`?`	Repeat previous backward search.

The specifications for our search are indicated by the second slash followed by the letter *h*: `/h`. The `h` is a modifier that specifies that the whole header is to be checked. In this case, it turned out that the `Organization:` field in the header had the phrase `AT&T` in it. There are a number of other modifiers that can be used also (see the "Searching for Articles by Pattern in *rn*" box). You can search backward (toward the beginning of the newsgroup) by using ? instead of `/`. A plain `/` or ? repeats the previous search.

The search options can be combined: for example, `/Unix/ar` means a forward scan for articles with `Unix` anywhere in the article (modifier `a`) and including the already-read-articles modifier (`r`).

Depending on the newsgroup, of course, such a search might find almost every article! Whole-article searches with the `a` modifier are necessarily slow. In most cases, the default search by subject works best.

Using Subject Mode

In addition to searching for subjects or other fields in articles within a newsgroup, we can also follow a discussion by finding the first article with a given subject and then searching the rest of the articles using that subject. (You may remember that you can get a list of subjects at the article level by typing =.) You can also start by searching for a subject with the pattern mechanism previously described. If you do so, however, make sure that you start at the beginning of the newsgroup (you can move there with `^`) in order to find the first article with that subject.

To enter *subject mode*, make the first article with your chosen subject current (by moving to it with an article selection or movement command) and then type `^N` (Control-n). This does two things: it tries to find the next article with the same subject as the current article, and it sets the subject mode. You can now move through all the articles on that subject. Let's see how this works:

```
End of article 158 (of 832)--what next? [npq] /ROM
Searching...
...200...250...300...350...400...450...500
Article 538 (672 more) in comp.sys.mac:
From: frankng@basser.oz (Frank Ng)
Subject: Re: Should 64K ROMs be supported?
Summary: The rest of us still use 64K ROMs
Message-ID: <849@basser.oz>
Date: 23 Dec 86 20:35:29 GMT
References: <476@runx.OZ> <1490@hoptoad.uucp> <907@ur-tut.UUCP>
<4939@reed.UUCP> <531@runx.OZ>
Organization: Dept. of Comp. Science, Uni of Sydney, Australia
Lines: 33
```

First we did a pattern search (`/ROM`) to find articles with `ROM` in their subjects. We found article 538. We then typed Control-n to set the subject mode:

```
--MORE--(29%) ^N
Article 540 (671 more) in comp.sys.mac:
From: dsc@izimbra.CSS.GOV (David S. Comay)
(SAME) Subject: Re: Should 64K ROMs be supported?
Message-ID: <43505@seismo.CSS.GOV>
Date: 24 Dec 86 14:24:03 GMT
References: <476@runx.OZ> <1490@hoptoad.uucp> <907@ur-tut.UUCP>
<4939@reed.UUCP><1986Dec19.114200.23189@utcs.uucp> <531@runx.OZ>
Sender: usenet@seismo.CSS.GOV
Reply-To: dsc@izimbra.UUCP (David S. Comay)
Organization: Center for Seismic Studies, Arlington, VA
Lines: 13
```

As you can see, rn found the next article with the subject **ROM**. Note that you can do this at the **MORE** prompt or after reading the article (at the end-of-article prompt). The rn program puts the word **(SAME)** at the start of the subject line to show that you are following a subject thread.

```
--MORE--(41%) q
End of article 540 (of 832)--what next? [^Nnpq]

Article 542 (670 more) in comp.sys.mac:
From: abbott@dean.Berkeley.EDU (+Mark Abbott)
(SAME) Subject: Re: Should 64K ROMs be supported?
Keywords: upgrades
Message-ID: lt]16703@ucbvax.BERKELEY.EDU>
Date: 24 Dec 86 16:40:33 GMT
References: <1986Dec19.114200.23189@utcs.uucp> <531@runx.OZ>
Sender: usenet@ucbvax.BERKELEY.EDU
Reply-To: abbott@dean.Berkeley.EDU (+Mark Abbott)
Distribution: net
Organization: University of California, Berkeley
Lines: 40
```

Here, we typed q at the **MORE** prompt to get to the end of the article without reading it. (We will have "more" to say on **MORE** when we cover article reading and the pager level later.) Notice that the prompt is now:

```
End of article 540 (of 832)--what next? [^Nnpq]
```

The default (the first command listed) is now **^N** (Control-n). This means that we can continue to follow our subject thread by just typing a space when this prompt turns up.

To leave subject mode, use one of the regular article movement commands. For example, typing n will put you back in the regular sequential mode—and then n will perform its normal function.

Besides finding articles you are interested in, subject searching can help you discard groups of articles that you do not want to read through. For example, we can use the k (kill) command to kill all articles with this same subject, that is, mark them as read:

```
--MORE--(24%) q
End of article 542 (of 832)--what next? [^Nnpq] k

Marking subject "Should 64K ROMs be supported?" as read.

Searching...
573     Junked
579     Junked
590     Junked
622     Junked
```

You can also use the ^P (Control-p) command to enter subject mode. It finds the *previous* article with the same subject as the current article. It then works like ^N.

More on the Pager Level

Now that we've learned how to navigate both in the .newsrc and within a newsgroup, let's look again at the paging commands for reading articles. As you know, typing a space at the MORE prompt lets you see more of the article. But you can also move to other parts of the article, and even scan the article text for a specified string. Here are some examples of pager-level commands:

```
Article 145 (632 more) in comp.lang.c:
From: m5d@bobkat.UUCP (Mike McNally )
Newsgroups: comp.sys.intel,comp.lang.c
Subject: Re: segments and Unix
Message-ID: <244@bobkat.UUCP>
Date: 21 Nov 86 14:20:20 GMT
References: <13802@amdcad.UUCP> <2327@ihlpa.UUCP> <407@intsc.UUCP>
Reply-To: m5d@bobkat.UUCP (Mr Mike McNally)
Organization: Digital Lynx; Dallas TX
Lines: 47

--MORE--(15%)    ←press space bar to read more
```

We've just displayed article 145. We are at the MORE prompt, which tells us that 15% of the article has been displayed so far. We press the space bar:

```
In article <407@intsc.UUCP> tomk@intsc.UUCP (Tom Kohrs) writes:
>       [ ... ]
>> The problem with doing this on a
>> 286, for instance is again the extreme overhead necessary to set up
>> (or check access permissions) on each data reference.
>
>In the 286 the hardware takes care of the overhead associated with
checking
>the access writes.  The time to do this is hidden in the pipeline.
>
>  tomk@intsc.UUCP                   Tom Kohrs
>                                          Regional Architecture Specialist
>                                          Intel - Santa Clara

The protection checks which involve already loaded descriptors are
indeed "free" (ignoring RISCy arguments along the lines that the chip
real estate and hardware sophistication could have been better used in
making instructions faster (and maybe curing my pet peeve, the
affection for AX felt by IMUL) (but I digress)).  However, a scenario
in which each individual object lies in its own data segment would
involve an LDS or LES or something before each reference.  Check your
handy iAPX 286 reference guide and see how long these instructions
take.  A long time, right?  While you're at it, ask your local Intel
rep why it's a bad idea to have too many code segments in a protected
```

Here we've displayed the next page of the article by typing a space at the **MORE** prompt. Now 50% of the article has been shown. This percentage is changed as you move through the article. (You can move forward only half a page by typing d or ^D.)

```
--MORE--(58%)    ← space bar pressed here
environment.

Don't get me wrong; I like the 286.  I strongly believe that it could
be used to great advantage in a machine like the Macintosh; that is, a
machine which is to run its own custom-designed OS.  Or, if you're so
inclined, I suppose the machine works just fine under iRMX (I'm not so
inclined...I'd like to more directly express my feelings here, but I
can't spell the noise I make when I think about RMX...sort of like
coming into work in the morning, pouring some coffee, taking a sip,
then realizing that you grabbed the wrong pot and got last night's cold
mouldy scum-laden black death...).  Of course, as I look through my
iAPX 386 Programmer's Reference Manual, I get warm feelings when I
think about stacks > 64K...

--
```

```
****                                                        ****
**** At Digital Lynx, we're almost in Garland, but not quite ****
****                                                        ****

Mike McNally                                  Digital Lynx Inc.
Software (not hardware) Person                Dallas  TX  75243
```

We've typed another space and have now seen most of the article (97%).

```
--MORE--(97%)   ←space bar pressed here
uucp: ...convex!ctvax!bobkat!m5             (214) 238-7474
End of article 145 (of 777)--what next? [npq]b
```

We've reached the end of the article: the what next? prompt. We decide to go back a page and reread part of the article. We do this by typing b:

```
>> The problem with doing this on a
>> 286, for instance, is again the extreme overhead necessary to set up
>> (or check access permissions) on each data reference.

--MORE--(58%) ^R
```

(Note: we did not show the entire screen in order to save space.) We have now gone back a page—nearly back to the beginning of the body of the article. Notice that a page is not the same as the screenfull of text that is presented when you type a space at the MORE prompt. It is more like a printed page.

Commands for Paging within an Article in *rn*

space	See next page of article.
b or ^B	Back up one page.
d or ^D	See next half page of article.
CR	See next line of article.
^R	Restart display of article from header.
v	Restart display with complete (verbose) header.
^L	Refresh (redisplay) the screen.
^X	Refresh screen, decrypt as "rot13".
q	Go to end of article. Don't mark as either read or unread.

At the MORE prompt you can also type ^R (Control-r) as shown in the last example. This restarts the article from the beginning of the header. If you ever want to restart an article and see the complete (verbose) header, type v.

Searching for Text in an Article

You have now seen that rn provides pattern-searching facilities at both the newsgroup and the article level. In fact, pattern searching can even be done at the pager level.

```
Article 454 (186 more) in comp.unix.wizards:
From: brandon@tdi2.UUCP (Brandon Allbery)
Newsgroups: comp.unix.questions,comp.unix.wizards
Subject: Multi-Spoolers
Message-ID: <126@tdi2.UUCP>
Date: 24 Dec 86 21:19:54 GMT
References: <161@ndmath.UUCP> <99@ems.UUCP>
Reply-To: brandon@tdi2.UUCP (Brandon Allbery)
Followup-To: comp.unix.questions
Organization: Tridelta Industries, Inc., Mentor, OH
Lines: 52
```

Let's say we've just been shown this article header. We're looking for a new spooling system for our System V UNIX machine. We don't want to wade through the whole article if it's about BSD because such a product probably won't work with our system. What we can do is search for occurrences of "System V" in the article. This should give us enough context about the relationship between this spooler and System V to determine whether we want to read the article in depth. We can use the g command, followed by a string, to search for the string System V in the current article:

```
--MORE--(14%) g System V
| System V's kind of spooling using the System V spooler. By correctly
| specifying printers and classes a user can send to a specific printer, or
| a specific class of printers.
----------------

--MORE--(79%) G
```

The g command, when used with a pattern, searches for that pattern in the article text. If it finds the pattern, the article is displayed with the line containing the pattern at the top of the screen. (We have omitted all but the first few lines to save space.) After reading about the System V spooler (which indicates that the author of this new spooler is at least using System V), we typed an uppercase G at the MORE prompt. This repeats the search with the previously specified pattern:

```
which currently (almost) runs under System V.  (I began writing it to solve
a perceived problem with the "lp" spooler:  it (1) lacks a forms handling
feature and (2) lacks a feature to automatically use the nearest free
printer
in a class to the person/program doing the spooling.)  It is as yet
incomplete,
but if you need something fast I can send you a shar file of what is
written;
what needs to be done isn't too much, if you want a "basic spooler" system
(parts I haven't started yet are a full pagination system and generic print
mode interpreters, but you could probably do without them; so could we).

--MORE--(87%)
```

We see that the author has almost completed a spooler program and is offering it to interested readers (we omitted some of the technical discussion). Our spooler search shows that you can use the pattern-searching commands to zero in on relevant parts of long articles, and thus speed up your reading.

Marking and Saving Articles

As you might expect, rn provides facilities for marking articles as unread and for saving them to a disk file. The m command marks the current article as unread. The M command marks the article as unread, but only after you leave the newsgroup. That way you can look at it in a later session but not keep bumping into it while you want to look for other things. Note that these and the following commands can be used at either the pager or the article selection level. This is useful because you can dispose of an article without having to finish reading it.

```
Article 533 (178 more) in comp.unix.questions:
From: chris@mimsy.UUCP (Chris Torek)
Newsgroups: comp.unix.questions,comp.unix.wizards
Subject: Re: Help on deciphering crash
Message-ID: <4914@mimsy.UUCP>
Date: 4 Jan 87 16:38:24 GMT
References: <3645@sdcrdcf.UUCP> <4891@mimsy.UUCP> <1419@cit-
vax.Caltech.Edu>
Organization: U of Maryland, Dept. of Computer Science, Coll. Pk., MD 20742
Lines: 60

--MORE--(16%) m
Article 533 marked as still unread.

End of article 533 (of 743)--what next? [npq] n
```

```
Article 534 (178 more) in comp.unix.questions:
From: mike@BRL.ARPA (Mike Muuss)
Subject: [Brint Cooper:  Pr man page improvement]
Message-ID: <2107@brl-adm.ARPA>
Date: 5 Jan 87 03:54:50 GMT
Sender: news@brl-adm.ARPA
Lines: 38

--MORE--(19%) M
Article 534 will return.
```

Notice the difference between the lowercase and the uppercase versions of the `m` command. When we used `m` with article 533, we were told that the article was still unread. When we used `M` with article 534, however, we were told that the article "will return" (not now, but the next time we are in the newsgroup).

Another way to keep an article for future reference is of course to save it to a disk file. The `s` command, when given with a filename, saves the current article to that file (complete with header). The default destination (if you give an ordinary filename) makes the article a file in your `News` directory. Various options discussed later can modify the directory used or the filename generated. The `w` command works like `s`, except that the article header is omitted. There are also uppercase forms of these commands: `S` and `W`. These are the same as their lowercase counterparts except that they use whatever shell you have set with the `SHELL` environmental variable, rather than the default shell `sh`. (This is of interest if you are using commands that work only with a certain shell. See the later section on UNIX commands from `rn`.)

Here are some examples of saving articles:

```
End of article 534 (of 743)--what next? [npq] n
Article 535 (177 more + 1 Marked to return)) in comp.unix.questions:
From: jerryp@tektools.UUCP (Jerry Peek)
Newsgroups: comp.unix.wizards,comp.unix.questions
Subject: Re: Can you stop it?
Message-ID: <2057@tektools.UUCP>
Date: 5 Jan 87 00:53:54 GMT
References: <3512@curly.ucla-cs.UCLA.EDU>
Reply-To: jerryp@tektools.UUCP (Jerry Peek)
Followup-To: comp.unix.questions
Distribution: usa
Organization: Tektronix, Inc., Beaverton, OR.
Lines: 30

--MORE--(28%)
End of article 535 (of 743)--what next? [npq] s unix.questions
```

```
File /uh/21/hrh/News/unix.questions doesn't exist--
        use mailbox format? [ynq] y
Saved to mailbox /uh/21/hrh/News/unix.questions


End of article 535 (of 743)--what next? [npq] n
Article 536 (176 more + 1 Marked to return)) in comp.unix.questions:
From: guy%gorodish@Sun.COM (Guy Harris)
Subject: Re: ulimit considered braindamaged?
Keywords: ulimit SysV irksome
Message-ID: <10943@sun.uucp>
Date: 5 Jan 87 08:40:59 GMT
References: <790@maynard.BSW.COM> <166@herman.UUCP>
Sender: news@sun.uucp
Lines: 12

--MORE--(36%)
End of article 536 (of 743)--what next? [npq] s unix.questions
Appended to mailbox /uh/21/hrh/News/unix.questions
End of article 536 (of 743)--what next? [npq]
```

In the first example, we gave the s command to save the article in a file called unix.questions. Since this was a new file, rn asked us whether to create it in regular or mailbox format. *Regular format* is simply a file with articles appended one after the other. *Mailbox format* is a file set up so that it can be read by mail with the -f option. This makes it easy to break out and work with (and even reply to) various articles saved in the same file. We chose mailbox format and then saved the next article. (Notice that this time the article was appended, and we were not asked again for the file format.) After saving a few more articles and then leaving rn, we later went back and looked at them with mail. (This assumes a Berkeley system; if you have System V, use mailx.)

```
$ cd /uh/21/hrh/News
$ mail -f unix.questions
"unix.questions": 4 messages 4 new
& headers
>N  1 tektools!jerryp Mon Jan 19 03:18  48/2024 "Re: Can you stop it?"
 N  2 news@sun.uucp Mon Jan 19 03:19  27/1130 "Re: ulimit considered
brainda"
 N  3 devon!paul Mon Jan 19 03:19  56/2509 "Re: ulimit considered brainda"
 N  4 ulysses!ekrell Mon Jan 19 03:20  45/1905 "Re: Remote File Sharing
(RFS)"
& p4
```

You can see that the articles have been stored as if they were received as mail.

They can now be displayed, saved individually, replied to, edited—anything you can do with mail.

Of course, there is the other side of the coin from saving or marking for future reference. This is marking articles as read so that you won't see them again. For example, after looking at the header of an article, you could decide that you don't want to finish reading it and that you want it to go away until you specifically ask for it. The `n` command, as we have seen, is the usual way to skip the current article, mark it as read, and get the next article. Sometimes, though, you want to skip to the end of the current article without going to the next one, so that you can issue other article-management commands. Using the `j` (junk) command marks the current article as read, and leaves you at the end of the article. No message will be displayed, but the article will be marked as read.

The `c` (catchup) command, which you saw at the newsgroup level, can also be used here.

Marking and Saving Articles in *rn*

`m`	Mark current article as unread.
`M`	Mark current article as unread, but not until the next time you are in the newsgroup.
`n`	Mark current article as read; skip to next article.
`j`	Mark current article as read; go to end of article.
`c`	Mark all articles in newsgroup as read.
`s filename`	Save currrent article to `filename`.
`S filename`	Save current article, using optional shell.
`w filename`	Same as `s`, except article header not saved.
`W filename`	Same as `S`, except article header not saved.

Replies

The commands for replying by mail to an article (`r` and `R`) and submitting a follow-up article (`f` and `F`) work in basically the same way as their `readnews` equivalents. They are a bit more verbose about what they are doing, however. Here's an example of submitting a mail reply to the following article, which was posted earlier as a test. (One good way to practice using mail is to first post a test article—see chapter 10 for how to post original articles—and then reply to your own article.)

```
Article 364 (143 more) in ba.test:
From: hrh@well.UUCP (Harry Henderson)
```

```
Subject: Article I posted as a test
Message-ID: <2439@well.UUCP>
Date: 20 Jan 87 22:28:03 GMT
Reply-To: hrh@well.UUCP (Harry Henderson)
Distribution: ba
Organization: Whole Earth Lectronic Link, Sausalito CA
Lines: 4

--MORE--(67%)  ←space bar pressed here
This is just a test
--
The opinions expressed are my own, but you're welcome to share them.
Harry Henderson (freelance technical editor/writer).
End of article 364 (of 364)--what next? [npq] r
```

(Notice that we've typed r to respond by mail.)

```
To: hrh
Subject: Re: Article I posted as a test
Newsgroups: ba.test
In-Reply-To: <2439@well.UUCP>
Organization: Whole Earth Lectronic Link, Sausalito CA
Cc:
Bcc:

(Above lines saved in file /uh/21/hrh/.rnhead)

(leaving cbreak mode; cwd=/uh/21/hrh)
Invoking command: Rnmail -h /uh/21/hrh/.rnhead
```

The rn program tells us which temporary file our message is being saved in for editing purposes. This information might be useful for recovering the message after a crash. A specialized version of mail called rnmail will be used to send the message.

```
Prepared file to include [none]:

"/tmp/rnmail8929" 9 lines, 181 characters
To: hrh
Subject: Re: Test of rn followup from end of newsgroup
Newsgroups: ba.test
In-Reply-To: <2439@well.UUCP>
Organization: Whole Earth Lectronic Link, Sausalito CA
Cc:
Bcc:
```

```
This is a test response to my test article.
:wq
"/tmp/rnmail8929" 10 lines, 224 characters

Send, abort, edit, or list? s
Append .signature file? [y] y
```

The program first asks if we want to include any already prepared text in our message. Our default editor is then called (usually `vi`), and we can edit the headers and write the message as usual. We can then abort (throw away the message), re-edit, list, or send the message. We told `rn` to send the message. The final question is whether we want to add our *signature file*. Signature files are described in chapter 10. They allow you to add a personalized "signature" and address information to your replies and original messages.

The `R` command would have worked in the same way, except that the article being replied to would have been included in the edit buffer, prefixed with a quoting character (by default `>`) showing that the lines were quoted. (We will give examples of proper use of quoting in chapter 10. For now, note that quoting can be abused: edit out any quoted lines that aren't needed to identify what you are responding to.)

Follow-ups

The follow-up `f` command normally works as it does in `readnews`, albeit with more verbosity. Here's what it looks like:

```
End of newsgroup rec.games.frp (145 articles still unread)

What next? [npq] f

(leaving cbreak mode; cwd=/uh/21/hrh)
Invoking command: Pnews -h /uh/21/hrh/.rnhead
```

You can see that the actual program used is called `Pnews`. It is similar to `postnews` (discussed in chapter 10, except that it is designed to be used automatically rather than interactively. The interface is provided by `rn`, which imparts some useful advice:

```
This program may post news to many machines.
Are you absolutely sure that you want to do this? [ny] y

Prepared file to include [none]:
```

The program asks if we wish to insert text that we may have already written or obtained elsewhere. Then it puts us in the buffer of our default editor:

```
"/tmp/article8880" 12 lines, 240 characters
Newsgroups: rec.games.frp
Subject: Designing a New Game
Summary: I want it to be educational but fun, too!
Reply-To: hrh@well.UUCP (Harry Henderson)
Followup-To:
Distribution: rec
Organization: Whole Earth Lectronic Link, Sausalito CA
Keywords: educational simulation
"/tmp/article8880" 12 lines, 240 characters
I would like to ask about your experiences in designing
educational software. I don't mean drill and practice stuff, but
software fun enough to sell as a game but educational enough to
be purchased by schools. What design elements contribute to this?
```

The article header is placed in the buffer for us to edit (see chapter 10 for more information on editing headers). We finish writing our article and exit the editor. We are then asked whether we want to send (post the article), abort (throw away the article), edit the article again, or list it on the screen:

```
:wq
"/tmp/article8880" 16 lines, 540 characters

Send, abort, edit, or list? s

(re-entering cbreak mode)
What next? [npq]
```

When the article is posted, we are returned to the prompt—the place we were when we started the follow-up.

The `F` command (follow-up with quoting) works like `f`, but it includes the text of the current article in your edit buffer, prefixed with quoting symbols (> by default). (In other words, `F` is to `f` as `R` is to `r`.) Quoting is further covered in chapter 10. For now, note that you should quote only enough to identify what you are responding to.

Responding to Articles in *rn*

- `r` Respond by mail to current article.
- `R` Respond by mail, including text of current article.
- `f` Post a follow-up to current article.
- `F` Post a follow-up, including text of current article.

More Special Features of *rn*

We have now covered a lot of material on rn. If you have mastered all the material so far, you already have a more powerful control over the news system than you had with readnews. At this point, you might want to practice the groups of commands that have been presented, until you are comfortable with them.

This section will present some other useful and powerful things that you can do with rn. We will not attempt to cover everything in the manual, but we will touch on the most interesting and important facilities. After you are comfortable with the program and the material in this chapter, it might be a good idea to read the manual entry for further ideas.

Regular Expressions

We have showed you a number of pattern-searching commands that can be used to search for articles. These commands in fact use a UNIX feature called *regular expressions*. Different UNIX commands support different sets of regular expressions: rn basically follows those recognized by the editor ed. If you have been using UNIX for some time, you are probably quite familiar with regular expressions. The ones used in this chapter are: ^ to match the beginning of a line (newsgroup name or line in an article) and $ to match the end of a line. For more examples of regular expressions, consult any good UNIX introduction (see Appendix E) or the UNIX manual entry for ed. In addition, rn supports some special regular expressions (see page 18 of the rn manual entry).

Macros

Macros are simply abbreviations for rn commands or groups of commands. You define a macro by typing the && command, followed by one or more characters for the abbreviation, followed by the command(s) that the abbreviation will stand for. For example

```
&& forget j
```

In this case, we were having trouble remembering that the way to mark an article as read is to use the j command for "junk." The macro definition in the preceding example sets the word "forget" equal to the letter "j." Whenever we type forget, a j will appear on the screen. We can then press Return and the j command will be executed.

Besides making commands easier to remember, macros can also save typing. Here are some examples:

```
******** End of newsgroups--what next? [npq] && gu g comp.unix.questions
******** End of newsgroups--what next? [npq] && oc o comp.sys
******** End of newsgroups--what next? [npq] && su s comp.unix.questions
******** End of newsgroups--what next? [npq] && sp s pc.questions
******** End of newsgroups--what next? [npq] &&

Macros:
gu      g comp.unix.questions
oc      o comp.sys
sp      s pc.questions
su      s unix.questions
```

As you can see, we happened to be at the end of a newsgroup. Macros can be defined with the `&&` command at almost any `rn` prompt. Typing `&&` by itself prints a list of the macros currently known to `rn`.

Here, we decided that macros beginning with `g` would be used to go to frequently read newsgroups. Thus, `gu` stands for the command `g comp.unix.questions`. Later we might add `gw` to go to `comp.unix.wizards`. We used macros beginning with `o` to get subsets of newsgroups with the `o` command. The macro `oc` will set a restriction to `comp.sys` groups.

We've used macros beginning with `s` to save articles to designated files. Here, `sp` will perform an `s` command to save articles on MS-DOS matters to the file `pc.questions`. Similarly, we defined an `su` macro to save UNIX questions.

You can see that we've created our own command shorthand system. Your ideas may be quite different from ours, but that is no problem. With macros, you can customize your `rn` interface. You can even use function keys on many terminals and map them to common commands.

Macros and the *.rnmac* File

Macros defined interactively as we did in the previous example are *not* saved by `rn` for permanent use, however. To make your macros permanent, simply create a file called `.rnmac` in your `home` directory, using your favorite editor. Put your macro definitions in this file (one per line). Now when you start an `rn` session, these macros will be automatically activated.

News Filtering with Kill Files

The `rn` program provides a number of facilities that you can use to customize your news reading environment. One of the most common things you might want to do is to have articles on certain subjects automatically marked as read when you enter a newsgroup. Given the tremendous volume of news available these days, there is no point in wading through 75 articles on something you are not interested in.

Using Macros in *rn*

1. To create a macro, use the following formula:

   ```
   && keys commands
   ```

   Type `&&`. Then type the characters that will designate the macro (`keys`). Type a space or a tab. Then type the commands to be substituted for the macro (`commands`). To execute the command, simply type the macro abbreviation, followed by Return. For example, `sp pc.questions` defines a macro, which, when you type `sp`, will save the current article to the file `pc.questions`. Any macros defined in the `.rnmac` file in your home directory will be loaded upon starting `rn`.
2. To obtain a list of current macros, type `&&` and press Return.

The mechanism that `rn` supplies for filtering out unwanted articles is called the *kill file.* This file contains one or more commands of the form:

```
/pattern/j
```

It means: Find articles that match this pattern and mark them as read immediately upon entering the newsgroup. This combination of a pattern and a command is actually a special case of a more general linking of patterns and commands that you will see in the section on `rn` batch commands. There are, in fact, two kinds of kill files. The *global kill file* is applied automatically to every newsgroup as it is entered. In addition, any newsgroup can have its own *local kill file.* This local file goes into action upon entry into that particular newsgroup.

There are three commands that are used to kill articles. The `k` command simply marks as read all articles with the same subject as the current article. It does not affect the kill file. The `K` command does the same thing as the `k` command, but it also adds the command to the local kill file for the current newsgroup. Thus, the command will be executed again each time that the newsgroup is entered.

The `^K` (Control-k) command is used to edit the kill files. When used on the newsgroup level, it edits the global kill file. If you use it within a newsgroup (on the article level), it edits the local kill file for that newsgroup. Let's see how this works:

```
Article 438 (299 more) in comp.unix.questions:
From: unllab@amber.berkeley.edu
Newsgroups: comp.unix.questions,misc.wanted
Subject: UVAX II DISK HELP
Message-ID: <2042@jade.BERKELEY.EDU>
Date: 22 Dec 86 08:19:04 GMT
```

```
Sender: usenet@jade.BERKELEY.EDU
Reply-To: unllab@amber.berkeley.edu()
Organization: University of California, Berkeley
Lines: 19

--MORE--(34%)k
Marking subject "UVAX II DISK HELP" as read.

Searching...
447 Junked
483 Junked
492 Junked
done
```

Here, we used k to kill all articles with the subject UVAX II DISK HELP. The numbers of the articles that matched the subject and that were killed, or "junked," were displayed. Such impromptu murder is handy for getting rid of developing discussions on topics of specialized interest that you don't want to follow.

```
Article 439 (298 more) in comp.unix.questions:
From: rlk@chinet.UUCP (Richard Klappal)
Subject: Re: foo
Message-ID: <962@chinet.UUCP>
Date: 21 Dec 86 17:56:29 GMT
References: <36@houligan.UUCP>
Reply-To: rlk@chinet.UUCP (Richard Klappal)
Distribution: usa
Organization: Chinet - Public Access Unix
Lines: 7

--MORE--(67%)K
Marking subject "foo" as read.

Depositing command in /uh/21/hrh/News/comp/unix/questions/KILL...done

Searching...
440     Junked
558     Junked
574     Junked
578     Junked
583     Junked
613     Junked
697     Junked
done
```

By using K, we got rid of the perennial discussion on the meaning of foo, a legendary USENET debate. (We won't go into it here; you can find it on the net for yourself!) Since we used the K command, the command was put in the local kill file for this newsgroup. (Notice from the pathname given by rn that this is at the bottom of a series of subdirectories going from your news directory down through directories based on the newsgroup name.) The matching articles were then marked as read.

```
Article 441 (290 more) in comp.unix.questions:
From: mouse@mcgill-vision.UUCP (der Mouse)
Subject: Re: echo (was $@ vs. $*)
Message-ID: <585@mcgill-vision.UUCP>
Date: 21 Dec 86 06:34:59 GMT
References: <181@haddock.UUCP> <106@quacky.UUCP><164@its63b.ed.ac.uk>
Distribution: world
Organization: McGill University, Montreal
Lines: 16

--MORE--(41%) ^K
Editing local KILL file:
/usr/ucb/vi /uh/21/hrh/News/comp/unix/questions/KILL
No lines in the buffer
"/uh/21/hrh/News/comp/unix/questions/KILL" 1 line, 11 characters /: *foo/:j
/BSD/:j
:wq
"/uh/21/hrh/News/comp/unix/questions/KILL" 2 lines, 23 characters
End of article 441 (of 743)--what next? [npq]
```

Here we used ^K (Control-k) to edit the local kill file. Notice that this file already had the foo kill command created earlier by the K command. We added one more kill command: /BSD/:j. This might be used by someone who doesn't want to read about BSD UNIX, perhaps a busy person who is committed to System V. Next time we enter this newsgroup, this is what happens:

```
Looking for articles to kill...

/: *foo/:j
/BSD/:j
457     Junked
496     Junked
510     Junked
521     Junked
522     Junked
626     Junked
647     Junked
```

```
679     Junked
686     Junked
708     Junked
712     Junked
732     Junked

[Type space to continue]
```

All of the articles with BSD in their subjects were marked as read. (It so happened that there were no `foo` articles to kill this time.)

```
******** End of newsgroups--what next? [npq] ^K
Editing global KILL file:
/usr/ucb/vi /uh/21/hrh/News/KILL
No lines in the buffer
"/uh/21/hrh/News/KILL" [New file]
/flame/j

:wq
"/uh/21/hrh/News/KILL" [New file] 2 lines, 10 characters

******** End of newsgroups--what next? [npq]
```

Here, we were at the end of a newsgroup, so we were back at the newsgroup level. Our `^K` (Control-k) command thus edited the global kill file. We added a command to delete all articles with `flame` in their subject. Unfortunately, there is no way to delete all articles that are filled with flaming opinions but don't have the word "flame" in their subject.

Global kill commands should be used rarely. First of all, they involve quite a bit of processing and are liable to cause an annoying pause when you enter each newsgroup. Also, words mean different things in the context of different groups. You may not want to kill an article on "flame retardant materials," for example. In general, it is better to use local kill files, and use commands that are specific enough to delete only the articles you don't want to see.

Batch Processing Commands in *rn*

We have already covered some useful commands for managing news articles as we read them. The main commands are:

- `m` Mark as unread.
- `M` Mark as unread the next time the newsgroup is entered.
- `j` Mark as read.

s Save to specified destination.

= Print subject lines.

In addition, there is the shell escape command, !, common to many UNIX programs. It is followed by a UNIX command that is processed by the shell.

These commands can actually be applied to a whole group of articles rather than just the current article. There are two ways to specify the group: by pattern and by numeric range. Let's look at patterns first.

The general form for the command is:

```
/pattern/modifiers:command{:command}
```

The first item in this command, pattern, is the same sort of string you have been using for finding newsgroups and articles. In addition, the pattern /^/ can be used to match *every* article in the newsgroup, since it matches the beginning of any line.

The second item, modifiers, is the same optional modifiers you have been using for article searches:

h Check article header only.

a Check the whole article,

r Also check articles already read.

Note that you can have more than one modifier by stringing the modifiers together.

The notation :command{:command} means that you can have one or more commands, separated from the modifiers and from each other by colons. Commands can be one or more of the article management commands already given (m, M, j, s, =) as well as the shell escape !. Some other commands may work in some situations: you can experiment to find out.

Here's an example of an rn batch command:

```
/pattern recognition/ar:j:s ai.news
```

This command looks for articles in the current newsgroup that have the phrase pattern recognition anywhere in the article (indicated by the a modifier). Even articles that have already been read will be accepted (this is indicated by the r modifier).

Articles that are found will first be marked as read (the j command). The article will then be saved (the s command) to the ai.news file.

Here's another example:

```
/^/ ¦ lpr:j
```

matches all unread articles (unread because there is no r modifier) and pipes them to the line printer command `lpr`. The (¦ command is shorthand for s ¦, that is, "save to a pipe.") The articles are then marked as read.

Let's look at some commands and how `rn` actually responds to them. First, we'll do a subject listing of our current newsgroup with the = command to see some available topics in `comp.lang.c`:

```
Article 524 (250 more) in comp.lang.c:
From: mouse@mcgill-vision.UUCP (der Mouse)
Newsgroups: comp.lang.c,comp.bugs.4bsd
Subject: Re: lvalues and ++
Message-ID: <583@mcgill-vision.UUCP>
Date: 21 Dec 86 06:19:51 GMT
References: <31da677c.809c@apollo.uucp>
Organization: McGill University, Montreal
Lines: 30

--MORE--(27%)=
  525 Re: Structure element offsets
  526 Re: Draft ANSI standard: const/volatile functions
  527 Re: Draft ANSI standard:  are chars signed?
  528 Re: Structure function returns -- how?
  529 Book to learn "C"
  530 Re: Structure element offsets
  531 Re: A Deficiency of the C Preprocessor
  532 Re: Portable code: identifier length
  533 Re: Draft ANSI standard: needs your tomatoes
  534 "C" on Atari looks pretty weird
  535 Re: A Deficiency of the C Preprocessor
  536 Re: A Deficiency of the C Preprocessor - (nf)
  537 Re: A Deficiency of the C Preprocessor - (nf)
  538 Re: "C" on Atari looks pretty weird
  539 Re: Is it really necessary for character values to be positive?
  540 Re: Bit-field pointers / arrays
  541 Re: Structure function returns -- how?
  542 Why static forward references?
  543 Re: Initializing variables (Was: Deficiency of Preprocessor)
  544 Re: Supplementary standards (Re: ANSI C -- nonrequired features.)
  545 Re: Bit-field pointers / arrays
  546 Re: A Deficiency of the C Preprocessor - (nf)
  547 Re: "C" on Atari looks pretty weird
[Type space to continue]
```

Let's say we are interested in the evolving ANSI standards for the C language. We see that there are some articles on that subject. Let's save them to a file:

```
End of article 524 (of 777)--what next? [npq] /ANSI/:s ansi.discussion
Searching...
526
File /uh/21/hrh/News/ansi.discussion doesn't exist--
        use mailbox format? [ynq]  ←space bar pressed here
Saved to mailbox /uh/21/hrh/News/ansi.discussion
527     Appended to mailbox /uh/21/hrh/News/ansi.discussion
533     Appended to mailbox /uh/21/hrh/News/ansi.discussion
544     Appended to mailbox /uh/21/hrh/News/ansi.discussion
done
```

(To save space we are including only the first few articles that rn reported on. Note that rn searches through the whole newsgroup, not just the small number of subjects we have displayed.)

The command /ANSI/:s ansi.discussion did the trick. Since we were searching for subjects, no modifiers were needed. Notice that rn still asks the usual questions: in this case, what format we wanted for our new save file.

```
Article 525 (249 more) in comp.lang.c:
From: mouse@mcgill-vision.UUCP (der Mouse)
Subject: Re: structure element offsets
Message-ID: <588@mcgill-vision.UUCP>
Date: 21 Dec 86 08:34:24 GMT
References: <1096@spice.cs.cmu.edu> <7377@utzoo.UUCP>
Organization: McGill University, Montreal
Lines: 24

--MORE--(31%) q
End of article 525 (of 777)--what next? [npq] /preprocessor/:j:s
preprocessor
Searching...
531     Junked
File /uh/21/hrh/News/preprocessor doesn't exist--
        use mailbox format? [ynq] y
Saved to mailbox /uh/21/hrh/News/preprocessor
535     Junked  Appended to mailbox /uh/21/hrh/News/preprocessor
536     Junked  Appended to mailbox /uh/21/hrh/News/preprocessor

done
```

In this example, we gave a command that found all articles with preprocessor in their subject. Each article was junked (marked as read) and then saved to the file preprocessor.

Automatic Batch Commands

Another nice thing that you can do is combine pattern-finding batch commands with the local kill file (discussed earlier in the section on kill files). If `K` is included with the command modifiers, the command is executed and then placed in the local kill file for the newsgroup. This means that, if you put a command like:

```
/preprocessor/K:j:s preprocessor
```

in your local kill file, each time that you enter the newsgroup, all articles with `preprocessor` in their subjects will be automatically marked as read and saved for you to read at your leisure.

As you can see, the combination of pattern matching, the application of a command to a set of articles, and the automatic operation of the kill file can be combined to automate a considerable amount of your news reading. This automation can be especially useful at low baud rates where you don't want to wait to read lots of individual lines. We have, in fact, shown you only the basics here. Advanced use of `rn` features could easily fill a book all by itself!

Numeric Batch Commands

You can also perform commands on a batch of articles selected by article number. To do so, use commands in this form:

```
range{,range} command{:command}
```

First, specify one or more ranges. A *range* is either a single article number or two article numbers separated by a hyphen (for example, `1-10` means articles 1 through 10). As you can see, more than one range can be specified: `1-5,7,11-15` would specify a total of 11 articles. The `command` is the same sort of command you used with previous patterns. Let's look at another article listing and see a few examples of numeric batch commands:

```
525 Re: Structure element offsets
526 Re: Draft ANSI standard: const/volatile functions
527 Re: Draft ANSI standard:  are chars signed?
528 Re: Structure function returns -- how?
529 Book to learn "C"
530 Re: Structure element offsets
532 Re: Portable code: identifier length
533 Re: Draft ANSI standard: needs your tomatoes
534 "C" on Atari looks pretty weird
538 Re: "C" on Atari looks pretty weird
539 Re: Is it really necessary for character values to be positive?
540 Re: Bit-field pointers / arrays
```

```
  541 Re: Structure function returns -- how?
  542 Why Static forward references?
  544 Re: Supplementary standards (Re: ANSI C -- nonrequired features.)
  545 Re: Bit-field pointers / arrays
  547 Re: "C" on Atari looks pretty weird
  548 Does \"volatile\" cover this?
  549 Incrementing after a cast
  550 Re: (unsigned)-1
  551 Re: Is it really necessary for character values to be positive?
  552 Re: Draft ANSI standard: needs your tomatoes
  553 Re: Reserved words in C
[Type space to continue]   ←space bar pressed here
End of article 535 (of 777)--what next? [npq] /529,549,553 s misc
```

Here we've spotted some articles we're interested in and saved them to the file `misc`. The `rn` program responds as follows:

```
529
File /uh/21/hrh/News/misc doesn't exist--
        use mailbox format? [ynq] y
Saved to mailbox /uh/21/hrh/News/misc
549     Appended to mailbox /uh/21/hrh/News/misc
553     Appended to mailbox /uh/21/hrh/News/misc
End of article 525 (of 777)--what next? [npq]
```

Let's look at one more example:

```
562 palindrome
563 Re: (unsigned)-1
564 Re: sizeof(((struct_type *)0)->member_name)
565 Request for Design Guides
567 Re: Is it really necessary for character values to be positive?
568 Re: Question about feof()
569 Re: Are the floating point routines on my machine broken?
570 Re: Pushing arguments onto the stack in C?
571 Re: Structure function returns -- how?
572 Re: Structure function returns -- how?
573 Are the floating point routines on my machine broken?
574 Re: 'register' type (was: bit-field pointers / arrays)
575 Re: Are the floating point routines on my machine broken?
576 I/O buffer size using lattice-C
577 Re: Why all this fuss about CTRL(X) ??
578 Re: Are the floating point routines on my machine broken?
579 Re: Machine readable version of ANSI draft
[Type space to continue]
```

```
End of article 525 (of 777)--what next? [npq] 562,571-572 ¦ pr > articles &
562
571
572
End of article 525 (of 777)--what next? [npq]
```

Here, we used a pipe command to send articles 562, 571, and 572 to the `pr` command to format them with page numbers and headers, saving the result in the file `articles` by output redirection. We used an `&` to place this UNIX command in the background so that we wouldn't have to wait for it to finish.

Percent Escapes

An `rn` feature mostly of interest to advanced users is the *percent escape* facility. The `rn` program keeps track of many items of information while it is running. These items include all the various parts of the current article, the current newsgroup, the filenames and directories currently recognized, and the values of various optional settings. These items can be accessed individually and used, for example, in shell escape commands. The value of the item is made available to the shell and can be passed to shell scripts, and so on. This means that you can write custom scripts that format and save parts of articles, for example. The `rn` manual lists three whole pages (pages 19–21) of percent escapes, and we must refer you to the manual for a complete discussion of them. Here are just a few examples of what you can do.

```
Article 461 (202 more) in comp.unix.wizards:
From: jsdy@hadron.UUCP (Joseph S. D. Yao)
Subject: Re: Vanilla 4.2 BSD sendmail problem
Summary: Loopback device
Keywords: mail, socket
Message-ID: <314@hadron.UUCP>
Date: 29 Dec 86 05:12:25 GMT
References: <490@ms3.UUCP>
Reply-To: jsdy@hadron.UUCP (Joseph S. D. Yao)
Organization: Hadron, Inc., Fairfax, VA
Lines: 28

--MORE--(31%) ! echo %s
Vanilla 4.2 BSD sendmail problem
--MORE--(31%) 461-470:! echo '%s' >> subjlist &
```

First, we gave the UNIX command `! echo %s`. This printed the subject of the current article. Next we used a more complex command. It first selected a range of articles (461– 470) and then executed a shell escape. The shell command used `echo` to append the subject `'%s'` to the file `subjlist`, performing the operation in the background. Note that %s is quoted to prevent the shell from getting confused by subjects containing characters with special meanings to the shell.

Command-Line Options

If you have mastered `readnews`, you know that it has a number of command-line options, or "switches," that can control such things as the directory in which saved articles will be placed. The `rn` program has almost every option that `readnews` has, and many more. These options can be set in one of four ways:

1. Put them on the command line when invoking `rn`.
2. Set them interactively by typing `&option name` while in `rn`.
3. Include them in the value of the environmental variable `RNINIT`.
4. Put them in a file whose name is assigned to the variable `RNINIT`.

For example, the `-v` option makes `rn` echo all commands that you type to it (something it does not ordinarily do). You could set this switch in several ways:

1. Invoke `rn` as follows: `rn -v`.
2. Type `&-v` at any `rn` prompt.
3. Use the shell command: `RNINIT="-v"; export RNINIT` (or `setenv RNINIT "-v"` in the C Shell).
4. Use the shell command `RNINIT=$HOME/switchfile; export RNINIT`, and put `-v` in a `switchfile` in your home directory (use a `setenv` command as shown above for the C Shell).

This last way provides a file that works in a way similar to the way `.mailrc` works with `mailx` (or `Mail` in BSD).

The available switches are described in detail on pages 14–18 of the `rn` manual. They are far too involved to cover in this book, but they cover these general features:

- Where `rn` looks for news and how it updates the `.newsrc`.
- Terse mode and type-ahead, useful for low baud rates.
- Echoing of commands.
- Specifying directories for saving files, and the format of saved files (mailbox or normal).
- Extent of header display and the fields displayed.
- Kind of scrolling and where new material appears on the screen.

Environmental Variables in *rn*

The rn program also provides a very generous assortment of environmental variables (see pages 22–27 of the rn manual). Although the defaults provided may be all you will want most of the time, we will list the most common environmental variables, organized by function, so that you can see what can be changed. See table 8-1. The variables can be set by the usual shell commands, for example:

```
EDITOR="usr/ucb/vi" ; export EDITOR     (Bourne Shell)
rs8]setenv EDITOR "usr/ucb/vi"          (C Shell)
```

The "options" line in the .newsrc used by readnews to set options is NOT recognized by rn, however.

Table 8-1. Some *rn* Environmental Variables

Variable	Description
	Parts of Articles You Write
NAME	Your full name (added to path).
ORGANIZATION	Name of your organization.
ATTRIBUTION	Description of quoted material in follow-ups, such as "so and so writes . . . ."
YOUSAID	Like ATTRIBUTION, but used for mail replies, such as "In article number you write . . . ."
	Location of Files and Directories
DOTDIR	Where to find dot files (such as .newsrc).
HOME	Your home directory (very commonly used in UNIX).
KILLGLOBAL	Where to find the global kill file.
KILLLOCAL	Where to find the local kill file.
MAILFILE	Where to check for mail.
RNINIT	Optional file containing switch settings for rn; put a slash followed by the filename as the first line of RNINIT if you want another file to be used instead.
RNMACRO	Location of file containing macro definitions.
SAVEDIR	Name of directory to save articles to by default.
SAVENAME	Name of file to save to if only directory given is Program Selections.
EDITOR	Name of your default editor.

Table 8-1. (cont.)

Variable	Description
	Location of Files and Directories
MAILPOSTER	Command used to run mail program for posting replies.
SHELL	Your preferred shell (for save commands, etc.).
VISUAL	Name of editor (could be used as an alternative to EDITOR).
	Terminal Definitions
TERM	Determines terminal type.
TERMCAP	Name of termcap file, or a termcap entry (BSD systems).

Summary

This chapter started by showing how you and rn interact to set up your .newsrc file. Then it looked at rn's three-tiered structure—newsgroup, article, and pager levels—and at the different commands for each level.

It explained some useful, advanced features of rn, such as macros, news filtering with global and local kill files, command-line options, and environmental variables.

This chapter has covered a large part of the functionality of rn, but by no means everything. Fortunately, you don't have to use more features than you are comfortable with. If you read more than a few news articles frequently, we think that you will benefit from rn's powerful news-filtering and subject-access facilities, even if you don't use many of the advanced features at first. You will probably appreciate being able to tailor your news reading environment and control your news flow as you become more involved with USENET.

In the next chapter, we will look at an alternative news reading program, vnews, which is easy to use if not nearly as powerful as rn. We will conclude this chapter with a reference listing of the three rn help displays.

The *rn* Help Displays

Here are the various help displays you can get from rn. You can use this listing as a quick reference section to save time at the terminal.

Newsgroup Level

Prompt: `******** n unread articles in group name--read now?`

Newsgroup Selection Commands:

y,SP	Do this newsgroup now.
.cmd	Do this newsgroup, executing cmd as first command.
=	Equivalent to .=<carriage return>.
u	Unsubscribe from this newsgroup.
c	Catch up (mark this newsgroup all read).
n	Go to the next newsgroup with unread news.
N	Go to the next newsgroup.
p	Go to the previous newsgroup with unread news.
P	Go to the previous newsgroup.
-	Go to the previously displayed newsgroup.
1	Go to the first newsgroup.
^	Go to the first newsgroup with unread news.
$	Go to the last newsgroup.
g name	Go to the named newsgroup. Subscribe to new newsgroups this way too.
/pat	Search forward for newsgroup matching the pattern
?pat	Search backward for newsgroup matching the pattern. (Use * and ? style patterns. Append r to include read newsgroups.)
l pat	List unsubscribed newsgroups containing pattern.
m name	Move named newsgroup elsewhere (no name moves current newsgroup).
o pat	Display only newsgroups matching pattern. Omit pat to unrestrict.
a pat	Like o, but also scans for unsubscribed newsgroups matching pattern.
L	List current .newsrc.
&	Print current command-line switch settings.
&switch	{switch} Set (or unset) more command-line switches.
&&	Print current macro definitions.
&&def	Define a new macro.
!cmd	Shell escape.
q	Quit rn.
^K	Edit the global KILL file. Use commands like /pattern/j to suppress pattern in every newsgroup.
v	Print version.

Article Level

Prompt at start of article: `Article n (n more) in group name article header`

Prompt while reading article: `--MORE--(n%)`

Prompt at end of article: `End of article n (of n)--what next? [npq]`

Note: article level commands work at any of these prompts. Pager level commands work at the `--MORE--` prompt.

```
Article Selection Commands:

n,SP                    Scan forward for next unread article.
N                       Go to next article.
^N                      Scan forward for next unread article with
                        same subject.
p,P,^P                  Same as n, N, ^N, only going backward.
-                       Go to previously displayed article.
number                  Go to specified article.
range{,range}           Apply one or more commands to one or more
command{:command}       ranges of articles. Ranges are of the form:
                        number ¦ number-number.  You may use . for the
                        current article, and $ for the last article.
                        Valid commands are: j, m, M, s, S, and !.
/pattern/modifiers      Scan forward for article containing pattern
                        in the subject line. (Use ?pat? to scan back-
                        ward; append h to scan headers, a to scan en-
                        tire articles, r to scan read articles, c to
                        make case sensitive.
/pattern/modifiers:     Apply one or more commands to the set of arti-
command{:command}       cles matching pattern. Use a K modifier to
                        save entire command to the KILL file for this
                        newsgroup.  Commands m and M, if first, imply
                        an r modifier.
                        Valid commands are: j, m, M, s, S, and !.
f, F                    Submit a followup article (F = include this
                        article).
r, R                    Reply through net mail (R = include this
                        article).
s ...                   Save to file or pipe via sh.
S ...                   Save via preferred shell.
w, W                    Like s and S but save without the header.
¦ ...                   Same as s¦...
C                       Cancel this article, if yours.
^R, v                   Restart article (v=verbose).
```

^X	Restart article, rot13 mode.
c	Catch up (mark all articles as read).
^B	Back up one page.
^L	Refresh the screen. You can get back to the pager with this.
X	Refresh screen in rot13 mode.
^	Go to first unread article. Disables subject search mode.
$	Go to end of newsgroup. Disables subject search mode.
#	Print last article number.
&	Print current values of command-line switches.
&switch {switch}	Set or unset more switches.
&&	Print current macro definitions.
&&def	Define a new macro.
j	Junk this article (mark it read). Stays at end of article.
m	Mark article as still unread.
M	Mark article as still unread upon exiting newsgroup or Y command.
	[Type space to continue]
Y	Yank back articles marked temporarily read via M.
k	Mark current SUBJECT as read.
K	Mark current SUBJECT as read, and save command in KILL file.
=	List subjects of unread articles.
u	Unsubscribe to this newsgroup.
^K	Edit local KILL file (the one for this newsgroup).
q	Quit this newsgroup for now.
Q	Quit newsgroup, staying at current newsgroup.

Pager Level

Prompt: `--MORE--(<n>%)`

Paging Commands:

SP	Display the next page.
x	Display the next page decrypted (rot13).
d	Display half a page more.
CR	Display one more line.
^R,v,^X	Restart the current article (v=verbose header, ^X=rot13).

^B	Back up one page.
^L,X	Refresh the screen (X=rot13).
g pat	Go to (search forward within article for) pattern.
G	Search again for current pattern within article.
^G	Search for next line beginning with "Subject:".
TAB	Search for next line beginning with a different character.
q	Quit the pager, go to end of article. Leave article read or unread.
j	Junk this article (mark it read). Goes to end of article.
	The following commands skip the rest of the current article, then behave just as if typed to the 'What next?' prompt at the end of the article:
n	Scan forward for next unread article.
N	Go to next article.
^N	Scan forward for next unread article with same title.
p,P,^P	Same as n, N, ^N, only going backward.
-	Go to previously displayed article.

The following commands also take you to the end of the article.
Type h at end of article for a description of these commands:

    # $ & / = ? c C f F k K ^K m M number r R ^R s S u v w W Y ^ ¦

(To return to the middle of the article after one of these commands, type ^L.)

9

Reading News with *vnews*

In chapter 6, we mentioned that the three news reading programs do not all use the same kind of *interface*, or way of communicating with the user. The `readnews` program, as we have seen, does not use any particular terminal features but just prints lines one after the other. The `rn` program does use highlighting and other terminal features, but it is still essentially *line-oriented*. What does that mean? In a line-oriented program, the programs interact with you by following a sequence like this:

Prompt for next command.

Print lines in response to command.

Prompt again.

This sequence continues until you quit. Regardless of what is printed (an article header, part of the text of an article, information about a newsgroup, etc.), the lines simply scroll upward and gradually disappear. No information is kept permanently on the screen for reference.

In this chapter, we will look at a different way of doing things, one you may like better. The `vnews` (visual news) program, is a *screen-oriented* news reading program. It interacts with you like this:

Display a screen with context prompt and information.

Update screen in response to a command.

Prompt again with new context.

Why *vnews*?

The way that vnews handles a display has some real advantages. While the text you are looking at (an article header, the body of an article, etc.) changes with the command you give, vnews always keeps you informed about which newsgroup you are in, the numbers of the current and the last articles, and whether there is more text to be seen in the current article. You always know where you are. We think you will find that, even though the actual functions offered by vnews are very similar to those in readnews, the "feel" of the program is quite different.

Like rn, vnews may not be available on all systems that belong to USENET. Still, it is widespread and popular because of its ease of use. You may find that it is all the news program you need.

Terminal and Speed Considerations

Screen-oriented programs such as vnews can have some disadvantages, however. Like vi, vnews requires that you have, or are able to emulate, a terminal supported by your UNIX system. If you are using a simple dial-up connection without basic terminal functions, you won't be able to use vnews. Most users these days have terminal capabilities, however.

Even if you have a terminal, you have to "tell" the UNIX system about it. If you don't, vnews will probably exit with an obscure message about a particular terminal function not being defined. Should this happen, you need to tell UNIX what terminal you are using or emulating. If you are using the Bourne Shell, you can put these commands in your .profile file:

```
TERM=terminal type
export TERM
```

where terminal type is the name of the terminal you are using. For example, if you have a VT100:

```
TERM=VT100
export TERM
```

If you are using the C Shell, you would enter a line like this in your .login file:

```
setenv TERM VT100
```

As a general rule, if you have been running vi, you should be able to run vnews without further setup. That is because both programs use your defined terminal setting.

Another disadvantage of screen-oriented programs is that they tend to run slowly on slow systems. What do we mean by "slow"? It's a combination of two factors: how many users are on the system and how fast characters can be sent to you. On dial-up lines, a 1200-baud rate can be too slow, especially if there are a lot of users on the system. The best way to judge efficiency is to try the program for a while and see if you are spending a lot of time waiting for the screen to be updated.

Starting *vnews*

Now let's see how `vnews` works. Start up the program by typing the word `vnews`. The opening screen will look like figure 9-1.

The newsgroup in which you start will depend on whether you have a `.newsrc` file and on which newsgroups happen to have news. If you have been

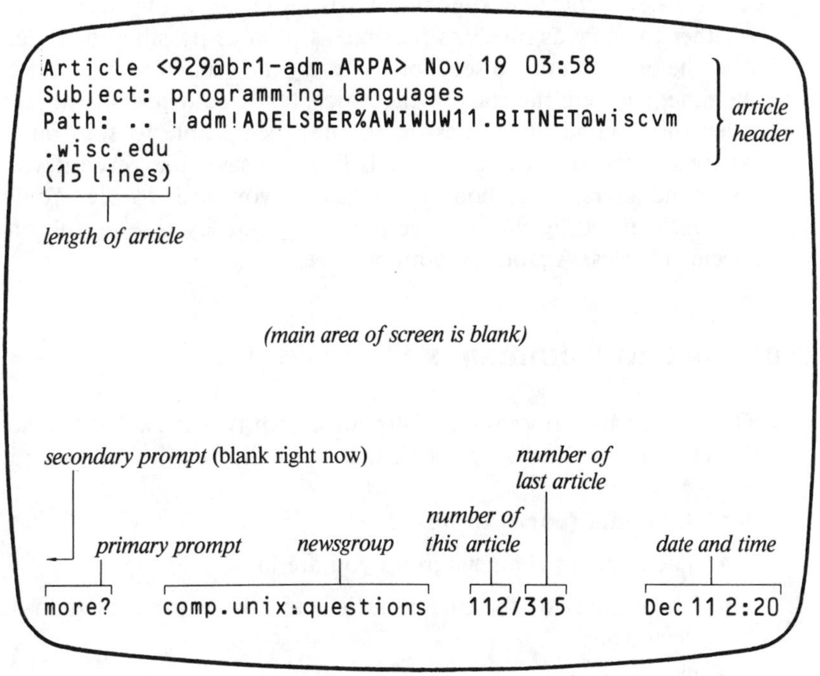

Figure 9-1. Screen display for **vnews**.

reading these chapters in order, you already have a `.newsrc` file. If you don't have a `.newsrc`, `vnews` will start one for you. It will do this without displaying any messages: there will simply be a pause of a few minutes. (We know that the lack of messages is puzzling, and we agree that it would be better if `vnews` gave you some idea what it was doing while it was constructing the `.newsrc`.)

The *vnews* Screen Display

If you look at figure 9-1, you will see that an article header is at the top of the screen, followed by the length of the article (15 lines in this case). A prompt line appears at the bottom of the screen. The `vnews` screen has two parts: the text area and the prompt area. When you start `vnews`, the text area contains the header for the first article found that meets the criteria in your `.newsrc` (or that you specified by command-line options or environmental variables). The header is actually only a part of the full header information for the article, but it gives you the parts you most often need: the article's unique ID number, its subject, and the path it took to arrive at your system.

The rest of the text area (the main part of the screen) is empty when you first reach a new article. A fundamental issue in designing news reading programs is whether to show as much as possible as soon as possible, or to let the user decide when he or she wants to see more. If everyone wanted to read most articles most of the time, showing the start of the article text would save keystrokes and time. But, given the volume of articles on the net, being able to skip quickly past articles whose subjects don't interest you is likely to save time, even if you have to issue a command to read the body of an article you wish to see. You may prefer `rn`'s approach of letting you browse the newsgroup by title or subject before reading specific articles. Again, try both and see.

Prompts and Commands in *vnews*

The prompt area in `vnews` actually consists of two lines. The *primary prompt* line is the very bottom line of the screen. It normally has the following information:

- A prompt (`more?` or `next?`).
- The name of the newsgroup you are in.
- The number of the current article and the number of the last article in the newsgroup.
- The current date and time.

In Figure 9-1, the prompt is `more?`. As we saw, `vnews` first shows only the header of a new article. The prompt is asking whether you want to see more on this article: in this case, the beginning of the actual article text. Typing a space or pressing Return at the `more?` prompt always shows you the next screenfull of text. If you read through an article and reach the last screenfull of text, the prompt changes to `next?` ("Do you want to see the *next* article?").

Note that the newsgroup and your place within it (via article numbers) are always shown, regardless of which part of an article you are looking at. This means that, unlike `readnews`, `vnews` does not require you to issue a special command to find out which newsgroup you are in and aproximately how many articles remain to be read in it.

By the way, `vnews` will also tell you if you receive mail during your news reading session. It will display the word `MAIL` at the end of the main prompt line for 30 seconds, and it will beep. This is simply an advisory signal, and you don't have to do anything about it unless you want to read your mail before continuing with news. Because `vnews`, in common with the other news reading programs, has a shell escape command (`!`), you can type `!mail` at the `vnews` prompt to read your mail (assuming your mail program is `mail`). When you exit `mail`, you'll be back in `vnews` without having lost your place!

There is also a *secondary prompt* line just above the main prompt line. Right now, it's blank. Certain commands require that you supply `vnews` with additional information, such as the name of a newsgroup or a file. The secondary prompt line is used for prompting for this information. It is also used to show error messages, such as the message that occurs when you ask to go to a newsgroup that does not exist.

Entering Commands in *vnews*

In chapter 7 you saw that commands entered in `readnews` had to be followed with a Return. This is not so for `vnews`. The `vnews` program normally acts on your keystrokes as soon as they are received. In this respect, `vnews` behaves like `vi` in command mode. Like commands in the other news reading programs, most `vnews` commands are single keystrokes, but there are some control character commands (that is, you must press the control key and type one other key). Most of your commands will not be echoed to the screen, so don't be alarmed if nothing appears to happen for a moment. (However, in our listings we will show the typed commands so that you can see which commands were given.)

Control-Character Commands

Note that notations such as `^B` are control-character commands. The caret (^) stands for the Control key. Thus, you would enter this command by holding down the Control key and typing the character *b*. By the way, we use capital letters for these commands to keep our notation consistent with the `vnews` documentation. You do not have to type capital letters for control-character commands. It is much easier to just press the Control key and type the lowercase letter. Case *does* matter for most of the other commands, however.

In addition, many commands take a *count*—a number telling vnews how many times to perform the command. You simply type the number, then the command. For example, the command ^F (Control-f) means to move forward one page in the current article. The command 3^F (a 3 followed by a Control-f) means to move three pages forward.

In a moment, we'll discuss all of these commands systematically and give examples of them.

vnews Commands and *readnews* Commands

If you read chapter 7, you will soon see that many of the commands used by vnews are the same as those used in readnews. The main difference is that vnews uses screen-oriented paging commands that are different from the line-oriented ones used by readnews. The prompting, as you have seen, is also different. And there are a few additional useful commands, such as the one that shows the "parent" article to which the current article is a response. To see a list of all the vnews commands and a brief explanation, type ? at any prompt, and you will see the display shown in figure 9-2.

```
Vnews commands:    (each may be preceded by a non-negative count)

CR Next page or article                   D  Decrypt a rot 13 joke
n  Go to next article                     A  Go to article numbered count
e  Mark current article as unread         <  Go to article with given ID
+  Go forward count articles              p  Go to parent article
-  Go to previous article                 ug Unsubscribe to this group
^B Go backward count pages                ^L Redraw screen
^N Go forward count lines                 v  Print netnews version
^P Go backward count lines                q  Quit
^D Go forward half a page                 x  Quit without updating .newsrc
^U Go backward half a page                c  Cancel the current article
h  Display article header                 H  Display all article headers
!  Escape to shell                        ?  Display this message
r  Reply to article using editor          K  Mark rest of newsgroup read
R  Reply--put current article in reply    b  Go back 1 article in same group
ESC-r Reply directly using mailer         m  Move on to next item in a digest
f  Post a followup article                s  Save article in file
N  Go to newsgroup (next is default)      w  Save without header
l  Display article
   (use after !, r, f, or ?)

[Press 1 to see article again]

more?              rec.games.board 4/11              Dec 16 3:24
```

Figure 9-2. The **vnews** help display.

Reading an Article

As we mentioned earlier, the prompt line begins with either `more?` or `next?`. Pressing Return or the space bar is a "yes" response to the prompt. In figure 9-1 we were looking at an article header. Pressing Return at the `more?` prompt changes the display to that shown in figure 9-3.

```
Article <929@brl-adm.ARPA> Nov 19 03:58
Subject: programming languages
Path: ..!adm!ADELBER%AWIWUW11.BITNET@wiscvm.wisc.edu
(15 lines)

We are setting up a new lab for teaching programming languages
and program language design. We have a micro-vax using UNIX 4.2
BSD. We urgently need compilers and interpreters (public-domain
or not too expensive) for general-purpose programming languages
such as ADA, Apl, C, CSP, FP, Hope, Lisp, Miranda, Modula, Occam,
Prolog, Smalltalk, Setl, Snobol, Sasl, etc.

Any help is appreciated.

Demuth, Technische Universitaet Wien
(College of Engineering, Vienna)

Please send your answers to:
adelsberawiwuw11 (bitnet, earn)

next?       comp.unix.questions 112/315       Dec 11 2:21
```

Figure 9-3. Display of article text.

Starting *vnews* and Reading Articles

`vnews options`	Start up `vnews` with possible options (discussed later). At the `more?` prompt, the following commands may be entered:
`Return` or `space`	Print text of current article.
`q`	Quit `vnews`; update `.newsrc`.
`x`	Quit `vnews`; don't update `.newsrc`.
`?`	Show help information.

The text of the article now appears on the screen. Note that the header area has not changed. There are two minor changes in the prompt area at the bottom of the screen. The prompt is `next?`, and the time has changed. As the line below the header indicates, this article is only 15 lines long, so it fits on one screen. Therefore, `vnews` asks if you want to see the next article. Of course, you may not want to move on to the next article yet, and you can still issue commands that affect the article you have just displayed, as we'll see later. Commands dealing with articles in the same newsgroup or with other newsgroups can be issued at either prompt.

Instead of pressing Return or the space bar (to see the next screenfull of text) at the `more?` or `next?` prompt, you can choose to quit `vnews`. Type `q` to quit and update your `.newsrc`, or type `x` to quit without updating the `.newsrc`.

Moving within an Article

There are of course many articles that are too long to fit on one screen. Figure 9-4 shows an article that is 37 lines long.

Note that the prompt in the lower left-hand corner of the screen is now `more(40%)?`, meaning that 40% of the full text of the article has been displayed so far. (The `vnews` program permits you to set a different pager if you want. We will discuss this later. Your system may use a different default pager, such as the System V `pg` program, so your prompt may be different.)

Commands for Moving within an Article in *vnews*

`Return` or `space`	See more of current article.
`^F`	Go forward (down) a page.
`^B`	Go backward (up) a page.
`^D`	Go forward (down) half a page.
`^U`	Go backward (up) half a page.
`^N`	Go forward a line.
`^Y`	Go backward a line.

(Note: to move more than one page or line, precede the command with the number of times you want to move.)

`^L`	Redraw the screen.
`h`	Go back to beginning of current article.
`H`	Print complete header information about article.

If you want to continue reading the text of the article, simply press Return or the space bar at the `more?` prompt. The next screenfull of text will be shown. Note that, although the header information at the top disappears (it's treated as part of the first page of the article), the most essential information (amount of text remaining to be seen, newsgroup, article number, last article number in newsgroup) is still shown on the bottom line. You still know where you are. (See figure 9-5.)

In `readnews`, you can return to the beginning of an article and reread it, but it's not easy to move back and forth within the article unless you specify a pager like `more` and use pager commands. In `vnews`, you can move around in the current article much as you would with `vi`'s long-range cursor movement commands. Indeed, if you know `vi`, you already know most of these commands!

For example, in the last listing we had reached the end of the article. Suppose we weren't sure about one aspect of the author's problem, and we wanted to go back and reread. Typing `^B` (Control-b) will move us back one page in the article, as shown in figure 9-6.

You can move "up" (backward) or "down" (forward) by a full page, a half page, or a line.

```
Article <3439@sdcrdcf.UUCP> Nov 18 17:06
Subject: Massive mysterious file system corruption on 4.2bsd
Path: ..!sdcrdcf!davem (David Melman @ System Development
Corporation R&D, Santa Monica)
Newsgroups: comp.unix.questions,comp.unix.wizards
(37 lines)

I have encountered a most mysterious and serious problem
on our UNIX 4.2bsd on a Vax 750.

The symptom is the string "Login timed out after 60 seconds", which
is being written seemingly arbitrarily to files throughout
all file systems. This includes binaries and DIRECTORIES.

I know this line comes from login.c if the user waits
more than a minute before finishing his password.

I have only one lead.
We have a DMZ-32 whose ports are connected to what we call a
Terminal Consentrator (TC) which in turn is connected to a custom lan.
Mistakenly, a couple of ports on this TC were configured as terminal-ports
instead of host-ports. They therefore carried on this infinite conversation

more (40%)?          comp.unix.questions 113/315       Dec 11 2:23
```

Figure 9-4. An article too long for one screen.

Special Reading Commands

Both `readnews` and `rn` require a special command to break a digest article into its component articles. (A *digest article* is a group of articles packed into one big article for space-saving and stylistic purposes.) The `vnews` program breaks down digest articles automatically, however. The `m` command is then used to move to the next article in the digest. Each article in the digest can be dealt with as though it were a separate article.

Jokes that are possibly offensive, as well as "spoilers" and clues, are often encrypted with a simple cipher. The command to decrypt an encrypted article is also the same as in `readnews`. The `D` command in `vnews` assumes that all encryption is "rot 13"; that is, that the encrypted letters are located thirteen alphabet positions past the original ones, rotating past the end of the alphabet if necessary.

Special Reading Commands in *vnews*

`m`	Move to next part of a digest.
`D`	Decrypt an encrypted article.

Filing the Current Article

The commands in `vnews` for saving the current article for later use are the same as in `readnews`. They do give us a chance to see how `vnews` uses the secondary prompt, however. Let's type `s` to save the current article. As soon as we press the `s` key, a prompt appears in the secondary prompt line:

```
file:
more? s             comp.unix.questions 135/335        Dec 12 2:42
```

(We'll omit all but the bottom of the screen in this and many of the following examples in order to save space.)

```
file: temp
more?               comp.unix.questions 135/335        Dec 12 2:42
```

Here, we typed `temp`, followed by a Return, at the `file:` prompt. (Note that, on the secondary prompt line, you *do* have to end your input with a Return so that `vnews` will know that you're done.) When we are finished, a message immediately appears to tell us what was done:

```
file: temp created
more?               comp.unix.questions 135/335        Dec 12 2:42
```

```
with the getty and login processes. For example, login would write "login:"
to the TC, the TC would respond "invalid command," then login would
prompt for a password and wait 60 seconds, and then write the incriminating
string "Login timed out after 60 seconds", and so on.

The DMZ driver is a 4.3 driver from Chris Torek.

Since directories also are being written on, something not allowed
by user processes, the kernel is suspect. My only guess is that
buffers are being screwed up somewhere and disk drivers (UDA50)
are writing bogus stuff out.

We are now rebuilding, hoping that the DMZ-TC cycling was responsible.

Please mail me any advice.
Thank-you.

David Melman
SDC - Santa Monica
A UNISYS COMPANY :^)

UUCP: {hplabs,ihnp4}!sdcrdcf!davem

next?              comp.unix.questions 113/315      Dec 11 2:25
```

Figure 9-5. Continuation of an article.

In this case, the `temp` file was created because it did not already exist. If the file had already existed, the message would have said "appended."

This kind of interaction is used with all `vnews` commands that require the user to type a string supplying further information (usually a filename, a newsgroup name, or an article number).

Commands to Dispose of Articles in *vnews*

`s filename`	Save articles (with header) to a file.
`w filename`	Save articles (without header) to a file.
`e`	Mark current article as unread.

```
is being written seemingly arbitrarily to files throughout
all file systems. This includes binaries and DIRECTORIES.

I know this line comes from login.c if the user waits
more than a minute before finishing his password.

I have only one lead.
We have a DMZ-32 whose ports are connected to what we call a
Terminal Consentrator (TC) which in turn is connected to a custom lan.
Mistakenly, a couple of ports on this TC were configured as terminal-ports
instead of host-ports. They therefore carried on this infinite conversation
with the getty and login processes. For example, login would write "login:"
to the TC, the TC would respond "invalid command," then login would
prompt for a password and wait 60 seconds, and then write the incriminating
string "Login timed out after 60 seconds", and so on.

The DMZ driver is a 4.3 driver from Chris Torek.

Since directories also are being written on, something not allowed
by user processes, the kernel is suspect. My only guess is that
buffers are being screwed up somewhere and disk drivers (UDA50)
are writing bogus stuff out.

more (70%)?          comp.unix.questions 113/315        Dec. 11 2:27
```

Figure 9-6. Moving back in an article.

Responding to an Article

The basic command for responding by mail to an article is `r`. It works exactly the same as it does in `readnews`. You are positioned in the default or the specified editor, and a header containing three lines (*To:*, *Subject:*, and *References:*) is constructed from the header of the article to which you are replying. As we will discuss in chapter 10, you should edit these lines if they are no longer appropriate (for example, if your response moves the discussion to a different subject).

The `R` command (found in `vnews` but not in `readnews`) works the same way, but it adds the text of the article to which you are replying to the message you are constructing. You should edit this text so that only enough of the article remains to identify the point in contention.

The `ESC-r` command puts you directly in the mailer rather than the editor. It is the same as the `rd` command in `readnews`, and is entered by pressing the Escape key and lowercase `r`. Using the `ESC-r` command speeds things up for quick messages, and getting the editor from most mailers is easy enough if you do need it.

The `l` command is useful when you have written something (a mail message or a reply article) or have used a shell escape to perform some UNIX commands. It restores the text of the current header or article to the screen.

Commands for Replying to Articles in *vnews*

`r`	Reply to article's author by mail.
`R`	Reply with article body included in reply message.
`ESC-r`	Reply directly in mailer, not editor.
`l`	Redisplay the article after follow-up or reply.
`c`	Cancel an article you have written.

Moving within the Newsgroup

The `vnews` commands for moving through the articles in a newsgroup are also similar to those used in `readnews`. Remember that if you are looking at the header of an article (the `more?` prompt) and don't want to read the article, you should type `n` to skip to the next article.

By now, you should be familiar with moving through the articles in a newsgroup. As we noted earlier, responding with a space or a Return to the `next?` prompt displays the header of the next article in the current newsgroup. The `b` command goes back to the previous article, as in `readnews`. The `-` command toggles to the previously displayed article, as in `readnews`.

The command to go to an article with the specified sequential number is a bit different. In `readnews`, you just type the article number. In `vnews`, you type the article number followed by `A` (it must be uppercase).

The `+` command for skipping a specified number of articles works the same as it does in `readnews`, but you first type the number of articles that you want to skip, then type the `+`. Like counts, article numbers precede the command involved.

```
more? 5+          comp.lang.c 197/517                Dec 21 5:50
more?             comp.lang.c 202/517                Dec 21 5:52
```

Here, we typed `5+` to move ahead five articles. (The count, 5, is echoed, but the command itself, `+`, is not.) Notice that the article number for the current article has changed from 197 to 202.

The rest of the commands are similar to their `readnews` counterparts, with some exceptions. First, there is a command, `<`, which allows you to jump to the article whose ID you specify. Remember that the ID is the one displayed in the header, not the sequential number within the newsgroup:

```
<954@zeus.UUCP
more? <              comp.lang.c 500/527                 Dec 22 11:31
```

As soon as we typed the `<`, it disappeared and then reappeared on the secondary prompt line as a prompt. We typed in the message ID next. If the article is found, it becomes the current article. This command is also case-sensitive; for example, `<954@zeus.uucp` will not match. One good use of this command is to save selected articles to a file for reading at your leisure. When you're ready to reply, you can go to the appropriate newsgroup with the `N` command (discussed later), issue a `<` command, and then use the reply commands to reply to the article.

Moving within the Newsgroup in *vnews*

`n` or `.`	Skip to the next article; don't print the current one.
`b`	Go back to the previous article.
`-`	Go back to the previous article shown (toggle).
`number A`	Go to the article with the specified sequential number.
`number+`	Skip forward the specified number of articles; record skipped articles as unread.
`p`	Show parent of current article.
`<`	Prompts for message ID; tries to find that article.
`K`	Mark as read the rest of the articles in the newsgroup; go to next newsgroup.
`ug`	Unsubscribe to current newsgroup.

The `p` command is interesting: it tries to find the "parent" of the current article. If the current article is a reply to another article, the *parent article* is the article to which it is a reply. If `vnews` finds the parent article, the parent becomes the current article and is displayed. If the parent article cannot be found, you are told so. Sometimes, for example, an article may have a parent that is no longer available because it is more than two weeks old and has been removed from the newsgroup. Here's how the `p` command works:

```
Article <3813@utcsri.UUCP> Fri 12:08
Subject: Re: ANSI C -- static forward references
Path: ..!utcsri!greg (Gregory Smith @ CSRI, University of Toronto)
(50 lines)
```

```
(blank lines here)

more? p               comp.lang.c 500/527              Dec 22 11:28
```

(We've left out the blank lines from the text area.) When we type `p`, `vnews` very briefly displays the article ID of the parent article (if found) on the secondary prompt line.

```
<114@decvax.UUCP>
more? p               comp.lang.c 500/527              Dec 22 11:28
```

Then the parent article becomes the current article:

```
Article <114@decvax.UUCP> Tue 15:29
Subject: Re: ANSI C -- static forward references
Path: ..!decvax!minow (Martin Minow @ Ultrix Eng. Group - Merrimack, NH)
(13 lines)

(blank lines)

more?                 comp.lang.c 447/527              Dec 22 11:29
```

The `p` command is useful for returning to the article that originally triggered a discussion. Sometimes, as in the preceding case, the parent article is itself a response to an earlier article. You can then use the `p` command with that article to continue tracing the discussion to the original parent. Unfortunately, there is no `vnews` command that will allow you to follow a thread of replies to a given article by moving forward.

Finally, note that the "unsubscribe" command for `vnews` is `ug`, not plain `u` as in `readnews`. This was done to make it harder to enter this command by mistake.

Moving between Newsgroups

The `N` command for moving to a new newsgroup works the same as in `readnews`:

```
group? comp.lang.c++
more? N               comp.lang.c 202/517              Dec 21 5:53
```

As soon as you type `N`, a prompt appears, asking for the group you want. You will be placed in the newsgroup `comp.lang.c++`, assuming it has news in it. If you simply press Return instead of specifying a group, you will be placed in the next newsgroup listed in your `.newsrc` file.

Moving between Newsgroups in *vnews*

`N`	Go to next newsgroup.
`N name`	Go to named newsgroup.

Shell Escape

Our miscellaneous (but useful) category includes the shell escape command, `!`, already discussed in connection with mail. As with `readnews`, this command has a built-in shell variable, `$A`, which is set to the name of the file containing the current article. Thus, you could, if you wanted to, type `!cp $A savefile`. This would save the current article to the `savefile` file, although the `vnews` command `s savefile` would be easier. If you type `!` without specifying a UNIX command, you get your default shell. You can type a Control-d when you're done entering commands to that shell, and you'll be back in `vnews`.

Options and Variables in *vnews*

The `vnews` program recognizes many of the same options and environmental variables used by `readnews`. If you are not sure how to use them, you may want to reread the general discussion of options and variables at the end of chapter 6 and also the description of `readnews` options and variables at the end of chapter 7.

Command-Line Options in *vnews*

The `vnews` command-line options are essentially a subset of those available in `readnews`. We will just list them here in the screened box; see chapter 7 for examples of how they work.

Note that these options can also be specified in the `options` line of your `.newsrc` or in the value of the `NEWSOPTS` environmental variable. If you are not clear about how to do this, see the end of chapter 6 and the options discussion for `readnews` in chapter 7.

Command-Line Options in *vnews*

`-n newsgroups`	Select named newsgroup(s).
`!newsgroups`	Omit named newsgroup(s).
`-t strings`	Select articles whose titles contain string(s).
`-a date`	Select articles posted after date specified.
`-r`	Show articles in reverse order (latest to earliest).
`-p`	Send everything found to standard output; don't wait for interactive commands.
`-x`	Ignore `.newsrc` file, show both read and unread articles.
`-u`	Update `.newsrc` every five minutes.
`-s`	Print site subscription list.
`-c`	Show first page of each article immediately (not just header).

Environmental Variables in *vnews*

The `vnews` environmental variables allow you to specify editor, pager, default news directory, and so on. These are nearly all the same as in `readnews`. As in `readnews`, you can also set the options given under command-line options to be the value of the variable `NEWSOPTS`. The screened box lists the environmental variables for `vnews`.

Most of these variables are the same as those in `readnews`, so we refer you to the options section of chapter 7 if you have questions or want to see examples of proper syntax. Remember that the way you set the variables depends on whether you are using the Bourne Shell or the C Shell. (The example of setting your terminal type at the beginning of this chapter shows the respective syntaxes for the two shells.)

The `NEWSARCHIVE` variable is not found in `readnews`. It is handy in `vnews` because it enables you to automatically generate an "author copy" of any article that you write. For example, the line:

```
NEWSARCHIVE = "sentnews" ; export NEWSARCHIVE
```

in your `.profile` file will cause copies of any articles you write to be placed in the file `sentnews`. If you don't give a value to `NEWSARCHIVE`, articles will be saved in the file `author_copy` in your home directory. Note that articles are appended to the specified file, not overwritten.

Environmental Variables in *vnews*

`NEWSOPTS`	Any of the preceding command-line options.
`EDITOR`	Pathname of default editor to use for replies.
`MAILER`	Pathname of default mailer to use for mailed replies.
`PAGER`	Pathname of pager to use for seeing the article text.
`NEWSARCHIVE`	File to send copies of articles you write.
`NEWSBOX`	File or directory name to use in saving articles.
`NEWSRC`	Filename to use as news record instead of `.newsrc`.
`NAME`	Full name to identify you in articles you write.
`ORGANIZATION`	Name of your organization to be used in articles you write.

The `NEWSRC` option is not found in `readnews` either. It specifies an alternative to `.newsrc`. It is useful if you want to switch between different sets of newsgroups and other options. For example, you might want to read all the `comp.` groups on company time, but the `rec.` and `soc.` groups on your own time.

Summary

The `vnews` program is a good alternative to `readnews` if you have a terminal and a fast enough line to use with it. It has most of the power of `readnews`, with a user interface that many people prefer. You might consider using it to introduce your colleagues to the joys of USENET. In light of our positive appraisal of `vnews`, you might wonder why we didn't choose it as the first news program to introduce in this book. The reason is that some sites may not have `vnews`, whereas `readnews` is everywhere that USENET is.

In chapter 10, you will learn how you can take a more active role in using USENET. We will show you how to post original articles on the net and how to write news that other people will be able to appreciate.

10

Posting News with *postnews*

The last three chapters concentrated on the mechanics of using the various news reading programs. This chapter features `postnews`, the program most commonly used for posting news articles. Before we begin our discussion of `postnews`, however, let's step back and look at the art of communication, USENET style.

Netiquette: USENET with Grace and Style

As we strive to master the technology of electronic writing and communication, it is easy to lose sight of the importance of the fact that we are communicating with other human beings. In any sort of written communication, including USENET, there are basic questions to be answered before our words are ready to give to the world. What audience are we trying to reach? How can we ensure that our article will be accessible to this audience? What is the best way to respond to others' communications? While we won't presume to teach you how to master the art of communication in this book, we will examine the unique matters of style and convention that aid communication on the USENET.

Like all communities, USENET has evolved a group of customs that many people will expect you to observe. These are not laws: the software will not eject you if you violate them, and the authorities will not break down your door in the night and confiscate your modem. In fact, there is a great deal of freedom of expression on USENET, as you have no doubt observed if you have been reading many newsgroups. Much of the value of USENET lies in the diversity of voices found there. USENET customs and practices are not a censorship of ideas, but rather a collective judgment about what is the best use of the net. Such judgment involves questions like these:

- Should I reply to an article by e-mail or by posting?
- How widely should I distribute my posting?
- Which newsgroup or newsgroups should I use for my posting?
- How can I make my article easy for interested people to recognize?
- How can I promote fruitful discussion rather than name-calling?
- How can I help conserve computer resources and keep phone costs down?

Where to Read about Netiquette

The collection of recommended practices for USENET is often called *net etiquette*, or *netiquette*. Although we will cover the basics of netiquette here, if you have not already done so, we strongly recommend that you read the standard articles on netiquette. These are kept permanently available on the net for the benefit of new users (and revised occasionally). Two such articles available at the time of writing are "A Primer on How to Work with the USENET Community," by Chuq Von Rospach, and "Everything You Always Wanted to Know about Network Etiquette (but didn't know whom to ask)," by Chris Andersen. These and other articles will provide a wealth of tips on netiquette as well as answers to common questions and bits of net trivia. A more general article on the use of USENET, "How to Read the Network News," by Mark Horton, also has useful advice. See Appendix D for some other good references on USENET matters, as well as references to the newsgroups where these articles can be found.

Much of this material is found in the newsgroup `news.announce.newusers`. The basic netiquette material is put in the special "newuser" groups in hopes that people new to USENET will read the articles before becoming active news posters. We recommend that you reread the articles and this chapter after you have been actively using USENET for a few weeks. Many of the tips and guidelines will make more sense after you have seen more of the typical problem situations.

Replying to Articles

A good way to practice your news writing is to reply to articles that interest you. If you have read the preceding chapters, you have learned that `readnews`, `rn`, and `vnews` all have commands that allow you either to reply directly to an article's author by electronic mail (e-mail) or to post a follow-up article that everyone can read. In fact, you may have already begun to reply to articles. Now we will look in greater depth at the why and how of replies.

The first question to ask is: "How should we reply to this article?" The basic rule for deciding how to reply is this: The reply should be by e-mail to the author unless the response is (1) likely to be of general interest to the readers of the newsgroup in question or (2) not likely to be duplicated by other responses.

How to Reply: Some Examples

The best way to see how this rule works in practice is to look at some typical situations. If you have been reading the news for a while, you probably have seen many examples of postings that can cause problems.

Want Ads

One kind of article that almost always calls for an e-mail response is the want ad. These postings are found in newsgroups such as `ca.wanted` (California items for sale or wanted) or `misc.wanted` (net-wide items for sale or wanted). Here's an example:

```
Subject: Car for sale
Keywords: 1981 Cadillac Eldorado
Newsgroups: ba.wanted,ba.general
--------
(9 lines) More? [ynq] y
1981 Cadillac Eldorado

Moon roof, digital, new Michelin tires, all extras. Immaculate,
runs great.

        $8995.
```

(By the way, we will be omitting personal information and information irrelevant to our topic (such as paths and organization names) from most of the examples in this chapter. We don't want to embarrass anyone whose article we've chosen to illustrate a problem in news writing. We also strongly doubt that the particular Cadillac offered in the example will still be available at the time you read this.)

There is no problem with the ad itself. It is clear and awaits the response of interested parties. The question is how to reply. If we want to start dickering for the car, an e-mail message or a telephone call (the author provided a phone number that we omitted) is obviously the way to go. Following the guideline given above, we can see that our interest in the car is not of general interest to other net users, so posting a follow-up article would be inappropriate.

Suppose, though, that we are somewhat interested in this car but want more information, such as what the car's gas mileage is, and whether the engine has been rebuilt. Should we post a reply article? Probably not. The reason is that if people get in the habit of posting reply articles asking for pieces of information about such want ads, there are likely to be many duplicate postings. Since it can take many days for an article to propagate through the net, it can be quite a while before everyone has seen the first follow-up query, let alone the author's reply. Many people might post queries thinking that the question has not occurred to anyone else. The result is that the newsgroup will become crowded, and it will become harder for people to flip through the want ads. By satisfying your need for information by posting a follow-up, you succeed only in making it harder for many other people to find information in the newsgroup. And remember that each posted article adds an increment to the telephone expense, CPU time, and storage space involved with each site.

Instead of posting a follow-up article, use the mail reply command of your news reading program and send an e-mail query to the author with your questions about the car. (In `readnews`, for example, you would use the `r` or `rd` command.) If the author receives several such questions, he or she can then post a single reply article making this additional information available to all interested parties. The result is that the net doesn't get cluttered up with dozens of articles asking what the mileage on this particular Caddy is, and this saves computer resources (for storing and processing the reply articles) and telephone charges (for transmitting the articles). It also saves human resources: people don't have to wade through a ton of replies on their way to the next substantial article. Keeping the volume of traffic in a newsgroup to a manageable size encourages people to read it. Important and interesting postings (such as yours!) are less likely to be lost in the noise. Keeping costs down and information content high encourages the backbone sites, which pay the largest cost for carrying a given newsgroup, to continue carrying the newsgroup. Everyone benefits.

Flames

A *flame* is the USENET term for an article that essentially involves an opinion held so strongly and fanatically that its author seems to be shouting rather than communicating. Since a flame is often a response to another article, we are discussing it in this section so that you'll know how to handle one without getting burnt. A typical flame might arise out of a situation like this. Some people on the net are having a nice, quiet discussion about future trends in MS-DOS when this article is posted as a follow-up to one of their articles:

```
Subject: Re MS-DOS trends for the future
Summary: MS-DOS is brain-damaged.
Newsgroups: comp.sys.ibm-pc,comp.os

     Why are you bothering to talk about the future of MS-DOS?
It has no future! It's brain-damaged. Only pea brains would
bother to develop MS-DOS software. Why are you wasting our time
with your drivel...
```

You can see that such responses don't promote a fruitful dialogue on operating systems, or any other subject for that matter. It's important to note that what makes this response a flame is not the fact that its author hates MS-DOS. Rather, it is the fact that he or she is making a personal attack on the author of the original article ("only pea brains"). Someone who held a similar opinion on MS-DOS could have written a much more constructive response that still made the desired points:

```
Subject: Re MS-DOS trends for the future
Summary: MS-DOS has a very limited future.
Newsgroups: comp.sys.ibm-pc,comp.os

     In my opinion, MS-DOS as we've known (and perhaps loved)
has in reality a limited future. The needs of multitasking large
memory systems can be better met by a derivative of UNIX,
particularly if it can run MS-DOS software as well...
```

You may or may not agree with this response, but further discussion seems possible. Therefore, the rule is: Don't post flames. If you really don't like someone personally, you can send them e-mail to that effect and take the consequences. Extensive flaming in a newsgroup can lead to readers staying away from it in droves, and perhaps to the group being dropped from the net.

This does not mean that you cannot express opinions forcefully, however. Again, you should be sensitive to the purpose of the newsgroup you are working in. Users of the `comp.` newsgroups, for example, usually expect a high standard of communication comparable to other professional communications, although perhaps not as stuffy. The `talk` groups are more freewheeling, especially the ones devoted to politics and philosophy. Opinions there are often more heated, and more frequently burst into flames. (One perennial battle is over abortion, another over the thought of Ayn Rand.)

Even (or especially) in the talk groups, each writer must take responsibility for his or her own words, watching the thin line between strong opinions and flames (see figure 10-1). The best advice seems to be: When in doubt, don't.

Criticizing Someone's Writing

A periodic problem on USENET is the self-appointed copy editor. Such persons pounce when they see an article such as this one:

```
Subject: Re XYZCo. UNIX implementation
Summary: We've tested our product extensively.
Newsgroups: comp.unix.wizards,comp.unix.xenix,comp.sys.ibm-pc

     In developing our version of concurrent DOS/UNIX for the IBM
PC we have taken great pains to insure compatability with
existing DOS and XENIX software. We have spent hundreds of hours
testing our product with leading products ...
```

Such articles are liable to generate replies like this:

```
Subject: Re XYZCo. UNIX implementation
Summary: You can't spell and your grammar's no good either.
Newsgroups: comp.unix.wizards,comp.unix.xenix,comp.sys.ibm-pc
```

```
> In developing our version of concurrent DOS/UNIX for the IBM
> PC we have taken great pains to insure compatability with

     It is clear you can't spell. The word is
"compatibility," not "compatability." Furthermore, you
don't "insure" something unless you are in the insurance
business, you "ensure" it ...
```

This is the infamous "spelling flame." The person who replied quoted the offending lines of the original and then pointed out the errors. While most of us want to encourage good grammar and proper spelling, this is not really an appropriate place or manner for doing so.

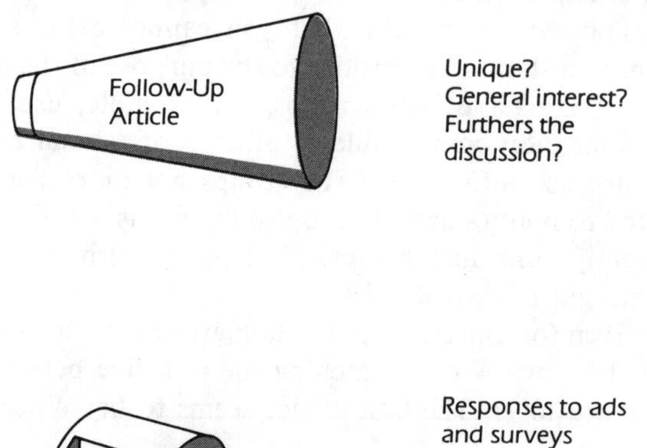

Figure 10-1. Where should a reply go?

Why is this a flame? It indirectly disparaged the author of the original article, but that is not the main problem. It is really an abuse of resources. The purpose of the newsgroups involved is the discussion of technical issues (UNIX, XENIX, IBM-PC, etc.). A "good" spelling flame can go on for dozens of replies and counter-replies. People who want to discuss UNIX implementations now have to wade through articles that contribute nothing to this discussion. Whether it is a matter of spelling, usage, or style, if you want to correct someone's writing, don't post the correction or criticism as a reply article. Send it by e-mail to the author in question. The latter may still not like you, but at least everyone else won't have to read about it.

By the way, it *is* a good idea to check your spelling (perhaps with the UNIX `spell` command), your grammar, and your presentation before posting. Besides keeping you from becoming the victim of a spelling flame, an article that shows careful writing is liable to make a better impression (possibly with that future employer . . .).

How Do You Kill the Troll?

Another kind of article that often generates wasteful responses is an article asking for specific information that many people are willing and able to provide. For example:

```
Subject: Disposing of the Troll in Dungeon of Despair
Summary: I can never get past the troll at the main gate.
Newsgroups: rec.games.misc

     I've never been able to get into the castle in the
"Dungeon of Despair" game, let alone into the dungeon. When I
confront the troll, sword in hand, it just laughs and cuts my
head off with its trusty axe ...
```

Well, hundreds of faithful Dungeon of Despair players happen to know that you can't kill the troll with something as mundane as a sword. You have to find the three-month-old Limburger cheese in the guardhouse cupboard, wave it under the troll's nose, throw it to the troll, and run past the troll while he is feasting on it. Of these hundreds of avid players, if only a dozen post follow-up articles to each such question, the newsgroup is soon filled with duplicate articles. There was nothing wrong with posting the original article. The information sought was of potential interest, given the subject matter of the newsgroup. But replies should go by e-mail to the author. After the author learns the answer, he or she can post a single reply article with the answer (or a summary of the answers).

The exception to this rule is if you want to discuss, say, the significance of the author's question rather than answer it. For example, you might reply to the preceding example with a follow-up article saying that you've sent e-mail to the author with the specific answer, but here's some general advice about monsters in Dungeon of Despair. You have thus turned the specific question into a matter of general interest about which a variety of opinions can be expressed. You have launched a new discussion. To summarize: Replies should be sent by e-mail if they involve personal business with the article author, or if they involve specific information liable to be supplied by many people. And the best place for flames is an asbestos waste basket.

When to Post Follow-up Articles

When should you post a follow-up article? Let's start with an example:

```
Subject: Accounting Software for Small Businesses
Summary: Seeking recommendations for small business accounting
software.
Newsgroups: comp.sys.mac
--------
     Can you recommend some good accounting software on the Apple
Macintosh that would be suitable for a small business that
processes about 500 transactions a week, and has a payroll of
five persons?
```

Here is a case in which there can clearly be more than one useful answer to the question. Further, it's a subjective matter where opinions can differ, and need to be justified. The discussion is likely to be of fairly general interest. Each contribution has the potential of shedding a little more light on the subject.

Now, let's say you are convinced that the Penny-Pincher Accountant program is the best solution to the author's needs. You post a reply article saying so, and why you think the program is a good choice. The article author sends you e-mail with some detailed questions about the product. Now it becomes a matter of judgment. If there's been a lot of discussion on accounting software in `comp.sys.mac` lately, you might conclude that the details are of general interest, and you might post another follow-up article. If you don't think there's a lot of interest, and the general trend of discussion lately has been desktop publishing products, you might want to continue the correspondence by e-mail. While guidelines can be useful, netiquette is ultimately a matter of sensitivity to others' needs and to the context of the newsgroup in which you are working.

Editing Headers in Follow-ups

Part of sensitivity to context is reading your follow-up in the light of what has been under discussion and where your posting may be taking the discussion. There are two areas in particular that may change as a result of the flow of the discussion: the subject and the newsgroup. Both of these appear as part of the article header, and are placed in the editor buffer for your use when you employ, for example, the `f` command in `readnews`. Let's consider a situation in which you might want to make some changes in these two header fields. Suppose you are replying to the following article, and the following header lines and text that you have written are in your editor buffer. (We'll ignore the distribution field and other fields for now.)

```
Subject: Re Information Hiding and Modularity in Ada
Newsgroups: comp.lang.ada
--------
     Many of the areas you have described are addressed by the
new C++ language, but in a much cleaner way. C++ preserves the
flexibility and control of the machine while providing
integration of data and functional structures, operator
overloading, etc. First, let's look at the "package"
concept...
```

After you wrote this response, you reread it (always a good idea!) and then considered what changes or additions might be appropriate to make in the header lines. You note that the subject has gone beyond a discussion of some Ada features to a comparative discussion of Ada and C++ with regard to how they address certain issues in language design. Thus, you went back to the headers and edited them:

```
Subject: Comparison of C++ and Ada: Modularity, Information
Hiding, and Packages
Summary: C++ provides a cleaner, leaner approach to these issues.
Keywords: Ada, C++, modularity, packages
Newsgroups: comp.lang.ada,comp.lang.c++,comp.compilers
```

You changed the subject to make it more descriptive of the content of your article. Browsers (and browsing is the main way people read news) will have a better idea of what your article is about and will be better able to decide if they want to read it.

You added `Summary:` and `Keywords:` lines to provide additional access to the article by people using the searching facilities of the news reading programs (particularly those of `rn`). These lines are optional, but they carry a lot of potentially useful information in a small amount of space, and we recommend using them.

Cross-Posting

Since your article discusses C++ at least as much as it does Ada, you added the newsgroup `comp.lang.c++` to the `Newsgroups:` line. And looking on the next page of the article, you saw that you had discussed some issues relating to compiler efficiency as well, so you also added `comp.compilers`. The article is now well described and is accessible from several vantage points. This is called *cross-posting*. Most articles (and replies) should be placed in only a single newsgroup. If something genuinely seems to belong in one or more groups, you can cross-post, but this adds somewhat to overhead on the net, so don't overpost.

On the other hand, the author of a cross-posted article sometimes specifies a single newsgroup for follow-ups. You will see this as a line that says `Followup-To:`, followed by the newsgroup name. This is an attempt to keep the discussion in one place. In this case, you don't have to worry about editing out any newsgroups on the `Newsgroups:` line; the software will automatically direct your follow-up to the specified newsgroup. See figure 10-2.

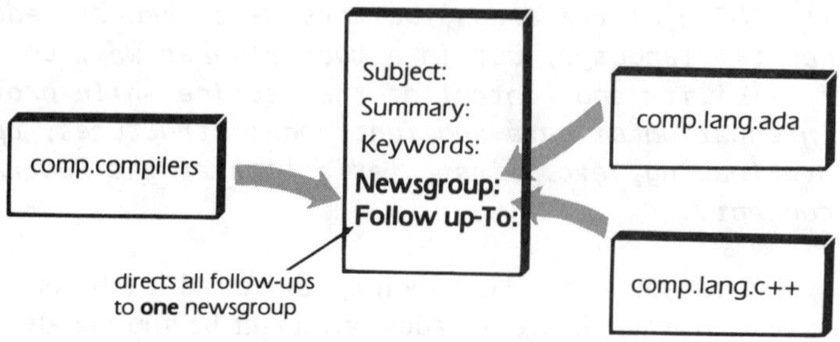

Figure 10-2. Cross-posting with directed follow-up.

When to Quote Articles in Follow-ups

You have probably noticed that portions of the article being replied to are usually included in the follow-up, typically preceded by the greater-than symbol, >. The follow-up command in most of the news reading programs gives you an opportunity to include a copy of the original article in your follow-up. For example, in `readnews`, the `f` command first asks for summary information and then asks if you want to quote the article you are replying to:

```
Please enter a short summary of your contribution to the discussion
Just one or two lines... (end with a blank line)
>   ←summary goes here
>
Do you want to include a copy of the article? y
OK, but please edit it to suppress unnecessary verbiage, signatures, etc.
```

If you say "yes," the lines of the original article, preceded by >, are inserted in your editor buffer, ready to be edited along with your reply. But `readnews` warns you that the entire article has been put in the buffer. The purpose of quoting is to provide a context for your reply (1) by showing what points in the original you are concerned with and (2) by refreshing the reader's memory about what the original said. There is much information now in the buffer that clearly does not contribute to this, such as header lines and possibly lengthy signature statements. In addition, there is probably material even in the body of the original that is not of immediate interest and that is not addressed by our reply. Thus, an important step in writing replies is to prune this extraneous material. Ideally, the result should be a summary of the relevant points in the original article, using a few well-chosen quotes.

It is discouraging to have to read through a lot of replies to an article, with each carrying a full set of quotes. If the topic is currently "hot" and other replies have kept the original in readers' minds, you can shorten your quoting because the context will be clear. Note that some of the Netnews software has implemented the *50% rule*, by which the software checks to see whether there are at least as many lines of your original material as there are lines of quoted material. It is easy to cheat this mechanism (such as by adding blank or near-blank lines), and it is not enforced universally. It is, however, a good guideline. If you find that you didn't have as much to say as you thought you did, perhaps the follow-up isn't necessary or e-mail would be better.

Here's an example of appropriate quoting using the preceding article:

```
Subject: Comparison of C++ and Ada: Modularity, Information
Hiding, and Packages
Summary: C++ provides a cleaner, leaner approach to these issues.
Keywords: Ada, C++, modularity, packages
Newsgroups: comp.lang.ada,comp.lang.c++,comp.compilers

> Thus Ada is the only language that provides an environment   ←quoted
> suitable for large software development projects where        material
> reliability is critical.
> Ada provides the powerful concept of packages...

Many of the areas you have described are addressed by the
new C++ language, but in a much cleaner way. C++
preserves the flexibility and control of the machine while
providing integration of data and functional structures, operator
overloading, etc. First, let's look at the "package" concept...
```

We quoted the conclusion of the original article and the first point we wanted to address, and then began our reply. Later, we can quote specific points from the original and intersperse them with our own comments.

There can be two or more levels of quoting. That is, if the article you are replying to is a response to an earlier article, it may already have some quoted material. Such levels of quoting are usually indicated automatically with > being the most recent material, >> being older material, and so on. Here's an example:

```
Subject: Re: Star Trek IV - Damaged Starship
Path: ..!sfsup!kumar (kumar @ AT&T Information Systems, Summit N.J.)
Newsgroups: rec.arts.startrek,rec.arts.movies,rec.arts.sf-lovers

> >> the Captain but he was played by an actor named Veejay   ←oldest
> >> Armitraj, a gentleman last seen by American moviegoers in   material
```

```
> >> the James Bond film "Octopussy." He played a secret service
> >> operative that assisted Bond while he was in India.
> >> The name of his character in Octopussy was incidentally, "Veejay."

Allan writes:

> Once and for all, the man's name is Vijay Amritraj. He
_IS_ a professional     ←article being replied to
> tennis player (ranked around #50 in the world). He has been both
> acting and playing professional tennis since his role in Octopussy.

For those who are interested, Vijay played a cop from India in the now
canned NBC series "The Last Precinct."
For those in the NY-NJ area, he now has a role in the Channel 11
syndication "What a Country!" on Saturdays at 6:00 pm.
```

Here, the lines beginning with **> >>** are from the oldest article. "Allan" responded to that article, and his response appears in the current response as quotes **>**. The author of the current article then has his or her say (in the lines not preceded by brackets). Many versions of the Netnews software provide an automatic identifying line that begins a quote with a phrase such as "So-and-so writes:". If this isn't the case with the article you are responding to, it's a good idea to add some identification for the earlier material you are quoting.

Checklist for Responding to Articles in *postnews*

- Should I use e-mail or post a response? If you decide to post a response, write your article and then check:
- Is the list of newsgroups still appropriate?
- Are the subject, summary, and keyword statements still appropriate?
- Have I quoted enough to identify the context but no more?
- Have I reread my response for spelling, grammar, and content?
- Did I say what I wanted to say, the way I wanted to say it?

Posting to Moderated Newsgroups

Some newsgroups do not directly accept postings of new articles. Postings for such groups are submitted to a moderator who reviews them for appropriateness. The advantage of such a group is that it considerably reduces the amount of irrelevant material you have to read through.

Many of these newsgroups were formerly identified by the prefix `mod.`, for "moderated," in the newsgroup name. This prefix is no longer used because it uses up part of the newsgroup name, which many felt was better devoted to topical information. For example, the newsgroup `mod.newprod` (moderated announcements of new products) is now called `comp.newprod` (new products under the "computer" topic). There are still moderated newsgroups, but you can no longer identify them simply from the newsgroup name.

The question then arises: how can one identify a moderated group, now that the `mod.` prefix is gone? By the time you read this, most USENET sites should be running new software that takes care of this problem. If you are using the 2.11 version of the Netnews software with the `vnews` or `rn` news reading programs, the word "moderated" will appear in the group heading to inform you that it is a moderated group. If you post an article to such a group, your posting will be sent to the moderator automatically. If you are running older software, you may need to find the name and UUCP address of the moderator for the group you are interested in. A list of moderators is usually kept in the newsgroup `news.announce` or `news.lists`. You then e-mail your submission to the moderator by using any UNIX `mail` program.

Posting Articles with *postnews*

Now you are ready to begin creating your own original news articles. Many of the considerations we have discussed concerning replies carry over into writing original news articles. We will continue our discussion shortly of netiquette as it relates to original articles. First, though, let's look at the mechanics of posting an original article and some of the basic decisions you need to make before posting.

The actual procedure for posting an original article is simple. Although there are several news *reading* programs of varying complexity, there is only one widely used news *writing* program—`postnews`. It is a line-oriented program like `readnews`, with very few options.

For our example of using `postnews`, we will write an article asking for some information about the Korn Shell (`Ksh`). In particular, we want to know whether `Ksh` runs on BSD UNIX. We have heard that this powerful new shell is available from AT&T, and so it seems quite possible that it works only with their System V implementation of UNIX.

Here's how we wrote and posted the article:

```
postnews
Is this message in response to some other message? n
Subject: Korn Shell on BSD
Keywords: Korn Shell, Ksh
```

We simply typed `postnews` at the UNIX prompt. The first question that postnews asks is whether the article is a response to another article. We replied "no." (We'll look at writing follow-up articles with postnews later. It is usually more convenient to do follow-ups from your favorite news reading program. All you have to do is position yourself at the article you are interested in and then give the appropriate command. You don't have to remember the article's ID number as you would with postnews.)

Using the Appropriate Newsgroup

For now, we'll assume that we aren't replying but are posting an original article. The next question that comes up is the newsgroup(s) to which we want to post our article:

```
Newsgroups (enter one at a time, end with a blank line):
The most relevant newsgroup should be the first, you should
add others only if your article really MUST be read by people
who choose not to read the appropriate group for your article.
But DO use multiple newsgroups rather than posting many times.

For a list of newsgroups, type ?

> comp.unix.questions
>
```

As you can see, postnews gives some advice about choosing the appropriate newsgroup. This advice might seem a little harsh. After all, there may be more than one appropriate newsgroup for an article, such as in the C++ versus Ada example given earlier. But in the vast majority of cases, the article will belong in one newsgroup. Sometimes it takes a little thought to figure out which one is best, however.

Cross-posting to several newsgroups may seem like a good way to reach the maximum number of people, but in practice other people on the net will view this negatively, especially if your posting causes a discussion in all the listed newsgroups. Remember that people resent having their time wasted.

Note that if you're not sure which group might be appropriate, you can get a list of newsgroups by typing a question mark. Actually it's better to print out the newsgroup list in /usr/lib/news/newsgroups (the path may be different at your site) and keep it handy while using postnews. What postnews does when you type ? at the Newsgroup: line is simply to pipe the newsgroups file through a pager (such as more). Another possibility is to look for appropriate newsgroups by doing a grep on the newsgroups file before using postnews. (Unfortunately, postnews doesn't have a shell escape.)

Since our subject matter here is a question about UNIX (the compatibility of Ksh with BSD), there are two possible newsgroups that come to mind:

comp.unix.questions and comp.unix.wizards. We chose the former because the question is not particularly technical or advanced. If we receive no replies, we can try comp.unix.wizards later, on the theory that the knowledge may be only in the hands of UNIX gurus who don't bother to read the "beginners" group. (It actually turned out that this wasn't necessary.) The wizards can be very helpful, but they're sometimes a bit touchy at being asked questions that appear beneath their dignity.

Specifying Distribution

A related question is how widely the article should be distributed. If there is doubt, preference should be given to the smaller distribution area. Some newsgroups already specify a limited distribution: ca.wanted, for example, which is limited to California, and ba.wanted, which is limited to the San Francisco Bay Area. Your site may also have special newsgroups that are distributed only to your site or to your company as a whole. (Of course, some of these can be quite large: AT&T for example.) But even general-purpose groups (those whose names begin not with a distribution prefix but with comp, rec, etc.) can be used with a restricted distribution by specifying that distribution to postnews. Thus, an article being posted to comp.sys.ibm-pc can be given a local distribution of ba, which means that the article will be distributed with the comp.sys.ibm-pc newsgroup, but only to readers in the San Francisco Bay Area. This is a perfect distribution for information about a local PC users group, for example.

```
Distribution (default='comp', '?' for help) : ?
How widely should your article be distributed?
local    Local to this site
well     Same as local.
ba       Everywhere in the San Francisco Bay Area
ca       Everywhere in California
usa      Everywhere in the USA
na       Everywhere in North America
net      Everywhere on USENET in the world
```

Here we typed a ? at the Distribution prompt to get a list of possible distribution areas. Yours will vary depending on your locality and possibly your workplace. The default provided is the prefix of the newsgroup specified earlier: in this case, comp. Since the distribution area for topical prefixes such as comp or soc is net-wide, and that seems appropriate for our general query, we accepted the default by pressing Return. We could have used a more local distribution (such as ca) and probably received enough replies, but we thought the answer to our question would be of wider general interest.

Writing the Article

We are now placed in our editor, which happens to be `vi` on our system. Lines for Subject, Newsgroups, and Keywords are provided from our responses to the earlier questions:

```
"/tmp/post017164" 4 lines, 85 characters)
Subject: Korn Shell on BSD
Newsgroups: comp.unix.questions
Keywords: Korn Shell, Ksh

~
I have read quite a bit about the Korn Shell (Ksh) lately.
I have seen it available on System V and XENIX.
Is there a version that will run on BSD systems?

:wq
"/tmp/post017164" 7 lines, 241 characters
```

At this point we are actually editing a temporary file with the uninteresting name of `/tmp/post017164` created by `postnews`. We write our article by appending it to the headers provided, check our work, and exit the editor normally. The `postnews` program then asks us what we want to do next:

```
What now?  [send, edit, list, quit, write] l
Subject: Korn Shell on BSD
Newsgroups: comp.unix.questions
Keywords: Korn Shell, Ksh

I have read quite a bit about the Korn Shell (Ksh) lately.
I have seen it available on System V and XENIX.
Is there a version that will run on BSD systems?
Please respond by e-mail.
```

The choices are:

Send Post the article to the newsgroup(s).

Edit Return to the editor and work on the article some more.

List Display the article again to check it.

Quit Leave `postnews`. Any article not posted or saved will be lost.

Write Save the article. You are prompted for a filename.

(Note: To enter these commands, type the first letter of the command and press Return.)

As you can see from the first line of the example, we gave the `list` command so that we could see the article one more time and check it for spelling errors and such. At that point we realized that we wanted to remind potential respondents to use e-mail, so we added "Please respond by e-mail." Next, we decided to save a copy of the article in our home directory for future reference:

```
What now?  [send, edit, list, quit, write] w
Filename? ksh.news.article
```

And, finally, we told `postnews` to post our article:

```
What now?  [send, edit, list, quit, write] s
Posting article . . .
Article posted successfully.
```

(There may be a pause of a moment or two before the posting is completed. If you read Part 3 of this book, you may be able to figure out much of what UUCP is doing behind the scenes to actually send out the article.

Checklist for Writing Original Articles in *postnews*

- Do I have the right newsgroup(s)?
- How widely should my article be distributed?
- What is my article really about (summary)?
- How might people look for my topic (keywords)?
- How and where do I want people to reply?
- Have I checked my spelling and grammar?
- Am I satisfied with what I have writtten?

Follow-ups from *postnews*

As we noted earlier, you can post a response article from `postnews` by answering "yes" (`y`) to the first question it asks. You are then asked for the newsgroup and the number of the article to which you are responding. This number is *not* the unique article ID, but the sequential number of the article within the group:

```
$ postnews
Is this message in response to some other message? y
In what newsgroup was the article posted? sci.space
Valid article numbers are from 96 to 309
```

```
What was the article number? 270
article /well/news/sci/space/270
From: stolfi@jumbo.dec.com (Jorge Stolfi)
Subject: Bucks from space (2)
Is this the one you want? y
Please enter a short summary of your contribution to the discussion
Just one or two lines ...  (end with a blank line)
>       Cheap spaceplanes mean low costs to orbit.
Do you want to include a copy of the article? n
```

After verifying that it has the right article, postnews asks you for the same information as that used by most of the other "respond" commands that we saw earlier: it asks you for a summary line and whether you want a copy of the article placed in the buffer. You are then placed in your editor buffer, ready to edit headings as necessary and write your response. The main difference between responding from postnews and responding from one of the news reading programs is that, for postnews, you need to know the newsgroup and sequential number of the article. Of course, this is no problem if you've printed out a copy of the article. If you haven't, you'd better find the article with one of the news reading programs, and write down the number before running postnews because, as we've noted, there is no way to get a shell and to cat or more a file from postnews. (You could also exit to the UNIX prompt and then use grep on /usr/spool/news if you remember a word or phrase to search for.)

Which way of responding is better? This is a matter of personal preference. Responding from a news reading program is easiest, since you don't have to keep track of numbers or other information. On the other hand, having some time pass between reading an article and responding helps promote good news writing. You can write your response at your leisure. Perhaps you can write it off-line and upload it. In any case, you have time for reflection and considered judgment, as well as self-editing.

There are two ways to gain such a breather before responding. In the first way, you can mark the article as unread while in the news reading program, and respond to it when it pops up again in the next session. In the second way, you can read and print out or save articles, and then use postnews later for responses. Using postnews does have the advantage of generally getting you to an article faster than if you did a "cold start" from a news reading program.

More about Writing News

We have now covered all the basic considerations of netiquette, as well as the mechanics of replying to and posting news. There are, however, a number of other things that come up in the net world. We will not try to cover them all here (you'll run into them in discussions on the net eventually), but we will touch on some of the more prominent ones.

Using Signatures

You have probably noticed that a number of articles have a concluding section consisting of a name, a phrase or two, and possibly a disclaimer: "The opinions expressed are not necessarily those of XYZ Corp." The signature often contains one or more network addresses, including alternate ones that people can use if they are easier than the path by which your article reached them. For example:

```
--
Gordon A. Moffett                                 {whatever}!amdahl!gam
 ~ How can I tell you ~
 ~ That I love you? ~
 ~ ... I can't think of the right words to say ~
--
[The opinions expressed, if any, do not represent Amdahl Corporation]
```

The signature gives you an opportunity to express a bit of your philosophy, to show some personality, and to provide a corporate disclaimer if you feel one is needed. Signatures of more than four lines are forbidden by recent versions of the Netnews software, however, because they take up space and reading time. Also, jokes are not recommended because they grow old fast.

To create a signature, simply create a file called `.signature` in your home directory with your favorite editor. Be sure to check it over for spelling errors, etc.

```
cat .signature
The opinions expressed are my own, but you're welcome to share them.
Harry Henderson (freelance technical editor/writer). ptsfa!well!hrh
```

This signature will now be automatically added to every article you post, whether original or follow-up. Here's what the signature looked like in a test article we created for viewing it:

```
Article 355 of 355, Fri 03:29.
Subject: Signature test
Keywords: test ignore
Path: hrh (Harry Henderson @ Whole Earth Lectronic Link, Sausalito, CA)
(5 lines) More? [ynq] y

    This is a test to see how my signature looks in a message.
--
The opinions expressed are my own, but you're welcome to share them.
Harry Henderson (freelance technical editor/writer). ptsfa!well!hrh
```

Collecting and Summarizing Responses

Let's return to our query concerning the Korn Shell on BSD. During the week or so following our posting, we received half a dozen replies (all by e-mail, as requested). Here are some excerpts as printed out from `mail`:

```
From: dual!decwrl!mips!hitz (David Hitz)
Message-Id: <8701020000.AA22437@mips.UUCP>
To: hrh
Subject: Re: Korn Shell on BSD
Status: R

Yes, Ksh should run on BSD. It's got lots of #ifdefs and looks like it
will run on just about anything. Under BSD it even has job control.

        mips!hitz

From ptsfa!dsp Sat Jan  3 09:34:12 1987
From: ptsfa!dsp
Message-Id: <8701031734.AA19453@well.UUCP>
To: well!hrh
Subject: Re: Korn Shell on BSD
Newsgroups: comp.unix.questions
In-Reply-To: <2281@well.UUCP>
Organization: Pacific * Bell, San Ramon, CA
Cc:
Status: R

In article <2281@well.UUCP> you write:
>I have read quite a bit about the Korn Shell (Ksh) lately. I have seen
>it available on System V and XENIX. Is there a version that will run
>on BSD systems?

Yes, it runs on Sun 3's, CCI's and a few other things. Got my copy from
the Toolchest 4-5 months ago.

I think it's supposed to run "out of the box" on most BSD systems.
---
David St. Pierre    415/823-6800  {ihnp4,lll-
crg,ames,qantel,pyramid}!ptsfa!dsp Minister of Disinformation
A hand in the bush is worth two anywhere else.
```

By the way, we can see that the author of the second message used a reply command that quoted part of our article and appended his signature.

The answer to our question, put briefly, appears to be "yes, `Ksh` can run on BSD." Whenever you ask for and receive useful information, it is a courtesy to the net to summarize the replies in a follow-up article of your own. This means that instead of there being a dozen replies on the net, there are two articles: your original and your follow-up or update. Here's how we did it in this case:

```
--------
Article 491 of 521: <2281@well.UUCP>
Subject: Korn Shell on BSD
Keywords: Korn Shell, Ksh
From: hrh@well.UUCP (Harry Henderson)
Path: hrh
Organization: Whole Earth Lectronic Link, Sausalito, CA
Newsgroups: comp.unix.questions
Date: 30 Dec 86 11:46:59 GMT
--------
(3 lines) More? [ynq] f
Please enter a short summary of your contribution to the discussion
Just one or two lines ...  (end with a blank line)
>        Ksh on BSD UNIX: summary of replies
>
Do you want to include a copy of the article? y
OK, but please edit it to suppress unnecessary verbiage, signatures, etc.
"/tmp/post022265" 11 lines, 395 characters
Summary: Ksh on BSD UNIX: summary of replies
References: <2281@well.UUCP>

In article <2281@well.UUCP>, hrh@well.UUCP (Harry Henderson) writes:
> I have read quite a bit about the Korn Shell (Ksh) lately. I have seen
> it available on System V and XENIX. Is there a version that will run
> on BSD systems?

~
"/tmp/post022265" 11 lines, 395 characters.
Your e-mail replies told me that Ksh (Korn Shell) should run on BSD.
Any of you who also thought it didn't run can now bug your system
administrators to get it :-)
:wq
"/tmp/post022265" 15 lines, 565 characters

What now?  [send, edit, list, quit, write] s
Posting article...
Article posted successfully.
```

You should be able to recognize what we did here. We found the article with a news reading program and then entered a follow-up to our own article. The information is now available to the whole net.

The strange symbol `:-)` after the last sentence in the article is called a "smiley face." (To see how it got that name, rotate the page clockwise 90 degrees!) It is a way of saying "I'm kidding" or "don't take this too seriously."

Using *test* Newsgroups

The previous example was posted to our local test group, `ba.test`. You can easily find the available test groups by doing `grep test /usr/lib/news/newsgroups`. Always choose the smallest (most local) test group for posting tests. Since you don't really want an audience, using the smallest group causes the least trouble. One day while reading news, we ran into this:

```
--------
Subject: test
Keywords: test
Newsgroups: comp.unix.wizards
--------
(1 lines) More? [ynq] y
this is  a test from ...
```

This person not only picked a regular (nontest) newsgroup, he picked `comp.unix.wizards` to do his testing. By now his terminal may very well have been turned into a frog . . . .

Short and to the Point

The next few examples illustrate some good news writing, as well as some other facets of USENET. Here's an example of a writer who gets to the point:

```
Article 418 of 491, Dec 19 10:59.
Subject: Wanted: termcap for Televideo 955
(7 lines) More? [ynq] y
Wanted: termcap for Televideo 955. AT&T UNIX System V.
Please Email.
Thank you.
--
/"""\ Jeffrey Mattox, Heurikon Corp, Madison, WI
¦0.0¦ {harpo, hao, philabs}!seismo!uwvax!heurikon!jeff  (news & mail)
\_=_/       ihnp4!heurikon!jeff  (mail)
```

Helping Shape the Net

Many things that eventually happen on USENET come about by popular demand. (Recall that chapter 6 described the grassroots nature of USENET and its development.) A continuing question is the appropriateness of a given newsgroup and whether a given topic belongs in a particular newsgroup. Discussions on the creation and use of newsgroups are best done within the group `news.groups`. This sort of "meta discussion," when carried on in a regular topical newsgroup, gets in the way of discussing matters of topical interest. Here's an example of a posting that advocates the use of a more local group devoted to discussion of UNIX:

```
Article 435 of 491, Dec 22 00:56.
Subject: California readers: comp.unix.* too big?  try ca.unix
Summary: ca.unix: use it or lose it
Path: ..!amdahl!gam (G A Moffett @ Amdahl Corp, UTS Products Group)
Newsgroups: comp.unix.questions,comp.unix.wizards,comp.unix.xenix,ca.news
(17 lines) More? [ynq] y
A newsgroup ca.unix has been created in California for those
of us who think comp.unix.* is too "noisy" and would like
to encourage better contacts with their neighbors. Because
it is local, you are likely to get a faster response than via
the world-wide comp.unix.* groups.

I encourage California readers of comp.unix.* to try instead using
ca.unix; otherwise it will be felt the experiment has been
a failure.
--
Gordon A. Moffett                                   {whatever}!amdahl!gam

[The opinions expressed, if any, do not represent Amdahl Corporation]
```

Creating a New Newsgroup

At some point in your USENET career, it is likely that you will feel that a given topic would be better addressed by having its own newsgroup. How are newsgroups created? In a way, it is like a candidate being nominated by a political party. Support must be marshalled for the "candidate" group. It helps to get some backbone site administrators who favor the idea. Whether the idea is likely to be favored depends greatly on whether the group addresses the perceived needs of enough people. If you have carefully looked over the available groups, and decide you want to start the ball rolling, first become familiar with the newsgroup `news.groups`, which carries discussion of the newsgroup scheme and possible ways to improve it. In that group you will probably find an article called "Procedures for Creating New Newsgroups," by David Taylor (possibly under a different title). (Other useful material on this subject may also be available in `news.groups`.) Mr. Taylor's article gives an excellent overview of how you can test your ideas and determine whether a new group will fly.

Mailing Lists: An Alternative to Newsgroups

An important alternative to newsgroups in some cases is the *mailing list*. Like a newsgroup, a mailing list is devoted to a particular topic. Unlike a newsgroup, however, it is not distributed to the whole network, or even a particular region. It is simply a list of electronic mail addresses maintained by the list coordinator. Any message that any member wants to send is mailed (using a regular UNIX mailer) to the coordinator, who in turn mails it to everyone on the list. Since the messages go only to those who have asked for them, the overhead is much lower than for a regular newsgroup. A mailing list is also a good way to test a proposed newsgroup topic. It is also useful for private discussions and for project-oriented working groups. A compilation of currently available mailing lists is usually available on one of the "newusers" groups, along with more instructions on how to establish your own mailing list.

The Line-Eater: A USENET Art Form

We will end our discussion of newswriting tips and techniques with something a bit whimsical. Perhaps you have been puzzled by a variety of odd first lines in articles on the net. They refer to a creature known as the "line eater," who says things like:

```
[Line-Eater Food]
[What Line-Eat####]
```

and so on. There originally *was* a "line eater" on the net—a bug in some versions of the news software that swallowed up the first line of an article when the line began with white space (spaces or tabs). As a result, people began putting a throw-away line at the beginning of each article. The bug is long gone, but the tradition remains. Perhaps you will devise a creative "line eater" line for the delectation of your fellow net users!

Summary

In this chapter you have learned the netiquette for follow-up and original articles, including the reasons why courtesy and sensitivity are important in UNIX communication through USENET. You've also learned tips and techniques for `postnews`, including how to reply to articles and what kinds of replies are appropriate in various circumstances. Flames, cross-posting, quoting, and signatures were other topics discussed.

Reading this chapter and the recommended net articles, and being sensitive to the concerns of the net as you read and post news, will make you a good news writer. Knowledge, entertainment, perhaps friendship, await. You may well find yourself spending considerable time on USENET. One good way to continue your exploration of USENET is to refer to Appendix D, which is a bibliography of important articles about USENET (many found on the net itself).

We have now extensively explored mail and news in our coverage of UNIX communications. The final part of this book explores the UUCP programs, and will help you use the powerful tools that underlie the world of UNIX communications.

Part

3

UNIX File Transfer: UUCP

Part 3 investigates *UUCP*, a collection of programs that provide the file transfer facilities underlying mail, news, and other UNIX communications programs. UUCP stands for *U*NIX to *U*NIX *CoPy*, and most of the UUCP programs start, quite logically, with the letters *uu*.

The next eight chapters demystify UUCP. They explain how to use the UUCP programs and discuss the important options available for them. Table 11-1 in chapter 11 lists each of the programs and briefly describes its function.

11

An Overview of UUCP

UUCP, which stands for *U*NIX to *U*NIX *C*o*P*y, is the ensemble of programs underlying the mail and USENET news programs. It is a system of low-level to midlevel programs that connect one UNIX machine to another and make such things as networks possible.

As figure 11-1 shows; UUCP is built from the bottom up. At the foundation of UUCP are the low-level programs `uucico` and `uuxqt`, which are never run by the average user. Next are the midlevel programs `uucp`, `uupick`, `uuto`, `uux`, and `uusend`, which are seldom run by the average user. At the top are `mail` and `postnews`, often run by the average user. These last two programs run the midlevel programs, which in turn run the low-level programs to do their jobs.

UUCP was first designed and implemented by M. E. Lesk of Bell Laboratories in 1976. It has undergone many revisions and improvements since then. The most notable of these is HoneyDanBer UUCP, written in 1983 by Peter Honeyman, David A. Norwitz, and Brian E. Redman. In this chapter and the following ones, we will explain how to use the *current* version of UUCP, as supplied with AT&T's System V Release 2 and the University of California's BSD 4.2 UNIX. Where appropriate, we will also illustrate the use of HoneyDanBer UUCP and show how it differs from the current UUCP.

The UUCP Programs

As a user, you can think of UUCP as a batch-processing environment that contains a set of related tools for such tasks as file transfer and remote execution of programs. To accomplish a task (such as a file transfer), a user posts requests into a spooling (temporary holding) directory. UUCP picks them up later for transmission to other sites. You have already done this indirectly if you have sent electronic mail or posted an

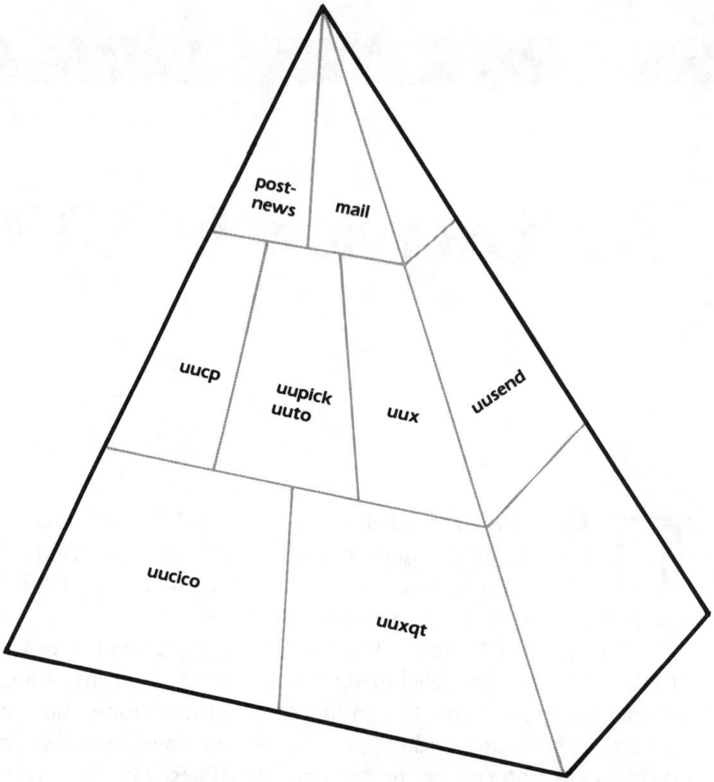

Figure 11-1. UUCP is built from the bottom up.

article on USENET. When you send a message with `mailx`, the message is handled on your behalf as a UUCP file transfer request. When you post an article with `postnews`, the article is also spooled for you as a UUCP request. In this, Part 3, you will learn how to create and manage UUCP requests like these directly.

Figure 11-2 provides an overview of the UUCP batch-processing system, showing the many programs in the UUCP environment and their place in the UNIX file structure. Don't worry now about the functions of these programs or the purposes of the various files: we will be covering them systematically in the following eight chapters. The main point for now is that UUCP is an ensemble of programs, shell scripts, and related files, grouped in several different subdirectories.

What Can UUCP Do for Me?

Table 11-1 on page 303 lists the UUCP programs and tells what each is used for. You can think of these programs as the tool kit used by higher-level UNIX mail and

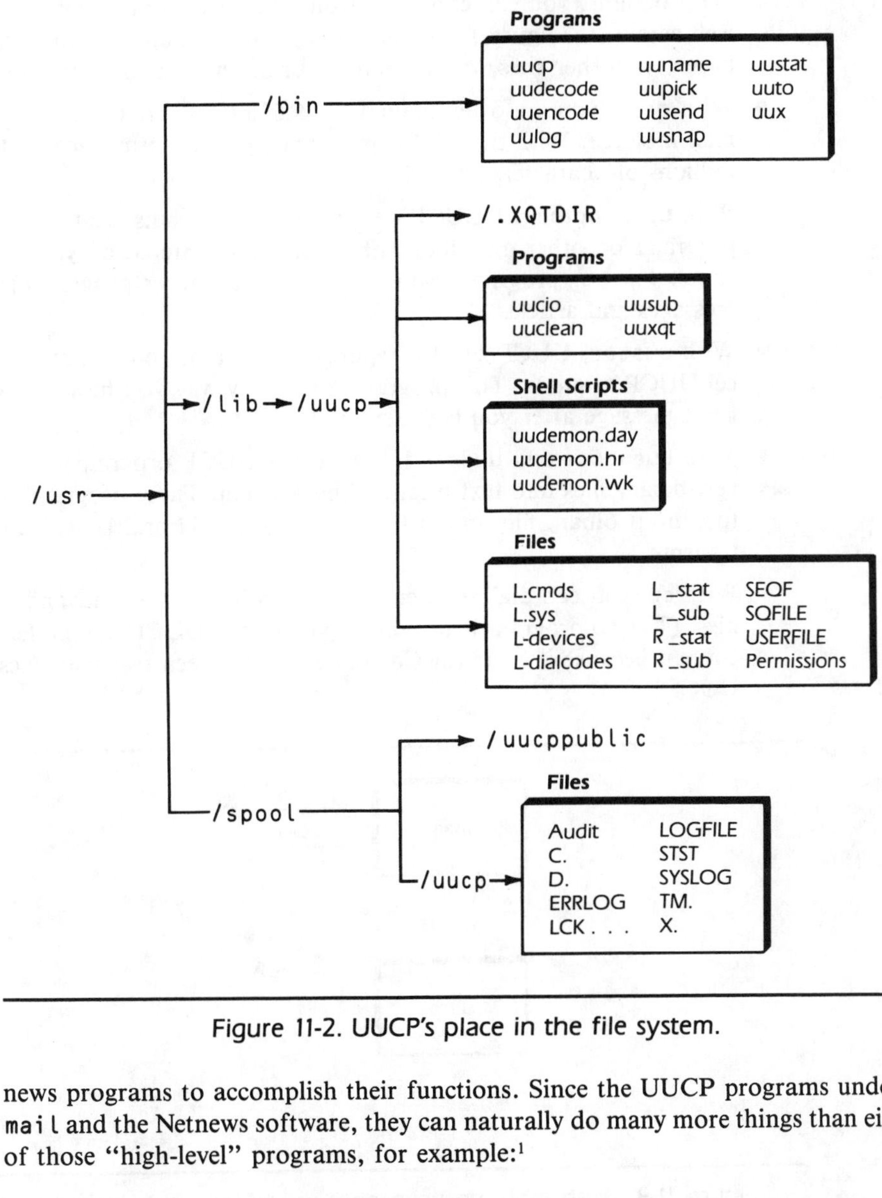

Figure 11-2. UUCP's place in the file system.

news programs to accomplish their functions. Since the UUCP programs underlie `mail` and the Netnews software, they can naturally do many more things than either of those "high-level" programs, for example:[1]

- With `mail`, you can send electronic messages only one way—*out* to other sites. On the other hand, with the **uucp** program, one of the UUCP ensem-

1. When we refer to `mail`, we mean any mail program, such as `mailx` (discussed in Part 1 of this book) or `/bin/mail` (see Appendix A). Although it is possible for mail or news programs to use something other than UUCP for file transfer, UUCP is in fact used in the majority of cases.

ble programs, you can copy files from other sites *in* to your machine as well as *out* (see figure 11-3). Additionally, with uucp, you can copy files between two other sites with a command run on your local machine.

- With mail, you are often limited to 65,536 (64K) characters per electronic mail message. With the UUCP programs, you can transfer files that contain millions of characters.
- With uux, another of UUCP's ensemble of programs, you can run (execute) programs on other machines with a command entered on your local machine. The uux program also enables mail and news programs to forward messages and articles.
- With uustat, UUCP's status reporting program, you can monitor and cancel UUCP requests. This program is the only way you have of cancelling a mail message after you have sent it.
- With uuencode and uudecode, two other UUCP programs, you can convert binary files into text files, and back again. These programs allow you to convert binary files into a form that both mail and UUCP are able to transmit.
- With cu, you can dial another UNIX machine, log into it, and transfer files. (The cu program is not really part of the UUCP ensemble, but we cover it because it establishes a connection between two machines via UUCP.)

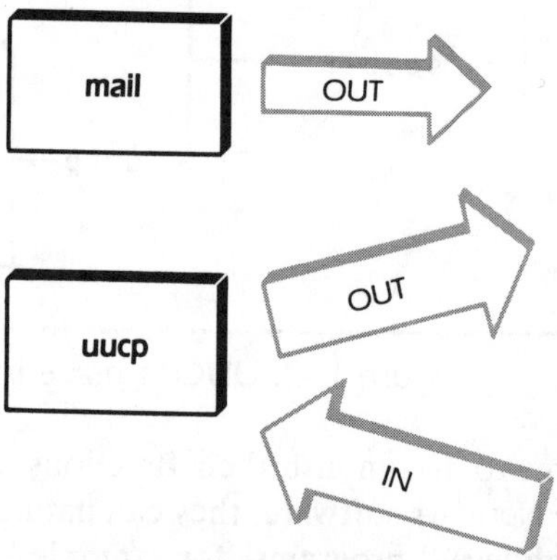

Figure 11-3. With **mail**, you can only send files out to other machines, and only tiny 64K files at that. With UUCP, you can copy files in as well as out, and those files can contain millions of characters.

This list could go on, but it suffices to give you a glimpse of some of the many things you can do with UUCP that you can't do with mail. The UUCP programs aren't intended to replace mail. Rather, they augment and extend the things you are able to do with UNIX in general.

Table 11-1. The Collection of UUCP Programs

Program	Description
uucp	Copies files between neighboring UNIX sites.
uusend	Copies files through a series or routing of UNIX sites to a remote UNIX site.
uuto	Sends files from your local site into the PUBDIR directory of a neighbor UNIX site.
uupick	Interactively retrieves files sent with uuto.
uux	Runs UNIX programs on other UNIX machines.
uulog	Views status of UUCP requests.
uustat	Views and modifies status of queued UUCP jobs.
uusnap	Views status of current neighbor site connections to your local machine.
uucico	Communicates with neighbor UNIX machines and disposes of queued UUCP jobs.
uuxqt	Handles received requests for programs to be executed.

How UUCP and *mail* Interact

To better understand the interplay between UNIX mail and UUCP, examine the simplified diagram in figure 11-4. Follow as we describe, for example, the sequence of programs that are triggered when you send an electronic mail message.

First, you run mail to compose, edit, and send your electronic message. Then, the mail program passes your submission to the rmail (restricted mail) program. The rmail program checks the "To:" line in your message to determine where it is being sent and then calls the uux program to queue a request for that message to be sent to the proper site. Sometime later—possibly immediately—the uucico program starts up. This is the real workhorse program of UUCP. It calls the remote site—or it is called by them—and starts a conversation with that site, transferring your message. If your message is being forwarded, the rmail program at the receiving site will go through this same process to pass your message to the next site specified by "To:".

The Concepts Underlying All UUCP Programs

There are four important concepts that underlie all the UUCP programs:

The Network UUCP, unlike `mail`, can communicate only with *neighbor* UNIX machines (machines that are directly connected to your local machine). We will illustrate use of the `uuname` program to find the names of those neighbor UNIX machines.

Queue and Spool All of the UUCP programs *queue* requests for files that are to be transferred. Those files are often *spooled* (copied to a temporary place) and then the copies are transferred at a later time.

Filenames The way that filenames are specified on neighboring UNIX machines differs from the way they are specified on your local machine. We will explain the correct ways to specify remote filenames and will warn you of pitfalls to avoid.

Permissions UUCP has many limits that govern what you can copy. We will show you how to find these limits on your machine, and we'll explain the importance of the PUBDIR public directory.

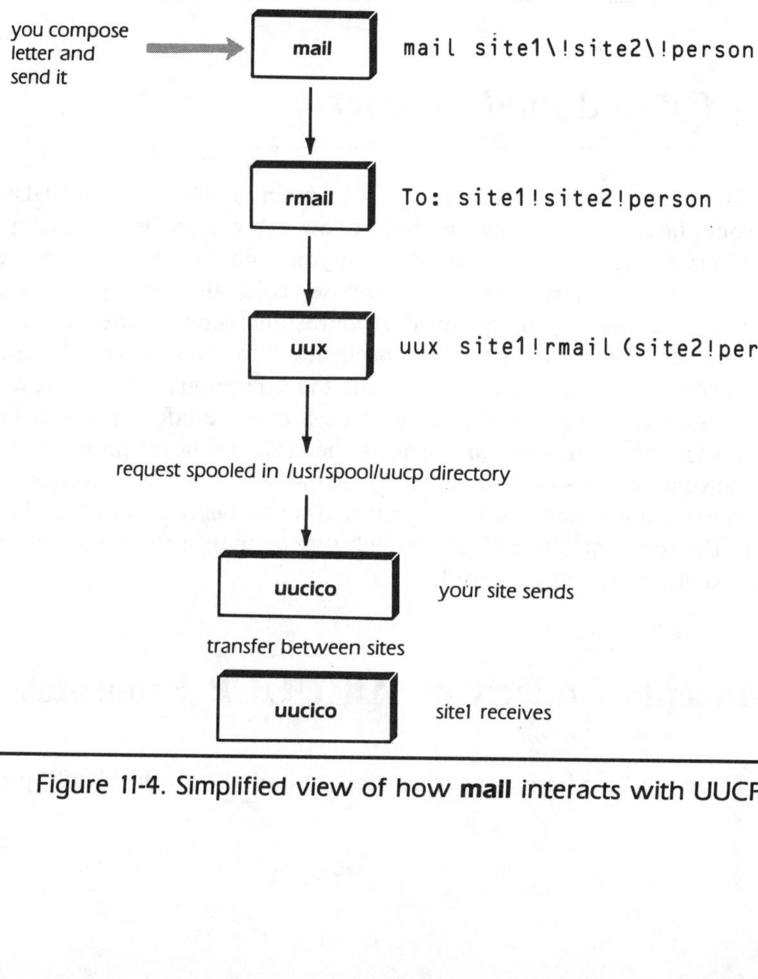

Figure 11-4. Simplified view of how **mail** interacts with UUCP.

UUCP's View of a Network

A UUCP network comprises two or more UNIX machines that are connected together in any of several common ways. Figure 11-5 shows one such network. The *hard-wired* lines (wiggly lines in the figure) are made by connecting the serial communications port of one machine directly to that of another. The *local network* (solid lines in the figure) can be any of several common LANs. *Dial-up* lines (dashed lines in the figure) are made by connecting a modem on your machine to a modem on another machine over telephone lines. UUCP includes software that enables your computer to make telephone calls (dial out). As you can see, UUCP is very flexible in its capability to work with many different kinds of physical connections between machines.

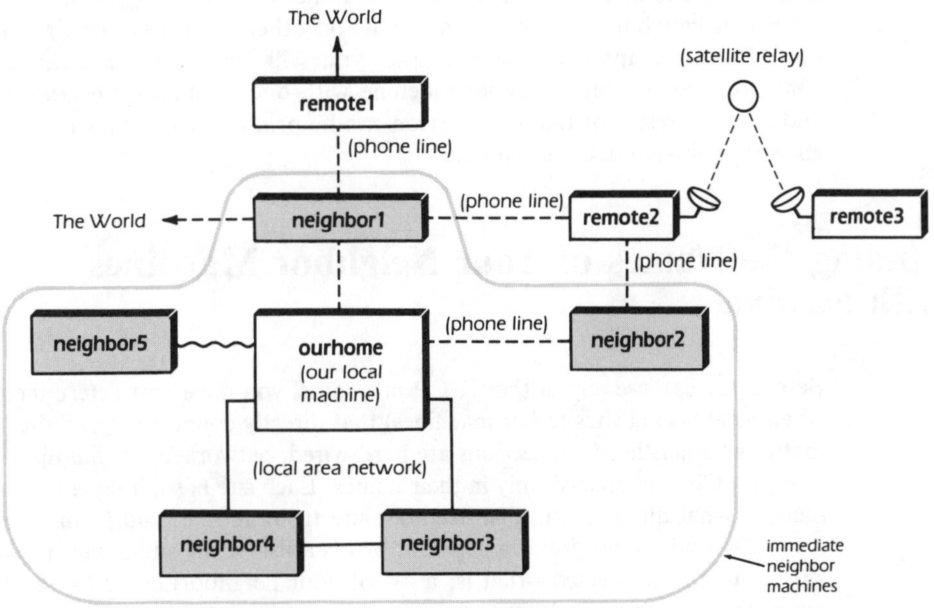

Figure 11-5. UUCP's view of a network.

Unlike `mail` and Netnews, which both view networks as worldwide, UUCP interacts *only* with its immediate neighbors. Examine figure 11-5 again. In this fictional network, our home machine is named `ourhome`. As you can see, our local machine is directly connected to the machines named `neighbor1`, `neighbor2`, `neighbor3`, `neighbor4`, and `neighbor5`. Because we are directly connected to those machines, they are our immediate neighbors.

Now examine figure 11-5 once again. Notice that our local machine `ourhome` is not directly connected to `remote2`. In order to interact with `remote2`, we need to go through either `neighbor1` or `neighbor2`. Because we are not directly connected to `remote2`, it is a *remote* site, rather than a *neighbor* site. In general, UUCP is not able to interact directly with remote sites.

Now this may seem like a serious limitation. After all, with `mail` you can send files to remote sites anywhere in the world. Within this limitation, however, lies one of UUCP's main strengths. Recall that all the UUCP programs can be thought of as low-level to midlevel programs. This means that they can be used as building blocks for high-level programs like `mail`. For example, look at figure 11-6. This figure shows how `mail` uses the midlevel UUCP program `uux` to forward its electronic messages from one UNIX machine to another. Forwarding is accomplished by having `uux` on each machine remotely execute `rmail` (restricted mail) on the next machine, which moves the message along step by step until it reaches its final destination.

Thus, although `mail` can be used to send files to remote sites anywhere in the world, it does so by forwarding from one neighbor site to another. It does this by using `uux`, one of the UUCP midlevel or building block programs.

This capability to execute programs on other machines turns out to be very powerful. In chapter 14, for example, you will learn how `uux` can be used to compare a file on one neighbor machine with one on another neighbor machine, and how the result of that comparison can be printed on your local machine—and all with a single UUCP command!

Finding the Names of Your Neighbor Machines with *uuname*

Before you can use any of the UUCP programs, you must first determine the names of all neighboring sites (other machines) that directly connect to your site. It doesn't matter whether those connections are hard-wired, networked, or dial-up. At the user level, UUCP is interested only in their names. Each site has a unique name, and that name is what differentiates one neighbor site from another and from yours.

The `uuname` program, when run, prints a list of the site names to which your site is directly connected—that is, a list of your neighboring UNIX machines. For example, in our fictional network, `uuname` would print the following:

```
uuname
neighbor2
neighbor4
neighbor1
neighbor5
neighbor3
```

Note that this list includes only the names of directly connected sites. The sites `remote1` and `remote2` are not listed because they are connected to `neighbor1`, but not to us (we are `ourhome`).

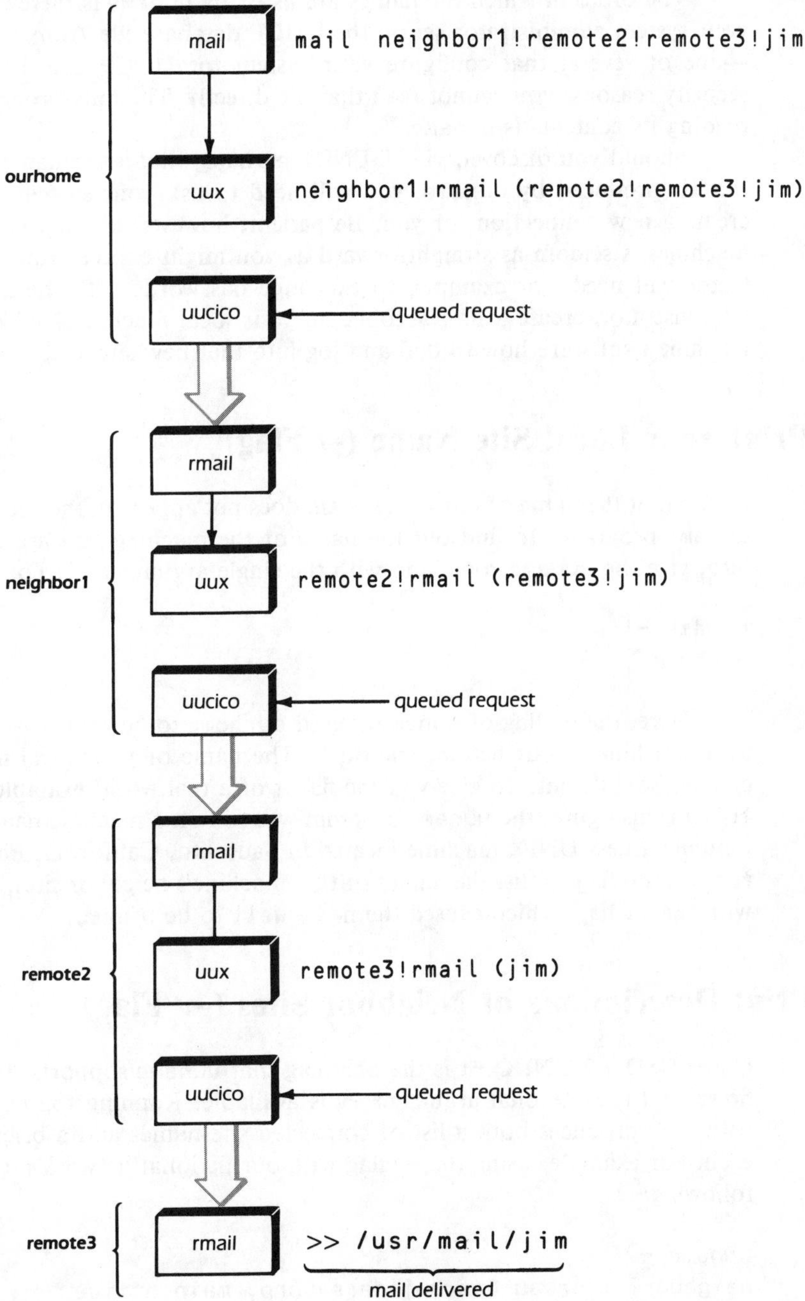

Figure 11-6. Simplified overview of how mail is forwarded.

The order in which the names are listed by uuname is merely a result of how your system administrator set up the UUCP database file /usr/lib/uucp/L.sys—one of several that configure your system for UUCP use. Unfortunately, for security reasons, you cannot read that file directly. The only program available for reading its contents is uuname.

Should you discover, via USENET perhaps, that a site name is missing from the list produced by uuname, you will need to ask your system administrator to create a new connection for you. Be patient, however, because connecting to new machines is seldom as straightforward as you might expect. Your system administrator will need, for example, to exchange passwords with the new site's system administrator, create a new account on your local machine, and teach your local machine's software how to dial and log into that new site.

Print Your Local Site Name (*-l* Flag)

Notice that the name of our own system does not appear in the list produced by the uuname program. To find out the name of the machine you are currently logged into, give the uuname command with the single argument -l. For example:

```
uuname -l
ourhome
```

Here, the -l flag of uuname caused ourhome to be printed—the name of our local machine in our fictional network. The name of your local machine will, of course, be different. To give you the flavor of a real world example, look at figure 11-7. In this figure, the uuname program was run on a machine named The WELL, a public-access UNIX machine located in Sausalito, California. First, uuname was run with no flags to list the names of that machine's neighbor sites; then, it was run with the -l flag, which caused the name well to be printed.

Print Descriptions of Neighbor Sites (*-v* Flag)

Under BSD 4.2 UNIX, -l is the only flag that uuname supports. Under System V, however, the additional argument -v is available. Running the uuname command with a -v produces both a list of connected site names and a brief description of each. For example, using the -v flag with our fictional network might produce the following:

```
uuname -v
neighbor2 Thoreau Dam Builders Corp, main office
neighbor4 Archives and Library
neighbor1 T&M Racing Equipment, South Bay
neighbor5 Jake's pc in computer room
neighbor3 The Editorial Pool
```

```
uuname
acad
aci
amiga
apple
cicomsys
cogsci
commem
copper
cosys
cpro
dual
eakins
esivax
forum1
iquery
hoptoad
hplabs
island
itivax
kdavis
lll-crg
lll-lcc
msudoc
m-net
micropro
notavax
picuxa
polliwog
portal
proper
ptsfa
r2d2
rencon
russs
simbrg
triton1
usenix
unicom
vanguard
vecpry
xanadu

uuname -l
well
```

Figure 11-7. A real example of **uuname**.

As a bonus, the -l and -v flags can be combined to produce a description of our home site:

```
uuname -l -v
ourhome Widgit Manufacturing, Inc.
```

Summary of *uuname* Flags

-l Display only the local site's name.

-v Display a one-line description following each listed site's name.

Is Yours a System V or BSD *uuname*?

To find out which version of uuname you have on your machine, the AT&T System V version or the UCB version, just enter the uuname command with an argument of -x (where x is any letter other than l or v). Under System V and its derivatives, you will see:

```
uuname -x
usage: uuname [-l] [-v]
```

Under BSD 4.2 and related versions of UNIX, you will see:

```
uuname -x
Usage: uuname [-l]
```

UUCP Requests Are Queued and Spooled for Later Transmission

Most UNIX programs perform their tasks at once and don't return you to your prompt until they are done. The UUCP programs, on the other hand, *queue* (schedule for later execution) requests for tasks to be done, and *spool* (make temporary copies of) files for later transmission. Although you get your prompt back at once with the UUCP programs, the task you expect to be done has merely been scheduled (queued) and not actually executed. That scheduled task is handled separately by the uucico program (chapter 18), at a time and in a manner arranged by the system administrator so as to have the least impact on system resources (perhaps late at night when the system has few users and telephone costs are at their lowest). The delay between the time you queue a UUCP request and the time it is handled by uucico can vary from a few seconds on local networks to several hours on public-access machines.

Whenever a queued UUCP request involves the eventual transmission of a file, UUCP software will usually spool a duplicate of that file and later transmit that duplicate, as illustrated in figure 11-8. The term "spool" is a common one in computing. To spool a file means to copy that file into a directory that has been set aside as a temporary holding place. For the UUCP programs, that temporary holding directory is called /usr/spool/uucp. When a file is transmitted by uucico, the duplicate that has been spooled in /usr/spool/uucp is transmitted and then removed. Your original file is left intact.

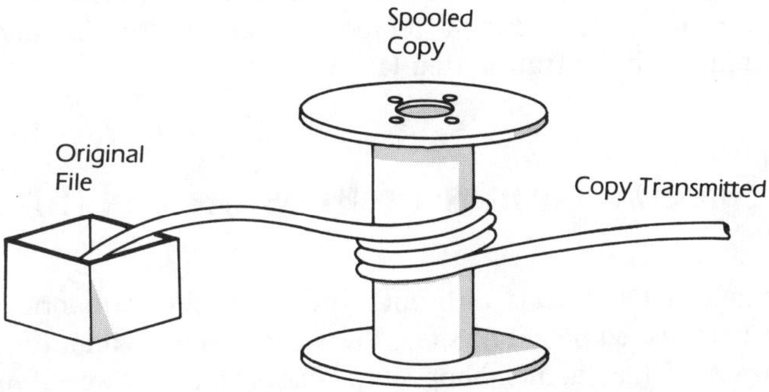

Figure 11-8. UUCP copies files into a spool directory and then transmits those copies instead of the originals.

In Part 1 of this book, which dealt with UNIX mail, you were given a glimpse of this queueing and spooling scheme. To illustrate, imagine sending an electronic mail message with the following:

```
mail neighbor1\!remote2\!duke
Subject: Thank You
Thank you for your brilliant suggestion at
yesterday's meeting. I'm looking forward to that
first paper!
^D
```

Here, you sent a letter through the neighbor site named neighbor1 to the user name duke at the remote site named remote2. You typed Control-d to send that letter, and immediately your prompt was returned. The immediate return of your prompt creates the illusion that your letter was transmitted. But that is just an illusion. In reality, the mail program has merely handed your letter to uux, one of the UUCP programs for processing. Nothing has left your local machine yet.

When uux gets a file to send, whether indirectly from mail or directly from a user, it spools that file and queues a request for the file to be transmitted. In the case of mail, the contents of your letter is the file that is spooled, and the queued request is to forward that letter to the remote site remote2 via neighbor1.

This example is intended merely to give you a feel for what queueing is and how spooling works. These concepts are somewhat more complex than we've indicated here. In chapter 18, the complete connection between mail and UUCP is spelled out in much greater detail. The reason we've introduced these concepts so early in our discussion of UUCP is to emphasize that *all* UUCP programs queue requests and spool files. In the following chapters, for example, we will make statements such as: "Here, uucp queued a request for the file . . . " and " . . . uux first spools a duplicate of . . . ." The first statement means that the uucp program is merely scheduling (queueing a request) for the file to be transmitted at a later time, and is not transmitting it immediately. The second statement means that the uux program is making a temporary copy of the file and that the copy, not the original, will be transmitted later.

How to Specify Names of Files on Neighbor Machines

Because UUCP deals with both your local site, ourhome in our fictional network, and connected neighbor sites, there is a special syntax (or form) for specifying the names of files at neighbor sites. The syntax for specifying a file on a neighbor machine differs from the way you normally specify a file on your local machine. Before discussing that difference, however, let's take a moment to review how files are specified on your local machine.

You are probably already familiar with UNIX's hierarchical file structure—directories and subdirectories. Table 11-2 shows most of the common ways available under UNIX for specifying files under this hierarchical scheme. These methods are

Table 11-2. How to Specify Filenames on Your Local Machine

Command	Meaning
file	File in current directory.
~/file	File in your home directory.*
~user/file	File in user's home directory.*
/path/file	Absolute location of file.
*.c	All files in current directory that end with .c.
temp*	All files in current directory that begin with temp.
??	All files in current directory of exactly two characters.
[ab].1	Files a.1 and/or b.1 in current directory.
file{.c,.h}	Files file.c and file.h.*

*Not the Bourne Shell.

the ones used on your local machine, and should be second nature by now. If you need to refresh your memory, refer to any of the introductory UNIX texts recommended in Appendix E. You will need to know how to specify filenames on your local machine in order to completely understand the discussion that follows.

Specifying a file on a neighbor machine is very similar to the way you specify a file on your local machine. One additional ingredient is needed, however, and that is the name of the neighbor machine. Figure 11-9 illustrates this procedure.

How to Specify a File on a Neighbor Machine

1. Type the name of the neighbor machine.
2. Type an exclamation point character (!) after the name.
3. Type the name of the file.

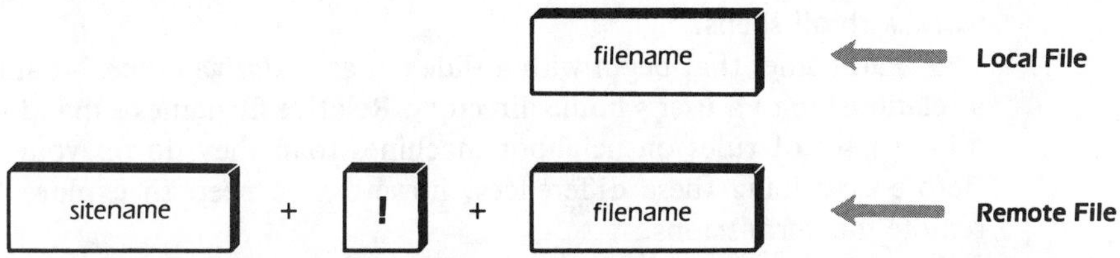

Figure 11-9. Neighbor filenames are specified by stating first the neighbor site's name, then an ! character, and lastly the filename.

The following example specifies the absolute location of a file on the neighbor machine `neighbor1`:

neighbor1!/path/file
↑
site

For a more specific example, consider the file `/usr/lib/unittab`, which is a list of units and their conversion factors, available on all UNIX machines. To specify this file on your local machine, you would enter:

/usr/lib/unittab
↑ ↑
path *file*

whereas to specify that same file on the neighbor machine named `neighbor1`, you would enter:

```
neighbor1!/usr/lib/unittab
↑         ↑        ↑
site      path     file
```

Be careful when using the `!` character under the C Shell and the Korn Shell. Both of these shells use the `!` as a history expansion character. To specify a neighbor site's name under these two shells, you must either escape the `!` by preceding it with a backslash, or surround the entire expression with single quote marks:

```
neighbor1!/path/file         (Bourne Shell)

neighbor1\!/path/file        ←backslash (C and Korn Shells)
'neighbor1!/path/file'       ←single quotes
```

Since the backslash is ignored by the Bourne Shell, we will escape the `!` character by preceding it with a backslash in all our examples. This will allow the examples to work with all shells.

Pathnames that begin with a tilde (~) are *relative names*—names that express a relationship to a user's home directory. Relative filenames expand under a slightly different set of rules on neighbor machines than they do on your local machine. Before describing these differences, however, we need to explore the concept of remote file permissions.

Remote File Permissions

For reasons of security, the ability to read from and write to files on machines other than your own is usually very restricted. This is understandable when you realize how hard it is to verify the honesty and integrity of outsiders whom you may never have met. The reasonable control of such outside access is one of the chief responsibilities of your UUCP administrator. Access can range from the very loose (in-house networks) to severely tight (public-access machines). At the middle ground, many sites allow users to access only files and directories they own, as well as the public directory.

The *public directory* is a specific one, owned by UUCP and called `/usr/spool/uucppublic`. This is UUCP's home directory. In both ordinary and HoneyDanBer UUCP, this directory is referred to by the name *PUBDIR*, for *PUB*lic *DIR*ectory. Take a moment now to examine the contents of the `uucppublic` directory and its permissions on your system. It should look something like this:

```
ls -al /usr/spool/uucppublic
```

```
drwxrwxrwx 1 root    512 Dec   6 12:02 .
drwxrwxr-x 1 root    512 Dec   6 12:01 ..
drwxrwxrwx 1 root    512 Dec   6 12:03 receive
...
etc.
```

Notice that uucppublic is readable, writable, and searchable by anyone.

On many machines, the uucppublic directory is the only directory into which, and from which, files may be copied. The degree of restriction is defined by your system administrator. The files /usr/lib/uucp/USERFILE, for ordinary UUCP, and /usr/lib/uucp/Permissions, for HoneyDanBer UUCP, contain one entry for each site to which your machine is connected. Each entry specifies the topmost directory allowed for copying files. For example, our fictional USERFILE might contain the lines:

```
uun1,neighbor1 /usr/spool/uucppublic/
jake,neighbor5 /
↑    ↑         ↑
login real     topmost
name  name     directory
```

From this file, we see that:

- The site neighbor1, who logs into our machine using the login name uun1, is severely restricted. This site's topmost directory is listed as /usr/spool /uucppublic—a reasonable restriction when you realize that neighbor1 is miles away and connected to us over public telephone lines.
- The site neighbor5, who logs into our system under the name jake, has access to everything—after all, "jake" is our system administrator and his pc is in the computer room. This site's topmost directory is /, which includes every subdirectory in the system.

In both examples, the topmost directory means the directory into which and under which files may be copied. In the case of neighbor1, this means that users at neighbor1 can copy files only into and out of the /usr/spool/uucppublic, or PUBDIR, directory on our machine, and into and out of subdirectories under that directory.

Another factor that limits what you may copy is the ordinary UNIX permissions. In addition to the restrictions defined in USERFILE, file access is further restricted by three simple rules:

1. For a file to be readable by any of the UUCP programs, whether on your local machine or on a neighbor machine, it must be readable by *anyone* (that is, at least mode 444 or -r--r--r--) and live in a directory that is readable and searchable by *anyone* (at least mode 555 or dr-xr-xr-x).

2. For a file to be written by any of the UUCP programs, whether on your local machine or on a neighbor machine, the directory that it will be written into must be readable, writable, and searchable by *anyone* (that is, at least mode 777 or `drwxrwxrwx`).
3. For both reading from, and writing into, all directories in the path leading to the specified directory must be readable and searchable by *anyone* (that is, at least mode 555 or `dr-xr-xr-x`).

The topmost directory listed in `USERFILE` and the preceding required permissions together form the limitations of what others may place into, and copy from, your local machine. Each of your neighbor machines has similar restrictions on what you may place into, and copy from, them. These restrictions are so fundamental to your use of the UUCP programs that they will be repeated throughout the chapters to follow.

The PUBDIR, or `/usr/spool/uucppublic`, directory is another key idea in UUCP. It is always permitted in `USERFILE`, and it always has the correct permissions that allow anyone to read files that are in it, and to write files into it. It is the one directory that is always available at all sites.

Relative Filenames

When you specify a relative directory to UUCP, using the tilde (~) character, it will expand to be a user's home directory. For example:

neighbor1\!~jane/list

This expression refers to the file `list` in the user `jane`'s home directory on the machine whose site name is `neighbor1`.

Like any ordinary user, the UUCP system also has a home directory. That home directory is the PUBDIR directory. Just as you can reference your own home directory by preceding your login name with a tilde character (e.g., `~jane`), you can reference UUCP's home directory by preceding its login name, `uucp`, with a tilde character:

neighbor1\!~uucp

Since the expression `~uucp` always yields UUCP's home directory, you can safely use it to reference the PUBDIR directory.

Note that the `~user` notation only works with the UUCP programs and the C and Korn Shells. It does not work with the Bourne Shell. With the Bourne Shell, you can specify a neighbor site's PUBDIR directory as:

neighbor1\!~uucp

because the UUCP software recognizes that notation. You cannot, however, specify your local PUBDIR as:

```
~uucp
```

because the Bourne Shell will not understand what you are talking about. Specifying local files with the `~user` notation works only with the C Shell, the Korn Shell, and UUCP software.

The use of the `~user` notation is common throughout all UUCP programs. It is a form of shorthand that makes neighbor site filenames clearer and easier to understand. In the chapters that follow, we will use this shorthand often, and we'll indicate where and when Bourne Shell users should be careful.

As a bonus, and only usable with the UUCP software, the expression `~uucp` can be expressed more succinctly as `~/`. That is:

```
neighbor1\!~uucp
```

and

```
neighbor1\~/
```

Both expressions describe the PUBDIR directory at the neighbor site named `neighbor1`.

Filename Expansion

It is possible to specify multiple files on a neighbor machine with a single expression. For example, the expression:

```
neighbor1\!~uucp/chap\*
```

refers to all the files that begin with `chap` that reside in the PUBDIR directory on the neighbor machine `neighbor1`. The use of the wildcard character `*` here is exactly the same as on your local machine (see figure 11-10). The only difference is that we've preceded it with a backslash character. The backslash prevents your local machine from recognizing the `*` and trying to expand it locally. Instead, the `*` is sent as-is to `neighbor1` and expanded on that machine.

Under UUCP, you are allowed to specify multiple files on a neighbor machine using either the wildcard character `*`, or the pattern-matching characters `?` and `[]` (see figures 11-11 and 11-12). To prevent the files from being expanded locally, however, you should always escape (precede) each with a backslash.

If you are not familiar with the use of these special characters, you should take a moment to review sh(1) in your UNIX manual, or csh(1) for the C Shell. The introductory UNIX books given in Appendix E also have detailed discussions of filename expansion and wildcards. Once you've learned to use wildcards, you'll wonder how you ever managed without them.

Figure 11-10. The wildcard character * matches anything—that is, zero or more characters.

Figure 11-11. The ? character matches any single character.

Figure 11-12. The [ ] characters are used to specify a range of characters that are to be matched; for example, **[C–E]** matches "C," "D," and "E."

Summary of Syntax for Use in Remote Naming

`/path/file`	Absolute location of file.
`~uucp/file`	File in PUBDIR directory.
`~/file`	File in PUBDIR directory (shorthand).
`~user/file`	PUBDIR/user/file.
`~/\*.c`	All files in PUBDIR directory that end in `.c`.
`~/\?`	All files in PUBDIR directory of exactly one character.
`~/\[ab\].1`	Files `a.1` and `b.1` in PUBDIR directory.

Summary of Uses and Caveats

The following is a brief summary of concepts we've explored in this chapter. Caveats are provided to illustrate variations, limitations, and possible pitfalls.

List names of neighbor machines

```
uuname
```

Caveat: The order is somewhat arbitrary. On some sites this list can be extremely long.

List name of your local machine

```
uuname -l
```

Specify the PUBDIR directory

```
/usr/spool/uucppublic
~uucp          ←except Bourne Shell
site\!~uucp    ←all shells
```

Topmost directory: listed in

```
/usr/lib/uucp/USERFILE
/usr/lib/uucp/Permissions    ←HoneyDanBer UUCP
```

File and directory permissions

To read:

```
File      mode 444 minimum (-r--r--r--)
Directory mode 555 minimum (dr-xr-xr-x)
Path      mode 555 minimum (dr-xr-xr-x)
```

To write:

```
Directory mode 777 minimum (drwxrwxrwx)
Path      mode 555 minimum (dr-xr-xr-x)
```

Summary

In this chapter you learned that UUCP views a network as being composed of immediate neighbor sites. You also learned how to use the uuname program to list both the names of those neighbor sites and the name of your own site. Finally you were introduced to some of the rules that govern all the UUCP programs. Included were the concepts of permissions and the use of wildcard characters and relative pathnames.

In the next chapter you will begin to use the actual UUCP programs. We will start with uucp, a program for copying files between and among neighbor UNIX sites. We will then show you uusend, a mail-like version of uucp for forwarding files through several sites to a remote UNIX site.

12

Copying Files with *uucp* and *uusend*

As we noted in chapter 1, we use the term "UUCP" (all caps) to refer to the set of communications tools that make up the UUCP system as a whole, and we use the term "`uucp`" (lowercase, in computer font) to refer to a specific program in the UUCP system. The name of the `uucp` program stands for *U*NIX to *U*NIX file *C*o*P*y. It is the main user program for copying files between two UNIX machines.

The `uucp` program has two notable advantages over `mail` for copying files:

1. The `uucp` program allows you to copy very large files. Whereas `mail` often limits you to sending files of 64K or fewer characters, `uucp` often allows you to copy files that are millions of characters long or longer.
2. With `uucp`, you can copy files from a remote UNIX machine *into* your local UNIX machine and you can send files *out* from your machine to a remote machine. With `mail`, you can only send files *out* from your local machine.

Earlier we mentioned that one disadvantage of `uucp` as compared to `mail` is that `uucp` can copy files only between two immediately neighboring UNIX machines. The `mail` program, however, can forward electronic messages through a series—or routing—of machines. This deficiency in `uucp` is made up for at most UCB UNIX sites and at some AT&T UNIX sites, with the addition of the `uusend` program. The `uusend` program understands `mail`-style addresses, and can be used to copy files through a series of UNIX machines.

In this chapter we will illustrate the ins and outs of using both `uucp` and `uusend`. Specifically, we will show you:

- How to transfer files between neighboring UNIX machines with `uucp`.

- How to send and receive mail notification of a successful file transfer with uucp.
- How to specify whether or not new subdirectories are to be created on a neighbor machine when uucp is used for copying.
- How to specify spooling, limit intermediate copies, and delay transfer.
- How to make uucp print out what it is doing, step by step.
- How to copy files through a series of UNIX machines by using uusend.

How to Use *uucp*

In this section, we will lead you through detailed examples of how to use the uucp program. We will show you how to use uucp to copy files from your local machine to a neighbor UNIX machine and back again. Copying files between neighbor UNIX machines will be covered also. Additionally, we will show you how to use all of the uucp options and flags, and we will illustrate many of the common variations for copying files with uucp.

Copying Files into a Neighbor Site's PUBDIR Directory

Recall from chapter 11 that files can be copied into the uucppublic directory (also called the PUBDIR directory) on any machine. The PUBDIR directory, as its name implies, is a public directory that is readable, writable, and searchable by anyone. Also, all the directories leading to it are readable and searchable by anyone. Because the PUBDIR directory is a standard UUCP directory found on all UNIX systems, it is the first place into which we will learn to copy a file using uucp.

The format for using uucp can be expressed as:

```
uucp from to
```

where from is the name of the file you want to send, and to is the place you are sending that file. We will begin by sending a file from your local UNIX machine to a neighbor UNIX machine. The files that you want to send from your local UNIX machine, from, are specified simply by stating their names. The place (neighbor UNIX machine) where you want to send those files, to, is specified as:

```
machine\!/path/file
```

Here, machine is the name of the neighbor UNIX machine (see uuname in chapter 11) to which you want to send the local file. The /path/file indicates the full path and the filename of the file on that neighbor machine into which you want the copy of the local file placed. Again, note that the \! separating the machine name from the /path/file may be more simply expressed as ! for Bourne Shell users. The \! notation will, however, work for all shells.

Before we show you an actual uucp command, take a moment to create the following file in your home directory. We will use this file in many of the examples that follow:

```
Hush-a-by lady, in Alice's lap!
Till the feast's ready, we've time for a nap.
When the feast's over, we'll go to the ball--
Red Queen, and White Queen, and Alice, and all!

Through the Looking-Glass
Lewis Carroll
```

If you were to call this file alice.txt, and you wanted to send it into the PUBDIR directory on the neighboring machine named neighbor1, you would invoke uucp with the command:

```
uucp alice.txt neighbor1\!~uucp
     ↑         ↑
     from      to
```

This command line tells uucp to copy the file alice.txt from your current directory and send that copy to the neighboring UNIX machine named neighbor1. It also instructs uucp to tell neighbor1 that it is to place the received copy into its home UUCP directory or PUBDIR directory. (It does this because of the notation ~uucp, which, as you saw in the last chapter, always refers to the public directory.) Just like UNIX's cp command, the uucp command to copy a file to a directory causes the new file to retain the name of the original file. If we could examine neighbor1's PUBDIR directory after our uucp request had been processed, we would find that a new file called alice.txt had been created there.

Recall from chapter 11 that uucp transfers do not happen immediately. In the preceding example, a request is queued for the file alice.txt to be copied to neighbor1, but the actual transfer may not take place at once. The delay between the time you queue your request and the time the file arrives at the destination machine can vary from a few seconds to several hours. If your machine is one of the slow ones, be patient.

How *uucp* Handles Errors

Usually, uucp does its work silently, but, when something does go wrong, it lets you know in one of two ways. Figure 12-1 is a block diagram showing the two ways that uucp reports errors to you.

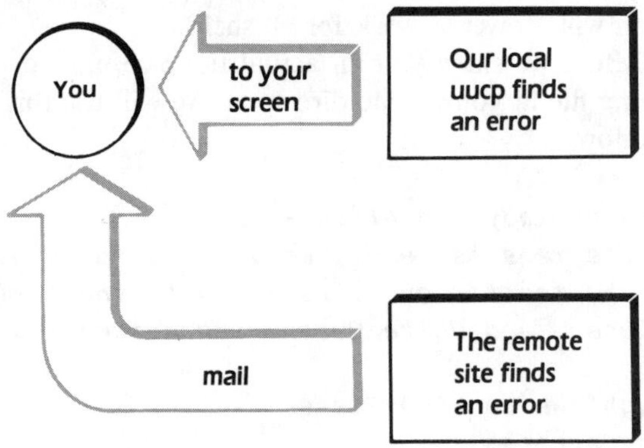

Figure 12-1. The **uucp** program reports errors to you in two ways.

1. If there is something wrong with your uucp transfer request—the outgoing file alice.txt doesn't exist, for example—you will see a diagnostic immediately:

```
can't get file status alice.txt
copy failed
```

2. If the request itself is okay, but some error occurs later after the request has been queued (something only the neighbor UNIX machine could discover, for example), you will receive an electronic mail message explaining your error:

```
From bill Fri Oct 31 12:00:00 1987
To: bill
Status: R

file /usr/bill/alice.txt, system neighbor1
can't copy to file/directory - file left in PUBDIR/user/file
```

In the second situation, the error message received by mail shows that you (bill) tried to specify UUCP's home directory using the absolute pathname /uucp /alice.txt instead of correctly using the relative pathname ~uucp. When the file alice.txt was transferred to neighbor1, the uucp program at neighbor1 tried to place it into /uucp/alice.txt on that machine. Since the directory /uucp probably doesn't exist on neighbor1 (or if it does, you lack write permission there), neighbor1's uucp placed the file instead into:

```
PUBDIR/user/file
```

or

```
/usr/uucp/uucppublic/bill/alice.txt
                    ↑         ↑    ↑
                 PUBDIR      user  file
```

as the message indicates.

Note that the filename listed in the mail received is the name of the file that was *sent* rather than that of the file you were trying to create on `neighbor1`. This can be confusing because you normally expect an error message to tell you the name of the file it *couldn't* deal with, the one on `neighbor1`, rather than the one it could deal with, the one on your local machine. This is one area in which HoneyDanBer `uucp` is a marked improvement over ordinary `uucp`. If you were to make the same mistake while using HoneyDanBer `uucp`, your mail would look more like this:

```
From uucp Fri Oct 31 12:00:00 1987 remote from neighbor1
To: ourhome!bill
Status: R

remote copy      [uucp job neighbor1D5bd2 (11/31-12:10:22)]
REQUEST: ourhome!/usr/bill/alice.txt --> neighbor1!/uucp/alice.txt
(SYSTEM: neighbor1) Can't create directory "/uucp"
```

This improved mail message shows more clearly that you (`bill`) incorrectly specified UUCP's PUBDIR directory as `/uucp`. The correct way to specify the PUBDIR directory is `~uucp`.

Mail Notification of a Successful Transfer (*-m* Flag)

Unless you tell `uucp` to do otherwise, it will perform a successful transfer without notifying you. Usually that's what you want, but there will be times when you will want to be notified that your copy succeeded.

By invoking `uucp` with the `-m` flag, you tell `uucp` to send you mail when the transfer is complete, even if there is no error. By way of example, let's create a new file to send and call it `walrus.txt`. This will give us two files to play with (we'll need them later):

```
'If seven maids with seven mops
Swept it for half a year,
Do you suppose,' the Walrus said,
'That they could get it clear?'
'I doubt it,' said the Carpenter,
And shed a bitter tear.
```

```
Through the Looking-Glass
Lewis Carroll
```

Again, we will use uucp to copy the file to the neighboring UNIX site neighbor1, but this time we will use the -m flag as an additional argument when invoking uucp:

```
uucp -m walrus.txt neighbor1\!~uucp
         ↑
         send mail to self on success
```

Note that the -m flag, as all flag arguments must when given to uucp, precedes any file or system specifications. That is, the form is always:

```
uucp flags from to
```

Since uucp merely queues a request, the actual transfer of walrus.txt may not happen right away. When it does (assuming the transfer was successful), you will receive an electronic mail message notifying you of that successful transfer:

```
From bill Fri Oct 31 12:10:23 1987
To: bill
Status: R

file /usr/bill/walrus.txt, system neighbor1
copy succeeded
```

Because you used the -m flag with uucp, you received an electronic mail message telling you that the copy was successfully received by the neighbor site neighbor1.

Copying from One PUBDIR Directory into Another

As you may recall from chapter 11, all UUCP programs require that specific permissions exist for any file that is copied:

- For a file to be copied (sent) from your local machine, or from a neighbor machine, it must be readable by anyone (i.e., at least mode 444 or -r--r--r--) and be situated in a directory that is readable and searchable by anyone (i.e., at least mode 555 or dr-xr-xr-x).
- For a file to be received (copied into a directory on your machine or on a neighbor machine), the directory into which it will be placed must be readable, writable, and searchable by anyone (i.e., at least mode 777 or drwxrwxrwx).

- For both copying from, and receiving into, all directories in the path leading to the specified directory must be readable and searchable by anyone (i.e., at least mode 555 or `dr-xdr-xdr-x`).

Additionally, on many machines—especially those set up as public-access machines and those involving government or industrial security—the PUBDIR directory is the only one into which, and from which, `uucp` may transfer files. (See figure 12-2.) Because of these restrictions, you have a greater likelihood of a successful transfer if you restrict your `uucp` activities to the PUBDIR directory.

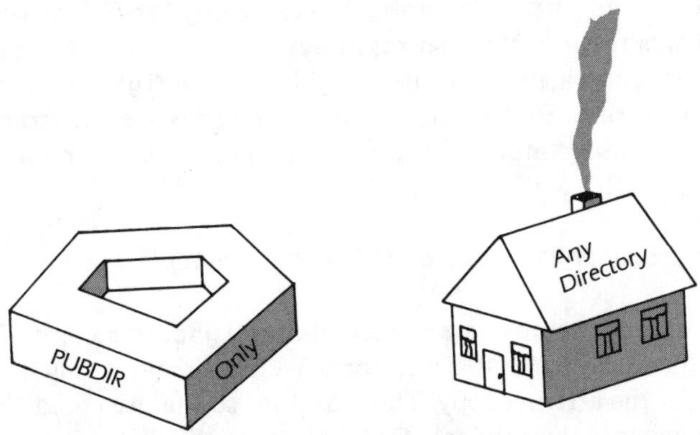

Figure 12-2. Sites that worry about intrusion usually restrict all outside access solely to UUCP's PUBDIR directory. Trusted and honest sites, on the other hand, are often allowed to access all directories.

Copy from Your PUBDIR Directory into a Neighbor Site's PUBDIR Directory

To illustrate how to transfer from your PUBDIR directory into the PUBDIR of a neighbor machine, we will transfer `alice.txt` once again. This time, two steps are required. First, copy `alice.txt` into your local PUBDIR directory:

```
cp alice.txt ~uucp                      ← C and Korn Shells
cp alice.txt /usr/spool/uucppublic      ← Bourne Shell
```

Then, transfer that duplicate using `uucp`:

```
uucp ~uucp/alice.txt neighbor1\! ~uucp
     ↑
     all shells
```

Notice that `~uucp` refers to UUCP's PUBDIR directory. This notation is built into all UUCP software, including `uucp`. Therefore, it can be used as part of `uucp`'s command line no matter which shell you are using. This is not true, though, for the cp command that we used to copy alice.txt into our local PUBDIR directory. Commands such as cp are handled completely by the shell. With such commands, you may use ~uucp only if you are using the C Shell or the Korn Shell. That shorthand is not available to users of the Bourne Shell.

Copy from a Neighbor Site's PUBDIR Directory into Your Local PUBDIR Directory

When using PUBDIR on both machines, the correct UNIX permissions are available on your machine as well as on neighbor machines. Because uucp can copy into as well as out of this directory, you can easily verify that what you sent to neighbor1 was received there successfully.

To copy a file from the neighbor site neighbor1's PUBDIR directory into your own site's PUBDIR directory, simply reverse the from/to arguments used in the previous example. (Of course, the file alice.txt must first exist in neighbor1's PUBDIR directory.)

```
uucp neighbor1\!~uucp/alice.txt ~uucp/alice.chk
```

In this example, we request that neighbor1's copy of alice.txt be copied into our local PUBDIR directory. We also request that the name alice.chk be used for the arriving copy. This was done so that we could check to see that the new copy matches the original. One way to do this is to use the diff program:

```
cd /usr/spool/uucppublic
diff alice.txt alice.chk
```

If the diff program doesn't print anything, then the two copies are identical.

If you find that permission is denied you when you try to uucp a file, remember that UUCP's PUBDIR directories are always available on all machines. If you can't copy a file directly into a remote user's home directory, you can always copy the file into PUBDIR on that user's machine. Later we will show you how you can have uucp automatically notify the user that a uucp-transmitted file has arrived.

Copying into Your Own and Other Directories

The PUBDIR directory is important because it is guaranteed to possess the correct permissions for UUCP. Beyond simple file permissions, it is almost always listed as usable in your system's USERFILE file (or in Permissions for HoneyDanBer UUCP). (See chapter 11.)

When UNIX machines are connected over some kind of local area network, the restrictions on which directories are usable for UUCP copying are often less strict than those on machines that are connected to the outside world. You will probably not be allowed to copy files into any directory, but you will certainly be able to copy files into your home directory. Let's see how this is done.

As a first step, create a subdirectory in your home directory called public and set its mode to 777 (readable, writable, and searchable by anyone):

```
cd
mkdir public
chmod 777 public
ls -ld public
drwxrwxrwx 2  bill    512 Nov 09 12:24 public
```

You could, of course, change your home directory to mode 777, instead of creating a special directory, but such a move would be terribly unwise because that would allow anyone to write into it. It is a much better idea to create a scratch subdirectory, like public, for receipt of uucp transfers.

Now that your scratch directory called public is set up, you can copy alice.txt from the neighbor site neighbor1 into it:

```
uucp neighbor1\!~uucp/alice.txt public
```

Again, uucp acts just like cp when a directory name is specified as a target. It places alice.txt, from the neighbor site neighbor1, into the directory public, a subdirectory in your home directory on your local machine.

There are several variations in the way you can specify the public directory relative to your home directory (assuming you are in your home directory):

```
$HOME/public
/usr/bill/public
~bill/public        ←not with Bourne Shell
~/public            ←not with Bourne Shell
./public
```

We prefer to use public because it is the most succinct and clear. You are free to choose whichever variation you prefer. It makes no difference to uucp. (See sh(1) or csh(1) in your UNIX manual for a more complete description of the variations available.)

At your site you might not be restricted to copying into an equivalent of the PUBDIR directory in your home directory. Any directory that is readable, writable, and searchable by anyone is a candidate. You should examine your system's USERFILE (or Permissions for HoneyDanBer UUCP) in /usr/lib/uucp to learn which directories have been set up by your system administrator as legal for uucp copying.

Notifying the Recipient with Mail (*-n* Flag)

Just as you can receive mail notification of a successful `uucp` transfer, you can also arrange for the recipient of the file on the destination machine to receive a similar notification. To do this, use the `-n` flag in much the same way you used the `-m` flag to send mail to yourself. The only difference is that the `-n` flag requires you to specify the recipient's *login name*:

```
-nname
```

Note that there must be no space between the `-n` and the login `name`.

For example, to copy `alice.txt` into the PUBDIR directory on the neighbor site `neighbor1`, and send mail both to yourself and to `john`, a user on `neighbor1`, you would type:

```
          send mail to john
          ↓
uucp -m -njohn alice.txt neighbor1\!~uucp
      ↑
      send mail to yourself
```

If the copy is successful, `john` will receive a letter much like the one you get. The only difference is that `john`'s mail will announce successful arrival rather than successful transmission:

```
/usr/spool/uucppublic/alice.txt from ourhome!bill arrived.
```

The name specified with the `-n` flag need not be that of the actual recipient. You might, for example, wish to notify the system administrator on the neighbor machine that you are experimenting with `uucp` by specifying `-nroot`.

Copying Multiple Files with *uucp*

The `uucp` program can be used to copy multiple files from your UNIX machine to a neighbor machine, and vice versa. The format for sending multiple files from your local site to a neighbor UNIX site is:

```
uucp file1 file2 file3 etc. machine\!directory
```

For example, to send both `alice.txt` and `walrus.txt` into the neighbor site `neighbor1`'s PUBDIR directory with a single `uucp` command, you would enter:

```
uucp alice.txt walrus.txt neighbor1\!~uucp
```

When listing multiple files on your local machine for sending with `uucp`, you are free to use any of the many conventions available on UNIX (see figure 12-3). In short, you may specify multiple files on your local machine in any manner permitted by your current shell environment and `uucp`.

A List of Files

`file1 file2 file3`

Absolute Pathnames

`/usr/you/public/file1`

Relative Pathnames

`~/file1`	in your home directory	← *not Bourne Shell*
`~user/file1`	in user's home directory	← *not Bourne Shell*
`../file1`	in parent of current directory	
`file1`	in current directory	
`./file1`	in current directory	

Wildcard Expressions

`*.txt`	all files ending in ".txt"	
`file?`	"file" followed by any single character	
`file[ab]`	"file" followed by "a" or "b"	
`file{.c,.h}`	"file.c" and "file.h"	← *not Bourne Shell*

Environmental and History Variables

`$FILES`	shell variable	
`!$`	last argument, previous command	← *not Bourne Shell*
`!23$`	last argument, command 23	← *not Bourne Shell*

Figure 12-3. How to specify multiple files on your local machine.

When specifying multiple files on the remote machine, the rules are much more limited. The format for copying multiple files from a neighbor UNIX site into your local machine looks like this:

```
uucp site\!/path/pattern directory
```

Here, `directory` is the name of a directory on your local machine into which you want the files placed. That directory must, like your `public` directory, possess the correct permissions for writing. The `site` and `path` in the example are what you have seen before: the site name of the neighbor UNIX machine from which you will be copying files, and the full pathname of the directory on that machine which contains those files. The `pattern`, however, is something new.

Since you can't list files on a neighbor machine using `uucp`, you need to instead specify multiple files by using a *pattern*. You may use any of the wildcard characters to construct that pattern. For example, to copy both `alice.txt` and `walrus.txt` from the neighbor site `neighbor1`'s PUBDIR directory into your `public` directory, you could execute the following:

```
uucp neighbor1\!~uucp/\*.txt public
                      ↑
                      wildcard character
```

Here, the expression `*.txt` expands on the neighbor site `neighbor1` to include all files in the PUBDIR directory there that end with the characters `.txt`.

Note that, just as with the ! character, you must precede any wildcard characters with a backslash. This is true for all shells. If you fail to use a backslash with the * in the preceding example, the shell on your local machine will try to match it to files on your local machine. By preceding the * with a backslash, you cause that * to be sent as-is to the neighbor site `neighbor1`. That site then uses the * to match files there, which is what you want.

The `pattern` for multiple files on a neighbor site can include other special characters in addition to the *. You can use a ?, which matches any single character, and the [] characters, which define a range of characters. Of course, all of these need to be preceded by a backslash as well. For example:

```
uucp neighbor1\!~uucp/alice.\* public
uucp neighbor1\!~uucp/chap\[0-9\] public
uucp neighbor1\!~uucp/chap\? public
```

The first example copies all files beginning with `alice` from the neighbor site `neighbor1`'s PUBDIR directory into our `public` directory in our home directory. The second example copies only those files that begin with `chap` and end with one of the single characters in the range 0 through 9. The last example copies any file that begins with `chap` and is followed by any single character.

When specifying multiple files on the remote machine, you are specifically prohibited from using the dot (.) and dot-dot (..) relative pathname expressions (for the current directory and the parent directory), and from using any of the environmental or history variables normally available from your shell. After all, the remote machine could hardly be expected to know about your local environment. For a complete description of filenames and the use of special characters, refer to sh(1) and csh(1) in your UNIX manual. Also see figure 12-4 for a summary of valid ways to specify files at a neighbor site.

Automatic Creating of Directories (*-d* and *-f* Flags)

Whenever `uucp` copies a file, it automatically creates any directories that are needed for the placement of that file:

```
uucp tortoise\!~/walrus.txt public/newdir/
                                          ↑
                                  this is a directory
```

This example queues a request that the file walrus.txt from neighbor site neighbor1's PUBDIR directory be copied into the subdirectory newdir in your local public directory. Since newdir doesn't exist in public, uucp will create it. Note that newdir has a trailing slash (/). This tells uucp that it is the name of a directory and not that of a file. Without the /, uucp would copy walrus.txt into (and create) a *file* called newdir, rather than creating a *directory* with that name.

Ordinarily, creation of directories as needed is just the behavior you want. Occasionally, however, you might prefer to prevent that creation. You might, for example, be sending a file to a friend who has asked you not to clutter his or her spool directory with unneeded subdirectories.

The -f flag has been provided by uucp to disable the automatic creation of directories:

```
uucp -f walrus.txt neighbor1\!~john/spool/alicedir/
     ↑
     don't create directories
```

This requests that the file walrus.txt be copied into the subdirectory spool/alicedir/ in user john's home directory at the neighbor site neighbor1. The -f flag tells uucp *not* to create the subdirectory spool/alicedir/ if it does not already exist.

The uucp program also offers a -d flag, which is used to specify that subdirectories *should* be created as needed. Since that is the default action

A List of Files

    file1 file2 file3

Absolute Pathnames

    /usr/you/public/file1

Relative Pathnames

~user/file1	in user's home directory	← *all shells*
~uucp/file	in PUBDIR directory	← *all shells*

Wildcard Expressions

*.txt	all files ending in ".text"
file\?	"file" followed by any single character
file\[ab\]	"file" followed by "a" and/or "b"

Figure 12-4. How to specify multiple files at a neighbor site.

anyway, -d is never used. In fact, the UCB version of uucp ignores that flag altogether!

Defining Types of Spooling (*–c*, *–C*, and *–s* Flags)

As we have seen, when you specify that a file is to be transferred with uucp, the file is not transferred immediately. Rather, a *request* that it be transferred is automatically queued for later execution by the low-level program uucico (see chapter 18). In addition to this queuing of your request, the file itself may be spooled (copied into a temporary holding directory), and the duplicate of your file later transferred instead of the original.

The uucp program offers three flags that can be used to specify the nature and location of this spooling:

-c The -c flag tells uucp not to spool the file at all. No duplicate is made of your file, and the original is later copied during the transfer.

-C The -C flag tells uucp to spool a duplicate of your file. That duplicate is later copied during the transfer.

-s The -s flag tells uucp which directory to use as the spool directory. The default spool directory is /usr/spool/uucp.

The -c flag, which prevents spooling (the default under AT&T UUCP), is useful when the file you are sending is not expected to change. Because no duplicate is made of your file, this request is processed swiftly. The larger a file is, the longer it takes to spool a copy of it, so it's clearly faster to avoid spooling.

The -C flag, which specifies spooling (the default under UCB UUCP), is handy for those files that will change between the time the request is made and the time the file is actually transferred. For example, suppose you are halfway through the writing of a new chapter and the editor asks for a copy right away. You can:

```
uucp -C chap5 neighbor1\!~editor/sample.chap
     ↑
     specify that chap5 be spooled
```

This command tells uucp to make a duplicate of the file chap5 in your current directory as it exists now, to place that duplicate in /usr/spool/uucp, and to send the duplicate rather than the original. Whenever uucp spools a duplicate, that duplicate is removed after it is transferred. Needless to say, requests using the -C flag will be processed somewhat more slowly than those using the -c flag. The main advantage here is that you know exactly what the editor will receive, whereas if you did not spool the file, the editor would get whichever version of the file existed at the time the request was later processed.

The -s flag is used to specify an alternative to /usr/spool/uucp as the place where duplicate files are placed. A possible application of this flag might be when you want to keep everything relating to a single project in a single place, including temporary copies destined for transfer to neighbor sites. For example, the request:

```
uucp -s~/book/spool -C chap5 neighbor1\!~editor/sample.chap
        ↑
        place the spooled duplicate here
```

tells uucp to spool a duplicate of chap5 and place that temporary duplicate into the subdirectory book/spool in your home directory. When the requested transfer eventually occurs, the duplicate in book/spool will be sent; then the duplicate will be removed.

Because the defaults for -c and -C differ between AT&T and Berkeley UUCP, you should always specify one or the other when the nature of spooling is of concern.

Summary of *uucp* Flags

-m	Sender receives mail notification of success.
-nuser	Recipient whose login name is user receives mail notification of arrival.
-f	Don't created needed directories.
-c	Don't spool copy of file.
-C	Do spool copy of file.
-sdir	Place spooled copy into directory named dir.
-esite	Execute this uucp request on the neighbor site named site.
-r	Queue but don't transmit.
-j	Print UUCP job number of this uucp queued job (chapter 15).
-x#	Print "verbose" or debugging output at level specified by the digit "#".

Advanced *uucp* Topics

There are a few functions of uucp that are extremely useful when needed but are beyond the needs of most users. We will discuss them here so that you know they are available if needed:

- The uucp program can be used for copying files between two neighbor machines, with the request being made on the local machine.
- The -e flag tells uucp to execute itself on a remote machine.
- The -r flag tells uucp to queue your request, and not to start uucico.
- The -x flag tells uucp to execute itself in a debugging, verbose mode. This provides an excellent mechanism for watching uucp in action.

Copying Files between Remote Machines

You have seen that uucp can be used to copy files from your machine to a neighbor UNIX machine and vice versa. It is also possible to use uucp to copy files from one neighbor UNIX site into another neighbor, or remote, UNIX site, with a request made on your local machine.

To do this, you simply need to specify both the from and to arguments to uucp in the site\!/path/file format, as:

```
uucp site1\!/path/file site2\!/path/file
     ↑                 ↑
     from              to
```

Imagine a situation in which each machine on your local area network had a directory called PUBDIR/archive that was available for the backing up of important files. If you had a document called doc in the PUBDIR/archive directory on the neighbor site neighbor3, and you wanted to copy a duplicate of that file into the PUBDIR/archive directory on the neighbor site neighbor1 (remember our local machine is ourhome), you could enter the following:

```
request made at our local site, ourhome
↓
uucp neighbor3\! ~uucp/archive/doc neighbor1\! ~uucp/archive/
     ↑                             ↑
     from                          to
```

This command tells our local uucp to copy the file doc from the neighbor site neighbor3's PUBDIR/archive directory into the neighbor site neighbor1's PUBDIR/archive directory. For transfers of this type to work, you must have permission to execute the uucp program on the neighbor site neighbor3 (see uux in chapter 14).

Executing *uucp* on a Remote Site (*-e* Flag)

The `-e` flag tells `uucp` to execute itself on a neighbor machine. The format for using the `-e` flag is:

```
-esitename
```

where `sitename` is the name of the neighbor machine on which you want the `uucp` command run. There must be no space between `-e` and `sitename`. For example:

```
request made at our local site, ourhome
↓
uucp -eneighbor3 \~uucp/archive/doc neighbor4\!~uucp/archive/
         ↑
         run this uucp command at site neighbor3
```

This is equivalent to the request in the previous example, when we copied a file between two neighbor sites. The entire request is copied to the neighbor site `neighbor3` and executed there as:

```
uucp ~uucp/archive/doc neighbor4\!~uucp/archive/
         ↑
         request run at site neighbor3
```

Just as with copying between neighbor machines, the `-e` flag requires that you have permission to execute the `uucp` command on the neighbor machine named by `-esitename` (see `uux` in chapter 14).

Queue But Don't Transmit (*-r* Flag)

Ordinarily, `uucp` will *try* to transfer your request as soon as you are done typing the command. It does this by executing the `uucico` program (see chapter 18), but `uucico` can be suppressed by using the `-r` flag.

For example, suppose you are sending a very large file to a friend whose login name is `lark`, and you want that friend to bear the cost of the phone call:

```
      notify lark via mail
      |           don't spool a copy
      ↓           ↓
uucp -nlark -c -r bigfile neighbor1\!~uucp/bigfile
                ↑
                don't transmit now
```

This command tells uucp to queue a request that the file bigfile on our local machine is to be sent to the neighbor site neighbor1. The -nlark tells uucp to notify the user named lark on the neighbor machine neighbor1 when the file arrives there, and the -c flag suppresses spooling of a duplicate. Finally, the -r flag tells uucp to simply queue the request and not to start uucico. The file will be transmitted later, either when neighbor1 calls us or when another user triggers a call by our site with uucp, mail, or postnews.

Watching *uucp* Work (–*x* Flag)

The uucp program is able to print out, for your edification, a step-by-step account of everything it trys to do. This feature is enabled by using the -x flag. The format for using the -x flag is:

```
-x#
```

where # is a digit from 1 through 9—the higher the digit, the more information uucp prints out.

It is difficult to give a general example for using the -x flag because the degree and the nature of output vary both with the digit (level) specified and with the version of UUCP you are running. The following example shows one possible kind of output. Notice line 8, where your request is actually queued:

```
1       uucp -x6 walrus.txt neighbor1!~uucp
2
3       ** START **
4       UID 123, User bryan,Ename () PATH /usr/bryan
5       file - walrus.txt
6       send file - 2
7       file - C.neighi2n6802
8       bryan neighbor1 (11/09-12:46-2021) QUE'D (C.neighi2n6802)
        etc.
```

Let's examine this output line by line.

Line 1: A uucp request is made to copy the file walrus.txt in the current directory of the local machine into a file of the same name in the PUBDIR directory of the neighbor site neighbor1. The -x6 tells uucp to produce its "verbose" output at level 6.

Line 2: Blank.

Line 3: The uucp program starts its verbose output.

Line 4: The user identification number (UID) of the user who is running uucp is 123. The user's login name (User) is bryan. There is no "effective" user name (Ename). The directory containing the local file to send (PATH) is /usr/bryan.

Line 5: The file is named walrus.txt.

Line 6: The file will be sent.

Line 7: The work file, created in /usr/spool/uucp, will be called C.neighi2u6802. That file will contain information about where and how walrus.txt will be sent.

Line 8: This is the status line placed into /usr/spool/uucp/LOGFILE (see chapter 15).

The diagnostic, verbose output produced by the -x flag and uucp gives you a rough overview of the steps that uucp goes through when spooling a request. The uucp program creates a number of work (C.), data, and status files in the process of spooling a request.

Copy through a Series of Machines with *uusend*

We noted earlier that uucp, unlike mail, copies only between directly connected (neighbor) machines. To overcome this deficiency, some UNIX sites provide a program called uusend.

The uusend program, like uucp, is used to copy files from your local UNIX site to a remote UNIX site. As a bonus, however, uusend accepts remote site specifications as:

```
uusend file site1\!site2\!site3\!/path/file
            ↑       ↑       ↑
```

a series of UNIX machines

Here, the path and file specifications are the same as those for uucp. The remote site, however, is not one site but three. In this example, file is first copied to site1—an immediate neighbor machine. That machine then copies file to site2, and site2 then copies it to site3. At site3, file is finally placed into /path/file.

Just as with mail, there is no unreasonable limitation to the number of sites through which a file may be forwarded in this way. We've shown you only three here, but you can use as many as are necessary (up to 256).

The rules for permissions for both the local file and the remote /path/file are identical to those for uucp, as discussed in the last chapter and reviewed earlier in this chapter. Where uusend and uucp differ is:

- The uusend program can forward files through a series of UNIX machines, whereas uucp cannot (see figure 12-5).
- The uusend program can only send files from your local UNIX machine to a remote UNIX machine. Unlike uucp, it cannot be used to copy files in the reverse direction.
- The flags used by uusend resemble those used by uucp, but they have different meanings and there are fewer of them.
- Only files may be sent with uucp. The uusend, on the other hand, can send what it reads through the standard input and pipes. We will expand on this shortly.

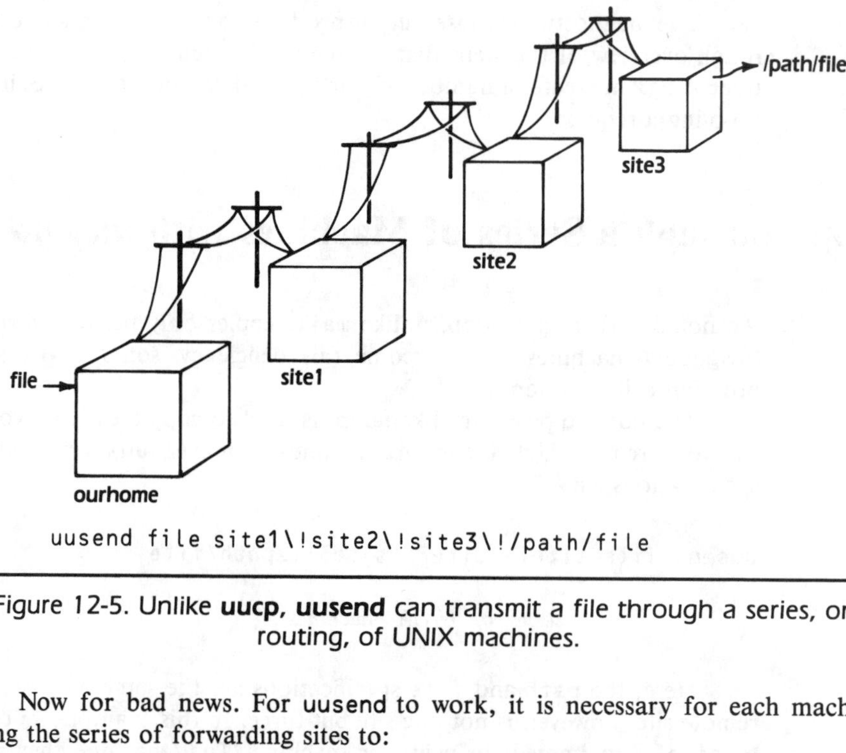


```
uusend file site1\!site2\!site3\!/path/file
```

Figure 12-5. Unlike **uucp, uusend** can transmit a file through a series, or routing, of UNIX machines.

Now for bad news. For uusend to work, it is necessary for each machine along the series of forwarding sites to:

- Have the uusend program available. Since most Berkeley UNIX sites have uusend, and most AT&T UNIX sites do not, the utility of uusend depends greatly on what flavor of UNIX your neighbors run. (If they are all academic institutions, chances are they run Berkeley UNIX.)
- Allow outside machines to run uusend. Even if a site possesses the uusend program, there is no guarantee that you will be allowed to access it for forwarding files.

So, how do you find out if you can use uusend to send files? First, you need to see if it is available on your local machine. Just type:

```
uusend
```

If you see the following Usage message, then you will know that uusend is available on your local machine:

```
Usage: uusend [-m ooo] [-r] -/file sys!sys!...!rfile
```

If uusend is available at your site, the next step is to determine if it is available to you at each of the sites you wish to copy through. To do this, you need to query each system administrator, by e-mail, with a message similar to this one:

```
Dear System Administrator:

I need to copy the following list of files
through your site to the destination site
site3. I hope to do this with uusend. Is that
program available for my use at your site?
...etc.
```

Then you must mail that message to each system administrator along the route you have selected:

```
mail site1\!root < message
mail site1\!site2\!root < message
mail site1\!site2\!site3\!root < message
```

Often, remote system administrators will allow you to access uusend for a brief period and for a good cause. If any site refuses you access, you should review mail routing (see chapter 4) for the techniques used to find an alternative series of machines.

Setting Permissions of Destination File (*-m* Flag)

One of the major weaknesses of uucp is that it always creates a destination copy that is readable by anyone. Ordinarily this is not a problem, but there will be times when you will want to transfer sensitive documents.

As an improvement over uucp, uusend offers the -m flag as a means to specify what permissions the destination file will possess. The format for the -m flag is:

```
-m ooo
```

Here, ooo is the *mode*, or permissions, that you want the transmitted file to have when it arrives at the remote site. The reason that the mode is printed as "ooo" is because the mode must be specified in octal notation. If you don't know how to specify a file's permissions in octal notation, refer to chmod(1) in your UNIX manual.

Consider the personnel director who needs to send a list of theft suspects to the Main Branch computer. She could use the -m flag with uusend as:

```
uusend -m 400 invest.list neighbor1\!remote2\!main\!/tmp
         ↑   ↑
```

set mode to read-only by owner

Here, a uusend request is queued to send the file invest.list and place that file into the /tmp directory on the remote UNIX site main. The -m 400 argument tells uusend to set the permissions of that copy on main to be readable only by its owner.

Feeding *uusend* through a Pipe (-)

Another advantage of uusend over uucp is that uusend can read from the standard input, whereas uucp cannot. This capability allows uusend to do more than simply transmit files. By using the pipe symbol (¦), you can cause uusend to transmit the output of other programs. As a bonus, you can also cause uusend to transmit characters that you type directly at your keyboard.

To cause uusend to read from the standard input, simply replace the source filename with a hyphen (-) character. That is, instead of specifying that uusend transmit a file directly as:

```
uusend filename site1\!site2\!site3\!/path/file
         ↑
```

transmit this file

you replace filename with a - character:

```
uusend - site1\!site2\!site3\!/path/file
       ↑
```

transmit standard input

thereby telling uusend to transmit what it reads from the standard input. Since the standard input ordinarily comes from your keyboard, this example would cause uusend to gather everything you typed, up to end-of-file or Control-d, and transmit that.

A more useful way to use uusend with the standard input is to connect the output of another program to the input of uusend by using a pipe. For example, suppose that an artist wants to transmit a graphics image. Because graphics images are usually stored in machine-specific image files, it is necessary to transform them into something portable before transmitting them. If the program to do that transformation were called gport, the artist could transmit image files with the following uusend command:

```
gport graphfile ¦ uusend - site1\!site2\!/path/file
```

Here, the output of gport is connected via a pipe, the ¦ character, to the standard input of uusend. The - character in place of a filename in the uusend command causes uusend to transmit what it reads from that standard input—the output of gport—to the remote UNIX site site2.

When using a - with uusend, it is always necessary to specify the file portion of /path/file. Because uusend is reading from its standard input, it has no idea what to name the copy it is transmitting.

Queue But Don't Transmit (*-r* Flag)

Ordinarily uusend will try to transfer your request as soon as you're done typing the command. It does this by executing the uucico program (see chapter 18), but this program can be suppressed by using the -r flag.

For example, suppose you are sending several files with uusend and want them all to be transmitted at once. You could:

```
uusend -r file1 neighbor1\!remote2\! ~/
uusend -r file2 neighbor1\!remote2\! ~/
uusend -r file3 neighbor1\!remote2\! ~/
uusend -r file4 neighbor1\!remote2\! ~/
uusend file5 neighbor1\!remote2\! ~/
```

This instructs uusend to queue requests that the first four files be transmitted into the PUBDIR directory on the remote UNIX site remote2. The -r flag causes those requests to be queued only and not transmitted. The last line in this example shows uusend being run without the -r flag. This both queues a request for file5 to be transmitted, and triggers the actual transmission of all five files.

Summary of *uusend* Flags

-m ooo	Set mode of destination file to be ooo, where ooo is octal.
-r	Queue but don't transmit.

Summary of Uses and Caveats

The following is a brief summary of the most common uses of the `uucp` and `uusend` programs. Caveats are provided to illustrate variations, limitations, and possible pitfalls.

Send `file` *to remote site: PUBDIR*

```
uucp file sitename\!~uucp/file
uusend file site1\!site2\!~uucp/file
```

Caveat: Target filename optional if same as source. UUCP's home directory (`~uucp`) may also be specified as: `/usr/spool/uucppublic` or `~/`.

Send `file` *to remote site: user's spool directory*

```
uucp file sitename\!~username/spooldir/file
```

Caveat: Target filename optional if same as source; `spooldir` must be mode 777 (`drwxrwxrwx`).

Send `file` *to remote site: absolute pathname*

```
uucp file sitename\!/absolutepath/file
```

Caveat: Target filename optional if same as source. All directories in `absolutepath` must be at least mode 555 (`dr-xr-xr-x`), with the final one mode 777 (`drwxrwxrwx`).

Send `file` *to remote site: PUBDIR to PUBDIR*

```
uucp ~uucp/file sitename\!~uucp/file
```

Caveat: Target filename optional if same as source. UUCP's home directory on either machine (`~uucp`), may also be specified as: `/usr/spool/uucppublic` or `~/`.

Send multiple files to remote site: PUBDIR

```
uucp filelist sitename\!~uucp
```

Caveat: The `filelist` may be specified in any manner that is legal for your shell. The target must be the name of a directory.

Send mail: to self

```
uucp -m file sitename\!path/file
```

Caveat: The `-m` ensures that mail will be received by the sender, indicating successful file transfer. The `uucp` program ordinarily tries to send mail to the sender only if there is an error in transmission.

Send mail: to recipient

```
uucp -nrecipient sitename\!path/file
```

Caveat: The `recipient` is the login name of someone on the remote site. There must be no space between `-n` and `recipient`.

Receive `file` *from remote site: PUBDIR to PUBDIR*

```
uucp sitename\!~uucp/file ~uucp/file
```

Caveat: Target filename optional if same as source. UUCP's home directory on either machine (`~uucp`) may also be specified as: `/usr/spool/uucppublic` or `~/`.

Receive multiple files from remote site

```
uucp sitename\!filelist ~uucp
```

Caveat: The `filelist` may contain only the special characters `*` and `?`, and the special operator `[]`. These must be backslashed or quoted to protect them from expansion locally. The target must be a directory, mode 777 (`drwxrwxrwx`).

Copy between remote sites

```
uucp sitename\!/path/file sitename\!/path/file
```

Caveat: Permission to execute `uucp` required on the first neighbor site.

Specify spooling with `uucp`

`-c`	Don't spool a copy. Do send original.
`-C`	Do spool a copy. Send copy, not original.
`-sspooldir`	Place copies into `spooldir`.

Summary

In this chapter you have learned how to copy files between neighboring UNIX machines with `uucp`, and through a series of remote UNIX machines with `uusend`. You have learned a host of rules that govern file and directory permissions, local filenames, and neighbor and remote UNIX site names. You have also learned how to send and receive mail notification, send and receive multiple files, specify spooling, and delay transfer.

In the next chapter we will explore two programs that make UUCP copying easier. Called `uuto` and `uupick`, these programs offer a simple and interactive means for copying files from one PUBDIR directory to another, and then retrieving those files.

13

Easy PUBDIR Copying with *uuto* and *uupick*

The uuto and uupick programs are available on many, but not all, UNIX systems.[1] Where provided, they form a simple, interactive method of transferring both files and directories to neighbor UNIX sites. To determine if they are available to you at your site, just type:

```
apropos uuto
```

This works on most UNIX systems. If the output of that command is:

```
uuto, uupick (1)   -- public system-to-system file copy
```

then they are indeed available for you to use. (If your site lacks the apropos command, you may alternatively try: man uuto, which uuto, whereis uuto, or, more simply and directly, uuto.)

The programs uuto and uupick are described as "public system-to-system file copy" because uuto transfers files into a neighbor site's PUBDIR directory, and uupick retrieves files from there. Remember that the PUBDIR directory—/usr/spool/uucppublic on most systems—is the one directory that is guaranteed to be available for all UUCP transfers.

The uuto program is used to send files:

- It can be used to send both individual files and directory hierarchies.
- The recipient is always notified by mail.
- The sender can also receive mail.
- Files can be spooled (see chapter 11) before being transmitted.

1. They are really Bourne Shell scripts. If you are interested, sh(1) in the on-line UNIX programmer's manual will help you to understand how they work.

The uupick program is used to retrieve files and directories that have been sent by uuto:

- It interactively allows you to view and accept or reject each file and directory received.
- It allows you to limit the selection of received files to those sent by a named neighbor UNIX site.

Starting *uuto*

The uuto program is used to send files or directory hierarchies to a user on another UNIX system. It is run by entering:

```
uuto file-or-directory remotesite\!user
```

Here, file-or-directory can be the name of any file or directory for which you possess ordinary read permission. In other words, if you can read a file, you can send it. If you can list (ls) a directory and can read all the files in it, you can send that directory and all the files in it.

For the examples in this chapter, remotesite will be our own system—a machine named ourhome; and user will be our login name—you. This will make demonstrating uupick easier because you will be able to receive files you've sent to yourself. The only difference in working with an actual remote site is specifying the remote site and file(s) correctly, following the rules given in the last two chapters.

To demonstrate uuto, we will first send a little-known but handy UNIX text file, /usr/lib/unittab, to ourselves. After that we will send a rather large directory that we will create by splitting up /usr/dict/words.

Sending a File with *uuto*

The format for sending a single file with uuto is:

```
uuto filename site\!user
```

where site, in this case, is the name of our own machine as provided by uuname -l (see chapter 11):

```
uuname -l
ourhome
```

and user is our own login name.

The file we are sending is /usr/lib/unittab, a human-readable list of common units of measure and their associated conversion factors, available on all UNIX machines. To send this file to yourself using uuto, simply enter:

```
uuto /usr/lib/unittab ourhome\!you
```

The uuto program uses a somewhat long pattern to describe where it sends files. In brief:

```
uuto file remotesite\!user
```

will send file into:

```
PUBDIR/receive/user/yoursite/file
```

on remotesite. In the case of our actual transfer of /usr/lib/unittab, uuto will send the file into /usr/spool/uucppublic/receive/you/ourhome/unittab.

The beauty of the uuto/uupick pair of programs is that uupick knows where to find the files sent by uuto, making it unnecessary for you to remember this long pathname. In figure 13-1, we show an overview of how uuto and uupick can be used to send (and receive) both the single file unittab and the whole directory /wordsdir (see the next section).

Sending a Directory with *uuto*

Before sending a directory and its contents with uuto, we will take a moment to create a directory to send. One of the pitfalls of UUCP, when copying files to yourself, is that UUCP preserves the permissions of the original file. Since UUCP owns everything it transmits, this means that, when sending files to yourself, you will receive files that you may not be able to remove. Just to be on the safe side, we will preset the permissions for the directory we are creating, so that we can later remove it.

To easily create a large test directory, we will fill it with many small files that have been split from the common UNIX file /usr/dict/words. This file is an alphabetized list of over 32,000 English words and proper nouns.

To create the test directory, which we will call wordsdir, enter the following:

```
cd
mkdir wordsdir
chmod 777 wordsdir
cd wordsdir
split - < /usr/dict/words
chmod 666 *
cd
```

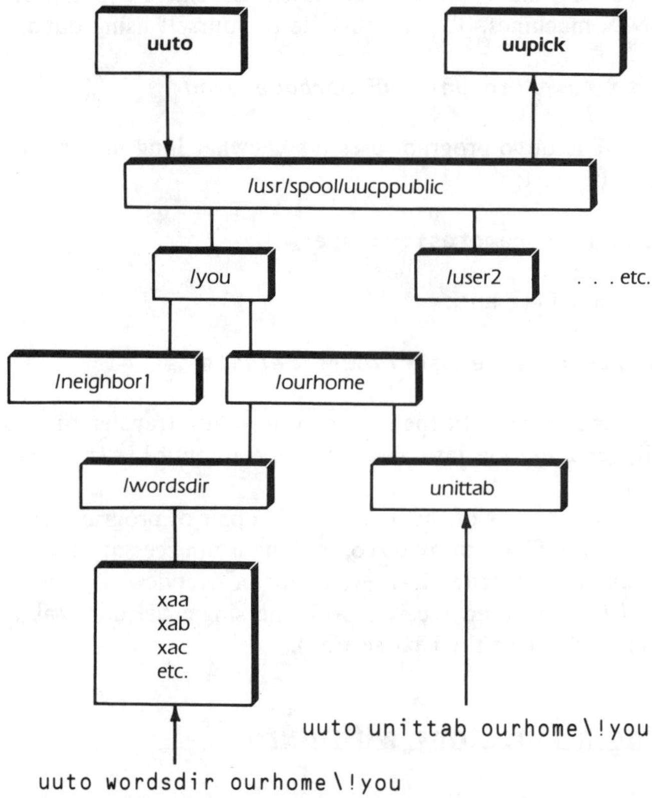

Figure 13-1. Overview of **uuto/uupick**.

Here, we create `wordsdir` and use `chmod 777` to make it readable, writable, and searchable by anyone. We then change to that directory with `cd` and use the `split` program to make many little files from the big file `/usr/dict/words`. (See figure 13-2.) Since `split` is reading from the standard input, it will create a series of 1000 line files called `xaa`, `xab`, etc. (See split(1) in the UNIX programmer's manual, volume 1.) Finally, we use `chmod 666` to change the permission of all those little files to be readable and writable by anyone.

Now to send `wordsdir`, we merely type:

`uuto wordsdir ourhome\!you`

This sends all the files in the directory `wordsdir` to you at your own site, `ourhome`. If `wordsdir` had contained any subdirectories, the files in those subdirectories would also have been sent.

Receiving Files and Directories with *uupick*

If you haven't already done so, take a moment now to create a subdirectory in your home directory for receiving files via UUCP (see chapter 2), and call it `public`. Recall that `public` should be made readable, writable, and searchable by anyone (i.e., mode 777 or `drwxrwxrwx`). Before running `uupick`, you should `cd` into `public`:

cd public

We do this because `uupick`, like all the UUCP programs, will copy files only into directories that are readable, writable, and searchable by anyone.

The `uupick` program is a breeze to run. Simply type its name:

uupick

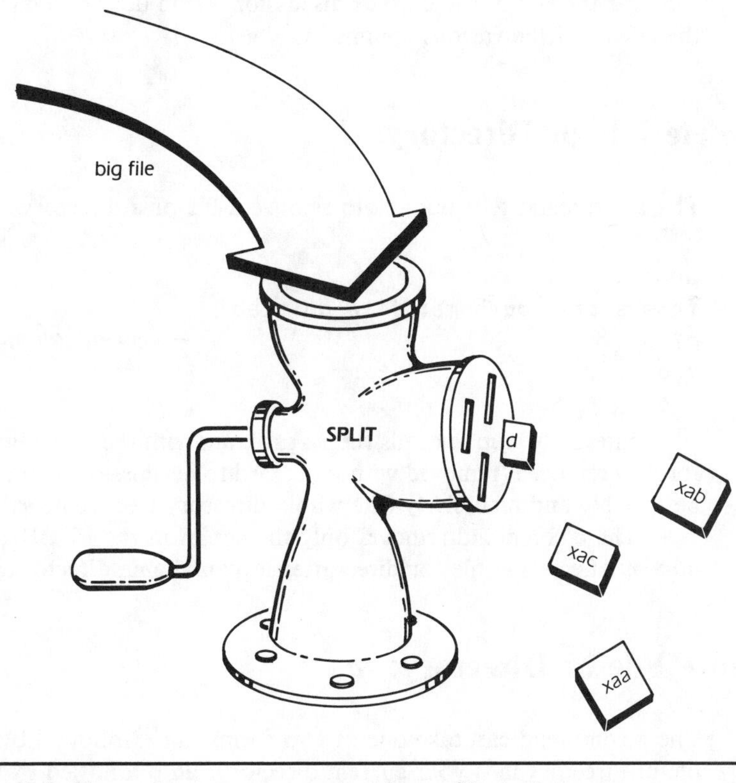

Figure 13-2. The split program reads a large file and creates many small files from it.

and, somewhat like mail, it will present you with the names of any files and/or directories that have arrived for you via uuto.

The name of each file or directory will be presented one at a time. The uupick program will then print a ? and wait for you to tell it what to do with each file or directory. The easiest command is just to press the Return key.

Pressing Return tells uupick to do nothing with that file/directory and proceed to the next. For the files we sent to ourselves with uuto, a do-nothing session with uupick would look like this:

```
uupick
from system ourhome: file unittab
?                                          ←press Return
from system ourhome: directory wordsdir
?                                          ←press Return
```

For each file or directory that uuto sent, uupick lists the site that sent it, tells you whether it is a file or a directory, gives you its name, and then waits for you to enter a command. (You will find a summary of all the uupick commands on page 355 near the end of the uupick discussion.) Run uupick again, and we will discuss the effects of the various commands.

Delete File or Directory: *d*

The d command tells uupick to remove a file or a directory.

```
uupick
from system ourhome: file unittab
b? d                                  ←you enter "d" to  delete
from ...
```

Internally, uupick calls the rm program with the -rf flags. It causes files to be forcibly removed (removed without regard to permissions), and causes directories to be forcibly and recursively (the whole directory tree) removed.

The d command removes only the copies in the PUBDIR directory, and it in no way affects any files or directories in your home directories.

Move File or Directory: *m*

The m command can take one of two forms: an m followed by a Return moves the file or directory into your current directory; an m followed by the name of another directory and a Return moves the file or directory into the directory specified. For example:

```
uupick
from system ourhome: file unittab
? m                                      ←move to current directory
from system ourhome: directory wordsdir
? m /tmp                                 ←move to /tmp directory
```

The `m` command causes the file `unittab` to be moved into the current directory, `public`. The command `m /tmp` causes the directory `wordsdir`, and all the files it contains, to be moved into the system directory `/tmp`, which is a safe, temporary directory that is available to all users and is readable, writable, and searchable by anyone.

Some versions of `uupick` use the `cpio` program to move files and directories. With this scheme, you may see something like the following when you use the `m` command:

```
uupick
from system ourhome: file unittab
? m
0 blocks
```

The `0 blocks` is meaningless, and can safely be ignored.

Move All Files or Directories from Same Site: *a*

The `a` command can take one of two forms, just like the `m` command. An `a`, followed by a Return, moves ALL the files or directories you have received from the currently displayed site (not just the file or directory currently shown) into your current directory. An `a`, followed by the name of another directory and a Return, moves all the files or directories you have received from the currently displayed site into the directory specified. For example:

```
uupick
from system ourhome: file unittab
? a
```

This tells `uupick` to move both the file `unittab` and the directory `wordsdir` (both having been previously sent from the same site, `ourhome`) into your current directory, `public`; whereas the following tells `uupick` to move both into the directory named `/tmp`.

```
uupick
from system ourhome: file unittab
? a /tmp
```

Print Contents of Files or Directories: *p*

The p command instructs uupick to display the contents of the file or directory currently shown. In the case of a file, the file's contents will be printed on your screen. In the case of a directory, the names of the files contained in that directory will be printed.

```
uupick
from system ourhome: file unittab
? p
                                    ←contents of unittab file printed here
```

or

```
from system ourhome: directory wordsdir
? p
xaa                                         ←filenames in wordsdir
xab                                           directory listed
xac
...etc.
```

Quit *uupick*: *q*

The q command allows you to exit uupick, leaving any unprocessed files for later disposition. The UNIX end-of-file character may also be used to exit. On most UNIX systems, the end-of-file character is Control-d.

```
uupick
from system ourhome: file unittab
? q                                 ←quit uupick
```

Run Program from *uupick*: *!cmd*

The !cmd command tells uupick to run the UNIX program whose name is cmd. After that named UNIX program has terminated, you are returned to uupick. In other words, this is a shell escape like those we have seen earlier with mail and news programs, and it uses the common UNIX convention of ! for a shell escape. The cmd is always run in your current directory. For example:

```
uupick
from system ourhome: file unittab
? m
from system ourhome: directory wordsdir
```

```
? !wc unittab
1256  5195  24012  unittab
?
```

Here, we first told uupick to move (m) the file unittab into our current directory. We then told uupick to run the UNIX program wc, which stands for word count. The argument given to wc was the name of the file whose words will be counted—unittab. The output of wc was (from left to right) the number of lines, words, and characters in the file. When wc was done, we were returned to uupick, where uupick resumed by waiting for a command telling it what to do with wordsdir.

Note: the !cmd command always runs programs using the Bourne Shell. To run C Shell scripts, you may have to invoke them as:

```
? !csh -c wc unittab
   ↑    ↑
```
tell C Shell to run one command; then exit

Getting Help: *

The * command instructs uupick to print a brief help message.

The *uupick* Commands

d	Delete the currently displayed file or directory.
m	Move the currently displayed file or directory into the current directory.
m dir	Move the currently displayed file or directory into the directory named dir.
a	Move all files and directories from the currently displayed site into the current directory.
a dir	Move all files and directories from the currently displayed site into the directory named dir.
p	Print the contents of the currently displayed file. List the names of the files in the currently displayed directory.
q	Quit uupick. End-of-file also quits (usually Control-d).
! cmd	Run the UNIX program named cmd and then resume uupick.
*	Get a Help summary of commands.

```
uupick
from system ourhome: file unittab
? *
usage: [d][m dir][a dir][p][q][cntl-d][!cmd][*][new-linerb]]
?
```

Improving *uupick*

Because uupick is a Bourne Shell script, it is possible to copy it into your home directory and modify that copy to suit your personal taste. Just copy uupick from /usr/bin into your home directory with:

```
cd
cp /usr/bin/uupick .
```

(The period . for the destination of cp is UNIX shorthand for "the current directory.") Thereafter, you can revise that copy using your favorite text editor and then run the revised copy instead of the original. (See PATH in sh(1) and csh(1) in the UNIX on-line manual for instructions on how to get your copy to run in place of the original.)

As suggestions for ways to improve uupick, consider the following:

1. Change p to print files using one of the screen-at-a-time programs, like more, pg, or less.
2. Change p to list directory contents in a more informative fashion, like ls -l or dtree -a. (Note that dtree is not part of regular UNIX. This useful command is distributed on USENET and shows a directory tree structure visually.)
3. Modify uupick so that it reprints the current file/directory after a p, !cmd or * command.
4. Rephrase the help command (*) so that it prints a full menu.
5. Modify uupick to handle directories as files; that is, to ask for disposition of each file in a directory, rather than requiring you to deal with directories as a whole.

Making these modifications requires knowledge of shell programming, which is beyond the scope of this book. See Appendix E for some recommended intermediate to advanced UNIX books that would be helpful for learning more about shell programming.

Restricting *uupick* to a Selected Sending System (*–s* Flag)

The uupick program ordinarily displays the names of all files and directories sent to you from all systems. There will be times, however, when you will want to dispose only of files and directories that were sent by a selected system. The uupick program provides for just this eventuality with the -s flag.

The -s flag requires a single argument—the name of the system in which you are interested. Just enter the system name after the -s, with a space between the two, as:

```
uupick -s system-name
```

In the case of our example, where we sent files and directories to our own system, we would say:

```
uupick -s ourhome
        ↑
        just list files and directories from this site
```

Here, we used ourhome because it is our home system in our fictional network. Of course, you may use the name of any system. If uupick doesn't know that name, it will exit immediately and print nothing.

Two *uuto* Flags

The uuto program accepts two flags as an argument. The -m flag is used to mail notification of success to the sender. The -p flag instructs uuto to spool (make a temporary duplicate) the file or directory you are sending, and to transmit that duplicate instead of the original.

Receive Mail (*–m* Flag)

Like uucp, uuto allows the -m flag to specify that it should send mail to the sender. The -m should precede the file/directory specification:

```
uuto -m wordsdir ourhome\!you
      ↑
      notify sender of success via mail
```

As an aside, note that whenever mail is to be sent to the sender, and the target is the sender's home machine, both uucp and uuto will ignore the -m flag. The rationale here is that you can easily look in the target directory and verify that the file was transmitted correctly. After all, this is your machine, so why bother to send mail?

Spool Original and Transmit Copy (*-p* Flag)

Like the -C flag of uucp, the -p flag of uuto tells uuto to make a duplicate of your original file or directory in a spool (temporary holding) directory and then to transmit that duplicate instead of the original. (See chapter 11 for a complete description of spooling and why it is used.)

The -p flag must precede the file/directory specification. It is used like this:

```
uuto -p wordsdir ourhome\!you
     ↑
     spool a duplicate and send that duplicate
```

Summary of *uupick* and *uuto* Flags

-s	Restricts uupick to files and directories sent by a selected system.
-m	Tells uuto to send mail to sender if transmission is successful.
-p	Tells uuto to spool a duplicate of a file or directory and transmit that duplicate instead of the original.

Summary of Uses and Caveats

The following is a brief summary of the most common uses of the uuto and uupick programs. Caveats are provided to illustrate variations, limitations, and possible pitfalls.

Send with uuto*: a file*

```
uuto file site\!user
```

Caveat: The file must be readable by anyone (e.g., mode 444), and the directory it is in must be readable and searchable by anyone (e.g., mode 555). Multiple files may be listed.

Send with `uuto`*: a directory*

```
uuto dir site\!user
```

Caveat: The files in `dir` must be readable by anyone (e.g., mode 444), and `dir` must be readable and searchable by anyone (e.g., mode 555). The `dir` directory may contain subdirectories.

Dispose of files with `uupick`*: all received files and directories*

```
uupick
```

Caveat: Files and directories may be moved only into a directory that is readable, writable, and searchable by anyone (e.g., mode 777).

Dispose of files with `uupick`*: by selected sending site*

```
uupick -s site
```

Caveat: If `uupick` doesn't recognize `site`, or if nothing was sent from `site`, it will print nothing and exit.

Summary

In this chapter you have learned how to send files and directories with the `uuto` program, and how to interactively retrieve files and directories sent by `uuto` with the `uupick` program. You have also discovered that these programs were really Bourne Shell scripts and that they could be copied, and those copies modified to suit your own requirements.

In the next chapter we will introduce you to the `uux` program. The `uux` program allows you to execute (run) programs on other UNIX machines and then view the output of those programs on your local machine.

14

Running Programs on Remote Machines with *uux*

The uux program—which stands for *U*NIX to *U*NIX e*X*ecute—provides a convenient way to run programs on neighboring UNIX machines. The uux program allows you to find, examine, and print files on another machine, using common UNIX commands such as ls, cat, and lp (or lpr). This chapter will illustrate these and other uses for uux, including how to:

- Find out which programs you are allowed to run on neighbor UNIX machines.
- Run simple programs on neighbor UNIX machines and view their output on your local machine.
- Run several programs, one after the other, on a neighbor UNIX machine, all with a single uux command.
- Use pipes for more complex chaining of programs on neighbor UNIX machines.
- Use a printer that is attached to another machine to print files located on your local machine.
- Receive, or prevent reception of, mail notifying you of successful execution of your uux request.
- Delay transmission of your uux request.
- Obtain a step-by-step listing of uux in action.

Because uux commands interact with UNIX more frequently than do uucp commands, you may wish to read this chapter with a good, introductory UNIX text close at hand. (See chapter 2 for a review of some basic UNIX commands and concepts.)

Which Programs Can You Run with *uux*?

Just as there are limits on what you may copy with uucp, there are limits on what you may execute with uux. At sensitive sites, like public-access UNIX machines, uux is usually limited to running only rmail and possibly rnews—restricted forms of mail and postnews. In local area networks, on the other hand, uux will often be allowed to run programs like who and lp. (The first program shows you who is logged onto a machine; the second prints files on a line printer.)

To find out which programs users on neighbor UNIX machines are allowed to run on your local machine, you can look in your system's L.cmds file:

```
/usr/lib/uucp/L.cmds
```

The L.cmds file is simply a list of programs, one program per line, that users at other UNIX sites are allowed to run on your local machine using uux. For example, a typical L.cmds file may look like this:

```
PATH=/bin:/usr/bin
rmail
rnews
lp
who
uusend
finger
```

This file specifies that users at other UNIX sites may run only the programs rmail, rnews, lp, who, uusend, and finger on your local machine. The first line in the file specifies that those permitted programs will be found in one of the two directories, /bin or /usr/bin.

The L.cmds file sets the rules for all outside sites, both trusted and not. If your machine is connected to the outside world, this file will contain few programs. If, on the other hand, your machine is connected only to others on a local area network, it may contain many programs.

Those of you running HoneyDanBer UUCP can also look in the Permissions file supplied with that system:

```
/usr/lib/uucp/Permissions
```

An advantage of HoneyDanBer UUCP over both System V UUCP and Berkeley UUCP is that it allows the restrictions of L.cmds to be further restricted by individual site name. A typical Permissions file might look like this:

```
LOGNAME=uun1 \               ! neighbor1 login name
COMMANDS=rmail:rnews
```

```
LOGNAME=uun3 \              ! neighbor3 login name
COMMANDS=ALL
```

This means that users on the neighbor site `neighbor1` are restricted to using only `rnews` and `rmail`, but users on `neighbor3` are allowed to run all the programs listed in the file `L.cmds`.

Unfortunately, there is no simple way to find out which programs you are allowed to run on a remote machine. The easiest way to find out is to mail an electronic letter to the administrator of a remote UNIX site, explaining that you are learning how to use `uux` and would like to know which programs are available to you. If you don't know the administrator's name, you can always mail to the user named `root`.

How to Run a Program Remotely

The `uux` program allows you to run a program on a neighbor UNIX machine with a command typed on your local machine. With `uux`, you can specify where that program's output is to go, and where that program's input is to come from. The format for using `uux` looks like this:

```
uux command-string
```

or, more specifically:

```
uux machine\!program "input-output-control"
```

where,

`machine`	is the name of the neighbor UNIX site on which you will run `program`.
`program`	is the name of the program that you wish to run on the neighbor UNIX site. This program must exist on that remote machine and you must have permission to run it.
`input-output-control`	is the redirection part of a UNIX command line. If `program` requires input, the input-output-control must use < to redirect that input from a file. If `program` produces output, the input-output-control must use > to redirect that output into a file. We will see examples of this redirection in the next section.

Like uucp, uux queues a request for the program to be run on the remote UNIX machine; and, like uucp, uux always sends you a mail notification if your program failed. See figure 14-1 for an overview of how uux works.

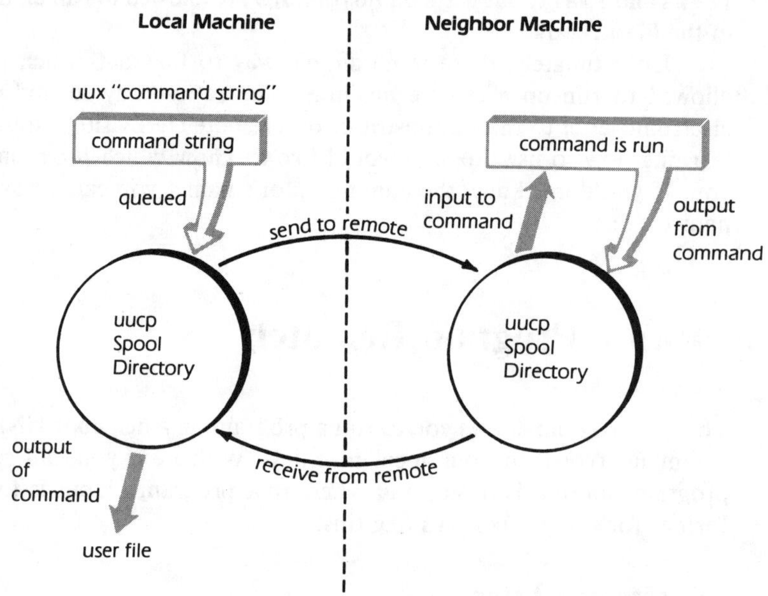

Figure 14-1. Overview of how **uux** works.

How to Capture a Remote Program's Output

Two useful programs for getting information about other users are who (found on all UNIX systems) and finger (found on BSD systems). The who program prints a list of all users that are currently logged in. The finger program displays an assortment of information about a particular user, such as last login date and full name. Both of these programs produce output, but neither requires any input. To run the who program on the remote UNIX site neighbor4, enter:

```
                         input-output-control
                                  ↓
uux  neighbor4\!who      "> neighbor4.who"
     ↑           ↑
     machine     program
```

This command queues a request for the program who to be run on the remote UNIX site neighbor4. The input-output-control, "> neighbor4.who", tells uux to redirect the output of the remotely executed who program into a local file named neighbor4.who.

The expression "> neighbor4.who" must be in quotation marks so that uux, not your current shell, handles the redirection of output. Omitting the quotation marks would result in the output of uux, rather than the output of who, being placed into neighbor4.who.

```
uux neighbor4\!who  > neighbor4.who      ←output of uux
uux neighbor4\!who "> neighbor4.who"     ←output of who
```

After the correctly constructed uux request has been executed on the neighbor UNIX machine, neighbor4, you will find that the file neighbor4.who has been created in your local directory and that it contains the output of neighbor4's who command:

```
george   tty3   06:51
joe      tty6   10:22
duke     tty9   09:15
etc.
```

At this point, you might wonder who joe is, never having seen that login name before. By running uux again, this time with the finger command, you can obtain some basic information about joe.

```
uux neighbor4\!finger joe "> neighbor4.joe"
```

Here, a uux request was queued to run the finger program on the neighbor machine neighbor4—giving the single argument joe to finger—and specifying that the result was to be placed into the file neighbor4.joe. When the uux request is finished executing at neighbor4, the file neighbor4.joe will be sent back to your local machine and placed into your current directory. That new file might then contain the following information about joe:

```
Login Name: joe          In real life: Joe Kerr
Directory: /usr/joe      Shell: /bin/csh
On since June 15 10:22:01 on tty6
Plan:
Like the name says, I seek to
inject humor into all situations.
```

For more information about the who and finger UNIX commands, see section 1 of the on-line UNIX programmer's manual.

Permissions Required for "> *file*"

Any file that is to receive the output of a remotely executed program must obey the same rules as those laid out for `uucp` copying in chapter 12. That is, for each file that is to receive the output of a remotely executed program:

- The directory in which the file will be placed must be readable, writable, and searchable by anyone (i.e., mode 777 or `drwxrwxrwx`).
- All directories in the path leading to the directory in which the file will be placed must be readable and searchable by anyone (i.e., at least mode 555 or `dr-xr-xr-x`).

If a file cannot be written for any reason, `uux` will leave the output of the remotely executed command in your local PUBDIR directory. The name of that file will be PUBDIR/yourname/yourmachine/file. For the previous example, improper write permission in your current directory would cause the file `neighbor4.who` to be left in:

```
                              your machine
                                   ↓
/usr/spool/uucppublic/jane/ourhome/neighbor4.who
                    ↑      ↑
                 PUBDIR  your name
```

Specifying the Local Filename

Recall that in the command:

`uux neighbor4\!who "> neighbor4.who"`

the input-output-control, `"> neighbor4.who"`, specifies that the output of the `who` program, when run on the neighbor site `neighbor4`, is to be placed—redirected—into the file named `neighbor4.who` on our local machine. In UNIX, the > symbol means "redirect into."

Because that input-output-control string is quoted, the filename `neighbor4.who` is interpreted by `uux` rather than by your local shell. The kinds of filenames that `uux` understands are much more limited than those understood by your shell. Thus:

```
"> neighbor4.who"              ←relative name
"> /usr/jane/neighbor4.who"    ←full pathname
"> ~jane/neighbor4.who"        ←jane's home directory
```

All three of these are legal, whereas the following are not:

```
"> ./neighbor4.who"           ← "." is illegal
"> ../neighbor4.who"          ← ".." is illegal
"> $HOME/neighbor4.who"       ←$HOME is illegal
"> !$/neighbor4.who"          ←!$ is illegal
```

The rules for specifying legal filenames with uux are the same as those for uucp. Specifically, you are prohibited from using the dot (.) and dot-dot (..) relative pathname expressions (for the current directory and the parent directory), and from using any of the environmental variables (like $HOME) or history expressions (like !$). After all, when uux is running the command on the other machine, it doesn't know anything about your original environment on your local machine.

To illustrate further, examine the following three legal uux requests:

```
uux  neighbor4\!who "> neighbor4.who"  ←if jane is in public
uux  neighbor4\!who "> /usr/jane/public/neighbor4.who"
uux  neighbor4\!who "> ~jane/public/neighbor4.who"
```

All three of these queue a request that the program who be run on the remote UNIX site named neighbor4, and that the output from that remote program's execution be placed into the file neighbor4.who in the user jane's public directory—a subdirectory in her home directory that is readable, writable, and searchable by anyone.

Note that the ~user form of shorthand is handled by uux and not by your shell, so it is available to all shells, including the Bourne Shell.

How to Place a Remote Program's Output into a Remote File

The redirection portion of uux's command line is not limited to placing program output into local files. By specifying the output file in the uucp style:

```
machine\!file
```

you can redirect that output into a file on any remote machine. For example, the following executes the who program on the remote UNIX machine neighbor4, and places the output of that program into the file PUBDIR/neighbor4.who on that same remote machine:

```
uux neighbor4\!who "> neighbor4\!~/neighbor4.who"
```

The file that is to receive the output can be on *any* machine to which the remote machine is connected, even if it is one to which our local machine is not connected. Although remote2 is connected to neighbor4, but not to us, we can still specify that the output of neighbor4's who program be placed into a file on that machine:

```
we are ourhome, and are not connected to remote2
↓                          ↓
uux neighbor4\!who "> remote2\!~/neighbor4.who"
                           ↑
                           file placed on remote2
```

Here, the uux program was run on our local machine, ourhome. It queued a request that the who program be run on the neighbor machine neighbor4. This uux request also specified that the output of the remotely executed who program be placed into a file called neighbor4.who in yet another remote site's PUBDIR directory, the one on the remote site remote2.

Note that the machine specified for receipt of a remote machine's program execution must be a site connected to that remote site, not merely one that is connected to your local site—although both may have connections in common.

Local versus Remote Names—What's Where

The uux program understands only a few methods of specifying file and program names. In general, names that do not contain the ! character are considered local. That is:

```
neighbor4.who
```

is interpreted as a local file. Also, program names that begin with the ! character are taken to mean that the program is on the local machine. Thus:

```
\!who
```

refers to the program who on the local machine. (Note that the ! still needs to be preceded by a backslash unless you are using the Bourne Shell.)

As a bonus—and for consistency—uux also recognizes filenames that begin with ! as being on the local machine. Thus:

```
\!filename
```

is interpreted as a *local* program or filename, whereas:

```
neighbor4\!name
```

is interpreted as a *remote* program or filename. To expand on this idea, examine the following two uux commands:

```
uux neighbor4\!who "> neighbor4.who"
uux \!who "> neighbor4\!~/neighbor4.who"
```

The first is what you've seen all along: The who program is run on the neighbor machine neighbor4, and the output of that program is placed into the local file neighbor4.who.

The second example, however, does just the opposite. The who program is run on our local machine, and the output of that program is sent into the remote file, PUBDIR/neighbor4.who, on the neighbor machine neighbor4.

The first example could alternatively have been written:

```
uux neighbor4\!who "> \!neighbor4.who"
                       ↑
                   local file
```

This form gives a consistency of style in that both the program and the filenames use the \! notation to indicate which machine each is on.

How to Run a Local Program with Remote Files as Input

Whenever you run a program with uux, and the program requires input, you must create that input by using the < character to redirect the contents of a remote file into the program. (The program cannot get standard input from the keyboard of the remote machine, since you are here, not there.) The format for the redirection looks like this:

```
uux program "< file"
```

To illustrate, let's use the lp program—it may be called lpr on your machine —to obtain a printout of a remote file using our local printer. The file we will print is a memo found in the user jane's public directory at the neighbor site neighbor4:

```
uux \!lp "< neighbor4\!~jane/public/newmemo"
       ↑                                ↑
    program                            file
```

In this example, we used the \!lp notation to tell uux that the program to be run is on the local machine. Since the lp program, without arguments, reads the standard input on our machine, we fed that input from the neighbor machine by using the < character.

If we wish, and if we are permitted to run the lp program on the neighbor site neighbor4, we can turn the preceding uux command around and print a local file on the neighbor machine's printer:

```
uux neighbor4\!lp "< \!localfile"
```

In both examples, the < character is used to feed the contents of a file into a program—lp.

Permissions for Input Files

Whenever a file's contents are to be fed into a program using uux, that file must possess certain permissions:

- The file itself must be readable by anyone (i.e., minimally 444 or -r--r--r--)
- The directory containing the file, and all directories in the path leading to that directory, must be readable and searchable by anyone (i.e., minimally 555 or dr-xr-xr-x).
- The directory containing the file must be listed as permitted in USERFILE (or HoneyDanBer's Permissions file).

How to Use Files as Arguments to *uux*

Some programs read files directly rather than reading from the standard input. One example is diff, a program that compares two text files and prints out any differences it finds between them. As a minimum, diff expects as its arguments the names of the two files to compare. The following illustrates the use of diff on your local machine to compare two local files:

```
diff chapter1 chapter1.backup
< chapter1
> chapter1.backup
45 c 45
< Not a cloud was in the sky:
---
> No cloud at all was in the sky:
```

Here, diff found that line 45 in chapter1 differed from line 45 in chapter1.backup.

Whenever you run a program using uux, and that program, like diff, requires that its arguments be filenames, you must specify three items:

1. The program name and the machine on which that program is to run.
2. The name of each file that is an argument, and the machine on which each file will be found.
3. Where the output of the program is to be placed.

For example, to run the diff program locally, with two remote files as its arguments, you might type the following:

```
uux \!diff neighbor4\!/tmp/ch1 neighbor3\!/tmp/ch1.bk "> \!diff.ch1"
                 ↑                      ↑                  ↑
          first remote file    second remote file  result of comparison goes here
```

In this example, the diff program on our local machine, ourhome, is used to compare two remote files: /tmp/ch1 at the neighbor site neighbor4 and /tmp/ch1.bk at the neighbor site neighbor3. The output of the diff program is placed into the file diff.ch1 in our current directory on our local machine.

Whenever files are used as arguments with uux, those files are first copied into a temporary directory on the machine that will run the program. The program is then run using those temporary copies as arguments. That is:

```
uux \!diff neighbor4\!/tmp/ch1 neighbor3\!/tmp/ch1.bk "> \!diff.ch1"
```

This statement will cause both ch1, from the neighbor site neighbor4, and ch1.bk, from the neighbor site neighbor3, to be copied first into a temporary directory at our local site, ourhome. The diff program will then be run locally to compare those copies. The output of diff will be placed into the file diff.ch1 on our local machine.

This procedure, although logical, opens the way for a potential pitfall. Since both files are copied to the same temporary directory, they must not have the same name. If they do, one will overwrite the other. That is, if in the previous example both files were called ch1, then both:

```
neighbor4\!/tmp/ch1
```

and:

```
neighbor3\!/tmp/ch1
```

will be copied into .XQTDIR/ch1 on our local machine, one overwriting the other—where .XQTDIR is the name of the temporary directory used by uux.

This problem occurs only when both files are from machines different than that on which the program is run. When a file is on the same machine as that on which the program is run, the original file is used and no copy is made. For example, if the `diff` program were run on the remote site `neighbor3`, the preceding files would be given to `neighbor3`'s `diff` as:

```
diff .XQTDIR/ch1 /tmp/ch1
```

resulting in no name conflict and no risk of overwriting.

How to Prevent *uux* from Copying an Argument

Unless told otherwise, `uux` will assume that all arguments containing a `!` character are the names of existing files. There are two situations in which this assumption might prove wrong:

1. When the argument is the name of a file that the program will create.
2. When the argument normally contains a `!` character, such as a mail address.

In both cases, the assumption that these are existing files is defeated by surrounding each with a pair of parentheses. For example:

```
(neighbor1\!jake)
```

This tells `uux` that `neighbor1\!jake` is not an existing file and therefore should not be copied.

Specifying Output File Arguments

One example of a program that takes as an argument the name of a file to create is the `ar` program. This program—which stands for *AR*chive—can be used to extract individual files from a library file. The format for using `ar` is:

```
ar x libraryfile extractedfile
```

where the `x` tells `ar` to extract the file named `extractedfile` from the library archive file named `libraryfile`.

If we were to run `ar` on a remote site, and wanted to have the extracted file sent back to us, we would enter the following:

```
uux neighbor3\!ar x neighbor3\!libfile "(ourhome\!extract)"
                             ↑                   ↑
                        library file       extracted file
```

This command tells uux to run the ar program on the neighbor site neighbor3, and it gives that program three arguments:

x — This tells ar to extract a file from a library.

libraryfile — The name of the library is libfile. Since libfile is on the same machine as that on which the program is run, uux will not make a copy. Instead, ar will operate on the original file that exists on neighbor3.

extractedfile — The file that ar is to create is extract. Since we want this file sent back to us on our local machine, ourhome, we specify it as ourhome\!extract. Since we do not want uux to try to copy the not-yet-existing file named extract from our machine, we enclose that name in parentheses. Note that any expression containing parentheses must be quoted to prevent those parentheses from being interpreted by your local shell.

The net result is that ar is invoked on neighbor3 as:

```
ar x libfile extract
```

and the resulting, newly created file extract is sent back to us at our local machine.

Specifying Arguments That Contain a ! Character

Some programs, such as mail, expect arguments that contain ! characters, for example, remote mail addresses. To run these programs using uux, you must surround those arguments with parentheses. For example:

```
uux neighbor3\!mail "(neighbor1\!jake)" "< neighbor3\!/tmp/ch1"
                     ↑
                     mail address, not a file
```

Here, the mail program is run on the neighbor machine neighbor3. The address where the mail is to be sent is neighbor1\!jake, but, since that address contains a ! character, we surround it with parentheses. This prevents uux from mistaking that address for a file and trying to copy it. Finally, the input to the remote mail program is redirected to come from /tmp/ch1 on the neighbor machine neighbor3.

The net result is that the user named jake on the neighbor machine neighbor1 will receive, via electronic mail, the contents of the file /tmp/ch1 from the machine named neighbor3.

How to Run Multiple Remote Programs with One *uux* Request

There are two ways to run multiple programs with a single uux request:

1. Programs can be run sequentially. That is, run one, and when it is finished, run the next.
2. Programs can be run simultaneously, with the output of one connected to the input of another through a pipe.

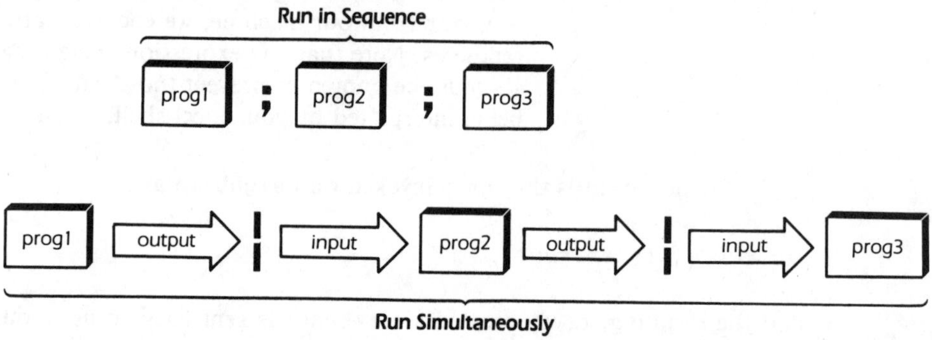

Figure 14-2. Programs run in sequence and simultaneously.

Running Multiple Programs Sequentially with *uux*

Multiple programs are run sequentially with uux the same way that programs are run sequentially under your shell—you simply separate one from the other with a semicolon on the same line:

```
prog1 ; prog2 ; prog3
```

This causes the program prog1 to be run first. When it is done, prog2 will be run; when prog2 is done, prog3 will be executed.

To run programs sequentially with uux, use the same technique:

```
uux "prog1 ; prog2 ; prog3 > file"
```

Notice a difference between this example and the others in this chapter. Previously, only the expression "> file" was quoted:

```
uux site\!program "> file"
```

Now the entire string of arguments to uux is quoted. The quoting is done for the same reason that the "> file" was quoted earlier: the semicolon (;) character has special meaning to the shell—it tells the shell to run programs sequentially. So, to ensure that uux, rather than the shell, is given the ; characters, we quote everything. To sum up, the following will not work:

```
uux prog1 ; prog2 ; prog3 "> file"
     ↑        ↑        ↑
```

run by uux *run by your local shell*

The correct syntax is:

```
uux "prog1 ; prog2 ; prog3 > file"
       ↑        ↑        ↑
```

run sequentially by uux on remote machine

As an example of running programs sequentially with uux, consider the need to uncompress a file at a neighbor site, have the size of that uncompressed file sent back to you, and then recompress that file again. This action is accomplished using the unpack, ls, and pack programs. Assuming you have permission to run them on a neighbor machine, you could make the following uux request:

prog1

```
                   ↓
uux "neighbor3\!unpack neighbor3\!/tmp/x.z ; \
ls -l neighbor3\!/tmp/x > \!x.len ; pack neighbor3\!/tmp/x"
↑                                   ↑
```

prog2 *prog3*

Note two things here: first, that the uux command was split into two lines by ending the first line with a backslash and a Return—a handy technique available to all shells; second, that only unpack, the first program of the three to be run sequentially, is prefixed with the neighbor3\! notation. Remember this important rule about uux: *When multiple program names are specified to* uux, *all the programs will be run on the machine specified with the first program name.*

When our request to uncompress, etc., the file x on the neighbor machine is processed, the following events take place:

- prog1 The unpack program is run on the remote site neighbor3 to uncompress the file x.z located in neighbor3's /tmp directory. Note that when unpack uncompresses a file, it strips off the .z, leaving, in this case, an uncompressed file named x in the /tmp directory.
- prog2 The ls program, with a -l flag, prints a long directory listing, including the length, of the file x in neighbor3's /tmp directory.

Since the first program was run on neighbor3, ls is also run on neighbor3 in accordance with the preceding rule. The output of the ls program is sent into the file x.len in our current directory on our local machine.

prog3 The pack program, running at the neighbor site neighbor3, recompresses the file x in neighbor3's /tmp directory. Note that when pack compresses a file, it adds a .z to the end of the file's name.

Running Programs Simultaneously with Pipes

When the pipe symbol, a ¦ character, is placed in a UNIX command line, the output of one program is connected to the input of another. That is:

```
prog1 ¦ prog2
```

causes the output of the program on the left, prog1, to be fed directly—piped—into the input of the program on the right, prog2. The ¦ character, for the same reasons as the ; character, requires that the entire uux command be enclosed in full quotation marks:

```
uux "prog1 ¦ prog2 > destfile"
```

Recall the example in which we ran the who program on the neighbor site neighbor1:

```
uux neighbor1\!who "> neighbor1.who"
```

Here, we queued a uux request for the who program to be run on the neighbor site neighbor1, and for the output of that program to be placed into the file neighbor1.who in our current directory on our local machine.

As an alternative, we can use the pipe character to cause the output of the who program to be mailed to us:

```
uux "neighbor1\!who ¦ rmail (oursite\!ourname)"
                    ↑
```

instead of "> neighborl.who"

The who program is run on the remote machine neighbor1, just as before, but the output of that program is piped into the input of the rmail program (also on the remote machine), instead of being placed into a local file.

The rmail program is a "restricted" form of mail that understands forwarding. The argument to rmail—(oursite\!ourname)—is the UNIX electronic mail address of the user who is to receive the output of the who program. Notice that the address is surrounded by parentheses. The parentheses prevent uux from thinking that oursite\!ourname is the name of an existing file. If the parentheses were omitted, uux would try to copy a file of that name and feed it into rmail—not the right thing to do!

Again, note that both progams are run on the same machine as that of the first program. That is, since who is the first program listed in the uux command, and it is run on the remote machine neighbor1, the rmail program will also be run on the remote machine neighbor1.

How to Feed Local Input through a Remote Program

As you've seen, remote programs that take input require you to specify where that input is to come from. The assignment of the input can be accomplished in either of two ways: by redirecting the standard input to come from a file, as:

```
uux site\!program "< site\!file"
```

or by connecting the output of one program to the input of another with a pipe, as:

```
uux "site\!prog1 | prog2"
```

The uux program provides yet a third way to feed input into a remote program. By using a lone hyphen (-) as an argument to uux, you are telling uux to read its local standard input and then to feed what it reads through a remotely run program:

```
uux - site\!program < localfile
```

Here, the - tells uux to read the local standard input—coming, in this case, from the local file localfile via the unquoted < in the command line. That input—the contents of localfile—is then fed through a program at the neighbor site by site\!program.

A common application for the - argument is that of printing local files using a printer and print program on a remote machine. The Berkeley print program is called lp and is the one we will use in the following example. (Under AT&T System V, you should use the lpr program.)

To print the local file walrus.txt using a printer on the neighbor machine neighbor1, queue the following uux request:

```
uux - neighbor1\!lp < walrus.txt
```

Note that the expression < walrus.txt is not surrounded by quotation marks because we want the local standard input connected directly to uux.

A slightly more complex example might better serve to illustrate the value of the - argument. In the following, the `nroff` program is run on the local machine to format a document (see figure 14-3). Rather than placing the formatted output of `nroff` into a file and then printing that file, as would be the case if we did:

```
nroff manuscript.n > file
uux - neighbor1\!lp < file
```

we use the pipe symbol (¦) to feed the output of `nroff` directly through `uux` and thus through the remote printer program `lp`:

```
nroff manuscript.n ¦ uux - neighbor1\!lp
```

This method has the advantage of allowing us to print our manuscript without having to create unneeded intermediate files.

For more information about the `nroff` program, refer to "nroff(1)" in volume 1 of the on-line UNIX programmer's manual, and to "An Introduction to nroff/troff" in volume 2 of the printed manuals.

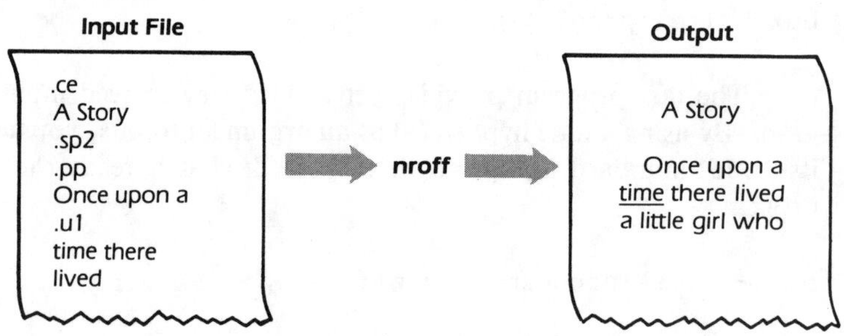

In **nroff**, special commands begin with a dot at the start of a line. Thus, **.ce** centers the next line and **.ul** underlines.

Figure 14-3. The **nroff** program formats text files based on special commands found in those files.

Special Characters and *uux*

As versatile as the `uux` program is, it is still not as versatile as your UNIX shell. It is able to understand and use only a small handful of special symbols. Here are the ones you've learned about so far in this chapter:

>	Place (redirect) output into the file whose name is the next argument.
<	Read (redirect) input to come from the file whose name is the next argument.
()	Prevent uux from interpreting the enclosed argument as a file to be copied.
;	Run a sequence of programs. When the first ends, begin the second, and so on.
¦	Run two programs simultaneously, connecting the output of the first to the input of the second.

The uux program is *unable* to understand or deal with the many special characters understood by most UNIX shells. The following characters may NOT be used as part of a uux command string:

>>	Append to file.	← *No*
<<	Redefine EOF.	← *No*
*	Wildcard character.	← *No*
[ ]	Range of characters.	← *No*
?	Match a single character.	← *No*

For example, let's say we want to print certain local files at a neighbor site and that these are called chap1, chap2, chap3, and chap4. The special notation for range of characters, [ ] is handy for this, as the simple phrase chap[1-4] yields all those chapters. But since uux does not understand this special notation, we cannot say:

```
uux "neighbor1\!nroff \!chap[1-4].n ¦ lp"
                                  ↑
                          uux won't understand this
```

Instead, we must pipe the output of nroff, from our local machine, through uux for printing at the neighbor site:

```
nroff chap[1-4].n ¦ uux - neighbor1\!lp
            ↑
    your shell understands this
```

In other words, we let our local shell, which *does* understand the special characters, provide the filenames to nroff, and we then pipe the output to uux for remote printing of the formatted files.

As a final word on special characters, note that each of the legal special characters (except the ! character) can be isolated from your local UNIX shell by surrounding it with full quotation marks. That is, all three of the following are equivalent:

```
uux neighbor1\!who "> neighbor1.who"
uux neighbor1\!who ">" neighbor1.who
uux "neighbor1\!who > neighbor1.who"
```

Each causes the output of the who program, coming from the neighbor UNIX site neighbor1, to be placed into the local file named neighbor1.who. The quotation marks cause uux, rather than your local shell, to interpret the >.

As an alternative to using quotation marks, you may isolate any single special character by preceding it with a backslash. The following, for example, is the equivalent of the preceding three examples:

```
uux neighbor1\!who \> neighbor1.who
                   ↑
```
backslash preceding special character

For readability, however, we will continue to use full quotation marks to isolate special characters from the local UNIX shell.

Two Sample Applications of *uux*

The bare-bones uux request is somewhat limited in what it can accomplish. As you have seen:

- The uux program can get files from anywhere, but it must run all programs on a single machine.
- The uux program recognizes only a handful of special characters.

To circumvent these limitations, it is often necessary to write special shell scripts that make uux simpler to use. In this section we will examine two of these shell scripts:

uuroff	A C Shell script that formats and prints files by using a remote machine's nroff program and printer.
uurecp	A Bourne Shell script that fetches selected recipes from where they are archived on a remote machine and then mails the recipes to you.

A C Shell Script as a Remote *nroff* Driver

On local area networks, there is often only one "good" printer that must be shared among several machines. In a large office, for example, there may be several IBM PC-AT's running System V/AT, each with an average-quality dot matrix printer, and one central VAX® with a high-quality daisy wheel or laser printer. For a user on one of the IBM PC-AT's, the C Shell script shown in figure 14-4 provides a simple means for getting high-quality, final draft printouts.

To use this C Shell script, first you must type it in exactly as shown, except for filling in the appropriate value for the `SITE` variable (that is, the actual name of the site where you want the printing to take place, rather than `neighbor1` as we have here). Next, you must make the script executable by entering the command:

```
chmod 755 uuroff
```

You can run this script in exactly the same way you would run `nroff`. That is, if you wanted to preview a formatted document—called `doc`, with an introduction and two chapters—on your terminal screen, you would enter:

```
nroff -me doc.intro.n doc.1.n doc.2.n
```

After you have previewed and revised your document, and you are ready for a final printout, you simply substitute `uuroff` for `nroff`:

```
uuroff -me doc.intro.n doc.1.n doc.2.n
```

The `uuroff` script, after checking the validity of each file, queues the following `uux` request:

```
cat doc.intro.n doc.1.n doc.2.n | uux - "neighbor1\!nroff -me | lp"
```

To run this script, you need permission to execute the `nroff` and `lp` programs on the neighbor machine `neighbor1`. In general, scripts like this are set up by the system administrator rather than the user, but this `uuroff` script does illustrate one way of extending and simplifying the use of `uux`. Note that there is some flexibility built into this script: you can change `ROFFPROG` to the name of a different formatting program (such as `troff`), and you can change `LPPROG` to the name of a different printing program (for example, `lpr` rather than `lp`), depending on what is available on the remote system).

The *uurecp* Script as a Remote Recipe Fetcher

On local area networks, there is often only one large hard disk that must be shared by several machines. A business, for example, may have several Sun Work Stations® running BSD 4.2 UNIX, each with a small, 40-megabyte disk, and one central VAX® that has perhaps three 450-megabyte Fujitsu Eagle hard disks.

```
#!/bin/csh

# uuroff -- a C Shell script.
# nroff files using nroff at a remote site and printing them there.

#
# Redefine the following to suit your site's requirements
set SITE=neighbor1
set FILES=""
set FLAGS=""
set ROFFPROG=nroff
set LPPROG=lp

if ($#argv == 0) then
        echo "usage: "$0" files flags"
        exit
endif

while $#argv != 0
        switch ($1)
          case "-*":
                set FLAGS="$FLAGS $1"
                breaksw;
          default:
                if (! -e $1) then
                        echo \"$1\": no such file or directory
                        exit
                else if (! -f $1) then
                        echo \"$1\": not a plain file
                        exit
                else if (! -r $1) then
                        echo \"$1\": not readable
                        exit
                else
                        set FILES="$FILES $1"
                endif
                breaksw;
        endsw
        shift
end

cat $FILES ¦ uux - "$SITE\!$ROFFPROG $FLAGS ¦ $LPPROG"
```

Figure 14-4. The **uuroff** program—a C Shell script.

In such a setup, the VAX, with all its disk space, is the machine on which most archived and collected materials would reside. It is probably also the one machine connected to USENET news.

One of the newsgroups distributed over USENET is the (now defunct) `mod.recipes` group. In our hypothetical network, the VAX would receive the weekly postings of recipes and would archive them. Each user at a Sun Work Station could then access and retrieve selected recipes using `uux`. The Bourne Shell script shown in figure 14-5 illustrates one method for retrieving those recipes.

```
#!/bin/sh
#
# uurecp -- fetch recipes from remote machine

#
# Redefine the following to suit your site's requirements
HERE='uuname -l'
THERE=vax
WHERE=/arch/recipes

if [ "$#" == "0" ]
        then echo "usage: "$0" recipe(s) or index" ; exit
fi

while [ "$#" != "0" ]
do
        uux "$THERE!rmail ($HERE!$USER) < $THERE!$WHERE/$1"
done
```

Figure 14-5. The **uurecp** script—a remote recipe fetcher.

To use this `uurecp` script, first type it in exactly as shown, except for filling in the appropriate values for **`THERE`** (the name of the remote site) and **`WHERE`** (the directory containing the archived files). Next, make `uurecp` executable by entering the command:

`chmod 755 uurecp`

It is then ready to invoke as:

`uurecp recipes`

where `recipes` is a list of filenames for recipe files archived on the remote VAX. Each selected recipe file will be mailed back to you. That is, for each selected file, `uurecp` will queue the following `uux` request:

```
uux "vax\!rmail (mysite\!myname) < vax\!/arch/recipes/recipe_file"
```

(with the appropriate site and filenames for your situation).

For the `uurecp` script to work, you need both permission to run `rmail` on the remote machine `vax`, and permission to read the files in `/arch/recipes` on that machine.

Again, for more information on writing shell scripts, see our listing of recommended UNIX books in Appendix E.

Some *uux* Options

In addition to the lone `-` argument, `uux` supports three other useful flags:

- `-n` Suppress mail notification.
- `-m` Place mail into a file.
- `-r` Queue the `uux` request, but don't transmit it yet.

Suppressing Mail Notification (*-n* Flag)

The normal behavior for `uux` is to send you mail notification whenever a failure occurs with your request. If you are queuing many `uux` requests, as with the `uurecp` shell script, you might find a sudden deluge of mail to be annoying.

The `-n` flag tells `uux` not to send you mail notification. The format for the `-n` flag is:

```
uux -n machine\!program "input-output-control"
```

Note that the `-n` flag is not supported by all versions of `uux`.

Placing Mail into a File (*-m* Flag)

The `-m` flag expands on what `uux` normally does. Normally, `uux` sends mail notification of remote execution failure. The `-m` flag tells it to also send notification of remote execution success. The format for the `-m` flag is:

```
-mfile
```

where `file` is the name of the file on your local machine into which you want notice of success placed. If `file` is omitted, then the notification of success will be sent to you directly via electronic mail. See figure 14-6.

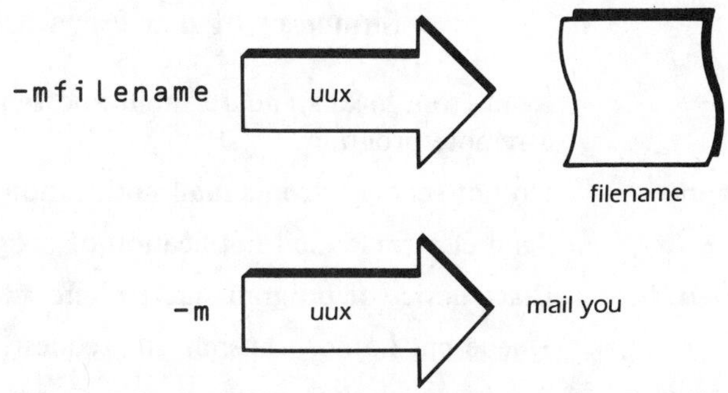

Figure 14-6. The **-m** flag is used in two ways: with a filename, it places notification of success into the local file named; without a filename, it sends notification directly to the user via UNIX mail.

These two ways to use the -m flag are invoked as follows:

```
uux -mfile neighbor1\!who "> neighbor1.who"
uux -m neighbor1\!who "> neighbor1.who"
```

Both of these examples queue a request for the who program to be run on the neighbor machine named neighbor1. They also request that the output of that program be placed into the local file named neighbor1.who. The -m flag in the first example tells uux to place any notification of success into a local file named file. The second example shows a -m flag with no file specified. This tells uux to send you electronic mail upon success.

Note that the -m flag is not available with all versions of uux.

Queue a Request But Don't Transmit (*-r* Flag)

Normally, UUCP software attempts to transmit a request as soon as it is queued. There will be times, however, when you will want to prevent your uux request from being transmitted immediately—perhaps your site has only one modem, and you don't want to tie it up with personal business.

Whatever your reason, uux provides the -r flag to prevent immediate transmission of a queued request. The format for the -r flag is:

```
uux -r machine\!program "input-output-control"
```

Note that the -r flag is not available with all versions of uux.

Summary of *uux* Flags

`-`	Read from local standard input and send that input through a remote program.
`-n`	Do not send electronic mail notification of program failure.
`-m`	Send electronic mail notification of program success.
`-mfile`	Place notice of program success into `file`.
`-r`	Queue but do not transmit `uux` request.
`-x#`	Produce verbose output for debugging; # is a digit from 1 through 9.

How to Watch It Happen (–*x* Flag)

For those interested in the inner workings of `uux`, the `-x` flag will make `uux` tell you all about what it is doing. It does this by printing verbose, or debugging, information. The format for using the `-x` flag is:

```
uux -x# machine\!program "input-output-control"
```

where # is any digit from 1 through 9—the higher the digit, the more information `uux` prints out.

In general, use of the `-x` flag is best left to your system administrator. The output produced by this flag contains references to subroutines inside `uux`. Full understanding of its output requires a thorough working knowledge of UUCP and its programs and internals. However, we are not saying that you should not use the `-x` flag. Go ahead and try it out. If you intend to pursue a deeper understanding of UUCP, examining the output produced by this flag is a fine place to start.

Summary of Uses and Caveats

The following is a brief summary of the most common uses of the `uux` program. Caveats are provided to illustrate variations, limitations, and possible pitfalls.

Execute remote program: output into local file

```
uux site\!program "> localfile"
```

Caveat: You need permission to run program at site. The localfile must be legal for copying into. See uucp's rules.

Execute remote program: output into remote file

```
uux site\!program "> site\!remotefile"
```

Caveat: You need permission to run program at site. The remotefile must be legal for copying into. See uucp's rules.

Execute remote program: input from local file

```
uux site\!program "< localfile"
cat localfile ¦ uux - "site\!program"
```

Caveat: You need permission to run program at site. In the first example, localfile must be legal for reading. See uucp's rules.

Execute remote program: input from remote file

```
uux site\!program "< site\!remotefile"
```

Caveat: You need permission to run program at site. The remotefile must be legal for reading. See uucp's rules.

Execute remote program: mail output

```
uux "site\!program ¦ rmail (site\!person)"
```

Caveat: You need permission to run program and rmail at site. The mail address must be surrounded by parentheses.

Compare remote files

```
uux \!diff site\!file1 site\!file2
```

Caveat: Both file1 and file2 must be legal for reading. See uucp's rules.

Print local files on remote machine's printer

```
cat files ¦ uux - site\!lp
```

Caveat: You need permission to run lp at site. Use lpr instead of lp for AT&T UNIX.

Summary

In this chapter you have learned how to use uux to run programs on neighbor UNIX machines. You have also learned many of the variations and options available for uux. You have seen that the uucp and uux programs are the real workhorses for copying and manipulating files between UNIX machines. You have also seen how these programs can be run from shell scripts to expand their versatility and power. Just as `uuto` and `uupick` are shell scripts for simplifying the use of `uucp`, the shell scripts like `uuroff` and `uurecp` can simplify the use of `uux`.

This chapter completes our coverage of the main "midlevel" UUCP programs. In chapter 15 we will explore the various programs that allow you to monitor and change the status of queued UUCP requests. We will show you what a UUCP job is, how to kill it before it is transmitted, and how to find out why a job is failing.

15

Status Reports and Job Control

Regardless of how you use the UUCP software—either directly with the `uucp`, `uusend`, `uuto/uupick`, and `uux` programs, or indirectly with `mail` and `postnews`—you'll sometimes want to check or modify the status of those requests. Within the UUCP family of programs, there are two programs that allow you to check the status of requests, and one that allows you to both check on and modify them. The three programs are `uulog`, `uusnap`, and `uustat`.

UUCP Status Checking and Job Control Programs

`uulog`	Examines UUCP's `LOGFILE` for general information.
`uusnap`	Gives a quick summary of machine activity (BSD UNIX only).
`uustat`	Examines UUCP's `L_stat` and `R_stat` files for information about specific jobs or machine status. The `uustat` program also kills and rejuvenates jobs.

In this chapter we will first show you what is meant by a UUCP job and how the UUCP database files are used to record the status of jobs. We will then cover the three programs just mentioned, detailing the proper use and potential pitfalls of each. We will also show you how to obtain UUCP job numbers from `uucp` and `uux`.

What a UUCP Job Is

A *UUCP job* is simply the collection of work created by a queued UUCP request. That collection can range from a simple task, like copying one file to another machine, to a complex one, like running the diff program to compare files from two neighbor machines. No matter how complex your UUCP request, it is a single UUCP job and has a unique UUCP job number associated with it.

Later in this chapter, we'll explain how a UUCP job number is assigned to a UUCP job. For the present, just remember that each queued UUCP request is a single UUCP job. For example:

```
uux \!diff neighbor1\!/tmp/ch1 neighbor3\!/tmp/ch1.bak "> ch.diff"
```

queues a uux request to compare two files, each of which is located on a different neighbor machine. Although this request involves copying files from both neighbor1 and neighbor3 and then running the diff program locally, it is still a single UUCP job.

On the other hand, the following uuto command appears to be a single UUCP request, but it is not:

```
uuto file1 file2 neighbor1\!jake
```

Remember that uuto is a shell script that queues a separate UUCP request for each file listed. In this example, two UUCP jobs are created—one for file1 and one for file2.

The UUCP Database Files

Whenever you queue a UUCP request, whether directly or indirectly, several pieces of key information about that request are added to one or more UUCP database files—LOGFILE, L_stat, and R_stat. Each request, as represented in these database files, is a single UUCP job. It is these database files that provide you with information about UUCP jobs.

UUCP Database Files

LOGFILE	Contains the status of calls made to, and received from, neighbor machines. Each line in this file includes the name of the user who made the request, the name of that user's machine, the date, and a brief status message. LOGFILE is located in /usr/spool/uucp.
L_stat	Contains the status of each machine connected to your system. Each line in this file includes a system name, the time of its last connection attempt, and a status code. The L_stat file is located in /usr/lib/uucp and stands for "Link Status."

R_stat	Contains the status of each queued job in your system. Each line in this file includes a job number, the name of the user who queued that job, that user's system name, the time the request was queued, the time the request was executed, and a status code. The R_stat file is located in /usr/lib /uucp and stands for "Request Status."

The three programs mentioned at the start of this chapter (uulog, uusnap, and uustat) all use these database files for information about UUCP jobs. The uulog program allows you to view the contents of LOGFILE. The uustat program allows you to view the contents of the L_stat and R_stat files, and translates the internal codes in those files into human-understandable messages. The uusnap program provides a "snapshot" of the L_stat file in table form.

Inside */usr/spool/uucp/LOGFILE*

Every time UUCP succeeds or fails in an attempt to call another system, it adds a one-line entry to LOGFILE. Also, whenever uucp or uux queues a request, a line of text describing that request is added to LOGFILE. During conversations with a neighbor UNIX system, another line is added, describing each major action taken by those machines.

Regardless of why a line is added to LOGFILE, each line is organized in the same way:

```
user system (date-time-pid) status (detail)
```

where,

user	is the login name of the user who made the request. This could be a pseudoname like news if an automatic program made the request.
system	is the name of the system on which user has an account. For outgoing requests, this will be your home system's name. For incoming requests, this will be the name of a neighbor system.
date	is the month and day, as MM/DD, on which this entry was placed in LOGFILE.
time	is the time, in 24-hour format, as HH:MM, at which this entry was placed in LOGFILE.
pid	is the process identification number (PID) of the program (user-run or automatic) that added this entry to LOGFILE.

`status` is a short message (e.g., `OK` or `FAILED`) that describes the outcome of the action described by this entry. (See table 15-1 for a description of possible status messages.)

`detail` is a short message (e.g., `startup` or `call to neighbor1`) that describes the action intended by this entry.

Table 15-1. *LOGFILE* Status Messages

Message	Meaning
`AUTODIAL (dev...)`	Modem is currently in use and not available.
`BAD LOGIN/ PASSWORD`	Your machine could not log into the neighbor machine. See your system administrator.
`BAD READ`	Could not read or write to a device. See system administrator.
`CALLBACK REQUIRED`	For security reasons, the neighbor system will verify your identity by calling you back.
`CAN NOT CALL`	The call failed because of a system problem. Another try will be made later.
`DIAL FAILED`	Either the phone was busy, or the neighbor site is down. Another try will be made later.
`FAILED (call to system)`	The modem was unable to dial for any of a number of reasons. Another try will be made later.
`FAILED (conversation complete)`	Conversation between our machine and the neighbor failed after a successful startup. The neighbor may have gone down, a program may have died, or the phone line may have simply hung up. Another try will be made later.
`FAILED (...tty#)`	A call-out device failure. See your system administrator.
`HANDSHAKE FAILED (LCK)`	A lock file exists and prevents you from calling out. Perhaps someone is using `cu`. If this persists, see your system administrator.
`NO CALL (detail)`	Generally, the system is just not scheduled to call out at this time. If detail is `MAX RECALLS`, see your system administrator.
`SUCCEEDED`	Connected to neighbor machine.
`TIMEOUT`	The remote system failed to answer within the time limit. Another try will be made later.
`OK`	Everything is okay.

A typical extract from LOGFILE might look like the following. (The numbers on the right are not part of the file—they are reference numbers that we'll use in the description that follows the listing.)

```
root ourhome (11/30-15:19-9257) XQT QUE'D (rmail jake)          1
root ourhome (11/30-15:19-9259) NO CALL (RETRY TIME NOT REACHED) 2
root ourhome (11/30-15:31-9512) SUCCEEDED (call to neighbor1)    3
root ourhome (11/30-15:31-9512) OK (startup)                     4
root ourhome (11/30-15:31-9512) REQUEST (S D.neighbB7160 D. ...  5
root ourhome (11/30-15:35-9512) REQUEST (S D.ourhomX7158 X. ...  6
root ourhome (11/30-15:37-9512) COPY (SUCCEEDED)                 7
```

Line 1: A request was queued to mail a letter from the user root, on the local machine ourhome, to the user jake, on the neighbor machine neighbor1 (implied by line 3 but not shown on this line).

Line 2: As of the time indicated, no call had been made to send the letter. Some sites limit how often calls can be made to any given neighbor site. This entry indicates that a previous call occurred too recently to allow another attempt.

Line 3: The local system, ourhome, succeeded in calling the neighbor system neighbor1 at the time indicated.

Line 4: The two machines have synchronized with each other, and transfer of data has begun.

Line 5: A data file (D.) was sent to neighbor1. This file contained the text of the letter.

Line 6: A data file (D.) was sent to neighbor1 as an execution file (X.). This file contained the action (rmail) that was to be applied to the first file.

Line 7: The copy (the sending of mail) was successful.

As you can see, the LOGFILE contains a wealth of information. Take a moment to view your own system's LOGFILE with cat or more. Note that a typical LOGFILE can contain thousands of lines, and size alone may make it difficult to locate particular lines describing your requests. Fortunately, UUCP provides a program for viewing selected lines in LOGFILE. That program is uulog.

Viewing *LOGFILE* with *uulog*

The uulog program allows you to view selected lines from UUCP's /usr/spool/uucp/LOGFILE. Since uulog's output can be several screenfulls of text, you should generally pipe its output through the more program, as:

```
uulog | more
```

The more program displays one screenfull of text at a time and then waits for a keystroke telling it what to do next. If your system lacks the more program, you can use either pg (usually found on System V machines) or less (distributed in USENET). Read your manual pages to find out how to advance to the next screenfull and how to quit.

In the absence of any flags, uulog displays only those lines that belong to you. Thus,

```
uulog
```

will cause uulog to display only those lines in LOGFILE that describe your own queued UUCP requests.

Specifying the User with *uulog* (-*u* Flag)

The -u flag tells uulog to display only those lines that belong to a specific user. The format for using the -u flag is:

```
uulog -uname
```

where name is the login name of a specific user. Note that there must be no space between -u and name. The following example requests only those lines in LOGFILE belonging to jake.

```
uulog -ujake
```

Such a request might produce the following:

```
jake ourhome (11/29-10:02-8611) XQT QUE'D (rmail ted )
jake ourhome (11/29-10:03-8664) SUCCEEDED (call to neighbor1)
jake ourhome (11/29-10:03-8664) OK (startup)
etc.
```

This output reveals that the user—jake on our system ourhome—is having mail that he sent to ted!neighbor1 transferred by UUCP.

Since what uulog, with a -u flag, really does is display all lines of LOGFILE beginning with the specified user name, the same result could have been accomplished with:

```
grep "^name" /usr/spool/uucp/LOGFILE
```

Figure 15-1 illustrates this use of the grep command.

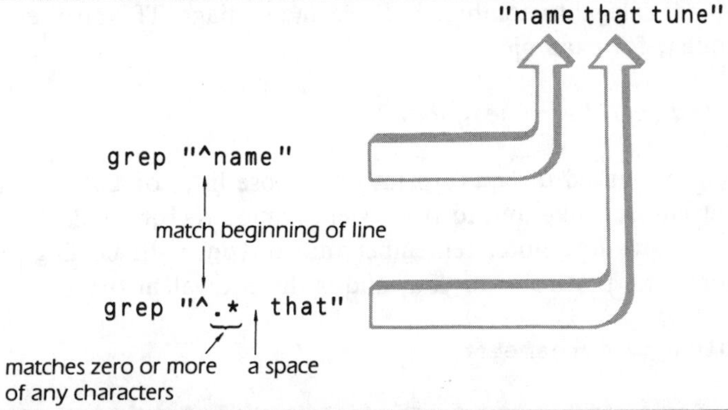

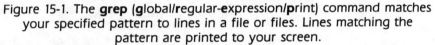

Figure 15-1. The **grep** (**g**lobal/**r**egular-**e**xpression/**p**rint) command matches your specified pattern to lines in a file or files. Lines matching the pattern are printed to your screen.

Specifying the System with *uulog* (*-s* Flag)

When the `uulog` program is run with the `-s` flag, it prints only those lines of `LOGFILE` that refer to a specified system name. The format for using the -s flag is:

```
uulog -ssystem
```

where `system` is the name of a specific system. Note that there is no space between `-s` and `system`. For example, the command:

```
uulog -sneighbor2
```

might display the following lines in `LOGFILE`:

```
news neighbor2 (11/29-05:16-7651) COPY (SUCCEEDED)
news neighbor2 (11/29-05:16-7651) OK (conversation complete)
uun2 neighbor2 (11/29-05:17-8233) news XQT (rnews)
etc.
```

This output shows that USENET news has arrived from the site named `neighbor2` and that the `rnews` program was executed at our site to handle that news.

The same output could be achieved by:

```
grep "^.* system" /usr/spool/uucp/LOGFILE
```

because the system name is always in the second column in `LOGFILE`.

It is legal to combine both `-u` and `-s` flags. This further narrows your range of inquiry, for example:

```
uulog -ujake -sneighbor2
```

Here, we asked `uulog` to print only those lines of `LOGFILE` that refer both to the user named `jake` and to the system named `neighbor2`.

As a final note, remember that `uulog`, with no flag arguments, prints only those lines that refer to you, and is the equivalent of:

```
uulog -uyourname
```

Summary of *uulog* Flags

`-uuser`	Display requests belonging to the user whose login name is `user`.
`-ssys`	Display requests belonging to the system whose name is `sys`.

Be Patient with UUCP

If `uulog` reveals that a request of yours has not yet been transferred to a neighbor site, don't queue another request. This will just have the effect of sending two requests. It is better to wait and let UUCP try again later. If the problem persists, you should contact your system administrator.

Status and Job Control with *uustat*

Every time you use `uucp` to copy a file, `uux` to request remote execution, or even `mail` to send an electronic mail message, you are queueing a UUCP job—that is, a request for some UUCP activity, or activities, to be performed on your behalf. The `uustat` program reports on, and allows you to affect, the status of these queued UUCP jobs. It can be used to:

- Examine the current status of all your UUCP jobs, both queued and recently completed.
- Kill (delete) UUCP jobs that have been queued but not completed.
- Examine the current status of all the UUCP jobs associated with a particular neighbor system.
- Examine the current status of all the UUCP jobs associated with a particular user.

- Examine the current status of any jobs that are newer than a specified number of hours, or older than a specified number of hours.
- Rejuvenate a job—that is, make it appear current because old jobs are automatically killed.
- Report on the current status of connections to neighbor UNIX machines.
- Summarize the current backlog of UUCP jobs by remote UNIX site name.

Explanation of *uustat*'s Output

When you run the uustat program it prints out a one-line description of every queued UUCP job. Remember that a UUCP job is the collection of activities that correspond to a single queued UUCP request. Each line of text that uustat prints will look like this:

```
jobnumber user system commandtime statustime status
```

where,

jobnumber	is the unique identifying number given by UUCP to each queued job.
user	is the login name of the user who ran the program that caused this job to be queued.
system	is the name of the neighbor UNIX system for which this job is targeted.
commandtime	is the date and time this job was queued. The time is in 24-hour format.
statustime	is the date and time that the last change in status for this job occurred. The time is in 24-hour format.
status	is a brief message explaining the current status of this job (see table 15-2).

In the absence of any flags, uustat prints information about only those jobs that belong to the current user. As an example, examine the following fictional output of the uustat command run by the user jake:

```
         user                        command time
uustat   ↓                           ↓
3471  jake   neighbor1 11/22-10:23  11/22-10:23  JOB IS QUEUED
3472  jake   neighbor3 11/22-11:21  11/22-11:22  COPY FINISHED
↑            ↑                      ↑            ↑
job number   system                 status time  status
```

Table 15-2. Meaning of *uustat* Status Messages

Message	Meaning
STATUS UNKNOWN: SYSTEM ERROR	Couldn't connect to neighbor site. The site may be down, its phone may be busy, or some other problem may exist. Retry later.
COPY FAIL	Modem hung up in midcopy, or some other problem aborted a transfer. Retry later.
LOCAL ACCESS TO FILE DENIED	Bad permissions on local machine (see chapter 11).
REMOTE ACCESS TO FILE DENIED	Bad permissions on the neighbor machine (see chapter 11).
A BAD UUCP COMMAND GENERATED	The program that uux tried to run is not one that is permitted.
REMOTE CAN'T CREATE TEMPFILE	Problem at neighbor site: disk full, hardware problems, etc. If this problem persists, contact the neighbor site's system administrator.
CAN'T COPY TO REMOTE DIRECTORY	Bad permissions on the neighbor machine. Directory not permitted in USERFILE (see chapter 11).
CAN'T COPY TO LOCAL DIRECTORY - FILE LEFT IN PUBDIR/USER /FILE	Bad permissions on the local machine. Directory lacks write permission for anyone, or not permitted in USERFILE (see chapter 11). File placed into PUBDIR instead.
LOCAL CAN'T CREATE TEMPFILE	Problem at local site: disk full, hardware problems, etc. If this problem persists, contact your local site's system administrator.
CAN'T EXECUTE UUCP	An attempt to forward a file, or remote-execute uucp with the -e flag, was not permitted.
COPY (PARTIALLY) SUCCEEDED	Some (possibly none) of the UUCP transfer succeeded before an unexpected problem caused an abort.
COPY FINISHED, JOB DELETED	The job is done. All is fine.
JOB IS QUEUED	Job has been placed into the UUCP queue for later transmission.
JOB KILLED	Job was killed.

Line 2 shows that the UUCP job number 3471 was queued by a user whose login name is jake, that this job is targeted for the neighbor UNIX machine named neighbor1, and that this job has been queued but not yet executed. Line 3 shows that the UUCP job number 3472 was also queued by jake. This one, however, was targeted for the neighbor UNIX machine named neighbor3. Here, the status shows that the job has been completed successfully.

Since each line of information produced by uustat corresponds to a single UUCP job, uustat is limited to reporting only the *current status* of any UUCP job. If you wish to observe the flow of information concerning any particular job, you will need to use the uulog program (described in the previous section) to look through all the entries for a given job.

Specifying Another User with *uustat* (*-u* Flag)

The uustat program provides the -u flag as a means of examining the UUCP status of jobs belonging to other users. The format for using the -u flag is:

```
uustat -uname
```

where name is the login name of any user having an account on your local machine. There must be no space between -u and name.

To view the current UUCP status of jobs belonging to, for example, the user news—the pseudouser who processes USENET news—you would type:

```
uustat -unews
```

which might produce the following output:

```
3844  news    neighbor2  11/22-12:01  11/22-12:10 COPY FAIL
```

Here, the user, whose login name is news, has queued a UUCP job, number 3844. That queued job is targeted for the neighbor UNIX machine neighbor2. The status shows that the last attempt to send this news to neighbor2 failed. Should repeated attempts continue to fail, the system administrator will have to intercede.

Specifying the System with *uustat* (*-s* Flag)

The uustat program provides the -s flag as a means of viewing the UUCP job status of selected remote UNIX sites. The format for using the -s flag is:

```
uustat -ssystem
```

where system is the name of one of the neighbor UNIX machines to which your machine is connected (see uuname in chapter 11). There must be no space between -s and system.

As an example, entering the uustat command with the -s flag, where system is neighbor2,

```
uustat -sneighbor2
```

might produce the following output:

```
3842  jake    neighbor2  11/22-11:55  11/22-11:55 COPY FINISHED
3844  news    neighbor2  11/22-12:01  11/22-12:10 COPY FAIL
3855  jake    neighbor2  11/22-13:15  11/22-13:15 COPY FAIL
```

Observe that at 11:55 a job was successfully transferred to the remote site named neighbor2. Beginning at 12:01, however, all jobs targeted for neighbor2 have begun to fail. This could mean that neighbor2's phone line is busy or that the site is down for some reason, but it could also mean that some new problem has developed with your site's UUCP software. So, it would be a good idea to rerun uustat, with the -sneighbor2 argument, in about an hour. If the problem persists, your system administrator should be notified.

Killing a Job with *uustat* (*-k* Flag)

To err is human, so uustat provides the means to undo what has been done, at least up to a point. The -k flag can be used with uustat to kill any UUCP job—as long as the job is your own and has not yet been completed.

You might want to kill one of your UUCP jobs for any number of reasons. Suppose you mailed an electronic letter to your boss complaining bitterly about being passed over for promotion. Just as you pressed Control-d to send that letter, a coworker leaned through the door and congratulated you on your promotion.

To kill the transmission of your letter, you must first run the uustat program, with no arguments, to find the UUCP job number of that letter and its status:

```
uustat
3518 bozo neighbor2 06/19-09:22 06/19-09:22 JOB QUEUED
↑         ↑                                     ↑
job       your name                             status
number
```

Recall that the uustat program, when run with no arguments, prints the status of only those UUCP jobs that belong to you. In the preceding example, your only job, the letter, has been queued but not yet sent.

To kill a UUCP job using uustat, you must give uustat a -k flag. The format for using the -k flag is:

```
uustat -kjobnumber
```

where jobnumber is the UUCP job number of the job you want to kill. There must be no space between -k and jobnumber.

To kill the job that is your letter, and thus cancel its transmission, rerun `uustat` as:

```
uustat -k3518
```

If you run `uustat`, again with no arguments, to confirm that the job has indeed been killed, you should see:

```
3518 bozo neighbor2 06/19-09:22 06/19-09:23 JOB KILLED (COMPLETE)
```

There are some common pitfalls to be aware of when you are trying to kill UUCP jobs:

- To kill a job (thereby preventing its transmission), the job must not have already been completed.
- If you have only one UUCP job queued, it is easy to know which job to kill. If you have several, however, you will be forced to run the `uulog` program, and search its more verbose output, to determine which of your jobs is the one to kill.
- If your UUCP job is targeted for a machine on a local area network (including your own machine), it is not likely that you will be able to kill the job before it is transmitted because local area network UUCP jobs are transmitted almost instantly.

Rejuvenating a Job with *uustat* (–*r* Flag)

Periodically, your system automatically runs UUCP maintenance software. That software kills and removes UUCP jobs that have been inactive for too long a period of time. Generally, this purging happens once a week, but at major sites, with lots of UUCP traffic, purging may happen more often.

UUCP jobs can sit idle for many reasons. Usually, they do so because a neighbor site is down for maintenance, or there is some temporary problem with the telephone lines. If a queued UUCP job of yours has been sitting idle for more than a day, the automatic UUCP maintenance software may kill and remove your job (see figure 15-2).

The `uustat` program offers the `-r` flag as a means of rejuvenating old and idle UUCP jobs. Rejuvenation of a UUCP job makes it appear fresh to the automatic UUCP maintenance software, so the job won't be removed.

The format for using the `-r` flag is:

```
uustat -rjobnumber
```

where `jobnumber` is the UUCP job number of the job you wish to rejuvenate. Note that there can be no space between `-r` and `jobnumber`.

Figure 15-2. Old UUCP jobs are automatically killed by UUCP maintenance software.

As an example of how and when to run the uustat command with the -r flag, consider the following output of uustat for the user jane:

```
uustat
4351 jane neighbor3 11/22-14:55 11/23-09:11 STATUS UNKNOWN: SYSTEM ERROR
                         ↑           ↑
                   command time  status time
```

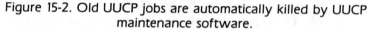

Notice that almost 24 hours have elapsed between the time the request was queued, commandtime, and the time the latest attempt to connect to the neighbor site neighbor3 failed. If jane wants to prevent UUCP from killing and removing her request, she can rejuvenate it with the -r flag:

```
uustat -r4351
uustat
4351 jane  neighbor3   11/23-10:01 11/23-10:01 JOB IS QUEUED
```

Here, the -r flag was used with uustat to make a tired, old UUCP job appear fresh and new. Obviously, if the job fails to be completed after another day has passed, continued rejuvenation is probably not useful—you will need to see your system administrator for help with the problem.

Getting Job Numbers from *uucp* and *uux* (*-j* Flag)

As you have seen, neither uustat nor uulog tells you much about what any particular UUCP job is supposed to be doing. There are several ways of figuring out which UUCP job number has been assigned to which UUCP queued request, but none of them is as easy as being told the job number directly.

Both the uucp and the uux programs have the ability to display the UUCP job number assigned to a request. To see the UUCP job number, just issue either of these commands using the -j flag. If you remember (or write down) this number, you can use it later with uustat to kill, rejuvenate, or view the status of that UUCP job.

An example of the -j flag used with uucp is:

```
uucp -j walrus.txt neighbor1!~/walrus.txt
job 6712
    ↑
    UUCP job number assigned to queued uucp request
```

An example of the -j flag used with uux is:

```
uux -j neighbor1\!who "> neighbor1.who"
job 6713
    ↑
    UUCP job number assigned to queued uux request
```

In both cases, the -j flag causes the UUCP job number assigned to the queued request to be displayed.

Viewing by Job Number with *uustat* (*-j* Flag)

When you know the UUCP job number, you can use the -j flag with uustat to view the status of a particular UUCP queued request. The format for using the -j flag is:

```
uustat -jjobnumber
```

where jobnumber is the number of the UUCP job for which you want the status displayed. There must be no space between -j and jobnumber.

For example, to post a request to send the file walrus.txt to the remote site neighbor1's PUBDIR directory using the uucp program, and then to view the status of that queued UUCP job, you might enter the following:

```
uucp -j walrus.txt neighbor1\!~/
job is 3452
uustat -j3452
3452 jane  neighbor1 11/23-10:01 11/23-10:01 JOB IS QUEUED
```

Note that a `-j` flag was used with the `uucp` program to make it display the UUCP job number assigned to its queued request.

Another way to use the `-j` flag with `uustat` is to use the word "all" instead of a UUCP job number:

```
uustat -jall
```

This format instructs `uustat` to print information about *all* UUCP jobs for which it has status. The `-jall` flag is usually combined with another flag, like `-o` (described next), to limit the range of information displayed to a manageable number of lines.

Limiting by Time with *uustat* (*-o* and *-y* Flags)

It is possible to limit the scope of information printed with `uustat`. The `-o` flag is used to limit `uustat`'s display to UUCP jobs *older* than a given time. Conversely, the `-y` flag is used to limit `uustat`'s display to UUCP jobs *younger* (newer) than a given time.

The format for using the `-o` and `-y` flags is:

`-ohour` ←*older than* hour *hours*
`-yhour` ←*newer than* hour *hours*

For both flags, `hour` is a number of hours, such as 12. For both flags, there must be no space between `-o`, or `-y`, and `hour`.

The chief use for the `-o` flag is to limit `uustat`'s output to include only old UUCP jobs. This flag is handy when you've been generating lots of UUCP queued requests, for example, and wish to check the status of those UUCP jobs that are older than a couple of hours:

```
uustat -o2
3452 jane  neighbor1 11/23-10:01 11/23-10:04 COPY FINISHED
3459 jane  neighbor3 11/23-10:02 11/23-11:56 STATUS UNKNOWN
```

Here, the first UUCP job, `3452`, has been transmitted successfully, but the second UUCP job, `3459`, has suffered transmission failure for the last two hours. It may be that the site `neighbor3` is down and not accepting UUCP transmissions. If this UUCP job gets too old without a successful transfer happening, it can be rejuvenated with the `-r` flag of `uustat` (discussed earlier). If the problem persists, your system administrator should be advised.

The `-y` flag for `uustat` is used to limit `uustat`'s output to include only the most recent UUCP jobs. It is handy when `uustat`'s output runs to more than a screenfull of information, and you wish to limit that output to only the most recent UUCP jobs.

In the following example, the `-y` flag is combined with the `-jall` flag of the previous section to limit the display of *all* UUCP jobs to only those queued within the last hour:

```
uustat -y1 -jall
```

Here, the `-y1` argument specifies that `uustat`'s output is to be limited to information about UUCP jobs that have been queued within the last hour. The `-jall` flag was used to specify that all UUCP jobs are to be displayed—that is, UUCP jobs for all users and all sites. So, the subset of jobs for all users and all sites that have been queued within the last hour is selected and displayed.

Displaying Numbers versus Text for Status with *uustat* (*-v* and *-O* Flags)

On some systems the `status` field in `uustat`'s output is printed in understandable text:

```
9112 jake  neighbor1 11/19-20:15 11/19-20:15 JOB QUEUED
                                             ↑
                                             status
```

On other systems, though, the `status` field is printed as a numeric code:

```
9112 jake  neighbor1 11/19-20:15 11/19-20:15 04000
                                             ↑
                                             status
```

If your site is one of those that prints the `status` field in numeric code form, you may use the `-v` (more verbose) flag with `uustat` to force it to print the `status` in readable text. For example, if `uustat` prints the following:

```
uustat
9112 jake  neighbor1 11/19-20:15 11/19-20:15 04000
```

you can use the `-v` flag to obtain:

```
uustat -v
9112 jake  neighbor1 11/19-20:15 11/19-20:15 JOB QUEUED
```

For machines that normally print `status` in text, the `-O` flag can be used to convert the text to a numeric code:

```
uustat
```

```
9112 jake  neighbor1 11/19-20:15 11/19-20:15 JOB QUEUED
uustat -O
9112 jake  neighbor1 11/19-20:15 11/19-20:15 04000
```

For the more technically oriented, the numeric code for `uustat` status is an octal representation of flag bits. These flags are used internally by `uustat` to represent each UUCP job's status.

Sumary of *uustat* Flags

`-uuser`	Display status of queued UUCP jobs owned by `user`.
`-ssite`	Display status of queued UUCP jobs destined for the neighbor UNIX machine named `site`.
`-jjobn -jall`	Display status of queued UUCP job whose UUCP job number is `jobn`. If the job number is `all`, display the status of all queued UUCP jobs.
`-kjobn`	Kill the queued UUCP job whose UUCP job number is `jobn`.
`-rjobn`	Rejuvenate the queued UUCP job whose UUCP job number is `jobn`.
`-ohour`	Display status of UUCP jobs that were queued more than `hour` hours ago.
`-yhour`	Display status of UUCP jobs that were queued less than `hour` hours ago.
`-v`	Convert octal status message codes into readable text.
`-O`	Convert readable text status messages into octal codes.
`-msite -Msite -mall`	Display connection status and times for the neighbor UNIX site whose name is `site`. If `site` is `all`, display connection status and times for all neighbor UNIX sites connected to your local site.
`-q`	Summarize backlog of queued UUCP jobs by neighbor site connections.

Displaying Status of Machine Accessibility with *uustat* (*-m* and *-M* Flags)

In addition to displaying information about the status of UUCP jobs, `uustat` can also display information about the status of connections between your machine and connected neighbor UNIX machines. This is done by using the `-m` or the `-M` flag. Both flags mean the same thing and may be used interchangeably.

The format for using the `-m` flag is:

```
-msitename    ←status for machine sitename
-mall         ←status for all machines
```

where `sitename` is the name of a neighbor UNIX site to which your site is connected (see `uuname` in chapter 11). If `all` is specified, then information about all neighbor UNIX sites that are connected to your site is printed.

The output of `uustat` with the `-m` flag is one line of information per neighbor UNIX site:

```
systemname  statustime   status
```

where,

`systemname`	is the name of the neighbor UNIX site for which this line provides status information.
`statustime`	is the date and time that the status information in this line was last updated.
`status`	is a description of the current state of this neighbor site. (Table 15-3 gives the meaning of the various status messages.)

A typical application for the `-m` flag with `uustat` would be to see why a UUCP job destined for a particular site had failed to be transmitted:

```
uustat -mneighbor3
neighbor3   11/15-20:22  WRONG TIME TO CALL
```

Here, transmissions to the neighbor UNIX site `neighbor3` are failing because our system administrator has placed a restriction on the times our machine may call `neighbor3`. The status message means that an attempt was made to call `neighbor3` at a time that was not permitted.

Summarizing Jobs for All Neighbor Sites with *uustat* (*-q* Flag)

The `uustat` program provides one final variation in the information it can display. The `-q` flag tells `uustat` to display information, in summary form, about queued

Table 15-3. Meaning of *uustat -m* Status Messages

Message	Meaning
`BAD SYSTEM`	The neighbor site specified is not known by the UUCP software.
`WRONG TIME TO CALL`	Calls to neighbor site restricted to certain periods of time. This is not a permitted time.
`SYSTEM LOCKED`	A call is already in progress with the neighbor site, or a lock file was not properly removed.
`NO DEVICE AVAILABLE`	UUCP couldn't find a free modem on which to call out. Local area network hardware is busy.
`DIAL FAILED`	Couldn't connect to neighbor site: remote site is down, remote site's phone is busy, or modem is broken.
`LOGIN FAILED`	Connected but unable to log into neighbor site: phone noise, hang-up during login, password or login name changed on neighbor site.
`HANDSHAKE FAILED`	The `uucico` programs couldn't synchronize to begin their conversation and exchange of data (see chapter 18).
`STARTUP FAILED`	The `uucico` programs lost synchronization before conversation or failed to agree on a protocol (see chapter 18).
`CONVERSATION IN PROGRESS`	Currently connected to neighbor UNIX site and in process of exchanging data.
`CONVERSATION FAILED`	The `uucico` programs lost synchronization during conversation: phone noise, software died (see chapter 18).
`CONVERSATION SUCCEEDED`	Exchange of files with remote site is completed. No more business.
`CALL SUCCEEDED`	Finished talking with neighbor site. Total success. All is fine.

UUCP jobs for all neighbor sites. Because the `-q` flag causes a descriptive header to be printed, the listing produced by `uustat` is fairly easy to understand:

```
uustat -q
```

```
System      # jobs # file          earliest            latest
neighb         1      2     Sat Nov 15 10:15 Sat Nov 15 10:30
neighb         4      9   **Sat Nov 14 22:43 Sat Nov 15 09:30
neighb         0      0
```

where,

- `System` is the name of the neighbor UNIX systems for which information is provided. Notice that the names are truncated to print only the first six characters. This is one good reason why site names should be unique in their first six characters.
- `# jobs` is the number of queued UUCP jobs that are destined for each neighbor site.
- `# file` is the number of files held in the UUCP spool directory that need to be transmitted to each neighbor site.
- `earliest` is the date and time of the earliest (oldest) untransmitted job. If the earliest is preceded by `**`, then it is more than 24 hours old.
- `latest` is the date and time of the latest (newest) untransmitted job.

If your machine is currently connected to one of the neighbor sites listed, an additional field will be printed following the `latest` field. This extra information is the date and time that the current connection was made to that neighbor site. If the date and time are preceded by `**`, then the connection has been continuous for more than 24 hours. This usually means that a lock file needs to be removed by the system administrator. (A *lock file* is an empty file that is created by software to let other programs know that some shared resource is busy. Those other programs will then either wait for that lock file to be removed before proceeding, or exit and run again later.)

UCB's *uusnap* Program

Under BSD UNIX, yet another UUCP status reporting program is available. Called `uusnap`, this program behaves very much like the `-q` flag for the `uustat` program. It prints a summary of the current status of connections to all neighbor sites. The `uusnap` program is usually used to examine UUCP backlogs and to diagnose UUCP system problems.

The `uusnap` program takes no arguments and is used simply as:

uusnap

It prints one line of information for each neighbor site connected to your machine:

```
sitename  #cmds #data #xqts  message
```

where,

`sitename`	is the full name of the neighbor site.
`#cmds`	is the number of UUCP command files. These files, one per UUCP job, contain instructions about which neighbor site to contact, the type of transfer, and where to place the transferred file via `uucp`.
`#data`	is the number of UUCP data files. These files, up to 20 per UUCP job, contain the actual data (copy of a file) that is to be transferred via `uucp` or `uux`.
`#xqts`	is the number of UUCP execute files. These files, one per UUCP job, contain instructions about remote command execution via `uux`.
`message`	is the current status of the neighbor site. Information may be printed giving the time remaining before UUCP can retry a call, or the number of times UUCP has tried to call and failed. If this field is empty, then UUCP is not currently connected with this site.

A typical display produced by the `uusnap` program might look like this:

```
uusnap
neighbor1  1 Cmds  2 Data      ---   CONVERSATION
neighbor3  4 Cmds  8 Data  1 Xqts
```

This display shows first that we are currently connected to the neighbor site `neighbor1` and that one command and two data files are being transmitted. Second, it shows that the remote site `neighbor3` still has a backlog of command, data, and execution files.

Note that the `uusnap` program prints out status only for neighbor sites that have UUCP jobs queued, rather than for all sites.

Summary of Uses and Caveats

The following is a brief review and summary of the most common uses of the `uulog`, `uustat` and `uusnap` programs. Caveats are provided to help illustrate variations, limitations, and possible pitfalls.

View `LOGFILE`*: select by user login name*

```
uulog -uname
```

Caveat: The `name` is the login name of a user on your system. There must be no space between `-u` and `name`.

View `LOGFILE`: *select by site name*

```
uulog -ssite
```

Caveat: The `site` is the name of one of the neighbor UNIX sites to which your machine is connected. The `-u` and `-s` flags may both be used to further narrow `uulog`'s output. There must be no space between `-s` and `site`.

Get UUCP job status: select by user login name

```
uustat -uname
```

Caveat: The `name` is the login name of a user on your system, or a neighbor site's login name. There must be no space between `-u` and the `name`.

Get UUCP job status: select by site name

```
uustat -ssite
```

Caveat: The `site` is the name of one of the neighbor UNIX sites to which your machine is connected. The `-u` and `-s` flags may both be used to further narrow `uustat`'s output. There must be no space between `-s` and the `site`.

Get UUCP job status: select by job number

```
uustat -jjobnumber
```

Caveat: The `jobnumber` is a number, assigned by UUCP, that describes a particular UUCP job; `-jall` will print the status of all UUCP jobs. There must be no space between `-j` and `jobnumber`.

Change UUCP job status: kill a job

```
uustat -kjobnumber
```

Caveat: The `jobnumber` is a number, assigned by UUCP, that describes a particular UUCP job. The `-k` deletes a UUCP job and all the temporary files associated with that job. There must be no space between `-k` and `jobnumber`.

Change UUCP job status: rejuvenate a job

```
uustat -rjobnumber
```

Caveat: The `jobnumber` is a number, assigned by UUCP, that describes a particular UUCP job. The `-r` makes an old job appear to be a new job to UUCP. There must be no space between `-r` and `jobnumber`.

View remote site status

```
uustat -msitename
uustat -mall
uustat -q
uusnap
```

Caveat: The first request summarizes the connection status for the neighbor site `sitename`. The second summarizes the connection status for `all` neighbor sites. The last two summarize the command backlog for all active neighbor sites.

Summary

In this chapter you have learned what a UUCP job is and how to examine and change the status of a UUCP job. You have also learned how to obtain a summary of jobs, connection status, and job backlog for neighbor UNIX sites.

In chapter 16 we will explore two special problems that arise when using `uucp`. First, we will show you several approaches to sending directory hierarchies. Then, we will discuss the problem encountered when sending binary files, and provide a solution.

16

Copying Archives and Binary Files

As you become more comfortable with the UUCP ensemble of programs, you will find yourself using them more and more often for routine tasks. Eventually, you will want to attempt some activities for which UUCP was not originally designed. In this chapter we will try to anticipate two of the more common problems that people encounter when using UUCP for advanced tasks, and we'll offer solutions to those problems. Specifically, we will provide help in the following areas:

- Copying directory hierarchies. We will show you three methods for using `uucp` to transfer the contents of a directory, including the contents of all its subdirectories.
- Transferring binary files using `uucp` and `mail`. We will show you how to convert a binary (non human-readable) file into a text (human-readable) file and how to convert that text file back into a copy of the original binary file. We will also provide you with a listing for a mini `uudecode` program.

Transferring Directory Hierarchies with *uucp*

The `uucp` program is limited in that it can send only *files* between one UNIX machine and another. It cannot send directories as such, although it can create any directories needed to put a file in the destination system's file structure, as you saw in chapter 12. This limitation runs contrary to the natural use of UNIX's hierarchical file system, where files and directories are organized in a branching fashion. As an example, examine figure 16-1. Notice how the user named `george` has arranged the files that constitute his current book. The introduction—called

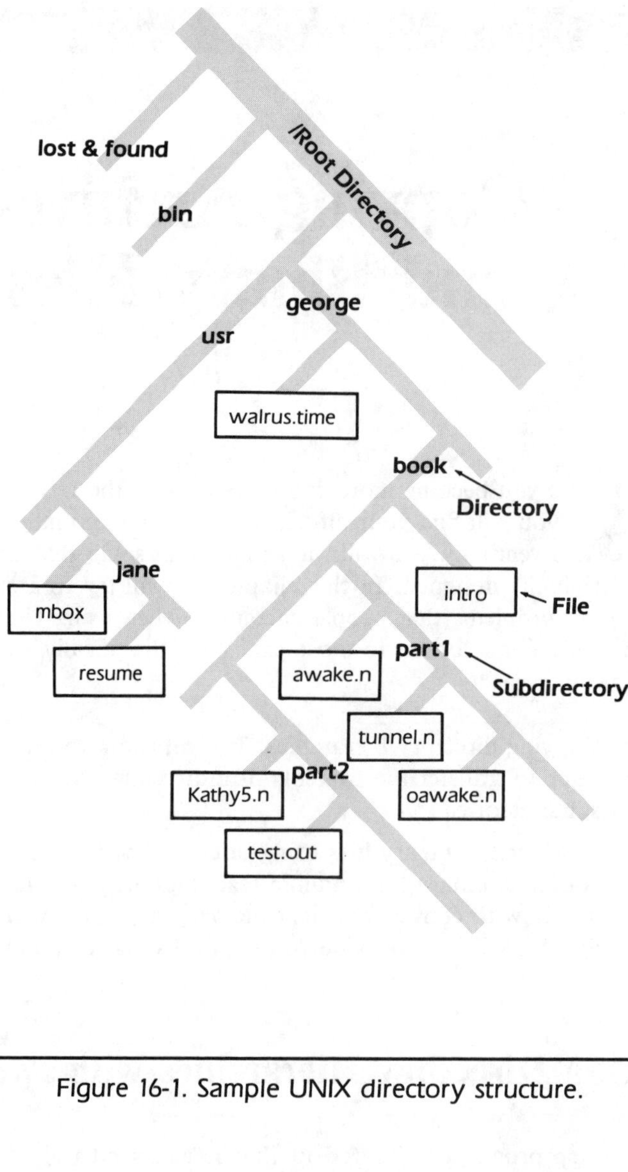

Figure 16-1. Sample UNIX directory structure.

`intro`—is in the directory `book`, and the rest of the chapters are arranged in subdirectories corresponding to parts of that book. (If you are unclear about how UNIX uses directory branching for its file structure, you may wish to review chapter 2 of this book, or consult one of the beginning UNIX books listed in Appendix E.)

To illustrate some limitations of both uucp and uuto for sending directory hierarchies, we will send copies of the files in /usr/george/book from our local machine into the PUBDIR directory of the remote machine named neighbor1. This includes the file intro and all the files in the subdirectories part1 and part2.

To send these files with uucp, you would type the following:

```
cd /usr/george/book
uucp intro part1/*.n part2/*.n neighbor1\! ~/
```

Here, we use the shell's wildcard character to specify that only those files in the subdirectories part1 and part2, having names ending in .n, be sent—this prevents the file part2/test.out from being sent.

The preceding uucp request, if successful, will place those files into neighbor1's PUBDIR directory as:

```
PUBDIR/intro
PUBDIR/part1/awake.n
PUBDIR/part1/tunnel.n
etc.
```

To send the same files using the uuto program, but this time including part2 /test.out, you would enter the following:

```
cd /usr/george/book
uuto intro part1 part2 neighbor1\! ~/
```

Since uuto is really a shell script, this uuto request actually generates a separate uucp request to transfer each file. These files will arrive on the neighbor site neighbor1 as:

```
PUBDIR/george/ourhome/intro
PUBDIR/george/ourhome/part1/awake.n
PUBDIR/george/ourhome/part1/tunnel.n
etc.
```

Here, george is the name of the user who sent the files, and ourhome is the name of his machine.

Either approach, uucp or uuto, is workable, but each has some disadvantages:

- Since uucp can handle only files, it requires you to specify, as part of the command line, every file that is to be transferred. Although wildcard characters make this easier, this limitation requires that you know how to specify every file, no matter how many there are and no matter how far the subdirectories may extend.

- Since uucp transfers one file at a time to a neighbor site, it is possible for some files to transfer while others fail. Recovering from this kind of failure requires you to examine the success of each file individually, resending on a case-by-case basis.
- Since uupick is not available at all sites, there is no guarantee that you can easily retrieve files sent with uuto. In the absence of uupick, files will have to be copied and moved individually at the remote site.

The disadvantages of using uucp and uuto to send directory contents are not too severe when only a few files are involved, but a better approach is needed when the number of files becomes large, or when the number and depth of subdirectories becomes complex. This better approach is to package a large or complex directory structure into a single file and then to send that package. This approach has two advantages over that of sending files individually with uucp or uuto:

1. A single packaged file is easier to handle at the remote site. The user there can copy or move a single file with a single command, even in the absence of a uupick program.
2. Transmission failure on a single packaged file means that only that one file need be resent. It is much easier to monitor the status of a single UUCP job with uustat (see chapter 15) than it is to monitor the status of many UUCP jobs.

In this section we will explore three ways of packaging a directory into a single file. We will discuss the strengths and weaknesses of each and suggest alternative ways of using each.

Three Ways of Packaging a File for UUCP Transmission

tar	Standing for "*T*ape *AR*chive," this program creates a single file that is easily unpackaged using tar at the remote site. Despite its name, tar is not limited to use with tapes.
cpio	Standing for "*C*o*P*y-*I*n-copy-*O*ut," this program creates a single file that is easily unpackaged using cpio at the remote site.
shar	Standing for "*SH AR*chive," this program creates a single file, in Bourne Shell script form, that is easily unpackaged using /bin/sh at the remote site.

Package Directories with *tar*

Although the `tar` program stands for "*T*ape *AR*chive," it is not limited to use with tapes. By using the `f` directive to specify a file instead of a tape drive, you can force `tar` to package a directory, and its contents, into a single file. The result is a file that can later be easily unpackaged using `tar` at the receiving site.

To package a directory and its contents using `tar`, merely run `tar` as:

```
tar cf - directory > packagedfile
```

↑ *directives* ↑ *to standard output*

Here, the directive `cf` is a combination of two directives: the `c` tells `tar` to create a new archive; the `f` tells `tar` to send that archive into the device whose name is the next following argument, in this case `-`. When the device is specified as `-`, `tar` sends its output to the standard output. The `>` in the command line causes the standard output to be redirected into the filename `packagedfile`. The `tar` program recursively archives the directory named `directory`, packaging all the files in `directory`, as well as the contents of all the subdirectories in `directory`, as well as any subdirectories to those subdirectories, and so on, all into `packagedfile` (see figure 16-2).

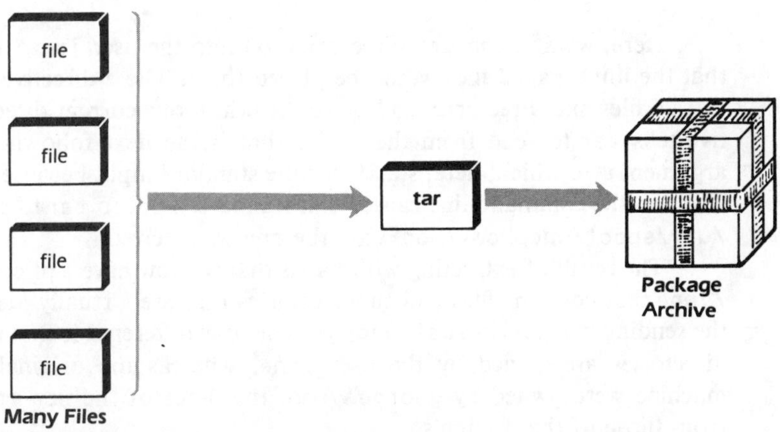

Figure 16-2. The **tar** program can be used to archive or "package" many files into a single file for transmission with **uucp**.

For example, to package the contents of the directory `/usr/george/book` (figure 16-1) using `tar`, you would type:

```
cd /usr/george
tar cf - book > booktar
```

This command tells tar to create a new archive and send that archive to the standard output. The > causes that output to be redirected into the file booktar. The tar program recursively archives the directory book, thus archiving the file intro and all the files in the subdirectories part1 and part2 into the single file named booktar. The resulting file, booktar, can now be sent to the neighbor site neighbor1 with the uucp command:

```
uucp booktar neighbor1\!~/
```

This command queues a request for the file booktar, our packaged tar archive, to be copied into the PUBDIR directory on the neighbor site named neighbor1.

When the file is received by neighbor1, it can be easily unpackaged using the tar program at that site:

```
cd /usr/jane
tar xf - < /usr/spool/uucppublic/booktar
     ↑  ↑
     |  standard input
directives
```

Here, we first changed directory (cd) into the user jane's home directory so that the unpackaged files would be placed there. The x directive for tar tells it to extract files and directories and place them into our current directory. The f directive tells tar to read from the device that is the next following argument. That argument is -, which, here, stands for the standard input because we are extracting. The < in the command line causes that standard input to tar to come from the file /usr/spool/uucpbook/booktar, the one we received.

The result of extracting with tar is that we now have a directory book in /usr/jane that contains files and subdirectories that are virtually identical to those on the sending machine in /usr/george. The only difference is that these new files and directories are owned by the user jane, whereas the originals on the sending machine were owned by george. Also, the dates of the new copies are different from those of the originals.

One pitfall to avoid when using tar to package a directory is that of specifying the directory using a full pathname:

```
tar cf - /usr/george/book > booktar
         ↑
         full pathname
```

When tar at the remote site tries to unpackage this, it will try to create directories and files using the full pathname of each. That is, if you unpackage with:

```
cd /usr/jane
tar xf - < /usr/spool/uucppublic/booktar
```

the tar program will unpackage by attempting unsuccessfully to create:

```
/usr/george/book
/usr/george/book/intro
/usr/george/book/part1
/usr/george/book/part1/awake.n
etc.
```

instead of attempting to unpackage by creating:

```
book
book/intro
book/part1
book/part1/awake.n
etc.
```

There are ways to override this problem on the remote site, but it is is best avoided in the first place by specifying only relative directory names at the sending site.

There are many other directives available for tar, such as v for verbose, that can make packaging and unpackaging easier. Consult "tar(1)" in your UNIX manual for details.

Transfer Directories with *cpio*

The cpio program stands for *CoPy In* copy *Out*. Unlike tar, cpio is not able to package directories directly. Instead, it reads a list of file and directory names and creates a package based on the contents of that list. The fact that cpio can package from a list is an advantage over tar when you wish to package selected files and subdirectories.

There are many ways to create a list of files for cpio. Probably the easiest is by using the find program. To create a list of the files in the directory /usr/george/book, for example, using find, you simply enter the following:

```
cd /usr/george
find book -print > booklist
```

This command tells find to recursively descend the directory book and, for each file or directory it finds there, to output (-print) its name. The output of find is redirected, using the > command-line argument, into the file booklist.

Running the preceding example would produce the file `booklist` that might contain the following lines:

```
book
book/intro
book/part1
book/part1/awake.n
etc.
```

That file can now be edited to exclude anything you don't want packaged; then `cpio` can be run to create a package of only those files and directories remaining in the list.

The `cpio` program expects its list of files to come from the standard input. It then gathers those files into a package that it always sends to the standard output. Because of this, the command to package the files listed in `booklist` using `cpio` looks like:

```
cpio -oc < booklist > bookcpio
           ↑          ↑
      list of files   packaged archive
```

The `-oc`, in the preceding example, is not one flag but two. The `o` tells `cpio` to output an archive based on the list of files it reads from its standard input. The `c` tells `cpio` to use ASCII header information instead of binary so that `uucp` will be able to transmit it.

The `cpio` program reads a list of files from `booklist` (see figure 16-3). Since `cpio` always reads from the standard input, that file is fed into `cpio` by using a < in the command. The < redirects `cpio`'s standard input to come from the file `booklist`.

The archive created by `cpio` is always sent to the standard output. By using > in the command line, we redirect that standard output into the file `bookcpio`—our packaged archive file.

Once a directory has been packaged using `cpio`, it can be sent with `uucp`:

```
uucp bookcpio neighbor1\! ~/
```

This command queues a request for the file `bookcpio`—our packaged archive of the `book` directory—to be sent into the PUBDIR directory at the neighbor site `neighbor1`. When the package arrives on `neighbor1`, it can be unpackaged with `cpio` on that machine. The procedure for doing that looks like:

```
cd /usr/jane
cpio -icd < /usr/spool/uucppublic/bookcpio
```

As you might have guessed, `-icd` is not one flag, but three. The `i` tells `cpio` to unpackage from its standard input. The `c` tells `cpio` that header information in the

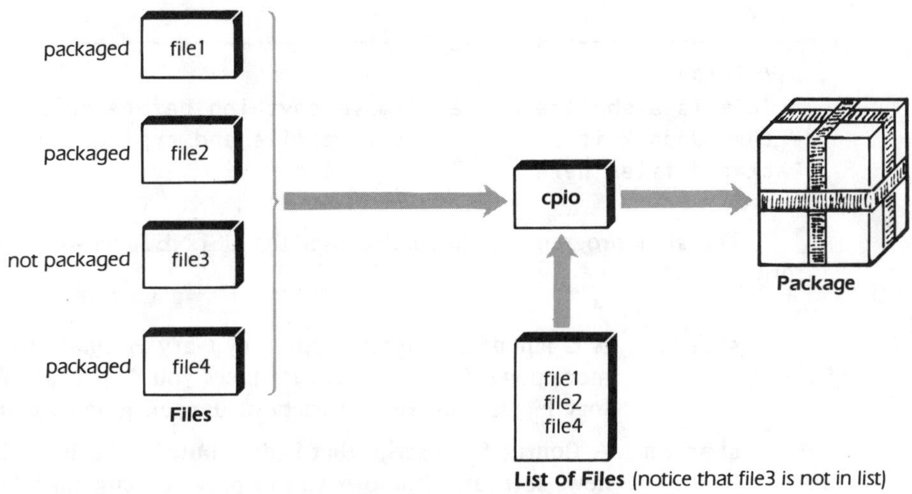

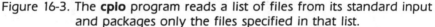

Figure 16-3. The **cpio** program reads a list of files from its standard input and packages only the files specified in that list.

input archive will be in uucp-transmittable, ASCII form. The `d` tells `cpio` to create directories as they are needed.

Since `cpio` unpackages from its standard input, we use `<` in the command line to attach that standard input to the file `/usr/spool/uucppublic/bookcpio`, the packaged archive we received from the remote site.

As with `tar`, avoid specifying files with full pathnames when you are creating your list of files for `cpio`. If you specify a file as `/usr/george/book`, that is how it will be packaged. This will cause `cpio` on the unpackaging machine to attempt to create the directory `/usr/george/book`, and this may not be possible.

For additional information about `cpio` and `find`, refer to your UNIX manual.

Transfer Directories with *shar*

Standing for *SH ARchive*, `shar` produces a packaged file that can be unpackaged on any machine by using the command:

```
sh package
```

The `shar` program is distributed periodically, and in a variety of forms, over USENET news. Readers of the USENET groups `comp.sources.unix` will recognize this form of packaging immediately. (More information on ways to download special types of files from USENET can be found in Appendix C.)

Traditionally, files that are `shar` archives look something like this:

```
Introductory text and electronic mail headers appear
here.
------------------<CUT HERE>----------------------
#!/bin/sh
# This is a shell archive. Remove anything before this line,
# then unpack it by saving it in a file and typing "sh file".
Packaged files here.
```

The shar program, as distributed over the USENET network, exists in two forms.

- `shar.c` A C language program written by Gary Perlman that is the more powerful of the two. It allows you to package full directory hierarchies with a variety of unpackaging schemes.
- `shar.sh` A Bourne Shell script that is distributed with the USENET news software. It allows you to package only plain files within a single directory.

Using the *shar* Program

This version of shar, written by Gary Perlman, is specifically designed as a tool for packaging files and directories for transmission via uucp and mail. Designed for portability, the resulting package can easily be unpackaged at the receiving remote UNIX site by typing the command line:

sh file.shar

Here, file.shar is the name of the packaged file created by shar, and sh is the Bourne Shell program.[1] This command line may also be run from the C Shell and Korn Shell, with no change.

The shar program supports a host of capabilities and options that allow you to customize a package to your own personal taste:

- It can recursively descend directories. The package created will make directories and descend into them as part of the unpackaging.
- It will not overwrite existing files with the same name when unpackaging. You can turn off this feature with the -s flag.
- It is able to convert full pathnames, like /usr/george/book, into relative pathnames like book.

1. The Bourne Shell is a program like any other. When run from any shell, including itself, as in the example, it reads the file that is its argument, treating the lines of text in that file as shell commands.

- It can perform a character count of unpackaged files to help ensure that there were no transmission errors.
- It can preserve permissions so that copies have the same UNIX permissions as the originals.
- It can use sed for unpackaging, thus minimizing the chance that mail will gobble characters during transmission.
- It understands uuencode (discussed later) and can create a package that will automatically be decoded with uudecode. This enables you to package binary files.

Package with *shar*

Creating a package of files and directories for transmission is easy with shar. In its simplest form, you run shar like this:

```
shar files > package.shar
```

Here, files is one or more file and/or directory names. The > character in the command line causes the standard output of shar to be placed into the file package.shar. The resulting package, package.shar, can then be transmitted as:

```
uucp package.shar neighbor1\!~/
```

or

```
mail site\!site\!person < package.shar
```

Once the transmitted package is received at the remote UNIX site, it is unpackaged by typing:

```
sh package.shar
```

Note that if the packaged file was received via UNIX electronic mail, the mail header will have to be stripped off before the package can be fed through sh.

Convert Full Pathnames to Relative Names (*–b* Flag)

You were previously warned to avoid using full pathnames when packaging with tar or cpio because problems arise when those packages are unpackaged at the remote site. If a file is specified as /usr/george/file in the package, for example, the unpackaging process will try to create the directory /usr/george and probably fail.

This problem can also occur with `shar`, but, fortunately, `shar` can be told to convert full pathnames into relative pathnames. This is done by using the `-b` flag:

```
shar -b /usr/george/file > george.shar
```

The `-b` flag will cause the package `george.shar` to contain instructions for unpackaging that will cause `/usr/george/file` to be unpackaged as `file`.

Check File Sizes When Unpackaging (*-c* Flag)

As a simple kind of error-checking, the `-c` flag can be used with `shar`. The flag causes the created package to contain instructions for verifying that the number of characters in each unpackaged copy of a file matches the number of characters in the original. The `-c` flag can be used as:

```
shar -c part1/*.n > part1.shar
```

Here, the expression `*.n` is expanded by your shell to include all files in the subdirectory `part1` that end with the characters "`.n`". Those files are packaged by `shar` into the file `part1.shar`. The `-c` flag causes `shar` to also include, in that package, instructions for checking the character counts of the originals against the character counts of the unpackaged copies.

At the receiving end, unpackaging will look something like this:

```
sh part1.shar
awake.n
error transmitting 'awake.n' (should have been 473 characters)
tunnel.n
```

When `shar` creates its original package, it adds a newline character to the end of any line that doesn't have one. This can cause the original and the duplicate to differ by one or more characters. If the `-c` flag has been used for packaging, those added newlines will be announced during unpackaging, as:

```
sh part1.shar
awake.n
a missing newline was added to 'awake.n'
error transmitting 'awake.n' (should have been 473 characters)
tunnel.n
```

As further protection, the `-c` flag will also cause `shar` to indicate the number of control characters in a file. This is handy because `mail` programs frequently remove control characters from files.

```
sh part1.shar
awake.n
5 control characters may be missing from 'awake.n'
error transmitting 'awake.n' (should have been 473 characters)
tunnel.n
```

Change How Much *shar* Prints (*-v* Flag)

The -v flag, when used with shar, causes the created package to contain instructions that print an informative description of each step taken during the unpackaging process. The -v flag can be used as:

```
shar -v part1/*.n > part1.shar
```

Here, the expression *.n is expanded by your shell to include all files in the subdirectory part1 that end with the characters *.n. Those files are packaged by shar into the file part1.shar. The -v flag causes shar to also include, in that package, instructions to print, step by step, what is being done during the unpackaging.

When part1.shar is unpacked with:

```
sh part1.shar
```

the following output will be produced:

```
creating directory 'part1'
entering directory 'part1'
extracting 'awake.n' (471 characters)
error transmitting 'awake.n' (should have been 473 characters)
extracting 'tunnel.n' (768 characters)
done with directory 'part1'
```

Define Your Own End-of-File String (*-d* Flag)

The internal technique used by shar to unpackage files looks like this:

```
cat << SHAR_EOF > 'filename'
...
contents of file here
...
SHAR_EOF
```

The << in the example tells the cat program to read every line up to, but not including, the line SHAR_EOF. The > redirects the output of cat into the file named filename.

The -d flag is provided with shar for those rare times when the file you are sending contains the line SHAR_EOF (this chapter for example). The -d flag allows you to redefine that end-of-file string:

```
shar -d "New_EOF" files > package.shar
```

This command tells shar to create a package containing lines having the form:

```
cat << New_EOF > 'filename'
...
contents of file here
...
New_EOF
```

where New_EOF is used to delimit cat instead of the default SHAR_EOF.

Make Permissions Match Original (*-m* Flag)

When a shar package is unpackaged with sh, the read, write, and execute permissions of each extracted file and directory are set to match those of the user who is unpackaging. Generally, this means that all files will be created with read and write permissions enabled, and all directories will be created with read, write, and search (execute) permissions enabled.

For those times when the files you are sending need to retain specific permissions when they are unpackaged, shar provides the -m flag. The -m flag tells shar to make up a packaged archive that contains instructions for resetting the permissions of extracted files and directories to match those of the packaged originals.

For example, suppose you are sending a copy of your résumé to a friend for criticism. You have made the file containing the résumé mode 600 so that it will be readable and writable only by you. If you were to package that file with shar and not use the -m flag, there is a chance that your friend might unpackage it and leave it readable by anyone. Use of the -m flag prevents an indiscreet disclosure.

```
ls -l resume
-rw------- 2   george  1281 Nov 22 15:19 resume
shar -c -m resume > resume.shar
```

Here, the file resume is mode 600 (-rw -------) readable and writable only by its owner. The -c flag is used to verify that the correct number of characters is packaged, and the -m flag to ensure that it will retain its narrow permissions when it is later unpackaged with sh:

```
sh resume.shar
extracting resume (1281 characters)
ls -l resume
-rw-------- 2 friend      1281 Nov 30 09:33 resume
```

So, `friend` now owns the file, but the permissions are analogous to your original ones. That is, the original can be read (or written) only by you, and the copy can be read or written only by `friend`.

Use *sed* for Unpackaging (*-p* Flag)

Ordinarily, `shar` unpackages by using the `cat` program:

```
cat << SHAR_EOF > filename
...
contents of file here
...
SHAR_EOF
```

The `<< SHAR_EOF` tells `cat` to print all lines up to, but not including, the line `SHAR_EOF`. The `> filename` causes `cat`'s output to be placed into the file named `filename`.

When sending a file via `mail`, you risk having that file modified by the `mail` programs at remote UNIX sites. Specifically, if your file contains any lines that begin with one of the `mail` header keywords—like "From" or "Path"—you may find those lines modified in transit. To avoid this problem, `shar` provides an option to use the `sed` program in place of `cat`. The `sed` program (*S*tream *ED*itor) is used by `shar` to insert and strip special characters from the beginning of each line of your file. This is done by using the `-p` flag with `shar`:

```
shar -p special_characters
```

Here, the `special_characters` are the characters you want inserted at the head of each line of each file packaged with `shar`. For example, suppose you wanted to send a file called `walrus.time` that contained the following lines:

```
The time has come, the Walrus said
To talk of many things.
```

The line beginning with the word "To" might be modified in transit by `mail`. To prevent this, you can use the `-p` flag of `shar` to insert an "X" character at the head of each line:

```
shar -p X walrus.time > walrus.shar
```

The -p flag, followed by X, causes shar to produce a package, for later unpackaging, that unpackages with sed, like this:

```
sed 's/^X//' << SHAR_EOF > walrus.time
XThe time has come, the Walrus said,
XTo talk of many things:
SHAR_EOF
```

The sed program, like cat, reads all the lines up to, but not including, the line SHAR_EOF. As with cat, the > redirects the output of sed into the file walrus.time. Unlike cat, however, sed uses the additional expression 's/^X//' as a rule for transforming each line it reads. This rule tells sed that, for every X character beginning a line (/^X/), it is to substitute (s) "nothing" (//), thus deleting the leading "X" from each line (see figure 16-4). (If you are unfamiliar with sed, consult one of the intermediate to advanced UNIX books described in Appendix E.)

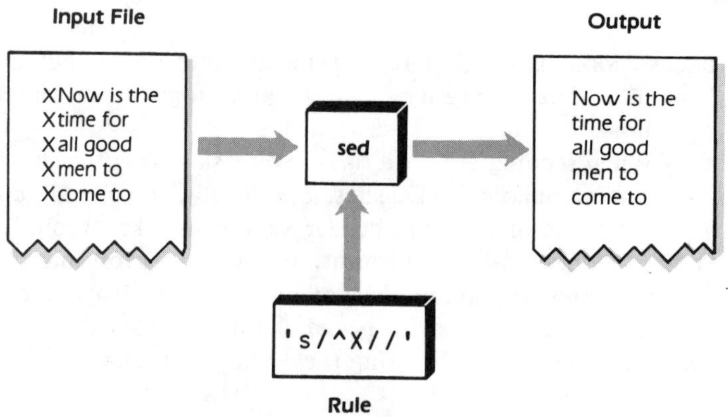

Figure 16-4. The **sed** (**s**tream **ed**itor) program reads a file and performs transformations on that file based on a rule you have specified.

Turn On All Options (-*a* Flag)

Since many of shar's flags are almost always used, shar provides the -a flag as a kind of shorthand. Using the -a flag is the equivalent of using all the following flags together:

```
-v -c -b -p pressing the tab and X keys simultaneously.
```

Turn Off All Options (*-s* Flag)

For "quick and dirty" unpackaging, shar provides the -s flag. This flag causes shar to create a package that will unpackage with all checking and extra output inhibited.

Additionally, the -s flag turns off shar's overwrite checking. Normally, shar will not overwrite a file that already exists. When shar tries to unpackage a file and that file already exists, it will normally print the message:

```
will not over-write existing file 'walrus.time'
```

The -s flag prevents this checking and allows files to be overwritten even if they already exist. This is useful when you want to send a package of updated files.

Other kinds of checking can be turned back on by using additional flags after the -s flag in the command line:

```
        "quick and dirty"
        ↓
shar -s -c walrus.time > walrus.shar
           ↑
           but check character count
```

Package Binary Files (*-u* Flag)

Binary files are files that contain nonprinting characters, usually files that are executable programs. Text files that contain control characters can also be thought of as binary files. To facilitate the sending of binary files, shar provides the -u flag.

The -u flag causes shar to create a package with uuencode that will later be unpackaged with uudecode. The uuencode program converts binary files into files that contain only printable text characters. The uudecode program converts them back to the original binary files. Both of these programs are discussed in detail later in this chapter.

Files containing control characters, like WordStar documents, are good candidates for packaging with the -u flag of shar, since mail often removes WordStar's control and "high-bit set" characters from files during transmission. The only disadvantage of using the -u flag is that it requires the receiving UNIX site to have uudecode available for unpackaging. The uuencode program is not required when creating the sent package because shar encodes internally.

Summary of *shar* Flags

`-a`	Turn on all checking and extra output. This flag is the equivalent of: `-v`, `-c`, `-b`, `-p`, and pressing the tab and `X` keys simultaneously.
`-b`	Change full pathnames into relative pathnames.
`-c`	Check size of unpackaged file versus size of original file with `wc`.
`-d New_EOF`	Use `New_EOF` in place of `SHAR_EOF` to delimit `cat` or `sed` when unpackaging.
`-m`	Make protection modes of unpackaged files match those of the originals.
`-p prefix`	Begin each line with `prefix` and use `sed` to unpackage files.
`-s`	Turn off all checking and extra output. Disable overwrite checking.
`-u`	Create a package that will be unpackaged at the receiving site with `uudecode`.
`-v`	Print additional information about what is happening during unpackaging.

Rolling Your Own *shar.csh* and *shar.sh*

A potential drawback of the `shar` program is that it is distributed over the USENET network and does not come with UNIX, so it may not be available at your site. If that is the case, it is a simple matter to make up a mini `shar` of your own.

Figures 16-5 and 16-6 show two small shell scripts that can be used in place of the full `shar`. They lack the fancy flags that `shar` has, but they will suffice for the more modest needs encountered when packaging files for transmission with `mail` and `uucp`.

The `shar.csh` shell script (shown in figure 16-5) is designed for use with the C Shell. It should be typed exactly as shown and saved under the name `shar`. You should then:

```
chmod 755 shar
rehash
```

Before running this mini `shar`, you must make it executable with `chmod` and then let your C Shell environment know it is there with `rehash`.

Bourne Shell. It should be typed exactly as shown and saved under the name shar. You should then:

chmod 755 shar

Before running this mini shar, you must make it executable with chmod.

```
#!/bin/csh
echo "echo -------------------CUT HERE---------------------"
echo "echo This is a shar file. To unpack, remove everything"
echo "echo above and including the line 'CUT HERE',"
echo "echo save in a file, and unpack with 'sh file'."
foreach i ($*)
        echo "echo extracting $i"
        echo "sed 's/^X//'<< 'SHAR_EOF' > $i"
        sed 's/^/X/' $i
        echo "SHAR_EOF"
end
```

Figure 16-5. A mini **shar** C Shell script, **shar.csh**.

```
:
echo "echo -------------------CUT HERE---------------------"
echo "echo This is a shar file. To unpack, remove everything"
echo "echo above and including the line 'CUT HERE',"
echo "echo save in a file, and unpack with 'sh file'."
for i
do
        echo "echo extracting $i"
        echo "sed 's/^X//'<< 'SHAR_EOF' > $i"
        sec 's/^/X/' $i
        echo "SHAR_EOF"
done
```

Figure 16-6. A mini **shar** Bourne Shell script, **shar.sh**.

Transferring Binary Files with *uucp* and *mail*

There are two kinds of files that can be thought of as binary files:

1. Text files that contain control characters.

2. Files that contain non-ASCII data. (Executable programs are files of this type.)

All files under UNIX are composed of a linear sequence of bytes. For text files, each byte contains one character. For executable programs, each byte can contain either part of a program instruction or embedded text characters (see figure 16-7).

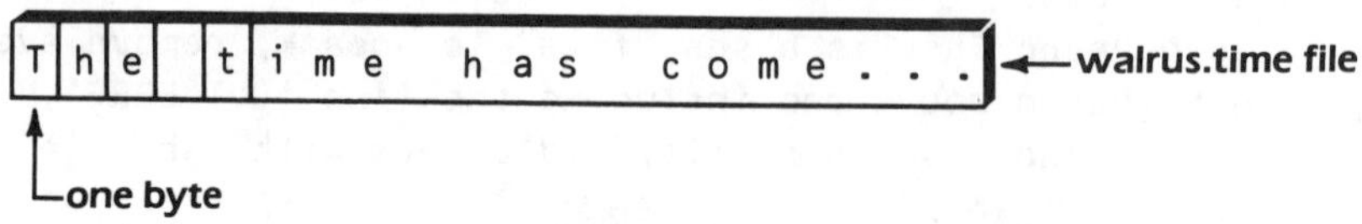

Figure 16-7. A file as a stream of bytes.

Ordinary text characters are represented in ASCII, with values ranging from 0 to 127. In figure 16-8, you can see that only 7 bits are needed to represent any ASCII character. Binary data, on the other hand, can range in values from 0 to 255 for each byte, and require 8 bits.

When data is transmitted with UUCP, it is often transmitted using only the lower 7 of a byte's 8 bits, depending on the hardware used. Unfortunately, binary files that use all 8 bits for information will suffer a severe loss if their eighth bit is stripped off during transmission.

In addition to UUCP's 7-bit transmission, some mail-forwarding programs also strip control characters. Control characters are those ASCII characters whose values are less than 32, or equal to 128 (the newline character, whose value is 10, and the tab character, whose value is 9, are not treated by mail as control characters). But what are considered control characters in a text file are perfectly valid values in a binary file, so stripping off control characters would destroy the usefulness of the binary program.

To prevent catastrophic distortion when transmitting binary files, and to prevent control characters from being stripped by mail, UUCP offers the uuencode and uudecode programs. The uuencode program converts any file into a stream of transmittable, 7-bit ASCII characters. The uudecode program converts a uuencoded file back into its original form.

How to *uuencode* a File

With the uuencode program, you can copy any file so that the duplicate is in a form suitable for transmission with uucp or mail. The uuencode program takes two arguments: the name of the file to be encoded and the name that file is to have when

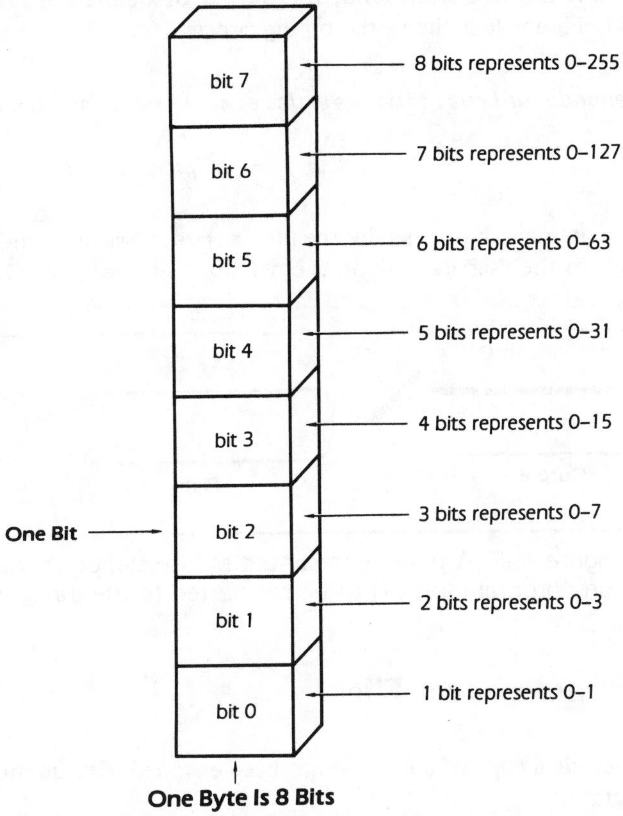

Figure 16-8. One byte of information.

it is decoded. The **uuencode** program always sends its encoded output to the standard output. The format for using **uuencode** is:

```
uuencode inputfile destfile > encodedfile
```

where **inputfile** is the name of the file to be encoded, and **destfile** is the name that the file should have when it is later decoded—usually the same name as that of the original. The **encodedfile** is the name of the resulting encoded file—the one that can be transmitted with **uucp** or **mail**.

For example, to **uuencode** the file **walrus.time** from the previous section, you would type:

```
uuencode walrus.time walrus.time > walrus.uu
```

The resulting file, **walrus.uu**, can be transmitted with **uucp** or **mail**, and later converted back to a copy of the original with **uudecode**.

As a bit of shorthand, the output of uuencode can be piped directly into mail. Figure 16-9 shows the piping process.

```
uuencode walrus.time walrus.time ¦ mail neighbor1\!george
                                 ↑
                             pipe symbol
```

This command both encodes the file walrus.time and sends that encoded copy, via mail, to the user george on the neighbor site neighbor1.

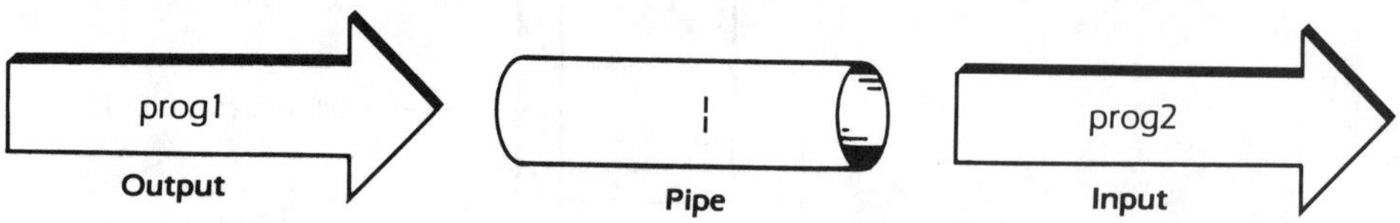

Figure 16-9. A pipe, represented by the symbol ¦, causes the output of one program (prog1) to be connected to the input of another (prog2).

How to *uudecode* a File

To decode a copy of a file that has been encoded with uuencode, use the uudecode program:

```
uudecode encodedfile
```

The uudecode program will decode encodedfile and create a copy of the original file. The permissions of the created copy will match those of the original. The name of the created copy may, or may not, match that of the original. The name will be the one specified by the destfile argument to uuencode at the sending site.

To decode the file walrus.uu, you would type:

```
uudecode walrus.uu
```

This will create a file named walrus.time—a name previously specified by the uuencode program—that is identical to the original.

The uudecode program starts decoding at the first line in encodedfile that starts with the word "begin," and stops decoding at the first line following "begin" that starts with the word "end." For this reason, it is possible to uudecode files that have been received via UNIX electronic mail without having to strip off any mail headers or trailing lines.

Rolling Your Own *uudecode*

A serious drawback to the uudecode program is that it is available only with BSD UNIX and AT&T System V systems that provide UCB enhancements. If your site lacks uudecode, you can use the mini decode program listed in figure 16-10.

Type in the program listing for decode.c exactly as shown and save it under the name decode.c. Then compile that program by typing:

```
cc -o decode decode.c
```

This creates an executable program, named decode, that can be used to decode uuencode files. The decode program reads the encoded file from the standard input and writes the decoded file to the standard output. It is used as:

```
decode < encodedfile > decodedfile
```

This command decodes the file encodedfile and creates the file decodedfile, which is a duplicate of the original.

Summary of Uses and Caveats

In this section we offer a summary of the more common ways to use the programs you have learned about in this chapter. Where necessary, we also outline any pitfalls that should be avoided.

Package files and directories with tar

```
tar cf - dirs_or_files > package.tar
```

Caveat: The directories and/or files listed in dirs_or_files should be specified as relative pathnames.

Unpackage files and directories with tar

```
tar xf - < package.tar
```

Caveat: Use cd to change to the directory in which you want to unpackage the package.tar files before running this tar command.

Create a list of files for cpio

```
find dir -print > listofiles
```

Caveat: The directory specified by dir should be stated as a relative pathname.

```
#include <stdio.h>

main () /* a filter to decode a uuencoded file */
{
        char buf[BUFSIZ], *gets();
        int gotstart = 0, nchars, off, i;
        setbuf (stdout, 0);
        while (gets(buf) !=NULL) {          /* find "begin" */
                if (strncmp(buf, "begin", 5) == 0) {
                        ++gotstart;
                        break;
                }
        }
        if (! gotstart)
                exit(0);

        while (gets(buf) !=NULL) {          /* process file */
                nchars = (int)(buf[0] - ' ');
                if (nchars == 0) break;
                for (off = i = 1; i < nchars; i += 3, off += 4)
                        decode(nchars - i + 1, &buf[off]);
        }
        return (0);
}

decode( cnt, cp )
int cnt; unsigned char *cp;
{
        unsigned char obytes[3];
        int i;

        obytes[0] = obytes[1] = obytes[2] = 0;
        for (i = 0; i < 4; i++)
                *(cp + i) -= ' ';
        obtyes[0] =  (*cp << 2);
        ++cp;
        obytes[0] |= (*cp >> 4);
        obytes[1] =  (*cp << 4);
        ++cp;
        obytes[1] |= (*cp >> 2);
        obytes[2] |= (*cp << 6);
        ++cp;
        obytes[2] |= *cp;
        cnt = (cnt < 3) ? cnt : 3;
        for (i = 0;i < cnt; i++)
                putchar (obytes[i]);
}
```

Figure 16-10. Mini **uudecode** program, **decode.c**.

Package files and directories with `cpio`

```
cpio -oc < listofiles > package.cpio
```

Caveat: The directories and files listed in `listofiles` should be stated as relative pathnames.

Unpackage files and directories with `cpio`

```
cpio -icd < package.cpio
```

Caveat: Use `cd` to change to the directory in which you want to unpackage the `package.cpio` files before running this `cpio` command.

Package files and directories with `shar`

```
shar -a dirs_or_files > package.shar
```

Caveat: The `-a` flag enables all diagnostic output, the use of `sed`, and error-checking.

Unpackage `shar` *files and directories with* `sh`

```
sh package.shar
```

Caveat: If `package.shar` is from a stranger, inspect it for questionable commands before feeding it to `sh`.

Encode with `shar`

```
shar -u dirs_or_files > package.uushar
```

Caveat: The recipient at the remote site must have access to `uudecode` in order to unpackage `package.uushar`.

Encode with `uuencode`

```
uuencode filename destname > filename.uu
```

Caveat: If the user at the remote receiving site lacks `uudecode`, send that user a copy of `decode.c` from figure 16-10.

Decode with `uudecode`

```
uudecode filename.uu
```

Caveat: The `uudecode` program ignores mail headers and any trailing lines in `filename.uu`.

Mail binary files with `uuencode` *and* `mail`

```
uuencode filename destname | mail site\!user
```

Caveat: See your `mail` manual to find out how to add a subject line.

Summary

In this chapter you have learned how to package files and directory hierarchies for transmission with `uucp` and `mail` by using the `tar`, `cpio`, and `shar` programs. You have also learned how to convert binary files into text files with `uuencode` so that they could be sent with `uucp` or `mail`, and how to convert those files back again with `uudecode`.

In the next chapter we will discuss the `cu` program—a simple telecommunications program supplied with all versions of UNIX.

17

Calling Out with *cu*

All UNIX machines offer a telecommunications program of modest abilities. Called cu, for "Call UNIX," it allows you to dial out and log into another machine, including non-UNIX machines (see figure 17-1). The cu program is not as powerful as any of the many modern telecommunications packages. It doesn't support xmodem protocols. It doesn't transfer binary files. It isn't menu-driven. In short, it's somewhat primitive. On the other hand, it's easy to learn and is supplied with *every* UNIX system. For that reason alone, you'll be glad you learned how to use it.

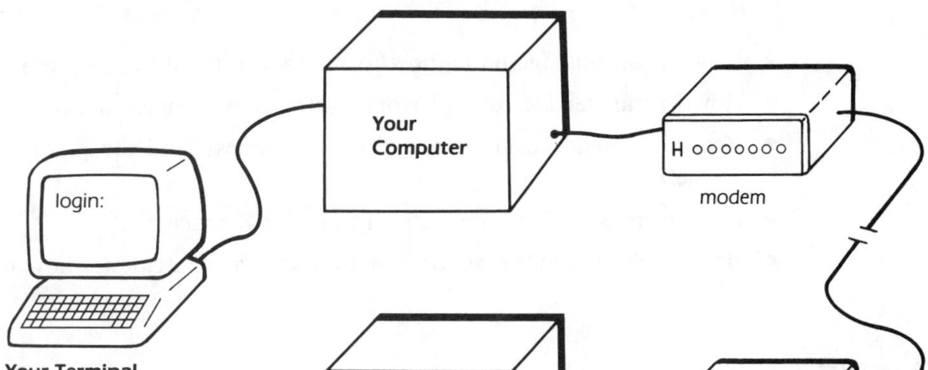

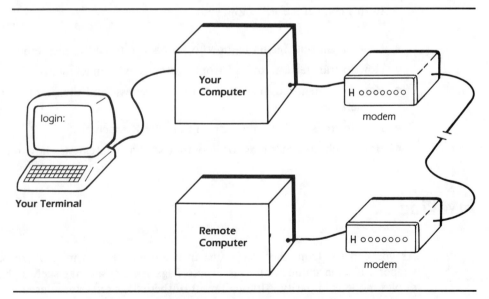

Figure 17-1. The **cu** program enables you to log into a remote computer and use that computer as though it were your own.

Now for some bad news. Because cu is able to dial out on telephone lines and is adept at calling long distance, you will likely find it either unavailable or severely restricted at some sites. Those most likely to restrict cu are public-access UNIX sites and companies fearful of user abuse. For example, consider the user who makes two-hour calls with cu to an electronic bulletin board on the opposite coast. If the calls are personal ones, the user's employer will likely curtail his or her future use of cu, and may even remove the cu program from the system entirely!

To find out if cu is available at your site, enter:

```
cu -x
```

If the response is:

```
usage: cu [-s speed] [-a acu] [-l line] [-h] [-o|-e]
[-r file] telno | "dir"
```

or something similar, then cu is available at your site, and you have permission to run it. On the other hand, if the response is:

```
cu: Permission denied
```

or any other error message, then you lack access to cu. You may still want to read this chapter to learn how cu works, since you may some day buy your own UNIX-capable microcomputer.

In this chapter we will show you:

- How to call out, including how to set baud rate and duplex mode.
- How to transfer files to and from another UNIX machine.
- How to suspend cu, take care of other business, and then resume cu where you left off.
- How to transfer files to and from non-UNIX machines.
- How to observe cu's diagnostic output so that you can see how cu operates.

Invoking *cu*

As you can see from the usage line in the example showing cu's response, cu supports a large number of flags. These flags specify settings such as baud rate, duplex mode, and parity. Although most of these flags are seldom used, you should learn what each means for those times when you will need one.

Summary of *cu* Flags

`-s speed`	Use modem whose baud rate matches `speed`.
`-t tty#`	Use modem attached to TTY line #.
`-n`	The `cu` program asks for number to dial.
`-e`	Set even parity on outgoing characters.
`-o`	Set odd parity on outgoing characters.
`-h`	Set half-duplex communications.
`-t`	Map CR to CR/LF on incoming lines of text.
`-r file`	Create a recording of session in `file`.
`-d`	Produce debugging output.

To run `cu` in its simplest form, you merely tell it the telephone number and let it handle everything else:

```
cu 9876543
    ↑
    telephone number
```

This command tells `cu` to locate the first available modem—without regard to baud rate—and dial the number **9876543**. If no lines are available, you will see the message:

```
connect failed: line problems
```

Usually this means that all lines are currently in use. If you repeatedly get this message, you should contact your system administrator, since this message can also mean that your system has not been set up properly.

Specifying a Baud Rate with *cu* (–*s* Flag)

If you have a mixture of modems, say 300, 1200, and 2400 baud, `cu` will assume that you want a 300-baud modem unless you tell it otherwise. (In fact, it will assume 300-baud even if you don't have a 300-baud modem.) The `-s` flag is used with `cu` to specify the baud rate you want. When used, it should always precede the telephone number. The space between `-s` and `speed` is optional:

```
cu -s 2400 9876543
    ↑
    specify baud rate (speed)
```

This command tells `cu` to locate a modem that is capable of 2400-baud communication and to dial out on that modem. If the system does not have a 2400-baud modem, you will see the mesage:

```
No line known at 2400 baud
```

The solution here is to simply try another speed, such as 1200.

Selecting a Line with *cu* (*-l* Flag)

When you know to which TTY line (UNIX terminal connection) a modem is attached, you can specify that line in lieu of a speed. If, for example, your only 2400-baud modem was attached to `/dev/tty9`, you could tell `cu` to use that modem by using the `-l` flag, followed by the name of that `tty line`:

```
cu -l tty9 9876543
      ↑
  specify tty (line)
```

To specify a `tty line`, use its name and omit the `/dev/` prefix. The space between the `-l` and the `tty line` is optional.

The `-l` and `-s` flags can be used together. When both `speed` and `tty line` are specified, as in:

```
cu -s 2400 -l tty9 9876543
```

`cu` checks to see that the requested speed on the requested line is indeed available and, if so, dials the number.

Dialing Manually with *cu*

The `cu` program knows how to dial only a small handful of modem brands. If it finds a modem that it does not know how to dial out on, it will print the message:

```
Connect failed: unknown dialer type
```

When this happens, you will have to interact directly with the modem's built-in software in order to dial. Most modern modems contain software that allows you to instruct them to dial a telephone number by typing special character sequences at your keyboard. For example, the Ventel modem allows you to get its attention by pressing the Return or Enter key twice on your terminal. You can then dial by typing a "k" followed by the number. Hayes and compatible modems, on the other hand, use "atdt," for ATtention, Dial, Tone, followed by the number.

To access a modem for direct interaction, you simply specify a `tty line` without a telephone number:

```
cu -l tty9
```

Note, however, on some systems, you may have to add the word "dir" following the `tty line`:

```
cu -l tty9 dir
```

Consult your UNIX manual to see which form is used by your system.

If `cu` is able to connect to the modem associated with the `tty line`, you will see the message:

```
Connected
```

and you may take control of the modem through its built-in software (see figure 17-2). Just type the correct characters at your terminal that cause your modem's software to dial out. You will of course need to consult your modem's manual to find out which characters to type.

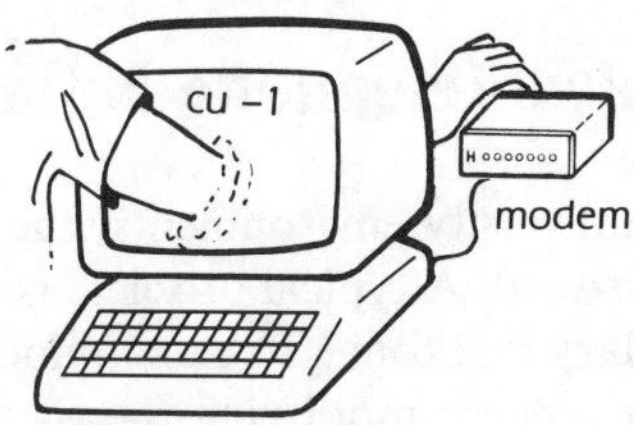

Figure 17-2. The **-l** flag of **cu** allows you to access directly the modem's software.

Calling by System Name with *cu*

Some versions of UNIX, including AT&T System V, allow you to dial out by giving a system's name to `cu`. Where this feature is supported, you may specify the name in place of the telephone number:

```
cu -s 1200 neighbor1
           ↑
```
system name in place of telephone number

The system name, `neighbor1`, must be one of those recognized by UUCP (see uuname in chapter 11). When you specify the system's name, rather than a telephone number, you are *not* allowed to specify the tty line with the -l flag.

Getting *cu* to Ask for a Number (*-n* Flag)

As a security feature, some versions of UNIX, including AT&T System V, provide the -n flag, which instructs cu to ask you for the telephone number.

Whenever you run a command under UNIX, it is possible for others to observe which arguments you gave that command by using the ps program. If the telephone number you are dialing is of a sensitive nature, you might prefer to hide it from accidental (or otherwise) disclosure. When you run cu and provide the -n flag, cu will prompt for the telephone number, rather than requiring you to include it in the command line:

```
cu -s 1200 -n
Number: 9876543
↑        ↑
cu prints  you type
```

Pressing Return instead of typing a telephone number will cause cu to exit.

Handling Complex Telephone Numbers with *cu*

In business and university environments, the process of accessing an outside line is seldom straightforward. A typical problem is that callers must first dial "9" and then wait for a secondary dial tone. To accommodate this process, the cu program offers two special characters for modifying the way a telephone number is interpreted:

- = The = character tells cu to wait for a secondary dial tone before proceeding with its dialing.
- \- The - character tells cu to pause for approximately 4 seconds before proceeding with its dialing.

By way of example, the following command instructs cu to dial "9" and wait for a secondary dial tone. It then tells cu to dial the three-digit access code "123" and wait 8 seconds (two - characters). Finally, it tells cu to dial the rest of the telephone number:

```
            wait for second dial tone
            ↓
cu -s 1200 9=123--9876543
                ↑↑
                pause four seconds (for each hyphen)
```

A common mistake is to begin the telephone number with a - character:

```
cu -s 1200 -9876543
            ↑
            wrong
```

The cu program will mistakenly think that **-9876543** is an unrecognized flag and will exit with an error message.

Setting Parity with *cu*

Parity is used by modems to signal each other that the count of "set bits" in any transmitted character is either even or odd. If the count is odd, then it is "odd parity," and if it is even, the count is "even parity." Parity is a primitive form of error-checking: an error may change the parity value and thus be detected. If this error-checking is not used, it is "no parity."

Normally, cu sends characters to the remote machine using "no parity." For those remote machines that require either even or odd parity, cu offers corresponding -e and -o flags:

- -e The -e flag tells cu to generate even parity for all characters sent to the remote machine.
- -o The -o flag tells cu to generate odd parity for all characters sent to the remote machine.

You may specify one or the other of these flags, but not both. To dial out using even parity, you would type:

```
cu -e -s 1200 9876543
   ↑
   use even parity
```

whereas for odd parity, you would type:

```
cu -o -s 1200 9876543
   ↑
   use odd parity
```

And, of course, for no parity—the UNIX default—simply use no flag, just as we've been doing all along.

Interacting with the Remote Machine

Regardless of which arguments you gave to `cu` when you ran it, a successful connection will be announced with the message:

```
Connected
```

From this point on, you are no longer talking to your own computer. Instead, you are talking to the remote computer you just called.

Logging into the Remote Machine

The login procedure on the remote computer will depend on the computer called. You already know how to log into a UNIX system:

```
login: bryan
Password:
Welcome to ...
```

Logging into any system via `cu` is no different than logging into that system directly when using your own modem and terminal.

Adjusting Modes with *cu*

There are two common problems that you might encounter when trying to log into a remote system.

1. *duplex* If the characters you type are not displayed on your screen, then the remote system is running in *half-duplex* mode.
2. *newline* If the lines that you see printed by the remote system are printed one on top of the other, then the remote site is using a *newline* that your system doesn't understand.

If either of these problems occurs, you will have to disconnect from `cu` (see the next section) and rerun `cu` using one, or both, of the `-h` and `-t` flags.

Set Half-Duplex Mode (*-h* Flag)

There are two possible kinds of *duplex*: *half* and *full*. In full duplex, the standard—default—for UNIX, the *remote* machine will echo each character that you type, thereby printing each character on your screen. In half duplex, *your* machine must echo each character you type because the remote machine will not, and, again, what you type will be printed on your screen (see figure 17-3).

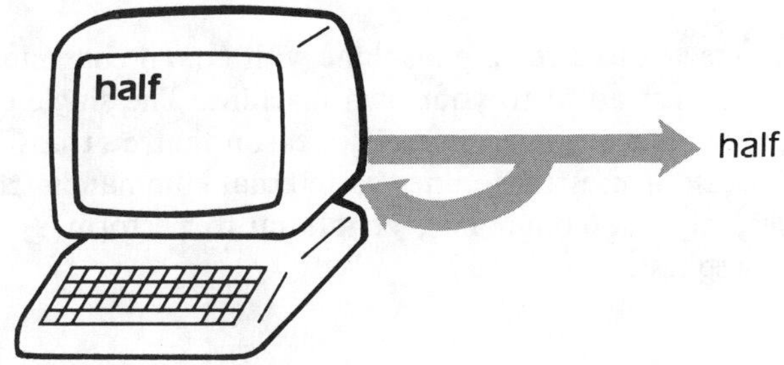

In half duplex, your local terminal echoes each character back to your screen.

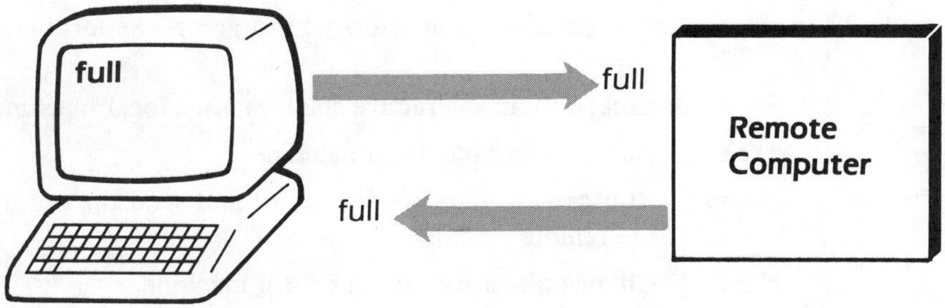

In full duplex, the remote machine sends each character that it receives back to you.

Figure 17-3. Half and full duplex.

The -h flag tells cu to start up in half-duplex mode:

cu -h -s 1200 9876543
↑
use half-duplex mode

Change Newline Mapping with *cu* (*-t* Flag)

Ordinarily, UNIX expects the two-character combinations of Return (Control-m) and newline (Control-j) to be used for moving the cursor to the left margin and down one line. Some systems, however, send only a Return and not a newline.

The -t flag tells cu to translate Returns received from the remote machine into the two-character combination understood by your UNIX machine:

cu -t -s 1200 9876543
↑
translate newlines

The Special Meaning of Tilde

Once you have connected to a remote machine with cu, all characters you type are sent to that machine instead of to your own machine. The single exception is the tilde character (~) when it begins a line. The reason that cu traps lines beginning with a tilde is because it uses those lines as internal commands from the user to itself. These lines, or tilde commands, enable cu to perform a wide variety of functions at your request.

Accessing the Local System (~!, ~$, ~%cd)

There are four tilde functions that allow you to access the local system:

`~!`	Escape to an interactive shell on your local machine.
`~!cmd`	Run cmd on your local machine.
`~$cmd`	Run cmd on your local machine and send the output of cmd to the remote machine.
`~%cd`	Change directory on your local machine.

Escape to Shell (~!)

Any line beginning with ~!, followed by a Return, will cause cu to provide you with a temporary, new UNIX shell within which to do work. This shell will be the same type (e.g., Bourne Shell or C Shell) as the one that was running before you ran cu. Thus, if you ran cu from the C Shell, you will be provided with a C Shell; if you ran cu from the Bourne Shell, you will be provided with a Bourne Shell. Whichever shell you get, it will be a new shell and not your original shell. For C Shell users, this means that you will be starting a brand new history.

Imagine that you are looking for a file on the remote machine and that the location of that file is contained in a letter in your current directory on your local machine. You can escape to a shell with ~!, read the letter, then quit that shell, and return to cu:

```
                                              ←in cu here
~!                                            ←escape to shell
more letter                                   ←view the letter
Hi,
The file you want is in /uh/twg/tips.
exit                                          ←exit the shell
                                              ←back in cu here
```

The way to exit the local shell and return to cu varies, depending on the shell you escaped to. You exit the C Shell by typing `exit`. You exit the Bourne Shell by typing `^D` (Control-d).

Run a Program Locally (*~!cmd*)

Any line beginning with `~!`, followed by a UNIX command (`cmd`), will cause `cu` to run that command on the local machine. When the command is done running, you will be returned to `cu` at the point where you left off.

Imagine yourself composing a letter using a text editor on the remote machine and needing a phone number from a file of phone numbers on your local machine. The `~!cmd` command allows you to run the `grep` program, for example, to search that file on the local machine and then return to `cu` where you left off:

```
great colors! Call them at        ←in editor via cu
~!grep o-rama phonelist           ←run grep locally
Paint-o-rama 876-5432
Bowl-o-rama 765-4321
876-5432 for a sample book.       ←back in editor
```

Send Output to Remote Machine (*~$cmd*)

Any line beginning with `~$`, followed by a UNIX command, will cause `cu` to run that command on the local machine, and send the output of that command to the remote machine just as if it were something you typed. When the command is done running, you will be returned to `cu` at the point where you left off.

Suppose you are talking to someone on the remote machine using `write` (see Appendix B). The other person asks to see a file you have on your local machine. You can run the `cat` program on the local machine by using the `~$cmd` function. The output of `cat` will be sent to the remote machine, and thus to the other person. When `cat` is done, you will again be returned to `cu`:

```
the carpenter, of course -o                           ←other user
nope, the walrus. I have the quote in                 ←you reply
a file, I'll send it ... hold on...
~$cat quotes/walrus.didit                             ←you send file
"He ate more than the Carpenter, though," said
Tweedledee. "You see he held his handkerchief in
front, so that the Carpenter couldn't count how
many he took: contrariwise."
Hah! Told you so -o                                   ←you conclude
Got me *again*!! -o                                   ←other user
```

Change Directory (*~%cd*)

Any line beginning with `~%cd`, optionally followed by the name of a directory, will cause `cu` to change to that directory and remain there. If the optional directory name is omitted, ~%cd will change to your home directory. After the new directory has been set, cu continues at the point you left off.

This feature is most often used in combination with other cu functions. For example, you might want to have a particular selection of files available during a conversation. Rather than specify quotes/thisfile, quotes/thatfile, and so on, you can simply change to the quotes directory with:

```
~%cd quotes
```

From then on, you specify thisfile and thatfile directly.

Pausing and Resuming *cu*

One of the nicer features offered by UNIX is the capability to stop (suspend) a program, perform other tasks, and then resume the stopped program where you left off.

The cu program offers two equivalent means of stopping it:

~^Z	Temporarily stop cu.
~%pause	Same as ~^Z.

The first command is a tilde, followed by a Control-z and a Return. The second command has an identical effect but is somewhat easier to type.

Once cu is stopped, you are returned to the shell from which you originally ran cu. There, you can take care of as much business as you need to. When you are ready to resume cu, simply type fg:

```
~%pause                                          ←suspend cu
Stopped
mail jake                                        ←send a letter
Subject: missing files
I am missing "Masterlist" here, please fix.
mail biff                                        ←send another letter
Subject: Where's Masterlist?
Did you delete "Masterlist"?
fg                                               ←return to cu
(cu)
```

The ~%pause differs from the ~! we discussed earlier in that ~%pause returns you to your original shell—with your history intact for C Shell users—whereas ~! provides you with a brand new shell. Which one you choose is a matter of personal taste and style.

Disabling *XON* and *XOFF* with *cu*

It is possible for `cu` to receive characters from the remote machine faster than it can display them to your screen. When the backlog gets large enough, `cu` sends an `XOFF` character to the remote system telling it to stop sending. After `cu` has caught up, it sends an `XON` character to the remote system telling it to start sending again.

The mnemonics `XOFF` and `XON` (also called DC3 and DC1) stand for "Control-s" and "Control-q", respectively. Control-s means to stop sending. Control-q means to resume or start sending.

Unfortunately, some programs use `XOFF` and `XON` for different purposes than stopping and starting character flow. A prime example is the `emacs` text editor, which uses Control-s to begin a search. When running `emacs` on a remote machine via `cu`, it is a good idea to disable `XON/XOFF` or you may find yourself searching through text at unexpected moments.

The `~%nostop` function in `cu` causes the automatic sending of `XON/XOFF` to be cancelled. Some versions of `cu` make this cancellation permanent, whereas others allow a second `~%nostop` to turn `XON/OFF` back on. (See "cu(1)" in your on-line UNIX programmer's manual, vol. 1.)

Sending a Tilde to the Remote Machine with *cu*

Any line you type that begins with a tilde (`~`) character will be interpreted internally by `cu` and will not be sent to the remote machine. All other lines will be sent directly to the remote machine as though you were typing them directly into that machine.

Fortunately, few lines begin with a tilde in the course of ordinary interaction with a computer. A few programs, however, require that special command lines begin with a tilde. A prime example is `mailx`. When composing a letter on your local machine with `mailx`, it is possible to review what you've written so far with the command:

```
~p
```

If you are composing that letter with `mailx` on a machine you've logged into via `cu`, however, typing `~p` will cause `cu` on your local machine to print:

```
Use '~~' to start line with '~'
```

and send nothing to the remote machine. Just as the message says, the solution here is to type two tildes when you wish to actually send one:

```
~~p
```

Chaining Machines

Once you are logged into a remote machine via cu, there is nothing to prevent you from logging into a third machine by running cu on that remote machine. This chaining of cu's is common among people having accounts on several UNIX machines. There is no theoretical limit to how many machines can be chained in this way, but for each additional machine you will find that the characters you type are being echoed more and more slowly.

The chief difficulty in handling multiple cu programs in a chain like this is specifying on which machine a tilde function will execute. Unfortunately, there is no simple way of keeping track. Observe:

```
Sys1   → cu   → Sys2   → cu   → Sys3

Sys3: uuname -l                 ←last machine
system3
Sys3: ~!uuname -l               ←caught locally
system1
Sys3: ~~!uuname -l              ←middle machine
system2
```

The prompt is Sys3 because the chained cu's have been used to log us into system3. The first uuname prints the name of that system, as you would expect. The second uuname is run with the ~! function. The single tilde is caught by our local machine, causing the uuname program to be run locally and system1 to be printed. The last uuname is run with ~~!. The first tilde is stripped off by our local machine, and the result, ~!, is sent to the second machine. That machine sees the ~! function as being meant for itself, so it runs uuname and prints system2.

Disconnecting *cu*

To disconnect from cu and hang up the dial-out line, use the ~. function. That is, begin a line with ~. followed by a Return:

```
              ←in cu here
~.
Disconnected
              ←back in original shell here
```

You should log off the remote machine before disconnecting cu because some accounting systems will bill you improperly if you don't actually log off. For many remote machines, however, this is unnecessary.

Summary of *cu* Tilde Functions

`~~`	Send line that starts with a ~.
`~!`	Escape to new interactive shell.
`~!cmd`	Run `cmd` on local machine.
`~$cmd`	Run `cmd` on local machine and send output of `cmd` to remote machine.
`~%cd`	Change directory on local machine.
`~^Z`	Suspend `cu`. Resume with `fg`.
`~%pause`	Same as `~^Z`.
`~%nostop`	Disable XON/XOFF flow control.
`~.`	Disconnect from `cu`. Hang up line.
`~%put from to`	Send file to remote machine.
`~%take from to`	Receive (take) file from remote.
`~>:file`	Place received characters into `file` (only available on some versions of `cu`).
`~>`	End `~>:file` capture (only available on some versions of `cu`).

Transferring UNIX Files

The `cu` program contains functions for transferring files from your local UNIX machine to a remote UNIX machine, and for transferring files from a remote UNIX machine into your local UNIX machine:

`~%put`	Transfer file from local machine to remote machine.
`~%take`	Transfer file from remote machine to local machine.

These functions should not be confused with similar functions provided by more powerful telecommunications programs like `kermit`. These functions can be used only to transfer text files, they work only when you are calling another UNIX machine, and they provide no form of error-checking. Figure 17-4 compares `~%take` and `~%put`:

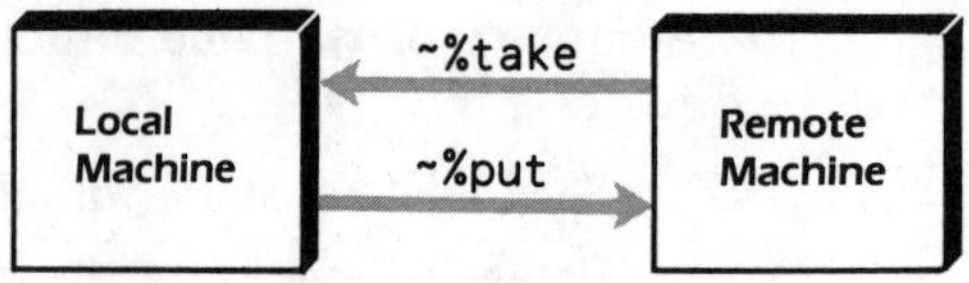

Figure 17-4. Direction of **~%take** versus **~%put**.

Sending with *~%put*

The format for using the ~%put function is:

```
~%put fromfile tofile
```

where fromfile is the name of the file on your local machine that you wish to transmit to the remote machine, and tofile is the name you wish to give that file on the remote machine. If tofile is omitted, then fromfile will become the name of the file on the remote machine.

```
~%put walrus.didit walrus.dupe                 ←you type
stty -echo; cat - > walrus.dupe; stty echo     ←cu sends
4 lines/193 characters
                                               ←all done
```

The line following ~%put was sent to the other system by cu as a UNIX shell command line. You can see that, for ~%put to send a file, the receiving remote machine *must* be running UNIX. Specifically, it must:

- Know how to run the stty program with a -echo flag to turn off echoing of characters.
- Know how to run the cat program with a - flag to specify that cat is to read from the standard input.
- Support the use of > for redirecting the output of cat.
- Know how to run the stty program with an echo argument to turn back on the echoing of characters.
- Support multiple commands in a single command line, where each is separated from the others by a ; character.

When ~%put is finished transferring the file, it prints the number of lines and characters that were transferred.

There is a minor pitfall to beware of when using ~%put: *If the file you are sending contains any Control-d characters, you should edit them out before send-*

ing. The Control-d character is UNIX's end-of-file character. Including it in a sent file will cause `cat`, and thus `~%put`, to finish prematurely.

Receiving with ~ *%take*

The `~%take` function is used to transfer files from the remote machine into your local machine. The format for using `~%take` is:

```
~%take fromfile tofile
```

where `fromfile` is the name of a file on the remote machine that you want transferred into your local machine, and `tofile` is the name you want the copy on your local machine to have. If `tofile` is omitted, then the file on your local machine will have the same name as `fromfile`.

For example, to copy the file `mbox` from the remote machine and place it into a file with the same name on your local machine, you would enter:

```
~%take mbox
stty -echo;mesg n;echo '~>':mbox;cat mbox;echo '~>';mesg y;stty echo
~>:mbox
20 lines/576 characters
```

As you can see, the line following `~%take` that is sent to the remote machine by `cu` —also printed to your screen—is somewhat more complex than the one that followed `~%put`. Here is what the elements in this line mean:

`stty -echo`	Turn off echoing of characters.
`mesg n`	Turn off permission for others to write to your terminal. This command protects your terminal from being written to by users on the remote machine and prevents others from calling you with `write` or `talk` and thus scrambling the file being received.
`echo '~>':file`	Send the expression `~>:file` back to the local `cu` program. This expression tells `cu` to start receiving a file named `file`.
`cat file`	Use the `cat` program to read the file named `file` and print the contents of that file to its standard output. Since your local `cu` is connected to that standard output, it receives that file.
`echo '~>'`	When `cu` receives a line consisting of the expression `~>`, it knows it is finished receiving.

`mesg y`	Turn back on permission for others to write to your terminal.
`stty echo`	Turn back on echoing of characters.

There are two minor pitfalls to beware of when using `~%take`:

1. If the file you are receiving contains tabs, and you want to prevent those tabs from being converted into spaces you should run:

   ```
   ~!stty tabs
   ```

   before running `~%take`.
2. If the file you are receiving contains the line:

   ```
   ~>
   ```

   you should insert a space in front of the tilde before copying the file.

Capturing Data with Non-UNIX Machines

The `cu` program was never intended to be used for calling non-UNIX machines—`~%put` and `~%take`, for example, have mechanisms that are clearly UNIX specific. However, transferring files from non-UNIX machines, though tricky, is not impossible.

In this section we will show you:

- How to make a recording of your `cu` session by using the `-r` flag.
- How to simulate `~%take` using `~>:file` and `~>`.
- How to capture a `cu` session by using the `tee` and `script` programs.

Capturing into a Recording File (*-r* Flag)

A recent addition to the `cu` program gives it the capability to create a recording of your `cu` session. That is, you can create a file that will contain everything you type and everything printed by the remote machine, even if that machine is not running UNIX. This new feature is not available on all versions of UNIX. Check your manual before trying it.

To create a recording file of your `cu` session, use the `-r` flag when you first run `cu` (see figure 17-5). The format for using the `-r` flag is:

```
-rfile
```

where, `file` is the name of the file you want the recording placed into. Note that there must be no space between the `-r` and `file`. Thus, to record a `cu` session and place that recording into the file `cu.recording`, you would type:

```
cu -rcu.recording -s 1200 9876543
    ↑
    record cu session in file named cu.recording
```

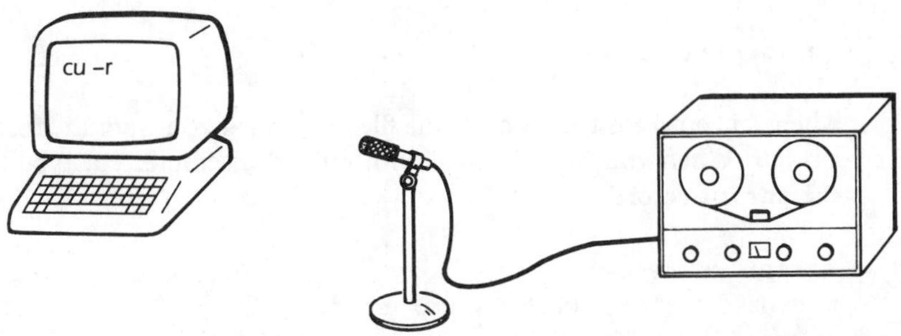

Figure 17-5. The **-r** flag is used with **cu** to create a recording file that will contain a record of everything you type and everything the remote site sends.

Capturing with Redirection

Another way to capture a session with a non-UNIX machine is by tricking `cu`. Recall that the `~%take` function does its job by getting the remote UNIX machine to send the sequence:

```
~>:filename
contents of file sent here
~>
```

This simple mechanism is easily emulated by inserting a line with `~>:filename` into the file at its head, and a line with `~>` into the file at its end. You then simply send the file by using `cat` or `type`, or whatever command is available on the remote machine to display text. The `cu` program will think it has asked for the file and will obligingly capture it for you. Note that the `filename` in the function `~>:filename` is the name of the file into which you want the transferred text placed on your local machine.

This trick works only if you have some way of editing the file on the remote machine. Another drawback is that not all versions of `cu` allow themselves to be tricked in this way. Experiment—it's a handy technique if you can get it to work.

Capturing with *tee* and *script*

If your version of `cu` lacks the `-r` recording flag, there are two alternative methods still available to you for capturing files. Both of these capture the entire `cu` session, placing a copy of everything you type, and everything the remote machine sends, into a file.

The first alternative is `script`, a program available under Berkeley UNIX. The `script` program can be used to save into a file a complete record of any UNIX session. To use it with `cu`, simply type:

```
script filename
```

where `filename` is the name of the file into which you want the record placed. Then run `cu`. When you have finished with `cu` and disconnected, type Control-d to end the `script` record:

```
script cu.record                          ←start script
Script started, file is cu.record
cu -s 1200 9876543                        ←start cu
                                          ←cu session here
~.                                        ←end cu
Disconnected
^D                                        ←stop script
```

If your system lacks the `script` program, you can emulate it by using the `tee` program. The `tee` program is a "pipe fitting," in that it reads from the standard input and produces two identical copies of its output. One copy of its output goes into a file you name; the other copy goes to the standard output—your screen (see figure 17-6).

To use `tee` with `cu`, you must pipe the output of `cu` into `tee`:

```
cu -s 1200 9876543 | tee cu.recording
```

Here, the output of `cu`, instead of going to your screen, is sent (piped) through the `tee` program. The `tee` program takes the output of `cu` and splits it. One copy goes into the file `cu.recording`, and the other goes to your screen.

Nothing special needs to be done to end the `tee` recording. The `tee` program ends automatically when you disconnect from `cu`.

Watching It Happen (*-d* Flag)

The `cu` program allows a user to watch its actions as it tries to connect to, and disconnect from, a remote machine. It does this by displaying debugging informa-

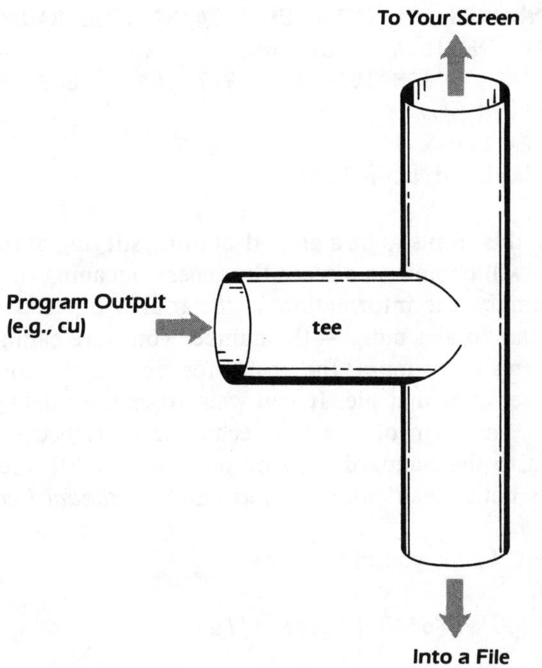

Figure 17-6. The **tee** program is a pipe fitting.

tion. Although this debugging output is intended primarily for system administrators, you too can make use of it.

The most common use of cu's debugging output is to discover why it is unable to make a connection. If, for example, you don't use the -d flag, you might encounter something like this:

```
cu -s 1200 9876543
Connect failed: dialer hung
```

Here, cu was unable to connect—that much is clear—but what does "dialer hung" mean? This is where the debugging mode of cu comes to the rescue. To enable the debugging output, use a -d flag when running cu:

```
cu -d -s 1200 9876543
call find_dev(, , 1200)
call connect(tty6,,9876543,1200)
dialup: searching for a ACU dialer
AUTODIAL ACU
Dialing 9876543
Using ventel
```

```
calling 9876543 -> 9876543
wanted $ ^M^JVEN-TEL 212-PLUS 1.34^M^J1200 BAUD^M^J$got that
wanted DIAL: ^M^JDIAL: got that
wanted ONLINE ^M^J^M^JDIALING .9876543    BUSY ^M^J$got ?
venDial failed
DIAL tty2 FAILED
Connect failed: dialer hung
```

At first, this seems to be a great deal of mystifying output. If you look closely, however, you will be able to discern the general meaning of this debugging output. More importantly, the information in the fourth line from the bottom tells you exactly why the "dialer hung"—the number you were calling was BUSY!

On systems that support the `-r` flag for creating a recording file, the output of `-d` is not placed into that file. If you want to capture debugging output, you will have to use a variation on the `tee` technique described earlier. Since debugging output is sent to the standard *error* output, you need to use a special pipe symbol that connects both the *standard output* and the *standard error output* to the `tee` program.

For the C Shell, you must type:

```
cu -d -s 1200 9876543 |& tee file
                      ↑
                      pipe standard output and standard error output
```

For the Bourne shell, you must type:

```
cu -d -s 1200 9876543 2>1 | tee file
                      ↑
                      connect standard error output to standard output
```

Summary of Uses and Caveats

In this section we offer a summary of the more common ways to use the `cu` program. Where necessary, we also outline any pitfalls that should be avoided.

Dial out at 1200 baud: dial a number

```
cu -s 1200 number
```

Caveat: The `number` must be all digits, except for the equal sign (=) which tells `cu` to wait for a secondary dial tone, and the hyphen (-) which tells `cu` to wait about 4 seconds.

Dial out at 1200 baud: dial modem directly

```
cu -s 1200 -l tty#
```

Caveat: The # in tty# is the number of a TTY in the directory /dev. You'll need to ask your system administrator which ones are connected to dial-out modems.

Dial out: call a system by name

```
cu systemname
```

Caveat: The systemname is the name of one of the remote sites connected to your site. Use the uuname command to find the names of those sites.

Send a tilde

```
~~
```

Caveat: To send a line beginning with a tilde to the remote machine, type two tildes.

Copy a file: from remote to local

```
~%take fromfile tofile
```

Caveat: The fromfile is the name of the file on the remote machine that you want copied into your local machine. If tofile is given, the local filename will be tofile; otherwise, it will be fromfile. Only text files may be copied. Use stty tabs to preserve tabs.

Copy a file: from local to remote

```
~%put fromfile tofile
```

Caveat: The fromfile is the name of the file on the local machine that you will send to the remote machine. If tofile is given, the remote file will be named tofile; otherwise, it will be named fromfile. Only text files may be sent.

Execute a command: local

```
~!command
```

Caveat: The command is any UNIX command. You see the output of the command, but that output is not sent to the remote machine. You are returned to cu when the command is completed.

Execute a command: local, send output to remote

```
~$command
```

Caveat: The command is any UNIX command. You see the output of the command, *and* that output is sent to the remote machine. You are returned to `cu` when the command is completed.

Stop `cu`

`~^Z`

or

`~%pause`

Caveat: Stops (suspends) `cu` and exits to the shell from which you originally ran `cu`. Resume `cu` with the `fg` command.

Summary

In this chapter you have learned how to use the `cu` program. In addition to learning how to dial remote machines, you have learned how to transfer files with `~%put` and `~%take`, and how to interact with your local machine from within `cu`.

As we stated at this chapter's beginning, `cu` is not a full-blown telecommunications package. If you have more sophisticated needs—like multiple file transfers or error-checking—you should explore professional packages, like `xmodem` or `kermit`.

In the next, and final, chapter about UUCP, we will take you on a tour. Beginning with `/bin/mail`, we will show you, step by step, what happens as an electronic message passes from your site to a neighbor site. Included is a discussion about the low-level UUCP programs `uucico` and `uuxqt`.

18

Putting It All Together

Up to now, we've been looking at individual UUCP programs. In this chapter, we will show you how many of these programs interact to perform a more complex activity. We'll give you a tour, of sorts. Beginning with the UNIX `mail` program, we'll show you each step that is taken by UUCP in the complex process of transmitting an electronic mail message to a neighbor site. This tour will cover one "hop" in the multihop mailing of a `mail` message—the transmission of that message from the first to the second of a chain of sites leading to the message's final destination.

Along the way, you'll meet two new UUCP players:

`uucico` Standing for *U*NIX to *U*NIX *C*opy *I*n *C*opy *O*ut, this is the real workhorse of any UUCP transmission. The `uucico` program is the only one that actually communicates with neighbor UNIX sites. It is the one that dials out over a telephone modem. It "converses" with another `uucico` program, running at that other site, and together they handle the transfer of data.

`uuxqt` Standing for *U*NIX to *U*NIX e*X*e*Qu*T*e, this is the program that executes, on the remote machine, the command you specified by running `uux` on your local machine. In other words, if you use `uux` to run `cat`, `uuxqt` will execute `cat` on the remote machine.

These are the final two programs that form the ensemble of programs called UUCP. The entire ensemble is listed on the next page.

Our tour is organized into seven steps. All but the first two correspond to one of the UUCP programs. Figure 18-1 shows the typical sequence of programs that are triggered each time you mail an electronic message. It looks complicated, and it is complicated—when studied in detail. What we present here, however, is the big picture—a simplified overview. We've distilled the essentials and limited our view so that you can more easily see how all the pieces fit together.

Review of UUCP Software

uucp	Copy files between neighbor sites.
uusend	Copy files through several sites to a remote site.
uuto	Copy files to a neighbor site's PUBDIR directory.
uupick	Retrieve files sent with uuto.
uux	Execute programs on other UNIX machines.
uustat	Examine and modify UUCP job status.
uucico	Transmit and receive all files.
uuxqt	Execute the program requested by uux.

Step 1: We Send an Electronic Mail Message

Regardless of the bells and whistles that distinguish any one mail program from the others, they all do the same basic things:

- Allow you to specify to whom the electronic message is addressed or destined.
- Allow you to enter the text, or body, of your message.
- Allow you to send your message.

These are the three key elements that define how and where your electronic mail message will eventually be transmitted. For example, look at the following session with the simplest of the mail programs, /bin/mail:

```
/bin/mail site1\!site2\!morgan              ←to whom
I bet you haven't any idea the number       ←text to send
of programs that have to be run just
to send this letter to you.
^D                                          ←send it
```

Here, we have specified three key elements: first, that this electronic message is destined for the user morgan on the remote UNIX machine site2 (site1 is our neighbor, and site2 is a remote machine); second, that the message body contains three lines of text; and, third, that this message is to be sent or transmitted

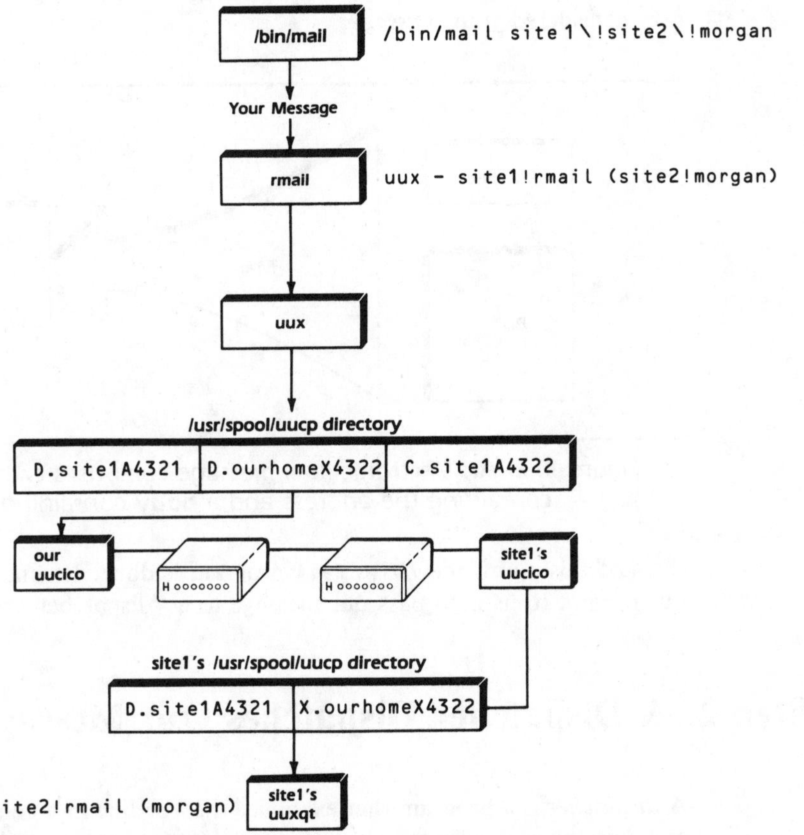

Figure 18-1. How **mail** is transmitted.

(remember that we could have cancelled this message and not sent it by typing Control-c).

When we've concluded our session with `/bin/mail`, it combines the first two of these elements ("to whom" and the "text to send") into a single file. That file looks like this:

```
To: site1!site2!morgan
From bryan

I bet you haven't any idea the number
of programs that have to be run just
to send this letter to you.
```

The first two lines form the *header* of the message. The last three lines form the *body* of the message. The header is always separated from the body by at least one blank line (see figure 18-2). This entire file, the combination of header and body, is now considered your *message*.

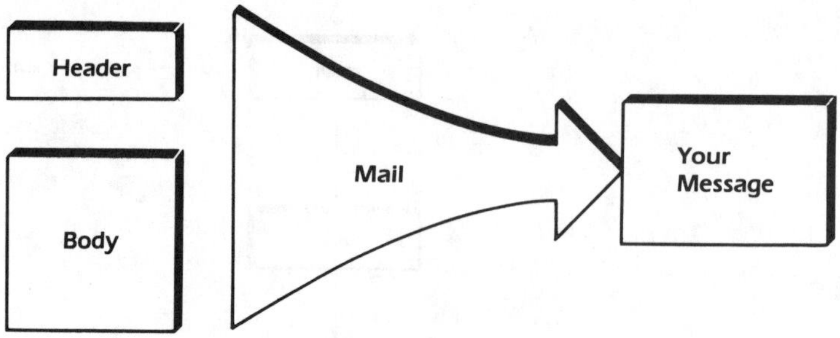

Figure 18-2. An electronic mail message comprises two parts: a **header** containing the address and a **body** containing the text.

At this point, the `/bin/mail` program is done. Its final act before returning our prompt to us is to pass our message to a "dispatcher program."

Step 2: A Dispatcher Dispatches Our Message

A *dispatcher* is a program that examines the `To:` line in an electronic mail message and determines the proper means for transmitting that message. The most common dispatcher, and the one we will discuss, is the `rmail` program—a restricted form of `/bin/mail` that understands forwarding. Another popular dispatcher program is `sendmail`. One advantage `sendmail` has over `rmail` is that `sendmail` knows how to send messages over many kinds of networks, whereas `rmail` can send messages only over the UUCP network. We won't discuss `sendmail` here (remember, we promised to keep this tour simple); instead we will focus on the `rmail` program and its interaction with UUCP.[1]

When the `rmail` program is handed (via its standard input) an electronic mail messsage, it first looks inside the body of that message for a line of text beginning with the expression "To:":

```
To: site1!site2!morgan
    ↑
    first site
```

1. The `sendmail` program, written by Eric Allman, is a powerful and complex dispatcher program, deserving an entire book of its own.

The first step in forwarding an electronic mail message is to send it to the first site in this list of sites. Here, `site1` is the first site, followed by `site2`.

The `rmail` program doesn't care if `site1` is a *directly connected site*—one of those connected to our local machine. All `rmail` does, once it has found the `To:` line, is to add some information to the `From` line and then run the `uux` program.

The `From` line in our message header is:

```
From bryan
```

It contains information for the eventual recipient. In this case, the `From` line tells the recipient `morgan` that the message is from `bryan`. Unfortunately, simply saying that the message is from `bryan` is not sufficient because `morgan` is a user on a remote machine. For this reason, `rmail` must add some additional information to the `From` line:

```
From bryan Sat Nov 09 1987 09:15 PST remote from ourhome
           ↑                                     ↑
```

date the message was sent *original sending site*

As figure 18-3 shows, `rmail` first adds the current date and time. It then adds the words "remote from," followed by the name of our local site, `ourhome` (the name of the site from which this message originated).

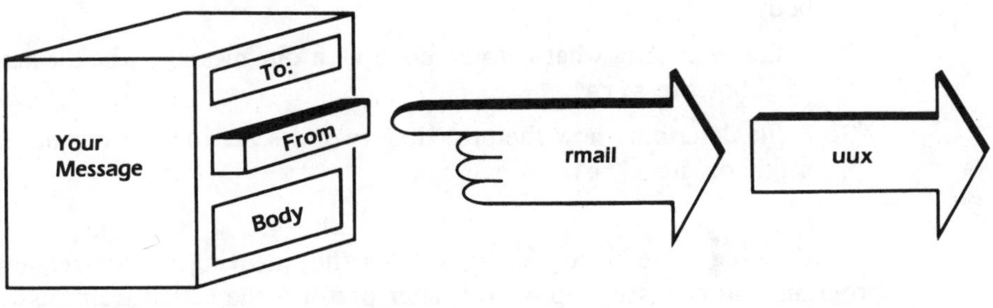

Figure 18-3. The **rmail** program annotates the "From" line in your mail message and then passes the entire message to **uux**.

Once `rmail` has both found the `To:` line and annotated the `From` line, its final task is to run `uux` to queue a request for the messsage to be transmitted to `site1`. It runs `uux` with a command that looks like this:

```
uux - site1!rmail (site2!morgan)
```

which we will explain in a moment. Having passed our message to `uux`, the `rmail` program exits.

Step 3: A *uux* Request Is Queued to Transmit Our Message

Recall from chapter 14 that you use the uux program to request execution of other programs on other UNIX machines. Such a request has the form:

```
uux - site1!rmail (site2!morgan)
```

This request tells uux to do a number of specific things. The command site1!rmail tells it to run the rmail program at the neighbor site site1. The parentheses surrounding (site2!morgan) tell uux that this is an *argument*—an electronic mail address—for rmail, and not the name of a file to be copied. Finally, the hyphen (-) tells uux to read from its standard input and feed what it reads into the rmail program at site1. The standard input to uux, because uux was run by rmail in the previous step, contains our message—both the header and the body.

Once uux has read in the entire message, it proceeds to queue a request (see chapter 11) for the message to be transmitted to site1. To queue a request, uux creates three files in UUCP's *spool* (temporary holding) directory, /usr/spool/uucp. The three files are:

1. A file containing the electronic mail message, the header as well as the body.
2. A file describing what is to be done with our message when it arrives at the neighbor site site1.
3. A file describing how the preceding two files are to be transmitted to the neighbor site site1.

Creating these three files constitutes the queueing of our request. Another program, uucico (see Step 4), will later perform the actual transmission of these files to site1. Figure 18-4 shows the three files (two data files and one command file) created by uux to process the request.

As you can see from figure 18-4, the three files are not labeled the same. Two are data (D.) files, and one is a command (C.) file.

C. *Command*, or "work," files contain instructions that tell uucico which files to transmit, where to transmit them, and in which order to transmit. Files to be received and programs to be executed can also be specified.

D. *Data* files contain an exact copy of the files to be transmitted. Data files can also contain instructions for the other sites' uuxqt program.

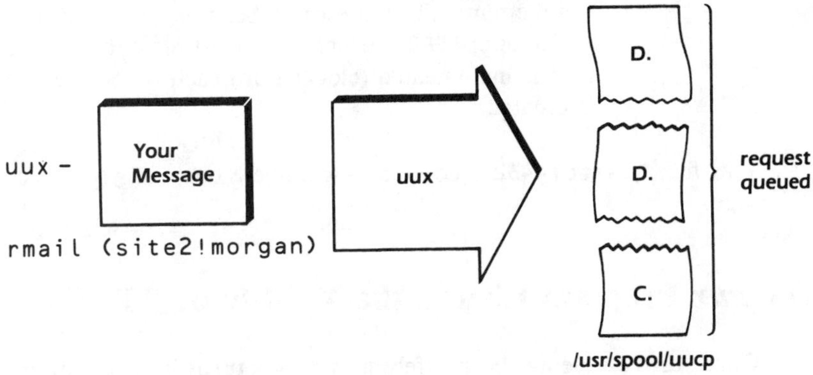

Figure 18-4. A **uux** request is queued when **uux** has completed the creation of its temporary files in UUCP's spool directory.

The First File Created by *uux* Contains Our Message

The first file created by uux in UUCP's /usr/spool/uucp directory contains the text of our electronic mail message. Like all of UUCP's temporary files, this file is given a somewhat cryptic name:

```
D.site1A4321
```

Don't be alarmed. As you will see, this kind of filename makes sense once you understand it. The meaning of the components that make up this name are:

- `D.` The `D.` means that this is a "Data" file—our message is considered data.
- `site1` The `site1` is the first seven, or fewer, letters of the name of the neighbor site, `site1`, that is to receive this data. If that site were instead called "ucbvax," the filename would be `D.ucbvaxA4321`.
- `A` The `A` means that this is an "A" grade file. The grade determines the order in which files will be sent to the remote site.[2] Grades run from "A" through "Z" and then from "a" through "z." "A" runs first and is the default for uux.
- `4321` The digits following the grade (here `4321`) form a unique number

2. Although available on System V and BSD UNIX, the grade is ignored. The new HoneyDanBer UUCP, however, uses grading as it was originally intended. (For more information about HoneyDanBer UUCP, contact AT&T and ask for documentation on their Network Communications System.)

used by UUCP to help ensure that every temporary file has a unique name. The latest number used is stored in the file /usr/lib/uucp/SEQF, which is a small file containing a single number that is incremented (clocked up) each time a new UUCP spool file is created.

This file, D.site1A4321, contains a complete copy of your electronic mail message.

The *uux* Program Checks the Validity of "To:"

Once our message has been safely stored, uux turns its attention to the name of the neighbor site site1. It looks in the file /usr/lib/uucp/L.sys to find the names of all the neighbor UNIX sites to which our UNIX machine is connected. If uux finds that site1 is *not* listed in that file, it sends us a message describing the problem and then exits. Otherwise, it continues to queue our rmail request by creating the next two temporary files.

The Next File Created by *uux* Describes the Actions to Be Performed on the First

The next temporary file that uux creates is also located in the /usr/spool/uucp directory. This file contains a description of what is to be done with the first file—our message—when it reaches site1. Like that first file, this description file has a somewhat cryptic name:

```
D.ourhomeX4322
```

The contents of this D. file describe the specific actions that must be taken by the remote site1's uuxqt program (we'll soon see how uuxqt works) in order to run the rmail program there. The meanings of the components that make up this name are:

D.	The D. means that this is a "Data" file.
ourhome	The ourhome is the first seven letters of our local site name, ourhome.
X	The X means that this is an "X" grade file. Files that contain execution instructions are always grade X.
4322	The 4322 is a unique number used by UUCP to ensure that every temporary file has a unique name.

The lines contained in the file D.ourhomeX4322 look like this:

```
U bryan ourhome
F D.neighA4321 /usr/spool/uucp/tmp
I /usr/spool/uucp/tmp site1
C rmail (site2!morgan)
```

The first letter in each line indicates the kind of information the line contains. Each line contributes information that will be used by uuxqt at site1 when it processes our electronic mail message:

- U The U (User) line says that the user named bryan on our local machine, named ourhome, queued this uux request.
- F The F (File) line says that the file D.neighA4321—the temporary file that contains our message—will be called /usr/spool/uucp/tmp when it gets to site1.
- I The I (Input) line says that the file /usr/spool/uucp/tmp will be used as input to the rmail program and that this file is located on the site site1.
- C The C (Command) line says that the rmail program will be run. The parentheses surrounding the (site2!morgan) mean that site2!morgan is a mail address and not a file.

When this *execution* file is later sent to the remote machine, the D. that begins its name will be changed to an X. These execution instructions begin as ordinary data here at our local site but will become real instructions when they reach the remote site. Remember this concept—it is an important one that we will mention again when we describe the uuxqt program.

The Last File Created by *uux* Describes the Transmission of the First Two Files

The last of the three temporary files created by uux contains instructions that describe how the first two files are to be transmitted to site1 (see figure 18-5). Like the first two files, this file also has a somewhat cryptic name:

```
C.site1A4323
```

This C. file contains information for uucico (the transmission program we'll describe in Step 4). The meanings of the components that make up this name are:

- C. The C. means that this is a "Command" file—also called a "work" file.
- site1 The site1 is the first seven, or fewer, letters of the name of the receiving site, site1.

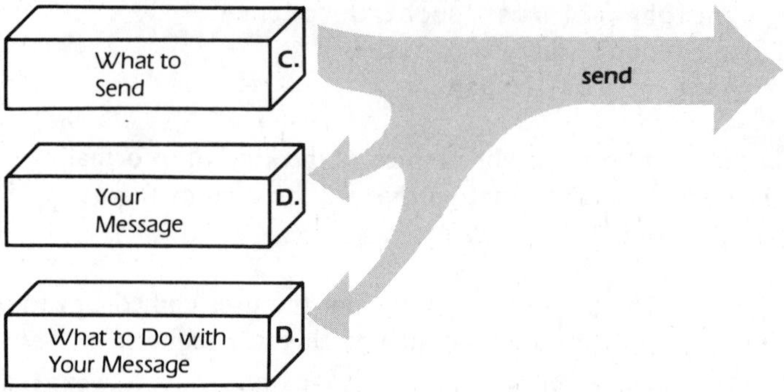

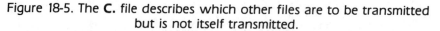

Figure 18-5. The **C.** file describes which other files are to be transmitted but is not itself transmitted.

A The **A** means that this is an "A" grade job.

4323 The **4323** is a unique number used by UUCP to ensure that each temporary file has a unique name.

The lines in this `C.` file tell `uucico` (see Step 4) how to transmit the other two temporary files. For our example, those lines are:

```
S D.site1A4321    D.site1A4321    bryan - D.site1A4321    0666
S D.ourhomeX4322 X.ourhomeX4322 bryan - D.ourhomeX4322 0666
↑ ↑               ↑               ↑     ↑ ↑               ↑
```

do *from file* *to file* *who* *flags* *send file* *mode*

The individual fields in each of these lines mean:

do Instructions for transmission. The `S` means to send a file to the neighbor site.

from file The name of the file to send. In the first line, it is the file containing our `mail` message. In the second line, it is the file of instructions for `uuxqt` on the remote machine.

to file The name that the *send file* will be given when it arrives on the remote machine. Notice that the instructions file in the second line will become an `X.` (execution) file when it arrives at the remote site, `site1`.

who The name of the user who queued this request.

flags The flags that were used when `uux` was run. No flags were used, so this is a lone hyphen `-`.

send file The full pathname of the file to be sent. In the case of UUCP temporary files, this name is the same as the one in the *from file* field.

mode The UNIX mode (permissions) that the file will be given at the receiving site. Here it is 0666—readable and writable by its owner, group, and anyone else. (See "chmod(1)" in the on-line UNIX programmer's manual for details on modes.)

The *uux* Program Exits

The creation of the three temporary files by uux results in queueing a request for our electronic mail message to be sent to the neighbor site site1. This is the end of uux's involvement. As it exits, it runs the uucico program. Our mail message is now ready to be transmitted.

Step 4: The Local *uucico* Transmits Our Message

The uucico program, which stands for *U*NIX to *U*NIX *C*opy *I*n *C*opy *O*ut, is the real workhorse of the UUCP ensemble of programs. This is the program that actually communicates with other UNIX machines, transmitting and receiving files. We have characterized it as a "low-level" program because it is a program that is seldom, if ever, run by ordinary users. Other than being run by your system administrator as part of UUCP debugging, the uucico program is run only by higher-level programs.

In chapter 11 we explained that queued UUCP requests are not necessarily transmitted at once. The delay can vary from a few seconds on local area networks, to several hours at public-access UNIX sites. The reasons for this delay are attributable to a variety of factors:

- The remote UNIX site—the one with which uucico will try to communicate—may not be accepting calls. It may be "down," or its phone may be busy.
- Another uucico process at our site may already be communicating with the remote site we want—remember that UNIX is a multitasking machine and that several uucico processes can be running at the same time.
- The system administrator may have specified times when the system may and may not communicate with a particular remote site, and this may not be one of the permitted times.
- If uucico fails, it merely exits. It will not be run again until: (1) the other site calls us; (2) another user on our site runs mail, postnews, uucp, or uux; (3) automatic system software (see "cron(8)" in the on-line UNIX

programmer's manual) runs `uucico` at some regularly scheduled interval; or (4) your system administrator runs `uucico` manually.

At those times when `uucico` can be run, and is run successfully, it calls up a neighbor UNIX site and transmits your electronic mail message. This communication and transmission is composed of nine distinct parts:

Part 1 Look through the spool (the temporary holding directory, `/usr/spool/uucp`) for work to do. Work is signalled by the existence of `C.` files.

Part 2 Call up the neighbor site using a telephone modem, local area network software, or any of several other mechanisms that we won't discuss here.

Part 3 Log into the neighbor UNIX site.

Part 4 Start up a conversation with the other site. This conversation is with another `uucico` program running at that other site.

Part 5 Agree with the remote `uucico` on which protocol will be used for transmission.

Part 6 Transmit the files listed in the `C.` file.

Part 7 See if the other UNIX site has any files it wishes to send us. If it does, the two `uucico` programs reverse roles.

Part 8 Perform housekeeping. The temporary files are deleted; the `LOGFILE` (see chapter 15) and other status files are updated.

Part 9 Look for more work to do (`C.` files). If any are found, repeat the whole process. If there is nothing more, exit.

Part 1: *uucico* Looks for Work

When `uucico` is run at our site—no matter by whom—it first looks through its `/usr/spool/uucp` directory for any work to do. Recall that work is signalled by the existence of files beginning with `C.`, designating a command file. Also recall from the previous step—where `uux` created its three files—that `C.` files contain instructions describing which files `uucico` is to transmit and how it is to transmit them. In the case of our electronic mail message, `uucico` would find the file:

```
C.site1A4323
  ↑
site name
```

The second part of this filename is the name of the other UNIX site with which `uucico` is to communicate, `site1`.

Part 2: *uucico* Connects to the Other UNIX Site

Once `uucico` has determined the name of the other UNIX site—the one it has work for—it looks in the file `/usr/lib/uucp/L.sys` to determine how to go about setting up communications with that site. The `L.sys` file contains one line of information for each neighbor site to which our site is connected. Unfortunately, that file is not readable by anyone but your system administrator because it contains login names and passwords for those other UNIX sites. For the purposes of our tour then, we will illustrate with a hypothetical `L.sys` file. One line in that file might look like this:

```
site1 Any,10 tty2 1200 9876543 ogin:-\n-ogin: ourhome word: jabberwok
↑     ↑      ↑    ↑    ↑       ↑
```

site name   *times*   *port*   *speed*   *phone number*   *how to log in*

This line in `L.sys` tells `uucico` how to dial the neighbor site `site1`. Specifically, this line tells `uucico` the following information:

site name — This field is the entry for `site1`, the neighbor UNIX site to which we are sending our electronic mail message—the site for which a `uux` request has been queued.

times — The *times* information tells `uucico`, first, that it is allowed to call `site1` at `Any` time of the day and, second, that it may retry a call no sooner than `10` minutes after its last failure. The `Any` can be replaced with a list containing days of the week and time intervals during those days. For example, `Sa|Su0000-0600,60` means to call only on weekends between midnight and 6:00 a.m., and not to retry more often than once per hour.

port — This field tells `uucico` that it is to use the modem connected to /dev/`tty2`. This is equivalent to the `cu` flag argument `-l tty2`, as described in chapter 17. For local area networks, this field might contain the word "NET," or some similar variation.

speed — The *speed* tells `uucico` that it will be calling on a 1200-baud modem. This is equivalent to the `cu` flag argument `-s 1200`, as described in chapter 17. For local area networks, this field may be omitted.

phone number — This is the telephone number that `uucico` is to dial in order to connect to `site1`. For local area networks, this field may be omitted.

how to log in This field tells uucico how it should log into the site site1. We will discuss this cryptic-looking command shortly.

Using the information provided by the L.sys file, uucico dials—or uses special local area network hardware—and connects to the other UNIX site, site1 in our example. If that connection is successful—the other site's modem answered the phone—uucico will attempt to log into the other UNIX machine. Otherwise, it will exit and another attempt will be made later. How soon that next attempt will be made is determined by the *times* entry. In our example, the next attempt will be no sooner than in ten minutes.

Part 3: *uucico* Logs into the Other UNIX Site

Once our local machine and the neighbor UNIX machine, site2, have connected (via modem or local area network hardware), our local machine will try to log into that neighbor machine. The last part of the line in L.sys, the *how to log in* part, describes the sequence of events that uucico must expect to receive from the other site. It also describes what it must send in order to log in. There are four parts here, beginning with what to expect:

```
ogin:-\n-ogin: ourhome word: jabberwok
↑              ↑       ↑     ↑
expect         send    expect send
```

First, uucico expects to receive from the other UNIX site the characters "ogin:"—covering both the case of "Login:" and "login:". This is a compound expectation because it comprises three subfields, each separated by a - character. If uucico receives anything other than ogin:, this subfield information tells it to send the newline character, specified as \n, and again wait to receive ogin:. If, at this point, uucico receives anything other than ogin:, it exits. In a real L.sys file, this repeated expectation of ogin: will be far more complex than what we've shown you here. For example, a site may print a "Welcome" message before printing the login prompt, or the baud rate may have to be adjusted by sending a break signal. This complexity is one of the reasons it is difficult for your system administrator to set up connections to new UNIX sites. "Tuning" this first field can take a lot of experimentation and time.

Next, assuming that we received ogin: from site1, uucico will send the word "ourhome" to that other site and then wait to receive word:. The string "word:" is the tail part of both "Password:" and "password:". If anything other than word: is received, uucico exits. Otherwise, it sends the password string (for our example, jabberwok) to the other UNIX machine.

Part 4: Our *uucico* Starts Up a Conversation with the Remote Site's *uucico*

When our site logs into another UNIX machine, instead of being given a Bourne Shell or a C Shell, it is given the program uucico on that other site as its login shell. From this point on, then, our local uucico will be talking to that other uucico program running on the other UNIX site, site1. To help keep the two uucico programs distinct from each other, we will refer to the one on our local machine as the Master uucico, and the one on the other UNIX machine, site1, as the Slave uucico. We didn't pull these names from a hat. They correspond to the roles that each program plays in its conversation and exchange of data, and are the actual terms used by UUCP (see figure 18-6).

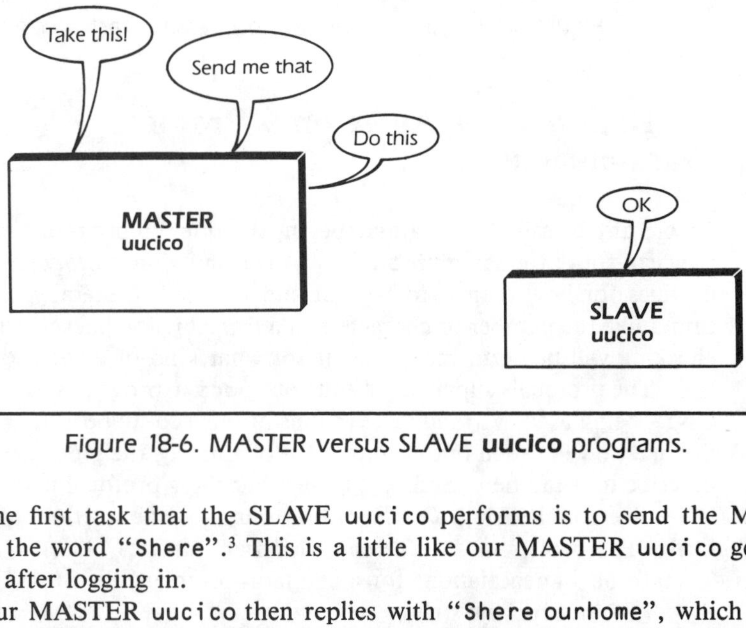

Figure 18-6. MASTER versus SLAVE **uucico** programs.

The first task that the SLAVE uucico performs is to send the MASTER uucico the word "Shere".[3] This is a little like our MASTER uucico getting its prompt after logging in.

Our MASTER uucico then replies with "Shere ourhome", which tells the SLAVE uucico that our real site name is ourhome (see figure 18-7). It does this because the name we used to log in is not necessarily the same as our real site name. Often, a site will have all out-site UNIX machines log in using a common name like uuoutside, and this convention helps to differentiate them.

After both uucico programs have greeted each other, they must negotiate a common "protocol" for the transmission of files.

3. The actual words transmitted by uucico are somewhat more complex than what is shown here. They include special control characters that we have elected to omit for simplicity.

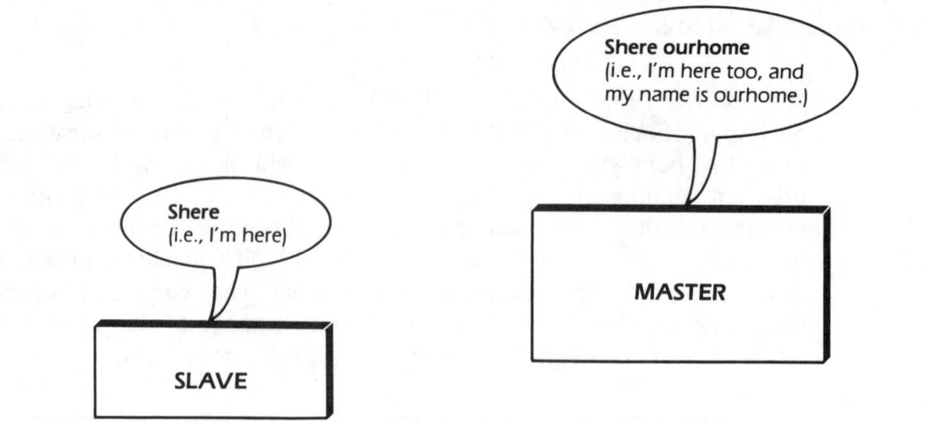

Figure 18-7. The two **uucico** processes start a conversation.

Part 5: Both *uucico*s Agree on a Protocol for Transmission

Before any transfer of data may begin, the `uucico` programs must determine that they can speak the same "protocol." A transmission *protocol* is an agreed-upon set of rules for how data is to be sent and received. Generally, a protocol describes things like the number of characters in a transmission packet, whether or not error-checking will be performed, and, if so, what kind of error-checking will be used.

The protocols supported by various `uucico` programs vary with the version of UNIX being used. Virtually all versions of `uucico` support the *g* protocol, so that is the one we will use in our example. Unfortunately, the *g* protocol is too complex to describe in detail here. Suffice it to say that the *g* protocol performs a "checksum" style of error-checking. (You can find out more about the *g* protocol in "Packet Driver Protocols," G. L. Chesson, Bell Laboratories 1986.)

To begin negotiations for a common protocol, the SLAVE `uucico` sends our MASTER `uucico` the string:

```
Pgn
 ↑
```
protocols that the SLAVE knows

Here, the `P` means "protocol," and `gn` tells our MASTER `uucico` that the SLAVE `uucico` has available only the `g` and the `n` protocols (the `n` being a common *network* protocol).

If our MASTER `uucico` has either of these two protocols available, it replies by specifying which it elects to use:

```
Ug
↑
```
MASTER selects to use protocol "g"

Here, the U means "use," and the g tells the SLAVE uucico that our site wishes to use the g protocol. Since we are the MASTER uucico, that is the protocol selected.

Part 6: Our *uucico* Transmits Its Files

Once the MASTER uucico and SLAVE uucico have agreed on a protocol, the transfer of files can begin. The MASTER uucico looks in its C. file—C.site1A4323 in our example—to see which files it should send. Recall that this file contains two lines of instructions:

```
S D.site1A4321    D.site1A4321    bryan - D.site1A4321    0666
S D.ourhomeX4322 X.ourhomeX4322 bryan - D.ourhomeX4322 0666
```

The C.site1A4323 file tells the MASTER uucico to first send the file named D.site1A4321 to the other site, site1; that file contains the text of our electronic mail message. After that file has been sent, it next tells the MASTER uucico to send the file D.ourhomeX4322. This second file, however, will be given the name X.ourhomeX4322 when it arrives on the other site; this file contains instructions for the other machine's uuxqt program, telling it what to do with the first file (see figure 18-8).

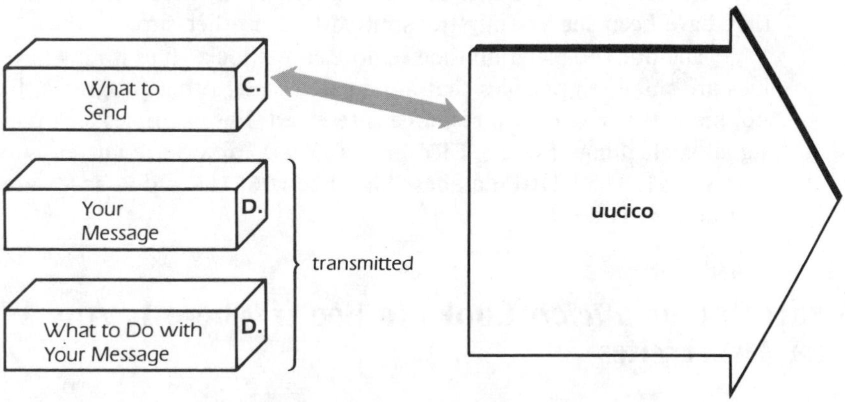

Figure 18-8. The work phase of **uucico**.

This sending of files is called uucico's *work phase*. In addition to sending files, the MASTER uucico can also be told to receive files. If there were files to receive in our example, there would be lines in the C. file that began with the letter *R*.

After all of the MASTER uucico's C. files—for the site site1—have been processed, our MASTER uucico asks the other site's SLAVE uucico if it has any work of its own.

Part 7: Does the Other UNIX Site's *uucico* Have Anything for Us?

If the other site's SLAVE uucico has any work—that is, if it has any C. files in its own /usr/spool/uucp directory—the roles of our two programs will reverse. The MASTER uucico will become the SLAVE uucico, and the SLAVE uucico will become the MASTER uucico.

After the roles have reversed, files will again be transmitted following the same steps as when our site was the MASTER. This time, however, the other site's uucico will be the MASTER and will call the shots.

When all work is done by both sites, the current MASTER uucico—whether our site or the other site—sends the word "OO" for "Over and Out." The SLAVE uucico replies with an "Over and Out" string of its own, and the two disconnect from each other—hang up the phone.

Part 8: Our *uucico* Performs Housekeeping Tasks

After our local machine has disconnected from the other UNIX site, it does some housekeeping. Never one to be sloppy, uucico removes the temporary files that were created by uux earlier. There is no reason to keep those files around because they have been successfully transmitted to the other site.

The uucico program then removes any "lock" files it may have created. *Lock* files are small, empty files that are created to let other programs, like uucico and cu, know that a common resource is reserved. For example, lock files are created to signal such things as: the TTY line is in use, or we are currently communicating with site1. The UUCP database files, like LOGFILE and R_stat, are then updated, and uucico is done.

Part 9: Our *uucico* Looks to See If There Is Any Work for Other Sites

There are two ways uucico can be run: it can be given a site name, in which case it will handle work only for that site and then exit; or it can be run with no site name specified. In the latter instance, uucico, when it is done with one site, will examine its /usr/spool/uucp directory to see if there are work (C.) files spooled for any other sites. If it finds any, it will go through this entire process all over again, for each of those other sites.

Our Electronic Mail Message Has Been Sent

At this point, our electronic mail message has been successfully transmitted to the first site specified in its `To:` header line, `site1`. This ends our machine's involvement with that message. To see what happens next, we need to move to the other UNIX machine.

Step 5: The Remote *uucico* Receives Our Message

In the previous step of our tour, our local `uucico` transmitted two files to the neighbor machine, `site1`. Now we have moved to `site1` to continue our tour. When the `site1`'s `uucico` received those two files, it placed them into its own `/usr/spool/uucp` directory. The first one it received was named:

```
D.site1A4321
```

This file contains the copy of our electronic mail message.

A second file was received and stored under the name:

```
X.ourhomeX4322
```

Recall from Step 3 of our tour that this file contains instructions for this `site1`'s `uuxqt` program. It was called "`D.ourhomeX4322`" when it was at our home site, and its name was changed to "`X.ourhomeX4322`" when it arrived here at `site1` (see figure 18-9).

Before `site1`'s `uucico` program exits, it looks through its `/usr/spool/uucp` directory for any execution (`X.`) files. For each one it finds—here it will find our `X.ourhomeX4322` file—it runs the `uuxqt` program to process the instructions contained in those files.

Step 6: The Remote *uuxqt* Runs Our *uux* Request

The first task that `uuxqt` (*U*NIX to *U*NIX e*X*e*Q*u*T*e) does is to examine the `X.` file it was given. In our example of sending electronic mail, `uuxqt` will find the following lines of text in our file `X.ourhomeX4322`:

```
U bryan ourhome
F D.site1A4321 /usr/spool/uucp/tmp
I /usr/spool/uucp/tmp site1
C rmail (site2!morgan)
```

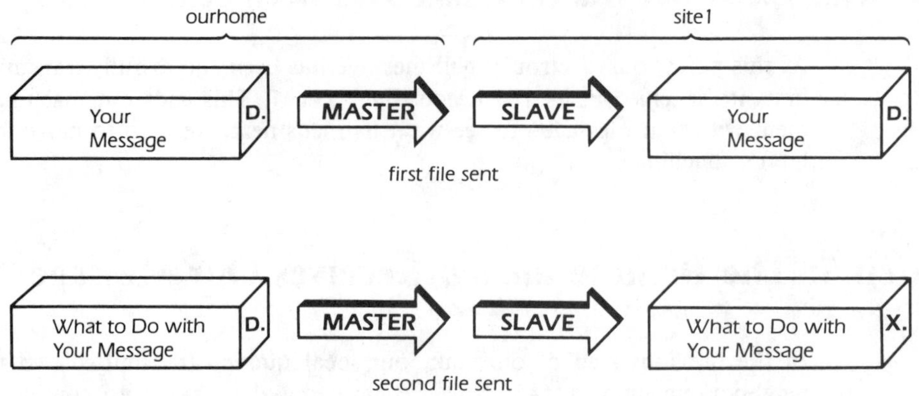

Figure 18-9. A **D.** file that contains instructions for **uuxqt** (the second file here) is renamed "**X.**" when it arrives at the SLAVE **uucico's** site.

The line beginning with `C` tells `uuxqt` that it is to run our `rmail` program (remember we are now on `site1`). The `uuxqt` program looks in its `L.cmds` file (see chapter 14) to determine if `rmail` is indeed a program that it is allowed to run. If the `rmail` program is not allowed, `uuxqt` will send mail to the user listed in the `U` line—`bryan` at the site named `ourhome`—advising him of that fact. Fortunately, for our example, the `rmail` progam is permitted, as it virtually always is.

The next thing our `uuxqt` program does is to move all the files listed in the first part of each `F` line:

```
F D.site1A4321 /usr/spool/uucp/tmp
```

into its `/usr/spool/uucp/.XQTDIR` directory (see chapter 14). For our example, that's the file `D.site1A4321`—the one that contains our electronic mail message. When `uuxqt` moves a file into its `.XQTDIR` directory, it renames that file to the name specified in the second part of the `F` line. To `uuxqt`, the name `/usr/spool/uucp/tmp` is a special one. It tells `uuxqt` to make up a new filename that begins with "tmp" and ends with a unique number, so that the new name is unique in its `.XQTDIR` directory. For our example, we'll assume that it made up the name "`tmp1234`".

After `uuxqt` is finished moving all necessary files into its `.XQTDIR` directory and renaming them, it is ready to immediately run the program listed in the `C` line:

```
C rmail (site2!morgan)
```

This example tells `uuxqt` to run the `rmail` program and to give that program the single argument `site2!morgan`—the electronic mail address. There is one piece of information missing, however, and that is the text that `rmail` is to send. The `I` line:

```
I /usr/spool/uucp/tmp site1
```

tells `uuxqt` that it is to feed the file `/usr/spool/uucp/tmp` into the `rmail` program. Recall that `/usr/spool/uucp/tmp` is a special file to `uuxqt`, and has just been transformed by `uuxqt` into `.XQTDIR/tmp1234`—and this is the file that contains our electronic mail message. Also recall that we are now on `site1`, having moved here from `ourhome` so that we could continue with our tour.

The final invocation of `rmail`, then, by `uuxqt`, looks like this:

```
rmail site2!morgan < /usr/spool/uucp/.XQTDIR/tmp1234
```

Look carefully at this command and remember that we are now at `site1`. Our system is being told to run the dispatcher program `rmail` once again, this time to send our electronic mail message to yet another remote machine, `site2`. That message is in the file named `tmp1234`, in our `.XQTDIR` directory, where it was placed earlier by `uuxqt`.

Step 7: The Remote *rmail* Forwards Our Message

We have come full circle. The `rmail` program on `site1`, just like the one back on our home machine, `ourhome`, will dispatch our electronic mail message to the next site, `site2`. Let's review how this is done and see how this new `rmail` differs from the earlier one.

This `rmail` program reads the text of an electronic mail message from its standard input. The `<` in the command:

```
rmail site2!morgan < /usr/spool/uucp/.XQTDIR/tmp1234
```

feeds the file `tmp1234`, from the `.XQTDIR` directory, into `rmail`'s standard input. That file contains the text of our electronic mail message.

Our earlier `rmail`, after it had read the entire message, looked into that message for a line beginning with the expression "`To:`". This `rmail`, however, is given an address, `site2!morgan`, as its argument. It too looks for a `To:` line, however, and, if it finds one, replaces that original one:

```
To: site1!site2!morgan
```

with the new one—the one taken from its argument:

```
To: site2!morgan
```

Finally, this `rmail` runs the `uux` program to queue a request for that electronic mail message to be sent to the next site in our chain of sites, `site2`:

```
uux - site2!rmail (morgan)
```

and the whole cycle starts over again.

Summary

In this chapter you were given a tour—a simplified but comprehensive glimpse—of how electronic mail messages are sent from one machine to another. You also saw how the low-level programs `uucico` and `uuxqt` operate, and how the high-level, midlevel, and low-level programs all interrelate.

This chapter ends our coverage of the UUCP progams. The inner-workings of UUCP are much more complicated than what you've seen here. We've given you just the flavor of UUCP, enough to use its programs comfortably and in everyday situations. If you hunger for more, there are a number of advanced references available. Those texts are listed in the bibliography (Appendix E).

During the course of this Part 3, you've learned how to use a host of new programs, ranging from the simple to the cryptic. Of the simpler programs, you have discovered how to use `uucp` to copy files between neighboring UNIX machines, and how to use `uusend` to send files through a series of UNIX machines to a remote UNIX site. You have also seen how `uuto` and `uupick` can be used for easy copying of files between the PUBDIR directories of neighboring UNIX sites.

With the more complex program `uux`, you have learned how to run programs on neighboring UNIX machines. You have discovered many handy applications that use the `uux` program: how to print local files on a neighbor machine's printer, how to compare files located on different neighbor machines, how to use `uux` to back up files, and much more. Of the more common UUCP programs, `uux` is the most difficult to learn, but the most rewarding to use.

Along the way, you have also learned how to view and modify UUCP job status with `uustat` and how to package directory hierarchies with `tar`, `cpio`, and `shar`. You have also learned what binary files are, and how to convert them to text files and back again with `uuencode` and `uudecode`. As a bonus, you were provided with the listing for a mini `uudecode` program called `decode.c`.

At the complex and cryptic end of the UUCP ensemble of programs, you have found `uucico` and `uuxqt`. In a tour, you saw how these low-level programs interrelate with the midlevel program `uux`, and how that program interrelates with the high-level program `/bin/mail`.

Although you won't use these other programs often—as often as `mail`, for example—should the need arise, you'll be glad you learned how to use the UUCP ensemble of programs.

Where Can You Go from Here?

First, be sure that you've tried out the examples in this book at your terminal. That is the only way to become truly comfortable with the programs discussed. You may want to reread some of the chapters to make sure you really understand the concepts presented (this is particularly true of the UUCP section, since UUCP is unavoidably technical). If you have trouble with some of the UNIX concepts that underlie our discussions, review chapter 2 and investigate the beginning UNIX books listed in Appendix E.

If you need to learn how to use `/bin/mail` (probably because it is the only mail program on your machine), see the `/bin/mail` tutorial in Appendix A. To learn about UNIX's *interactive* facilities for talking to other users in real time, see Appendix B on `write` and `talk`. For an overview of some additional UNIX communications facilities that are particularly useful for downloading program code, see Appendix C on `xmodem`, `kermit`, and other protocols. To delve further into the workings of USENET, see Appendix D for information sources. To learn more about UNIX, see Appendix E, a bibliography of books about UNIX.

We look forward to communicating with you on UNIX!

Appendices

A

A */bin/mail* Tutorial

This appendix explains how to use /bin/mail, the electronic mail program that was developed with the original UNIX system from AT&T. (It's also available on all subsequent versions of UNIX.) If you have System V or Berkeley UNIX, you should use mailx (Mail) instead—it's more convenient and has many more options (see chapters 3 through 5). However, if you have an old version of UNIX, /bin/mail may be the only mail program on your system.

The /bin/mail program is located in the /bin directory, hence its name. With /bin/mail, you can perform all the essential operations you need to do with mail (send, receive, and store messages). However, /bin/mail is somewhat awkward and lacks many of the features of the more advanced mail programs.

In the sections that follow, you'll learn how to:

- Send messages.
- Create messages using one of the UNIX editors.
- Read messages.
- Delete messages.
- Save messages.
- Forward messages to other users.
- Issue UNIX commands while in /bin/mail.
- Call up /bin/mail with command-line options.

If electronic mail is new to you, read the first part of chapter 3 to get an overview of this form of communication. Other sections in chapters 3 through 5 also pertain to /bin/mail. We'll refer you to these as they come up in the text.

Sending Messages with */bin/mail*

Sending messages is almost exactly the same in `/bin/mail` as in `mailx`. You type the word `mail`, a space, and then the login name of the person receiving the message. For instance, to send a message to a user named `chesley`, enter:

mail chesley ←*press Return*

The Simple Message Editor

When you press Return, you'll see the cursor move down to the next line; `/bin/mail` has placed you in a basic editor that allows you to enter your message. Type your message text, pressing Return at the end of each line. Your message might look like this:

```
Hi Chesley,

I'm just learning to use the mail program...it seems to be
pretty easy; ha, this is a test!  Please send me a reply to let
me know if you received this message.

Talk to you later,

Heather
```

If you make a mistake, use the backspace character to move the cursor left and erase the incorrect characters. Try both the Backspace key and Control-h to see which works. (Some older "hard-copy" terminals use the pound sign (#) for erasing characters.) Now retype the line correctly. Some systems also allow you to delete the entire line with Control-x or the @ key.

As you can see, this message editor has severe limitations. After you press Return, the computer saves the line you've just typed; you can no longer change it with the message editor. If you notice a mistake on the first line while you are on the second line, you're stuck: there is no way to return to a previous line to correct it. You might add a line of explanation later in your message:

```
Oops! I meant "zoology" not "zoobirds" in line 1.
```

If the mistake is serious, you can cancel the entire message and start over, as we'll explain shortly. Or you can compose the message with a more powerful editor as explained later in this section. The moral: use the default editor for "quick and dirty" messages. For messages that are longer or that need more polish, we'll show you how to bypass the limited default editor.

Sending Off the Message

When you have finished writing your message, press Return (to make sure that you're on a new line). Now type a single period and press Return again, like this:

```
mail chesley

Chesley --

Just checking to see if we're still on for Italian dinner
tomorrow night.

Heather    ←press Return

           ←type a period and press Return
EOT        ←UNIX responds
```

The single period is not inserted in the message; it merely tells the program that your message is complete. After you press Return the last time, UNIX displays EOT (end of transmission). This means that UNIX accepted your message and sent it on its way.

Instead of a period, you can type Control-d:

```
mail chesley

Kelley's out of town til the end of the month. He's
asked me to stand in for him while he's gone. Please
call when you have a few minutes free.

Heather    ←press Return

^D         ←press Control and d keys simultaneously
EOT        ←UNIX responds
```

Be careful—once you send a message with Control-d or a single period, there's no easy way to recall it. It's like dropping a letter in the mailbox. (There is a way to cancel *some* mail messages after the mail program has accepted them but before they are actually sent. However, the procedure is too cumbersome for most users. If you are interested, see chapter 15.)

Cancelling a Message

You can cancel a message while you're still writing it by issuing an *interrupt* character. On our system, Control-c generates an interrupt character. Some systems accept the Delete key instead.

After you cancel the message, you are returned to the UNIX prompt. The cancelled message is temporarily saved in the file `dead.letter` in your home directory. This file is used to hold the latest cancelled or undeliverable message. If you cancel another message (or if a message you send can't be delivered), it will replace the existing contents of `dead.letter`.

Sending Mail to Several People

It's easy to send the same message to more than one person at once—just add the login names of the additional recipients to the `mail` command line, for example:

```
mail chesley alan kemar
```

will send the message you create to `chesley`, `alan`, and `kemar`.

Sending Messages to Other UNIX Systems

So far, we've assumed that you're sending messages to users who are on the same UNIX computer as you. You can send messages to users on other UNIX systems as well.

If your system is directly connected to a computer named `hplabs`, you can send a message to a user on `hplabs` with a command like:

```
mail hplabs!username
```

where `username` is the person's actual user ID.

You can also route a message from computer to computer until it reaches the desired user. You would use a command such as:

```
mail hplabs!nike!sunybcs!username
```

For a complete explanation, see "Sending Messages to People on Other Computers" in chapter 4.

Limitations of */bin/mail*

In `mailx` you can escape from the default message editor by typing a tilde (~) in the first column. You then have access to the tilde commands described in chapter 4. These commands allow you to insert a file into the message, edit the message with another editor, issue a UNIX command, and so forth.

Unfortunately, `/bin/mail` doesn't respond to tilde commands. Once you are in the message editor, you are stuck there. This means that if you want to use a more powerful editor to compose your message, you have to call it up ahead of time.

Sending Mail from a UNIX Editor File

To overcome the limitations of the /bin/mail message editor, you can create a message with any of the text editors on your system (for example, ed, ex, or vi). Once you're satisfied with the text, save it as a file and exit the editor program. To send the file to another user, enter a command such as:

```
mail huxley < text_file
```

where text_file is the name of the file you've created. The redirection character (<) tells the mail program to take its input from the file text_file and send it as a regular mail message.

Preparing Messages on a PC

If you use a PC as a terminal for a UNIX system, you can prepare messages with your PC word processor rather than with the UNIX editors. Writing messages off-line can save you money if you pay phone-line charges for communicating with the UNIX systems. You can learn more about this in chapter 4, "Sending Messages Written on Your PC." You can read about transferring files between PCs and UNIX systems in Appendix C.

Reading Your Mail

If you have received messages, you are greeted with the following notice when you log into your UNIX system:

```
You have new mail.
```

To read your messages, enter:

```
mail
```

at the UNIX prompt. If mailx or Mail is on your system, you may have to call up /bin/mail with:

```
/bin/mail
```

The screen will display the most recent message that you have received. It will look something like this:

```
>From bea Sun Mar 22 19:55:57 1987
Received: by well.UUCP (4.12/4.7)
        id AA00461; Sun, 22 Mar 87 19:54:38 pst
Date: Sun, 22 Mar 87 19:54:38 pst
From: bea (Bart Anderson)
Message-Id: <8703230354.AA00461@well.UUCP>
To: cricket

If you're looking for free-lance work, you might try Kalimera
Software in Yellow Springs. They want C programmers and people
who can document C programs. Good luck!

?
```

The first seven lines in the preceding message are *header lines*. The header lines tell who the message is from, how it came to you, when it was received, and so forth.

Following the message, you'll see the `/bin/mail` prompt—a question mark (?). At this prompt, you enter a command to tell `/bin/mail` what to do with the message currently displayed. You can read, send, delete, or forward any messages you've received. Table A-1 lists the commands available in `/bin/mail`; we'll discuss them one by one.

Table A-1. Commands in */bin/mail* for Reading Messages

Command	Use
`Return`	Display next message.
`+`	Display next message (same as Return).
`-`	Display previous message.
`?`	Display a list of `/bin/mail` commands.
`*`	Display a list of `/bin/mail` commands.
`d`	Delete this message and display the next.
`m user(s)`	Forward this message to specified `user(s)`.
`p`	Display the current message again.
`q`	Quit the mail program (deleted messages are lost).
`s file`	Save this message in the specified file.
`w file`	Save this message (without header) in the specified `file`.
`x`	Exit the mail program (all messages, even those you've deleted, are left intact).

Displaying a Summary of Commands: *?* and *

Entering a question mark (?) or an asterisk (*) displays a summary of the commands available. (Some systems will accept either character.)

Displaying Messages: *Return* or +

In `/bin/mail`, it's simple to display the messages you've received. Press Return at the `/bin/mail` prompt and the next message will be displayed. (Entering + does the same thing.) To temporarily stop the display of a message, type Control-s. Type Control-q to resume the display. If you want to stop the display of a message and return to the ? prompt, type Control-c. You can examine all your messages in this way. The latest messages are displayed first, then the earliest (see figure A-1).

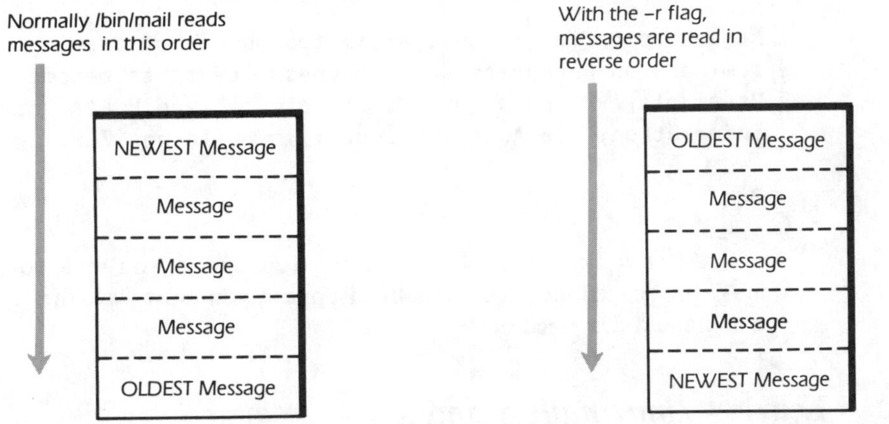

Figure A-1. In **/bin/mail**, the latest messages are displayed first.

On some systems, you can reverse the order in which you see messages by using the `-r` option:

```
mail -r
```

The `-r` option is useful if you receive a number of messages on the same topic and you want to read them in chronological order.

Rereading Messages: *p* and –

If you want to reread a message that you've already displayed, you have a choice of two commands. Entering *p*

displays the current message again (for instance, if it's a long message that has scrolled off the screen).

To display the *previous* message, enter a minus sign:

-

Deleting Messages: *d*

Just as you receive junk mail in your regular postal mailbox, you will probably receive some "junk" electronic mail. Perhaps a friend has sent you an electronic message on which you've already followed up. If you have such messages in your electronic mailbox, you can delete them. To delete the message you've just displayed, type d at the ? prompt, as in this example:

```
Mega Corporation now has a limited number of openings in its
seminars on Corporate Consciousness. Learn to become a real
"team player" and a good "corporate citizen." For more
information, see Audrey DeLucchi in Building 47LF.
```

? *d*

After you delete messages with the d command, you're not quite finished. To make the deleted messages actually disappear, you must leave the program with the q command described next.

Leaving */bin/mail*: *q* and *x*

As in the mailx program, you can leave /bin/mail in two ways. If you quit the program by entering:

q

all the messages you've deleted with the d command are lost from your system mailbox. You are then returned to the UNIX prompt ($ or %). (On some systems, messages that you have saved to other files are also removed from the system mailbox by the q command.)

On the other hand, if you exit the program with:

x

no messages are lost from your system mailbox—even if you have used the d command.

Use q if you want /bin/mail to go ahead and delete the messages you've marked as deleted. Use x if you are having second thoughts and don't want any of your messages to disappear.

Saving Messages: *s*

The simplest way to save the message you've just displayed is by entering:

```
s
```

at the ? prompt. The message is appended to the default file named mbox (mailbox) in your home directory. The problem with this simple method is that mbox soon grows large and unwieldy. Messages from different users on all subjects are saved together in mbox with no order or organization.

> *Warning*: On many UNIX systems, mbox files are not protected; anyone on the system can examine them. To keep other people from looking in your mbox file, enter the command:
>
> ```
> chmod go-rwx mbox
> ```

To better organize your messages, save them to files with meaningful names. You can save the current message in a file named for the sender:

```
s carmela
```

or in a file named for the subject matter:

```
s pascal_class
```

In this way, you can conveniently organize your messages without cluttering your mbox file.

Reading Messages in Files Other Than the System Mailbox: *-f* Option

When you receive messages, they are put into a special file called your *system mailbox*. This file is located in different places in different systems. In System V, it's /usr/mail/login (where login is your user name). On Berkeley UNIX and some other versions, it's in /usr/spool/mail/login. Figure A-2 shows how /bin/mail interacts with these and other files.

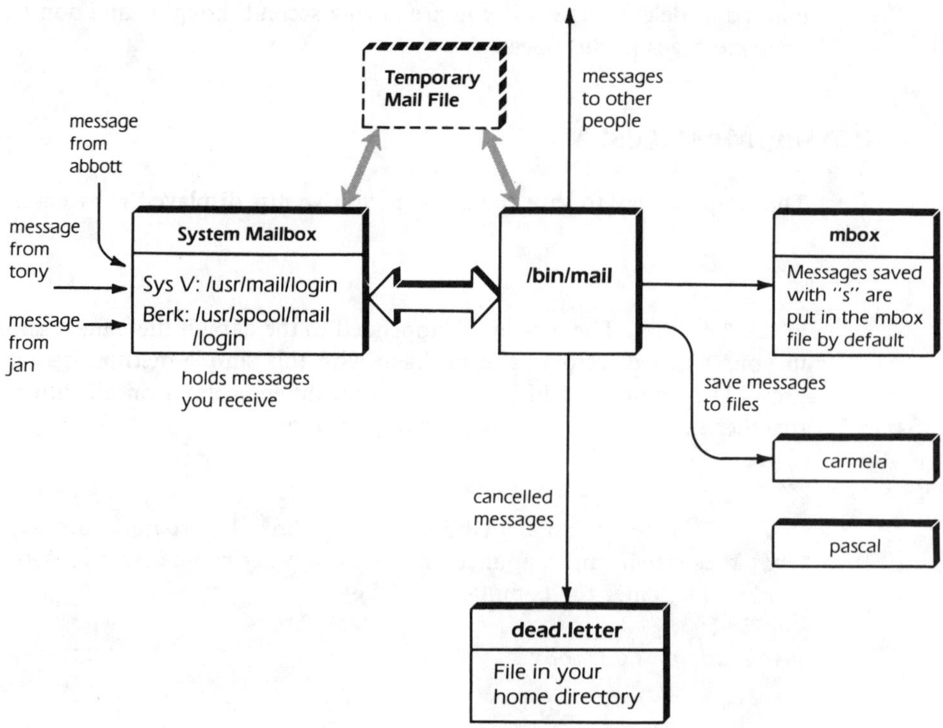

Figure A-2. The **/bin/mail** program and the files it uses.

When you call up the /bin/mail program, it normally reads the messages in your system mailbox. However, you can read messages in other files by using the -f option. To read the default mbox file, call up the program with:

```
mail -f mbox
```

To read the messages in the file bookproject, enter:

```
mail -f bookproject
```

You can use all the usual /bin/mail commands to read, delete, forward, and save messages in these files.

Saving Messages without Headers: *w*

As you've seen, each message is preceded by several lines of header information. The header lines tell the name of the sender, the time the message was received, and other, more cryptic, information. If you want to save the message to a file, but *without* the header information, use the `w` command. For example:

```
w delta_proj
```

This command saves the current message to the file `delta_proj`, but without the several header lines. In all other respects, `w` is the same as `s`; if no file is named in the command line, the current message is saved to `mbox`.

Forwarding Messages to Other Users: *m*

Suppose you've just displayed a message about the status of the Delta Project. If you want the user `mck` to get a copy of the message, you can forward it to `mck` with the command:

```
m mck
```

at the `?` prompt. It's just as easy to forward messages to multiple users. To do so, enter a line like:

```
m heather chesley mck
```

and the mail program sends the current message to users `heather`, `chesley`, and `mck`.

Issuing UNIX Commands: *!*

When you're in the `/bin/mail` program, you'll often want to issue a regular UNIX command. For instance, you might want to display your files with the `ls` command or review a file with the `cat` command. You can enter a UNIX command at the `/bin/mail` prompt by prefacing it with an exclamation mark. For instance, to see the contents of the file `worksked`, enter:

```
!cat worksked
```

After the file is displayed, you are returned to the `/bin/mail` prompt.

Other */bin/mail* Command-Line Options

We've already seen that, with some systems, calling up the `/bin/mail` program with the `-r` option allows you to see the messages in reverse order (first in, first out).

We've also seen that the `-f` option followed by a filename allows you to examine the messages in that file. These and several other options are listed in table A-2.

Table A-2. Command-Line Options for */bin/mail*

Option	Effect
`-e`	No messages are displayed. If a user has mail, a value of 0 is returned; otherwise, 1 is returned. This option is used to test for the presence of mail.
`-f filename`	The `/bin/mail` program reads messages in the file specified instead of in the system mailbox. If no file is specified, the `mbox` file is read.
`-p`	All mail messages are displayed one after the other, without waiting for user commands.
`-q`	The `/bin/mail` program will terminate if an interrupt character (Control-c) is entered. Without this option, an interrupt character stops only the current message from being displayed.
`-r`	Mail messages are displayed in reverse order; the first message received is the first displayed, etc.
`-t`	The message being composed will be preceded by a list of all the users to which the message is being sent.

Caveat

The `/bin/mail` program on your system may differ slightly from the one described here. For example, messages that have been saved with the `s` command may be deleted from the system mailbox when you `quit` the program. Also, not all the command-line options in table A-2 may be available on your system.

Summary

If your UNIX system doesn't have the `mailx` program, you will have to use the less sophisticated `/bin/mail` program to send and receive electronic messages.

To send a message with `/bin/mail`, enter `mail login`, where `login` is the name of the mail recipient. You will be placed in `/bin/mail`'s simple message editor to create the message. End the message by entering Control-d or a period on a new line. You can send a text file as a message with a command like `mail username < filename`.

You can send messages to several users at once with a command like `mail` `user1 user2 user3`. You can send a message to a user on another UNIX system with a command like `mail computername!user`.

To read messages sent to you, enter `mail` at the UNIX prompt. The most recently received message will be displayed, followed by the `/bin/mail` prompt—a question mark (?). At this prompt, you can delete (`d`) the current message, forward it to another user (`m username`), or save it to a file (`s filename`). To display the next message, press Return. Entering `p` displays ("prints") the current message, and entering a minus (`-`) displays the previous message.

To leave `/bin/mail`, enter `q` if you want the "deleted" messages to disappear from the system mailbox. Enter `x` if you want the system mailbox to stay as it was, retaining even the "deleted" messages.

We have shown you the highlights and main commands in the `/bin/mail` program. While `/bin/mail` is no competition for `mailx` and other recent mail programs, you can still use it to perform the basic tasks of electronic mail.

B

On-Line Communications

Most of the time you will be using mail programs such as `mailx` or `Mail` to communicate with other users. These mail programs are convenient to use because the recipients don't have to be on-line at the same time you are. They can read your messages and send you replies at their convenience. However, at times you may want to communicate with other users directly and interactively—in "real time"—rather than waiting for them to receive your mail messages. This appendix describes several of the programs available under UNIX for such on-line communication:

- The `write` command (AT&T and Berkeley UNIX), a line-oriented program that causes the text you type to be immediately displayed on the terminal of another user. The `write` command allows two people to type messages back and forth to each other while connected to a UNIX system, and thus hold an on-line conversation.
- The `talk` command (Berkeley UNIX only), a screen-oriented program similar to `write`.
- The `mesg` command, a program that can be used to prevent others from interrupting you with `write` or `talk`.
- The `chat` command, one of the most recent UNIX programs for on-line communications.

Sending Messages with *write*

The first step in on-line communication is to see who else is on the system. You can find out by entering the `who` command. You will see a display like this:

```
doris    ttyh1   Dec 11 15:44
tracy    ttyh2   Dec 11 15:47
rachael  ttyh3   Dec 11 16:02
flynn    ttyh4   Dec 11 16:02
gilles   ttyh5   Dec 11 16:39
bea      ttyh6   Dec 11 16:39
ray      ttyh9   Dec 11 16:38
wowbag   ttyi1   Dec 11 15:21
```

This display lists all users currently logged onto the system, the terminal each is using, and the time and the date that each user logged on.

Let's say your login name is `wowbag`, and you want to get in touch with Doris Miller (who has the login name `doris`). You can send a message to her from your keyboard by entering:

`write doris`

Doris would normally hear a beep from the speaker in her terminal and see:

```
Message from wowbag on ttyi2 at 16:41 ...
```

On your (`wowbag`'s) screen, the cursor moves down one line and you can type your message. As usual, the characters you type are echoed to the screen. At the end of each line, you press Return and the line of text is sent to Doris's terminal and displayed.

When you are finished with your message, type Control-d (^D) to leave the `write` program. The characters `EOF` will appear on Doris's terminal to mark the end of the message. The message might look like this to Doris:

`I made popcorn in the microwave--do you`
`want to take a break and share it with me?`
`wowbag`
`EOF` ←*Appears when the sender types Control-d; signifies end of message*

Holding Two-Way Conversations with *write*

In the previous example, we sent just one message and then left the `write` program. While this can be useful for getting another user's attention, it is not the most interesting use of `write`. The `write` program can also be used for an actual conversation between two users.

To carry on a conversation, you do not type Control-d at the end of your message and exit the `write` program. Instead, you type `-o-` ("over") to signify the end of a thought and let the other person know that it is his or her turn to type. You might enter:

```
hello doris
Doris--slight emergency.
Can I borrow your toolkit?
-o-    ←-o- shows that you are finished with your thought (don't type ^D yet)
```

At her terminal, Doris sees the message displayed, and can reply by issuing the command:

```
write wowbag
```

She then types her message, also ending it with `-o-` to show that it's your turn to talk.

```
Sure. The toolkit is in the usual place.
What broke this time?
-o-
```

The two people type back and forth, using `-o-` to separate their messages. The use of `-o-` corresponds to the pauses in spoken conversation. Without such a convention, one person's text might appear in the middle of the text being typed by the other person, making a hash of the `write` conversation.

When you are finished with the conversation, you indicate it to the other person by typing `-oo-` ("over and out"). Finally, press Control-d to actually exit from the `write` program.

```
Nothing broke, just a loose cable,
Doris. But Mr. Big wants it fixed now.
-oo-   ←"over and out"
EOF    ←appears when the sender types ^D
```

Since `-o-` and `-oo-` are just conventions and not part of the program, you are free to ignore them or create your own conventions. We recommend you use them, however.

If you want to get a taste of how `write` works, try issuing the `write` command to yourself. (For example, if you have the login name of `wowbag`, type `write wowbag` at your terminal.) See what happens as you type your message. Type Control-d as usual to exit the `write` program.

Writing to Users on Other UNIX Systems

The `write` program allows you to converse with people logged onto other UNIX systems that are connected to yours (such as in a LAN—local area network). You may need help from the system administrator or a knowledgeable user to show you how to find out who is on the other system(s). To `write` to a user on another system, use a command such as this:

```
write utopia!amy
```

This command lets you start a conversation with user `amy`, assuming that she is logged onto the `utopia` system and that your system is connected to `utopia`.

Running Other UNIX Commands While in *write*

Sometimes you may want to use other UNIX commands while you are still in the `write` program. To perform a UNIX command, you can escape temporarily from the `write` program without disconnecting from the other user. Just type an exclamation mark at the beginning of a line, followed by the UNIX command. For instance, suppose the person you are conversing with wants to know if you have a certain file. You can get a list of your files while using `write` by typing:

```
!ls
```

Preventing Interruptions: *mesg*

When you are in the middle of a task, it's unnerving to be interrupted by a `write` message. You hear a beep from your terminal and see strange text appearing in the middle of your screen. (Note that although the `write` message makes the screen display confusing, it doesn't actually affect the file you're working on.) You can keep other people from interrupting you with `write` messages by using the `mesg` (message status) command. Typing `mesg` by itself tells you the current message status (whether or not you'll receive `write` messages). The default status is `y` (yes, accept messages). Typing `mesg n` tells the system you don't want to accept `write` messages. Typing `mesg y` means you want to accept `write` messages again.

A typical sequence of commands is:

```
mesg      ←checks your message status
is y      ←"yes" status (accept write messages)
mesg n    ←prevents incoming write messages
mesg      ←checks message status again
is n      ←status is now "no"
```

When you log off the computer, the `mesg` setting reverts to the default of "yes." This means that you must issue the `mesg n` command every time you log into the system if you want to prevent interruptions. You can automate this chore by adding the `mesg n` command to the list of commands in the file that your system executes whenever you log in: `.login` for the C Shell or `.profile` for the Bourne Shell.

The `mesg n` command also prevents interruptions by the `talk` program, described next.

Communicating with *talk*

If you are on a Berkeley UNIX system, you can communicate with others by using `talk`, a more sophisticated alternative to `write`. While `write` is line-oriented, `talk` is screen-oriented and requires that the system be set to handle the specific cursor-addressing of your terminal. (If you are already using other screen-oriented programs such as the `vi` editor, you probably have the settings you need. Otherwise, ask your system administrator or another knowledgeable user for help.)

The `talk` program gives you a split-screen interface, in which one user has the upper screen and the other has the bottom. Both can type at the same time, so you don't have to worry about taking turns. A `talk` conversation is set up much as a `write` conversation. If the other person is currently on the system, contact the person with a command like:

```
talk rachael
```

The other person sees a display like this:

```
Message from Talk_Daemon@grumpy at 16:45 ...
talk: connection requested by wowbag@grumpy
talk: respond with:  talk wowbag@grumpy
```

This display tells user `rachael` that user `wowbag` wants to talk with her. The string "`@grumpy`" means that `wowbag` is on the UNIX system called `grumpy`. If that is the same system `rachel` is on, she doesn't have to use the system name. She just types:

```
talk wowbag
```

If `rachael` and `wowbag` are on different UNIX systems (for instance, if they are on two systems connected by a local area network), she must identify the system that `wowbag` appears on. The syntax for specifying a user on another system can be any of the following:

```
user@system
system!user
system.user
system:user
```

Thus, if `wowbag` were on a system called `sneezy`, `rachael` could type:

```
talk wowbag@sneezy
```

What *talk* Looks Like

Once a `talk` connection has been established between the two users, both their screens clear. Each screen is divided into two halves by a horizontal line of dashes in the center. One person's text appears in the top half of the screen; the other person's text appears in the bottom. Unlike `write`, `talk` allows both people to type simultaneously, since text is displayed in different windows. You don't have to worry about taking turns—you can type as the spirit moves you. Still, the conventions `-o-` and `-oo-` are useful to keep the order of the conversation clear. A typical `talk` conversation looks like this (note that the bracketed numbers represent the order of the conversation):

```
[1]Rachael?
-o-

[3]I saw you on the system (by typing who), and Gilles told me
you had a question for me.
-o-

[5]No, sorry. No time for brochures. I just started at Maxwell
Systems and I'm still getting my bearings. I've never worked in
a big corporation before.
-o-

----------------------------------------------------------------------

[2]Yes, I'm here.
-o-

[4]Gilles is right. I've been trying to get hold of you. I need
to know--do you want to work on the modem brochure?
-o-

[6]I've never been in a big corporation either. I've done some
free-lance work for them, though. The pay is usually good, but it
takes *months* to get them to agree on what they want!
-o-
```

In `talk`, when the text reaches the bottom of either window, the cursor jumps to the top of that window and begin to overwrite existing text. (Typing Control-l redraws the screen.) In other words, each user's window acts like a complete terminal screen.

To exit the `talk` program, issue the interrupt character for your system (typically, Control-c).

The `talk` program is a definite improvement over `write`, since you don't have to worry about your text interfering with the other person's text. However, neither `talk` nor `write` is soon going to replace human speech. A significant drawback is that conversation with these programs is *s–l–o–w* because you are limited by typing speed, and sometimes by system response time (if there are a lot of users on the system.)

A New Form of On-Line Communication: *chat*

We'll finish this appendix with a brief look at one of the newer programs for UNIX, `chat`. The `chat` program was developed by David Taylor (who recently wrote the `elm` mail program and authored the article "All about UNIX Mailers"—a survey of UNIX mail programs—in *UNIX Papers*, Indianapolis: Howard W. Sams, 1987). Although not yet widely available, `chat` contains several improvements over the older on-line communications programs and gives an idea of how much is possible for on-line conversations. To begin with, `chat` allows several people on the same computer to converse simultaneously (`write` and `talk` limit you to two-way conversations).

Each user chooses a *chat-name*, which identifies all messages subsequently typed by that user. A `chat` conversation looks like this:

`[ian]` *You're surprised that the schedule slipped?*

`[gilles]` *I don't understand how you do things here. Out in the field if we gave a customer a date, we hustled to meet it. Here in headquarters, dates don't seem to matter.*

`[doris]` *Large organizations develop laws of their own, which defy rational analysis.*

Among the dozen or so commands available in `chat` is one to insert a file into the conversation. You use the redirection indicator (<) like this:

```
< old_jokes
```

The file named `old_jokes` then appears in the conversation. You can save the text of a discussion to a file by using another redirection indicator (>). For example, this command:

```
> grouptalk.209
```

saves a record of the conversation to the file named `grouptalk.209`.

Summary

Use the `write` command to send quick messages to someone who is currently on-line, or to hold two-way conversations. To prevent others from interrupting you with `write` or `talk` messages, enter `mesg n`. If you are on Berkeley UNIX, you can hold two-way conversations with a more sophisticated, screen-oriented program called `talk`. Conversations with several users are possible with the new `chat` program.

C

UNIX to PC Communications with *kermit*, *xmodem*, and *arc*

This appendix will briefly discuss two more communications programs, `kermit` and `xmodem`, and the public-domain archiving program `arc`.

The `kermit` and `xmodem` programs are presented here because they have two important characteristics:

1. They allow communication between UNIX and a variety of non-UNIX systems.
2. They have built-in error-correction procedures.

Unlike the programs discussed in the main part of the book, `kermit` and `xmodem` are not part of UNIX and are not written specifically for UNIX systems. Rather, they are implemented on a great variety of computer systems: indeed, there is scarcely a brand of computer that does not have implementations of them. They are also found on many UNIX machines; `kermit` is the more common, but `xmodem` is increasingly available.

Since many people who use UNIX also use MS-DOS® computers, Macintosh™ computers, or computers with other operating systems, it is desirable to be able to transfer files back and forth between UNIX and non-UNIX systems. This is easily done with these versatile communications programs.

Error-Free Transmission

Suppose you want to transfer files between a microcomputer and a UNIX system. If you have a modem and communications software, you can dial up a UNIX system, log in, and use the *terminal emulation* feature of your communications software to allow your microcomputer to simulate one of the terminal types recognized by the

UNIX system. Terminal emulation usually includes the capability to "capture" to a disk the data that appears on the screen. Thus, you could transfer a file by doing something like this:

(On UNIX System)	(On Microcomputer)
	dial command, phone number
ID and password prompts	type in ID, password
	"capture filename"
$ cat filename	(data appears on screen)
$	"close buffer"
	file written to disk

The actual commands used on the microcomputer vary with the software used, of course. The idea is that when you say "capture filename" at the micro, all incoming data from the UNIX system is saved in a buffer in the micro's memory. It is then written to the disk file specified, either immediately or after the buffer is closed.

This is a handy way to transfer short text files. But sometimes there is a need for *error-free* transfer of files. Telephone lines are not 100% reliable and accurate for transferring data. Most of the time the characters that arrive at the destination are the ones that were sent, but errors creep in. (If you use dial-up lines to access your UNIX system, you are familiar with the "garbage" characters that show up on the screen from time to time.)

Suppose, for example, you displayed and captured a text file and then found a line like this in it:

```
When in the couqse of huma@ events
```

You could still figure out what you were reading. But suppose you captured a C program source file that ended up with a line like this in it:

```
pj_ntf ("Hello, world");
```

(instead of the original `printf...`). Well, that wouldn't be too bad. When you tried to compile the program, the compiler would give you an error message, and you could fix it. But now suppose the program you received had the wrong number for initializing a variable, or the wrong location in an array of data. The compiler won't complain, but the program will not run correctly. The error could be so serious that the program crashes completely, or the error could be more subtle. Finally, suppose you transfer a binary (machine-code) file? There would be no easy way for you to examine the file for errors, even if you were willing to spend hours doing so.

For this reason, *error-correcting protocols* were developed. Such a protocol, in simplified terms, works like this: The communications program on the source machine sends a block of data (such as 128 bytes). Along with the block, it sends a number derived by adding the values of all the bytes sent. The destination machine has a communications program that understands the same protocol (it need not be the same program). This program adds the incoming block of bytes and compares the number it gets to the number it received with that block of data. If the numbers match, the receiving program sends back an acknowledgment (usually a special character or sequence of characters) that is the equivalent of "Okay, it checks. Send me the next block."

If the number calculated from the bytes in the block does not match the number sent with the block by the source machine, some sort of error has occurred. Perhaps one or more characters were garbled in transmission. In this case, the receiving program sends back a message that translates to "Something was wrong with that block. Send it again." The block of data is sent repeatedly until it is received correctly, some specified number of attempts is made, or a specified period of time passes.

Actually, there are several ways of obtaining a sum of the bytes to be checked; we will not discuss the details or differences among them here. The checksum method used by standard `xmodem` and by `kermit` is about 99.6% accurate, whereas a more recently developed method, `xmodem` with `CRC` (cyclic redundancy check), is perhaps 99.9% accurate. Although no method of transmission is perfect, using such error-correcting protocols means that most programs will be received exactly as they were sent.

The *kermit* Program

In the not-so-good old days when there were only big computers, intercomputer communication, when it existed, was usually accomplished by proprietary software that worked only with a particular model or family of computer. The coming of UNIX with its philosophy of portability helped break down the barriers to computer communication. Indeed, as you have seen, UNIX communications programs such as the UUCP programs can run on any machine that runs UNIX.

In the early 1980s, however, as microcomputers became common, a need developed to find a way to transfer files between larger machines and microcomputers. But most microcomputers did not run UNIX. The `kermit` program was developed by Bill Catchings, Frank da Cruz, and Vace Kundakci at Columbia University as a way for students to move files between the central campus computing center and their personal computers. (The name `kermit` is not an acronym, by the way. It is named for the famous frog on "The Muppet Show," and is used by permission.)

It is important to note that `kermit`, like `xmodem`, which we will discuss later, is not a single program. Rather, it is a standard *protocol*, or agreed procedure for intercomputer communication. One `kermit` program might be written in the C language on a big UNIX machine; another version of `kermit` might be written in 8088 assembly language for the IBM PC; and yet another `kermit` might be written in 6502 assembler and found running on Apple IIs. While some of these `kermit` programs may offer features not found in others, and their commands and syntax may differ slightly, all of them implement the same basic protocol. Thus, they can all understand each other. This is after all the whole point: the ability to transfer files and provide other services without having to worry about differences in hardware architecture or operating system. So, when we refer to `kermit` in the rest of this discussion, we mean "a program that implements the `kermit` protocol."

Transferring Files with *kermit* between a Micro and a UNIX Machine

The `kermit` program has a variety of features that make it quite a versatile program. We will deal here only with establishing the connection and doing basic file transfers. To find out which features are available on your `kermit`, check the manual entry for the version of `kermit` on your UNIX system. (You may have to ask the system administrator where this is. Remember that `kermit`, like the Netnews software, is not part of standard UNIX.) If your UNIX system does not have `kermit`, or you do not have `kermit` for your microcomputer, it is easy to obtain. Most university computing centers and many large bulletin boards (including USENET) have several versions of `kermit` available, usually with enough documentation to get you started.

The following sections will explain how to use `kermit` to transfer files between a microcomputer and a UNIX machine. On the micro end, we will use the MS-DOS version of `kermit`, called `mskermit`. If you use another version, you will find that the commands are very similar, if not identical. The main difference will be in the form of filenames allowed by your micro's operating system.

Starting *kermit*

You can use another communications program to dial the UNIX system and log in. Then you are ready to run `kermit`. At your micro, type:

```
A>mskermit
IBM-PC Kermit-MS V2.27
Type ? for help

Kermit-MS>connect

[Connecting to host, type Control-] to return to PC]
```

When the Kermit-MS> prompt appeared, we typed connect. This means that anything we type will now be sent directly to whatever is at the other end of the cable connected to the machine's RS-232 port—usually a modem. Then kermit reminds us that if we want to type a command that will be read by kermit rather than sent out the RS-232 port, we need to prefix our command with an *escape sequence*. In the preceding example, typing ^] (press Control and type a right square bracket) will momentarily take us out of "connect mode" so that we can type a kermit command. For example, to obtain a list of available commands, we can use the kermit "help" command like this:

```
                  ←we type ^] from connect mode (it is not echoed)
Kermit-MS>help    ←enter a kermit command
BYE               CLOSE             CONNECT           DEFINE
DELETE            DIRECTORY         DO                EXIT
FINISH            GET               HELP              LOCAL
LOG               LOGOUT            PUSH              QUIT
RECEIVE           REMOTE            RUN               SEND
SERVER            SET               SHOW              SPACE
STATUS            TAKE
```

(We will cover only a few of these commands here.)

Dialing with *kermit*

You can use kermit itself to make the connection. First make sure your modem is turned on. Then run kermit and give the connect command:

```
A>mskermit
IBM-PC Kermit-MS V2.27
Type ? for help

Kermit-MS>connect

[Connecting to host, type Control-] to return to PC]
```

At this point, kermit is connected to your modem. Anything you type is sent to the modem. Therefore, if you type your modem's dialing command, your modem will dial out:

```
ATDT5551234
```

This assumes that your modem uses the Hayes command set. For other modems, you will have to look up the correct code. If the UNIX system answers, you can then type in your normal login ID and password.

Sending a File from a Micro to the UNIX System

The kermit program uses a pair of commands to perform file transfers. The kermit on the system *sending* the file uses the send command; the kermit on the system *receiving* the file uses the receive command.

Notice that while we can run kermit on the micro to log onto the UNIX system, we need to have a kermit already running on the UNIX system before we can transfer files. Assuming we are connected to the UNIX system and have logged in, we can of course type any UNIX commands that we want the remote system to execute.

We want to start kermit running on the UNIX system in receive mode, since we are sending a file to the UNIX system.

```
$ kermit r
```

(Note that kermit does not use the usual notation for UNIX flags. There is no hyphen in front of the r.)

A few not very meaningful characters will appear on the screen as kermit starts to run. You can ignore them. The next step is to go back to the kermit running on the micro so that we can tell it to send the file. Remember that we use the Control key plus] to give commands to our local kermit:

```
                                      ←type ^]
Kermit-MS>send c:chapter1
```

The form of the filename used with the send command depends on the operating system used on the micro. Here, we're using MS-DOS and sending the file chapter1 on drive c:.

The file transfer now begins. Our local kermit (the one running on the micro) will keep us informed of the progress of the transfer:

```
           File name: chapter1
   KBytes transferred: 4
  Percent transferred: 100%
             Sending: Completed

    Number of packets: 57
    Number of retries: 0
           Last error: None
         Last warning: None

Kermit-MS>
```

When the sending is completed, you will be signalled (usually by a beep). At this point you issue a connect command to reconnect to the remote system and continue your session. You can exit your local kermit with the exit command, which will return you to the micro's operating sytem. Usually you want to do this only after logging off the remote system, however.

Sending a File from the UNIX System to a Micro

For this next dance, the partners change roles. Now the kermit on the UNIX system will be in send mode, while the kermit on the micro will be in receive mode. Let's say we want to send the file unix.install.notes from the UNIX system to our micro.

First, we start the sending process on the UNIX system by typing:

```
kermit s unix.install.notes
```

Then, we type Control-] (^]) to issue the receive command to our local kermit:

←type ^]

```
receive b:notes
```

The filename is optional. If we don't give one, the local kermit will try to use the UNIX filename (but see the next section). Again, we will be kept informed of the progress of the transfer:

```
          File name: B:notes
  KBytes transferred: 4

          Receiving: Completed

   Number of packets: 57
   Number of retries: 0
          Last error: None
        Last warning: None

Kermit-MS>
```

Note that the percentage is not given when the local kermit is receiving, because it doesn't know how long the file will be until it receives the last block.

While you are sending or receiving files, most kermits allow you to type:

Control-x To stop sending the current file and move on to the next one, if any.

`Control-z`	To stop sending the current file and not send any further files.
`Control-c`	To return to local command mode without notifying the other `kermit`.
`Control-e`	To send an "error packet" to the other `kermit` to try to reset it to command level so that you can start everything over.
`Return`	To tell the other `kermit` to resend the current packet (note that retries are usually automatically attempted by `kermit` when errors occur).

Batch Transfers and Filenames

UNIX `kermit` understands the standard UNIX wildcards for specifying multiple filenames. Thus, you can use the command

kermit s chap?

to send `chap1`, `chap2`, `chap3`, and so on. The `kermit` on the micro needs only the receive command. You do not have to specify the names of the files being received:

kermit r

The files will be saved separately as they are received.

Whether you can use wildcards at the micro end of the transfer depends on your micro's operating system. With MS-DOS `kermit`, for example, you can use the regular MS-DOS wildcard characters, except that you must use = instead of ? because the question mark is used by `kermit` as the help command. For example:

`send chap=.bak` ←*send chap1.bak, chap2.bak, etc.*

`send *.c` ←*send all files ending in ".c"*

A cause for occasional confusion is the fact that `kermit` will sometimes change the name of a file when it is saved at the destination. The most common example is when a UNIX file having a name with more than eight letters is sent to an MS-DOS system. For example, in the earlier example, if we had said

receive

at the micro, without a filename, `kermit` would normally use the name that the file has in the UNIX system and would save the file to the default drive. But a name such as `unix.install.notes` would be saved as `unix.ins`. There are two reasons for this. First, the filename is too long for MS-DOS, which has a maximum filename length of eight characters plus a three-character extension. When the MS-DOS `kermit` encounters the first period in the UNIX filename, it thinks that an extension is coming and uses the first three characters after the period. Second, some `kermit`s will put a period on the end of the names of files uploaded to the UNIX system if the filename doesn't already contain a period.

Setting *kermit* Parameters

The `kermit` program has a number of variables (parameters) that can be set to control the mode of communication and other aspects of the program's behavior. If you give `kermit` the `status` command, it will show you the current parameters:

```
Kermit-MS>status
 HEATH-19 emulation On                    Local echo Off
 Baud rate is 1200                        Parity SPACE
 Escape character: ^]                     Session logging Off
 Flow control: XON/XOFF                   Handshake used: none
 File destination: DISK                   Default disk: C:
 Warning On                               Ring bell after transfer
 Discard incomplete file                  EOF mode: NOCTRL-Z
 Send cntrl char prefix: #                Receive cntrl char prefix: #
 Receive start-of-packet char: ^A         Send start-of-packet char: ^A
 Receive timeout (seconds): 13            Send timeout (seconds): 8
 Receive packet size: 94                  Send packet size: 80
 # of send pad chars: 0                   # of receive pad chars: 0
 Timer Off                                8-bit quoting will be done
                                          with: &
 End-of-line character: ^M                Block check used: 1-CHARACTER-
                                          CHECKSUM
 Communications port: 1                   Debug mode Off
```

Consult your `kermit` documentation for a full description of what these parameters do and how to set them. We will show just a few here:

```
set baud 1200
```

The `set` command is used to set `kermit` parameters. As with other `kermit` commands, if you are in connect mode, you must first escape by typing `^]`. Here are some other examples of setting `kermit` parameters:

```
set default-disk b:     ←use drive b: by default
set heath19 on          ←emulate the Heath 19/VT 52 terminal
```

`set local-echo on`	←*echo incoming characters locally (needed if sender is half-duplex)*
`set parity odd`	←*use odd parity*
`set warning on`	←*give warning on duplicate filenames*

Notice that there are parameters enabling you to do terminal emulation (the types of terminals available will vary). You may also need to change the baud rate and parity to match those used by the remote system.

The `warning` parameter, when set on, will tell you when you already have a file with the same name as the incoming file. It will rename the incoming file to avoid collision. If `warning` is off, the existing file is deleted.

Other *kermit* Features

The `kermit` program has other features besides those we've just discussed. For example, `mskermit` allows you to preset parameters in an initialization file, `mskermit.ini`, which is read in when `mskermit` is run. You can also assign strings to function keys, which is handy if you use `kermit` to dial out. Some `kermits` also offer *server mode*, which provides a more powerful and flexible way of doing file transfers. See your `kermit` documentation for a full explanation of the `kermit` features.

UNIX to UNIX *kermit*

The `kermit` program can of course be used to transfer files between two UNIX systems. In this case, the UNIX `kermit` is run on both systems. See the UNIX `kermit` documentation for details. We will show just one possible scenario here:

Your Machine	*Other Machine*
`$ kermit clb /dev/tty01 1200`	←*start kermit with specified port and speed*
`Kermit: connected`	
`dial out and log in`	←*See chapter 17 on cu*
`start kermit in receive mode on other machine`	→*$ kermit r*
`^c`	←*escape to command mode*
`Kermit: disconnected`	
`kermit slb /dev/tty01 1200 chap1`	←*tell local kermit to send*

See the UNIX kermit documentation for a full list of options. Again, note that the options are not prefixed by hyphens and that the values for the options follow the last option, and are given in the same order as the options. Thus, the command

```
$ kermit clb /dev/tty01 1200
```

(typed at the UNIX prompt) means:

c Enter "connect mode."

l Use the specified TTY line (/dev/tty01).

b Use the specified baud rate (1200).

The *xmodem* Program

The second communications program we will look at is xmodem. The xmodem program was orginally developed in the micro world using the CP/M operating system, where it is sometimes known as the "Christensen protocol" after its originator Ward Christensen. In one form or another, it is the most common protocol used for uploading and downloading programs from thousands of computer bulletin boards, and it is available for most microcomputers.

Unlike kermit, which is usually a stand-alone program on micros (although it can be part of a larger software package), xmodem on micros is normally part of a communications software product such as PC-Talk. You will have to consult the documentation for your micro communications software to find out how to initiate an xmodem file transfer from the micro end. On the UNIX end, xmodem is usually a stand-alone program (it may be called xm). You will also need to consult your UNIX manual for documentation on your particular version of xmodem.

Unfortunately, xmodem is neither as common on UNIX systems as kermit, nor as standardized. To complicate matters, not all versions of xmodem found in communications software for micros follow the standard, and this sometimes causes transfers to fail because of timing problems.

To illustrate the use of xmodem between a UNIX system and a micro, we will briefly introduce a version used under BSD UNIX on The WELL (Whole Earth 'Lectronic 'Link). Remember that your version is likely to be different.

The general form for starting xmodem on the UNIX machine is:

```
xmodem transfer = mode options filename...
```

The transfer = mode is one of the following:

st Send text.

`sb` Send binary.

`rt` Receive text.

`rb` Receive binary.

We will not cover the options here; they are used to select particular variants of the `xmodem` protocol, packet sizes, and other features. You should compare the options available on your UNIX `xmodem` with those supported by your micro communications software. You may not have to use any options.

The last item you must specify is a filename. If your `xmodem` supports what is called a "batch mode," you can use wildcards and multiple filenames. Again, you will have to see which batch modes, if any, are supported by the software at both ends. Two common ones are **MODEM7** and **YMODEM**.

Here is a possible scenario for downloading a file from a UNIX system to a micro via `xmodem`:

Micro	*UNIX System*
(dial up with communications software and log in)	
(give command to activate xmodem)	*$ xmodem st chapter1*
	xmodem announces completion
(return to connect mode; continue session)	

We dialed up and logged in. Then, at the UNIX prompt, we ran the `xmodem` program and told it to send the text file `chapter1`. The `xmodem` program displays a message that will look something like this:

```
XMODEM Version 3.2b -- UNIX-CP/M Remote File Transfer Facility
File chapter1 Ready to SEND in text mode
Estimated File Size 1K, 1 Records, 30 Bytes
Estimated transmission time 2 seconds
Send several Control-X characters to cancel
```

Next, at the micro, we give the command to start `xmodem` from the communications package. With a program such as PC-Talk, we would type `alt r` for "receive," and then the filename with a specifier meaning "use `xmodem`."

```
==RECEIVE A FILE==
Use =X or =B after File Name for Binary or XMODEM
   specification:b:chapter1=x
Changing to 8 BITS with PARITY=N for Binary or XMODEM
```

```
===========================
==RECEIVE WITH XMODEM==

**Holding for Start..
```

While xmodem is doing the transfer, you will see a numbered list of the blocks transmitted. You will also see reports of any problems, such as an incorrect checksum.

```
Receiving Block # 1 - verified
Receiving Block # 2 - verified
(rest of blocks)

**End of File - verified
```

Sending a file from the micro to the UNIX system would be similar, except that the xmodem command on the UNIX system might be:

```
$ xmodem rb prog1
```

Here, we are telling the UNIX xmodem to receive (r) a binary (b) file and save it as prog1. From the micro, we would give the appropriate command to send a file using xmodem.

Handling Special File Formats

Before sending a file from a UNIX system to your micro, you should check to make sure that it isn't in one of the special file formats described in chapter 16. If it is a shar file, you should use the shell command to unpack it into its component files:

```
sh filename
```

and then download the files. If the file is encoded with uuencode, you will need to use uudecode to decode it before transmission unless you have a CP/M-80 or MS-DOS uudecode program on your micro (these are available from user groups and the public-domain archive at SIMTEL20.ARPA).

Files whose names end in .z are probably compressed by the UNIX compress utility. You will need to uncompress the file with:

```
uncompress filename
```

or

```
compress -d filename
```

Finally, you may run across files with the extension .arc. These are created by the arc program, a public-domain archiving program found widely in the micro world and on some UNIX systems. If you have a micro version of arc, you can download the .arc file and then "unpack" it on the micro with:

```
arc -e archive_name
```

Programs for de-arcing archived libraries are available for UNIX systems in the archive at **SIMTEL.20.ARPA**. Ask your system administrator or local downloading guru to obtain a copy for your system. To obtain instructions on how to do this, send a mail message containing the text "send help" to **ARCHIVE-REQUEST @SIMTEL20.ARPA**. Note that not all versions of arc can read each others' archives, so you may have to do some experimenting.

D

Sources for Information about USENET

Sources for information about USENET can be found in the reference books and articles described in Appendix E, as well as in the individual manuals for the various Netnews programs. Probably the best source for finding out more about USENET, however, is USENET itself. It contains many articles, written by knowledgeable people, on various aspects of USENET. In addition, many lists and statistics about the net are maintained by various contributors. We will note here some of the more important newsgroups that you should check for useful information.

Notice that some of the group names, particularly those beginning with `mod.`, may be different by the time you read this. Particular articles may be no longer available, and certainly there will be many additional interesting articles. Also, some articles are posted to more than one newsgroup. For example, the list of active newsgroups is found in both `mod.announce.newusers`, since it is obviously of interest to new users, and `mod.newslists`.

Basic Information and Articles for New Users

Newsgroup: *mod.announce.newusers*

We noted in chapter 6 that the `mod.announce.newusers` newsgroup should be the first one you read. It has many informative, basic articles. We recommend that you read the ones listed here, but there are others worth reading also.

Horton, Mark. "Rules for Posting to USENET."

Guidelines for deciding when posting is appropriate, and which kinds of postings to avoid.

"List of Active Newsgroups."

An alphabetical list of all currently active newsgroups with one-line descriptions of their contents.

"List of Moderators."

A listing of the names of the moderators for all moderated newsgroups (those to which contributors cannot post directly) and addresses to which articles can be sent for submission to these groups.

"List of Publicly Accessible Mailing Lists."

Mailing lists available to the public. (A mailing list is something like a mini-newsgroup. Each article submitted is sent to everyone on the mailing list. Mailing lists are useful for topics that are too specialized for a newsgroup. They also provide a way to test interest in a topic before setting up a full-fledged newsgroup.)

Offutt, Jeff. "Hints on Writing Style for USENET."

A guide to the basics of good writing, with particular emphasis on writing for the USENET medium.

Schwarz, Jerry. "Answers to Frequently Asked Questions."

Many beginners post questions like "What does UNIX stand for?" To help the curious, and reduce the number of such postings, this article answers a range of questions about terms and procedures for doing various things with USENET.

Von Rospach, Chuq. "A Primer on How to Work with the USENET Community."

The basic article on good net practice and "netiquette."

Lists of Statistics about USENET

Newsgroups: *mod.newslists, news.lists*

List-making seems to be a very popular activity among USENET contributors. In the `mod.newslists` and `news.lists` newsgroups you can find lists of newsgroups by popularity, estimated cost per user, traffic volume, and other criteria. (You can also find lists of the *least* popular newsgroups.) To give you a sample of the lists found in these newsgroups, here are the forty most "popular" newsgroups at the time of writing:

```
Article 360 (9 more) in mod.newslists:
From: reid@decwrl.UUCP (Brian Reid)
Newsgroups: mod.newslists,news.lists,news.groups
Subject: TOP 40 NEWSGROUPS IN ORDER BY POPULARITY (MAR 87)
Message-ID: <9021@decwrl.DEC.COM>
Date: 2 Apr 87 19:08:15 GMT
```

Sender: reid@decwrl.DEC.COM
Organization: DEC Western Research Laboratory, Palo Alto, Calif., USA
Lines: 54

A companion posting explains the statistics and the algorithms that produced them.

```
+-- Estimated total number of people who read the group, worldwide.
|     +-- Actual number of readers in sampled population
|     |     +-- Propagation: how many sites receive this group at
|     |     |    all
|     |     |     +-- Recent traffic (messages per month)
|     |     |     |     +-- Recent traffic (kilobytes per month)
|     |     |     |     |     +-- Participation ratio
|     |     |     |     |     |    +-- Cost ratio: $US/month
|     |     |     |     |     |    |    /reader
|     |     |     |     |     |    |        +-- Share: % of
|     |     |     |     |     |    |        |    newsreaders
|     |     |     |     |     |    |        |    who read this
|     |     |     |     |     |    |        |    group.
V     V     V     V     V     V    V        V
```

1	25000	1961	86%	142	2024.8	5	0.36	16.1%	net.sources
2	23000	1801	95%	47	2114.3	2	0.41	14.8%	mod.sources
3	22000	1660	95%	7	56.7	0	0.01	13.6%	mod.announce.newusers
4	20000	1537	89%	168	250.6	8	0.06	12.6%	misc.consumers.house
5	18000	1359	94%	104	209.5	5	0.05	11.2%	misc.jobs
6	17000	1336	94%	15	79.7	0	0.02	11.0%	mod.conferences
7	17000	1321	96%	551	1013.3	32	0.27	10.8%	comp.sys.ibm.pc
8	17000	1276	87%	501	626.1	29	0.17	10.5%	rec.humor
9	16000	1214	97%	382	624.4	23	0.18	10.0%	comp.unix.wizards
10	16000	1200	93%	4	3.9	0	0.00	9.8%	mod.announce
11	15000	1187	84%	21	90.3	1	0.03	9.7%	net.sources.games
12	15000	1116	95%	2	3.5	0	0.00	9.2%	mod.newprod
13	14000	1097	97%	61	118.2	4	0.04	9.0%	comp.sources.d
14	14000	1061	96%	301	492.9	21	0.16	8.7%	comp.unix.questions
15	14000	1048	85%	45	213.9	3	0.07	8.6%	net.sources.bugs
16	13000	1022	96%	131	172.3	10	0.06	8.4%	misc.wanted
17	13000	976	94%	62	104.5	4	0.04	8.0%	comp.misc
18	12000	958	96%	204	324.2	17	0.12	7.9%	comp.lang.c
19	12000	931	96%	72	126.0	6	0.05	7.6%	comp.graphics
20	12000	929	97%	90	114.0	7	0.04	7.6%	comp.sources.wanted

21	12000	897	88%	95	111.9	7	0.04	7.4%	misc.forsale
22	12000	887	97%	21	36.9	1	0.01	7.3%	news.misc
23	12000	885	95%	5	241.6	0	0.09	7.3%	mod.computers .ibm-pc
24	11000	882	96%	567	738.4	51	0.30	7.2%	comp.sys.mac
25	11000	854	94%	18	30.8	1	0.01	7.0%	mod.compilers
26	11000	844	95%	50	112.2	4	0.05	6.9%	mod.telecom
27	11000	837	94%	38	104.5	3	0.04	6.9%	mod.os
28	11000	824	95%	277	680.8	25	0.28	6.8%	comp.arch
29	11000	824	95%	70	218.5	6	0.09	6.8%	mod.recipes
30	11000	812	97%	70	154.2	6	0.06	6.7%	news.groups
31	11000	809	86%	72	116.0	6	0.05	6.6%	comp.os.minix
32	10000	785	95%	58	257.9	5	0.12	6.4%	comp.ai
33	10000	784	96%	24	347.2	2	0.16	6.4%	comp.bugs.4bsd .ucb-fixes
34	10000	783	88%	987	1884.6	98	0.85	6.4%	soc.singles
35	10000	768	81%	247	398.2	24	0.18	6.3%	comp.windows.x
36	9800	756	88%	427	657.5	43	0.30	6.2%	rec.arts.movies
37	9700	746	96%	111	157.0	11	0.07	6.1%	comp.text
38	9700	743	95%	112	245.1	11	0.11	6.1%	mod.ai
39	9600	737	96%	4	52.3	0	0.02	6.0%	mod.newslists
40	9400	723	96%	17	34.5	1	0.02	5.9%	mod.computers. workstations

USENET Practices, Use of Newsgroups, and News Software

Newsgroups: *news.misc*, *news.groups*, *news.software.b*

General discussion of USENET practices (such as what should be posted, how to quote material, how to use copyrighted material, etc.) can be found in `news.misc`. Discussion of *where* something should be posted, or of what is appropriate for particular newsgroups, is found in `news.groups`. Proposals for establishing new newsgroups are often found here as well.

The `news.software.b` newsgroup has information on new releases of version B of Netnews, including bug reports and suggestions for improvement.

News Configuration and Administration

Newsgroups: *news.admin, news.sysadmin, news.config, news.newsites*

Although the information in these groups is mainly of interest to news administrators, browsing through some of the articles will give you an insight into the kinds of problems that can occur in distributing the news. Theoretically, `news.sysadmin` is for system administrators, and `news.admin` is for news administrators, but the topics frequently overlap, and at many smaller sites the same person fills both roles.

The `news.config` newsgroup mostly contains announcements about sites that are having problems or that will be unavailable for a time. The `news.newsites` newsgroup contains announcements about new USENET sites.

E

Some Recommended Books and Articles

Readers of this book may wish to read more about the UNIX operating system. Fortunately, a number of good books are available on such topics as:

- Beginning UNIX.
- UNIX shell programming.
- UNIX system administration.
- UNIX communications programs.

The following list is an annotated bibliography of selected UNIX books. While the list is by no means complete, the books are ones that we have found to be especially helpful.

UNIX Books for Beginners

Pasternack, Irene, and The Waite Group. EXPLORING THE UNIX ENVIRONMENT, 332 pages. New York: Bantam, 1985.

A very understandable presentation of all the material that most users will ever need to know. Excellent for the beginner or casual user.

Waite, Mitchell, Donald Martin, Stephen Prata, and The Waite Group. UNIX PRIMER PLUS (#22028). 416 pages. Indianapolis: Howard W. Sams, 1983.

Covers both BSD and System V UNIX. Similar to UNIX System V Primer.

——. UNIX SYSTEM V PRIMER (#22570). rev. ed. 456 pages. Indianapolis: Howard W. Sams, 1987.

Contains all the essential information that beginners need to use UNIX System V, including UNIX utility commands, the various UNIX editors, and compiler programs under UNIX. Designed to provide easy, step-by-step instruction.

General Reference Books

AT&T Bell Laboratories. THE UNIX SYSTEM USER'S GUIDE. 544 pages. Englewood Cliffs, NJ: Prentice-Hall, 1986.

This manual is that rare creature, a readable book from a corporate environment.

AT&T Information Systems. THE UNIX SYSTEM USER'S MANUAL. 637 pages. Englewood Cliffs, NJ: Prentice-Hall, 1986.

A reference manual for UNIX commands, plus material of interest to programmers and system administrators.

Prata, Stephen, Donald Martin, and The Waite Group. UNIX SYSTEM V BIBLE (#22562). 528 pages. Indianapolis: Howard W. Sams, 1987.

Covers all the basic and advanced UNIX utilities, providing the detailed discussion and examples that are sorely lacking in the standard UNIX manuals.

University of California. UNIX USER'S MANUAL. 4 vols. Berkeley: University of California Press, 1984.

This is the manual for Berkeley (BSD) UNIX.

UNIX Programming and Advanced UNIX

Fiedler, David, and Bruce Hunter. UNIX SYSTEM ADMINISTRATION. 320 pages. Hasbrouck Heights, NJ: Hayden, 1986.

A good introduction to system administration, with many helpful examples and shell scripts.

Kernighan, Brian, and Robert Pike. THE UNIX PROGRAMMING ENVIRONMENT. 368 pages. Englewood Cliffs, NJ: Prentice-Hall, 1984.

A classic from Bell Labs, and a must for programmers. Not for the casual user.

Prata, Stephen, and The Waite Group. ADVANCED UNIX: A PROGRAMMER'S GUIDE (#22403). 484 pages. Indianapolis: Howard W. Sams, 1985.

A thorough introduction to shell scripts, system calls, and C programming with UNIX.

Sage, Russell G., and The Waite Group. TRICKS OF THE UNIX MASTERS (#22449). 414 pages. Indianapolis: Howard W. Sams, 1987.

A UNIX "guru" shows you tricks, tips, and techniques for getting the most out of UNIX and for customizing your environment. Also includes much material of interest to system administrators. For intermediate to advanced users and programmers.

The Waite Group. UNIX PAPERS (#22578). 544 pages. Indianapolis: Howard W. Sams, 1987.

Tutorials and discussions of state-of-the-art developments in many aspects of UNIX, including communications, utilities, programming, and system implementation. For intermediate to advanced users and programmers.

USENET, UUCP, and Other Networks

Articles from Bell Laboratories

Chesson, G. L., "Packet Driver Protocols." Bell Laboratories, 1986.

Norwitz, D. A., and M. E. Lesk. "A Dial-Up Network of UNIX Systems." Bell Laboratories, 1978.

———. "Uucp Implementation Description." Bell Laboratories, 1978.

Articles from Other Publications

Allman, Eric. "Interview with Peter Honeyman." *UNIX Review*, January 1986.

LaFave, Sandra A. "Installing Netnews," parts 1 and 2. *UNIX World*, November and December 1986.

Hoskins, Josiah C., and John S. Quarterman. "Notable Computer Networks." *CACM, ACM*, 1986.

Brief descriptions of several dozen different computer networks and protocols.

Reiken, Bill, and Jim Webb. "HoneyDanBer UUCP: Bringing UNIX Systems into the Information Age," parts 1 and 2. ;login: USENIX Association Newsletter, 1986.

Describes the popular HoneyDanBer extension to uucp.

Thomas, Rebecca. "Bringing Up UNIX Systems Communications: A Case Study." *UNIX World*, June 1986.

Toxen, Bob. "Linking Up with the Outside World." *UNIX Review*, September 1984.

Books on UUCP and USENET

Stigliani, Joan. UUCP MANAGEMENT GUIDE. Masscomp Computer Corp., 1985.
(Also see Appendix D for information on USENET available as USENET news articles.)

Todino, Grace. USING UUCP AND USENET: A NUTSHELL HANDBOOK. O'Reilly & Associates, 1986.

Todino, Grace, and Tim O'Reilly. MANAGING UUCP AND USENET: A Nutshell Handbook. O'Reilly & Associates, 1986.

The *kermit* and *xmodem* Programs

Sources for *kermit*

da Cruz, Frank, and Bill Catchings. KERMIT PROTOCOL MANUAL. Protocol Version 3. New York: Columbia University, 1983.

da Cruz, Frank, Daphne Tzoar, and Bill Catchings. KERMIT USER'S GUIDE. 4th ed. New York: Columbia University, 1983.

"Kermit: A File-Transfer Protocol for Universities." *Byte*, June and July 1984.
Describes the philosophy and design decisions involved in creating `kermit`*, and shows how the data packets are constructed, transmitted, and received.*

Sources for *xmodem*

"Picking the Proper Protocol." *PC Magazine*, June 11, 1985.
Briefly discusses several protocols and checksum methods, and compares their accuracy and features.

Index

S

V

W

X

Z